BEST PRACTICES
IN ASSESSMENT
FOR SCHOOL AND
CLINICAL SETTINGS

BEST PRACTICES IN ASSESSMENT FOR SCHOOL AND CLINICAL SETTINGS

H. Booney Vance, Editor

Clinical Psychology Publishing Co., Inc.
4 Conant Square
Brandon, Vermont 05733

Library of Congress Cataloging-in-Publication Data
Best practices in assessment for school and clinical settings / H. Booney
Vance, editor.
    p. cm.
  Includes bibliographical references and index.
  ISBN 0-88422-114-8 : $49.50
  1. Handicapped children–Education–United States. 2. Handicapped
children–United States–Psychological testing. 3. Special education–
United States. 4. Educational tests and measurements–United States.
I. Vance, H. Booney, 1941-
LC4031.B43   1993
371.91'0973–dc20   91-75519
                                                                       CIP

Library of Congress Catalog Card Number: 91-75519
ISBN: 0-88422-114-8

[CPPC] 4 Conant Square
        Brandon, Vermont 05733

Cover Design: Sue Thomas

Printed in the United States of America

TABLE OF CONTENTS

CONTRIBUTORS

MaryAnn Demchak
Assistant Professor
Department of Curriculum
   and Instruction
University of Nevada, Reno
Reno, Nevada

Samuel A. DiGangi
Assistant Professor, Special Education
College of Education
Arizona State University
Tempe, Arizona

Sarah Drinkwater
Assistant Professor
Department of Curriculum
   and Instruction
University of Nevada, Reno
Reno, Nevada

G. Franklin Elrod
Associate Professor of Education
Eastern Oregon State College
La Grande, Oregon

Suzanne P. Faykus
Assistant Professor, Special Education
College of Education
Arizona State University
Tempe, Arizona

Annette M. Iverson
Assistant Professor
The University of Missouri
Rolle, Missouri

Susan James
School Psychologist
Johnson City, Tennessee

LaMont Johnson
Professor
Department of Curriculum
   and Instruction
University of Nevada, Reno
Reno, Nevada

Donald R. Jones
Director of School Psychology
   Program
Department of Human
   Development and Learning
East Tennessee State
   University
Johnson City, Tennessee

Belinda Lazarus
Assistant Professor
The University of Michigan-
   Dearborn
Dearborn, Michigan

Steven W. Lee
Assistant Professor
Department of Educational
   Psychology and Research
The University of Kansas
Lawrence, Kansas

Cleborne D. Maddux
Professor and Chair
Department of Curriculum and
   Instruction
University of Nevada, Reno
Reno, Nevada

Koressa Kutsick Malcolm
Psychologist
McDowell, Virginia

Lawrence E. Melamed
Professor of Psychology
Kent State University
Kent, Ohio

Kenneth W. Merrell
Assistant Professor
School Psychology Program
   Coordinator
Department of Psychology
Utah State University
Logan, Utah

Ted L. Miller
Associate Professor
Department of Special
   Education and Rehabilitation
University of Tennessee, Chattanooga
Chattanooga, Tennessee

Margaret R. Rogers
Assistant Professor of School
   Psychology
Loyola University of
   Chicago
Chicago, Illinois

David A. Sabatino
Professor and Chairman
Department of Human
   Development
   and Learning
East Tennessee State
   University
Johnson City, Tennessee

Steven K. Shapiro
Assistant Professor
Department of Psychology
Auburn University
Auburn, Alabama

Dennis G. Tesolowski
Clemson University
Clemson, South Carolina

H. Booney Vance
Director of Grants
Upper East Tennessee
   Educational Cooperative/
   East Tennessee State
   University
Johnson City, Tennessee

PREFACE

The major purpose of this book is to provide readers with insight into the ways in which psychologists conduct psychoeducational assessments in a variety of settings.

This book is based on the assumption that there are different approaches to assessment; however, applications such as actual case studies are stressed that show how real people obtain and use information from various settings and sources in order to maximize results. Examples and case studies illustrating the specific assessment-related procedures and techniques that a psychologist might employ on a job have also been provided.

Each contributed chapter in this book is written by a specialist(s) in the particular assessment instrument or strategy and gives a detailed and practical discussion of the assessment procedures and instruments along with a detailed case study. These chapters should inform readers of the scope, central issues, and best practices of the various assessment strategies covered in this volume. The references at the end of each chapter will direct the reader to the literature should he or she wish to pursue a topic further.

In addition to chapters on the more popular instruments such as the WISC-R/III and the Binet IV, the book includes chapters on preschool assessment, assessment of social skills, assessing conduct disorders, working with minority populations, as well as assessing vocational needs and skills. These chapters were deemed necessary since Public Law 94-142 has expanded educational services to cover children age 3 to individuals age 21. In each case, specialized assessment procedures, techniques, and instruments are needed.

This book is primarily intended for school psychologists, clinical child psychologists, educational diagnosticians, and others directly or indirectly involved in psychodiagnostic work. Educators of exceptional children will find the material helpful in their effort to provide comprehensive assessment. This book can be used as a graduate-level text in psychology and special education training programs. It will serve as an important resource for anyone involved in assessment.

A number of people have been generous with their time, energy, and wisdom during the writing of this book. I am especially grateful and indebted to the authors who contributed their expertise to the project.

A book can not be influenced more fundamentally than in the conception of the idea behind it. The idea for this book came from Dr. Gerald B. Fuller, President, Clinical Psychology Publishing Company. I am grateful to Dr. Fuller for his support and encouragement during this arduous project. I have learned much from my colleague and friend, Jerry. I am indebted to Jane Todorski for the excellent job she did as managing editor. Her help is greatly appreciated.

My family plays a very important and special part in my life and has provided continuous, much-needed support during the editing of this book. Thank you all for everything.

H. Booney Vance

1 DEFINING BEST DIAGNOSTIC PRACTICES

David A. Sabatino, H. Booney Vance, and Ted L. Miller

Diagnosis, assessment, or testing may be considered critical to disability determination—the very cornerstone in establishing school, clinical psychology, and rehabilitational services. Special education services begin with the identification of disabled students. The importance of diagnostic and assessment considerations is apparent if one examines the number of books, book chapters, journals, and journal articles written yearly that address the topic (Hospodka, Sedlak, & Sabatino, 1985; Sabatino, 1981). Virtually all students in psychology and special education, graduate and undergraduate programs, are mandated by certification requirements to undertake specific formal coursework in assessment. For some degrees, up to one third of individual training programs may be spent on characteristics and diagnostic considerations of various handicapped populations.

With the advent of the resource room model, and the rapid growth of clinical and school psychology in the 1960s and 1970s, whose primary function was to identify special education students, assessment became a principal function of these diagnosticians. Following the October 1977 mandatory IEP requirements for all handicapped students, the role of a special educator who had some understanding of assessment from the contributing disciplines became commonplace. Frequently the building principal's designee in many multidisciplinary and IEP follow-up meetings was a so-called "specialist," a person with a special education background who could work with each diagnostic team member to generate needed information. The diagnostic team was composed of professionals aligned closely to the field of special education. Most notable among this group were school psychologists, speech-language clinicians, and in some instances occupational or physical therapists, school social workers, and at times a range of medical specialty personnel.

It is clear that diagnostic and/or assessment practices should be an integral part of any contemporary human service program. But paradoxically, diagnostic and/or assessment practices are often poorly understood, frequently maligned, and the topic of endless professional disagreement (Glasser, 1981). The most frequent area of confrontation that occurs between or within the disciplines, and the single greatest area of confusion and argument with parents' advocates and between school-based teams and external service providers, concerns diagnostic considerations. A review of litigation in special education clearly supports this point. An examination of the litigation in special education over the past 20 years will illustrate that limited litigation has occurred over the type or amount of special educational service. A review of litigation in the past decade indicates that diagnostic and placement practices constitute the most frequent legal action (Martin, 1991).

Many psychologists (Reynolds, 1981; Sabatino, 1981) generally view assessment and diagnosis as one and the same. This very failure of psychologists to differentiate between these two practices leads to limitations in the descriptions of learning and behavioral characteristics of disabled children and adults and remains one of the most problematic aspects of the profession as it approaches the 21st century (Glasser, 1981). Indeed, there are clear signals that the contemporary trends in assessment are at best murky and at worst pejorative to students and professionals. If we consider only the past decade or so, criticisms of assessment practices have been pervasive and have arisen from numerous quarters both within and outside the profession (Bersoff & Hofer, 1990). According to these authors, the practice of school psychology has become so regulated by the courts, Congress, and state legislators that control has transferred from professional bodies to legislative bodies. Legislative control may tend to restrict the range of professional function.

The many arguments have ranged from critiques of various conceptual models, the value of diagnostics, the value of tests, and technical issues related to implementation of appropriate test administration practices. Certainly many of these arguments have merit, and proposals to modify inaccurate practices have ranged from minor to radical changes in contemporary practice, the latter including outright elimination of many formal assessment instruments and procedures.

The reality, however, is that assessment will continue to be a dominant force in the practice of school and clinical psychology, especially regarding the identification of special needs students. More succinctly, and in a predictive sense, we see two simultaneous thrusts: (a) an increased—not diminished—need for assessment information and (b) an evolution in assessment techniques and the resulting implications from these diagnostic data. These assumptions outline the purposes of this chapter and are designed to serve as an orientation and introduction to the reader.

CURRENT ASSESSMENT PRACTICES

First, in current diagnostic and assessment practices there appears to be massive confusion as to the difference between ascertaining a characteristic, assessing a hypothesis, and administering and reporting a test score. In some school systems, assessment has been divided into levels. All children who are referred obtain certain tests. Some of those initially referred do or do not obtain another level of assessment. In one sense, that is utilizing a combination of screening and comprehensive diagnostic practice.

Second, there is the issue of who needs what to answer which question. In reality, special education placement practices have been reduced to the routine administration of a few tests. The purpose is frequently not to determine a diagnosis, but to determine if a child meets a rather limited set of special education guidelines. The aftermath of such an approach is that children with handicaps are fit into pre-existing programs. There is little room for the true nature of diagnosis to be played out by clinicians: to build custom-tailored programs based on the unique needs of handicapped students who fail to interact successfully with the regular (basic) curriculum or display unwanted and inappropriate social behaviors.

The issue here is really much larger and has direct monetary connections. The emphasis in special education today is to provide a maximum amount of education in the regular classroom with or without modification for most handicapped students. That fact downplays the necessity and significance of diagnostics. Why look for uniquenesses in learning characteristics that require adaptation of the task to be taught and alteration to the instructional environment if special education administrators merely are seeking a response to an eligibility requirement? There are now school systems that forbid school psychologists to write custom-tailored recommendations, in which the school psychologist's function has been reduced to determining if selected eligibility requirements have been met. Frequently those requirements focus on the assessment of intelligence, reported as a summary score. As the profession moves more toward considering information-processing behaviors associated with learning and adaptive behaviors and as a general upswing in defining neuropsychological function continues, a growing informational gap is apparent between what school psychology can offer and what special education wants to hear. The result has been massive confusion between what constitutes screening, assessment, and diagnosis. We will attempt to clarify those issues.

CURRENT REVIEW OF DIAGNOSTIC PRACTICES

In a recent publication (Bowman, 1989) on the history of psychological assessment practice, it is noted that 2,000 years before Binet's monumental efforts the ancient Chinese were writing on the topics of memory and other mental abilities and the relationship of social class to test performance, as well as protesting the use of the same content for people from different provinces in China in tests used for personnel selection. One of the major distinctions between the use of very early tests and the use of those that followed Binet is that the early tests were used for one specific purpose: They were designed to assess memory, for example, and were not global measures of ability intended to measure several aspects. Binet himself was interested in describing specific traits or aptitudes that relate to learning. The development of the IQ concept was added by Terman in the American standardization of Binet's basic instrument. The logic applied was that if the subparts of intelligence (those factors that comprise it) are ascertained, the end product should be a usable global score. The question of how many different intelligences there are is quite another issue. At this juncture in the history of the human race on the planet Earth, the answer is yet unknown.

We repeat this history for one important reason. It illustrates how anxious we are to be able to simplify the complexities of human learning into a single predictor. The use of single predictors such as IQ scores sounds good in a criterion statement for determining eligibility for special educational services. It must be for that reason that various states address IQ as a definitive criterion and rely on highly suspect concurrent measures of academic achievement in discrepancy with one another (when frequently intelligence and achievement tests have common items) to distinguish among undifferentiated populations to define further undifferentiated subpopulations such as learning disabled children.

The aftermath of these current "testing practices" is questionable at best. For instructional and behavioral management purposes, a group of children is classified as learning disabled on the basis of the statistical relationship between two measures (a global standard score from an intelligence test and standard scores from achievement measures). Because the group has a common name, "learning disabled," there appears to be general speculation that some commonality exists (internal consistency) among the characteristics that define this subpopulation. Most any teacher of learning disabled children will contest these assumptions.

The reduction in the description of the unique behaviors associated with a student's learning and behavioral characteristics becomes lost in the effort to define people's traits objectively. In the astute words of Matarazzo (1990), ". . . objective testing and clinically sanctioned and licensed psychological assessment are vastly different, even though assessment usually includes testing" (p. 1000). Objective diagnosis derived from psychological assessment is impossible. Assessment requires a large measure of subjectivity. Tests do not derive diagnostic values, people do. The value of any test is no greater than the person using it. The inability to see beyond standardized observations and create other behavioral sampling conditions has become a major issue that is well addressed in one example, the absence of learner outcome and/or academic performance standards. We defy any diagnostician or multidisciplinary diagnostic group to write meaningful short- or long-term IEP goals, including enabling instructional activities, on the basis of IQ and achievement test data. These scores do not provide the basis for making instructional and behavioral management decisions about highly complex learner characteristics in disabled persons.

> As a consequence, an increasing number of attorneys recognize that even in our nation's most advanced centers for psychological assessment, the measurement of intelligence (or personality, memory, or other psychological functions) is not, even today, a totally objective, completely science-based activity. Rather, in

common with much of medical diagnosis, experience in our nation's courtrooms is forcefully making clear to psychologists that the assessment of intelligence, personality, or type and level of impairment is a highly complex operation that involves extracting diagnostic meaning from an individual's personal history and objectively recorded test scores. Rather than being totally objective, assessment involves a subjective component. (Matarazzo, 1990, p. 1000)

STRENGTHS AND WEAKNESSES

The modern school system is in a hurry to complete countless numbers of evaluations of so-called classified disabled children in brief time periods. To accomplish this feat, they prescribe limited numbers of commonly administered tests as if diagnosis and assembly line production were one and the same. Two of the most frequently administered tests are the Wechsler Intelligence Scale for Children - Revised (WISC-R; Wechsler, 1974) and the Bender Visual Motor Gestalt Test (BVMGT; Bender, 1978). In response to the criticism raised as to how to obtain more from diagnostic data, the test results are to be summarized in terms of *their* strengths and weaknesses.

The *their* in the last sentence is a key word. What is being described is not the child's performance against some model of how people process information but rather a contrast of the "test's" subtest structure. The real issue here is that this disastrous system of examining psychometric properties is confused with trait measurement of learner characteristics. Learner characteristics being described cannot exceed those that the tests being administered measure. The assumption appears to be that those limited behaviors ascertained by these commonly administered instruments relate to "best practices" in intervention.

SCREENING VS. COMPREHENSIVE ASSESSMENT

If a person has a strength on the WISC-R Vocabulary subtest, but weaknesses in language usage on WISC-R subtests as displayed in Similarities or Comprehension subtests, does that finding provide some usable guide to the establishment of an IEP? The answer is that without further diagnostic hypothesis development, very little is known about the learner on the basis of these subtest comparisons obtained from screening (assessment) procedures. The routine administration of any instrument, no matter how valid or how reliable, does not suggest that it has inherent diagnostic value. Assessment is the determination that a criterion contained in the screening process is or is not present. Do all disabled persons have some type of measured cognitive strength or weakness? Probably not. Do all disabled persons generate a range of scores on commonly administered psychological instruments? No, they do not. Then the search for strengths and weaknesses from scores resulting from routine administration of tests—a screening procedure—makes very little sense, especially when clinical rules as opposed to statistical applications are applied for determining what a strength or weakness is.

PSYCHOLOGICAL SCREENING

What, then, is the alternative to screening procedures that define psychometric strengths and weaknesses? An alternative is to use observational and screening data to develop systematic hypotheses, in keeping with scientific method, as a nomological net that will permit reporting how children learn most efficiently and most effectively. The difference between screening and diagnosis is that a test battery is imposed in screening and the criterion has been established that will define how the generated data are to be used. That is exactly the process when school psychologists routinely use prescribed instrumentation to answer predetermined questions such as, Is this child eligible for special education entry? To use that same screening data in deriving answers to diagnostic questions related to the establishment of appropriate interventions is not possible. What is possible is to use that screening data to suggest what clinical hypothesis should be pursued through comprehensive assessment.

We treat special education eligibility and placement as if it were an intervention. The diagnostic value of any assessment procedure begins with declaring eligibility and the concomitant placement of children into various forms of special educational programs and services. If the only decision to be made is to determine if a "special educational service" is needed, then countless professional resources are misused in "diagnosing" for which no specific pedagogy exists (Hilliard, 1979). This may be what Reschly (1978) meant when he suggested that "Consensus on theoretical or research criteria and agreement on practical implications has not been achieved" (p. 25). The value of diagnostic decisions in developing intervention strategies has been layered over with artifacts that appear to offer

some assurances that all is well. However, most of these so-called procedural safeguards, such as multidisciplinary assessment, student outcome
criteria, development of placement options, and effective intervention
programs, are being met in name only. Support for this statement will be
offered in the summary of this chapter.

WHAT IS DIAGNOSIS?

Diagnosis is decision making. The value of diagnosis must be seen in
the interventions offered. A test score is not a diagnosis; comparisons of
test scores are not diagnosis. Diagnosis with handicapped populations is
defining disability in type and amount in order that appropriate levels and
intensity of intervention may be offered. Reschly (1978) discussed the
level of inference used in the predictions made about individuals based on
diagnoses of minimal brain damage and/or learning disabilities. As he
pointed out, the "assessment which results in a high level of inference is
usually not related to intervention, and is, therefore, of questionable
benefit to individuals" (p. 38). In this case, and in others, a prediction
orientation can no longer be supported. These types of decisions based on
prediction are often helpful to the school but are often damaging to the
individual and misleading to others. Reynolds (1975) wrote some time ago
that

> . . . consequently, schools require a decision rather than simple
> prediction [orientation]; they need one that is oriented to indi-
> viduals rather than institutional payoff. In today's context, the
> measurement technologies ought to become integral parts of
> instruction, designed to make a *difference in* the *lives* of *children*
> and not just a prediction about their lives. (p. 15)

Does the assessment process as it currently exists serve to discriminate
further among children by using bureaucratic criteria that may act as a
rejection process for the very student who needs, or can profit from
assistance the most? Are we, or do we continue to be, weather forecasters
reporting sometime after the storm has occurred, rather than learning and
behavioral problem solvers? The answer to this question is important
because it dictates how we use assessment data.

REORIENTING THE DIAGNOSTIC PROCESS

The traditional approach in the assessment of children with learning problems has emphasized the use of formal (standardized) tests. These standardized observational procedures are administered to children in small rooms, by examiners with little other observational or record-based data on the child who is being assessed. The procedure lasts 2–3 hours and results in a written report that may not communicate with either teachers or parents. The wide availability of formal tests, the relative ease of administering them, and the use of normative data are some of the major reasons why these tests have been used extensively within schools creating a test-taking traditional practice. Recently, however, there has been a growing dissatisfaction among many behavioral scientists and educators who have questioned the sole usage of formal tests to assess children. Questions concerning the overgeneralization of standardized test results and the low reliabilities of many formal tests have been expressed. For example, the ever popular BVMGT has a stability factor of .33 to .66. This means that this instrument may report errors in visual motor perceptual development that will not be ascertained on repeated measurement.

The major concern with most standardized tests remains the very minimal amount of specific instructional and behavioral management information that they provide. Very little data that might be directly applied to instructing the child is obtained by the teacher (Fuchs & Fuchs, 1991). Instead, the results usually include a general quantitative score (e.g., percentile, grade score), which is used to compare the disabled student to normal children's performance on the same tasks under the same conditions. The quest has become one of finding information more directly related to specific academic behaviors and the types of interventions and level of instructional activity that are essential in preparing an appropriate educational program.

In attempting to supplement the results of formal tests with more behaviorally oriented information, many psychologists have included different types of informal assessment procedures in the evaluation process. Teacher-made tests and various observational techniques have been widely used to combat the problems associated with formal assessment. However, these procedures have their share of problems associated with imprecision. Informal assessment techniques must meet the same criteria for use as do formal procedures or they are worthless in reliably pinpointing specific skill strengths and weaknesses. Observations and informal tests should be used in a teacher's ongoing instructional program as a matter of course.

The search is for a reasonably scientifically sound process by which schools may apply educational and behavioral assessment as a means for planning instructional interventions. Often, improper emphasis has been placed on the grade-equivalent and age-equivalent scores that are obtained from formally published tests. Children are referred to as having an arithmetic age-equivalent score of 7-2, for example, or as reading at a 2.4 grade level. We think that the emphasis upon exact scores incorrectly accentuates the least valuable information in terms of planning interventions for children with a specific learning problem. The detailed information that actually leads to the formulation of the particular score is more important to the teacher. For example, the fact that a teacher knows which letter sounds are known by a child and which sounds are missed on a standardized reading test will probably be more helpful than the teacher's knowledge of the child's grade-level scores. This descriptive skill information provides the teacher with basic data for teaching the child, whereas grade-level scores are usually too general to use in planning specific teaching sequences.

The specific skills approach to assessment is recommended among professionals because of its applicability to various clinical and educational strategies. The information obtained from a specific skills assessment outlines the precise nature of a child's learning and behavioral difficulties in terms of skill strengths and weaknesses. This information is then used as direct intervention to overcome particular difficulties.

The arguments of formal assessment versus informal assessment are not new. The professional literature pronounced (prematurely) the death of formal assessment in the 1970s. Some of those who made such pronouncements have since grown wealthy on the proceeds from the sale of standardized tests. The truth remains that the gross annual national sales of standardized assessment instruments increase yearly. What, then, has happened to the search for the test-curriculum tie-in, and why doesn't the lure of prescriptive curriculum entry and continuous performance monitoring appeal to the profession? One needs data to answer such a question, and the data reside in the predominant practices in the field. Data from special educators taken during a summer special education institute over the past 2 years make one truth self-evident: Experienced special educators, in response to questions on formal and informal assessment practices, are aware of the pitfalls of formal assessment. They see little value in traditional assessment practices and realize that a major gap exists in going from formal assessment data to IEP objectives and the curriculum-enabling steps to achieve those objectives.

CURRICULUM-BASED ASSESSMENT

With all the confusion that exists over assessment practices, there has been a major movement to de-emphasize formal assessment practices (standardized procedures) in favor of informal assessment procedures. One current fad, and it can be measured by the number of chapters that address it in this text, is to utilize curriculum-based assessment materials drawn from the very content of any specific instructional material. The primary rationale for redirecting the assessment process from psychometric standardization to curriculum-based measures is that interventions taken directly from the curriculum achieve greater immediate impact on the task to be learned.

Advocates also argue that there are many other advantages from the use of informal tests which draw their items directly from the curriculum content in use with a child (Howell, Kaplan, & O'Connell, 1979). By using test items that lock directly into the content of a curriculum already in use) psychologists will know precisely how a student can perform on any particular page, skill, output measure, or competency they want to assess. The major argument is that teachers can use the curriculum as the basis for a prescriptive entry and will not need to start on page one, lesson one or proceed in any lockstep manner. Thus, the proponents for curriculum-based assessment justify the time required to make a test and administer it in the time gained in learner efficiency and learner effectiveness.

The more prescriptive in terms of an exact entry point, the greater the amount of content to be covered. The more prescriptive the entry point, the more assurance the teacher will have that the student can master the material and enjoy the success of accomplishment. The more prescriptive the approach, the greater the need for continuous student monitoring. The more feedback students obtain, the greater their success rate. The more data a teacher has on how a student is interacting with curriculum tasks, the faster it can be modified, sped up, or slowed down. The arguments for curriculum-based assessment and curriculum-based management are the very ones used by the current group of educational reformists who advocate performance testing of learner outcomes (Finn, 1991).

Frisby (1987), in an excellent review of curriculum-based assessment, outlines four distinguishing components: (a) student assessment in the classroom, (b) short duration testing, (c) frequent and repeated measurement, and (d) graphed data to allow for monitoring of student progress. Gickling and Havertape (1981) have set down a number of sensible rules in the development of teacher-made tests. They see curriculum as simply a neutral or insignificant occurrence if it does not bring a competitive learner success. They view the failure to interact successfully with the curriculum as producing children who become curriculum casualties.

The goal of all instructional delivery is to provide effective and efficient instruction. Instruction must be capable of challenging students while not overwhelming them and be provided at the students' learning rate (cognitive tempo) while examining optimum learning conditions. The major difficulty is that too frequently students with poor academic achievement (rule-learning skills) often face insurmountable curriculum tasks. These students are left but one choice and that is to pull away from this frustration. As a result they do not achieve the rewards of success, and progress toward skill development is lost in frustration and even anger.

Gickling and Thompson (1985) have established decision rules for teacher-made tests. Students are required to generate typical classroom performance responses to the test items (i.e., read out loud, write response, figure math problems) at high levels of mastery rates (ranging from 75% to 95% correct). The student's cognitive tempo is also considered. What is sought is a smooth, regular flow of response to questions. Normally (Gickling & Thompson, 1988), teacher-made tests are short, requiring 2-3 minutes after the initial entry decisions are made (initial tests may be slightly longer). The simplistic beauty of their approach is that teachers make curriculum decisions on a ratio of known to unknown test items, with the criterion set to ensure entry-level success.

THE ADVANTAGES OF CURRICULUM-BASED ASSESSMENT

Curriculum-Based Assessment Defined

Curriculum-based assessment is defined (Deno, 1987) as ". . . any set of measurement procedures that use direct observation and recording of a student's performance in the local curriculum as a basis for gathering information to make instructional decisions" (p. 41). The breadth of that definition is the major advantage. Curriculum-based assessment is a road map for entry into any curriculum—curriculum being defined as any formal (adapted) plan of study or school culture in which de facto or hidden rules for learning must be known by the student in order to be successful.

Curriculum-based assessment unlocks the range of curriculum possibilities and suggests that a full range of different teaching materials should be included, not just one text in one subject area. This includes a full range of both commercial and teacher-made materials; hence the notion of prescription. Curriculum through the use of curriculum-based assessment can be any material, used in a number of different teaching approaches to accomplish the objectives.

Curriculum is viewed as a series of enabling steps, and the smaller the step the better. The smaller the step, the more control over the task to be learned. The more control over the task to be learned, the quicker the control for learning—defining what is and is not learned can be moved to the student. The more control students have over task and environment, the greater their ownership. Until learned helplessness and amotivational disorders are decreased, a simple repetitive remediation of commercially available text materials will not be effective.

Nelson (1989) examined the use of curriculum-based language assessment and came up with four curriculum-based questions that make a great deal of sense. We have modified these to be slightly more inclusive than language function or development.

1. What kinds of achievement or behavioral skills does a child need to interact successfully with any particular curriculum? A criterion-referenced question.

2. What type of academic or behavioral skills or rule-learning strategies does the child have in interaction with any curriculum content?

3. What are the immediate academic or behavioral skills or rule-learning strategies that a student needs next (immediate) to succeed on a specifically defined aspect of the curriculum?

4. What modifications can be made in the amount of curriculum taught; how it is taught (presented); the requirements for specified aspects (rules or approaches) to be learned; the requirements for examinations (tests) to be taken; changes in student strategies, practice, or approach (learning behaviors or characteristics); and changes in teaching strategies, practices, or approaches that will benefit the student?

This final point is critical. Wesson et al. (1988) draw a powerful observation based on a finding from their research on curriculum-based measurement: Student learning rates and teacher behaviors are predictably stable. There appears to be a strong relationship between the consistency of teaching practice and what is taught, how it is taught, and student learning rate. Does teacher behavior make a difference? In the words of these researchers, and we echo wholeheartedly, "To be successful in effecting change in those relationships [teacher to student relationships] interventions that more strongly impact teacher behavior must be developed" (p. 342).

In the past, one of the major values of special education was that it offered alternative curricula for simplified goals to students not interacting successfully with the regular curriculum. Curriculum-based assessment may restore this practice.

Curriculum-Based Assessment Maximizes Teacher Contact in Time on Instructional Task

Curriculum-based assessment is determining which small, sequentially arranged aspect of any curriculum content (word recognition, reading comprehension, reading vocabulary, etc.; which aspect of math calculation or math reasoning) the student is having difficulty completing. It is a process that emphasizes the interaction between the child and the task to be learned.

Curriculum-Based Assessment Provides Students Corrective Feedback on What They Are and Are Not Learning

Practically all the studies on learning rate (Brophy & Good, 1986) show that acceleration occurs when students have corrective feedback. The logic is simple. When students continue to make errors they do not know they are making, we may be inadvertently reinforcing unwanted learning; we may be contributing to learning that is incorrect. Learning research certainly suggests that optimum learning takes place when students receive immediate and frequent corrective feedback on any response they make. Fuchs and Fuchs (1986), in a meta-analysis of systematic monitoring of student progress, have noted an average gain of .7 standard deviation for handicapped students where continuing data-based management is applied. In performance that means the students would function at the 76th percentile instead of the 50th percentile.

The advantage of technology, from the simplest teaching machine to the most sophisticated interactive system, is that technology can be programmed to offer the learner immediate corrective feedback. Teachers do not always have that opportunity.

Any time that the curriculum is examined in such a way that small, tightly sequenced steps can be taken, then corrective feedback specific to a small segment of what is to be taught is available. The smaller the curriculum segment to be learned, the quicker it can be learned.

Curriculum-Based Assessment Provides Successful Entry and Monitors Continual Progress Made by Students

If the teacher-made test items used in curriculum-based assessment are used concurrently across the curriculum as the student progresses in measuring that progress, the curriculum-based assessment practice has been altered and is one of curriculum-based monitoring or management. The value of curriculum-based management is that it continuously raises the question of the value of the objective(s) being taught and the value of the instructional activities that are known as enabling steps in achieving those objectives. The point in using curriculum-based management is simple: The longer the time between examining the progress made in response to any instructional objective, less feedback is available to either student or teacher. The fewer times that objectives are pulled up to see what progress has been made, the fewer times we ask if the objective was appropriate and continues to be appropriate. Then, too, the objective may be appropriate, but the instructional activities (enabling steps) needed to reach or achieve it are not the right ones, or at least not the right ones for that student.

Studies on the value of IEPs reveal a mixed bag. The concept of long- and short-term goals, and the specification of activities to achieve those goals, provides the basis for accountability. It should assure students, parents, and the educational community that long-term (independent living and competitive employment) goals are known and in place. Curriculum-based management also assures us that short-term goals (objectives) to achieve those long-term ones are also in place; that the short-term goals may be appropriate or they may be the wrong ones; that activities to achieve the objectives may lend themselves to learning efficiency or they may not. Research on IEPs frequently indicates that the IEPs written when the student goes into the program are the very ones that are still in place 6 years later. This is particularly true in the junior and senior high schools.

Curriculum-Based Assessment Overcomes the Conversion of Nebulous Findings from Formal Assessment into Immediate Curriculum Content Steps

Several times in this chapter we have raised the issue of a probable major pitfall in the use of formal test results. Let's say the school psychologist assesses a child for eligibility determination. In the process she or he administers a test and receives an IQ or aptitudinal measure in some area of cognitive function. In addition, achievement test scores are obtained. These data provide a basis for understanding in either perceptual or language learning what a child may be able to do (aptitudinal measures). Using the global IQ scores, we sometimes describe predicted achievement levels, those grade levels in academic areas that the child should be able to achieve. Academic achievement tests are performance measures of functional accomplishment. The achievement test is designed to depict what a child knows in some specific area of academic achievement (i.e., word recognition, reading vocabulary, reading word meaning, sentence or paragraph comprehension). Academic achievement data provide a picture of what the student has achieved to date and therefore we often refer to it as an actual level of achievement.

With predicted and actual levels of achievement we can describe levels of under- or overachievement. These are arbitrary concepts and merely suggest relative learning reference points. A number of people over several years have attempted to use relative learner aptitudinal data (IQ) and academic achievement data to establish curriculum entry. The results from most of these formal test-curriculum entry procedures have not stood up well. Cognitive tests, which are language loaded, may suggest language learning level and rate; a combination of formal tests of visual and auditory perception may suggest areas of learner preference (i.e., auditory perceptual discrimination, or auditory perceptual retention, visual perceptual discrimination, or visual perceptual retention). Knowledge of academic achievement level may offer diagnostic planners information on where to initiate instruction or, better yet, on what levels curriculum-based assessment can begin. It would seem that the results from formal assessment as we have used them make some sense as a first step in developing where the informal assessment process may begin. In that sense formal assessment serves a purpose in addition to determining eligibility for special education services. The task then is two-fold: to facilitate the relationship between formal and informal assessment and to extend both practices forward in such a manner that the results from each process are usable in arriving at a diagnostic whole. In the future one thing that may be necessary is that each of the diagnosticians expand his or her current role. They may screen children for eligibility and then develop more comprehensive assessment roles. It may be that current assessment practices need only a modest nudge to enter into the next era.

Curriculum-based assessment and curriculum-based measurement are decision-making processes. Curriculum-based assessment works with four components and is designed to provide data on what instructional content and curriculum level should be taught as established in instructional objectives and instructional activities. It examines the relationship between learner characteristic, task to be learned, learning environment, and teacher behaviors. Curriculum-based measurement is designed to provide continuous pupil–curriculum interactive data to determine the efficiency and effectiveness of the instructional objectives and instructional activities, assisting the curriculum decision maker in knowing when curricular modification is necessary (Shinn, Rosenfield, & Nancy, 1990).

Is curriculum-based assessment a diagnostic process, or is it an educational assessment practice? It does not diagnose a pathogenic or etiological condition that explains disability or a disabling condition. It is curriculum based, not learner characteristic based. It does promote information critical to socio-family situations, brain–behavioral relationships, or possible causation in a learning problem. A clinician may use the best practices available in curriculum-based assessment only to learn that the child consistently failed to retain anything she taught him. The curriculum was assessed properly; the child was not. (For example, in one case it was later learned that the client had a clinically significant substance abuse habit that was destroying his memory.) Diagnosis of learning and behavioral dynamics may include curriculum-based assessment, but curriculum-based assessment is at best a single entity in the complex diagnostic process, and is not a best diagnostic practice for that reason.

WHAT DEFINES BEST DIAGNOSTIC PRACTICES?

What will happen in the public schools with special education assessment practices in the next 10 years? Two forces are being directed now and will increasingly be emphasized in the immediate future: (1) an increased employment of technology and (2) the return of performance-based practices or accountability. A third force is gathering speed like a brewing thunderhead. With the increase in technology, the business and industrial community will become more knowledgeable about schools and curriculum. They will be making much of the technology we use and the programs that the technology depends on. With the notion of waivers, parents' choice, and site-based management growing with regularity as well, the future for privatization of education draws much nearer, much more rapidly than earlier predictions would have suggested.

The reason this chapter considers these factors is that a few years ago assessment and diagnostic practices were driven by the search for "best practices." That no longer seems true. The courts, the federal government, parents, business/industry, and state and local government have much to say about what is done and how it gets done, including assessment and diagnostic practices. When we entered the profession many years ago as school psychologists, it was customary to peruse professional journals and view the profession in terms of what it established as "best practices." It is clear today that the courts and governmental practices have taken over that role.

The future being described will bring the same litigation to intervention that was brought since the 1960s to assessment. However, the litigation may well hold up the prognostic statements leading to the choice of intervention, the time (efficiency question) that a specific intervention requires, and/or the effectiveness question, the amount of learning that can be achieved.

THE NEXT FIVE YEARS

Over the next 5 years we predict that five major changes will occur that will describe major trends in the field.

Diagnosis Leading to Prognosis

The amount of money spent on psychological assessment is astronomical and growing annually. The percentage of the dollars spent on clinical assessment will require greater justification in the near future. A number of state human service agencies have already begun to devise means by which expenditures are not simply doled out on a per handicapped child or disabled adult basis. Client information will give way to the question of what specific intervention is needed to assist the person to function in a specified environment. The answer to the needed intervention will become the diagnostic question.

Although money spent on special education and rehabilitation is the driving force behind the question, the question itself is a good one and one that has been neglected. It will require that diagnostic teams go beyond the establishment of eligibility as a declaration of services and the receipt of state or federal monies. It will require that a prognostic statement be made that a client's handicapping condition be established in terms of the type and amount of disability.

Type of Disability

Today eligibility requirements are unidimensional. The view is that either the client does or does not have a presenting behavioral problem that reduces his or her functioning in society. Tomorrow, given that we already know many complexities exist among the types of handicapping conditions, the issue of type of handicap will be raised against requirements for service. The model is present in the American insurance industry. Insurance companies do not pay the same amount for toenail surgery as they do for open heart surgery.

Tomorrow state and federal governments will require diagnosticians to outline the interventions required at either fixed or negotiated costs. A child with mental retardation as a primary condition will receive a fixed-cost instructional program. But if that child has sensory (visual and/or hearing), gross or fine motor, or speech problems, then the need for additional specialized interventions will be added. Costs for services will be directly related to the types of services needed.

Today modern medicine saves more children who in years past might not have survived. Today more children are born to parents who have, through poor health practices, environmental toxins, or a long-term health problem, the capability to create conditions for their children that will require long-term management. The result is that more children come to school with multihandicapping or serious handicapping conditions. Education cannot be looked at as a stand-alone intervention; it really never was. To be effective, education must draw from a full range of therapies—

occupational, physical, speech and language, orthoptic, perceptual-cognitive training, counseling, behavioral management, behavioral therapy, other systems of psychotherapy, surgery, medication, and the promise of technology, including rehabilitation engineering.

The multidimensionality of the questions to be asked will determine what sets of interventions are required to realize the goals of education. The very definition of education will change as well. Education in the immediate future will not be defined as reading, writing, and arithmetic. It will be defined as the career interests or career-related ability patterns needed to obtain independent living and competitive employment success.

The difference between the present and the future is that today we establish eligibility for handicapped services based on guidelines that contain minimal entry-level criteria. Tomorrow, the criteria will be related to the type of intervention needed to reduce or eliminate the effects of disability on the child and family.

Amount of Disability

Dealing prognostically with type of intervention sought will probably not work until at least a second dimension, amount of handicapping condition, is configured into the equation by psychologists. Simplistically, psychologists can describe each type of intervention requirement against some level or amount of disability. The reason is that a mild handicapping condition or behavioral problem will require less intervention time than would a severe disability. More sophisticated measures of amounts of disability will be found. Some better prognostic statement than mild, moderate, and severe will be obtained, but for our purposes we can use those as the amount dimensions and see the surface of the question expand simplistically.

Using a simple type and amount of disability paradigm, learning and behavioral disabilities in the future will be described by psychologists in greater diagnostic detail. Specific information-processing behaviors and inappropriate behaviors will be diagnostically detailed. No longer will the clinician be expected to describe global behaviors such as visual motor perceptual function, but specific perceptual and cognitive behavioral variables will be broken into the smallest unit that either theory or method of measurement will permit. Prognostic estimates for the type of intervention needed and the amount of intervention needed will be based on more precise measures. Therefore, considerations in regard to a wide range or band of specific learner characteristics or information processing behaviors will be addressed.

The need in the schools for neuropsychological procedures will be fully established, and neuropsychological descriptions will replace global predictive measures. Both medical and vocational rehabilitation are now neuropsychological predictors instead of IQ. There are several reasons for this, including the fact that many educators and psychologists do not view biological/neurological conditions as relevant to the treatment process and, accordingly, "biological causes for disability have increasingly become of less concern to the practicing special educator" (Senf, 1979, p. 52). The issue may be broader than the often discussed treatment interaction effect, for it is questionable whether the tests now administered relate to brain functioning in the way many neurologists would suggest (Reed, 1974). As Senf (1979) indicated, this linkage is essentially an issue of demonstrating construct validity, for the neuropsychologist must demonstrate that there is a linkage rather than merely claiming so. Many of the psychoneurological assessment instruments are still at the experimental stage and cannot yet demonstrate a precise relationship (Samuels, 1974).

Whether neuropsychology can prove itself worthwhile is a problematic question. How can the already full curriculum of special education and the assessment load placed on school psychologists be stretched even further? How can the teachers and school psychologists engaged in these programs master enough information about neurology and neuropsychology to feel comfortable about the specialty? These questions remain unanswered, yet there are reasons to believe that the approach may ultimately prove beneficial. Reynolds (1981), for example, suggested that the neuropsychological paradigm offers an approach to aptitude–treatment interactions that is built upon strong theories of the outcome of the assessment process. Fuller and his colleagues (Fuller & Friedrich, 1975; Fuller & Lovenger, 1980; Vance, 1981) have found reason to believe that some tests (particularly the Minnesota Percepto-Diagnostic Test) are very useful in screening children with reading handicaps as well as subgroups of handicapping etiologies. What seems to be appearing is exciting improvement in the past dismal state of psychoneurological assessment.

This is the juncture where formal and informal assessment converge. The strengths of both standardized and task-situational assessment will be required. The future will require efficient use of and therefore well-justified (and probably much more expensive) interventions. The role of brain and behavior, especially learning behaviors, will breathe life into the now anoxemic multidisciplinary practices. The question of what drugs expand or contract memory, language learning, or reading comprehension will bring education, medicine, and the behavioral sciences together in a team relationship dependent upon one another for answers and interventions. Once again the crude role that technology plays today will be significantly impacted by instrumentation that would sound like it is from the year 2000 and beyond. But this technology will be upon us before the year 2000, in a magnitude and with capabilities that even today seem remote.

Diagnostic Dimensions

Assessment and gathering of test data as necessary prerequisites to establishment of disability determinations will continue to be major roles for psychologists. Will assessment practices continue only to be all-or-nothing decisions? Simply that a client meets eligibility or does not? That practice presents a major flaw. Human disability is a relative concept, relative to the task and environment. Franklin Delano Roosevelt was none the less an effective president post polio with the loss of lower extremity function than he was before the onset of this condition. Had FDR been a logger in the Pacific northwest, his disability would have required vocational rehabilitation—he would have been handicapped given the tasks to be performed and the environment in which he would have had to perform those tasks. The answer, then, is that assessment practices will cave into diagnostic practices in search of specific hypotheses.

Anyone who thinks disability is not a relative concept need only examine the performance dimensions of mental retardation, learning disabilities, or behavioral disorders. The relative importance of the class, the school, the material to be learned, the amount of emotional support, or the amount of internal vs. external control has more to do with academic learning than IQ ever did. Learning disability has never been a unidimensional characteristic that described a given child. It describes a general undifferentiated, undiagnosed condition. It describes a collection of possible factors that may explain why learning does or does not occur, or occurs at a given efficiency or effectiveness.

Learning disability requires comprehensive perceptual-cognitive, emotional, and control factor diagnosis. Behavioral disorders require similar differential diagnosis, as do mental retardation and the other handicapping conditions of today.

The current problem with assessment as practiced by many psychologists who seek to establish disability against stated criteria is that it fails to raise either etiological or ecological questions. If the client is either sick or well, disabled or not disabled, there is little reason to ask those questions relative to determining the learner's efficiency or effectiveness in various perceptual or in cognitive functions; or determining the amount of emotional support needed to regain reasonable levels of motivation to achieve academically; or in identifying what the control issues are in the use of intellectual function and emotionality as the person displays these other two factors. Diagnosis asks questions that require the development of hypotheses. In that regard it promotes a detailed understanding of how children use their emotionality or intellectual function in response to a certain task in a specified environment.

Differential Diagnosis

One of the foreseeable changes in diagnostic practices is that psychologists will begin to measure learner characteristics and behaviors with as much zeal as we have administered tests in the past. Today psychologists test the test. Tomorrow psychologists may ascertain some given characteristic in an effort to determine how much behavior is usable, what rate of learning will be required for a specific intervention to be effective, and under what conditions the client will respond to interventions. Today we establish reliability of instruments and establish validity of scores that often attempt to find simplistic global or specific measures of some trait according to a predefined method of measurement. Psychologists often administer tests as if our lives, or the lives of those served, depend on them, and treat the scores as if they were true scores defining some critical aspect of a person, if not the person him- or herself.

The time may be drawing to a close on these testing practices and on the use of scores to define whatever it is that such a test measures. What we need are scientific applications, a search for reliability, to determine just how well psychologists are able to define a condition and address its uniqueness in terms of specific interventions.

The question that you have surely formed by now is, Why do we continue to follow the assessment rituals that have become centerplace in our practices? The answer is simple: It often fits the client. When all the interventions look the same, there is no need to differentiate diagnostically among the specific characteristics in the population. Diagnostic differentiation of the population begins when the sensitivity of the interventions requires it. How soon is that? Just about now.

SUMMARY:
CHANGES IN MEASUREMENT TECHNOLOGY

Today behaviors may be measured by means of observations, tests, rating scales, and so on. Many of these procedures, particularly tests, are derived from a set of principles collectively termed *psychometric theory.*

For our current purpose, psychometric theory can be uncritically defined as a set of formal operational rules by means of which behavior is quantified and made interpretable. But it is important to note the word *theory,* for theory invariably emphasizes the use of assumptions, basic ideas that may be modified or discarded when their value is for some reason diminished. Although modifications to theory should occur only after rigorous evaluation, there are data that suggest this event is occurring in traditional measurement approaches. In fact, many of the assumptions of the classic psychometric model have recently been severely criticized, and through these criticisms traditional measurement approaches have been shaken. This chapter has suggested that very important attributes of tests, such as reliability and validity, have been drastically de-emphasized, while attention was directed to using tests to determine if a criterion is achieved by the client in his or her test performance. Other authors (Vance & Stone, 1990) have suggested that the continued refinement of contemporary approaches is inefficient (i.e., a point of diminishing returns between input effort and outcome benefits has been reached).

Still other authors have argued for more drastic alternatives. Howell, Kaplan, and O'Connell (1979) have challenged the traditional psychoeducational model, based upon traditional psychometric theory, and found evidence in favor of a behavioral model, simplistically defined here as a focus upon totally observable behaviors. The psychoeducational approach is seen as ineffective and, for many educational purposes, untenable. In contrast, Feuerstein and his colleagues (e.g., Feuerstein, Rand, & Hoffman, 1979) have reached a similar conclusion regarding current assumptions and practices but have proposed fundamentally differing alternatives. Feuerstein et al. (1979) argue that traditional approaches are static, characterized by stimulus-bound right or wrong responses that summate to allow an estimate of what the student can do, not how the student achieves the particular accomplishment. In contrast, a dynamic model purposefully explores the nature of behaviors and the fundamental interventions needed to correct the inappropriate behavioral response or disability. Moreover, the dynamic model employs interventions during testing, a procedure perhaps shocking to some psychologists trained in the administration of standardized norm-referenced tests!

Changes in measurement technology are inevitable and will appear as will new theoretical models of learning and behavior. This is particularly true of aptitudinal and personality measures, and the much needed next generation of technologically administered and scored informational processing behaviors. As late as the mid-1970s the color cathode ray tube was a rarity, the voice synthesizer was primitive, and the remarkable silicon chips that make microprocessors possible were in their early stages of development and were frighteningly expensive. Today, these technological developments are so commonplace that probably every reader of this paragraph owns more than one of these components. Indeed, computer systems that would have cost tens of thousands of dollars but a few years ago are now available for far less than the cost of a used automobile. So, what we are witnessing is the development of procedures for collecting, monitoring, and evaluating information that are inexpensive and capable of tasks far beyond those of paper-and-pencil procedures.

Electronics make possible a wide range of measurement, such as brain-evoked potential, that heretofore was impossible with paper-and-pencil procedures. They will allow a more comprehensive analysis of performance which, if imputed directly, would save considerable time. In short, it is entirely feasible that technology will greatly alter and expand the range of possibilities in clinical diagnosis. Coupled with changes in our basic conceptual models of human behavior, it may be surmised that powerful assessment devices may be developed within the next few decades: devices that will record brain function in response to specific tasks; devices that will record stress in response to task, presenter, and environment; devices that will record multiple behavior samples relating to biological and behavioral aspects in relationship. Standardization, like the global measures it provides, will be viewed as a significant historic event. Learning of specific tasks and the quality and quantity of behavioral responses will be interindividual as we work to achieve tasks and environments that promote the quality of human performance, function, and response.

REFERENCES

Bender, L. (1978). *A visual motor Gestalt test and its clinical use.* New York: American Orthopsychiatric Association. Research Monograph No. 3.

Bersoff, D., & Hofer, P. T. (1990). Legal regulation of school psychology. In T. Guktin & C. Reynolds (Eds.), *The handbook of school psychology* (pp. 939-963). New York: John Wiley.

Bowman, M. L. (1989). Testing individual differences in ancient China. *American Psychologist, 44,* 857-993.

Brophy, J. E., & Good, T. L. (1986). Teacher behavior and student achievement. In M. C. Wittrock (Ed.), *Handbook of research on teaching* (3rd ed., pp. 368-374). New York: Macmillan.

Deno, S. L. (1987). Curriculum-based measurement. *Teaching Exceptional Children, 20,* 41.

Feuerstein, R., Rand, Y., & Hoffman, M. B. (1979). *The dynamic assessment of retarded performances: The learning potential assessment device, theory, instruments, and techniques.* Baltimore: University Park Press.

Finn, C. E. (1991). *We must take charge: Our schools and our future.* New York: Free Press.

Frisby, C. (1987). Alternative assessment committee report: Curriculum-based assessment. *CASP Today, 36,* 15-26.

Fuchs, L. S., & Fuchs, D. F. (1986). Effects of systematic formative evaluation: A meta-analysis. *Exceptional Children, 53,* 199-208.

Fuchs, L. S., & Fuchs, D. F. (1991). Curriculum based assessment: A review. *Diagnostique, 4,* 28-41.

Fuchs, L. S., Fuchs, D. F., & Hamlett, C. L. (1984). Effects of instrumental use of curriculum-based measurement to enhance instructional programs. *Remedial and Special Education, 5,* 43-51.

Fuller, G. B. (1984). The Minnesota Percepto-Diagnostic Test—Revised manual. *Journal of Clinical Psychology* (Monograph Supplement).

Fuller, G. B., & Friedrich, D. (1975). Three diagnostic patterns for children with reading problems. *Academic Therapy, 10,* 219-231.

Fuller, G. B., & Lovenger, C. (1980). Personality characteristics of three subgroups of children with reading disabilities. *Perceptual and Motor Skills, 50,* 303-308.

Gickling, E. E., & Havertape, J. (1981). *Curriculum-based assessment (CBA).* Minneapolis, MN: National School Psychology Inservice Training Network.

Gickling, E. E., Shane, R. L., & Croskery, K. M. (1989). Assuring math success for low-achieving high school students through curriculum-based assessment. *School Psychology Review, 18,* 81-87.

Gickling, E. E., & Thompson, V. (1985). A personal view of curriculum-based assessment. *Exceptional Children, 52,* 205-218.

Gickling, E. E., & Thompson, V. (1988). *Curriculum-based assessment with Ed Gickling.* Philadelphia, PA: Temple University School Psychology Program.

Glasser, R. (1981). The future of testing: A research agenda for cognitive psychology and psychometrics. *American Psychologist, 36,* 923-936.

Hilliard, A. G. (1979). Standardization and cultural bias as implements to the scientific study and validation of intelligence. *Journal of Research and Development on Education, 2,* 47-58.

Hospodka, V., Sedlak, R. A., & Sabatino, D. A. (1985). Introductory texts in special education: An analysis of citations. *The Journal of Special Education, 19,* 158-175.

Howell, K. W., Kaplan, J. S., & O'Connell, G. Y. (1979). *Evaluating exceptional children: A task analysis approach.* Columbus, OH: Merrill.

Martin, R. (1991). *Litigation in special education.* A presentation to West Virginia Special Educators, Morgantown, WV.

Matarazzo, J. D. (1990). *Psychological assessment versus psychological testing: Validation from Binet to the school, clinic, and courtroom.* Washington, DC: American Psychological Association.

Nelson, N. F. (1989). *Curriculum-based language assessment and intervention.* Washington, DC: American Speech-Language-Hearing Association.

Oakland, T., & Matuszek, P. (1977). Using tests in nondiscriminatory assessment. In T. Oakland (Ed.), *Psychological and educational assessment of minority children* (pp. 52-70). New York: Brunner/Mazel.

Parker, J. D. (1972). There is more to Q than the I: The appropriate use of standardized intelligence tests. In R. C. Schafer (Ed.), *The legal and educational consequences of the intelligence testing movement: Handicapped and minority group children* (pp. 53-86). Columbia, MO: University of Missouri Press.

Reed, H. B. C. (1974). Biological defects and special education: An issue in personnel preparation. *Journal of Special Education, 1,* 9-35.

Reschly, D. F. (1978). *Non-biased assessment and school psychology.* Des Moines, IA: Department of Public Instruction, State of Iowa.

Reynolds, C. R. (1981). Neuropsychological assessment and the habilitation of learning: Consideration in the search for the aptitude X treatment interaction. *School Psychology Review, 10*(3), *343-349.*

Reynolds, M. C. (1975). Trends in special education: Implications for measurement. In M. D. Reynolds & W. Hivehy (Eds.), *Domain-referenced testing in special education* (pp. 161-183). Minneapolis, MN: University of Minnesota.

Sabatino, D. A. (1981). A five year analysis of four selected special education periodicals. *The Journal of Special Education, 15,* 373-388.

Samuels, S. J. (1979). An outside view of neuropsychological testing. *Journal of Special Education, 1,* 57-61.

Senf, G. M. (1979). Can neuropsychology really change the face of special education? *Journal of Special Education, 1,* 51-52.

Shinn, M. R., Gleason, M., & Tindal, G. (1989). Varying the difficulty of testing materials: Implications for curriculum-based measurement. *The Journal of Special Education, 23*(2), 223-233.

Shinn, M. R., Rosenfield, S., & Nancy, K. (1990). *Curriculum-based assessment: A comparison of models.* Reston, VA: ERIC Clearinghouse on Handicapped and Gifted Children.

Vance, H. B. (1981). Intellectual factors of reading disabled children. *Journal of Research and Development in Education, 4,* 11-24.

Vance, H. B., & Stone, J. (1990). A critical review of the PPVT-R: An appraisal. *Diagnostique, 15,* 149-160.

Wechsler, D. (1974). *Wechsler Intelligence Scale for Children Revised manual.* San Antonio: The Psychological Corporation.

Wesson, C., Deno, S. L., Mirkin, P. K., Skiba, B., King, R., & Sevcik, J. (1988). A causal analysis of the relationships among ongoing curriculum-based measurement and evaluation, the structure of instruction, and student achievement. *The Journal of Special Education, 22*(3), 17-22.

2 BEST PRACTICES IN INFORMAL ASSESSMENT

Ted L. Miller

Assessment procedures vary on a number of dimensions including purposes, procedures, personnel responsible for the assessment, and location of the assessment activity. Guerin and Maier (1983) have proposed that informal assessment is distinct from formal assessment in terms of a number of specific dimensions: setting of assessment, data interpretation, technical quality, statistics, and reporting format. Assessment instruments developed within these general orientations may be directed at numerous purposes in the educational process, including screening, identification, diagnosis, and measurement of the outcomes of instruction. Often there is a close alignment with the measurement of specific educational achievement. Thus these devices are frequently directed at the measurement of specific facts, i.e., basic skills. There is reason to believe that this limited focus will become more lenient. Cole (1990) recently suggested that two foci have dominated the conceptualization of educational achievement: (a) an emphasis on basic facts and skills and (b) a growing interest in the achievement of higher order thinking skills and advanced knowledge. Cole indicates that these emphases are currently at odds and in need of integration if a proper conceptualization of educational achievement is to be established. Although informal assessment is increasingly directed toward the measurement of higher order thinking skills, the former continues to be the dominant view of informal measurement activities. This characteristic reflects the behavioral-based, criterion-referenced assessment structure (Popham, 1978) that is often associated with informal assessment. Integration of the two approaches described by Cole has been most notable through the incorporation of the work of Bloom and his colleagues (Bloom, Engelhart, Furst, Hill, & Krathwohl, 1956). In fact, the phrase "higher order thinking skills" (or sometimes "critical thinking skills") is often associated in informal testing with an effort to integrate the work of Bloom et al. into the basic measurement network. In the main, these efforts have been limited and remain secondary in the day-to-day use of informal measures.

This chapter will first discuss the techniques of informal measures of educational achievement in response to the measurement of student acquisition of basic facts and skills. Next, effort will be directed at illustrating the use of these techniques by specific content domains. Finally, the chapter will address concerns and changing pedagogical orientations that may direct the refinement of future informal assessment techniques.

WHY USE INFORMAL ASSESSMENT?

Teachers and other professionals routinely utilize informal assessment techniques. These techniques have generally had criterion-referenced scoring systems, been utilized in direct instructional approaches, and frequently were developed for the measurement of a specific student's progress toward mastering a specific task, that is, formative evaluation (Guerin & Maier, 1983; Scriven, 1967). Thus configured, such tests are extremely useful. They are sensitive to small changes in instructional outcomes and they can be readily developed where no adequate formal instrument is available. Thus informal tests can accomplish some important educational functions well, especially the monitoring of progress or measurement of changes in specific learning outcomes.

These positive attributes of the devices do not limit use to special education. But, because of student characteristics, the behavioral instructional methods generally accepted in special education, and the unique instructional content that is necessary for many exceptional learners, special education is an educational activity that is ideal for informal assessment techniques. The professional has two essential options to meet these demands. The first of these is to develop procedures that are unique to particular events and conditions. The second is to utilize procedures that are not unique but have been configured to meet some specific conditions.

INFORMAL ASSESSMENT APPROACHES

Any number of assessment paradigms can be adapted for use in the informal assessment process. Luftig (1989) suggests seven methods that are frequently employed in informal assessment: observations, checklists, rating scales, questionnaires, interviews, inventories, and teacher-made tests. Luftig's enumeration of approaches that may be considered informal is a useful departure point for discussion. But it is arguable that the order of utilization in actual practice may vary and that other approaches might be added to this list. Shapiro (1984), for example, describes self-monitoring techniques in a manner that implies that these methods could be considered as informal assessment approaches. Further, Salvia and Ysseldyke (1991) simply describe informal assessment as any procedure that is not norm referenced. Despite the difficulty in reaching agreement regarding techniques that can be considered informal assessment devices, the teacher-made, criterion-referenced achievement test must certainly be among the least equivocal. Because it is also among the more commonly used devices, a discussion of the approach is in order.

Informal Achievement Tests

Gronlund (1988) emphasizes the achievement test as essential for measuring classroom outcomes and defines the format based upon the purposes of the test: placement, formative evaluation, diagnostic evaluation, or summative evaluation. In Gronlund's view, the function of the test has dramatic effects upon both sampling considerations and specific item characteristics. Thus an informal achievement test that is designed to be group administered and to measure the progress of students in routine instruction will be quite different from one that is designed for remediating those students who failed the first test. Despite these considerations, Gronlund insists that all informal achievement tests must meet certain criteria:

1. Achievement tests should measure clearly defined learning outcomes.

2. Achievement tests should be concerned with all intended learning outcomes.

3. Achievement tests should measure a representative sample of instructionally relevant learning tasks.

4. Achievement tests should include the types of test items that are most appropriate for measuring the intended learning outcomes.

5. Achievement tests should be based on plans for using the results.

6. Achievement tests should provide scores that are relatively free from measurement errors. (pp. 8-10)

For Gronlund, the heart of any informal test is the interaction of learning outcomes (instructional objectives) and content. The intersection of these elements is displayed in the *table of specifications*. During test construction the table is very valuable for assuring content validity, proper item sampling, level of questioning (from simple knowledge to more complex mental activities), format of specific test items, and other key elements. Figure 2.1 illustrates a table of specifications that might be used with a classroom test. As may be seen, learning outcomes are paired with the content outline and the sample size is noted. This particular outline has also been designed to reflect differing levels of learning as proposed by the hierarchical structure of Bloom et al. (1956). That is, the students are presumably being measured for knowledge, comprehension, and application of the content.

An informal achievement test such as the above is especially valuable in the determination of students' learning of typical classroom topics of instruction. In principle, it can be applied to the measurement of a great many unique learning outcomes. The format does not lend itself well to any measurement topic in which the learning outcome cannot be well specified or the content cannot be agreed to. Further, the process is rather exacting and requires the test developer to allocate a considerable amount of planning and development time to the process. Finally, the process is not efficient for measuring single event learning outcomes. If the instructor wishes to measure the student's ability to accomplish a single discrete task, the process is unnecessary and one simply defines the outcome and the conditions under which the outcome should occur. These conditions are

FIGURE 2.1. *Table of Specifications for a Classroom Test*

OUTCOMES / CONTENT	KNOWS			COMPREHENDS PRINCIPLES	APPLIES PRINCIPLES	TOTAL NUMBER OF ITEMS
	TERMS	FACTS	PROCEDURES			
Role of Tests in Instruction	4	4		2		10
Principles of Testing	4	3	2	6	5	20
Norm Referenced versus Criterion Referenced	4	3	3			10
Planning the Test	3	5	5	2	5	20
Total Number of Items	15	15	10	10	10	60

Note. From *How to Construct Achievement Tests* (4th ed.) (p. 23) by N. E. Gronlund, 1988, Englewood Cliffs, NJ: Prentice Hall. Copyright 1988 by Allyn & Bacon. Reprinted by permission.

then established and the student's ability to complete the task is observed. For example, the format would be fully acceptable for determination of students' ability to demonstrate knowledge, comprehension, and application of geographical facts about a particular country. It would be unnecessary in merely requesting the student to name the capital of Costa Rica.1

A number of authors (e.g., Evans, Evans, & Mercer, 1986; Salvia & Hughes, 1990; Taylor, 1989) have provided substantial descriptions of the concept of *curriculum-based assessment*. This approach has been heavily emphasized in the recent literature; for example, volume 52, issue 3 of *Exceptional Children* (1985) was devoted to this topic. But, in fact, "Curriculum based assessment (CBA) is a new term for a teaching practice that is as old as teaching itself: using the material to be learned as the basis for assessing the degree to which it has been learned" (Tucker, 1985, p. 199). More recently, Salvia and Hughes (1990) have stated that CBA must have six capabilities: curricular match, direct measurement of pupil performance, evaluation of pupil progress on specific objectives as well as more general goals, frequent administration, provision of valid inferences about instructional modification, reliability, and sensitivity to small but important changes in pupil performance. These criteria represent a refinement of the essential characteristics described by Gronlund (1988). The reader is encouraged to investigate the applications that have been devised, especially for exceptional populations (Evans et al., 1986; Idol, Nevin, & Paolucci-Whitcomb, 1986; Salvia & Hughes, 1990; Tindal & Marston, 1990).

Performance Testing

The measurement of many aspects of student learning outcomes in special education is not compatible with the traditional purposes of informal testing. That is, tests of knowledge, such as those described above, measure student skills indirectly. The examiner is left to assume that the appearance of conditions in real-life situations will evoke correct responses. This may be a poor assumption, particularly with exceptional students who may have difficulties not only in remembering but in recognizing the conditions that specify the elicitation of learned behaviors. Accordingly, performance tests attempt to measure skill outcomes in ecologies that are close to the conditions within which the skill will

1 The capital of Costa Rica is San Jose.

ultimately be used. Unfortunately, performance tests are not adequately utilized because they can be much more difficult to prepare and score and because ". . . our past emphasis on norm-referenced measurement has made indirect measurement acceptable" (Gronlund, 1988, p. 85). The emphasis in special education on specific skill development makes performance testing a procedure of choice wherever feasible.

A performance test can be thought of as an increasingly accurate simulation of a real event. The realism of the simulation can vary from a paper-and-pencil abstraction to completion of the actual activity. The degree of realism is often dictated by expense or safety concerns, and the learner often experiences a series of evaluations in which successive tests are increasingly reflective of the actual situation. Gronlund notes that such tests can focus more on the student's knowledge of procedure than on the student's product or a combination of both. Generally, about four levels of realism are required. First, paper-and-pencil tests are designed that place emphasis upon the application of previously learned facts. A second level is often referred to as an identification test, and at this level the student may identify anything from tools to probable sources of malfunctions. The third step is simulated performance (e.g., calculating appropriate change with student customers in a classroom-based store purchase). In the final step, the student actually carries through the specified activity in a totally, or certainly near totally, realistic manner.

A good illustration of the performance examination sequence occurs in driver education. Usually students learn conventional information such as the meaning of signs, followed by the specific capabilities of components of an automobile. This is usually followed by brief, supervised excursions on a closed course. Finally, the student operates the car in real traffic situations. Few teachers would risk omission of the first three steps because the learning of essential prerequisite skills is assured and transfer of these skills can be judged in limited and carefully monitored fashion.

As might be suspected, performance testing is somewhat subjective to score and it is considerably more difficult, and sometimes risky, for the teacher to produce the conditions for testing, at least at the upper levels of the test. Time and money are often factors. But, performance testing should be viewed as an essential form of informal testing for at least two reasons. First, it is the only way that the instructor can be certain that skills are appropriately transferred to the locations in which they are needed. Second, by close observation of the students, the instructor can gain insight into the legitimacy of the trained task. This assures that the skills that are taught are valuable in actual application.

Observation Strategies

No discussion of informal assessment can neglect the use of teacher observation. However, because the procedures outlined here are well known, only a brief outline is offered. Guerin and Maier (1983) dichotomize observation into methods that may be considered direct and those that may be considered indirect. Direct measures demand a high level of specificity of behavior, employ observation of the student's activities at the time they are occurring, and result in an immediate and precise record. *Direct observation* is usually used for describing prespecified, directly observable behaviors. *Indirect observation* procedures often have a format which results in information that is a summary of prior experiences. These procedures are generally used to obtain an overview of less specific, perhaps less readily observable, behaviors.

There are many variations of techniques of direct and indirect observation. The simplest form of direct observation is the *sequence sample* (sometimes called anecdotal record) in which the observer notes instances of specific types of behaviors as these happen to be observed. The observer attempts to note all that appears after the behavioral event and to the extent possible reconstruct all that occurred prior to the event. A more specific adaptation of this approach has been termed *functional analysis* (Bijou & Peterson, 1970). According to Drew, Logan, and Hardman (1988) the approach is founded in behavioral analysis and is especially applicable for assessment in early childhood. (See Bergan, 1977, for more specific rationale.) Direct observation is employed in the setting in which the identified behavior is of concern (i.e., artificial clinical settings are not used). Drew et al. (1988) note that behavior is usually recorded with respect to behavioral deficits or excesses and inappropriate stimulus control. The result is a record that specifies the precise elements of the intervention program. The approach would appear to be exceptionally useful with severe handicapping conditions.

In *chronolog recording*, the observer details a description of all events that are ongoing for a particular time frame. Properly constructed, this report yields a detailed description of the events as they occurred. *Frequency or duration recordings* note the numbers of occurrences or the length of occurrences of specific predetermined behaviors during some specified time and in some specified location. Finally, in the *trait sample technique*, specific predetermined trait characteristics are recorded, usually by frequency. This is a closed system in which the behaviors have been prespecified, often on the basis of some heuristic model. Techniques such as these have been extensively applied to the analysis of teacher-pupil interaction and the observer's task is to specify not only the behaviors but the sequence of the behaviors. These approaches are sometimes termed *observational systems* (e.g., see Simon & Boyer, 1974). A very sophisticated variation, currently more likely to be used in the laboratory than in the classroom, has been termed the *lag sequential approach* (Sackett, 1979). In this approach, relationships among behaviors—not strictly absolute quantities of behaviors—can be statistically ascertained. An example of the lag sequential approach may be found in Slate and Saudargas (1987).

Each of these direct observation approaches has specific strengths and weaknesses. The techniques vary in suitability for the specific circumstances in which data are to be collected, ease of use in terms of observer training, level of attainable reliability and validity, and so forth. One variation of these approaches lies less in specific techniques than in the responsibility of the examinee. That is, the examinee may sometimes be the observer. Such self-observation (Mahoney & Thoreson, 1974; Meichenbaum, 1979; Watson & Tharp, 1989) may be extremely useful in monitoring behaviors such as time maintained in concentrating on task. These procedures have generally gained favor in altering student behavior but they are also useful for monitoring behavior prior to some intervention.

All of these approaches are techniques of analysis that must be specified for a particular case. The practitioner must become familiar with and adept in using and adapting the various possibilities to the peculiarities of specific settings. Guidelines for the use of all of these procedures are readily available. And, because observation strategies are often the basis for evaluating the effects of behavioral assessment (Bellack & Hersen, 1988), single subject research (Tawney & Gast, 1984), and classroom management strategies (Alberto & Troutman, 1990; Kazdin, 1980; Walker & Shea, 1988), practical descriptions can be found in textbooks devoted to these topics.

Indirect approaches to observation are no less common in availability of technique and appearance in practice. All of these procedures are dependent upon the recall and judgment of the observer. The approaches can be used to examine developmental history, current life circumstances, or an inventory of beliefs or attitudes (Guerin & Maier, 1983). Commonly, indirect observation takes place with one of the following procedural formats: *checklists*, in which the observer simply indicates yes or no to some query; *category ratings*, in which the observer selects a word or phrase that best characterizes him or her or some event; *forced choice items*, in which the observer must select a response that is not gradiated (for example the rater is forced to indicate "always" or "never" and is limited to these choices); responses that indicate some level on a continuum of possibilities (e.g., "agree," "somewhat agree," "disagree"). Many instruments are available or the teacher can develop instruments specifically oriented to a particular circumstance.

Indirect measures have the advantage of being able to evaluate a broad range of behaviors and to investigate topics of interest that may not be readily observable. Typically, the approaches are used to summarize impressions that have been gathered over some lengthy period of time. Additionally, the approach is generally less cumbersome to the observer. In fact, in self-report variations of indirect measures, the client-student completes the form independently. Despite these advantages, the techniques may be susceptible to erroneous reporting by the student either purposefully or by errors in judgment, or errors may occur in the reporting process. Pigford (1989), for example, has recently criticized the use of behavioral checklists for the purposes of teacher evaluation. Among the more prominent of Pigford's concerns was the reduction in adequacy of information and the misleading outcomes that can arise from a data technique that de-emphasizes subtleties in the interest of expediency. In the face of such concerns, indirect measures such as checklists have often been considered best utilized when reserved for initial clinical investigations. However, rating scales in particular have recently demonstrated a much more sophisticated technology (Martin, 1988) and some of these concerns are at least partially diminished. In particular, Martin (1988) noted that the vast improvements which have taken place since 1975 have allowed rating scales to become the most often used measurement device for verifying and determining the degree of social maladjustment.

One special approach to indirect observation is the personal interview. Although interviews may be described as indirect, some elements of the direct observation are present in that the interviewer observes the student face to face and in so doing has some opportunity to judge the information that is supplied. Structured interviews have been advocated for use with academic evaluation (Gable & Henderson, 1990; Howell & Kaplan, 1980;

McLoughlin & Lewis, 1990; Zigmond, Vallecorsa, & Silverman, 1983) and the technique has been used to measure learning aptitudes, career-vocational goals, adaptive behavior, social emotional concerns, and other domains of interest. Good interviewing practices require considerable training, and the practitioner completely unfamiliar with the approach is encouraged to seek formal training. Excellent descriptions of the essentials of interviewing can be found in Guerin and Maier (1983), Martin (1988), and McLoughlin and Lewis (1990).

Ecological Analysis

In recent years a growing recognition has emerged that student behavior is closely linked to environmental influences. This recognition has been linked to the emerging emphasis and success of the behavioral orientation in assessment and programming, but a variation of this orientation has been termed *ecological analysis*. As noted by Wallace and Larsen (1978), the professional who employs an ecological perspective attempts to view the child in relationship to the total environment, or rather environments, as opposed to discrete influences. Much of the rationale for this approach is drawn from ethological studies and more recently ecological psychology. For some, the theoretical underpinnings and practical assessment procedures associated with ecological assessment are little more than a modified approach to traditional behavioral methods (Baer, 1977). For others, the approach may be thought of as a partial departure in the emphasis of assessment and eventually the conceptualization of treatment strategies (Rogers-Warren & Warren, 1977; Scott, 1980; Willems, 1974). A number of concepts are relatively unique to ecological analysis of behavior. For example, Scott (1980) defined the behavioral setting, a key concept of ecological analysis, as a collection of time, place, and object properties that demonstrate a standing pattern of behavior. A specific classroom might be identified as such in that it contains object properties unique to it and displays a standing pattern of behavior at some particular time (e.g., arithmetic instruction). The ecologist would suggest that this standing pattern of behavior displays similarity from one occasion to the next and that persons entering this setting would tend to blend in (i.e., adopt behaviors that are characteristic of the setting's major structure). In ecological analysis, observation of these setting characteristics is considered to be essential if the behavior of an individual is to be properly described, characterized, and understood.

Simeonsson (1986) has identified components of the behavioral and ecological approaches that are held in common. Both strategies rely on systematic observation as the primary means of assessment (although observation approaches vary in focus, precision, and methodology). Both approaches may be considered age irrelevant, i.e., the identical procedures may be used regardless of the child's age or handicapping conditions. Finally, all data are criterion referenced. Simeonsson (1986) notes that "the value of ecological and behavioral approaches is that they provide means whereby the contextual and functional influences of the environment can be assessed" (p. 99). However, the procedures and assumptions of the methods diverge somewhat at this juncture. Simeonsson notes that whereas ecological methods focus on the context of the behavior, behavioral approaches focus on stimulus–behavior relationships. Ecological analysis places great emphasis on nonobtrusive observation, whereas behavioral methods emphasize measurement under conditions of experimental control. Whereas behavioral methods operationalize behavior prior to observation, the ecological approach produces inferences only after all recordings have been completed. Finally, the ecological approach views patterns and sequences of behavior as the primary unit of analysis. The behavioral approach usually measures frequency or duration of a particular behavior.

The data collection procedures that are associated with ecological analysis are neither simple nor efficient to apply. Data collection generally begins with a long narrative record, often accomplished from a transcribed tape recording. The intent of the record is to describe thoroughly the events that the child is undergoing. The record is extensive and comprehensive, but it is not at this stage evaluative. Generally, several records are collected, resulting in many pages of descriptive text. The evaluator then attempts the process of *unitization*, that is, structural units of naturally occurring behaviors are identified and characterized. These activity units (AUs) are identified by beginning and ending points of behavior sequences and the collected AUs are then categorized. Typical AU titles might be *talks with classmates, stares out window, runs from wall to wall, attempts to attract teacher's attention,* and so on. Ultimately, a summary of the AUs is developed, often by percentage of time that the student is engaged in them.

Although the methods of ecological analysis are complex and time consuming, the procedure does tend to reveal insights into student behavior that may otherwise be overlooked. The evaluator may discover proportions of time that are devoted to specific behaviors, or identify specific environmental antecedents to specific behaviors. These data can help establish areas in which an emphasis on behavioral change should be considered. The data can also be invaluable for the identification of components of the environment supporting erroneous behaviors. Moreover, the data are unique in that no prestructured elements are specified, and unnoticed or unanticipated elements of behavior can emerge without the transducer or filtering process (Barker, 1965; Schoggen, 1978) imposed by more traditional structured, obtrusive data collection procedures. For readers with a particular interest in ecobehavioral analysis, excellent resources are provided in Benner (1992) and Schroeder (1990).

A Comment on General Informal Assessment Approaches

These approaches provide a significant expansion of the data collection procedures that are available to practitioners through formal methods of data collection. Care must be taken in the selection of appropriate procedures, and the development of specific measurement instruments must be based upon sound guidelines. "Informal" should not imply technically inferior. The value of well-developed informal measures is increasingly being recognized. Tidwell (1980), for example, emphasized the importance of the appropriate use of informal assessment for one group of professionals. Noting that school psychologists are well known as test givers by teachers, the author also suggested that "they *are not* seen by classroom teachers as providing the kind of information that is helpful to teachers in their day-to-day instructional struggles" (p. 210). Tidwell's arguments proceed to support the notion that "informal assessment can not only alter the *image* of school psychologists so that they are perceived as more useful, but it can also actually *make them more useful and effective* professionals" (p. 210). Tidwell suggests several reasons that support the use of informal assessment, including instructional payoff, facilitation of a consulting orientation between school psychologists and teachers, and supporting the needs of parents by involving them in the overall assessment process. However, Tidwell also emphasizes the very real concern that informal procedures must meet appropriate quality standards. As noted by the author, a primary reason for the development of formal procedures was that informal tests had generally failed to guarantee appropriate quality standards.

There may be many reasons why informal tests have so often been found to be inappropriately constructed, including a lack of technical sophistication on the part of test developers. However, because the instruments are so idiosyncratic—often utilized on only one or at most a few occasions—there may be strong inclination to devote less than adequate energy to development. This is unfortunate because, as Tidwell suggests, the procedures are exceptionally useful for many tasks and related considerations in assessment. In fact in some instances, at least as defined here, informal approaches may constitute not only the best but the *sole* available means of collecting useful information.

How might this be resolved? Several considerations might be effective in resolving this qualitative dilemma. The assessment specialist should always exercise care in the selection (or development) and use of informal techniques. Additionally, the specialist should incorporate findings with corroborating evidence including available formal assessment data. On occasions where formal and/or multiple informal procedures do not provide similar perspectives on the assessment outcomes, differences should be carefully inspected and reconciled. These precautions can help eliminate the likelihood of drawing conclusions that are *a priori* invalidated as a result of faulty assessment devices. Models for data integration have been provided by Bornstein, Bornstein, and Dawson (1984), Bott (1990), Evans et al. (1986), Luftig (1989), Salvia and Hughes (1990), Simeonsson (1986), and other authors. These models typically demand multiple points of evidence, consideration of the validity of the information, and consensual validation of conclusions through the use of multiple professionals' input. Following the guidelines in these models will help assure that faulty conclusions are not drawn on the basis of improper assessment approaches or practice.

ASSESSMENT DOMAINS

Although each of the above basic techniques can be applied to many domains of assessment, if appropriate care is taken to assure the use of qualitatively adequate procedures, specific approaches tend to be especially adaptive to certain instructional content. Also, some basic procedures are combined or modified for the assessment conducted in specific domains. The following is intended to provide a brief synopsis of the procedures most commonly used within some domains of assessment–

school personnel encounter. Specialized approaches are described where warranted.

Reading

The assessment of reading, as is the case with many academic areas of instruction, commonly involves both formal and informal procedures. However, unlike some areas of academic instruction, a very significant number of formal measures are available (Salvia & Ysseldyke, 1991), although some of the procedures generally described as formal measures do, in fact, also display characteristics associated with informal techniques. For example, several published oral reading tests are technically inadequate for use as formal measures but may be useful when employed to respond to issues more characteristic of informal assessment (Salvia & Ysseldyke, 1991). Whether these instruments are best considered formal or informal is problematic for the evaluator because the use of a device for reaching a decision that its technical merits cannot support is a major technical blunder. Thus, because of the importance of reading, its multiple conceptualizations as a process (Tindal & Marston, 1990), the numbers of measurement instruments available, and the sometimes blurred distinction between formal and informal assessment devices noted above, readers with particular interest in reading assessment are strongly encouraged to begin their study with a thorough examination of the conceptualization of the reading process and devices fully accepted as formal measurement techniques.

As might be expected, such remarkable controversy makes a discussion of reading assessment difficult and more or less satisfactory depending upon the perspective one holds on the activity termed reading. Many, but certainly not all, discussions of reading assessment emphasize devices designed to assess (a) word attack/word sequence (sometimes simply decoding) and/or (b) reading comprehension (usually divided into subcomponents such as literal and inferential comprehension). But, Tindal and Marston (1990), among others, do not agree that this traditional view remains an effective construct. These authors cite extensive research to support their contention that reading is best conceptualized as a unitary model "in which the focus is not on identifying separate subskills of the reading process" (p. 143). Obviously, such a dramatically modified approach, if generally accepted, has extensive implications for virtually all current formal and informal assessment procedures. For the present time, however, many reviewers continue to discuss reading along the dichotomy outlined above. Recent years have, however, demonstrated an increasing theoretical interest in and corresponding measurement emphasis directed towards the assessment of comprehension as opposed to decoding.

In this vein, Luftig (1989) has provided an excellent overview of the procedures commonly used in the measurement of reading. A staggering array of procedures (generally considered formal) include reading tests, oral reading tests, diagnostic reading tests, reading comprehension tests, and criterion-referenced tests. Informal measures include: observations, informal reading inventories, error analysis, checklists, and the cloze procedure. McLoughlin and Lewis (1990) expand this list of informal procedures to include diagnostic reading procedures and criterion-referenced tests. Salvia and Hughes (1990) discuss curriculum-based assessment of reading and emphasize the concept of performance measures applied to various aspects of reading assessment. As may be seen, there does not appear to be consensus regarding which procedures can be considered informal measures of reading. Some of the more generally accepted are briefly described below.

Criterion-Referenced Tests

The practitioner can certainly construct useful criterion-referenced tests along the lines described earlier in this chapter. Additionally a number of very useful, published criterion-referenced tests of reading are available to the practitioner. Among the more popular of these devices are the BRIGANCE Diagnostic Comprehensive Inventory of Basic Skills (Brigance, 1983) and System FORE (Bagai & Bagai, 1979). Other systems are described and evaluated for specific technical merit in Luftig (1989), McLoughlin and Lewis (1990), and Salvia and Ysseldyke (1991).

Observations

Observation strategies can also follow many of the general approaches outlined earlier in this chapter. However, many other approaches that will be mentioned in this section contain, as a part of the procedure, elements that could be termed observation. Informal inventories, error analysis strategies, the cloze procedure, and other methods include some elements of observation. Observation may also be used to monitor student time on task and other variables involving reading. The teacher may, for example, count the number of occasions that a student leaves the seat during a reading lesson, or the number of questions asked or the duration of apparent reading activity before undertaking the completion of some other task. These procedures may be more or less direct and they may be more or less specific in behaviors that are measured. Additionally, in some cases the teacher may find it useful to utilize self-monitoring (i.e., direct the student to observe and record personal behavior).

In practice, observation may be more directed to the analysis of decoding than to the analysis of comprehension, but this is certainly not always the case. When a teacher notes answers to questions that parallel reading assignments, the teacher is employing a form of observation. Variations of this approach are fairly abundant. One interesting illustration of the use of observation to assess comprehension can be found in a subtest (Reading/Understanding) of the Kaufman Assessment Battery for Children (Kaufman & Kaufman, 1983). Although the KABC is a formal test, the basic approach could be readily adapted to measure specific instructions of importance or possibly to gauge comprehension levels. The subtest requires students to read a passage and then pantomime the statement. For example, the statement might request that the child pretend to mix up some paint. The examiner then observes the child's actions to determine if the directions were understood. This approach uses observation effectively and in a manner that children seem to enjoy.

As may be seen, observation is a useful and integral part of the assessment of reading. The evaluator is certain to utilize observation techniques whether independently or as part of other informal approaches.

Checklists

Observation procedures must be directed (i.e., focused upon critical points that are to be measured). Checklists are often utilized for this function. In the measurement of reading there may be several ways that we can think of the function of checklists. First, there are checklists that are focused primarily on decoding skill, usually organized by skills to be learned at particular grade levels. Similarly, checklists are available that focus on comprehension in similar manner. Sometimes a more or less integrated network is offered within a single checklist. Finally, because reading is so fundamental for success in academic activities, checklists exist to examine attitudes directed toward reading and cognitive development in relationship to reading behaviors. Useful checklists can be found in Evans et al. (1986), Guerin and Maier (1983), Hammill (1987), McLoughlin and Lewis (1990), and many other texts.

The practitioner must be careful to examine checklists for their suitability for a particular use. For example, it is very important to use curriculum skill checklists that are in parallel with the curriculum that is taught (curriculum-based assessment) or to use attitudinal indices that are developmentally appropriate.

Informal Reading Inventories

Informal reading inventories (IRIs) are among the most popular and common informal devices for assessing the reading proficiency of children, adolescents (Olson & Gillis, 1987), and adults (Cheek, Kritsonis, & Lindsey, 1987). Despite the popularity of IRIs, some authors (e.g., Anderson, 1986; McKenna, 1983) have pointed out technical weaknesses that should be carefully considered by users of these devices. These criticisms include small samples of behavior, standardization inadequacies on published examples, or varying estimates of passage difficulty (e.g., variations in the formats of the published test such as the types of errors that are scored and the degree of curriculum parallel that is apparent). As a result, it is impossible to assume that responses on one test necessarily relate strongly to results from another test, a significant problem if the examiner wishes to equate outcomes (McKenna, 1983). Spache (1981) has also questioned the logic of inferring silent reading capacity from measures of oral reading. Published examples of the IRI have been provided by Burns and Roe (1989), Ekwall (1986), Silvaroli (1986), and others.

Structurally, virtually all forms of the IRI contain a graded word list and a series of graded word passages. The latter are established for grade-level representativeness using any of several procedures to estimate reading level (e.g., Fry, 1972). Generally, the word lists are used to establish quickly the level of the passages that should be used to begin oral reading by the student (Duffelmeyer, Robinson, & Squier, 1989). The student then reads passages aloud while the teacher scores oral reading errors using unique symbols to denote specific types of predesignated errors. Subsequent examination for oral reading miscues (i.e., consistent patterns of inappropriate reading responses) is termed *error analysis* (Luftig, 1989). At the end of specific passages, students are asked to answer questions that provide indication of comprehension of the material. Generally, questions are stated in such fashion that a number of possible types of comprehension can be assessed. Finally, based upon specific criteria (that vary from test to test), the student is profiled for levels at which reading can be conducted independently or considered useful for instruction (but will require assistance) and frustration, and levels of reading that should not currently be attempted. In some cases, specific tests may include listening comprehension, a level at which the student cannot read but can profit from others reading the materials aloud. IRIs thus attempt to estimate suitability of reading materials for particular students, describe decoding errors that are made in oral reading, and estimate comprehension by level and type (e.g., literal and inferential).

IRIs contain an intrinsic diagnostic face validity and can be useful if outcomes of the devices are not overgeneralized. The instruments do have significant technical deficiencies and therefore some degree of measurement error. For this reason the teacher is often well advised to utilize reading materials that are known to have been or that will be used by the child. Reading difficulty formulas (for estimating paragraph reading difficulty) can be found in many locations including Evans et al. (1986). An analysis of considerations for text selection for adolescent students has been offered by Olson and Gillis (1987), while a discussion of considerations in the use of the IRI (and other informal assessment devices) with adults has been provided by Cheek et al. (1987). Any of the oral reading error guidelines that are available can be used, and an excellent summary of guidelines for evaluating comprehension can be found in Luftig (1989) and Nessel (1987). Although somewhat time consuming, teachers and other diagnosticians can often benefit from constructing personalized IRIs. But, whether commercial or personally developed IRIs are utilized, the approach is not difficult to use and the diagnostician should encounter little trouble attaining proficiency.

Cloze Procedure

The cloze procedure was first introduced by Taylor (1953), although the technique seems to have been popularized by Bormuth (1968). In any case, the approach is used to determine the suitability of reading material of known grade level for a particular student. To use the procedure, one popular approach (variations exist in the development of the approach, see Tindal & Marston, 1990, pp. 168-169) advises the teacher to select passages at known grade level; each passage is approximately 250 words in length. Every fifth word is then blocked out and, in a typed copy of the sample, equal length lines are inserted for the missing words. According to Bormuth (1968), if the student supplies between 44% and 57% of the missing words the passage is at the student's instructional level. Levels above this indicate that the passage is acceptable for independent reading. There is debate regarding the meaning of these results, Tindal and Marston (1990), for example, presented a summary of studies which suggest that the outcomes of the cloze procedure are only moderately correlated with teacher judgments of grade placement and more traditional measures of reading comprehension. A part of this discrepancy may reside in two factors. First, the cloze procedure is based upon a quite different view of achievement than most contemporary measures, drawn as it is from the gestalt psychology concept of closure. Second, regardless of the merits of the general approach, variations in the technique for conducting the cloze procedure are certain to introduce additional variance in the comparisons of scores with estimates of performance drawn from other sources. As a result there is a concern for the validity of the procedure; in fact, Tindal and Marston indicate that there are questions as to exactly what the test does measure. Still, there is a considerable amount of research on the cloze technique and many researchers appear to feel that the approach is a valuable, if perhaps eccentric, measure of reading comprehension.

Categorizing Errors in Reading (Error Analysis)

Morsink and Gable (1990) have proposed a system for evaluating student reading proficiency based upon systematic analysis of the student's errors. In effect, the process is a logical extension of several procedures and is made up of several steps. Step one requires the examiner to initiate a systematic sampling technique in order to identify error patterns. While the student reads orally, the teacher notes errors but does not correct them (Salvia & Hughes, 1990, have referred to this process as *topological analysis*). The process may be conducted with materials of several levels of difficulty, and both qualitative and quantitative information is acquired. Typically patterns of decoding errors are noted, but it is quite likely that the examiner will also wish to conduct measures of comprehension, perhaps utilizing miscue analysis (Goodman & Burke, 1972). Step two is retesting to confirm that any original patterns of errors are in fact standing patterns and not simply the result of carelessness or anxiety. Step three is a structured interview of the student during which faulty approaches to decoding are verbally conveyed. If the student is unresponsive, the evaluator may ask specific questions based upon the assumptions formulated on the basis of the original testing. Step four is the construction of a record of findings as a basis for initiating instruction and, logically, a baseline by which to evaluate instructional effects.

Performance Measures

Salvia and Hughes (1990) have described a procedure termed *perform-ance measures*. This is a sequence that first assesses the student's ability to pronounce letters and groups of letters in isolation and follows the skill sequence to end with the student pronouncing words in passages that are taken from the school readers. According to these authors, the emphasis is on both accuracy and speed. A specific seven-step sequence of perform-ance measures is outlined: "fluency in saying sounds in isolation, fluency in saying nonsense words, fluency in saying phonetically regular words, oral reading accuracy and rate on passages from text, fluency in saying prefixes and suffixes in isolation, fluency in saying endings, prefixes, and suffixes with nonsense root words, fluency in saying words that can be analyzed structurally" (Salvia & Hughes, 1990, pp. 128-132). This ap-proach appears to be an easily devised technique that can readily be adapted from classroom materials and appears to yield useful informal assessment results.

Retellings, Think Alouds, and Dictated Stories

A number of unique approaches to assessment of specific aspects of reading are available in the literature. Three are presented here.

Retellings of stories are, as the name implies, restatements or rewritten versions of an original story. According to Kalmbach (1986), retellings have been used for at least 60 years as a means for the assessment of a variety of topics, the most prevalent of which is comprehension, especially reading comprehension. Although the approach may be more associated with the laboratory as a research tool rather than the classroom as a diagnostic tool, Kalmbach argues that the devices are useful to teachers if, "instead of comparing retellings to original stories, teachers analyze the structure of retellings as stories" (Kalmbach, 1986, p. 327). In particular, Kalmbach suggests that teachers can learn about the points that students see in stories and the problems that students are having organizing the various elements contained in the story. The author provides considerable detail in the use of the procedure and offers illustrations that would be of value to the practitioner attempting to conduct this interesting approach to the measurement of reading comprehension.

Wade (1990) indicates that even informal assessment devices have received criticism as too narrow in their emphasis on mastery of serially related discrete skills. The author points out that research in comprehension and metacognition suggests that reading is a very complex process that exceeds a conceptualization of it as simply a collection of discrete skills. *Think alouds* are "verbal self-reports about . . . thinking processes—to obtain information about how they attempt to construct meaning from text" (Wade, 1990, p. 442). Wade provides an overview of the processes involved in comprehension, a taxonomy of different types of comprehension that might be found, and a discussion of instructional approaches as well as an assessment of the strengths and weaknesses of the approach. The article is constructed in sufficient detail that the reader could reasonably expect to attempt to implement the approach. Think alouds appear to be a useful approach typical of some evolving concerns of informal assessment that will be discussed in some detail later in the chapter.

Agnew (1982) emphasizes that young children are often not aware of the technical features of reading, that is, the code conventions that make reading possible. In Agnew's view, *dictation* (a part of the whole language approach) provides a means by which the teacher can probe the child's understanding of these conventions. As might be expected, the process begins with the development of a story by a child or by a group of children. A seven-step procedure is then placed in motion. The steps in this procedure are relatively simple to accomplish and appear to be capable of yielding interesting and valuable information. The reader is referred to Agnew (1982) for examination of specific details of the process.

Mathematics

Mathematics assessment is generally considered to be more "clearcut" than is reading assessment (Salvia & Ysseldyke, 1991, p. 422). In formal testing this translates into fewer diagnostic tests and more similarity between those tests that are available. Diagnostic tests usually sample content, operations, and applications and, in general, most informal tests measure mathematics achievement in one or more of these areas. As noted by VanDevender and Harris (1987), informal techniques are necessary for pinpointing exactly what the student has learned and precisely what is to be taught.

Luftig (1989) suggests that at least the following approaches can be used in the assessment of mathematics: prerequisite abilities (including intelligence measures and developmental readiness; see Guerin & Maier, 1983, for an excellent discussion of these dimensions), formal assessment devices (including diagnostic tests and other commercially prepared tests), criterion-referenced tests, and, finally, informal procedures. Luftig indicates that the following may be considered informal measures: mathematical inventories (of which at least five are widely available), checklists, interviews, and error analysis. McLoughlin and Lewis (1990) include the concepts of probes and questionnaires. The reader has been introduced to many of these general approaches through previous discussion, particularly in the assessment of reading.

Mathematics Inventories

Inventories are especially useful in assessment conducted in this domain because there is generally more agreement on specific skills to be learned and specific sequences of introduction. Luftig (1989) notes that it is often advisable for the teacher to create the inventory from the particular curriculum because this will nearly assure a match between assessment and the skills that are taught. If the practitioner chooses to accept a model rather than create a sequence through curriculum analysis, Guerin and Maier (1983) have provided a useful if somewhat abbreviated skill sequence, while more detailed skill hierarchies can be found in Bartel (1986), Enright (1983), Reisman (1978), and other sources. A very thoughtful and useful content taxonomy was developed by Tindal and Marston (1990) based upon the work of Glennon and Wilson (1972). In this case the authors provided an integrated model of assessment that is in parallel with the taxonomy, and specific guidelines for assessment practice are provided. Figure 2.2 provides a representation of the content taxonomy (p. 238) and Figure 2.3 depicts the assessment model developed by Tindal and Marston (1990, p. 241).

Checklists

Checklists are effective for providing the practitioner a quick method for evaluating the completion of some specific task by a student or for

FIGURE 2.2. *Example of a Content Taxonomy in Mathematics*

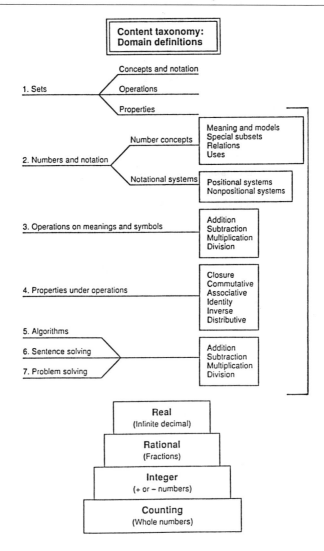

Note. From *Classroom Based Assessment: Evaluating Instructional Outcomes* (p. 238) by G. A. Tindal and D. B. Marston, 1990, Columbus, OH: Merrill. Copyright 1990 by Charles Merrill. Reprinted by permission.

FIGURE 2.3. *The Model of Assessment Developed by Tindal and Marston (1990)*

Grade 1
Numbers to 10
Addition and subtraction facts to 6
Addition and subtraction facts to 8
Addition and subtraction facts to 10
Place value to 100
Time and money
Addition and subtraction facts to 12
Geometry and fractions
Addition/subtraction of 2-digit numbers
Measurement
Addition/subtraction facts to 18

Grade 2
Addition and subtraction facts to 10
Place value to 100
Addition and subtraction facts to 14
Addition and subtraction facts to 18
Place value to 1,000
Time and money
Addition of 2-digit numbers
Subtraction of 2-digit numbers
Geometry and fractions
Measurement
Addition/subtraction of 3-digit numbers
Multiplication

Grade 3
Addition and subtraction facts
Numeration and place value
Addition
Subtraction
Time and money
Multiplication facts
Division facts
Measurement
Multiplication facts
Division
Fractions and decimals
Geometry

Grade 4
Addition and subtraction facts
Numeration
Addition and subtraction
Multiplication and division facts
Graphing
Multiplying by 1-digit numbers
Dividing by 1-digit numbers
Measurement
Fractions and mixed numbers
Multiplying by 2-digit numbers
Dividing by 2-digit numbers
Decimals
Geometry

Grade 5
Numeration
Addition and subtraction
Multiplication
Dividing by 1-digit numbers
Dividing by 2-digit numbers
Graphing
Number theory and fractions
Addition and subtraction of fractions
Multiplication and division of fractions
Measurement
Addition and subtraction of decimals
Multiplication and division of decimals
Geometry
Ratio and percent

Grade 6
Numeration
Addition and subtraction
Multiplication
Division
Graphing
Number theory and fractions
Addition and subtraction of fractions
Multiplication and division of fractions
Addition and subtraction of decimals
Multiplication and division of decimals
Measurement
Geometry
Ratio and percent
Integers

Grade 7
Addition /subtraction of whole numbers
Multiplication/division of whole numbers
Equations
Addition and subtraction of decimals
Multiplication and division of decimals
Number theory
Addition and subtraction of fractions
Multiplication and division of fractions
Ratio and proportion
Percent
Measurement
Geometry
Perimeter, area, and volume
Probability and statistics
Integers

Grade 8
Whole numbers and operations
Decimals
Number theory
Fractions
Solving equations
Geometry
Ratio
Percent
Measurement
Perimeter, area, and volume
Integers
Rational numbers
Probability and statistics
Real numbers and the coordinate plane
Right triangles, similarity, trigonometry

indicating those skills that are already mastered (i.e., for maintaining a record of student accomplishments). Checklists are technically most accurate and defensible as assessment devices when they are used in parallel with skill hierarchies as described in mathematics inventories such as those mentioned above. In using checklists, the practitioner should exercise care to be certain that (a) the correct skills in the correct sequence are being investigated, (b) behaviors are sampled more than once thus minimizing errors in the judgment of student competency, and (c) the skill hierarchy is followed with precision.

Interviews

Ginsburg (1987) has described a flexible interviewing technique that appears to be very useful in the assessment of mathematics. The author notes that the technique "has great potential for instructional assessment" (p. 443) and is "an enormously powerful technique for identifying students' thinking and learning processes" (p. 459). Ginsburg considers flexible interviewing to be a complex process that has four components: establishing rapport, discovering thinking processes and strategies, describing how these processes operate, and ascertaining levels of competence. Helpful guidelines that would allow a reader the opportunity to attempt the approach are presented (Ginsburg, 1987, pp. 443-460).

Error Analysis

Error analysis is described in nearly all discussions of the informal assessment of mathematics. The procedure has long been utilized and in some ways is a counterpart to oral reading analysis procedures described earlier. There are several variations of error analysis; one of the currently most comprehensive discussions is offered by Ashlock (1990). Citing the work of Roberts (1968), four categories of errors were identified: wrong operation, obvious computational error, defective algorithm, and random response. Roberts (1968) noted that the largest proportion of errors were the result of defective algorithms except for students in the lowest quartile. (These students made more random responses, a probable indication of near total failure to learn the algorithms.) Ashlock provides some discussion on the patterns of errors that are often seen as well as reasoned estimates of why the particular error patterns emerge. Guidelines for instructional practices that will help prevent the appearance of defective algorithms and other inappropriate learning are also included. However the most important part of this book for the current discussion lies in its presentation of children's error patterns in a format that is designed to instruct the reader to detect algorithmic errors. The text also includes a useful bibliography for assessment of mathematics.

Questionnaires

Questionnaires are useful when students can read and write at an appropriate level. The format may be sentence completion or it may require the student to provide a response to a complete statement. It seems possible that potential assessment concerns could be addressed ranging from specific skills that the student can or cannot accomplish to attitudes regarding mathematics and mathematics instruction.

Despite the efficiency that is possible with questionnaires (they can be group administered, for example), there are at least two potential drawbacks. First, we must make the assumption that students can read and write at a satisfactory level. They must be able to comprehend the question and formulate an accurate response, and this is certainly not always the case. Second, we must be relatively assured that the student is motivated to answer the questions in a satisfactory manner. Some students may be so disenchanted with the necessity of composition that responses are abbreviated and inaccurate—anything to get the task done. Thus, in many cases, the assurance of acceptable validity implies that the evaluator should forgo questionnaires and conduct interviews.

Thinking Aloud and Building Sentences

VanDevender and Harris (1987) describe two techniques somewhat similar to those described by Kalmbach (1986) and Wade (1990) for reading instruction. *Thinking aloud* simply requires the student to describe the steps in the algorithm that are being applied to solve the problem. The strategy not only spares the evaluator the deductive process of determining the error from work samples but may also provide insight into the student's cognitive strategies for solving the stated problems.

The authors also describe a process termed *building sentences*. In this process, the student sometimes uses wood blocks to illustrate the meaning of problems, or the student may be required to verbalize the steps in the solution of word problems. In either case the practitioner has the opportunity to investigate the student's thought processes relative to solving the problem.

Written Language

McLoughlin and Lewis (1990) note the complexity of written language and the fact that the development of the skill is late in the communication sequence that begins with speech. Further, they note that written language is related to but quite distinct from other forms of communication, especially in that writing is a solitary act that eliminates all immediate possibility for clarification that can emerge from spoken language (e.g., restatements that occur as a result of the facial expressions of a receiving individual). There are certainly many skills involved in the development of written messages. First, the writer must conceptualize a message, whether that be a note reminding the writer to purchase cat food or the far more complex task of constructing a good letter to the manufacturer convincingly describing the quality of the cat food. Part of the conceptualization may require research of specific information essential to completion of the thoughts that are to be developed. The writer then must have several skills that are essential to the final written message. These include knowledge of grammar, punctuation, spelling, production of script (by hand or the use of the keyboard), and possibly vocabulary (though assessment of vocabulary is often conducted in terms of receptive language skills and reading). Considering the complexity of these components, and there are likely others, it is little wonder that written communication is generally considered to be one of the most advanced human skills.

Although many of these areas are assessed, two factors need be considered. First, many of the components are judged in a very informal manner. Judgment of the theme or content of written production, whether for creativity or adequacy of the message, for example, is generally very subjective. Why is one author's style particularly appealing? Why is a book eloquent to one and obscene to another? Such complex issues, even with classroom compositions, are often difficult to address. Thus, point two, much assessment of written composition tends to emphasize the somewhat more mechanical aspects that include spelling, grammar, punctuation, and production of script. We will concentrate here on a few illustrations in the measurement of spelling and written expression.

Spelling

A number of approaches are often attempted to facilitate the assessment of spelling. These include work samples (that is, error analysis conducted on work samples). Another approach is to use informal inventories of words, often drawn from classroom texts, to determine the student's ability to spell a selected group of words. The words may be selected based upon specific configuration of structural components (i.e., specific vowel sounds or syllabication patterns). Teachers may also use observation strategies, interviewing techniques or the cloze procedure, or teacher-made criterion-referenced tests can be developed. It is apparent that many of the basic techniques used in the assessment of reading and mathematics are similarly useful in the assessment of spelling.

Written Expression

As is the case with spelling, the informal assessment of written expression generally consists of adaptations of techniques that have previously been discussed. These include rating scales and checklists, sample analysis, and observation, including observations for interest in writing. A few features of writing are unique; measures of fluency [often using thought (T) units], sentence analysis by structure and type (Polloway & Smith, 1982), and specialized vocabulary analysis (Cartwright, 1969; Polloway & Smith, 1982) are among these.

SUMMARY ON DOMAIN-BASED INSTRUMENTS AND SOME CONCERNS FOR USE

As this review has made clear, there has been an enormous increase in the development, professional acceptance of, and actual application of informal assessment devices within the past few years. Some of this has probably resulted from disenchantment with formal approaches, at least for many educational purposes, and the litigious atmosphere that has painfully exposed the devices' limitations. This review has been limited to a very few of the assessment domains in which these instruments have been applied. For example, informal procedures have been developed and adapted for preschool assessment, vocational education assessment, assessment of communication-interaction in the classroom and social behavior, and learning strategies assessment. The latter (and, to a somewhat lesser extent, preschool assessment) is particularly interesting as it represents the informal assessment of aptitudes as opposed to the more typical use of informal procedures in the measurement of specific skills. This implies that the domains—interests—associated with informal assessment are steadily expanding.

The professional should be aware that informal practices are not always above professional skepticism. Some of the approaches described in the current chapter are better researched and technically more sound than are others. Some are simply not adequate for many assessment purposes. There is a danger that, in sincere efforts to improve educational measurement, informal procedures will be used inappropriately, or worse, the apparent simplicity of the devices will foster use without appropriate scrutiny. In fact, professionals must use selection and development procedures that represent the best of our current understanding of the approaches. To do otherwise is to assure eventual criticism and disregard for informal procedures. In this regard, there are many precedents for the appropriate utilization of tests. (See, for example, Salvia and Ysseldyke, 1991, especially chapters 2 and 3.) And, fortunately, there are an increasing number of well-written, up-to-date, technically accurate guides in the form of textbooks. This was not the case only a few years ago. The reference section of this chapter thus provides an excellent resource to guide the practitioner in the proper development of and appropriate use of informal measurement devices.

Future Directions

Speculation about the future of informal testing is, at best, risky. As an assumption that may be useful in examining this question, we may consider that tests of any nature will inevitably follow the course of change in educational practice. Certainly, specifying the course of educational change is itself very difficult, in part because reforms of schooling appear to be unending (Cuban, 1990). However, much reasoned speculation has been conducted in this area, more so than with tests in particular, and many guidelines have been suggested. Therefore, if we examine dimensions that seem likely to affect education, we may be able to speculate reasonably about the future directions of informal assessment.

In the following section three considerations for reform in education— admittedly out of many that might be considered—are briefly described. These are: the changing population of public education, consideration of the meaning of educational achievement, and the appropriate philosophical foundation for modern curricula. Possibly the future will prove some of these considerations to have been important in the development of informal measurement techniques.

The Changing School Population

Although schools do continually reform curricula, administrative arrangements, and the like, schools remain social institutions that accept in one way or another the students who arrive there. Of course there are massive differences in schools and the populations that they serve. However, if we look at the projected aggregate of students, it is apparent that the population enrolled in the schools of the next decade will be quite different from the current population. Pallas, Natriello, and McDill (1989) have examined the nature of the changing population of schools in the United States, noting that the numbers of disadvantaged children, those at greatest risk for educational failure and requiring specialized methods of instruction, will increase dramatically by the year 2020. The authors contend that failure to plan effective instruction, which must surely imply relevant measurement techniques, will threaten the very economic structure of the nation.

Exactly how these changing demographics will affect informal testing is unclear, although cultural and ethnic diversity implies that a broader array of curricular and instructional techniques be used and that, in turn, implies alternative assessment models. Current procedures are seen to be nonadaptive for many students, and a part of the failure in school may be attributable to the curricula and to the testing procedures that accompany them. In this regard, the current infatuation with school reform—if it continues—must address these changing demographics or face the prospect of constructing reforms appropriate for a greatly diminished, and in some cases absent, population. Although demographic trends don't readily suggest the specific areas of change in either curricula or testing patterns, they do imply that change will continue and perhaps require quite diverse alterations from contemporary models and approaches.

What Is the Meaning of Educational Achievement?

Cole (1990), as mentioned earlier in the chapter, has indicated a concern that achievement in schools can be considered in at least two ways:

mastery of facts and mastery of higher order thinking skills. Cole suggests that contemporary education is a product of behavioral psychology and has been so since the late 1960s. Demands for accountability were instrumental in accelerating the trend, as well as the apparent simplicity and precision of approach. This proved very attractive to practitioners and those responsible for documenting the schools' viability. In this climate the public view of accountability has become linked to students' knowledge of facts—or lack of it. That students cannot identify the capital of Costa Rica is taken in the public's view as proof of significant failure in the educational system.2

The achievement of higher order thinking skills has a long tradition that fell into disarray during the 1960s and 1970s but reemerged in the late 1970s and the 1980s. According to Colt, there are a number of conceptualizations of higher order thinking skills including those based on philosophical traditions (e.g., Dewey, 1900, 1956; Broudy, 1988), more recent input from cognitive science (e.g., Glaser, 1984), and others. Cole notes that these two orientations—facts versus thinking skills—have dominated educational achievement concepts in recent years. In Cole's view, neither is sufficient and a number of steps for integration are offered. One step, "the need to more clearly relate our conceptions to both the short-term and long-term purposes and goals of schooling" (p. 5), serves to illustrate the need for rethinking our priority in the use of informal achievement measures and perhaps the need to develop different models of informal testing altogether. Cole places the issue in perspective with this question: "What do we remember from our high school or college education that makes us different, educated people today?" (p. 6). It seems to this author that our current techniques would have difficulty identifying a student's progress toward long-term goals such as this; in fact, reliably and validly assessing judgments based upon memory and personal analysis might prove difficult: Is what I recall actually what was most important to me? Cole speculates that most educators believe in the importance of long-term

2 The point here is not to imply that students do not need to know the capital cities and other relevant facts of world geography. However, it can be suggested that such isolated facts are not particularly valuable and are easily forgotten if not embedded in a useful context. Consider the degree of complexity involved, and insight to be gained, from a test question that requires a student to describe differences between San Jose and Washington, DC, and to relate those differences to their personal lives. This important distinction between these levels of learning seems to have been omitted in many public discussions of reform.

goals and yet focus on more immediate short-term goals, with a loss to students and schools. A part of the reason for this must be the recent emphasis on behavioral approaches, but a part of any change toward this orientation will require considerable modifications to our existing informal assessment framework.3

Criticism of Curriculum-Based Assessment Models

Informal assessment devices have a number of characteristics, many noted earlier in this chapter. One of the most often cited is the manner in which the tests are in better parallel with the curriculum (i.e., many informal tests embrace the concept of curriculum-based assessment). CBA is, in turn, directly supported by the concept of direct instruction. The efficiency of direct instruction has been repeatedly shown in the measurement (usually by informal measures) of the acquisition of basic facts and skills and has become nearly the standard procedure advocated for the instruction of exceptional students. Most of the informal assessment procedures described in this chapter are best suited to these approaches. However, these approaches have recently been criticized by Heshusius (1991) in an elaborate review of the assumptions and purposes of the models. Heshusius suggests that CBA/DI is "not a model of assessment and instruction for human learning, but an isolated set of measurement and control procedures that are superimposed on but are unrelated to the human phenomena that they claim to assess" (p. 315). Heshusius asserts that in the CBA/DI models measurement demands dictate the information to be learned: "one determines desired learning outcomes a priori so that they can be atomized, sequentialized, and quantified by the adult mindset to report, presumably, valid knowledge claims" (p. 318). Continuing, the author demonstrates that the direct instruction model is a manifestation of the Newtonian/Bacon paradigm that extols control as one essential element of reality and knowing—in Heshusius' view to the detriment of both learners and teachers. Ultimately, Heshusius finds other characteristics— the atomization of information, emphasis on quantification and insistence on control, as well as belief in objectivity, prediction, and uncertainty—to be clear indicators of direct instruction's development from a mechanistic, positivist conceptualization of science. This, as he notes, is a view that

3 Note that the above point may well be related to Cole's concern for the development of worthy long-term goals, and implications for the structure of informal measures.

has reached disfavor with many distinguished scholars (e.g., Bronowski, 1965) as a worthwhile means for conceptualizing scientific inquiry. (Interestingly, Cziko, 1989, has recently criticized the positivistic/mechanistic tradition as a paradigm for educational research.)

In effect, Heshusius (1991) calls into question the instructional outcome of the curriculum-based approach, and with it, many of the assumptions that currently undergird informal assessment. If the critique provided by the author were accepted by education, assessment would change dramatically. In Heshusius' view, the "reconstruction of assessment" (p. 324) would demand (among other features): valid indicators of learning (i.e., learning grounded in "personal purpose"; p. 325); be more holistic in nature; reflect the social nature inherent in learning; and be more varying of format and domain (e.g., include intuitive and kinetic learning). That educators are concerned with many of the issues raised by Heshusius seems clear. In fact, as noted by the author, a significant number of special educators have provided statements that support in some manner the points listed here.

The concepts advocated by Heshusius seem to suggest an emerging need for what could be termed qualitative measures in measurement and evaluation of educational activity. Eisner (1991) has recently written at length regarding the nature of qualitative evaluation and the necessity for using the approach in future efforts to conclude educational success. Many of the characteristics of qualitative assessment are opposites of the more traditional models; for example, there is far more interest in holistic measures, and in more personalized, global outcomes from the learning process. An illustration of how such processes might evolve can be found in the literature associated with Arts PROPEL, a program that "seeks to assess growth in and learning in areas like music, imaginative writing, and visual arts, which are neglected by most standard measures" (Gardner & Hatch, 1989, p. 7). The personnel directing this program have explored a number of qualitative assessment devices that may illuminate a part of the course of future advances in informal assessment. One of these, the portfolio (or sometimes process-folio), has been skillfully used on a number of occasions to document changes in students' thought processes. The results of these efforts are not yet sufficiently consolidated to provide a wealth of tools available to the practitioner. Moreover, the philosophies behind them may seem decidedly foreign, vague, and difficult to incorporate in many existing educational settings. However, data continue to emerge and, increasingly, scholars are turning their attention to these models. The outcome of that attention bodes for great change in the nature of instruction, and with it, informal assessment. Heshusius' contention that CBA/DI are nearing the end of their influence as curricular models is a statement that should receive serious contemplation from those interested in the future of informal assessment.

SUMMARY

This chapter has sought to provide an overview of contemporary informal assessment devices and representative illustrations of specific techniques utilized in the assessment of several domains of interest. Other devices exist, and a number of domains of assessment of potential interest were not covered due to space considerations. Readers need to be aware that many excellent resources are available, often by content area, and the minimal time directed to identification of these resources can lead to a plethora of useful ideas and procedures.

The final section of the chapter used three considerations for educational reform as a means to explore changes in future measurement approaches that may occur. As a result of these projections, the chapter suggests that informal assessment is likely to be rethought and restructured to include elements drawn from the cognitive psychology and qualitative measurement traditions.

REFERENCES

Agnew, A. T. (1982). Using children's dictated stories to assess code subconsciousness. *The Reading Teacher, 35*, 450-454.

Alberto, P. A., & Troutman, A. C. (1990). *Applied behavior analysis for teachers: Influencing student performance* (3rd ed.). Columbus, OH: Merrill.

Anderson, B. (1986, April). *A report on IRI scoring and interpretation.* A paper presented at the International Reading Association Convention, Philadelphia.

Ashlock, R. B. (1990). *Error patterns in computation: A semi-programmed approach* (5th ed.). Columbus, OH: Merrill.

Baer, D. M. (1977). A note on the absence of Santa Claus in any known ecosystem. In A. Rogers-Warren & S. F. Warren (Eds.), *Ecological perspectives in behavioral analysis* (pp. 33-36). Baltimore: University Park Press.

Bagai, E., & Bagai, J. (1979). *System FORE handbook.* North Hollywood, CA: Foreworks.

Barker, R. (1965). Explorations in ecological psychology. *American Psychologist, 20*, 1-14.

64   BEST PRACTICES IN ASSESSMENT

Bartel, N. B. (1986). Problems in mathematics achievement. In D. D. Hammill & N. R. Bartel (Eds.), *Teaching children with learning and behavioral problems* (4th ed.) (pp. 178-223). Boston: Allyn & Bacon.

Bellack, A. S., & Hersen, M. H. (Eds.). (1988). *Behavioral assessment: A practical handbook* (3rd ed.). Elmsford, NY: Pergamon.

Benner, S. M. (1992). *Assessing young children with special needs: An ecological perspective*. White Plains, NY: Longman.

Bijou, S. W., & Peterson, R. F. (1970). The psychological assessment of children: A functional analysis. In P. McReynolds (Ed.), *Advances in psychological assessment* (Vol. 2, pp. 63-78). Palo Alto: Science & Behavior.

Bloom, B., Englehart, M. B., Furst, E. J., Hill, W. H., & Krathwohl, D. R., (1956). *Taxonomy of educational objectives: The classification of educational goals. Handbook 1. Cognitive domain*. New York: Longman Green.

Bormuth, J. R. (1968). Cloze test readability: Criterion reference scores. *Journal of Educational Measurement, 5,* 189-196.

Bornstein, P. H., Bornstein, M. T., & Dawson, B. (1984). Integrated assessment and treatment. In T. H. Ollendick & M. Hersen (Eds.)., *Child behavioral assessment: Principles and procedures* (pp. 223-243). New York: Pergamon.

Bott, D. A. (1990). Managing CBA in the classroom. In J. Salvia & C. Hughes (Eds.). *Curriculum based assessment: Testing what is taught* (pp. 270-294). New York: Macmillan.

Brigance, A. H. (1983). *BRIGANCE Diagnostic Comprehensive Inventory of Basic Skills*. North Billerica, MA: Curriculum Associates.

Bronowski, J. (1965). *Science and human values.* Hew York: Harper & Row.

Broudy, H. S. (1988). *The uses of schooling.* New York: Methuen.

Burns, P. B. & Roe, B. D. (1989). *Burns/Roe Informal Reading Inventory: Preprimer to twelfth grade.* Boston: Houghton Mifflin.

Cartwright, G. P. (1969). Written expression and spelling. In R. Smith (Ed.), *Teacher diagnosis of educational difficulties* (pp. 68-91). Columbus, OH: Merrill.

Cheek, E. H., Kritsonis, D., & Lindsey, J. D. (1987). Informal reading assessment strategies for adult readers. *Lifelong Learning: An Omnibus of Practice and Research, 10*(7), 8015.

Cole, N. S. (1990). Conceptions of educational achievement. *Educational Researcher, 19*(3), 2-7.

Connolly, A. (1988). *KeyMath—Revised.* Circle Pines, MN: American Guidance Service.

Cuban, L. (1990). Reforming again, again, and again. *Educational Researcher, 19*(1), 3-13.

Cziko, G. A. (1989). Unpredictability and indeterminism in human behavior: Arguments and implications for educational research. *Educational Researcher, 18*(3), 17-25.

Dewey, J. (1900/1956). *The school and society.* Chicago: The University of Chicago Press.

Drew, C. J., Logan, D. R., & Hardman, M. L. (1988). *Mental retardation: A life cycle approach* (4th ed.). Columbus, OH: Merrill.

Duffelmeyer, F. A., Robinson, S. S., & Squier, S. E. (1989). Vocabulary questions on informal reading inventories. *The Reading Teacher, 43*(2), 142-148.

Eisner, E. W. (1991). *The enlightened eye: Qualitative inquiry and the enhancement of educational practice.* New York: Macmillan.

Ekwall, E. E. (1986). *Ekwall Reading Inventory* (2nd ed.). Boston: Allyn & Bacon.

Enright, B. E. (1983). *ENRIGHT Diagnostic Inventory of Basic Arithmetic Skills.* North Billerica, MA: Curriculum Associates.

Evans, S. S., Evans, W. H., & Mercer, C. D. (1986). *Assessment for instruction.* Boston: Allyn & Bacon.

Fry, E. (1972). *Reading instruction for classroom and clinic.* New York: McGraw Hill.

Gable R. A., & Henderson, J. M. (Eds.). (1990). *Assessing students with special needs: A sourcebook for analyzing and correcting errors in academics.* New York: Longman.

Gardner, H., & Hatch, T. (1989). Multiple intelligences go to school: Educational implications of the theory of multiple intelligences. *Educational Researcher, 18*(8), 4-10.

Ginsburg, H. P. (1987). Assessment techniques: Tests, interviews and analytic teaching. In D. D. Hammill (Ed.), *Assessing the abilities and instructional needs of students* (pp. 441-462). Austin: Pro-Ed.

Glaser, R. (1984). Education and thinking: The role of knowledge. *American Psychologist, 39,* 93-104.

Glennon, V. J., & Wilson, J. W. (1972). Diagnostic-prescriptive teaching. In National Council for Teachers of Mathematics: *The slow learner in mathematics: The 35th yearbook.* Reston, VA: NCTM.

Goodman, Y., & Burke, C. (1972). *Reading Miscue Inventory: Manual of procedure for diagnosis and evaluation.* New York: Macmillan.

Gronlund, N. E. (1988). *How to construct achievement tests* (4th ed.). Englewood Cliffs, NJ: Prentice Hall.

Guerin, G. R., & Maier, A. S. (1983). *Informal assessment in education.* Palo Alto: Mayfield.

Hammill, D. D. (Ed.). (1987). *Assessing the abilities and instructional needs of students.* Austin: Pro-Ed.

Heshusius, L. (1991). Curriculum-based assessment and direct instruction: Critical reflections on fundamental assumptions. *Exceptional Children, 57,* 315-328.

Howell, K., & Kaplan, J. J. (1980). *Diagnosing basic skills: A handbook for deciding what to teach.* Columbus, OH: Merrill.

Idol, L., Nevin, A., & Paolucci-Whitcomb, P. (1986). *Models of curriculum-based assessment.* Rockville, MD: Aspen.

Kalmbach, J. R. (1986). Getting at the point of retellings. *Journal of Reading, 29,* 326-333.

Kaufman, A. S., & Kaufman, N. L. (1983). *Kaufman Assessment Battery for Children, Interpretive Manual.* Circle Pines, MN: American Guidance Service.

Kazdin, A. E. (1980). *Behavior modification in applied settings* (rev. ed.). Homewood, IL: Dorsey.

Luftig, R. L. (1989). *Assessment of learners with special needs.* Boston: Allyn & Bacon.

Mahoney, M. J., & Thoreson, C. E. (1974). *Self-control: Power to the person.* Monterey, CA: Brooks.

Martin, R. P. (1988). *Assessment of personality and behavior problems: Infancy through adolescence.* New York: Guilford.

McKenna, M. C. (1983). Informal reading inventories: A review of issues. *The Reading Teacher, 37,* 670-678.

McLoughlin, J. A., & Lewis, R. B. (1990). *Assessing special students* (3rd ed.). Columbus, OH: Merrill.

Meichenbaum, D. (1979). *Cognitive behavior modification: An integrative approach.* New York: Plenum.

Morsink, C. V., & Gable, R. A. (1990). Errors in reading. In R. A. Gable & J. M. Hendrickson (Eds.), *Assessing students with special needs: A sourcebook for analyzing and correcting errors in academics* (pp. 46-62). New York: Longman.

Nessel, D. (1987). Reading comprehension: Asking the right questions. *Phi Delta Kappan, 68,* 442-445.

Olson, M. W., & Gillis, M. K. (1987). Text type and text structure: An analysis of three secondary informal reading inventories. *Reading Horizons, 28*(1), 70-80.

Pallas, A. M., Natriello, G., & McDill, E. L. (1989). The changing nature of the disadvantaged population: Current dimensions and future trends. *Educational Researcher, 18*(5), 16-22.

Pigford, A. B. (1989). Evaluation by checklist: Debating the effectiveness. *NASP Bulletin, 73*(520), 81-84.

Polloway, E. A., & Smith, J. E., (1982). *Teaching language skills to exceptional learners.* Denver: Love.

Popham, W. J. (1978). *Criterion referenced measurement.* Englewood Cliffs: Prentice Hall.

Reisman, F. K. (1978). *A guide to the diagnostic teaching of arithmetic* (2nd ed.). Columbus, OH: Merrill.

Roberts, G. H. (1968). The failure strategies of third grade arithmetic pupils. *The Arithmetic Teacher, 15,* 442-446.

Rogers-Warren, A., & Warren, S. F. (Eds.). (1977). *Ecological perspectives in behavioral analysis.* Baltimore: University Park Press.

Sackett, G. (1979). The lag sequential analysis of contingency and cyclicity in behavioral interaction research. In J. Osofsky (Ed.), *Handbook of infant development* (pp. 623-634). New York: Wiley.

Salvia, J., & Hughes, C. (1990). *Curriculum based assessment: Testing what is taught.* New York: Macmillan.

Salvia, J., & Ysseldyke, J. E. (1991). *Assessment* (5th ed.). Boston: Houghton Mifflin.

Schoggen, P. (1978). Ecological psychology and mental retardation. In G. P. Sackett (Ed.), *Observing behavior: Theory and application in mental retardation* (Vol. 1, pp. 108-142). Baltimore: University Park Press.

Schroeder, S. R. (Ed.). *Ecobehavioral analysis and developmental disabilities: The twenty-first century.* New York: Springer-Verlag.

Scott, M. (1980). Ecological theory and methods for research in special education. *Journal of Special Education, 14,* 279-294.

Scriven, M. (1967). The methodology of evaluation. In R. E. Stake (Ed.), *Curriculum evaluation* (pp. 58-73). American Educational Research Association Monograph Series on Evaluation, No. 1. Chicago: Rand McNally.

Shapiro, E. S. (1984). Self-monitoring procedures. In T. H. Ollendick & M. Hersen (Eds.), *Child behavioral assessment: Principles and procedures* (pp. 148-165). New York: Pergamon.

Silvaroli, N. J. (1986). *Classroom reading inventory* (5th ed.) Dubuque, IA: Brown.

Simeonsson, R. J. (1986). *Psychological and developmental assessment of special children.* Boston: Allyn & Bacon.

Simon, A., & Boyer, E. G. (Eds.). (1974). *Mirrors for behavior III: An anthology of observation instruments.* Wyncott, PA: Communications Materials Center.

Slate, J. R., & Saudargas, R. A. (1987). Classroom behaviors of LD, seriously emotionally disturbed, and average children: A sequential analysis. *Learning Disabilities Quarterly, 10,* 125-134.

Spache, G. (1981). *Diagnosing and correcting reading disabilities.* Boston: Allyn & Bacon.

Tawney, J. W., & Gast, D. L. (1984). *Single subject research in special education.* Columbus, OH: Merrill.

Taylor, W. L. (1953). Cloze procedure: A new tool for measuring readability. *Journalism Quarterly, 30,* 414-438.

Taylor, L. (1989). *Assessment of exceptional students: Educational and psychological procedures* (2nd ed.). Englewood Cliffs: Prentice Hall.

Tidwell, R. (1980). Informal assessment to modify the role and image of the school psychologist. *Psychology in the Schools, 17,* 210-215.

Tindal, G. A., & Marston, D. B. (1990). *Classroom-based assessment: Evaluating instructional outcomes.* Columbus, OH: Merrill.

Tucker, J. A. (Ed.). (1985). Curriculum based assessment. *Exceptional Children, 52,* 199-298.

VanDevender, E. M., & Harris, M. J. (1987). Why students make math errors. *Academic Therapy, 23*(1), 79-85.

Wade, S. E. (1990). Using think alouds to assess comprehension. *The Reading Teacher, 43,* 442-451.

Walker, J. E., & Shea, T. M. (1988). *Behavior management: A practical approach for educators* (4th ed.). Columbus, OH: Merrill.

Wallace, G., & Larsen, S. C. (1978). *Educational assessment of learning problems: Testing for teaching.* Boston: Allyn & Bacon.

Watson, D. L., & Tharp, R. G. (1989). *Self-directed behavior: Self-modification for personal adjustment* (5th ed.). Pacific Grove, CA: Brooks.

Willems, E. P. (1974). Behavioral technology and behavioral ecology. *Journal of Applied Behavioral Analysis, 7,* 151-165.

Zigmond, N., Vallecorsa, A., & Silverman, R. (1983). *Assessment for instructional planning in special education.* Englewood Cliffs: Prentice Hall.

3 BEST PRACTICES IN THE VOCATIONAL ASSESSMENT OF SPECIAL NEEDS LEARNERS

G. Franklin Elrod and Dennis G. Tesolowski

OVERVIEW: DEFINING VOCATIONAL ASSESSMENT

Many terms have been used in labeling the assessment of vocationally related skills. Terms such as *career assessment, vocational evaluation,* and *vocational assessment* are often used synonymously. In practice, however, these three terms refer to processes that have distinct origins, definitions, and purposes. The following section provides a brief overview of each of these processes.

Career Assessment

Career assessment involves an examination of an individual's progress along a career development continuum. Just as there are stages in, for example, cognitive development, language acquisition, and reading proficiency, so too are there stages to career development. Career development is viewed as a lifelong process wherein individuals assume various roles from birth through the preschool years and elementary education, to secondary schooling and postsecondary education, continuing into one or more vocations, and ending with the retirement years.

Career development models (see, for example, Brolin, 1978, 1983, 1989; Clark & Kolstoe, 1990; Halpern, 1985; Kokaska, Gruenhagen, Razeghi, & Fair, 1985) take a holistic view of an individual's "career," focusing not only on vocational roles (e.g., "employee"), but also on the other roles that a person assumes during a lifespan. These other roles could include, for example, "student," "parent," "citizen," "volunteer," and "homemaker." It follows, therefore, that career assessment encompasses the totality of this holistic career experience, examining functional, personal, and social skills, as well as occupational readiness.

Vocational Evaluation

Emanating primarily from the field of rehabilitation, vocational evaluation focuses on a narrow set of outcomes. Rather than the holistic, paid and nonpaid roles that comprise a career assessment model, vocational evaluation is conducted "to determine individual competencies, needs, and adjustments for placement in a work environment" (Veir, 1987, p. 214). Vocational evaluation as a separate entity has drawn from the fields of psychology, vocational and industrial education, occupational therapy, military training, medicine, and workshop settings. Stated in another manner, vocational evaluation has as its primary function the identification of an individual's physical, mental, and emotional abilities, limitations, and tolerances in order to predict his or her current and future employment potential and adjustment. The goals of vocational evaluation can be summarized as seeking to answer the following four questions:

- Is the individual ready to decide on a vocational training curriculum?

- If so, which course or program of study is best suited to the individual?

- If not, which of the individual's weaknesses need strengthening?

- What plan would promote changes in the individual or the environment to enhance the individual's decision on a vocational training program? (Roberts, 1970)

Thus, vocational evaluation addresses various domains, all directed at facilitating the progress of an individual toward job training and eventual job placement. Vocational evaluation, therefore, often involves the use of simulated or actual work settings to gain a better perspective of specific tasks (e.g., sorting, alphabetizing) that may be relevant to success on a particular job.

Vocational Assessment

Expanding on the domains of vocational evaluation, while retaining an occupational orientation, vocational assessment affords equal weight to traditional educational variables. In other words, the examination of academic and sociobehavioral variables is viewed as an integral part of the process of determining vocational program placement by identifying needed support services and curricular adjustments with the ultimate goal of facilitating job training and placement. Thus, vocational assessment has been defined as "a comprehensive process conducted over a period of time, involving a multidisciplinary team . . . with the purpose of identifying individual characteristics, education, training, and placement needs, which provide educators the basis for planning an individual's program" (Dahl, Appleby, & Lipe, 1978, p. 103).

Major distinctions among vocational assessment (the theme of this chapter) and the other two diagnostic approaches discussed above are:

- vocational assessment is not as holistic as career assessment (i.e., nonpaid roles are rarely the focus);

- vocational assessment is a more ongoing process than vocational evaluation, often extending from the beginnings of secondary schooling through actual job placement; and

- vocational assessment gives equal weight to educational variables (which is also true of career assessment).

Due to its multidisciplinary nature, the vocational assessment process may be completed by a variety of professionals including regular and special educators, guidance counselors, school administrators, and vocational educators. Parents can also lend valuable information to this assessment process. It should be emphasized that data gleaned from vocational assessment should not be used merely to screen students from a vocational program, but should also provide insight as to how some vocational courses may be adapted, or support services provided, to enhance students' potential for success (Elrod, 1987a).

Historical Perspective

A form of vocational assessment was introduced more than 2,300 years ago when Plato proposed a series of tests for the guardians of his ideal republic (Odiorne & Miller, 1971). Situational work evaluation techniques were also mentioned by Gideon in the Biblical book of *Judges*, Chapter 7, when he selected 300 warriors to fight the Midianites (Jaffee, 1965; Tesolowski & Morgan, 1980).

Based on more recent history, however, the systematic study of work potential seems to have spanned a period of approximately 65 to 75 years, beginning with World War I. Neff (1968) identified the following four approaches to vocational assessment:

- mental testing,
- job analysis,
- work samples, and
- situational assessment.

Any history of vocational assessment must necessarily focus on legislative enactments, which in turn drive programs and specific themes. Key legislation with provisions focusing on vocational assessment and training can be subdivided into categories representing fields from which they have emanated. Three fields that have had a major impact on vocational assessment are vocational education, rehabilitation, and special education (Phelps & Frasier, 1988). These three categories are discussed below from a historical perspective, along with the umbrella civil rights provisions for persons with disabilities mandated through the Americans with Disabilities Act (U.S. Congress, 1990a).

Vocational Education

The early years of the 20th century in the United States constituted an era of growing industrialization, expanding agricultural production, and increasing immigration of workers from other lands. A continuing and urgent need for a well-trained work force was a major impetus for the enactment of the Smith-Hughes Act (U.S. Congress, 1917). This Act was the outcome of the work of the Commission on National Aid to Vocational Education, which viewed vocational training as a necessary ingredient to "democratize the education of the country" (Commission on National Aid to Vocational Education, 1914, p. 12).

Another major event that prompted a renewed interest in vocational education was the Soviet Union's successful launching of Sputnik in 1957. Concerns surfaced that students in schools in the United States were lacking in technical knowledge. These concerns were translated into action through the passage of the National Education Act (U.S. Congress, 1958). This Act emphasized the need for occupational training by earmarking funds for the preparation of skilled technicians, supporting students interested in higher education, and providing $15 million for the construction of area vocational education programs (Nystrom & Bayne, 1979).

During the early to mid-1960s, the key historical event that occupied much of the energy of the United States was the civil rights movement. It suddenly became clear that equal occupational opportunities were only valid if supported by comprehensive vocational training. Thus, the Vocational Education Act (U.S. Congress, 1963) was passed with the intent of opening vocational programs to disadvantaged populations through the provision of more vocational guidance and career planning services. This Act also provided funds for developing programs for students with academic, social, or other disabilities that were of such severity so as to impair their chances of completing regular vocational education programs.

In 1968, through the Vocational Education Amendments (U.S. Congress, 1968), monies were set aside to be used expressly for disadvantaged and disabled populations. As a result, a state would have to spend at least 10% of its total federal vocational education allotment on programs for disadvantaged students, and one half of that 10% total on programs for students with disabilities. These earmarked funds were enacted to bolster the Vocational Education Act of 1963, which, by itself, did not achieve the desired gains for these target student populations.

The Carl D. Perkins Vocational and Technical Education Act (U.S. Congress, 1984) is the only legislative enactment that mentions vocational assessment (Veir, 1987). Although continuing on the theme of providing for vocational programs for disabled and disadvantaged populations, the Perkins Act mandates "an assessment of the interests, abilities, and special needs of [a disabled or disadvantaged] student with respect to completing successfully the vocational education program" (U.S. Congress, 1984).

The most recent vocational education legislative initiative has under-scored the linkage between traditional academics and vocational training. The Carl D. Perkins Vocational and Applied Technology Education Act Amendments (U.S. Congress, 1990b) promote a shift in vocational educa-tion from a job-skills orientation toward a vehicle for learning academics and thinking skills, and for linking thought to action (Wirt, 1991). Increasingly, therefore, vocational assessment must be viewed as a key bridge to this linkage.

Thus, from the turn of the century, vocational education has had a goal of offering contemporary training for all students, including those with disadvantages or disabilities. Legislation emanating from that field has enunciated this theme. With the passage of the Carl D. Perkins Act of 1984, and the subsequent amendments of 1990, the assessment of vocational skills has now become an integral component of the overall assessment menu available for use with students.

Rehabilitation

With the passage of the Rehabilitation Act of 1973 (U.S. Congress, 1973), the federal government broadened the concept of rehabilitation from focusing primarily on the outcome of competitive employment to also including intermediate outcomes such as sheltered or homebound employment (Phelps & Frasier, 1988). Of course, the most noteworthy sections of the Rehabilitation Act (i.e., Sections 503 and 504) promote affirmative action and antidiscriminatory policies, respectively, on behalf of persons with disabilities.

However, the Act also authorized the use of an individualized written rehabilitation program (IWRP) which required:

- a statement of long-range rehabilitation goals and related objectives;

- a statement of specific rehabilitation services to be provided;

- projected dates for initiation and duration of services;

- objective evaluation criteria; and

- where appropriate, a detailed explanation of the availability of a client assistance project. (Phelps & Frasier, 1988, p. 14)

Thus, the guidelines for development of the IWRP, which closely parallel those for development of the individualized education plan (IEP), either directly or indirectly implied the necessity for some form of assessment to be conducted. If individualized goals and objectives were to be provided, these provisions would have to be based on the needs of an individual client. Thus, it would have been necessary to conduct an assessment of a client's vocational abilities and limitations. In addition, the IWRP guidelines specifically mention that "objective evaluation criteria" be developed to assess a client's progress toward rehabilitation. Such an evaluation would necessarily involve an ongoing vocational assessment of a client's skills relative to the skills the client possessed prior to commencement of the individualized rehabilitation program.

New directions in rehabilitation and training were initiated with the passage of the Rehabilitation Act Amendments (U.S. Congress, 1974) and the Rehabilitation, Comprehensive Services, and Developmental Disabilities Amendments (U.S. Congress, 1978). The 1974 Amendments provided for community service employment and projects for training persons with severe disabilities in "real work settings" (Phelps & Frasier, 1988, p. 16). The Amendments of 1978 strengthened affirmative action provisions for persons with disabilities. This strengthening was so pronounced that these Amendments have been interpreted as entitlements that permit persons with disabilities to receive services as a right rather than as a privilege (Kiernan & Payne, 1982).

The contributions of the field of rehabilitation have augmented and, in some cases, preceded efforts from education in the vocational preparation of persons with disabilities. In general, while providing a foundation of antidiscrimination and affirmative action, rehabilitation legislation established the basis for IWRP development. These guidelines both directly and indirectly promoted the use of assessment and evaluation in working with individual clients.

Special Education

The Education for All Handicapped Children Act (EAHCA) (U.S. Congress, 1975) established a foundation for providing a free, appropriate, public education for all students with disabilities. This Act also includes vocational education under the rubric of the "education" that must be free, appropriate, and public (Hursh & Kerns, 1988). Under guarantees of the EAHCA, the provision of "least restrictive environment" (LRE) is most pertinent to vocational assessment. By linking the concept of LRE with the concept of vocational education, the thrust of vocational assessment, therefore, should: (1) identify a student's strengths and limitations relative to vocational training and (2) promote, to the greatest extent possible, the education of students with disabilities in the least restrictive vocational setting.

The Education of the Handicapped Act Amendments (U.S. Congress, 1983) initiated the allocation of grants for developing model programs for secondary special education and transition services. This initiative was directed at reducing high levels of unemployment among individuals with disabilities while enhancing better service coordination among the various agencies (including schools) that provide job preparation and occupational orientation services (Phelps & Frasier, 1988).

A policy thrust from the U.S. Office of Special Education and Rehabilitation Services in the mid-1980s (see Will, 1984) prompted the development of educational programs that would foster the occupational outlook of students with disabilities. At approximately the same period of time, several statewide follow-up studies underscored the need for better preparation of students with disabilities for the world of work (Edgar, Levine, & Maddox, 1986; Hasazi, Gordon, Roe, Hull, Finck, & Salembier, 1985; Mithaug, Horiuchi, & Fanning, 1985). As a result of this policy initiative and these follow-up studies, special educators became more cognizant of incorporating career, prevocational, and vocational goals and objectives into students' individualized education plans. Thus, the assessment of variables relative to these three domains emerged as a programmatic influence, which currently continues to be evidenced.

The most recent special education legislation is the Individuals with Disabilities Education Act (IDEA) (U.S. Congress, 1990c). With regard to assessment practices, IDEA establishes that "transition services" must be based on an individual student's needs, which encompass that student's vocational interests. Furthermore, IDEA stipulates that a student's individualized education plan (IEP) must provide a statement of needed transition services, beginning no later than age 16 and continuing annually thereafter. For students who might possess more serious disabilities, the transition statement can begin on the IEP at age 14 or younger.

Civil Rights

The theme of serving Americans with disabilities has been revitalized with the passage of the Americans with Disabilities Act (ADA) (U.S. Congress, 1990a). This Act is intended to extend and protect the civil rights of Americans with disabilities. It is hoped that this Act will end the unjustified segregation and exclusion of these persons from the mainstream of American life. Congress, in enacting this piece of legislation, focused on the fact that 43 million Americans have one or more physical or mental disabilities and that this number is increasing as the population as a whole ages. Furthermore, Congress had to come to terms with the fact that Americans with disabilities often encounter discrimination in such critical areas as employment, housing, public accommodations, education, transportation, communication, recreation, health services, voting, and access to public services. The "bottom line" of ADA is to provide legal recourse for discrimination against persons with disabilities, just as is currently available for discrimination based on race, color, sex, national origin, religion, or age. Justin Dart, Chair of the President's Committee on Employment of People with Disabilities, indicated that the ADA establishes "a clear and comprehensive prohibition of discrimination on the basis of disability" (Dart, 1990, p. 1).

With regards to assessment, Section 102, Title 1, of the ADA specifically directs employers to use tests that measure the job skills of an applicant, rather than reflect the applicant's disability. It follows, therefore, that vocational assessment conducted in the educational setting should focus on the student's skill level while addressing adaptations that can facilitate successful completion of vocational training.

ASSESSING VOCATIONAL SKILLS: FORMAL ASSESSMENT

Work Sample Evaluation

Historical Background

The relatively short history of work sample evaluation is described in Pruitt's (1977) text. He stated that the first work sample, developed by Munsterberg at the turn of the century, was a model of a street car designed to try out prospective operators for the Boston Railroad Company. The second oldest reference by Pruitt indicated that a standardized work sample was developed in the late 1920s to select garment machine operators (Treat, 1929).

During the past 50 years, literally thousands of noncommercial work samples have been developed in rehabilitation facilities throughout the United States. However, the first commercial work evaluation system, commonly referred to as The TOWER System, was developed by the Institute for the Crippled and Disabled (1959) in New York. This system was formally titled TOWER: Testing, Orientation and Work Evaluation in Rehabilitation. Since the early 1970s, numerous commercial work sample systems have been developed by private entrepreneurs and through government-sponsored funding.

Definition of a Work Sample

Nadolsky (1977) stated that numerous definitions of the term *work sample* are available and that the essential components of these definitions are consistent with one another. In a discussion of standardized work samples, Anastasi (1961) stated:

the [work sample] task set for the subject is similar to the work he is to perform on the job. The representativeness of the behavior sample and the closeness with which the task duplicates actual job conditions are essential considerations. For practical expediency, work samples are sometimes presented in the form of "miniature," "analogy," or "simulated" tests. (p. 468)

When discussing the work sample approach to vocational evaluation, Neff (1968) defined a work sample as "a 'mock-up'—a close simulation—of an actual industrial operation, not different in its essentials from the kind of work a potential worker would be required to perform on an ordinary job" (p. 178).

Finally, a working definition was created by Task Force Number 7 of the Vocational Evaluation Project (1975) as a part of the "Glossary of Terms Used in Vocational Evaluation." This Task Force defined a work sample as:

A well defined work activity involving tasks, materials, and tools which are identical or similar to those in an actual job or cluster of jobs. It is used to assess an individual's vocational aptitude, worker characteristics, and vocational interests. (p. 92)

Commercial Work Samples

The definition of the term *work sample* has established the parameters for using simulated tasks that are closely associated with occupations in the labor market. Numerous commercial work samples have been developed since the early 1970s. Generally, activities included in work sample systems are designed to be as realistic as possible, to reflect the actual work to be performed.

Benefits Associated with Work Samples

Students with special instructional needs (e.g., disadvantaged students and students with disabilities) can benefit from participating in work sample activities because these activities provide practical, hands-on experiences that cannot readily be assessed by written industrial tests or through on-the-job observation in actual work environments (Neff, 1968). Work samples often incorporate tools, technology, and standards associated with actual employment. In addition, work sample technologies are usually designed to emphasize psychomotor (performance) skills rather than cognitive (verbal or written) skills. Professional educators working as evaluators in this process are able to observe the actual work-related performance of students with special needs. It is possible to gather useful information about students' work capacity, manipulative skills, interpersonal skills, physical abilities, and work habits. It is extremely important for this information to be utilized when identifying students' strengths and limitations, determining appropriate vocational program placement, establishing realistic career goals, identifying the need for program or equipment modifications, and for placing students in jobs in the labor market (Sarkees & Scott, 1986).

Advantages of Using Commercial Work Samples

One of the primary advantages of using commercial work samples in the assessment process is that they tend to motivate students with special needs. This high level of motivation is attributed to the similarity of work sample procedures to actual job tasks. The students appear to enjoy participating in psychomotor-oriented tasks much more than pencil-and-paper tasks. Neff (1968) indicated that the virtue of the work sample approach is its strong reality orientation, its close simulation of actual work demands, and the unparalleled opportunity it affords to observe actual work behaviors in a reasonably controlled setting.

By observing the performance of special needs students on work sample technologies, skilled evaluators can acquire useful data to assist them in predicting functional levels associated with occupational abilities, aptitudes, attitudes, tolerances, and limitations. Students are required to participate in hands-on experiences and often must exhibit the ability to follow verbal directions. The ultimate advantage for students with special needs is the potential for selecting an appropriate vocational education program, and eventually acquiring an appropriate job in the local community (Sarkees & Scott, 1986).

Availability of Commercial Work Samples

Numerous commercial work sample technologies are available. Researchers and authors such as Botterbusch (1987), Pruitt (1977), Sarkees and Scott (1986), and Scarpati (1989) have reported the specific advantages and disadvantages of many individual work sample systems. The most comprehensive comparison of vocational assessment and evaluation systems was conducted by Botterbusch (1987). His publication, entitled *Vocational Assessment and Evaluation Systems: A Comparison*, compares 21 commercially produced work sample systems. This source, which is "must" reading for anyone who wants to learn more about the advantages and disadvantages of work sample systems, is available through:

Ronald Fry, Director
Materials Development Center
Stout Vocational Rehabilitation Institute
School of Education and Human Resources
University of Wisconsin—Stout
Menomonie, WI 54751.

Table 3.1 displays corporate names and addresses for selected commercial work samples, dexterity tests, and work simulators. It is suggested that these companies be contacted for specifics on validity, reliability, and use of the samples listed.

A Vision of Work Sampling Technologies of the Future

Several corporations that produce and market "work simulators" have been included in Table 3.1. These high-technology work simulators, which appear to have evolved from work sampling technology,

TABLE 3.1. *Corporate Names and Addresses for Selected Commercial Work Sample Technologies*

Corporation/Address	Work Sample Names
Attainment Company P.O. Box 103 Oregon, WI 53575	Work Skill Development Package
Baltimore Therapeutic Equipment 7455-L New Ridge Road Hanover, MD 21076-3105	Bolt Box Assembly Tree
Baltimore Therapeutic Equipment 1202 Bernard Drive Baltimore, MD 21223	BTE Work Simulator, Model WS10 BTE Work Simulator, Model WS20
Career Evaluation Systems, Inc. 7788 Milwaukee Ave. Niles, IL 60648	Career Evaluation System
Easy Street Environments Health Services Marketing, Ltd. 6908 East Thomas Road, Suite 201 Scottsdale, AZ 85251	Work Hardening, Office and Factory Modules
Dr. Edward Hester University of Kansas Lawrence, KS 66045	Hester Evaluation System
ICD Rehabilitation and Research Center 340 East 24th St. New York, NY 10010	TOWER Worksamples Micro-TOWER
Jastak Associates 1526 Gilpin Ave. Wilmington, DE 19806	Wide Range Employment SampleTest (WREST)
Loredan Biomedical, Inc. 1632 DaVinci Ct., P.O. Box 1154 Davis, CA 95617	LIDO WorkSET
McCarron-Dial P.O. Box 45628 Dallas, TX 75245	McCarron-Dial Work Evaluation System

continued

New Concepts Corporation 2341 S. Friebus Ave., Suite 14 Tucson, AZ 85713	Singer Worksamples
Piney Mountain Press, Inc. P.O. Box 333 Cleveland, GA 30528	Skills Assessment Module Prevocational Assessment Screen
Prep, Inc. 1007 Whitehead Road Ext. Trenton, NJ 08638	Coats Worksamples
Physio-Tek, Inc. P.O. Box 190 Martinez, CA 94553	Human Engineering Center
Psychological Corporation 1001 Polk Street San Francisco, CA 94109	Crawford Small Parts Bennett Hand Tool
S.A.V.E. Enterprises P.O. Box 5871 Rome, GA 30161	Systemic Approach to Vocational Evaluation
Talent Assessment, Inc. P.O. Box 5087 Jacksonville, FL 32247	Talent Assessment Program

The Work System
Lake Forest Health Services
31740 Franklin Fairway
Farmington Hills, MI 48018
	The Work System:
	  Work Simulations
	  for Sustained Productivity

Valpar International Corporation
P.O. Box 5767
Tucson, AZ 85703-5767
	Valpar Component
	  Worksamples
	MESA Computerized
	  Screening Tool
	Valpar 17

Vocational Assessment Consultants P.O. Box 64401 Virginia Beach, VA 23464	Vocational Assessment System

Vocational Research Institute
  Jewish Employment and
  Vocational Service
1528 Walnut Street, Suite 1502
Philadelphia, PA 19102
	JEVS Worksamples

Work Evaluation Systems	WEST 1 & 2 Lifting
Technology	WEST 3 Comprehensive Weight
1950 Freeman	WEST 4 Upper Extremity
Long Beach, CA 90804	WEST Bus Bench
	WEST Tool Sort
Work Recovery, Inc.	ERGOS Work Simulator
2341 S. Friebus Ave., Suite 14	
Tucson, AZ 85713	

---

seem to be on the "cutting edge" of vocational evaluation and assessment procedures. Futuristic work simulators are expanding the boundaries of traditional work sampling technologies and curriculum-based assessment procedures. They are making it possible to gather more valid data related to many of the following critical vocational assessment areas: vocational interests and values, career awareness, physical skills, functional academic skills, aptitudes and worker traits, specific vocational skills, work behaviors and attitudes, learning style, related functional living skills, career decision-making skills, job-seeking skills, and personal understanding of oneself and the world of work (Peterson & Peterson, 1986).

The Critical Aspect of Collecting and Using Valid Data

Data collected through the vocational assessment process are generally used to determine the direction of each special needs student's adult life. More specifically, this information is used to identify in which vocational education program a student will be allowed to participate and, possibly, to ascertain that student's eventual job placement when he or she exits the school system. Certainly, the importance of this information is magnified when the lifelong ramifications of these decisions are reflected upon. The concern about using valid data on which to base decisions has led to the evolution of work simulators. This new breed of work sampling technology focuses on the concept of "physical/functional capacities assessment."

Although educational agencies (i.e., the public schools) may not be assessing students to determine whether or not they should be hired, they are making decisions that will very likely affect the entirety of these students' adult working lives. After all, decisions are being made that relegate individual students to specific vocational education programs and, possibly, eventual job placement. Consequently, the importance of using objective, valid data, based upon actual occupational standards, is critical to the assessment process.

Physical/Functional Capacities Assessment

Work sampling technologies and curriculum-based vocational assessment rating instruments have often focused on collecting useful data related to physical/functional abilities. However, the data generated through these processes are often subjective. In work simulator approaches, physical/functional capacities assessment is a highly structured, interdisciplinary, individualized evaluation program designed to provide a benchmark of the individual's physical/vocational functioning. It includes a baseline assessment of physical performance that is related to the physical and functional demand factors defined by the U.S. Department of Labor (Work Recovery, 1988, p. 4). Drawing from the fields of ergonomics (i.e., the science of maximizing comfort on the job) and engineering, work simulator technology has resulted in a system that focuses on the examinee by considering the educational and emotional factors and the aptitudes, interests, attitudes, and other relevant data needed to become a successful worker.

The ERGOS Work Simulator (Work Recovery, Incorporated, 1989), for example, has five component units that are used to collect functional capacities assessment data. These components are:

1. Strength measurement simulation;
2. Whole body range of motion simulation;
3. Work endurance simulation;
4. Standing work tolerance simulation; and
5. Seated work range and upper extremity simulation. (Brandon & Snyder, 1989, p. 215)

The work simulator approach provides a step toward more valid and reliable assessment data. The more valid and reliable that vocational assessment can become, the more confidence we can have in predicting vocational potential. As a whole, formal vocational assessment is evolving toward this more valid and reliable assessment process.

INFORMAL ASSESSMENT

An option to the norm-referenced instrumentation of formal assessment, criterion-referenced informal assessment has gained in popularity in recent years. A rationale for using informal assessment procedures often focuses on its economic advantages, ease of administration, and is direct application to instruction (Elrod, Isbell, & Braziel, 1989). Specific objectives of informal vocational assessment have been identified as including:

- the identification of students with learning problems,

- diagnosis of students' academic strengths and limitations;

- gleaning of information to assist in curricular and instructional modification;

- the assistance in the identification of appropriate classroom materials based on needed classroom skills; and

- the use of classroom teachers or other personnel familiar with the curriculum in the design of the assessment instrument (Wisconsin Vocational Studies Center, 1980)

Classroom-Based Techniques

Informal assessment techniques can address prevocational skills that influence success in vocational training and vocationally related skills that have direct bearing on vocational achievement. Work habits, occupational interests and knowledge, academic skill level, and personal-social skills can be assessed informally. Classroom-based assessment techniques are those practices that evaluate a student's *typical performance* rather than *optimal performance* as might be gleaned in a more formal testing situation (Tindal & Marston, 1990). Classroom-based assessment can be conducted by regular and special educators, with ongoing evaluation being conducted by vocational educators. Parents may also be a part of the informal vocational assessment intake process.

As displayed in Table 3.2, academic and occupational skills can be self-assessed in an informal fashion. By using a simple Y (yes) or N (no) response mode, elementary-age children can self-report their own perceptions regarding their academic skills and work habits. The behaviors identified in Table 3.2 are applicable to both school and work situations (Elrod et al., 1989). Such a scale can be paired with self-monitoring

TABLE 3.2. *Sample Student Academic/Occupational Self-Evaluation Scale*

Academic/Occupational Skills		
I enjoy keeping my desk neat.	Y	N
I enjoy writing letters to my friends.	Y	N
I enjoy answering questions in class.	Y	N
I like to do crossword puzzles.	Y	N
I like to play sports.	Y	N
I can count money easily.	Y	N
I like to think about what I will be when I grow up.	Y	N
I plan my own schedule.	Y	N
I enjoy taking care of others.	Y	N
I like to watch adults at work.	Y	N
I enjoy talking on the telephone.	Y	N
I like to run.	Y	N
I enjoy going to new places.	Y	N
I like people to count on me.	Y	N
I like to learn about inventors.	Y	N
I can draw maps well.	Y	N
I enjoy earning money.	Y	N
I like to save money.	Y	N
I complete all my homework.	Y	N

Note. From "Assessing Transition-Related Variables from Kindergarten Through Grade 12: Practical Applications" by G. F. Elrod, C. H. Isbell, and P. M. Braziel, 1989, *Diagnostique, 14,* p. 253. Copyright 1989 by the Council for Educational Diagnostic Services. Adapted by permission.

behavioral techniques. Although not a vocational assessment, per se, such an evaluation, if conducted with preadolescents, can assist in building critical work habits that will later have a direct bearing on a student's potential for vocational success. If necessary, the teacher conducting the assessment may read the scale items to account for lower reading skill levels of all or some of the children in the class.

An important, but nonetheless neglected, aspect of classroom-based vocational assessment is teacher self-evaluation. Assessment of vocationally related skills should not be simply an annual activity for reporting purposes. The information gleaned from such assessment practices must be incorporated into instruction at all grade levels. Table 3.3 provides a teacher self-evaluation scale that can be used weekly or monthly as a reminder to infuse career/vocational concepts into the existing curriculum (Elrod, et al., 1989). A modified version of this scale can be used to facilitate a carryover of instruction in vocationally related skills with parents.

TABLE 3.3. *Example of Teacher Self-Evaluation Scale*

Self-Evaluation Scale Items	Rating				
I integrate transition-related skills with basic skills objectives.	1	2	3	4	5
I encourage parental involvement in curricular decisions.	1	2	3	4	5
I select classroom activities that are applicable to real-life settings.	1	2	3	4	5
I use a concrete approach in demonstrating problem solving.	1	2	3	4	5
I use a "hands-on" approach to teaching.	1	2	3	4	5
I maintain a classroom environment that stimulates independence.	1	2	3	4	5
I am consistent with my behavior management.	1	2	3	4	5
I implement student self-management techniques.	1	2	3	4	5
I create opportunities for group interaction.	1	2	3	4	5
I seek support of other professionals with regard to program planning.	1	2	3	4	5
I assign classroom duties to promote proper work attitudes.	1	2	3	4	5

Rating scale: 1 = Almost never; 2 = Occasionally; 3 = About half of the time; 4 = Usually; 5 = Almost always.

Note. From "Assessing Transition-Related Variables from Kindergarten Through Grade 12: Practical Applications" by G. F. Elrod, C. H. Isbell, and P. M. Braziel, 1989. *Diagnostique, 14,* p. 254. Copyright 1989 by the Council for Educational Diagnostic Services. Adapted by permission.

Determining a student's vocational interests has been identified as a key dimension of vocational assessment (Veir, 1987). Although outstanding commercially produced vocational interest scales exist, such as the AAMD-Becker Reading-Free Vocational Interest Inventory (Becker, 1975), the Self-Directed Search, Form E (Holland, 1985), and the Wide Range Interest and Opinion Test (Jastak & Jastak, 1974), the classroom teacher, through a structured interview process, can assess a student's career interests. As presented in Table 3.4, a series of questions addressing vocational preferences and student knowledge about those preferences can indicate a degree of career maturity (Elrod et al., 1989).

Although the evaluation instrument exemplified in Table 3.5 may not appear to be vocational in nature, it is actually a component of the Alternative Learning Program (ALPs) Assessment Battery (Looslie, 1991) of the Union County (Oregon) Educational Service District. As an informal

TABLE 3.4. *Sample Vocational Interest Interview Questions*

---

1. What job would you like to have when you finish your education?
2. Do you like to work (play) inside or outside?
3. Do you like to work (play) alone or with others?
4. Do you like to have it quiet when you work (play)?
5. Would you be willing to move in order to get a job?
6. Would you mind working in the evenings or on weekends?
7. Would you mind receiving further training to become a better employee or receive a promotion?
8. What kind of yearly salary do you feel is reasonable?
9. Would you prefer a desk job or a job where you can use your physical skills?
10. Would you prefer working for a large company or a small business?

Note. From "Assessing Transition-Related Variables from Kindergarten Through Grade 12: Practical Applications" by G. F. Elrod, C. H. Isbell, and P. M. Braziel, 1989, *Diagnostique, 14,* p. 255. Copyright 1989 by the Council for Educational Diagnostic Services. Adapted by permission.

---

diagnostic tool, the ALPs Battery is composed of three domains: reading, mathematics, and language arts. These three skill areas are each requisite competencies to success in the ALPs course for students with behavior disorders. The content of the program is a school-based production enterprise that includes manufacturing, advertising, sales, and reinvestment of profits. Therefore, reading, mathematics, and language arts are essential skills for success in the ALPs curriculum. As a pretest, the ALPs Battery can determine the support that each student will need to complete the program successfully. The ALPs Battery is also correlated with skills that the students will need if they elect to take the General Education Diploma (GED) examination. Thus, traditional academics, in the case of the ALPs course, are viewed as essential for competent performance in the school-based enterprise.

In a pure sense, a program such as ALPs is not considered a vocational program. It is not a course designed to prepare students for a specific occupation (e.g., plumbing, drafting, or welding). However, some students, such as those with behavior disorders, are typically underrepresented in traditional vocational programs. Thus, it can be argued that because a program such as ALPs does, in fact, prepare students for the world of work in a generic sense, it *does* constitute some degree of vocational training. And, if ALPs can be perceived as a generic vocational program promoting generalizable vocational skills (Greenan, 1983), then the ALPs Battery can be perceived as informal vocational assessment.

TABLE 3.5. *Selected Items from ALPs Assessment Battery*

Mathematics:

6) 4038   7) $2.69 + $3.74 =
    2379
    +401   34) 8 5/12 − 3 2/3 =

39) Sam has 4 coins in his pocket: a 50 cent piece, a quarter, a dime and a penny. How much money does Sam have in change?

44) Terry applied for a typing job that required a typing speed of at least 65 words per minute. She was given a 6 minute timed typing test. Terry typed 348 words. How many words per minute did Terry average on this test?

Language Arts:

Choose the option that makes the sentence correct.
___2. ___both excellent softball players.
   a. Their
   b. Theirs
   c. They're

___3. The President talked, laughed, and _____.
   a. he was joking.
   b. joked.
   c. he joked.

Choose the correct sentence.
___2. a. Sandy, will you please give me a call?
      b. Sandy will you please give me a call?
      c. Sandy, will you please give me a call.

Reading:

[The following items are based on reading passages.]

Select the correct response.

___2. If you follow the advice in the passage, what does the author predict will happen?
      a. The car will break down within a week.
      b. You will save money by buying a new car.
      c. You will have found a good mechanic.
      d. You will never break down.
      e. You will have found a car worth buying.

continued

___4. The main purpose of this passage is to:
  a. give factual information about buying a car.
  b. tell you which model of car to buy.
  c. get you to look under the hood carefully.
  d. get you to hire a mechanic.
  e. warn you about used car salesmen.

Source: Courtesy of Alternative Learning Program, Union County Educational Service District; Island City, OR. Used with permission of Ms. Kathy Looslie, Coordinator, Alternative Learning Program.

Curriculum-Based Vocational Assessment

Curriculum-based vocational assessment (CBVA) has been defined as "a continuous process used to answer questions about the instruction and special service needs of individual students as they enter into and progress through specific vocational education programs" (Albright, Cobb, Sarkees, & Kingsbury, 1989, p. 144). Thus, rather than a program screening device, or a pre- and posttest procedure, CBVA is an ongoing process evaluating not only student progress, but also the effect of specific instructional interventions. The distinguishing features of CBVA have been identified as:

1. a response to the information needs of personnel
   - during the selection and planning of a student's vocational program;
   - as the student progresses through the program; and
   - during the transition of the student from school to competitive employment or postsecondary education;
2. an assessment activity tied directly to the student's vocational education curriculum;
3. a collaboration of personnel responsible for providing vocational instruction and special services to the student;
4. the use of criterion-referenced, performance-based, and direct procedures for determining student achievement;
5. an adaptation to community-based training environments at both the secondary and postsecondary levels. (Albright et al., 1989, p.144)

Although CBVA has been defined and various approaches offered (see, for example, Albright & Cobb, 1988; Ianacone & Leconte, 1986; Stodden, Meehan, Bisconer, & Hodell, 1989), the "operationalizing" of CBVA is still open to interpretation. Two factors influence this openness. First, by definition, CBVA is a *process*, not a single, standardized assessment instrument or test battery. This process may vary based on the type of vocational program, setting, and personnel. Second, by nature, CBVA is *flexible* and can be adapted, not only across vocational courses, but to community work sites, as well. Variables influencing this flexibility include: instructional pedagogy, availability and type of equipment used in instruction, adopted course text (if any), and desired outcomes (i.e., course adaptation, identification of student strengths and limitations, and community placement).

The development of a foundation of an established process on which to base CBVA, therefore, can enhance its application and exportability. As an alternative assessment approach, curriculum-based assessment has been applied to academic skills (Fuchs, Deno, & Marston, 1983), individualized education plan goals and objectives (Fuchs & Fuchs, 1986), regular classroom instruction (Bursuck & Lessen, 1985), and the screening and referral process (Marston, Mirkin, & Deno, 1984). Such alternatives provide established processes and procedures from which CBVA can be developed and applied across vocational programs and community work sites.

A curriculum-based assessment approach proposed by Bursuck and Lessen (1987) is particularly pertinent to CBVA applications. The reasons for the relevance of this approach are:

- the use of task types (e.g., see/write, hear/write behaviors) with which to categorize competency behaviors;

- the development of probes based on the categorized competency behaviors;

- the use of a "work habits" assessment domain; and

- the application of ecological assessment through an environmental inventory.

The following section, therefore, applies the Bursuck and Lessen model to CBVA. Using a vocational course in General Metals, specific competency behaviors are identified and categorized into task types. This categorization is followed by work habit variables that can be assessed, and dimensions of the classroom environment that can be examined for adaptation purposes. General Metals is a competency-based course providing the student with the knowledge and skills necessary for employment in various metal manufacturing technology occupations (e.g., casting, sheet metal, gas welding, soldering, and ornamental iron work).

Task Types

The curriculum-based assessment model proposed by Bursuck and Lessen (1987) includes four task-types: see/write behaviors, see/say behaviors, hear/write behaviors, and think/write behaviors. These four task-types are applied, below, to the General Metals course. A fifth task-type, learn/perform behaviors, is added to the model to reflect the performance nature of vocational education courses.

As depicted in Table 3.6, a course in General Metals includes several see/write competency behaviors. Some of these behaviors (e.g., those involving arithmetic computations) can be instructed in the special class and reinforced in the vocational class. Thus, CBVA can assist in detecting generalizable skills (Greenan, 1983, 1987) that are applicable across various vocational course offerings. The results of CBVA with the General Metals course indicate substantial amounts of written work, more so than may be imagined by most special educators or diagnosticians. Additionally, a behavior such as "copy notes from a class demonstration" is a skill uniquely different from taking lecture notes in a traditional class setting. Although this latter note-taking skill is often taught in the special class, there is less emphasis on gleaning important information from in-class demonstrations. In such an instance, while this skill is taught in a special class, the vocational instructor, using verbal and visual cues, can underscore important points during the demonstration of the skill itself.

Table 3.7 displays see/say competency behaviors for General Metals. Some of these behaviors (e.g., "orally convert fractions to decimals") can be converted into in-class probes whereby the instructor can quickly assess a student's knowledge or application of a procedure.

As shown in Table 3.8, some of the hear/write behaviors may also be taught in a special class (e.g., "list safety rules," "spell related terms"). It is noteworthy that CBVA clearly defines the importance of safety in a vocational course such as General Metals. A mention of safety is found in four out of the five domains used as task-type categories.

TABLE 3.6. *See/Write Behaviors for General Metals Course*

Copy a drawing with dimensions.

Copy safety rules.

Identify in writing various metals (e.g., brass, bronze).

Draw a ruler depicting increments of 1/64".

Indentify in writing:
  Measuring tools.
  Layout tools.
  Cutting tools.
  Filing tools.

Identify in writing metal-working machinery.

Compute in writing:
  Multiple digit addition with regrouping.
  Multiple digit subtraction with regrouping.
  Multiple digit multiplication with regrouping.
  Multiple digit division with regrouping.
  Addition of fractions with unlike denominators.
  Subtraction of fractions with unlike denominators.
  Conversion of fractions to decimals.
  Addition of decimals.
  Subtraction of decimals.

Copy notes from class demonstrations.

TABLE 3.7. *See/Say Behaviors for General Metals Course*

Orally identify safety rules.
Orally recite procedures for starting and stopping metal-working machinery.
Orally recite procedures for proper operating of metal-working machinery.
Orally identify techniques for bending, cutting, and filing machine work.
Orally convert fractions to decimals using charts.
Orally identify drill and tap sizes from charts.

Think/write behaviors, indicating that a novel outcome is expected from the synthesis of prior knowledge, are displayed in Table 3.9. An interesting factor related to the think/write behaviors (both of which involve drafting) is that other identified skills (e.g., "proper line weight" and "correct labeling and dimensions") are prerequisites to success. Thus, an initial examination of curricular requirements in a

TABLE 3.8. *Hear/Write Behaviors for General Metals Course*

List safety rules from memory.
Spell related terms from dictation.
Write class lecture notes.
List machinery-operating procedures from lecture.

TABLE 3.9. *Think/Write Behaviors for General Metals Course*

Draft a drawing of metal assembly.
Draft parts of a product to be manufactured.

TABLE 3.10. *Learn/Perform Behaviors for General Metals Course*

Demonstrate safety rules in shop setting.
Demonstrate proper welding procedures.
Perform proper procedures in using metal-working machinery.
Demonstrate proper techniques for:

Casting.
Forming.
Bending.

Exhibit proper procedures when finishing a product.

TABLE 3.11. *Spelling Probe from General Metals Course*

abrasive	copper	oxidation
adhesion	corrosion	pewter
alloy	ductility	
aluminum	embossing	
anvil	ferrous	
beryllium	forge	
brazing	galvanized	
chisel	malleability	
cohesion	metallurgy	

given vocational class may spawn the need to assess (and teach) prerequisite behaviors.

Due to the application and performance nature of vocational education, a fifth competency behavior domain of learn/perform was added to the four domains proposed by Bursuck and Lessen (1987). These learn/perform behaviors (shown in Table 3.10) focus on a demonstrated synthesis of knowledge, much of which combines behaviors from the other four competency domains. Thus, "demonstrate proper techniques for casting" can be viewed as a synthesis of, among others, the following:

- see/write behaviors:
  - copying safety rules;
  - identifying various metals; and
  - copying notes from class demonstrations;
- see/say behaviors:
  - orally identifying safety rules; and
  - orally converting fractions to decimals;
- hear/write behavior:
  - listing safety rules.

Using information gained from the task-type analysis, assessment probes are designed to evaluate specific competencies. Table 3.11 provides a listing of 20 terms from the General Metals course that are incorporated into a spelling probe. These same terms can be used to assess knowledge of key concepts. Some probes that are performance-based in nature may have a timed element derived from industrial standards.

Work Habits

Beyond the assessment of tasks related to specific vocational courses, CBVA should evaluate a student's work habits across several settings. As portrayed in Table 3.12, work habits and behaviors can be assessed through the use of a Likert-type scale wherein specific behaviors are targeted. To glean the generalizability of these behaviors, it is suggested that such an evaluation be conducted simultaneously in different settings. For example, on a given day, a regular teacher, a special education teacher, a vocational instructor, and an employer (if work experience is an option) can complete the same rating scale on a specific student. Thus, evaluated behaviors can be assessed across various environments in which the student is expected to perform. Although the rating scale shown in Table 3.12 is teacher designed, there are some prepackaged, researched work habits assessment tools that are available. (See Rosenberg & Tesolowski, 1979; Rusch, Schutz, Mithaug, Stewart, & Mar, 1982.)

TABLE 3.12. *Work Habit Rating Scale*

Student: _____
Date: _____ Evaluation Site: _____
Rater: _____

Work Behavior	Rating
1. Dresses appropriately.	1 2 3 4 5
2. Is well groomed.	1 2 3 4 5
3. Attends class (work) regularly.	1 2 3 4 5
4. Is punctual.	1 2 3 4 5
5. Demonstrates initiative.	1 2 3 4 5
6. Works well independently.	1 2 3 4 5
7. Works well with peers.	1 2 3 4 5
8. Works well with authority figures.	1 2 3 4 5
9. Is receptive to constructive criticism.	1 2 3 4 5
10. Shows pride in work.	1 2 3 4 5
11. Keeps neat work area.	1 2 3 4 5
12. Completes tasks on time.	1 2 3 4 5
13. Asks questions, if needed.	1 2 3 4 5
14. Accepts new responsibilities.	1 2 3 4 5
15. Solicits additional tasks (duties) when finished with a task (duty).	1 2 3 4 5

Rating scale: 1 = Never observed; 2 = Observed sometimes; 3 = Observed about half the time; 4 = Observed often; 5 = Always observed.

Note. From "Assessing Transition-Related Variables from Kindergarten Through Grade 12: Practical Applications" by G. F. Elrod, C. H. Isbell, and P. M. Braziel, 1989, *Diagnostique*, 14, p. 257. Copyright by the Council for Educational Diagnostic Services. Adapted by permission.

Ecological Assessment

Evaluating the vocational environment in which a student performs can facilitate that student's success in that environment. Uses of ecological assessment have been identified as:

- the identification of instructionally relevant variables that can be influenced by the teacher or supervisor;

- the determination of whether a particular vocational course or work experience site is suitable for a given student; and

- the distinguishing of achievement problems that are student-centered or teacher-centered. (Bursuck & Lessen, 1987)

Thus, appropriate vocational ecological assessment should evaluate both teacher (supervisor) behaviors and student behaviors in an antecedent/behavior/consequence manner (Bursuck & Lessen, 1987). Some of the variables included in the assessment device in Table 3.13 have been determined to correlate positively with academic achievement (Anderson, Evertson, & Brophy, 1979), success in vocational training (Elrod, 1987b), and job performance (Salzberg, McConaughy, Lignugaris/Kraft, Agran, & Stowitschek, 1987).

Specific alterations in the Bursuck and Lessen (1987) ecological assessment device were incorporated into the instrument displayed in Table 3.13. To make the instrument more applicable to vocational programs, the terms *teacher* and *supervisor* are used interchangeably to address work experience situations in which an employer/supervisor would be the focus of the evaluation, rather than a teacher. Also, instead of focusing solely on academic responses (i.e., correct/incorrect answers), the vocational environment would necessarily include *performance* of skills. Thus, both successful and unsuccessful performance scenarios are used. It should be noted that the device displayed in Table 3.13 reflects only a partial ecological screening, focusing primarily on student–teacher (supervisor)–peer behaviors in successful and unsuccessful situations. Other variables that can be assessed via an ecological survey would include: (a) the physical setting of the vocational course/work site, (b) the worker/student-supervisor/teacher ratio, (c) the type of equipment needed, and (d) specific type of clothing that might be necessary on the job (e.g., steel-toed work boots).

By using a model of CBVA that incorporates curricular task evaluation, work habits assessment, and an ecological screening, the evaluator can gain a knowledge of variables that directly affect a student's potential for success in a specific vocational program. At various times in the ongoing assessment process, the evaluator must use the gathered data to address these decision points:

1. Is the vocational course suitable for the student?
2. If so, what skills does the student need for successful course completion?
3. Can skill deficits be strengthened?

TABLE 3.13. *Ecological Assessment Instrument for Vocational Programs*

1. Teacher (supervisor) response to successful performance:
___a. immediate reinforcement
___b. delayed reinforcement
___c. no reinforcement

2. Student response to successful performance:
___a. positive
___b. negative
___c. no response

3. Peer response to student's successful performance:
___a. positive
___b. negative
___c. no response

4. Teacher (supervisor) response to unsuccessful performance:
___a. immediate corrective feedback
___b. delayed corrective feedback
___c. modeling of correct performance
___d. requiring of student to imitate correct performance
___e. no corrective feedback
___f. punishment/sarcasm

5. Student response to unsuccessful performance:
___a. guessed
___b. self-correction
___c. gave up
___d. attempted alternative response:_____
___e. sought assistance from:_____
___f. became negative/hostile

6. Peer response to student's unsuccessful performance:
___a. positive/encouraging
___b. negative/discouraging
___c. no response

4. Can these skills be taught cooperatively between vocational and special education?

5. Can the vocational course be adapted to assist the student in overcoming these skill deficits?

CASE STUDY

Assessment of vocational skills must be translated into valid annual goals and short-term objectives on an individual student basis. A thorough vocational assessment report should address interests and aptitudes with prescriptions as to prospective vocational education approaches. A student's strengths and limitations related to training in a specific vocational program must be clearly defined.

TABLE 3.14. *Vocational Assessment Case Study*

Anytown High School
1234 Pinewood Avenue
Anytown, USA

Date: January 22, 1991

Student: John Doe
Age: 15
Grade: 10

Examiner: P. Smith
Evaluation Dates: January 10, 11, 14, 1991

Assessment Devices Used:
        Vocational Interest Assessment System I(VIAS)
        New Concepts Engine Service Work Sample
        New Concepts House & Industrial Wiring Work Sample
        Apticom: Aptitudes E, F, K, M, & P

Background Information:

John Doe is a student with learning disabilities who is mainstreamed for all but one period of the school day. He is a likable young man who is cooperative and presents himself well in public. John's parents divorced when he was 10 years of age, and he is currently living with his mother. He has one younger

continued

sister, 11 years old, who is also living at home with the mother. John is an athletic young man, who possesses an interest and skill in working with his hands. John's work history includes a summer job as a stock boy with Miller Hardware, and a part-time kitchen helper at the high school.

Strengths:

With regard to John's relative strengths, the following characteristics are pertinent:
- excellent attendance
- punctual
- neat appearance
- cooperative with peers, authority figures
- seeks assistance as needed
- good mechanical ability

Limitations:

John's relative limitations are as follows:
- poor conceptualization skills
- poor attention span
- low frustration tolerance
- does not work well under pressure
- lacks self-confidence
- slow work pace

Primary Learning Mode:

John acquires material most effectively when it is presented through an audio/visual means (e.g., a film), or though actual "hands-on" instruction.

Assessment Results:

Vocational Interests:

Results of the VIAS showed that John demonstrated a high degree of interest in the following areas:
- electrical/electronics
- trade and industrial - mechanical
- engineering technology

Test Performance:

New Concepts Engine Service Work Sample:
This work sample measures the ability to learn and perform several of the basic tasks commonly performed in mechanical repair jobs. The tasks explored in this work station most closely resemble those performed by Automobile Mechanics, DOT #602.261-010. Both time and accuracy scores should be taken into consideration as they relate to recommended jobs.

Accuracy . . . . 5 errors
Time . . . . 107 minutes

New Concepts House & Industrial Wiring Work Sample:
This work sample measures the ability to learn and perform several of the basic tasks commonly performed in entry-level jobs in the wiring trades. The tasks explored in this work station most closely resemble those performed by an Electrician's Helper, DOT #829.684-022. Both time and accuracy scores should be considered as they relate to recommended jobs.

Accuracy . . . . 6 errors
Time . . . . 205 minutes

Apticom: Aptitude E
Measures the ability to move the hand and foot in coordination with each other in accordance with presented visual stimuli.

Results . . . . . 54th percentile

Apticom: Aptitude F
Measures the ability to move the fingers and manipulate small objects with the fingers rapidly and accurately.

Results . . . . . 91st percentile

Apticom: Aptitude K
Measures the ability to coordinate eyes and hands or fingers rapidly and accurately in making precise movements with speed. Ability to make a movement response accurately and quickly.

Results . . . . . 60th percentile

Apticom: Aptitude M
Measures the ability to move the hands easily and skillfully. To work with the hands in placing and turning motions.

Results . . . . . 54th percentile

continued

Apticom: Aptitude P
Measures the ability to perceive pertinent detail in objects or in pictorial or
graphic material. To make visual comparisons and discriminations and see
slight differences in shapes and shadings of figures, and widths and
lengths of lines.

Results   . . . . 56th percentile

Physical Demands Reported:
The physical demand level of John's profile indicates a level of lifting
50 pounds maximum with frequent lifting and/or carrying of objects
weighing up to 25 pounds. This level may be re-verified on specific
job sites.

Analysis of Test Performance:

Engine Service Work Sample:
   Accuracy: John's near average accuracy score suggests that he
should not require more supervision than most trainees or workers.
His score also indicates an ability to learn and perform fairly accurately a multistep process through a combination of verbal instructions, hands-on learning, and learning strategies applications. John
may also benefit from training if a higher level of accuracy is required
for satisfactory job performance. His accuracy suggests that he
should be comfortable working with hand tools, such as those used
in mechanical repair jobs.
   Time: John's slightly below average time score suggests that he would
benefit from practice in learning to perform tasks of this nature quickly. He
might also benefit from training to achieve the level of speed required for
satisfactory job performance. John's score also suggests that he may not
be comfortable working with hand tools, such as those used in mechanical
repair jobs, at least at present.

House and Industrial Wiring Work Sample:
   Accuracy: John's low score suggests that he will likely require more
supervision than most trainees or workers. His score also indicates that he
would benefit from practice in learning to perform a multistep process
accurately. John would also benefit from training to achieve the higher level
of accuracy required for satisfactory job performance. His accuracy also
suggests that he is not comfortable working with small hand tools used in
entry-level wiring trades.
   Time: John's near average score suggests that he felt fairly comfortable with the task. His score also reflects a tendency to try to work quickly

in performing work-related tasks. John's score also suggests that he should, with development of accuracy, eventually be comfortable with small hand tools used in entry-level wiring occupations.

Apticom: Aptitude E
John's score suggests that he has the aptitude to work fairly comfortably at tasks that require skilled or easy coordination of the eyes, hands, and feet, such as is required of workers operating machines such as sewing machines, fork-lifts, and motor vehicles.

Apticom: Aptitude F
John's excellent score suggests that he has the aptitude to work very comfortably at tasks which require fast or accurate finger movement, such as is required of bank tellers, electronics workers, or data-entry operators.

Apticom: Aptitude K
John's score suggests that he has the aptitude to work fairly comfortably at tasks that require rapid and accurate coordination of the eyes, hands, and fingers in making precise movements with speed. This level of aptitude is required for a person to work comfortably as a telephone answering service operator, clerk typist, stenographer, veterinarian, librarian, audit clerk, mail clerk, clothes designer, illustrator, general duty nurse, calculating machine operator, bindery worker, coding clerk, restaurant manager, forester, diesel mechanic, automobile painter, or forester aide.

Apticom: Aptitude M
John's near average score suggests that he has the aptitude to work fairly comfortably at tasks that require skillful or easy hand movement, such as is required of electronics mechanics, sheet metal workers, electronics assembly workers, printer compositors, surgical technicians, or machine packagers.

Apticom: Aptitude P
John's near average score suggests that he has the aptitude to perceive pertinent detail in objects or in pictorial or graphic material. However, this score also indicates that he may encounter some difficulties in making visual comparisons and discriminations in very fine shapes, shadings of figures, and widths and lengths of lines. This higher level of aptitude is needed in interpreting dental x-rays, photographic materials or flight charts.

continued

Summary and Recommendations:

For vocational training and work, John's strengths consist of:

1. An ability to learn and perform a multistep process fairly accurately, using hand tools for mechanical repair jobs.
2. An ability to learn and perform fairly quickly work tasks using hand tools for entry-level jobs in the wiring trades.
3. Good form perception.
4. Good motor coordination.
5. Excellent finger dexterity.
6. Good manual dexterity.

For vocational training and work, John's limitations consist of:

1. A need for practice in learning to perform quickly when working with hand tools for mechanical repair jobs.
2. A need for extended practice in learning to perform a multistep process accurately, using small hand tools for entry-level jobs in the wiring trades.
3. Fair eye-hand coordination.

As depicted in Table 3.14, a vocational evaluation report should be readable and reflect specific test results. If, as in the case study shown, formal assessment batteries are used, the tests and subtests should be briefly described as to their content and the specific skills assessed. Results should relate to specific occupations and job listings in the Dictionary of Occupational Titles (DOT) (U.S. Department of Labor, 1977).

The subject (John Doe) described in the case study is a student with a mild disability. He possesses enough skills that, with minimal support services, he can be educated in the least restrictive vocational setting. In addition to the summary and recommendations noted in the case study, a multidisciplinary examination of the assessment results can delineate roles and responsibilities of vocational, regular, and special education.

In John Doe's case, for example, some of his limitations can be addressed in the special class and reinforced in both vocational and regular education. John's first limitation focuses on his work pace. Although the results specifically target a mechanical orientation, work pace can be taught and reinforced in other settings, as well. An annual goal on John's individualized education plan might be written as follows:

John Doe will decrease the length of time it takes him to complete an assigned task.

This effort to influence John's work pace can also be reinforced in the regular classroom. Cooperating regular teachers can monitor the time it takes John to complete assignments given in class. These regular teachers can also reinforce on-time task completion by providing verbal or visual cues as reminders of expired time or off-task behaviors. Parents can even monitor John's on-time task completion performance at home.

John's second limitation, performing a multistep process when using hand tools for entry-level wiring jobs, provides another opportunity for multidisciplinary cooperation. The special educator and vocational educator can cooperatively design a learning strategy wherein each step of the hand tool use process can be identified and applied to a mnemonic device to facilitate recall of the steps. Such a strategy development process has been used to promote acquisition and application of steps in improving academic performance (Deshler, Schumaker, & Lenz, 1984; Deshler, Schumaker, Lenz, & Ellis, 1984) and classroom participation (Ellis, 1989) among students with learning disabilities. Strategy instruction has also been applied in teaching steps to successful job interviewing (Julian, 1987).

As stated earlier in this chapter, the primary purpose of the vocational assessment of students with disabilities is to support their education in the least restrictive vocational setting. Thus, cooperation among special, regular, and vocational education can enhance a student's progress toward successful completion of a vocational training program.

FUTURE DIRECTIONS

As the field of vocational education evolves to reflect a more technically oriented job market, so too will the nature of vocational assessment change to meet this evolution. The skills needed for success in technological fields will, increasingly, be less distinguishable from more traditional academic subjects. A major factor that will continue to differentiate vocational education will be its application of those academic skills in a work environment. The outmoded notion that students who cannot perform successfully in traditional subject areas will be able to find a haven in vocational education will simply not be valid. Success in vocational education will increasingly depend on the possession of the requisite academic and social skills and work behaviors that reflect the needs of a more information processing–oriented society. Recent educational reform efforts have made the erroneous assumption that students already possess the necessary work habits (as identified in Table 3.12) and only need more intensive academic or vocational preparation. To the extent that the instruction of work habits is ignored in new curricular policy thrusts, these well-intentioned reform initiatives will produce less than hoped for outcomes. It has been documented, for example, that the excellence that Asian-American students display in our nation's schools is a result of a work ethic that has eclipsed the work habits of non-Asian-American students (Butterfield, 1990).

As vocational education becomes more like traditional education, and vice versa, the abdication of responsibility for vocational assessment (which is currently viewed as the primary domain of vocational education) will be less justifiable. It will be more incumbent upon regular educators, special educators, counselors, and school psychologists to participate actively in the vocational assessment process. To emphasize this point, a study by Tesolowski and Wichowski (1984) found that instructors and counselors were making vocational placement decisions on available work sample results even though neither group had sufficient training in vocational assessment to interpret the test outcomes accurately. Only through a truly multidisciplinary assessment approach will the abstract nature of certain traditional school subjects be minimized through relevant vocational applications, and will proper vocational program placement decisions be implemented. This multidisciplinary approach will require a collaborative theme to vocational assessment, which means that more than just vocational education must be involved in this assessment process.

The authors would like to express their appreciation for the assistance of Mr. Ray Minge, Consultant for Vocational Special Needs Education, Union County (OR) Educational Service District, and to the New Concepts Corporation of Tucson, Arizona, in the development of this chapter.

REFERENCES

Albright, L., & Cobb, R. B. (1988). Curriculum based vocational assessment: A concept whose time has come. *The Journal for Vocational Special Needs Education, 10*, 13-16.

Albright, L., Cobb, R. B., Sarkees, M. D., & Kingsbury, D. (1989). Formative field test evaluation of a curriculum-based vocational assessment training program. In G. F. Elrod (Ed.), *Career education for special needs individuals: Learning, earning, contributing* (pp. 143.152). Reston, VA: Division on Career Development of the Council for Exceptional Children.

Anastasi, A. (1961). *Psychological testing* (2nd ed.). New York: Macmillan.

Anderson, L. M., Evertson, C. M., & Brophy, J. F. (1979). An experimental study of effective teaching in first grade reading groups. *The Elementary School Journal, 72*, 193-223.

Becker, R. L. (1975). *AAMD-Becker reading-free vocational interest inventory.* Washington, DC: American Association of Mental Deficiency.

Botterbusch, K. (1987). *Vocational assessment and evaluation systems: A comparison.* Menomonie, WI: University of Wisconsin—Stout, Materials Development Center.

Brandon, T. L., & Snyder, L. (1989). Work Recovery Center, Piedmont Hospital, Atlanta, Georgia. In L. Ogden-Niemeyer & K. Jacobs (Eds.), *Work hardening—State of the art* (pp. 209-221). Thorofare, NJ: Slack.

Brolin, D. E. (1978). *Life centered career education: A competency based approach.* Reston, VA: The Council for Exceptional Children.

Brolin, D. E. (1983). *Life centered career education: A competency based approach* (rev. ed.). Reston, VA: The Council for Exceptional Children.

Brolin, D. E. (1989). *Life centered career education: A competency based approach* (3rd ed.). Reston, VA: The Council for Exceptional Children.

Bursuck, W. D., & Lessen, E. I. (1985). Curriculum-based assessment: Increasing the participation of regular educators in mainstreaming. *ICEC Quarterly, 34*, 25-26.

Bursuck, W. D., & Lessen, E. (1987). A classroom-based model for assessing students with learning disabilities. *Learning Disabilities Focus, 3*, 17-29.

Butterfield, F. (1990, January 21). Why they excel. *Parade Magazine*, 4-6.

Carl D. Perkins Vocational Education Act of 1984. (PL 98-524).

Clark, G. M., & Kolstoe, O. P. (1990). *Career development and transition education for adolescents with disabilities.* Boston: Allyn and Bacon.

Commission on National Aid to Vocational Education. (1914). *Report of the Commission on National Aid to Vocational Education* (together with hearings held on the subject). U.S. House of Representatives, 63rd Congress, Second session, Doc. No. 1004. Volume 1, p. 12. Washington, DC: Government Printing Office.

Dahl, T., Appleby, J., & Lipe, D. (1978). *Mainstreaming guidebook for vocational educators teaching the handicapped.* Salt Lake City: Olympus.

Dart, J. (1990, Fall). ADA: Landmark declaration of equality. *Worklife: A Publication on Employment and People with Disabilities, 3*, 1.

Deshler, D. D., Schumaker, J., & Lenz, B. K. (1984). Academic and cognitive interventions for LD adolescents: Part I. *Journal of Learning Disabilities, 17*, 108-117.

Deshler, D. D., Schumaker, J., Lenz, K., & Ellis, E. (1984). Academic and cognitive interventions for LD adolescents: Part II. *Journal of Learning Disabilities, 17*, 170-179.

Edgar, E., Levine, P., & Maddox, M. (1986). *Statewide follow-up studies of secondary special education students in transition.* Working paper of the Networking and Evaluation Team, Child Development and Mental Retardation Center, University of Washington, Seattle.

Ellis, E. S. (1989). A metacognitive intervention for increasing class participation. *Learning Disabilities Focus, 5,* 36-46.

Elrod, G. F. (1987a). Transition-related assessment: The foundation of preparation for postsecondary success. In G. F. Elrod (Ed.), Transition-related assessment [Monograph]. *Diagnostique, 12,* 127-130.

Elrod, G. F. (1987b). Academic and social skills pre-requisite to success in vocational training: Perceptions of vocational educators. *The Journal for Vocational Special Needs Education, 10,* 17-21.

Elrod, G. F., Isbell, C. H., & Braziel, P. M. (1989). Assessing transition-related variables from kindergarten through grade 12: Practical applications. *Diagnostique, 14,* 247-261.

Fuchs, L. S., Deno, S., & Marston, D. (1983). Improving the reliability of curriculum-based measures of academic skills for psychoeducational decision making. *Diagnostique, 8,* 135-149.

Fuchs, L. S., & Fuchs, D. (1986). Curriculum-based assessment of progress toward long-term and short-term goals. *Journal of Special Education, 20,* 69-82.

Greenan, J. P. (1983). Identification and validation of generalizable skills in vocational programs. *Journal of Vocational Education Research, 8,* 46-71.

Greenan, J. P. (1987). Generalizable skills instruction. In G. B. Meers (Ed.), *Handbook of vocational special needs education* (2nd ed., pp. 157-174). Rockville, MD: Aspen.

Halpern, A. S. (1985). Transition: A look at the foundations. *Exceptional Children, 51,* 479-486.

Hasazi, S. B., Gordon, L. R., Roe, C. A., Hull, M., Finck, K., & Salembier, G. (1985). A statewide follow-up on post high school employment and residential status of students labeled "mentally retarded." *Education and Training of the Mentally Retarded, 20,* 222-234.

Holland, J. L. (1985). *The Self-Directed Search—Form E.* Odessa, FL: Psychological Assessment Resources.

Hursh, N. C., & Kerns, A. F. (1988). *Vocational evaluation in special education.* Boston: College-Hill Press.

Ianacone, R. N., & Leconte, P. J. (1986). Curriculum-based vocational assessment: A viable response to a school-based service delivery issue. *Career Development for Exceptional Individuals, 9,* 113-120.

Institute for the Crippled and Disabled. (1959). *TOWER: Testing, orientation, and work evaluation in rehabilitation.* New York: Author.

Jaffee, C. L. (1965). Assessment centers find management potential. *Bell Telephone Magazine, 44,* 18-24.

Jastak, J., & Jastak, S. (1974). *Wide range interest and opinion test.* Wilmington, DE: Guidance Associates of Delaware.

Julian, M. (1987, March). *Strategy applications to enhance interviewing skills.* Paper presented at the annual Conference of the South Carolina Division on Career Development, Columbia, SC.

Kiernan, W. E., & Payne, M. E. (1982). Hard to train: A history of vocational training for special needs youth. In K. P. Lynch, W. E. Kiernan, & J. A. Stark (Eds.), *Prevocational and vocational education for special needs youth* (pp. 15-42). Baltimore: Paul H. Brookes.

Kokaska, C. J., Gruenhagen, K., Razeghi, J., & Fair, G. W. (1985, October). Division on Career Development's position statement on transition. In D. E. Brolin (Ed.), *Proceedings of the International Conference on the Decade of the Disabled: Transition to work and adult life* (p. 28). Reston, VA: Division on Career Development, Council for Exceptional Children.

Looslie, K. M. (1991). *ALPs assessment battery.* Island City, OR: Union County Educational Service District.

Marston, D., Mirkin, P., & Deno, S. (1984). Curriculum-based measurement: An alternative to traditional screening, referral and identification. *Journal of Special Education, 18,* 109-117.

Mithaug, D., Horiuchi, C., & Fanning, P. (1985). A report on the Colorado statewide follow-up survey of special education students. *Exceptional Children, 51,* 397-404.

Nadolsky, J. N. (1977, July). *The use of work samples in the vocational evaluation process.* Paper presented at the Rehabilitation Forum on Systems of Vocational Evaluation, Rehabilitation Services Education, Auburn University, Auburn, AL.

Neff, W. S. (1968). *Work and human behavior.* Chicago: Aldine.

Nystrom, D. C., & Bayne, G. K. (1979). *Occupation and career education legislation* (2nd ed.). Indianapolis: Bobbs-Merrill.

Odiorne, G. S., & Miller, E. L. (1971). Selection by objectives: A new approach to managerial selection. In W. L. French & D. Hellriegel (Eds.), *Personnel management and organization development: Fields in transition* (pp. 218-236). New York: Houghton Mifflin.

Peterson, M., & Peterson, D. (1986). Assessment: A resource in vocational instruction of special needs students. *The Journal for Vocational Special Needs Education, 8,* 13-16.

Phelps, L. A., & Frasier, J. R. (1988). Legislative and policy aspects of vocational special education. In R. Gaylord-Ross (Ed.), *Vocational education for persons with handicaps* (pp. 27-48). Mountain View, CA: Mayfield.

Pruitt, W. A. (1977). *Vocational (work) evaluation.* Menomonie, WI: Walt Pruitt Associates.

Roberts, C. L. (1970). Definitions, objectives, and goals in work evaluation. *Journal of Rehabilitation, 36,* 13-15.

Rosenberg, H., & Tesolowski, D. G. (1979). *Florida International diagnostic-prescriptive vocational competency profile.* Chicago: Stoelting.

Rusch, F. R., Schutz, R. P., Mithaug, D. E., Stewart, J. E., & Mar, D. K. (1982). *The vocational assessment and curriculum guide.* Seattle: Exceptional Education.

Salzberg, C. L., McConaughy, E. K., Lignugaris/Kraft, B., Agran, M., & Stowitschek, J. J. (1987). Behaviors of distinction: The transition from acceptable to highly valued worker. *The Journal for Vocational Special Needs Education, 10,* 23-28.

Sarkees, M. D., & Scott, J. L. (1986). *Vocational special needs* (2nd ed.). Alsip, IL: American Technical Publishers.

Scarpati, S. (1989). Assessing vocational abilities. In H. L. Swanson & B. L. Watson (Eds.), *Educational and psychological assessment of exceptional children* (2nd ed.) (pp. 309-337). Columbus, OH: Merrill.

Stodden, R. A., Meehan, K. A., Bisconer, S. W., & Hodell, S. L. (1989). The impact of vocational assessment information on the individualized education planning process: Supporting curriculum-based assessment. *The Journal for Vocational Special Needs Education, 12,* 31-36.

Task Force Number 7, Vocational Evaluation Project. (1975). Glossary of terms used in vocational evaluation. *Vocational Evaluation and Work Adjustment Bulletin, 8,* 85-93.

Tesolowski, D. G., & Morgan, T. E. (1980). Selecting educational administrators: The assessment center technique. *NASP Bulletin, 64,* 107-115.

Tesolowski, D. G., & Wichowski, C. P. (1984). Perceived equity of admission standards and practices utilized in public occupational education programs. *Journal of Industrial Teacher Education, 21,* 25-42.

Tindal, G. A., & Marston, D. B. (1990). *Classroom-based assessment: Evaluating instructional outcomes.* Columbus, OH: Merrill.

Treat, K. (1929). Tests for garment machine operators. *Personnel Journal, 8,* 19-28.

U.S. Congress. (1917). Smith-Hughes Act.

U.S. Congress. (1958). National Education Act.

U.S. Congress. (1963). Vocational Education Act, Public Law 88-210.

U.S. Congress. (1968). Vocational Education Act Amendments of 1968, Public Law 90-576.

U.S. Congress. (1973). Rehabilitation Act of 1973, Public Law 93-112.

U.S. Congress. (1974). Rehabilitation Act Amendments of 1974, Public Law 93-516.

U.S. Congress. (1975). Education for All Handicapped Children Act, Public Law 94-142.

U.S. Congress. (1978). Rehabilitation, Comprehensive Services, and Developmental Disabilities Amendments, Public Law 95-602.

U.S. Congress. (1983). Education of the Handicapped Act Amendments, Public Law 98-199.

U.S. Congress. (1984). Carl D. Perkins Act, Public Law 98-524.

U.S. Congress. (1990a). Americans with Disabilities Act, Public Law 101-336.

U.S. Congress. (1990b). Carl D. Perkins Vocational and Applied Technology Education Act Amendments, Public Law 101-392.

U.S. Congress. (1990c). Individuals with Disabilities Education Act, Public Law 101-476.

U.S. Department of Labor. (1977). *Dictionary of occupational titles.* Washington, DC: Author.

Veir, C. A. (1987). Vocational assessment: The evolving role. In G. D. Meers (Ed.), *Handbook of vocational special needs education* (2nd ed., pp. 213-255). Rockville, MD: Aspen.

Will, M. (1984). *OSERS programming for the transition of youth with disabilities: Bridges from school to working life.* Washington, DC: Office of Special Education and Rehabilitative Services.

Wirt, J. G. (1991). A new federal law on vocational education: Will reform follow? *Phi Delta Kappan, 72,* 425-433.

Wisconsin Vocational Studies Center. (1980). *Puzzled about educating special needs students?* University of Wisconsin, Madison: Author.

Work Recovery, Incorporated. (1988). *ERGOS training manual.* Tucson, AZ: Author.

Work Recovery, Incorporated. (1989). *ERGOS work simulator.* Tucson, AZ: Author.

4 DEVELOPMENTAL ASSESSMENT: EVALUATION OF INFANTS AND PRESCHOOLERS

Koressa Kutsick Malcolm

A request to assess a child who has not reached school age often strikes fear in the hearts of psychoeducational diagnosticians. Few clinicians receive specialized training in infant and preschool assessment. As such, instruments available for this purpose are not familiar tools. Many of the tests look cumbersome and complicated with all their attendant toys and objects. Examiners may recall vague information that these instruments were flawed in terms of validity, reliability, and other statistical components. In many cases, examiners just do not know which tests they should administer. To make matters worse, there are the preschool children themselves. These children typically do not have prior experience in sitting still for any type of structured activity. They squirm and grab at all the assessment toys. They want to work on the floor and not at a table. They refuse to give back a particular test object. Their articulation skills may be so poor that their speech is unintelligible. You ask them to do something and they look at you as if you are from another planet. Many won't separate from their parents in order to go to the evaluation room. These factors have led some psychologists, diagnosticians, speech pathologists, and other educationally based professionals to exclaim, "I don't know what to do with these little guys."

Reports have been filed stating that a certain young child was "untestable." The first premise of this chapter is that there is no such thing as an untestable child. Some children, especially the very young child who might possess a variety of handicapping conditions, pose greater challenges to the assessment process than do others. Nevertheless, they can be evaluated. The purpose of this chapter is to discuss guidelines, issues, techniques, and instruments relevant to the evaluation of young children. A review of the history of preschool assessment will also be discussed. It is hoped this information will provide the evaluator of preschoolers with an appropriate framework for completing developmental assessments.

HISTORY OF PRESCHOOL ASSESSMENT

Interest in the assessment of the developmental status of infants and preschool-aged children can be traced to the turn of the 20th century. The creation of instruments for preschool assessment follows the general history of psychological testing. Early attempts to examine intellectual functioning of young children were undertaken in order to gather data for theories of cognitive development that were emerging during the late 1800s and early 1900s. Educational, governmental, and military needs to classify individuals for training purposes fostered the development of techniques to assess ability. Binet and Simon, in the first decades of the 1900s, pioneered intelligence testing with the development of the early Binet Scales. Hall and Gesell, with their clinics for the study of child development, sparked continued interest in the assessment of young children. Terman and Merrill (1937) revised the Binet Scales and included items that were developed for preschool-aged children. The number of published assessment instruments has increased dramatically and continually since the 1930s.

During the 1940s, instruments specifically designed for the assessment of infants and preschoolers emerged. Two of the most used tests of that era were the Cattell Infant Intelligence Scale (Cattell, 1940), which was designed for children ages birth through 2 years, and the Leiter International Performance Scale (Leiter, 1948), for children ages 2 to 18. For the next several years, researchers examined the predictive nature of such instruments. Little correlation was found between scores on infant and preschool tests and later school success.

Serious attention to the special assessment needs of the preschool child was not achieved until the 1960s. With the advent of Head Start and other early intervention programs came the need to mark and follow the developmental status of large numbers of children. By 1971, over 120 preschooler and kindergarten tests had been developed (Hoepfner, Stern, & Nummedal, 1971). Unfortunately, flaws in statistical properties, standardization procedures, and measurement practices plagued many of these instruments.

The Head Start program of the 1960s marked the beginning of an era of governmental and legislative actions that have had major impacts on the education of children in the United States. Federal mandates especially influenced the development of special education for handicapped children and created an incredible demand for instruments assessing intelligence and academic performance. Public Law 94-142, the Education for All Handicapped Children Act, passed in 1975, set the stage for widespread efforts to educate all handicapped children. PL 94-142 held that public school systems must provide free and appropriate educational services for handicapped individuals ages 3 to 21 in the least restrictive environment. Initial and follow-up evaluations of these individuals were mandated by this law. In 1986, the federal government enacted PL 99-457, The Education of the Handicapped Act Amendments, which extended the intent of 94-142 to children from birth.

The diagnosis of handicapping conditions in school-aged and pre-school-aged children has led to a multimillion dollar test publishing industry. Advances in test construction are leading to larger and more comprehensive test batteries with statistical properties that far surpass the early psychometric tests. The development of good preschool tests has lagged behind those for older children. The 1980s, however, marked the beginning of newfound interest and effort directed at the improvement and development of preschool assessment instruments.

MAJOR INSTRUMENTS

For the past two decades, four instruments have dominated the field of developmental assessment: the Bayley Scales of Infant Development (Bayley, 1969); the McCarthy Scales of Children's Abilities (McCarthy, 1972); the Stanford-Binet Intelligence Scales (Terman & Merrill, 1973); and the Wechsler Preschool and Primary Scale of Intelligence (Wechsler, 1967). The latter two tests underwent revising in 1986 and 1989, respectively. The revisions are likely to hold dominant positions in the assessment of preschool children.

Extensive and comprehensive reviews of the Bayley, McCarthy, Binet, and Wechsler scales are available in a number of sources (for example, Sattler, 1982, and Anastasi, 1988). In order to allow space for discussion of other useful, but less well publicized preschool tests, only brief descriptions of these instruments will be presented in this chapter.

The Bayley Scales

The Bayley Scales of Infant Development were constructed to assess the mental, motoric, and behavioral functioning of children ages birth through 2½ years (Bayley, 1969). There are three major components of this scale. The most commonly utilized is the Mental Scale. Items in this scale tap sensorimotor functioning, early receptive and expressive language, object manipulations, learning, and memory. The Motor Scale is similar in format and administration procedures to the Mental Scale. It taps fine and gross motor functioning. The Infant Behavior Record, the third component of the Bayley, is an examiner-completed checklist and questionnaire which organizes observations of the child's social and emotional functioning. Single standard scores, which have a mean of 100 and standard deviation of 16, are computed for the child's performance in the Mental and Motor Scales. Reliability and validity information for the Bayley has been amassed by numerous studies (for example, Ramey, Campbell, & Nicholson, 1973; Gottfried & Brody, 1975; Matheny, Dolan & Wilson, 1976; Berk, 1979) since the test's publication. Both reliability and validity are adequate for a test of its kind. As with most infant tests, the predictive validity of the Bayley for functioning in later stages of childhood and adulthood is limited. The Bayley is best used as a measure of an infant's current developmental status. It is a well-respected instrument and has been utilized to judge the validity of other infant tests (Roszkowski, 1989).

Administration of the Bayley requires thorough familiarity with the large number of assessment items comprising the scale. Examiners should have knowledge of general measurement principles and techniques as well as knowledge of child development. One drawback of the Bayley for many practitioners is that the scale does not yield separate domain scores for abilities tapped by the mental and motor scales. Bayley asserted that infant abilities were so intermeshed that they can not be separated into discrete factors or domains. In an age where a child's eligibility for preschool special education services depends on documentation of delays in at least one area of functioning, examiners often have wished for separate Bayley domain scores. Some researchers (Haskett & Bell, 1978) have developed alternative scoring systems for the Bayley that provide for recategorization of items into separate functional clusters and identification of a child's strengths and weaknesses. The most parsimonious of these systems is one developed by Reuter and Craig (1976), which separates the Bayley items into five domains: cognitive, language, social, fine and gross motor. Examiners can chart the child's performance and graphically represent strengths and weaknesses with little difficulty.

McCarthy Scales of Children's Abilities

The MSCA is a comprehensive developmental battery that assesses the intellectual and motor development of children ages 2½ to 8½ years. The test is composed of 18 subtests, which are organized into five scales. These scales include the Verbal Scale, which taps a child's verbal expression and conceptual thinking; the Quantitative scale, which measures a child's understanding of numbers; the Perceptual-Performance Scale, nonverbal response activities that assess a child's ability to reason without words; a Memory Scale, which assesses short-term auditory and visual memory; and the Motor Scale, which addresses the child's fine and gross motor functioning. Scores on the first three of these scales combine to form the General Cognitive Index (GCI), an overall measure of a child's current developmental status. The GCI has a mean of 100 and a standard deviation of 16. Each of the five domain scores carries means of 50 and standard deviations of 10.

Psychometric properties of the McCarthy are good. The test was standardized on 1,032 children stratified by race, geographic region, father's occupation, and urban-rural dimensions as reflective of the 1970 census. Reliability data for the MSCA are strong. Test-retest coefficients for the GCI and separate subscales run in the .90s. Internal consistency ranges from the high .70s to low .90s for the five scales and GCI (McCarthy, 1972, p. 34). The validity of the MSCA has been established in numerous publications (for example Nagle, 1979; Davis & Walker, 1976; Gerken, Hancock, & Wade, 1978). Correlations with other instruments such as the

WPPSI and Stanford-Binet Scale Form L-M generally range from the low .70s to low .80s.

The administration of the MSCA usually takes 60 to 90 minutes. This is a long time to maintain a small child in structured activities. What helps keep a child on task is that the motor subtests are placed in the middle of the battery and allow the child to walk, jump, skip, toss and catch beanbags, and stretch a bit. The majority of tasks comprising the McCarthy are very child oriented. The puzzles, blocks, pictures, and xylophone typically can hold a child's interest. The activities also move along quickly, which helps to keep a preschooler on task.

Kaufman (1977) outlined the major limitations of the MSCA. He felt the administration of the test required a great deal of clerical work and was difficult to learn. In addition, he cited the following weaknesses in the test relevant to practitioners:

1. The MCSA could only be administered by a psychologist.
2. The test lacked items that require social comparisons or judgments.
3. The motor scale is not a stable measure after age 6½.
4. There was no sufficient ceiling for children over the age of 7.
5. The score range of the McCarthy is 50 to 150, so it is not a good measure to use with children who are functioning at or below trainable levels of mental retardation, or who are highly gifted.
6. There is not enough of a base for the youngest children. The test seems too difficult for children under 3 years of age.

Kaufman also had found that a 15-point discrepancy exists between the GCI and Full Scale WPPSI IQs and Binet-LM IQs for LD children, with the GCI being lower. If the McCarthy is used as a measure of ability in the diagnostic process of determining whether or not a child is learning disabled, an evaluator would not be as likely to uncover a significant ability–achievement split as if the WPPSI was used. In turn, a number of children who would have been found eligible to receive special education services if the Wechsler test had been used would go without services. Kaufman does not recommend the use of the MSCA in the evaluation of LD children.

Despite these limitations, the MSCA has held a prominent place in the assessment of young children. The test's 1972 publication date will probably indicate a need for revision in this decade.

Wechsler Preschool and Primary Scale of Intelligence and Wechsler Preschool and Primary Scale of Intelligence - Revised

One of the four major preschool assessment batteries to undergo a recent revision is the Wechsler Preschool and Primary Scale of Intelligence. A downward extension of the Wechsler Intelligence Scale for Children - Revised (1989), perhaps the most commonly used test of intellectual ability in school-aged children, the WPPSI was published in 1967 for use with children ages 4 to 6½ years. In 1985, The Psychological Corporation began a review of the strengths and weaknesses of this test which led to the revision of the WPPSI-R.

The WPPSI-R, published in 1989, maintains a striking similarity to the old WPPSI. Those who worked on the development of this revision wanted a final product that was a close relation to the original version, so that users would find it easy to pick up and master, yet one that would reflect improvements in test procedures and measurement theory. The WPPSI-R maintained 48% of the WPPSI items. There were five major changes in the test. These included: An expansion of the age range from 3 years to 7 years, 3 months; larger, more colorful artwork; addition of an object assembly task; the development of a crack-back manual; and a redesign of the record form, which now highlights examiner information and provides a tear-away score sheet so examiners can easily remove this sheet from the rest of the test to save file space.

The WPPSI-R consists of 12 subtests that comprise Performance and Verbal scales. The Performance Scale consists of six subtests, including: Object Assembly, Geometric Design, Mazes, Picture Completion, and Animal Pegs. The Verbal Scale contains the Information, Comprehension, Arithmetic, Vocabulary, Similarities, and Sentences subtests. Each of the WPPSI-R subtests has a mean of 10 and a standard deviation of 3. The Performance, Verbal, and Full Scale IQ scores, like all of the Wechsler Tests, carry a mean of 100 and a standard deviation of 15.

The WPPSI-R was standardized on 1,700 children who were randomly selected and reflective of the 1986 U.S. census in terms of region, age, gender, ethnicity, and parental education and occupation levels. Norm sets were broken into 17 groupings for ages 3-0 to 7-3. Reliability data cited in the manual are good. Internal consistency correlations were generally above .80 for all age groups. Test-retest reliabilities for the scaled scores ranged from .88 to .91! Test-retest coefficients for the individual subtests were not as strong, however. These ranged from .52 for Mazes and .59 for Object Assembly to .82 for Picture Completion. Construct, concurrent, and discriminant validity are reported in the WPPSI-R manual. Clean two-factor performance and verbal solutions have been obtained in factor analytic studies of the WPPSI-R. (For those familiar with factor structures of the WISC-R, it is interesting to note that the WPPSI-R has not been found to carry the freedom from distractibility factor.) This factor structure was felt to lend good support to the construct validity of the test. In terms of concurrent validity, correlations between the WPPSI and WPPSI-R have been in the mid-.80 range, between the Stanford-Binet IV (Thorndike, Hagen, & Sattler, 1986) and WPPSI-R in the .80 to .90 range. Low moderate correlations have been found between the WPPSI-R and Kaufman Assessment Battery for Children. In terms of discriminant validity, it was generally found that children who scored low on the WPPSI-R also scored low on other tests of ability. There is little information available regarding the predictive validity of the WPPSI-R, due to its recent publication date.

The administration of the WPPSI-R generally takes 75 minutes. At times, the process of the administration of this test becomes quite tedious. This is especially true for the Block Design subtest, which with its demonstrations, second trials, and ceiling rules seems to go on forever. It is very difficult to keep a young child interested in the WPPSI-R, even with the improvements in graphics and materials.

Two changes noted in the WPPSI-R will have ramifications for its use in the identification of special needs children. One of these changes is that the IQ score range has been expanded. The WPPSI-R yields IQs from 41 to 160, whereas the WPPSI range was 55 to 155. This change will allow the WPPSI-R to be useful in the identification of children who possess abilities in the trainable range of mental retardation. It also seems that the WPPSI-R yields less inflated IQ scores than did the WPPSI. A recent study by Kaplan (in press) found for a group of thirty 4½ to 5½ year-old children that the WPPSI yielded a mean Verbal score of 123, mean Performance score of 124, and a mean Full Scale score of 126, whereas for the same group of children, the mean WPPSI-R Verbal score was 117, the mean Performance score was 114, and the mean Full Scale score was 118. The greatest ramification of this factor will be felt in the diagnosis of young, learning disabled children. With lower WPPSI-R IQ scores, it may be more difficult to document ability–achievement splits. As such, fewer young children may be diagnosed as learning disabled.

Even though the changes in the WPPSI-R reflect advances in test and measurement practices, the instrument still has some weaknesses. The most relevant of these for the practitioner are:

1. There are no specified directions for adapting testing procedures to fit a child's handicapping condition and still maintain the integrity of the standardization of the test.

2. Even though some subtests allow examiners to demonstrate items to a child, the test does not provide sample teaching items which are often   necessary and useful when working with children who have little experience in formal educational or testing activities.

3. The WPPSI-R has a limited item floor. Some children can obtain a raw score of 0 (which means they could not do any of the items in the subtest) and still obtain a scaled score as high as 6. Because of this, the WPPSI-R may not yield an accurate measure of abilities in lower-functioning children.

Despite its faults, the WPPSI-R does mark advances in test construction. Early reviews of the test hold that it may become the best measure of abilities of preschool children available. Time will tell if this will be the case.

Stanford-Binet

Since 1937, the Stanford-Binet has been the instrument of choice for the assessment of a young child's abilities. The major reason for this was that it was perhaps the most extensive battery available for preschool-aged children in its day. The 1937 Binet Scales extended its age range down to a 2-year-old level (Terman & Merrill, 1937). Items appropriate for children ages 2 to 5 were added to this version. Twenty-three years later in 1960, a revision of the scales was undertaken. Items and normative data were updated, and the test incorporated the deviation IQ as the index of intellectual ability.

During the 1960s, 1970s, and early 1980s, the 1960 Stanford-Binet (known as Stanford-Binet Form L-M) was a primary measure of abilities in preschool children. Test items were organized in 6-month intervals based on developmental age appropriateness for the youngest of children and then by year intervals after age 5.

Items at the preschool level were very much based on activities young children typically encounter, such as block stacking or bead stringing. The Stanford-Binet Form L-M (SB-LM) yielded a single IQ score for a child. This became a source of criticism of the SB-LM because the test tapped more than one area of functioning. It was difficult to determine a child's strengths or weaknesses in specific ability areas from his or her test performance on the SB-LM. It was also difficult to determine the impact of a child's particular handicapping condition on his or her test perform-ance because only one overall score was obtained and items were not separated by domains. Examiners would almost have to "guesstimate" the ability level of a child who could not perform particular kinds of items due to a physical handicap. Despite these weaknesses, the test items for young children contained materials they enjoyed (small cars, blocks, beads, tiny household objects). Administration of the test was quick at this age level and relatively reliable, and valid test scores were obtained.

In 1986, the SB was again revised and termed the Stanford-Binet IV (Thorndike, Hagan, & Sattler, 1986). A wide variety of content was retained from the SB-LM, but the test authors updated, reorganized, and added items. The SB-IV yields four area scores as well as an overall measure of intelligence. The area scores include: Verbal Reasoning, Ab-stract Visual Reasoning, Quantitative Reasoning, and Short-Term Mem-ory. Fifteen separate tests now comprise the SB-IV. Not all children are administered all 15 tests. Authors of the SB-IV developed an adapted-levels approach for examiners to follow in selecting appropriate subtest starting points for administration. Examiners begin the administration of the SB-IV with the vocabulary subtest. A child's score on this test indicates which other subtests are administered and what level is an appropriate starting point for that child so that beginning items are neither too easy nor too difficult.

The SB-IV composite score has a mean of 100 and standard deviation of 16. Each of the area scores also has this mean and standard deviation. Raw scores on the 15 individual tests are converted to a "standard age score" with a mean of 50 and standard deviation of 8.

Reliability data for the composite and area scores are good for a test of this magnitude. Kuder-Richardson and test-retest reliabilities are at and above the .90 range. The reliability of the individual subtests, however, is not as strong, ranging from .73 to .97 for KR-20 reliabilities and .28 to .83 for test-retest coefficients. Similar patterns were noted for the validity of the SB-IV when compared to other tests. The SB-IV area and composite scores correlated moderately highly to highly with other measures of abilities (i.e., WISC-R, WPPSI). The individual subtests did not fare as well. The ramifications of the reliability and validity data available on the SB-IV for examiners are that use of the area and composite scores for describing a child's abilities is most acceptable. Interpretation of strengths and weaknesses at the subtest level may not yield accurate descriptors of a child's functioning status.

In terms of its appeal to young children, the SB-IV seems to have lost some of the attractiveness older versions of the test possessed. Fewer objects are available for the child to manipulate. Children do not seem as interested in the tasks presented. Many examiners have lamented how few items a lower-functioning preschooler might be given for test scores, and how raw scores of 0 can yield even low average test results. Because of these factors, the SB-IV may be of less value as a measure of abilities in preschoolers than were its predecessors.

NEWER DEVELOPMENTAL ASSESSMENT BATTERIES

Changes in federal and state laws that created or expanded special education services for handicapped infants and preschoolers brought greater needs for assessment tools appropriate for this population. Within the past few years, a number of new tests have been developed for the young child. Many of these instruments may rival the traditional developmental tests in terms of their utility and value in the diagnostic assessment of children from birth through age 5. The most promising of these tests are presented below.

Miller Assessment for Preschoolers (MAP)

Published by The Psychological Corporation in 1982, the Miller Assessment for Preschoolers (Miller, 1982) is one of the most comprehensive of the newer developmental batteries. This test is appropriate for children ages 2 years, 9 months through 5 years, 8 months. Sensorimotor and cognitive abilities are tapped by the test. Five developmental indexes are yielded for a child's performance. The Foundations Index provides information about the child's motor and sensory functioning. The Coordination

Index examines gross, fine, and oral motor functioning. The Verbal Index, the index probably most similar to traditional measures of ability, consists of items that measure auditory and visual memory, sequencing, comprehension, association, and verbal expression. The Non-Verbal Index, one of the most valuable of the tests, provides information about a child's memory, sequencing, visualization, and mental manipulations that do not require verbal response. This index would be particularly useful with a child whose severe articulation or language delays interfere with his or her performance on tasks requiring verbal responses to demonstrate cognitive functioning. The final index of the MAP is the Complex Tasks Index. Test items in this grouping require a child to interpret visual-spatial information that is presented in a variety of ways. Test items that comprise the MAP have a strong neurological basis and are similar to activities found on neuropsychological batteries.

The MAP was standardized on 1,200 preschoolers stratified by age, race, sex, geographic location, socioeconomic levels, and urban/rural residence. Adequate reliability and validity data are provided in the manual; however, additional research is needed to strengthen this data. Percentile scores are available for a child's overall test performance and for the five performance indexes.

The test activities of the MAP are very appealing to children. Tasks are presented in a game format. Test administration is generally completed in less than 30 minutes. The clinician will need to spend a good bit of time becoming familiar with the testing procedures and materials as all the objects that are appealing to a young child take some management on the examiner's part to present to the child correctly. Individuals who would be eligible to administer the MAP include psychologists, master's-level educators, educational diagnosticians, program coordinators, preschool specialists, preschool speech pathologists, and others trained in test/measurement theory and practice and in early childhood development.

The MAP is a rather unique preschool assessment battery. It offers some different information and taps different functioning areas than do other batteries of its kind. The MAP would be a good addition to a battery of tests given to young children. It is also has good research potential.

Battelle Developmental Inventory (BDI)

The Battelle Developmental Inventory (Newborg, Stock, Wnek, Guidubaldi, & Svinicki, 1984) is a standardized assessment battery for children from birth to 8 years. It is becoming a popular test among teachers of handicapped infants and preschoolers as the BDI is one of the few comprehensive batteries that yields standard scores. The BDI consists of 341 items grouped into five domains: Personal-Social, Adaptive, Motor, Communication, and Cognitive. The domains are separate entities. An evaluator may choose to administer all five or any of the separate domains depending on need. A screening test composed of 96 of the total test items is also available.

Administration of the BDI incorporates a number of data-gathering techniques. Direct assessment of the child; parent, caregiver, or teacher interviews; and observations of the child in a home or center setting can be the sources of data collected about the child's ability to perform any of the test items. A three-point scoring system (0 for no response or no opportunity to perform the action; 1 for partial or sometime performance; and 2 for a full, complete response) allows examiners to identify emerging skills and develop educational strategies to foster these. Administration time is estimated at less than 1 hour for children under the age of 3 years and 1½ to 2 hours for children over age 3. Testing may be completed during several sessions to save fatigue on the child and examiner. Some evaluation teams even assign various BDI domains to be administered by different team members.

The BDI was standardized on 800 children (a relatively small sample) who were representative of 1981 U.S. census data for race and sex and who resided in 24 states and four geographic regions of the United States. Children with high- and low-incidence handicapping conditions were included in the standardization group. Reliability and validity information reported in the manual are modestly adequate, although additional data are needed regarding these dimensions of the test. A number of derived scores can be obtained for each of the test domains including percentiles, z scores, T scores, deviation quotients, and normal curve equivalents. One weakness of the BDI, however, is that the norm tables report scores only to a deviation quotient of 65. The manual describes procedures for computing lower scores; however, this opens the possibility of calculation errors.

The BDI contains one feature that is very useful for those who must assess children with particular physical handicapping conditions. Test instructions carry specific information as to how an item can be adapted for a physically, visually, or auditorily impaired child. These adaptations can theoretically be made without interfering with the normative character of the test.

One aspect of the BDI that needs to be addressed is that the test can be purchased with or without test materials. Buying the test without the stimuli certainly cuts down on cost. Those using the test gather their own materials per specifications for each item. Gathering one's own test materials, however, would seem to lead to problems regarding standard administration and raise questions regarding validity of test scores. Subtle changes in materials might alter the difficulty of an item. In such cases, examiners would have to be cautious when comparing their subjects' test performance to those of other children in the normative sample. Even when a complete test kit is bought, examiners may still need to purchase materials such as a beeper ball, as a few items necessary to adapt a test activity for a handicapped child are not included.

The BDI is a useful instrument for the identification of strengths and weaknesses in young handicapped children in order to aid in program development. It can also be used to chart a student's progress and to help determine the effectiveness of educational interventions. The format of the test lends itself well to the development of individual educational plans. Because of these applications, the BDI is finding a place among the tests educators of preschool handicapped children routinely use.

Cognitive Abilities Scale (CAS)

One of the most difficult-aged children to test is the 2- to 3-year-old. Because the child is too old and developmentally advanced for infant tests, such as the Bayley, and too young for the tasks required of the preschool batteries, such as the McCarthy, it is very difficult to obtain precise measures of the 2-year-old's functioning status.

Noting this problem in her own work with children, Bradley-Johnson (1987) developed an assessment instrument specifically designed for the 2- to 3-year-old. The Cognitive Abilities Scale (Bradley-Johnson, 1987) provides for a norm-referenced assessment tool to be used in the diagnosis of developmental delays and to ascertain a child's skill acquisition in five basic areas. These areas include: Language, Reading, Mathematics, Handwriting, and "Enabling Behaviors." The Language subtest assesses a child's ability to use and understand spoken words. The Reading subtest measures readiness skills such as handling a book, picture identification, and listening comprehension. The Mathematics subtest assesses various quantitative concepts and early rote and rational counting. The

Handwriting subtest assesses prewriting skills such as early drawing of shapes and lines and pencil grasp. The Enabling Behaviors subtest is less achievement oriented than the first four tests. This subtest taps a child's auditory and visual memory.

Administration of the CAS can be accomplished within a 30- to 45-minute time frame. Materials required for administration include a manual, a record booklet, various toys, a picture book, and a story book provided as manipulables for the assessment of the child. Although the materials are a bit cumbersome to access, as they are stored in a cloth bag, the use of objects helps keep this age child interested in the testing procedure.

The CAS provides percentiles and standard scores. The overall test score has a mean of 100 and a standard deviation of 15. The subtests have means of 10 and a standard deviation of 3. Five hundred thirty-six children comprised the norming sample and were representative of sex, residence, parent occupation, ethnicity, and age characteristics of the U.S. population. The reliability and validity data available for the CAS are adequate, although like so many of the tests for young children, additional information is needed in these areas.

Although not a thorough battery, the CAS may find a use as a bridge between the infant and preschool tests. It would be a good test to include when evaluating a 2- to 3-year-old child.

ASSESSMENT OF ACHIEVEMENT IN THE PRESCHOOL CHILD

Until recent years, assessment of achievement in children who were not yet in kindergarten was an unheard of concept. With needs to document delays for special education preschool placements and for program evaluation, this area of assessment has come to light.

The assessment of achievement in preschool-aged children generally involves tapping their acquired knowledge of preacademics or readiness skills. This knowledge includes color and shape recognition and quantity and quality dimensions. As the child approaches kindergarten age, this knowledge may also include prereading and prewriting skills such as letter identification, name printing, and various drawing tasks. Only a few individually administered tests of achievement are available specifically for the preschool-aged child. A number of these are presented below.

Bracken Basic Concept Scale (BBCS)

The Bracken Basic Concept Scale (Bracken, 1984) is probably the most comprehensive individually administered achievement test for young children. A total of 258 concepts (not all of which are administered to a single child) are assessed by this scale. Items are grouped into seven subscales. These include a School Readiness Composite, which will be discussed below as it plays a role in the testing procedure of this scale. Other BBCS subtests include Direction/Position, Social/Emotional, Size, Texture/Material, Quantity, and Time/Sequence, all of which measure concepts as their titles imply. A screening test is also available in the Bracken Basic Concept Scale.

The administration of the Bracken is very simple and straightforward. Materials needed include the manual, stimulus booklets, a record booklet, and a pen or pencil. The stimulus materials are pictorial and are presented in an easel format, which aids in administration. There is no need to fumble through boxes and test kits for manipulables. Not having concrete objects to manipulate can make this test somewhat boring to very young children. The test moves along quickly, however, which helps keep children on task. Responding is limited to requiring the child to point to one of four quadrants that pictorially represents a particular concept named by the examiner. For example, if the examiner asks, "Show me which is big," the child would point to one of four choices which demonstrates the concept "big." The manual discusses phrasing and prompts examiners may use to help children understand the required task. For example, it would be permissible to encourage a child to "look at all the pictures and to choose the best answer" and to "look at this picture, this picture, and this one, and this one" in order to attempt to elicit the correct response from a child.

The diagnostic scale of the Bracken begins with six separate subtests which comprise the School Readiness Composite Scale. These subtests tap the child's knowledge of colors, letters, numbers, shapes, directions, and positions. The child's combined raw score on these subtests determines a recommended starting level for administration of the subsequent scales. Basals on the subsequent tests are established by working from the starting point and moving backwards or forwards as necessary until three consecutive passes are achieved.

Ceilings are established once three consecutive failures are obtained. Raw scores on these subtests can be used to obtain standard scores (with a mean of 100 and standard deviation of 15), percentiles, and age equivalency. Responses are recorded by marking the appropriate circle in each item responding to (1) for pass and (0) for no pass and selecting the appropriate response 1, 2, 3, 4 or writing in a response as appropriate. The author of the test recommends drawing slash marks through the circles, but coloring them in works well.

The BBCS was normed on 1,109 children who were representative of U.S. population demographics. Reliability and validity information for the test provided in the manual is adequate, but based on small sample sizes. Additional information is needed to support the validity and reliability of the BBCS.

The Bracken may be utilized by a number of professionals and paraprofessionals within school and clinical settings who are trained in basic psychoeducational test administration and interpretation. This would include educational diagnosticians, teachers of special education students, school and clinical psychologists, and speech and language pathologists.

One of the most useful features of the BBCS is that it lends itself well to the development of individualized education plans (IEPs). A checklist is provided that allows examiners to mark which of the concepts a child has mastered. Recommendations for concepts that need to be developed stem nicely from this list and are readily understandable by parents as well as professionals. This list can also be used to chart the progress a child has made from pre- and postinterventions; therefore, it could also serve as a program evaluation and child progress documentation tool.

The BBCS represents a positive step in the developmental history of preschool assessment instruments. It should prove to be a useful addition to diagnostic batteries used with young children. Its greatest value will probably come in its role of documenting a young child's level of pre-school knowledge acquisition for use in identifying ability–achievement discrepancies.

Boehm Test of Basic Concepts - Preschool Version

Another norm-referenced test of general achievement in the preschool-aged child is the Boehm Test of Basic Concepts - Preschool (Boehm, 1986). The Boehm - Preschool taps 26 basic receptive vocabulary and grammar concepts that a 3- to 5-year-old child typically encounters in his or her world. This test is a downward extension of the Boehm Test of Basic Concepts.

Administration of the Boehm takes approximately 15 minutes and is easily accomplished. Children are asked to point to a picture that best represents a concept presented by an examiner. Scoring is a simple pass/no pass system. Raw scores yield percentiles and T scores.

The Boehm - Preschool was standardized on 433 children, a small sample, but one that did represent race, region, and socioeconomic dimensions proportionate to those of the U.S. population. Reliability and validity information presented in the manual is good, although somewhat limited in terms of sample size and number of studies conducted.

The Boehm is a good instrument to use to screen children who might be in need of additional testing to determine if they need special education services. It would also be a useful tool to use to supplement the educational portions of evaluations conducted with children ages 3 to 5 years.

Learning Accomplishment Profile

The Chapel Hill Project in North Carolina generated a series of assessment tools useful in documenting the educational needs of young children. These instruments include the Early Learning Accomplishment Profile (E-LAP; Glover, Perminger, & Sanford, 1978) for children birth through 3 years; the Learning Accomplishment Profile - Revised (LAP; Stanford & Zelman, 1981) for children ages 3 to 6; and the Learning Accomplishment Profile-Diagnostic Edition (LAP-D; LeMay, Griffin, & Sanford, 1977) for children 3 to 5 years of age. These are criterion-, rather than norm-referenced tests.

The various versions of the LAP are best used by those who work with a child in an educational program. The developers of these tests advocate their use as pre- and postmeasures of a child's developmental status. They are good measures to use for program effectiveness evaluations. The tests were not designed as tools to diagnose handicapping conditions or to determine eligibility for special services, although they are frequently inappropriately used for such purposes.

The technical data available for the LAP tests are questionable. The tests were constructed based on "expert review" of the type and age appropriateness of items. The LAP-D manual does offer some reliability data, which are promising but limited.

Administration of the LAP tests requires rather extensive examiner familiarity. The test materials are numerous and it takes practice to become familiar with their manipulation and presentation. The administration time for the LAP tests varies by child, but typically involves an hour for a complete administration. The LAP subtests tap similar areas of a child's functioning. These areas include fine and gross motor skills, cognitive, language, self-help, and social-emotional.

Brigance Diagnostic Inventory of Early Development

Another criterion-referenced instrument available to those who work with preschool children is the Brigance Inventory (Brigance, 1978). The Brigance can be administered to children from birth through age 7. This test covers a number of developmental tasks including: gross and fine motor functioning, self-help skills, speech/language skills, and general knowledge. For older preschoolers and young primary grade students, the Brigance also taps basic readiness skills such as reading common signs, printing upper- and lower-case letters, and early numerical knowledge.

Some of the materials necessary to administer the Brigance must be gathered by examiners. Some that are simply printed matter are provided. Technical data available regarding the Brigance are limited. Criterion-referenced tests typically do not present the elaborate details of the test's development as do the norm-referenced tests.

Perhaps the most useful feature of the Brigance is that its response booklet allows for the continuous assessment of a child. An examiner can use one response booklet to record a child's performance during numerous administrations of the test. Different colored pens or pencils can be utilized to chart the child's progress over administrative sessions. In a glance, examiners can note what skills a child has acquired over time.

ASSESSMENT OF EMOTIONAL STATUS IN PRESCHOOLERS

The evaluation of a preschooler's emotional status should focus on his or her social skills, temperament, attachment to others, frustration tolerance, and general behavior patterns. Unfortunately, measures of these attributes are almost nonexistent for the very young child.

A few experimental tests exist for the assessment of an infant's emotional status. Some limited tests are available for older preschoolers. These will be highlighted below. For the most part, however, examiners will need to rely on observational data, analysis of related test data, parental responses to questionnaires, and parts of various available tests in order to assess personality factors in children under the age of 5.

Social Competency

The reader may recall that most of the preschool tests reviewed in this chapter contained subtests or domains that addressed social functioning (for example, the Social-Emotional Scales on the BDI and BBCS). Examiners can combine these subtests and administer them to children in order to assess directly a child's knowledge of various social skills. Most of the tasks utilized in these tests involve a child's identification of facial expressions, moods depicted in various settings, and interactions between individuals. Sociograms, simple assessment tools that ask questions such as "whom would you eat lunch with," can be developed to fit an examiner's need. Such tools can be used with preschoolers, if administered in an interview format. The sociogram is helpful in determining which child may be least popular among his or her peers. These questions can also help document that a child's behavior or emotional difficulties are interfering with peer relationships.

More formalized measures of social competency in the preschool-aged child include the Kohn Social Competence Scale-Revised (Kohn, Parnes, & Rosman, 1979) for children ages 3-6 years, the California Preschool Social Competency Scale (Levine, Freeman, & Lewis, 1969) for children ages 4 through 6½, and the Children's Behavior Scale (Stott, 1962) for 4- through 6½-year-olds. The reliability and validity data on all three of these tests need development; however, the scales can provide some information as to the level of social skill development a young child has acquired.

Behavior

A few general behavior rating scales are available that were specifically designed for the child under age 5. One of the most widely used is the Preschool and Kindergarten Edition of the Burks' Behavior Rating Scale (Burks, 1977). This scale is composed of 105 items, which are grouped into 18 behavior domains addressing such aspects as the child's self-concept, anger control, intellectual functioning, aggressiveness, or dependency. The Burks Preschool can be completed by a parent, caregiver, and/or teacher. Responses from one individual or a number of individuals can be easily plotted to provide an overview of impressions of a child.

Another rating scale designed specifically for the young preschool child is the Preschool Behavior Questionnaire (PBQ; Behar & Stringfield, 1974). The PBQ is a teacher-completed scale consisting of 36 items. Three behavioral characteristics (hostile-aggressive, anxious-fearful, and hyperactive-distractible) are derived from this scale. The Preschool Burks and the PBQ have adequate reliability and validity data. Each can be used to determine general behavioral difficulties in young children.

One important factor to remember regarding the behavioral and emotional assessment of preschool-aged children is that such assessments should not be geared only toward the identification of characteristics of the child. The young child's social and emotional functioning is perhaps as dependent upon family and cultural variables as it is on more genetically predisposed characteristics such as temperament. Parental styles, socioeconomic conditions, discipline techniques, and parental expectations, to name a few, can have great impact on a child's emotions and behaviors.

Temperament

Temperament consists of the genetically determined components of a child's emotional nature. Included in this construct are the child's ability to adapt to change, response speed, general mood, pattern of sleep and wakefulness, and interaction style with others (Thomas, Chess, & Korn, 1977). Infant temperament scales have been used primarily for research purposes. These tools can provide examiners with general data regarding a child's basic personality structures. Data obtained from these scales can be used to assist parents in learning how to interact with their children, what discipline strategies may be most effective, and provide ideas for enhancing the child's social and emotional functioning.

ISSUES IN PRESCHOOL ASSESSMENT PRACTICES

Instrument Selection

One of the most important rules of thumb to keep in mind about choosing the instruments to evaluate a young child is that no one instrument will address all aspects of a child's functioning. Some of the larger batteries will tap a number of domains, but never all. For example, the WPPSI-R is reported to tap verbal and performance abilities; however, it does not have items that assess gross motor functioning. For the most part, examiners will find they need to combine subtests and tasks from a number of instruments in order to obtain comprehensive information about a child.

This becomes especially true of the child who possesses a handicapping condition that prevents his or her performance on certain parts of batteries, which in turn would cause full scale scores to be less than accurate representations of a child's functioning. A common example of this would involve a child between the ages of 2 and 5 who possesses a severe speech and language handicap. When choosing assessment tools for such a child, the examiner may not wish to select instruments that completely involve expressive language skills as a response format. Obviously a child who could not talk would not do very well on such instruments. Errors in diagnosis can be made if the handicapping condition is not taken into account when assessment instruments are selected, administered, and interpreted. A child who could not express her- or himself verbally might end up with test scores and diagnoses indicative of mental retardation, rather than of a speech and language impairment. Faulty recommendations and treatments could result that would limit effectiveness of interventions and cause the child more harm than good. A case illustration is provided below that demonstrates the selection of tests and parts of tests to address assessment needs of a young child.

> Ted is a 39-month-old child who has a medical diagnosis of Cerebral Palsy with involvement of the lower and upper extremities. He is not ambulatory, and he has no motor control in his right arm and hand. Ted does have some mobility in his left arm and hand which permits him to use a pointing response. Ted's vision, hearing, and expressive language skills appear to be intact.

In this case, because Ted is not ambulatory, gross motor assessment tasks requiring running, kicking, or ball bouncing would not be in order. His performance on tasks that involved complex fine motor movements would not provide a true image of his overall abilities because activities requiring these skills would measure the degree to which his physical handicap prevented him from completing these tasks rather than other aspects of his functional capabilities. Although you may want to know the extent of his physical limitations, you should not rely on object manipulation activities to obtain a complete view of this child.

For Ted, the most appropriate kinds of tasks that could be used to assess his potential for learning as well as his acquired knowledge would be those requiring verbal expression or limited physical dexterity, such as pointing to objects or pictures. In terms of specific instruments and subtests, the following would be appropriate tools to administer to Ted in the assessment of his abilities and skills:

Cognitive Functioning:	WPPSI-R: Verbal subtests Stanford-Binet IV: Verbal, Quantitative, and Memory subtests McCarthy Scales of Children's Abilities: Verbal, Quantitative, and Memory subtests (with the possible exception of tapping sequence, which involves a motoric response)
Pre-Academic Skills:	Bracken Basic Concept Scale Boehm Preschool Brigance Inventory of Early Development

An evaluator could attempt to administer some tasks that require minor object manipulations just to see what Ted would do with them (for example, perceptual performance items on the McCarthy such as block building and puzzle solving). As long as these tasks reflect the extent of the child's physical handicapping condition and this is communicated appropriately in a report, it would be acceptable to attempt to administer such items.

Another consideration related to the selection of appropriate assessment tools for young children is the possible need to move to lower levels of tests. This need may be encountered when it is not possible to acquire enough background information on a child prior to testing to estimate approximate functioning levels to guide test selection. The case of Mary is used to illustrate this point.

Mary was a 4-year, 8-month-old child referred to a local preschool handicapped program after her mother discovered educational services for young children were available. Although the child had been followed by public health agencies since birth, delays in functioning had not been noted. Mary's mother felt her daughter might "be a little slow" since her other child, a boy in kindergarten, was recently found eligible for special services.

Limited background data were available for Mary. Her medical re-cords indicated no significant physical or health factors. By the mother's report, Mary obtained developmental milestones at age-appropriate levels. Her chronological age was used to select the first instruments adminis-tered to her. These were the WPPSI-R and Bracken Basic Concept Scale.

It soon became evident that Mary's abilities and skills were at levels well below her chronological age. With the exception of Object Assembly and Comprehension on the WPPSI-R, Mary obtained raw scores of 0 on all other WPPSI and BBCS subtests. Given that the lower age limits on these instruments are 3 years 0 months and 2 years 6 months, respectively, examiners knew they needed to drop back and find tests that tapped functional abilities below these levels. With the administration of the WPPSI-R and BBCS, the examiners knew what Mary could not do but had no idea what she could do.

To continue the evaluation process, on subsequent assessment ses-sions, examiners pulled subtests from the McCarthy, lower age limit 2 years 6 months, and finally the Bayley Scales and Brigance inventories before accurate measures of Mary's functioning were obtained. Her devel-opmental delays were pervasive as she was found to be functioning at an 18- to 24-month range in all areas.

Rapport

Building and maintaining rapport with the preschool child involves different techniques from those used with older children. A young child is often fearful of strangers and unwilling to work with an examiner. As such, time must be spent gaining the child's trust. A good way to acquire this is to spend time together with the child in the presence of the mother and/or father. Typically an examiner can engage the parent in a structured inter-view and gather data about the family and child while giving the child a chance to become accustomed to the examiner.

In cases where a child is extremely reluctant to be alone with an examiner, there is no need to make the evaluation a traumatic experience. It is also rather pointless to try and test a child who is screaming for his or her parent. In these situations, a parent may be asked to sit with the child during the evaluation. The parent's presence is often enough to calm the child and allow him or her to work at the testing tasks. Before this arrangement is attempted, however, it is wise to discuss with the parent the fact that he or she cannot help the child to perform any of the requested tasks. It is very difficult for the parent to watch the child being evaluated, especially as the child reaches tasks he or she cannot do. By discussing the parent's role prior to the evaluation, an examiner can help ensure the test performance reflects the child's, not the parent's, functioning.

Home vs. Center Testing

When a child is not yet attending school, a question as to where to test a child arises. Many professionals prefer to have a child brought to their clinical setting. The advantages of clinics and other center-based evaluation rooms are that greater controls can be put on the environment. Generally when a center-based evaluation room is utilized, examiners can ensure that the room is quiet, relatively free of distractions, that furnishings are clean and child size, and that necessary testing materials are close at hand. Testing a child in a clinical setting can create problems, however. Young children often are frightened of new surroundings. They may be so fearful or guarded in the clinical setting that their test performances are adversely affected. A child not accustomed to new surroundings can also be so stimulated by the testing environment that he or she spends all his or her energies in exploratory behaviors. In either situation, the clinical setting creates barriers to ascertaining true measures of the child's functioning.

An alternative to a clinical evaluation site is testing in the child's home. On their home turf, children tend to be more spontaneous and outgoing. Time needed to build rapport and gain cooperation can be reduced when the examiner meets a child in the child's home setting. As such, test results may be less susceptible to a child's shyness, stranger anxiety, and other in vivo factors. Testing in the home, however, also carries limitations. Examiner safety is one. Unfortunately, many homes and neighborhoods are plagued with violence and crime. Examiners should never travel to homes where there are strong possibilities they could be harmed. In one situation, a mother who was contacted to set up the evaluation of her 3-year-old cursed the examiner profusely before she angrily agreed to set a date for the evaluation. Information about the mother indicated she had spent time in prison for attempted murder and drug-related convictions. Her older children had been removed from her custody, and she was fearful the 3-year-old was being evaluated to see if he would be taken away. In fact, the evaluation was being requested by the local school system to determine the child's eligibility for preschool special education services. Given the mother's phone manner and history of incarceration, the examiner requested a large male supervisor to accompany her to the child's home. Fortunately the mother was very pleasant and the evaluation occurred without incident. Risk to one's own safety should always weigh heavily in decisions regarding where to test.

Other adverse factors related to home testings are:

1. It is difficult to ensure adequate workplaces or table space at which to work.
2. Other children in the home may want to participate in the test activities. After all, they look fun.
3. Some children have few restraints placed on them at home and behave much less appropriately there than they would at a school or clinical setting.

The choice of where to test depends on personal preferences and pragmatic concerns regarding issues such as transportation for families and work space available in schools or clinics. For those who opt to do home testing, it is helpful to consider taking along some extra materials in addition to the tests themselves. A list of these materials includes:

1. a vinyl tablecloth that can be spread on a floor to provide a clean work area for babies or children and examiners;
2. a small folding table, such as a TV tray, in case the family does not have a table at which to work. A TV table with short legs can be put atop a table cloth and the child and examiner can sit on the floor and have adequate tabletop working space;
3. a box of toys, perhaps good used items, which can be left with the child who cries because you need to take away your test materials.

Criterion- vs. Norm-Referenced Testing

A debate has arisen as to whether or not criterion-referenced testing is more appropriate for preschool children than is norm-referenced testing. Some evaluators feel the use of norm-referenced tests leads to diagnostic labels that in turn set up certain expectations for a child. The decision as to what type of test is used depends on the assessment needs of the child and evaluator. When a child is tested to determine eligibility for a special program, norm-referenced tests should be the instruments of choice. These tests, by nature of their design, provide for a comparison of the child being tested to some predetermined norm. The comparison allows examiners to document specific delays and the magnitude of the delay. Norm-referenced tests also tend to have better defined statistical properties (such as reliability and validity) than do criterion-referenced tests. These data can be used to provide justification for a test's use in the diagnosis or classification of a child.

Criterion-referenced tests, such as the Brigance and LAP-D, are useful tests for examiners who simply want to mark the progress a child makes over time. These tests usually break skills into very specific actions. They also tend to be more direct in the assessment of particular skills. These features of criterion-referenced tests make them somewhat more appealing to educators who must develop specific education plans for a child and communicate with parents regarding details of a child's functioning.

SUMMARY

The assessment of a preschool-aged child poses challenges to examiners who may be more accustomed to working with older children. A number of new tests and revised versions of traditional instruments are helping evaluators face these challenges. Test developers are becoming more sensitive to the assessment needs of the young child. They are designing tests to tap a number of abilities and skills that are creative yet relatively fun for the child to take. Selection and proper administration of various batteries and parts of tests allow examiners to obtain complete reviews of a child's developmental status. Although some tests for preschoolers still need work to develop reliability and validity data, they hold great promise in the task of evaluating the young child.

IDEAL ASSESSMENT — CASE STUDY

Reason for Referral

Harry was referred for this psychoeducational evaluation after a preschool screening conducted by his school system indicated he might be experiencing significant developmental delays.

Background Information

Harry is a 4-year, 10-month-old child who currently resides with his biological parents. He has been attending a private preschool program in his community. Harry's teacher reported the boy experiences attending and off-task behavioral difficulties that are not typical of the other children in her program. Harry's medical history is significant for a number of risk factors. At the age of 18 months he began to experience severe seizures, which were found to be related to the presence of a right temporoparietal arachnoid cyst. A shunt was placed to drain fluid from the cyst, and his seizures were treated with phenobarbital. Reports from Harry's physician indicated that at the time of this evaluation, Harry is functioning medically as a normal child. Recent physical examinations indicated no significant neurologic findings; however, abnormal EEG spiking had been noted in previous hospital reports.

Behavioral Observations

Harry was asked to spend 3 days attending the preschool program for children with developmental disabilities in his local school district. Observations of Harry in this setting found him to be an energetic little boy. He initiated interactions with the other children and with adults. He played with a variety of toys and materials. Harry could use words and short sentences to express himself. It was noted, however, that he had some difficulty answering questions with appropriate responses. He could give related information, but not the specific content requested. Harry followed the routine of the classroom nicely and adjusted to group activities well. He appeared to be a happy, curious child.

Harry's evaluation was conducted over the course of 2 separate days in order to prevent him from becoming unduly fatigued by the assessment process. During the evaluation, Harry had some difficulty attending to structured activities. He was very distractible and he demonstrated an impulsive response style, even for his age. Harry displayed a bit of stubbornness as he would put his head down on his arms when he could not have his way. He responded quickly, however, to requests to comply with directions. Throughout the verbal segments of this evaluation, Harry demonstrated difficulty processing questions and retrieving appropriate information. Many times he would tend to give related, but inappropriate, content for questions.

Harry responded well to firm requests to comply with directions and to the use of positive reinforcement (stickers) for appropriate behavior and effort. His performance on the various tasks comprising this evaluation was felt to be a valid indicator of his abilities and skills.

Methods of Evaluation

—Wechsler Preschool and Primary Scale of Intelligence - Revised (WPPSI-R)

—McCarthy Scales of Children's Abilities (MSCA), The Memory & Motor Scales

—Bracken Basic Concept Scale (BBCS)

—Battelle Developmental Inventory (BDI) Personal-Social, Adaptive, & Communication Scales

—Burks' Behavior Rating Scale—Preschool & Kindergarten Edition

Results

Harry's WPPSI-R performance indicated he is experiencing significant delays in the development of intellectual abilities. His general functioning was found to be from 12 to 24 months behind levels expected given his chronological age. Harry's nonverbal abilities were found to be within a range of two to three standard deviations below means established for children his age, indicating significant deficits in this area of functioning. His verbal abilities were somewhat better developed as they were found to be in a range of one to two deviations below means for Harry's age. Specific intellectual weaknesses identified in Harry were found in the areas of perceptual-motor functioning, general information, and arithmetic reasoning.

The MCSA Motor and Memory subtests were administered to Harry in order to gain information about his abilities in these areas. His gross motor skills were found to be age appropriate. He demonstrated right-hand dominance. His balance and general coordination were good. Harry's fine motor functioning was found to be significantly delayed. He obtained an age equivalency of 3 years on all of his drawings. His work indicated perceptual-motor weaknesses consistent with his WPPSI-R performance. In terms of his memory, Harry demonstrated significant weakness in his ability to recall verbal information of any kind, be it words or numerical data. His performance on all of the tasks requiring short-term auditory recall of sentences, words, or numbers was at a 2-year developmental equivalency. When the memory tasks did not require a verbal response, Harry was able to give a stronger performance. His visual-memory was assessed to be at a 3½-year level.

Academic skill testing conducted with Harry indicated delays in a number of concept areas. His basic skills of color recognition, number concepts, and letter and shape identification, as measured by the BBCS, were at the first percentile for children his age. Harry did not consistently identify colors, letters of the alphabet, or shapes. He could not count rotely or rationally. Harry has not yet developed an understanding of concepts such as "different" and "same." His knowledge of social and emotional concepts, size dimensions, quantity concepts, textures, and materials was all at levels below the 10th percentile for his age. Strengths that Harry demonstrated involved his knowledge of directions (i.e., up, down) and knowledge of time (night, day). These strengths were within the low average range.

Harry's mother was asked to complete a Burks' Behavior Rating Scale in order to summarize her impressions of her son's behavior. From the information gathered on this scale, Harry's attention span, impulse control, and intellectual status were seen as his greatest areas of weakness. Harry's mother also indicated her son could be resistant to directions and authority. All other areas of his behavior and emotional and mental status were seen as being appropriate for his age.

Summary and Recommendations

The results of this evaluation indicated Harry is experiencing significant developmental delays in the areas of cognition, language, perceptual-motor functioning, and preacademic skills. These delays represented magnitudes of 25% to 50%. Harry's behavior is characterized by impulsivity, a short attention span, and a tendency to resist authority. He responds well to behavior management techniques. With his medical history and current levels of functioning, Harry would meet eligibility requirements for special education services available to preschool children. It is recommended that Harry participate in the preschool program for handicapped children. Other recommendations for Harry include:

1. Sharing the results of this evaluation with Harry's physician and the medical staff who monitor his physical and neurologic status, pending permission to do so. Harry's receiving preschool teacher and these professionals should communicate regularly in order to monitor the boy's developmental status and the possible effects of his medication and of his past medical problems on his learning experiences.

2. Harry's preschool program should emphasize language-building experiences to help him improve his functional communication competency.

3. Behavior management techniques designed to reinforce appropriate behaviors would be useful in building Harry's on-task behavior and his compliance with directions from those who work with him. A firm and consistent management style will also help reduce his resistance to authority.

4. Harry's parents should be provided a short list of activities each week that they can do at home to help build Harry's basic skills in color recognition, counting, etc.

5. Harry's parents should be encouraged to continue to allow their son to care for as many of his own needs as possible (such as grooming and dressing) to keep these skills strong.

SUGGESTED READINGS

Kaufman, A. S., & Kaufman, N. C. (1972). *Clinical evaluation of young children with the McCarthy Scales.* New York: Grune & Stratton.

Lichtenstein, R., & Ireton, H. (1984). *Preschool screening: Identifying young children with developmental and educational problems.* San Antonio, TX: The Psychological Corporation.

Paget, K. D., & Bracken, B. A. (1983). *The psychoeducational assessment of preschool children.* Orlando, FL: Grune & Stratton, Harcourt Brace, Jovanovich.

Vietz, P. M., & Vaughn, H. G. (1988). *Early identification of infants with developmental disabilities.* San Antonio, TX: The Psychological Corporation.

REFERENCES

Anastasi, A. (1988). *Psychological testing* (6th ed.). New York: Macmillan.

Bayley, N. (1969). *Bayley Scales of Infant Development: Manual.* San Antonio: The Psychological Corporation.

Behar, L. B., & Stringfield, S. A. (1974). A behavior rating scale for the preschool child. *Developmental Psychology, 10,* 601-610.

Berk, R. A. (1979). The discrimination efficiency of the Bayley Scales of Infant Development. *Journal of Abnormal Child Psychology, 7,* 113-119.

Boehm, A. E. (1986). *Boehm Test of Basic Concepts - Preschool version.* San Antonio: The Psychological Corporation.

Bracken, B. A. (1984). *Bracken Basic Concept Scale: Manual.* San Antonio: The Psychological Corporation.

Bradley-Johnson, S. (1987). *Cognitive Abilities Scale: An educationally relevant measure for two- and three-year old children.* Austin, TX: Pro-Ed.

Brigance, A. H. (1978). *BRIGANCE Diagnostic Inventory of Early Development.* North Billerica, MA: Curriculum Associates.

Burks, H. F. (1977). *Burks' Behavior Rating Scales: Preschool and kindergarten edition.* Los Angeles: Western Psychological Services.

Cattell, P. (1940). *The measurement of intelligence of infants and young children.* New York: The Psychological Corporation.

Davis, E. E., & Walker, C. (1976). Validity of the McCarthy Scales for Southwestern rural children. *Perceptual and Motor Skills, 42,* 563-567.

Gerkin, K. C., Hancock, K. A., & Wade, T. H. (1978). Comparison of the Stanford-Binet Intelligence Scale and the McCarthy Scales of Children's Abilities with preschool children. *Psychology in the Schools, 15,* 468-472.

Glover, M. E., Perminger, J. L., & Sanford, A. R. (1978). *Early Accomplishment Profile.* Winston-Salem, NC: Kaplan.

Gottfried, A. W., & Brody, D. (1975). Interrelationships between and correlates of psychometric and Piagetian scales of sensori-motor intelligence. *Developmental Psychology, 11,* 379-387.

Haskett, J., & Bell, J. (1978). Profound mental retardation: Descriptive and theoretical utility of the Bayley Mental Scale. In C. E. Meyers (Ed.), *Quality of life in severely and profoundly mentally retarded people* (pp. 327-352). Washington, DC: American Association on Mental Deficiency.

Hoepfner, R., Stern, C., & Nummedal, S. C. (1971). *CSE-ERIC preschool/kindergarten test evaluations.* Los Angeles: UCLA Graduate School of Education.

Kaplan, C. H. (in press). Bright children and the revised WPPSI: Concurrent validity. *Journal of Psychoeducational Assessment.*

Kaufman, A. (1977). *Clinical evaluation of young children with the McCarthy Scales* (rev. ed.). New York: Grune & Stratton.

Kohn, M., Parnes, B., & Rosman, B. (1979). *Kohn Social Competence Scale (revised).* New York: William A. White Institute of Psychiatry, Psychoanalysis, & Psychology.

Leiter, R. G. (1948). *International Performance Scale.* Chicago: Stoelting.

LeMay, D. W., Griffin, P. M., & Sandford, A. R. (1977). *Learning Accomplishment Profile - Diagnostic Edition.* Winston-Salem, NC: Kaplan.
Levine, S., Freeman, F. F., & Lewis, M. (1969). *California Preschool Social Competency Scale.* Palo Alto, CA: Consulting Psychologists Press.
Matheny, A. P., Dolan, A. B., & Wilson, R. S. (1976). Within-pair similarity on Bayley's Infant Behavior Record. *Journal of Genetic Psychology, 128,* 263-270.
McCarthy, D. (1972). *Manual for the McCarthy Scales of Children's Abilities.* New York: The Psychological Corporation.
Miller, L. J. (1982). *Miller Assessment for Preschoolers.* San Antonio: The Psychological Corporation.
Nagle, R. J. (1979). The McCarthy Scales of Children's Abilities: Research implications for the assessment of young children. *School Psychology Digest, 8,*(3), 319-325.
Newborg, J., Stock, J. R., Wnek, L., Guidubaldi, J., & Svinicki, J. (1984). *The Battelle Developmental Inventory.* Allen, TX: DLM-Teaching Resources.
Ramey, C. T., Campbell, F. A., & Nicholson, J. E. (1973). The predictive power of the Bayley Scales of Infant Development and the Stanford-Binet Intelligence Test in a relatively constant environment. *Child Development, 44,* 790-795.
Reuter J., & Craig, S. (1976). *Bayley Scales of Infant Development Kent Scales Profile* (First Chance Project Grant #0E6-0074-02678) Kent, OH: Kent Developmental Metrics.
Roszkowski, M. J. (1989). Review of the Bayley Scales of Infant Development. In J. C. Conoley and J. K. Kramer (Eds.), *Tenth mental measurements yearbook* (pp. 192-212). Lincoln, NE: The University of Nebraska Press.
Sattler, J. M. (1982). *Assessment of children's intelligence and special abilities* (2nd ed.). Boston: Allyn & Bacon.
Stott, D. H. (1962). Personality at age four. *Child Development, 33,* 287-311.
Terman, L. M., & Merrill, M. A. (1937). *Measuring intelligence.* Boston: Houghton Mifflin.
Thomas, A., & Chess, S. (1977). *Temperament and development.* New York: Brunner/Mazel.
Thomas, A., Chess, S., & Korn, S. (1977). Parent and teacher temperament questionnaire for children 3-7 years of age. In A. Thomas & C. Chess (Eds.), *Temperament and development* (pp. 247-284). New York: Brunner/Mazel.
Thorndike, R. L., Hagen, E. P., & Sattler, J. M. (1986). *Technical manual: Stanford-Binet Intelligence Scale* (4th ed.). Chicago: Riverside
Wechsler, D. (1967). *Wechsler Preschool and Primary Scale of Intelligence.* San Antonio: The Psychological Corporation.
Wechsler, D. (1974). *Wechsler Intelligence Scale for Children - Revised.* San Antonio: The Psychological Corporation.
Wechsler, D. (1989). *Wechsler Preschool and Primary Scale of Intelligence - Revised.* San Antonio: The Psychological Corporation.

5 ASCERTAINING INTELLECTUAL FUNCTIONING WITH BINET-TYPE INSTRUMENTS

David A. Sabatino

The purpose of this chapter is to acquaint the reader with several issues related to the assessment of intelligence in establishing "diagnostic best practices" with a limited selection of Binet-type instruments. The review is confined to intellectual diagnostic procedures with Binet-type tests, concentrating in detail on the 1986 Stanford-Binet, 4th edition. The chapter does not purport to develop theoretical cognitive structures in response to Binet's original thinking.

An overview of assessment practices with language-loaded instruments (verbal measures of vocabulary, language comprehension, and language concept formation) will be provided. The historical development and concerns that have plagued the ascertainment of verbal intelligence in handicapped children will also be briefly examined.

Highlighted in this chapter are the views that intellectual assessment is a standardized sampling of specific behavioral functions or tasks; that intelligence is composed of a number of specific cognitive traits or abilities; and that intelligence tests provide the user with task samples quickly and reliably under certain conditions. Three major points will be stressed:

—careful selection of intelligence tests must be made based on psychometric principles, the child's age and disabilities, and goals to be achieved by the assessment procedure.

—language-loaded intelligence test data comprise but one piece of information and do not serve to make placement or curriculum intervention decisions isolated from hypotheses related to how children use (function with) and develop language.

—most important, the selection of the appropriate diagnostic procedures (including the instrument of choice) and how the data are derived cannot exceed the skills of the test user. No test can be better than the person using it, and the best instrument available is as limited as is the user's ability to organize and address the implications derived from the behaviors being sampled.

ESTABLISHING BEST PRACTICES

The assessment of intelligence is the oldest and remains the most popular form of ascertaining abilities, especially with handicapped children. The assessment of intelligence occurs for a wide range of reasons, principal among these being the belief that intellectual assessment provides concurrently useful information in planning academic programs and has the capability of predicting future academic success. Therefore, it is not difficult to understand why special educators consider the determination of intelligence a central ingredient in developing a special education program placement decision and in addressing the type and amount of curricula interventions that would be most appropriate.

It has long been assumed that the amount of information that can be learned and the speed with which it can be learned are directly related to measured intelligence. If one studies the items that constitute most intelligence tests, they appear to be designed to use tasks that examine memory performance, vocabulary or word knowledge, motor speed and accuracy, language usage or comprehension, and other skills closely associated with academic learning. The very definition of intelligence is that it represents the ability to learn new information, that may be verbally abstract in nature, at an age-appropriate rate, while retaining it. That is probably why educators, more than psychologists, have valued the scores derived from intelligence tests. Operationally defined, whatever it is that an intelligence test measures, it does so quickly and conveniently.

It is correct to view intelligence tests as standardized behavioral sampling devices. In assuming that view, two things appear immediately as important: First, it might take a week or more to elicit reliable observational samples of the same tasks that an intelligence test can capture in 30 minutes to an hour. Second, observations or academic achievement test data place great emphasis on prior learning and present environmental conditions that may represent a serious bias. Intelligence tests may not be culturally fair, but they do permit a behavioral sampling procedure where cultural-linguistic effects or those of disability can be controlled to some degree.

This leads us to the major point in this chapter. There are critical differences in intelligence tests. The test(s) of choice must be selected based on the child's age, disabilities, cultural-linguistic learning, and other factors that guide the use of the information ascertained. Intelligence tests are selected samples of behavior; they attempt to measure a specific task, or human function, or theorized human trait. The use of test batteries applied routinely to the assessment of children, especially those with disabilities, is a poor and limited practice.

To reiterate: One major aspect of establishing best diagnostic practices is to match the intellectual measure to the hypothesized need for data; dependence on one instrument for most cases, or on some test battery, is not a best practice; and, *the bottom line is that an intelligence test is only as good as the person who administers and interprets the results.*

WHAT IS (ARE) INTELLIGENCE(S)?

Intelligence is frequently assumed to be a large, general factor rather than a subset of specific abilities or mental traits. Those who view intelligence as a global trait often view an IQ score as an absolute value. In contrast, many believe that an IQ is not an absolute value. Even the reliability of intelligence tests changes with the age of children, and measured intelligence with some groups of disabled children will generate highly erratic data. Test stability with preschool children is a very real issue; and, children with known central nervous system problems have been shown to generate irregular test results.

There is cultural and linguistic bias in all intelligence tests, and especially in those that are language loaded. Other factors exist that only careful individual administration of intelligence tests can partially control. That is the principal reason that only data derived from individual intelligence tests should be used in making academic and behavioral management decisions concerning handicapped children.

Beginning in the 1920s, both educators and psychologists noted that it is probably incorrect to talk about intelligence as a single factor and that the global use of a score, an IQ, was limiting and misleading. The major reason for limiting the dependence on intelligence as a specific concept was that many psychologists began to argue that the complexities of the human mind could not be boiled down to one score. In truth it is impossible to come up with an accurate description of educational placement or a curriculum intervention for handicapped children based solely on an IQ score.

The corrected term, argued for by a number of thoughtful scholars, should be *intelligence traits* or preferably a variety of specific *cognitive abilities*. An example of what is meant by cognitive abilities is seen when we examine any area of academic achievement. School success in subject areas related to reading and language usage appears to be related to verbal reasoning, language comprehension, and vocabulary development. In contrast, the ability to fix a car, plumb a house, or draw a blueprint would require a different type of intelligences or mental abilities.

Over time, numerous forms of intelligences have been hypothesized. One of the leading scientists in this area was Guilford. He hypothesized and, through research in developing test instruments, isolated over 128 different and specific cognitive abilities. In Guilford's (1967) report on the theoretical structure of the intellect, he described intelligence as an interactive cube, one side of which was operations, or thinking processes; one side was content, or where the mind describes what it is working with; and a third side was called products, or how the mind symbolically classifies and organizes information and references it later. Guilford's five mental structural operations were: cognition, memory, divergent production, convergent production, and evaluation.

It must be understood that we have little clear understanding as to what we erroneously allude to as native or natural intelligence. There appears to be a fairly high level of agreement among scholars who study intelligence that it is partly a factor of human genetics, which includes the health and development of the central nervous system. However, most researchers believe that intelligence is strongly related to what and from whom a person has the opportunity to learn. Intelligence is connected to what the environment offers, how rich it is in intellectual stimulation. It is clear in all developing central nervous systems that an extraordinary range of human cognitive abilities exists, and that an extraordinary amount of variance exists among the performance levels within each ability.

In the next section of this chapter, we will briefly review the relatively short history of intellectual assessment. Then the chapter will focus on what are currently considered best practices in Binet-type intellectual assessment. A list of things to do and things to avoid in intellectual assessment will be provided. Finally, and for the most part, the text will focus on types of intelligence tests and review a selected range of the more commonly used Binet-type tests. It is not the purpose of this chapter to represent an in-depth review on intellectual assessment or to offer a conclusive review of the issues. Rather, the intention is to provide an orientation to intellectual assessment using a certain class of instruments. To achieve that end the chapter will isolate and define in simple terms relevant intellectual assessment vocabulary and concepts.

THE GENESIS OF INTELLECTUAL ASSESSMENT

One aspect of human intelligence is the ability to communicate in several forms, using abstract symbol systems. Another aspect is the ability to reason, drawing from several abstractions simultaneously. Early psychologists drew conclusions about what constitutes intelligence, at least the intelligence that relates to academic achievement, purely from observation. There appeared to be several obvious factors. Memory for symbols and memory for language units were clearly one dimension. The human mind may have several forms of memory: for numbers, for letters, for places and things, for abstract detail, or for abstract language usage. Memory is an important consideration, and how memory is learned, how many different memory functions are possible, suggests that memory, like so many other human traits, is easy to talk about and much more difficult to understand.

There do appear to be intelligence traits associated with language learning, and those associated with learning form discrimination in single and multiple dimensions. Some people can read complex blueprints without ever being taught how. Others can take several drafting classes and never be very proficient at it. Some people cannot read music nor have they ever had a music lesson, yet they can play almost anything on dozens of different instruments by ear. Is that a form of cognitive ability? What of the person who has the ability to draw in the third dimension, making spatial relations details with a piece of charcoal, while his or her classmates cannot make a circle look like a ball? One person makes great recipes by tasting foods cooked by others, while another cannot make foods taste good even in the presence of great recipes.

One child learns complex abstract math faster than his or her agemates learn their times tables. Who said we were all born equal, except under the law? How do you explain reading readiness, and what appears to be the maturation of at least six essential skills that support beginning reading? And why is it that some students, in the presence of well-developed vocabularies and excellent language comprehension development, cannot learn to read? Is dyslexia the loss of one or more cognitive functions related to reading? If so, does an intelligence test define those functions? The early observers of intelligence(s) noted that some people have unusual talent to learn in one area. The study of the lives of great musicians, outstanding mathematicians, writers, and artists led early scientists concerned with the structure of the intellect to view it as comprising diverse abilities among people and in some cases within individuals as well. To say we are all different suggests that we differ intellectually. Other early observers saw giftedness as a factor and noted that gifted people perform many things, if not most things well. That led to the belief that intelligence is a summation of factors manifest as a general ability. These two points of view comprise the original beliefs and therefore arguments among early scientists concerned with the measurement of intelligence or cognitive structures. It is important that the reader understand that many of the theories and tests used to measure specific cognitive structures became tests of intelligence, i.e., the Binet-type instruments. Others, such as Werthmeimer's (1923) nine Gestalt (Bender Visual Motor Gestalt Test) designs developed to assess intelligence, became popular measures of a specific cognitive function (visual motor perceptual discrimination). If that seems confusing, simply remember that so is the common everyday interchange in terms between intelligence and cognitive abilities. To some, intelligence is a summation of cognitive measures. To others, it is a specific type of cognitive measure, and to still others, the two terms have no interchange at all. Lacking precision in the language of what it is that we think we ascertain (intelligence), it is little wonder that the world is confused.

Alfred Binet was not confused. He was not interested in defining intelligence or even measuring it except as an aspect of those cognitive functions that relate to academic learning. Yet Binet stands as a major French pioneer in intellectual assessment.

THE CONTRIBUTIONS OF ALFRED BINET

The contributions of Alfred Binet (in collaboration with Victor Henri, 1872–1980) are so crucial to intellectual assessment that it is important to discuss the impact this man's thinking had on the intellectual assessment movement. Binet devoted his life to the study of learning problems and how the human nervous system learns or, conversely, what abilities appear to function poorly in the case of academic failure. The French schools were attempting to identify consistently and therefore classify mentally retarded children and to program them in special education classes. As there was no consistent identification process, the children were inconsistently classified. Binet and physician Theodore Simon were commissioned to develop an instrument that would consistently classify children based on their abilities to profit from school. Binet and Simon were to develop a procedure that would reliably (generating stable results from one child to another) identify handicapped children (in this case, those who were mentally retarded).

Binet and Simon (1905) developed a test consisting of 30 different subtests to measure six specific abilities. The test was individually administered to children ages 3 to 13. What these two test authors offered the world was a comprehensive integration of different trait measures through specific subtests. This procedure of using subtests to measure a specific trait literally caught on and has continued up until the present time.

In the 1908 version, Binet and Simon placed items at an appropriate age level where 60% to 90% of normal children successfully possess items. This represented an important milestone and led to the concept of mental age. Binet's original six traits were: (1) memory, (2) attention to detail, (3) language comprehension and reasoning, (4) spatial relations (the ability to visualize objects in three dimensions), (5) general reasoning, or what Binet called reasoning, and (6) humor. Binet did not use the term IQ (intelligence quotient). That terminology was added later by Terman (1916). Binet's effort was to describe the development of specific traits by determining how children performed these subtests designed to measure those traits. What was to follow in the use of the Binet-type tests is simply a paradox.

Remember that Binet was interested in specific abilities. What soon occurred in America was that Binet's test was redesigned and standardized to generate an IQ score, and a single and global measure of intelligence would be used to classify children educationally. It is interesting that frequently great contributions begun to serve one purpose or represent a given theory are used for yet another purpose, a purpose that is the exact antithesis of what those contributions were initially developed to do. This is what happened to Binet's contribution, and is one reason that this French scientist's theories and work from the turn of the 20th century deserve rediscovery at the turn of the 21st century.

INTELLECTUAL ASSESSMENT IN THE UNITED STATES

In 1908, Henry Goddard, Director of Research at the Vineland Training School (for the mentally retarded) in Vineland, New Jersey, published the 1905 Binet test in English. In 1910, Goddard made some revisions of Binet's work and had standardized the administration of the test on American children. Goddard attempted to remain fairly faithful to Binet's theories of intelligence. The next revision, conducted by Stanford psychologist Lewis Terman, although an adaptation of Binet's test items, was constructed to meet the definition Terman (1916) had for intelligence. Terman believed that intelligence could be summarized as a person's ability to think abstractly. Therefore, Terman's 1916 edition of the newly named Stanford-Binet used the term *mental age* and generated IQ scores.

This scientifically developed test, with its rigorous standardization for that era, was extremely well received. In fact, to say that it was widely accepted and highly regarded would be an understatement. Early research on the Stanford-Binet (Bond, 1940) showed high positive relationships between IQ and reading comprehension (.73), so high that, literally, to know one was to know the other. The correlational studies to follow convinced the professional community that Binet had found the answer to predicting which child would not be able to profit from a regular school program.

Educators were so convinced that numerous states immediately began to use this test as the sole criterion for placement of mentally retarded children into special classes. The result was that by 1927, 11 years after Terman introduced it, 15 states required it to identify the mentally retarded. Those original classes for the mentally retarded in many states were called Binet classes. The enthusiasm for the Stanford-Binet created the belief that tests could be developed to diagnose almost anything. Today, it is interesting that educators are concerned about the inability of test results to relate to what or how to teach. It should be observed from this short historic overview that it was the profession that made that leap in logic, not the test developers.

As testing became more popular, it became impossible to separate diagnosis (Wolfensberger, 1965) from testing. The erroneous conclusions sent the professional community into a test development spree that would last until the current period. And it will continue until the professional community sees testing as distinct from diagnosis and ceases confusing the building of other (so-called better) diagnostic devices with procedures for determining and observing those behaviors that inhibit the learning and adjustment process in children. Later in this chapter, we will spend additional time discussing this confusion in practice.

Terman and Merrill (1937), in expanding the Binet instrument in items and age levels, gave the world the most popular intelligence test ever. Revisions occurred again in 1960, and by 1961 *American Psychologist* reported that thc Stanford-Binet was the most widely used of all tests, a position today occupied by the Wechsler scales. Terman and Merrill updated items, providing culturally sensitive test materials, and restandardized the 1960 edition in 1972 adding representative samples of minority children.

In 1986, a completely new version of the Binet appeared (Thorndike, Hagen, & Sattler, 1986) which, unlike the early versions and many revisions, was designed to reflect Binet's original constructs. This new version is rather complex and therefore perceived to be difficult to administer and score (Glutting, 1989). There were errors in the initial technical data, and it has received mixed reviews from the professional community. Reliability and validity considerations of the Stanford-Binet have always been excellent. The 1986 or 4th edition of the Binet (Binet IV) was no exception (Keith, Cool, Novak, White, & Pottebaum, 1988; Phelps, 1989; Phelps & Bell, 1988).

Content validity for the Binet tests has always been appropriate and so highly considered by the profession that it is generally used as a construct measure in the development of other instruments. Reported criterion-related validity coefficients tend to range from the high .40s to the low .70s. Predictive validity for language learning and reading, in particular, has always been outstanding, with correlations frequently reported in the .90s and going as high as .96. The American versions of the Stanford-Binet Intelligence Test, given some shortfalls in representative standardization and a heavy dependence on vocabulary and language development, is and remains one of the premier tests, frequently emulated but never duplicated. But, even the American versions did not do justice to the genius of Alfred Binet.

To summarize, Binet gave the world a theory of a few basic cognitive characteristics that appear to relate strongly to academic learning in children. The French pioneer's work was reinterpreted in the United States, and Lewis Terman, a Stanford University psychologist, reduced the ability of the Binet to describe human performance but augmented the statistical validity and standardization of the instrument, ensuring reliability. Standardization became important because it permitted the test to be used across specific populations in this country.

Terman needed a single score to work with statistically and therefore took Goddard's concept of mental age, or the level a child achieved across test items, and divided mental age by chronological age to determine IQ. IQ was a simplified and boiled down summation of an individual's cognitive development in the form of one score. It became misused as a descriptor of a person's intelligences. The result was that cognitive functions took a backseat to a performance quotation. Although that single score (IQ) was important for research, it did not provide for effective individual case management. Restated, an IQ score may consistently classify a child as mentally retarded and suggest that his or her learning rate and level are less than normal. The result suggests a special class. However, IQ scores do not sufficiently describe that child's cognitive function to permit specification of curriculum or other behavioral interventions.

Terman revised the Stanford editions of the Binet tests again in 1937, and 1960. The test was renormed in 1972. Although it was "the" test from 1917 to the mid 1960s, the Stanford revisions had several shortcomings. First, the normative structure made it primarily a children's test. It had only three adult levels and was not age sensitive to adult changes in mental function across the life span. Second, it was heavily language loaded. This means that it was a measure of verbal learning rate and retention. There was no corresponding nonverbal aspect; therefore, there was no verbal and nonverbal comparison.

NONVERBAL TEST DEVELOPMENT

What happened next was essentially initiated by a 20-year controversy over the use of Binet-type tests with young children, the deaf and sensory impaired, children with cultural linguistic pluralism and how it is effectively measured, and the need for an adult intelligence test. Most of what occurred was directly related to the theoretical view of how language developed in both normal and either culturally limited children or children with other handicaps. An initial discovery occurred when early psychologists attempted to use the Binet-type instruments (vocabulary and language-loaded tests) with deaf and hearing impaired children, in contrast, indicating the importance of normal language learning patterns in children.

In 1943, Samuel Hayes adapted the 1937 Stanford-Binet for use with the blind. Unfortunately, the Interim Hayes-Binet (Hayes, 1943) was never adequately standardized and its use was limited. The most commonly used test with blind children is the Verbal Scale of the Wechsler Tests. However, in 1970 Davis used the 1960 revision of the Stanford-Binet to develop the Perkins-Binet Intelligence Test for Blind Children. This well-standardized adaptation of the Binet instrument was issued in two forms. Form U was designed and standardized on children with usable residual vision. Form N was intended for use with totally blind children. These two tests have an age range from 5 to 15. Mental age and IQ scores are determined; and, these instruments use about 25% to 30% performance items.

In 1931 a New York psychologist, Pintner, had argued that language-loaded and verbal vocabulary-dependent tests unfairly penalized hearing impaired children. He recommended drawing a number of existing performance (nonverbal measures) test items into intelligence test measures for the deaf. The nation was busy admitting hundreds of thousands of new immigrants into the United States. These non-English-speaking people were administered performance tests of intelligence (nonverbal items) on Ellis Island. This was the first large-scale use of nonverbal intelligence tests. One test that was used was the Knox Cubes (Peterson, 1926), a test requiring persons to make block designs from 1" square cubes. This was a nonverbal measure of perceptual organization and required high levels of spatial ability. Manual motor rates of manipulation, including finger tapping speed and manual motor accuracy, were ascertained with non-English-speaking children and consequently the deaf. Other measures included the assembly of large wooden puzzles.

It was essential in the administration of tests to non-English-speaking children and sensory impaired children to ascertain their ability to develop language concepts. The task was to determine the ability of the child or person to develop language concepts when motor speech development was poorly developed or the ability to speak English was limited or their ability to hear was questionable. Nonverbal vocabulary and language conceptual abilities were ascertained by having people match, or pair, or construct pictures. One such test that was developed as a nonverbal language conceptual development measure with both mentally retarded and deaf children was the Leiter International Performance Scales (Leiter, 1948).

The Leiter and other such nonverbal measures of vocabulary or language conceptual development ascertain language concept learning by having the subject match cut-up pictures, or match similar conceptual items through graduated abstractness. Other such tests used with young children and those children with sensory or motor speech impairments were the Columbia Mental Maturity Scale (Burgemeister, Blum, & Lorge, 1972) and the French Pictorial Test of Intelligence (French, 1964).

Joseph French developed the Pictorial Test of Intelligence for use with sensory impaired or motor speech impaired children. It sampled five different cognitive functions: vocabulary, verbal comprehension, perceptual organization, spatial relations, and number relations. There are several Binet-type tests that do not include a vocal motor speech response. Most of these require a pointing response to a picture stimulus. One of the earliest collections of nonverbal performance tests was a preschool test, the Merrill-Palmer Scale of Mental Tests (Stutsman, 1931). Grace Arthur brought forth her collection of nonverbal measures in 1947 (Grace Arthur Performance Scales), and later, Marshall Hiskey (1955) provided the first learning aptitude–related test of intelligence for both hearing impaired and deaf children. Hiskey's test (Hiskey-Nebraska Test of Learning Aptitude) has 12 nonverbal subtests measuring such things as bead patterns, memory for color, picture identification, and spatial relations.

Performance tests are generally composed of items developed for a wide range of purposes. These nonverbal measures of intelligence generally do not relate well to verbal measures but have the decided advantage of not requiring aural understanding of the test items. The directions and vocal motor response format are frequently limited to pointing or manual motor manipulation as in the case of the Hiskey-Nebraska. These and other so-called nonverbal or performance tests were used with a wide range of people with hearing loss, cultural-linguistic differences, speech and motor handicaps, and in some cases orthopedic handicaps extensive in the upper extremities.

Weaknesses of these early performance tests were the limited range of cognitive abilities they sampled and the fact that these devices did not provide a good comparison to other existing verbal measures. They were never standardized on or developed to be used with the same population on which the early Binet scales were based. The result was that an IQ score on a nonverbal scale did not relate well to the master test, the Binet. Consequently, it was argued that nonverbal scales were poorly developed and even more poorly standardized. The professional community was skeptical of them and used them only when a Binet test could not be used. One problem with that approach was that deaf and other children were not assumed to be very intelligent because they simply could not take the best intelligence tests. Although the logic was incomplete, the attitude was prevalent and there are arguments in the literature throughout the 1930s up until the present time to that effect.

The shortcomings of the verbally loaded Binet instruments are the inability to ascertain central language formation free and independent of vocal motor speech responses. Although performance tests may not be precise in their ability to isolate and establish functional levels of central language formation, they at least control to some degree the verbal tests' dependence on receptive and expressive language function and vocal motor speech development. What was badly needed was an intelligence test for adults; and, it was hoped, one that would have two comparable scales, one a verbal measure and one a performance measure. What would be perfect, then, would be to see this adult measure reworked and made useful with children.

THE TWO SCALES OF DAVID WECHSLER

In contrast to Binet, Wechsler's work was principally with adults. What he wanted was a test that would measure adult intelligence, because the Binet did not do it well. Next he wanted a verbal scale and a nonverbal scale that would be statistically comparable, therefore designed into the same instrument. (See Chapter 8 by Jones and James on the Wechsler-type instruments.)

The Wechsler-type instruments for children (1958, 1974) were designed to stand in psychometric contrast to the Binet-type instruments. Both are individually administered, and the Verbal scale of the Wechsler measures many Binet concepts such as vocabulary, mathematical reasoning, memory, and the associative and mediational use of language through similarities and comprehension. The Verbal scale of the Wechsler and the 1960 Binet related quite well (generally in the high .80s). But, that is where the similarity ends. The early Binet-type tests (up until the most recent edition) provided one score, an IQ. The Binet uses the mental age concept given it by Terman. The Wechsler does not have a mental age and it provides the user with 13 subtests in two scales. Both scales provide an IQ.

What the Wechsler instruments attempt to measure are a large number of specific traits or abilities—in fact, some of the very abilities that Binet originally proposed as important. Wechsler's tests attempt to accomplish this by providing its user with two major subscales, one with verbal subtests and one with performance subtests. It is well standardized, easy to administer and score, has high reliability, and has over the past 20 years exceeded the Binet as the most popular test for these reasons.

Are the Wechsler scales a relatively perfect psychometric procedure? The answer would be no. For one thing, the subtests within each scale do not sample a wide range of specific abilities. However, many psychologists and special educators treat the individual subtests as if they were distinctly different subtests measuring distinct cognitive traits; they do not, however. Most of the Wechsler subtests in a particular scale relate quite highly and positively. The Wechsler scales provide within one instrument a two-scale device capable of measuring verbal and performance abilities. Is it a stand-alone cognitive measure as so many would-be users contend that it is?

CONFUSION IN PRACTICE

In 1961, Zigler noted that a major misunderstanding had occurred among the terms *diagnosis*, *classification*, and *labeling*. The fields of education and behavioral science were naturally attracted to testing as a means of classifying people, forgetting the intermediary step of diagnosis because of the example of medical science. Medicine organizes the symptoms of disease according to a diagnostic classification scheme. Tests are used in medicine to identify important contributing characteristics. Traditionally, medical diagnosis is the uncovering of these characteristics in order that a classification can be made. There are four questions that are raised in that process. They are:

1. Is the person different from the group called normal?
2. What is the degree of difference if it exists?
3. What group of people is he or she most like in characteristic, etiology, or symptomatology?

4. Can the origin of the difference be traced to its ultimate causation?

The truth is that global test scores reduce the descriptive characteristics of a particular person's behavior. In arriving at a child's learning or adjustment problem, no one procedure can tell enough of the story to provide a diagnosis. A test may provide a label used in classifying a child, but those data will not be useful in assisting teachers or others to know what to do with a particular child instructionally. Therefore, the professional community must make several initial choices in establishing the diagnostic process, such as determining how to test the child and what intelligence test to use. For example, should a single- or multiple-domain test be administered? Should it be administered in group or individual settings? Should it be a highly structured standardized procedure, or should it permit maximum decision making by the examiner? Should it be commercially prepared or should it be curriculum based, and very possibly teacher made? These issues are illustrated below.

A CASE STUDY

Use of the Binet IV is illustrated by the case study of a 10-year-old 4th-grade boy who repeatedly failed to read with comprehension under remedial conditions in a special education resource room. This boy was found by the psychological placement screening procedures required for special education to have normal verbal and performance intelligence on the Wechsler Intelligence Scale for Children - Revised and a reading word recognition grade level of 1.7 with a standard score of 76, a reading vocabulary grade level of 1.6 with a standard score of 71, and a reading comprehension grade level of 1.3 and a standard score of 69. He demonstrated, by the statistical discrepancy between intelligence and reading standard scores, the academic achievement deficit necessary to qualify for special education as a learning disabled student. He did not have any particular verbal strengths on the WISC-R, achieving standard scores of 10s, 11s, and 12s on the subtests of Similarities, Comprehension, and Vocabulary. His speech was clear, and his language expressive for his age. He had normal sensory hearing function and no visual acuity problems.

His arithmetic subtest performance on the WISC-R and his classroom grades in math were both very strong. He had a 13 scale score on the

Arithmetic subtest and received As in math at school each grading period. His writing was good and he had no gross or fine motor deficits. In fact, he was quite athletic.

Performance scores on the WISC-R indicated three strengths in Picture Recognition (scale score of 11), Picture Arrangement (scale score of 13), and Object Assembly (scale score of 12). His weaknesses were in Block Design and Coding. On those two WISC-R subtests he had subtest scores of 8 and 9, respectively. A scale score of 10 is average. Therefore, a 9 is still in the average range.

His Digit Span was also a 9 scale score. In short, the WISC-R does not have any clinical indicators that an information-processing deficit exists. The special education resource teacher administered the academic subtests of the Woodcock-Johnson Psycho-Educational Battery. She found that he had a reading comprehension problem based, in her opinion, on poor reading skills. She therefore recommended that he receive a basic developmental curriculum in a remedial, one-on-one format. The results of the remedial effort were not positive. The parents, in cooperation with the special education resource teacher and the regular class teacher, requested an IEP review meeting. At that point the school-based team recommended that a comprehensive psychological examination be obtained. They felt that the routine special education screening procedures, which frequently consist of a WISC-R, Bender Visual Motor Gestalt Test, and Human Figure Drawings, were inadequate.

In response, the school psychologist administered the Binet IV as a means of developing a clinical hypothesis that might then be further tested through observation and measurement. The administration of this instrument indicated normal language learning with high average vocabulary and language comprehension and verbal reasoning. Bead Copying and the discrimination and retention of visual perceptual detail were excellent. Arithmetic and math reasoning performance demonstrated above-average function.

A major difficulty was uncovered, however, on the Binet IV. This 10-year-old boy with average ability to recall digits generated below-average ability in retention for word units. The Wechsler Memory for Sentences and subtests 3 and 10 of the Detroit Tests of Learning Aptitude-2 (Hammill, 1985) confirmed this hypothesis.

The multidisciplinary team discussed this information processing deficit in verbal related memory for word units. Observations and hypothesis testing were conducted within the resource room using color and form cues, and tactile-kinesthetic multisensory techniques in combination were effective in bolstering memory for word units. Later a linguistic reading approach permitted transference back to a developmental curriculum. Using memory training routines and larger unit memory retention devices (chunking), this child was able to obtain grade-level performance in reading and maintain it.

This case illustrates at least three points in best practice procedures. First, the routine use of test batteries, a common practice in special education placement, is not a good substitute for the use of diagnostic procedures in response to specific clinical hypotheses. Second, rarely will one diagnostic procedure effectively test enough of the information-processing skills to be helpful in setting instructional objectives or recommending instructional activities. Third, the diagnostician is wise to consider a range of procedures in response to the referral information that should be driven by detailed observations. In this case, to assume that the memory for digits requires the same information-processing skills as does the retention for word units is incorrect.

STANFORD-BINET IV

Test Authors: Thorndike, R. L., Hagen, E. P., & Sattler, J. M.
Copyright Date: 1986
Test Publisher: The Riverside Publishing Company
　　8420 Bryn Mawr,
　　Chicago, IL 60631
Prices:

Item	
Examiner's Kit	$420.00
Guide for Administration and Scoring	$33.00
Technical Manual	$12.00
Examiner's Handbook	$21.00
Record Booklet (Package 35)	$37.50
IBM Program Kit	$294.00

Stated Purpose: This instrument is designed to ascertain general (verbal) reasoning in keeping with the original concepts of Binet. It generates four area scores and a composite score. The four area scores are: (1) verbal reasoning (2) abstract/visual reasoning, (3) quantitative reasoning, and (4) short-term memory. The principal purpose of this individually administered test of intelligence was to provide a "continuous scale for appraising cognitive development from age 2 to adult" (Thorndike, Hagen, & Sattler, 1986). The 4th edition (this edition) attempted to draw on the items from the earlier editions and even to utilize Binet's original concepts of intelligence. One of the major departures from the earlier versions of the Stanford-Binet has been the shift to an omnibus test arrangement instead of a spiral administration or age-scale format. The earlier Binet-type tests were intent on generating a mental age across tasks and therefore required that different tasks designed to measure different traits be administered at each age level. In contrast, Wechsler-type instruments were designed to determine the client's abilities within one task area (test or subtest area) before moving on to another. Clinicians have generally agreed, and there is research evidence to support the fact, that an omnibus test item arrangement produces higher mental development thresholds than does the spiral arrangement common to the pre-1986 Binet-type scales. In a spiral-item test, each subtest item is administered at a given age level along with items measuring other abilities. In an omnibus arrangement all items measuring a particular trait are given clustered together as a subtest. The omnibus arrangement also makes the tests easier to score and administer.

With the advent of Wechsler's children's tests, clinicians over the past 15 years generally agree that the Wechsler-type scales are easier to administer and interpret. There was a time, however, when the Wechsler scales were new to the field and clinicians generally claimed that the Binet-type instruments were more easily administered and interpreted. It may be possible that the type of test used primarily in an examiner's training is the one perceived to be the easiest to administer and score. It is therefore considered to be the more easily administered and scored, and is thus the most readily used.

The test authors for the Binet IV claim that maintaining the content and tasks within an age scale ". . . has usually succeeded in maintaining the interest of the examinees, particularly that of young children" (p. 8). It is the authors' contention that by retaining the variety of content and tasks of the earlier instruments and dropping the age scale, Thorndike et al. have successfully challenged a major fault in the earlier editions (3rd Edition, Form L-M) reducing ". . . intra-individual differences in cognitive abilities." The new edition no longer places such a stress on verbal abilities, especially at the upper age levels. This supposedly balanced assessment tool has been selected by clinicians, according to the authors (p. 9), as a diagnostic procedure that maximizes the study of cognitive abilities with gifted children, mainstreamed children having difficulties learning, and the mentally retarded. The authors point out that this test is designed to ". . . assess the kinds of cognitive abilities that years of research have shown are correlated with school progress" (p. 8).

Intended Population: People with normal sensory function (hearing and vision) in absence of dyskinesis, haptic or tactile disabilities, in the age ranges of 2 to adult, from a wide sample of African-American, White, and Hispanic cultures in the United States, where the principal linguistic structure is English. The instrument may not be the one of choice for subtrainable or developmentally young children. With the present revision (Binet IV), the psychologist has the capability of deleting from administration various tests (subtests), and even areas (assumed factorially related tests.)

Ease of Administration: Many of the complaints surrounding this instrument are concerned with the time required to administer it. Many psychologists contend that the instrument cannot be administered in less than 2 hours. The test authors found a mean time of 114 minutes required to administer the instrument. The test authors have addressed that problem to some degree by combining four subtests in a quick screening test. The mean time for the quick screening procedure is 34 minutes. Carvajal and Gerber (1987) report that the relationship between the quick scale procedure and full instrument was .90.

The second issue that apparently works against the popularity of this test is the difficulty in manipulating the materials in some of the subtests. It is an instrument that requires an experienced examiner well grounded and well versed in the 1986 Binet.

Ease of Scoring: The major strength of this scale is the psychometric theory upon which it is developed. Each subtest and each of the four areas produce a score, providing the user with individual and area trait measures. A composite score is also obtained.

The four area scores are composed of 15 tests. It may simplify the understanding of this instrument to review each of the subtests that constitute each area.

I. Verbal Reasoning Area
   1. Vocabulary
   2. Comprehension
   3. Absurdities
   4. Verbal Relations
II. Abstract/Visual Reasoning Area
   5. Pattern Analysis
   6. Copying
   7. Matrices
   8. Paper Folding and Cutting
III. Quantitative Reasoning Area
   9. Quantitative
   10. Number Series
   11. Equation Building
IV. Short Term Memory
   12. Bead Memory
   13. Memory for Sentences
   14. Memory for Digits
   15. Memory for Objects

Reliability: Test stability is .90 to .91 for the Composite Score, Verbal Reasoning is .87, Abstract/Visual Reasoning Area is .67, Quantitative Reasoning Area is .51, and Short Term Memory is .81.

Test-retest reliability on subtests ranges from .86 on the comprehension subtest to .46 on copying. K-R 20s ranged from .97 for 5-year-olds to .70 and .80 for 8-year-olds.

Validity: The test authors argue for the validity of their instrument on three bases: (1) First, correlational patterns among tests as clarified by factor analytic procedures, (2) the correlation of the test with scores on other tests deemed to be measures of the same or similar constructs, and (3) the performance of groups identified by indices as acceptable tests. The subtests within areas generally show intercorrelations in the .60s to .70s. Subtests between areas generally show correlations in the .40s to .50s. Factor analytic (Reynolds, Kamphaus, & Rosenthal, 1988) data do not appear to show reasonable clusters, and most of the variance loads on the highly verbal subtests. It is difficult to justify all four areas, and especially the Abstract/Visual Reasoning and Quantitative Reasoning.

The Binet IV Verbal Reasoning correlates .73 with the WISC-R Verbal Scales, .60 with the WISC-R Performance Scales, and .73 with the WISC-R Full Scales. The Binet IV Composite correlates .78 with WISC-R Verbal Scales, and .73 with WISC-R Performance Scales, and .83 with the WISC-R Full Scales.

Summary: Most of the reliability coefficients reported for the new Stanford-Binet (4th edition) and correlations with the 3rd edition were .80 and above (Hartwig, Sapp, & Clayton, 1986). Correlations between IQ scores and other tests with various populations have also suggested the test's uniqueness, while clearly measuring intelligence (Carvajal, Gerber, & Smith, 1987; Hayden, Furlong, & Linnemeyer, 1988; Krohn & Lamp, 1989). The 1972 and the 1986 editions are particularly useful in assessing language-related learning in children 5 through 8 years of age, free of cultural linguistic or sensory-language learning problems.

The most recent revision of the Binet (Binet IV) is, in keeping with the Binet tradition, a highly language-loaded verbal measure that seems to be strong with the late preschool and early school-age child. It should be an excellent test for identifying gifted children, and in determining the use of language and language-related skills in educable mentally retarded and possibly trainable mentally retarded populations (Lukens, 1988). It may be useful in exploring language learning–related problems with learning disabled children, especially in the presence of other nonverbal and language conceptual measures.

Currently the field is dependent on the Wechsler Scales. The newest edition of the Binet has been compared, maybe too much so, to the WISC-R. It does examine language learning more completely, offering memory for words and word unit subtests that the WISC-R does not. It may sample language more deeply and may not attempt to cover as broad a cognitive sampling as the WISC-R. It does augment the examiner's test repertoire and should be used for specific purposes more often than it is at present. It does not offer the parallel verbal and nonverbal structure common to the WISC-R that many wished it would. But why should it? It offers a different set of verbal and nonverbal language conceptual sensitive measures. This test can be used as a custom-built procedure designed to examine the language-related learning of children with educational problems. As such it can offer a great deal of hypothesis testing support. If the WISC-R has become the commonplace special education screening instrument, then the Binet IV offers a way out. It offers a return to intensive

language-learning diagnosis in combination with other diagnostic procedures that can intensify the description of the functional and developmental learning of language and its symbolic applications in academics.

SLOSSON INTELLIGENCE TEST FOR CHILDREN (SIT)

Test Authors: Slosson, R. L.
    Revised by: Nicholson, C. L., & Hibshman, T.
Copyright Date: 1963
Test Publisher: Western Psychological Services
    12031 Wilshire Blvd.
    Los Angeles, CA 90025
Prices: Score Sheets - pad of 50 - $19.50
         Norms Tables - 1 set $27.50/Manual 1-$24.00

Stated Purpose: A quick screening device useful for children and adults. It
is essentially a Binet-type vocabulary instrument measuring principally
the vocabulary factor.

Intended Population: It can be used with any individuals or groups, age
2 years to adult, who have English cultural experiences. Most of the
questions require verbal administration; therefore, it assumes usable
sensory hearing and no interfering vocal motor, delayed speech, or central
language deficits. The items administered to infants require attention,
grasping responses, and other motor activities.

Reliability: Test-retest reliability over 2-month intervals yields coefficients of .97.

Validity: The SIT suffers from several validity problems. The data regarding
its construction and development are nebulous; the standardization samples are
relatively undefined, and less than rigorous procedures were used in defining
them. As one would assume, interrelationships with Binet vocabulary are very
high (about .90). The ratio IQ makes the procedure suspect with older subjects.
The test has the distinction of appearing to be built using Gesell Developmental Schedule test items at the younger age levels, while appearing to use items
similar to the Binet vocabulary and language comprehension items at the
upper age levels. Correlations between the SIT and the Wechsler Full Scale
range from .54 to .93, between the SIT and Stanford-Binet, .76 to .90.

Ease of Scoring: Scoring is quick and very simple. The test provides a verbal age (mental age equivalent) and a verbal IQ. The test is designed to require only limited training for administration, scoring, or interpretation.

Ease of Administration: The major advantage of this instrument is that it can be administered by a qualified user, who in this case may be an educational diagnostician as opposed to a licensed psychologist. It can be administered in 10 to 30 minutes.

Summary: This test can be used by educational diagnosticians with only preliminary assessment training and limited psychometric information. Although it is quick to administer and easy to score, the user must take precautions in any interpretation, realizing that the SIT is primarily a screening device, not a diagnostic procedure. It can be used to determine expected grade level performance and, in combination with achievement tests, is a good yearly review tool to ascertain vocabulary growth and language comprehension development. It is not suitable for determining eligibility for special education; but with gifted children, for example, it could be used as one among several screening procedures to assist in the prereferral process. This is a crude screening device built to describe one or two Binet-proposed traits. It is not suitable for diagnosis.

PICTORIAL TEST OF INTELLIGENCE (PTI)

Test author: French, J. L.
Copyright Date: 1964
Test Publisher: Houghton Mifflin Company
One Beacon Street
Boston, MA 02108
Price: Kit - $175.00

Stated Purpose: This test is a further development of the Binet-type test set in a nonverbal response model. It employs an objective, multichoice response format, permitting children with speech and motor handicaps easier response and stimuli access. It was designed to measure vocabulary, verbal comprehension, perceptual organization, spatial relationships, and number relationships. There are six subtests designed to measure Picture Vocabulary, Form Discrimination, Information and Comprehension, Similarities, Size and Numbers, and Immediate Recall.

Intended Population: The test is principally used with normal and handicapped children 3 to 8 years of age. The PTI goes beyond the Ammons Full-Range Picture Vocabulary Test (Ammons & Ammons, 1948) and the Peabody Picture Vocabulary Test—Revised (Dunn, 1972, 1981) in terms of the sample of intellectual function it ascertains. These three devices tend to sample only vocabulary.

Ease of Administration: The procedure requires 45 minutes and can be administered by persons who have specific supervised training and proficiency administering Binet-type instruments. It is a restricted test and was designed for psychologists to administer. The test can be given in its entirety or short forms of varying numbers of subtests can be administered.

Ease of Scoring: Scoring is routine and simple. Each subtest provides a score, but the principal score is the composite.

Reliability: Test-retest reliability coefficients range from .88 to .92. Internal consistency runs from .81 to .90.

Validity: The subtest correlations with the total test are in the high .50s to the high .60s. It correlates at .77 with the Binet (1960), .67 with the Full Scale WISC, and .61 with the Columbia Mental Maturity Scale.

Summary: The most critical objection must be that after 28 years this test needs to be revised. The test author has spent some considerable time and energy gaining experience with difficult-to-assess handicapped children using this procedure. In so doing he has developed a technique that is responsive to children with upper extremity and motor speech problems. The instrument, like most performance scales, does take time to learn. The rather large cards and packets of smaller stimuli cards get out of order and are never where they should be. One of the major improvements in this otherwise well-thought-out and well-standardized test that is sensitive to several important academic areas of handicapped children's growth would be to spiral-bind both the response and stimuli materials. The green metal box is both a plus factor (it is durable) and yet it is not the world's most perfect test administration easel. The small support leg is never in the right position. Nitpicking aside, this instrument should be in every school psychologist's test cabinet.

COLUMBIA MENTAL MATURITY SCALE (CMMS)

Test Authors: Burgemeister, B. B. , Blum, I. L., & Lorge, I.
Copyright Date: 1954, Revised 1972
Test Publisher: The Psychological Corporation
    Harcourt, Brace, Jovanovich, Inc.
    555 Academic Court
    San Antonio, TX 78204-2498
Price: Kit - $346.50

Stated Purpose: This is an individually administered mental ability test that requires no verbal response and a minimum motoric pointing response on the child's part to match a pictorial shape, color, or other aspects of three, four, or five designs on 92 rectangular cards.

Intended Population: Children ages 3½ to 10 years.

Reliability: Split-half reliability ranges from .85 to .91; short-term test-retest reliability is in the mid-.80s.

Validity: It has been demonstrated to correlate .88 with 1937 Stanford-Binet, .39 with 1960 Stanford on nondisabled 4- to 5-year-olds, .73 with Otis Alpha nonverbal with deaf populations. The correlation with most verbal measures, including the earlier Stanford-Binet, ranges from .60 to .70.

Ease of Scoring: Record blanks make scoring an easy procedure, and conversion of raw scores to mental age is a simple task.

Ease of Administration: 15 to 20 minutes.

Summary: Carvajal, McVey, Sellers, Weyand, and McKnab (1987) reported on the relationship around the SB-IV, Peabody Picture Vocabulary Test—Revised, Columbia Mental Maturity Scale, and Goodenough-Harris Drawing Test on 23 third-grade children. The only moderate relationship was .60 between PPVT-R and the composite on SB-IV (SB-IV mean SAS was 113, PPVT-R standard score equivalent was 1.10). The verbal and language comprehension "g" factor provided low positive correlation with the Goodenough-Harris Drawing Test and the Columbia Mental Maturity Scale in a similar study. It is useful with both orthopedically handicapped and vocal motor speech-handicapped children.

TO BEST PRACTICES

The intent of this chapter has been to review the work of Binet and those who followed him, in their efforts to create intelligence tests that would consistently discriminate those children who have difficulty learning. A best practice is a perception of what constitutes an issue and how it can be appropriately ascertained and constructively managed. What is a best practice today, however, may simply be an opinion.

This chapter contains a brief description of selected Binet-type instruments. We have attempted to examine those that provide unique stimuli presentation and require nonverbal response forms. This chapter has cautioned those using such instruments to be aware of the risks involved in using language-loaded instruments. Although these instruments remain the best predictors of school success, they do depend on the student possessing intact sensory function, having the uninterrupted ability to form central language concepts, and generally having some motoric response mechanism in addition to free vocal motor speech. We spoke of the confusing but common practice of using scores from tests as the derived measures providing a diagnosis. Of all the notions stressed in this chapter, the most imperative are the beliefs that a test is as good and no better than the person using it and that a test score does not make a diagnosis. Diagnosis is derived by raising clinical hypotheses in a scientific format and then selecting from one's knowledge of diagnostic procedures those observational, formal, and informal procedures that will best address that request (hypothesis) for data. Tests are tools; they are not the diagnostician.

In conclusion, then, it is a diagnostic best practice to discount any notion that test scores, singularly or in combination, can derive a handicapping classification. Test scores serve somewhat to describe learner behaviors; but, test scores alone cannot determine the setting of an instructional or behavioral management plan. What good are they? Tests are standardized observations and, as such, they reduce the time and limit the need for creative response formation that less-structured observations would require. Is observation, then, or informal assessment better than formal assessment? No. All observation, formal or informal, must respond to the same requirements including reliability and validity.

Finally, where are we? We are attempting to bring the science of trait measurement into its infancy. How will that be done? It is being done each day by people all over the world, applying psychometric principles to what they hypothesize relates to how we learn, or how we process information.

What, then, is your role in the application and scientific processes? Will you blindly believe and practice as if numbers can reflect intelligence, or will you seek to define diagnosis as the process by which we attempt to understand and describe learning as the interaction between the learner, the task to be learned, and the environment?

REFERENCES

Ammons, R. B., & Ammons, H. S. (1948). *The Full-Range Picture Vocabulary Test.* Missoula, MT: Psychological Test Specialists.

Arthur, G. (1947). *A Point Scale of Performance Tests, Revised Form II.* New York: The Psychological Corporation.

Binet, A., & Simon, T. (1905). Methods nouvelles pour le diagnostic du niveau intellectual des anormaux. *L'Annee Psychologique, 11*, 191-244.

Binet, A., & Simon, T. (1908). Le developpement de l'intelligence chez les enfants. *L'Annee Psychologique, 14*, 1-94.

Bond, E. A. (1940). *Tenth grade abilities and achievements.* Teaching College Contributions to Education, No. 813.

Burgemeister, B. B., Blum, L. H., & Lorge, I. (1972). *Columbia Mental Maturity Scale.* San Antonio, TX: The Psychological Corporation, Harcourt, Brace, Jovanovich.

Carvajal, H., & Gerber, J. (1987). 1986 Stanford-Binet abbreviated forms. *Psychological Reports, 61*, 285-286.

Carvajal, H., Gerber, J., & Smith, P. D. (1987). Relationship between scores of young adults on Stanford-Binet IV and Peabody Picture Vocabulary Test-Revised. *Perceptual and Motor Skills, 65*, 721-722.

Carvajal, H., McVey, S., Sellers, T., Weyand, K., & McKnab, P. (1987). Relationships between scores on the general purpose abbreviated battery of Stanford-Binet IV, Peabody Picture Vocabulary Test-Revised, Columbia Mental Maturity Scale, and Goodenough-Harris Drawing Test. *Psychological Record, 62*, 127-130.

Davis, C. J. (1970). New developments in the intelligence testing of blind children. *In Proceedings of the Conference on New Approaches to the Education of Blind Persons.* New York: American Foundation for the Blind.

Dunn, L. M. (1972). *Peabody Picture Vocabulary Test.* Circle Pines, MN: American Guidance Service.

Dunn, L. M. (1981). *Peabody Picture Vocabulary Test-Revised.* Circle Pines, MN: American Guidance Service.

French, J. L. (1964). *Manual: Pictorial Test of Intelligence.* Boston: Houghton Mifflin.

Glutting, J. J. (1989). Introduction to the structure and application of the Stanford-Binet Intelligence Scale-Fourth Edition. *Journal of School Psychology, 2*, 69-80.

174   BEST PRACTICES IN ASSESSMENT

Goddard, H. H. (1908). The Binet and Simon tests of intellectual capacity. *Training School, 5*, 3-9.

Guilford, J. P. (1967). *The nature of human intelligence.* New York: McGraw-Hill.

Hammill, D. D. (1985). *Detroit Tests of Learning Aptitude-2.* Austin, TX: Pro-Ed.

Hartwig, S. S., Sapp, G. L., & Clayton, G. A. (1986). Comparison of the Stanford-Binet Intelligence Scale: Form L-M and The Stanford-Binet Intelligence Scale Fourth Edition. *Psychological Reports, 60*, 1215-1218.

Hayden, D. C., Furlong, M. J., & Linnemeyer, S. (1988). A comparison of the Kaufman Assessment Battery for Children and the Stanford-Binet IV for the Assessment of Gifted Children. *Psychology in the Schools, 25*, 239-243.

Hayes, S. P. (1943). A second test scale for the mental measurement of the visually handicapped. *Outlook for the Blind, 37*, 37-41.

Hiskey, M. (1955). *Hiskey-Nebraska Test of Learning Aptitude.* Lincoln, NE: University of Nebraska.

Keith, T. Z., Cool, V. A., Novak, C. J., White, L. J., & Pottebaum, S. M. (1988). Confirmatory factor analysis of the Stanford-Binet Fourth Edition: Testing the theory-test match. *Journal of School Psychology, 26*, 253-274.

Krohn, E. J., & Lamp, R. J. (1989). Concurrent validity of the Stanford-Binet Fourth Edition and K-ABC for Head Start children. *Journal of School Psychology, 27*, 59-67.

Leiter, R. G. (1948). *International Performance Scale.* Chicago: Stoelting.

Lukens, J. (1988). Comparison of the Fourth Edition and the L-M Edition of the Stanford-Binet used with mentally retarded persons. *Journal of School Psychology, 26*, 87-89.

Peterson, J. (1926). *Early conceptions and tests of intelligence.* Yonkers, NY: World Book.

Phelps, L. (1989). Comparison of scores for intellectually gifted students on the WISC-R and the Fourth Edition of the Stanford-Binet. *Psychology in the Schools, 26*, 125-129.

Phelps, L., & Bell, M. C. (1988). Correlations between the Stanford-Binet: Fourth Edition and the WISC-R with a learning disabled population. *Psychology in the Schools, 25*, 38-383.

Pintner, R. (1931). *Intelligence testing* (2nd ed.). New York: Teacher College Press.

Reynolds, C. R., Kamphaus, R. W., & Rosenthal, B. L. (1988). Factor analysis of the Stanford-Binet Fourth Edition for ages 2 years through 23 years. *Measurement and Evaluation in Counseling and Development, 21*, 52-63.

Slosson, R. L. (1963). *Slosson Intelligence Test for Children.* Los Angeles: Western Psychological Services.

Stutsman, R. (1931). *Mental measurement of preschool children.* Tarrytown on Hudson: World Book.

Terman, L. M. (1916). *The measurement of intelligence.* Boston: Houghton Mifflin.

Terman, L. M., & Merrill, M. A. (1937). *Measuring intelligence.* Boston: Houghton Mifflin.

Terman, L. M., & Merrill, M. A. (1960). *Stanford-Binet Intelligence Scale Form L-M.* Boston: Houghton Mifflin.

Thorndike, R. P., Hagen, E. L., & Sattler, J. M. (1986). *Technical manual: Stanford-Binet Intelligence Scale* (4th ed.). Chicago: Riverside.

Wechsler, D. (1958). *Measurement and appraisal of adult intelligence* (4th ed.). Baltimore: Williams & Wilkins.

Wechsler, D. (1974). *Wechsler Intelligence Scale for Children - Revised.* San Antonio: The Psychological Corporation.

Wertheimer, W. (1923). Studies in the theory of Gestalt psychology. *Psychology in the Schools, 4,* 32-36.

Wolfensberger, W. (1965). Diagnosis diagnosed. *Journal of Mental Subnormality, 11,* 62-70.

Zigler, E. (1961). Social deprivation and rigidity in the performance of feeble-minded children. *Journal of Abnormal Social Psychology, 62,* 413-421.

6 BEST PRACTICES IN COMPUTER-ASSISTED ASSESSMENT

Cleborne D. Maddux and LaMont Johnson

The decade of the 1980s was one of rapid growth in the implementation of computer technology in education and related endeavors such as psychology and counseling. One of the most rapidly growing uses of computing continues to be in the area of *assessment*. Many professionals have noted this trend. For example, Meier and Geiger (1986) suggest that "Human services professionals are witnessing an unprecedented growth in the automation of instruments for psychological and career assessment" (p. 29). Green (1988) asserts that "Small, versatile computers are changing the way tests are given, and changing the kinds of tests being given" (p. 223). Madsen (1986) predicts that during the next decade, computer-assisted testing will increase tenfold, while Johnson (1979) goes even further and predicts that by the next century, all testing will be done by computer.

There are probably several reasons for the rapid growth during the 1980s and 1990s in use of computers in assessment. Such factors as increasing case loads of human services personnel in the face of budget cuts in social programs (another trend of the eighties) undoubtedly played a role. Walker and Myrick (1985) allude to this factor and say of computers, "This new technology seems to have the potential to revolutionize the testing responsibilities of school psychologists, particularly those with heavy testing loads" (p. 51). Then, too, it was not until the eighties that powerful but inexpensive microcomputers first became widely available (Eberly & Cech, 1986).

Whatever the reasons for increased interest in incorporating computers into the assessment process, the growth trend is now well established. Jacob and Brantley (1987) surveyed 268 school psychologists and reported that 72% used computers in their assessment work. Further, of those who did not use computers at the time of the survey, many reported that they planned to use them in the future (33% planned to use them for data storage, 30% for test scoring, and 30% for report writing).

Another indication of the growing interest in the use of computers in assessment is the recent appearance of a number of new journals, including *Computers in Human Behavior, Computers in Human Services, Computers in Psychiatry/Psychology,* and *Computers in the Schools* (Kramer, 1988). In addition, the American Psychological Association's Committee on Professional Standards, in conjunction with the Committee on Psychological Tests has published *Standards for Computer-Based Tests and Interpretations* (APA, 1986).

HISTORICAL ROOTS OF COMPUTERIZED ASSESSMENT

Neither computerized assessment procedures in general, nor automated testing in particular, is new. One of the earliest proponents of automated testing was Sidney Pressey (1926, 1927). Pressey noted that objective tests, used widely in the military during World War I, were becoming commonplace in schools. Pressey feared that teachers would soon be overwhelmed by bookkeeping and other routine tasks related to administering and scoring these tests. To solve this problem, he developed an experimental testing machine to administer multiple choice items to students.

Pressey's device presented a question followed by several alternative answers. In the earliest version of the device, both question and answer appeared in a slot on the machine. Later versions had questions and alternatives on a printed page (Travers, 1967). Pressey also experimented with the machine's potential for instruction. Although many educators and psychologists were interested in Pressey's device, it was never widely implemented.

B. F. Skinner (1954, 1958) was responsible for the next cycle of interest in what came to be termed *teaching machines*. Skinner's machine differed from Pressey's in several respects, including the ability to handle *essay-type* questions:

> Material is printed in 30 radial frames on a 12-inch disk. The student inserts the disk and closes the machine. He cannot proceed until the machine has been locked, and, once he has begun, the machine cannot be unlocked. All but a corner of one frame is visible through a window. The student writes his response on a paper strip exposed through a second opening. By lifting a lever on the front of the machine, he moves what he has written under a transparent cover and uncovers the correct response in the remaining corner of the frame. If the two responses correspond, he moves the lever horizontally. This movement punches a hole in the paper opposite his response, recording the fact that he called it correct, and alters the machine so that the frame will not appear again when the student works around the disk a second time. Whether the response was correct or not, a second frame appears when the lever is returned to its starting position. The student proceeds in this way until he has responded to all frames. He then works around the disk a second time, but only those frames appear to which he has not correctly responded. When the disk revolves without stopping, the assignment is finished. (Skinner, 1958, p. 974)

Many others became interested in teaching machines. However, once again, the machines never really "caught on," although a number of different designs were successfully built and tested.

Although teaching machines were never widely implemented, the principles employed by Skinner and others (especially task analysis and reinforcement) were later applied to printed materials such as books and workbooks. The use of such materials came to be termed *programmed instruction*. The programmed instruction movement gained a considerable following, peaked during the early 1960s, and declined rapidly thereafter. Readers who are interested in the history of this movement are referred to excellent analyses by Osguthorpe and Zhou (1989), Gayeski (1989), Criswell (1989), and Skinner himself (Skinner, 1986).

At about the same time that programmed instruction gained its brief popularity, there were a number of experimental educational computing projects that incorporated assessment components. The PLATO Project and the Stanford Project were the most well known, as well as the most ambitious of these ventures.

The PLATO project (Programmed Logic for Automatic Teaching Operations) was developed at the University of Illinois, and this may have been the largest computer-assisted instructional and testing system ever developed (Burke, 1982). PLATO began as a single special student workstation connected to a large, mainframe computer. It evolved into a highly interactive network through which entire courses could be offered to many learners, each using the special PLATO terminal. Over a thousand separate PLATO programs were developed, and the system was installed on mainframe computers housed on a number of university campuses.

The Stanford Project was headed by Patrick Suppes and Richard Atkinson, and was aimed at improving instruction in math and reading. This computer project was to involve three levels, including: (a) drill and practice, (b) tutorials, and (c) questioning routines. The first two of these levels were successfully implemented, but the questioning routines were never perfected.

Projects such as PLATO and the Stanford Project were widely discussed and extensively written about but never widely used. One of the problems with such systems was their expense. Microcomputers did not exist, and these systems required use of a mainframe computer. Mainframes were immensely expensive; experienced frequent, costly breakdowns; required a large operational staff; and allowed few users at any one time. Therefore, rental of time on these machines was costly. The special workstations and telephone lines required were other expenses that most public school systems were unable or unwilling to accept. There were other problems, as well, including the fact that most teachers were unfamiliar with the technology involved and did not know how to make good use of such systems. Then, too, at about this time, federal support for educational research and development began to decline, making funding even more difficult.

Thus, although education and psychology have had a number of periods marked by interest in a variety of computerized assessment applications, it was not until recently that such applications have become widely and inexpensively available. With wide availability, however, have come a variety of real and potential advantages and disadvantages. This chapter will discuss these advantages and disadvantages and will provide some guidelines for educators and others who are contemplating the use of computerized assessment procedures. No attempt will be made to review specific software. Not only would a comprehensive review be far beyond the scope of a single chapter, but changes are occurring so rapidly that such a review would be out of date before it was published. Instead, the chapter will concentrate on providing guidelines to help assessment professionals make good choices of software that is currently available as well as software that will become available in the future.

SOME GENERAL PROBLEMS IN COMPUTING AND IN ASSESSMENT

Before beginning a discussion of the use of computers in assessment, it may be helpful to discuss general problems in each of these areas that may have important implications for those who would combine the two activities.

Some General Considerations Related to Computing

Few would argue that computers have enjoyed wide acceptance, approval, and implementation in business, the military, and in many other walks of life. There are many reasons for this near-universal acceptance, and space will not permit a comprehensive discussion. What is most relevant to the present discussion, however, is a lesson from cultural anthropology. Anthropologists have long realized that *successful technological change is always linked to the values a society endorses* (Kneller, 1965).

Americans associate computers with a variety of powerful values about work, including belief in the importance of (a) speed, (b) accuracy, (c) precision, and (d) the removal of human error from work activities (Maddux, Johnson, & Willis, 1992).

Because computers are perceived as promoting these goals, they were widely accepted, first by the military and business subcultures, and then sanctioned for use in schools by those who control school policy. (In this country, school boards are the most common controllers, and these boards are usually dominated by successful businessmen; Boocock, 1980.)

The point is that because Americans associate computers with these respected values, *they have a tendency to believe that computerizing an activity automatically improves it in some important way*. Weizenbaum (1976) has addressed this phenomenon:

It is important to understand very clearly that strengthening a particular technique—putting muscles on it—contributes nothing to its validity. For example, there are computer programs that carry out with great precision all the calculations required to cast the horoscope of an individual whose time and place of birth are known. Because the computer does all the tedious symbol manipulations, they can be done much more quickly and in much more detail than is normally possible for a human astrologer. But such an improvement in the technique of horoscope casting is irrelevant to the validity of astrological forecasting. If astrology is nonsense, then computerized astrology is just as surely nonsense. (pp. 34-35)

Thus, there is a tendency to believe that *whenever techniques are computerized, progress has been made.* Actually, computerizing often (but not always) streamlines or otherwise improves the way an idea is put into action. However, improving the way an idea is *operationalized* does not necessarily improve the idea itself. Computers may simply make it easier, faster, or more convenient to continue carrying out a bad idea. For example, if the analysis of discrepancies between verbal and achievement IQ scores does not contribute to accuracy in diagnosis or remediation, speeding up that analysis or improving the accuracy of the calculations by employing computers does not address the real problem.

The illusion of progress is dangerous because it may cause us *to neglect thinking about and evaluating the concepts that underlie our actions* and cause us to focus exclusively on "putting muscles on" existing techniques. Thus, although computers may or may not help us be innovative in our approach to *technique*, they have a tendency to make us more conservative and less likely to consider and adopt new *ideas*.

Another contributor to this phenomenon is the fact that computerizing requires considerable time, effort, and expense. Therefore, once this process is viewed as completed and computers are in place, there is often great reluctance to make even minor adjustments. It is not unusual for consultants to be told to make recommendations concerning changes in any and every aspect of an organization's functioning *with the exception of some aspect that has been recently computerized.* Administrators and workers alike often feel that too much time, effort, and expense went into a recent computer implementation to consider any changes for at least several years after the implementation was put into place.

These problems are related to a larger phenomenon we have called *The Everest Syndrome* (Maddux, 1984). This syndrome is characterized by the belief that computers should be implemented simply "because they are there." Those who indulge in this syndrome do so because they have neglected to ask what kinds of tasks *ought* to be submitted to computer solutions and assume that computers *should* be used to do whatever they *can* be made to do. Eberly and Cech (1986) refer to this problem: "Computer technology has been almost uncritically integrated into the counseling process" (p. 24). In this paper, we will attempt to make the case that although many assessment tasks *can* be turned over to computers, some clearly *should not* be computerized.

Some General Considerations Related to Assessment

There are a number of reasons why caution should be exercised in integrating computers and assessment. Standardized testing is currently misunderstood by the public and by many educators, parents, and other consumers of assessment results. Many people incorrectly assume that test scores are as highly accurate as are measurements of the physical world. As most assessment professionals realize, however, *the state of the art in psychological assessment is in its infancy.* (This can be appreciated in light of the fact that individual psychology is only about 100 years old.) Then too, psychologists, unlike physicists, do not make direct measurements of independently existing variables and are instead forced to measure behavior they believe is related to some hypothetical construct!

Why has this mistaken idea concerning the precision of test scores come to be accepted? There are undoubtedly many reasons, including the following:

1. In the Western world, many people suffer from what Papert (1980) has termed "mathophobia," or an unreasonable fear of mathematics. Because many people feel intimidated by numbers, and because scientists and others *have* developed highly accurate numerical descriptors for the physical world, some people assume that any psychological trait that has been quantified enjoys the same accuracy and precision as that reflected in the measurement of, for example, heat, weight, or distance.

2. The media contributes to an unrealistic valuing of the results of standardized testing. Television programs and movies often employ plots that imply that the state of the art in psychological testing is far more advanced than it really is.

3. Many people are aware of the great emphasis placed upon precision in standardization, administration, and scoring of formal tests. Such people erroneously assume that the results obtained from such techniques are as precise as the procedures used to produce them.

4. Assessment professionals have sometimes encouraged the overvaluing of tests. We have frequently failed to emphasize the tentative nature of test scores. We have, in fact, reinforced public misunderstanding by referring to IQ scores as if they were attributes analogous to eye color, by reporting observed scores rather than confidence intervals, and by otherwise overtly or covertly supporting the notion of the infallibility of testing.

Because testing is *already* highly overvalued, we should engage in careful thought before deciding to convert highly visible assessment procedures to computer implementation. Bringing computers into the process is almost sure to contribute further to the overvaluing of testing, because many people already associate precision, power, accuracy, and prestige with any activity carried out in whole or in part by computer.

COMPUTERS IN ASSESSMENT

There are a number of assessment-related tasks that are sometimes carried out partially or completely by computers. These include (a) administration of standardized tests, (b) scoring of test items, (c) arithmetic manipulation or transformation of test or subtest scores, (d) interpretation of test results, (e) production of test or assessment reports, and (f) storage of test scores or other assessment data.

Computer Administration of Standardized Tests

Professionals cite a number of reasons for wanting computer implementations of assessment instruments:

1. *Computer administration can save time.* Even a casual reading of the literature reveals that this is the most commonly cited advantage for using the computer to administer tests (e.g., Halpern, 1986; Madsen, 1986; Moe & Johnson, 1988; Olsen, Maynes, Slawson, & Ho, 1989; Ronau & Battista, 1988; Sampson, 1986; Schuerholz, 1984-1985; Sternberg, 1986; Turner, 1987; Walker & Myrick, 1985; Wise & Plake, 1989).

2. *Assessment personnel will be freed from routine data gathering* and will, consequently, be able to devote more time to more professional services with clients (Sampson, 1986).

3. *Test takers will gain a greater sense of control*, leading to more active, and less passive participation in the educational or counseling activity (Eberly & Cech, 1986).

4. *Precisely standardized administration procedures* will be guaranteed. Computers, can, for example, administer items at precisely timed intervals. Then, too, computers are patient and nonjudgmental. These factors could eliminate problems due to examiner bias (Eberly & Cech, 1986; Eller, Kaufman, & McLean, 1986; Schuerholz, 1984-1985).

5. *Access to testing* will be provided to handicapped individuals whose condition precludes traditional test formats (Becker & Schur, 1986; Schuerholz, 1984-1985).

6. *Most examinees have a good attitude* toward computerized testing and will be motivated to try their hardest (Ronau & Battista, 1988; Schuerholz, 1984-1985; Watkins & Kush, 1988).

7. *Computers will permit the development of new kinds of tests* (Turner, 1987; Wise & Plake, 1989). Such tests include those that will gather nontraditional data (such as response latency) as well as those employing animation or other nontraditional presentation or response modes.

Currently, there are two general types of computerized testing in use: (a) *computer-based (CB) tests*, and *computerized-adaptive (CA) tests*. Wise and Plake (1989) provide an excellent analysis of research findings related to each type. Computer-based testing refers to the use of the computer to administer a conventional test, which has often merely been transferred from paper and pencil to computer screen. Computerized-adaptive testing, on the other hand, refers to tests in which choice of the next item to be administered is made by reference to the examinee's performance on earlier items. Most computerized testing is presently available only in CB format (Turner, 1987).

It may appear that there would be few, if any problems involved in converting objective format tests from paper and pencil to computerized administration mode. Indeed, the actual *programming* to accomplish this conversion is relatively simple. However, there are many problems, including the following:

1. *There is accumulating evidence that the computer version of a test cannot be assumed to be equivalent to the original, paper-and-pencil version*. Indeed, Watkins and Kush (1988) suggest that "Translating conventional tests to a computer format simply duplicates the weaknesses of conventional testing methods while confounding them with new sources of error (e.g., keyboard unfamiliarity)" (p. 87). This is unfortunate indeed,

because lack of equivalence means that the computer version of the test *must be restandardized and renormed,* a costly and time-consuming process. Moe and Johnson (1988) administered both a paper-and-pencil and the computer version of a standardized aptitude test to 315 students in grades 8 to 12, then surveyed them about their experiences. Although the students were positive about the computer experience, more than half reported experiencing problems during the computerized testing. Sixty-three percent said their eyes got tired during the test, 39% indicated that the screen was too bright, and 27.6 % said there was glare on the screen. Furthermore, in the computer testing, girls were more likely to report nervousness than were boys, and girls reported having a wider variety of problems than did boys, even though there was no difference by gender in the amount of previous computer experience.

2. *Many kinds of tests do not lend themselves to computer implementation,* due to the nature of required communication with the examinee, or the crude state of the art of the technology (Schuerholz, 1984-1985). Many reading tests require the subject to read a passage orally and then respond to oral questions. Speech synthesis problems such as lack of sophistication and standardization also mitigate against immediate implementation.

3. *Many computerized testing programs do not permit the examinee to review previous questions and answers, will not allow the skipping of items, and do not permit returning to earlier items to change answers* (Ronau & Battista, 1988). Although research results are somewhat contradictory, there is evidence that scores on tests that do not permit skipping as well as review and revision of previous answers will be lower than scores on otherwise equivalent paper-and-pencil versions that do so permit (Wise & Plake, 1989).

4. *There is evidence that computerized tests are completed faster* than paper-and-pencil versions (Wise & Plake, 1989). Therefore, the computerized versions of timed tests will require different, probably shorter, time limits than does the traditional format.

5. *Standardization of administration can be compromised by lack of standardization of computers and peripherals* (Madsen, 1986). There is great variance in screen size, color, and resolution; keyboards; display fonts; furniture; and room lighting. Effects of such variables are unknown and are probably test-specific. Therefore, resolution of this problem will require separate norming and standardization of computer implementations. Sarvela and Noonan (1988) discuss these and a number of psychometric problems in computer assessment.

6. *Some computer tests employ flawed programs or poor error trapping procedures that result in program "crashes" during testing* (Walker & Myrick, 1985). Consumers should carefully check the software to be sure that the programming is accurate (correct order of items, proper spelling, accurate calculation of raw scores, etc.) and that it avoids other such problems.

7. *Computerized testing will require extensive equipment maintenance and staff training* (Jacob & Brantley, 1987; Madsen, 1986; Meier & Geiger, 1986)

8. *Computerized testing could dehumanize the assessment process* (Eller et al., 1986; Madsen, 1986; Sampson, 1986). One danger is that professionals will begin to rely excessively on computerized testing and approach the assessment process in a mechanical fashion. Subjects should be observed while using the computer, and professionals must be sensitive to subjects' general emotional state as well as attitudes toward computers. As Eberly and Cech (1986) point out, the computer should not be used to avoid subjective evaluation by the assessment professional.

We have no problem with the use of computers to administer tests, so long as the professionals are aware of the problems listed above and make every effort to deal with them. Given these problems, however, it should be remembered that most of the advantages we have listed are conjectural and have not been empirically established (Eberly & Cech, 1986). Given the experimental nature of this computer application, we advise great caution in its implementation.

Scoring of Test Items

Computerized scoring of "objective" items has been used successfully for years. We see little problem with the continuation of this practice. We can envision future problems in this area, however, as complicated scanning devices become more sophisticated. Such devices may eventually be employed to score short answer or even essay formats. We have summed up our objections as follows:

> Our objection to computerized scoring, however, is *when it usurps expert judgment in determining correctness of responses.* Most test manuals give considerable leeway to experienced examiners in judging correctness. Also, human examiners become expert at sensing when a child is too tired or inattentive to continue, or

when to probe a response. (Maddux, Johnson, & Willis, 1992, p. 68)

Arithmetic Manipulation or Transformation of Scores

Of all the possible uses for computers in assessment, this is the one we believe is most appropriate. Procedures such as calculating a subject's chronological age; summing the number of correct items; calculating z scores or other standard scores; transferring raw scores to grade equivalent or age equivalent scores through use of extensive tables; and plotting scores on a graph are tedious, boring, time-consuming, and error-prone tasks for humans. Computers, on the other hand, are ideally suited to performing such complicated, mechanical, rote activities.

Our only concern about this computer implementation is related to *accuracy of the program controlling these manipulations*. We have seen a number of such programs that contain errors that would lead users to erroneous conclusions about performance. This is compounded by the fact that many assessment professionals have a tendency to blindly accept as accurate results obtained from a computer program. Therefore, we recommend that purchasers validate software accuracy by comparing computer results to hand calculations known to be accurate (Maddux et al., 1992).

Interpretation of Test Results

This is one of the fastest growing applications of computers in the assessment process. In 1984, Krug located over 190 computer programs intended for test interpretation, and many more are available today. Kramer (1988) suggests that there are, for example, more than a dozen commercial programs for interpreting the WISC-R alone.

Of all computer applications in assessment, we find interpretation to be the most questionable. Interpretation of test results calls for a form of subjectivity often called *clinical judgment* or *professional expertise*. One reason that computers cannot be invested with good clinical judgment is that development of this skill in *people* is a mysterious, little-understood process. It seems to emerge from a synthesis of wide and varied experience, intelligence, common sense, factual knowledge, intuition, and a mixture of human affective qualities such as compassion, empathy, and wisdom. Computers are ill-suited to make diagnostic and other decisions about human beings because they lack both human intelligence and the human affective qualities. Furthermore, computers cannot be invested with human intelligence nor these affective qualities, because human experiences are required in their formation. Weizenbaum (1976) refers to the dilemma faced by those who would invest computers with intelligence:

> I have argued that the individual human being, like any other organism, is defined by the problems he confronts. The human is unique by virtue of the fact that he must necessarily confront problems that arise from his unique biological and emotional needs. . . . No other organism, and certainly no computer, can be made to confront genuine human problems in human terms. And, since the domain of human intelligence is, except for a small set of formal problems, determined by man's humanity, every other intelligence, however great, must necessarily be alien to the human domain. (p. 223)

The formal problems to which Weizenbaum refers are the rare ones that *do* yield to computer solutions, and are referred to by Dreyfus and Dreyfus (1988) as *structured problems*. Structured problems are those for which there are sequential, step-by-step, convergent solutions. These solutions yield to IF-THEN strategies, a paradigm developed for computers. Examples include warehouse inventory control, mathematical processes, delivery truck routing, optimal weight distribution of objects in cargo holds of airplanes, and other such problems. Dreyfus and Dreyfus (1988) say of structured problems, "Here the goal and what information is relevant are clear, the effects of decisions are known, and verifiable solutions can be reasoned out" (p. 20).

Unfortunately, nearly all important human problems are *unstructured* and do not yield to IF-THEN logic, or straightforward, sequential thinking of any kind. Examples of unstructured problems in everyday life include riding a bicycle, identifying a faint odor, and recognizing a human face. Such problems are characterized by "a potentially unlimited number of possibly relevant facts and features[;] and the ways those elements interrelate and determine other events is unclear" (Dreyfus & Dreyfus, 1988, p. 20). It is precisely such problems that are the stuff of nursing, counseling, and alas, of assessment itself.

Computer programs have been developed that are *attempts* to invest computers with human expertise. Such programs are known as *expert systems* and are part of a larger effort known as *artificial intelligence*. So far, such "intelligence" is artificial indeed, and Dreyfus and Dreyfus (1988) suggest that the effort to apply artificial intelligence to unstructured problems is one of the great commercial failures of this century. Many companies dedicated to developing expert system software have either gone out of business or changed their focus. Dreyfus and Dreyfus (1988) maintain that although there has been limited success in creating expert systems for structured problems, no one has even come close to writing a program that can emulate the kind of complex human expertise necessary for the solution of the vast majority of important (and unstructured) human problems.

Yet this is precisely what would be required if the plethora of interpretation programs on the market were to do their jobs as well as a human expert. Kramer (1988) conducted an analysis of interpretation programs and concluded that:

> They often make general statements about the client that would apply to almost every human being (a phenomenon referred to as the "Barnum effect"); and they often suggest specific remedial strategies that go far beyond published data on the efficacy of the original test. (p. 147)

Perhaps because of the above shortcomings, Jacob and Brantley (1987), in their survey of 268 school psychologists, found that 33% reported problems with such programs and 57% anticipated future problems.

Not only do commercial programs exist to interpret individual tests, but there are a rapidly growing number of programs designed to accept test scores and other data about a student, and to then produce the student's legally mandated *individual education program (IEP)*. The IEP contains a diagnosis as to whether the student qualifies for special education or the handicapping condition he or she is suffering from, and even determines long- and short-term instructional goals!

The requirement for an IEP to be written for every special education student is one of the great educational experiments of our time. The intent of the law that requires it (Public Law 94-142) was that the IEP be written by an interdisciplinary team of experts during a problem-solving meeting including the child's parents and, when appropriate, the child him- or herself.

The potential for abuse through the use of expert systems for the writing of IEPs can be seen in the following endorsement of computer IEP programs by Guilbeau (1984): "In the old days—a couple of years ago—it took educators . . . as much as an hour to develop and prepare IEP's . . . . Today, IEP development . . . requires only five to 15 minutes for each student" (p. 43).

Is there any doubt at all that an IEP program used in this fashion violates the letter and spirit of the law, which calls for the careful consideration of evidence, professional debate among experts, consultation with parents, and the reaching of eventual consensus concerning the best course of action?

The suggestion that IEPs be written in 5 to 15 minutes per student calls to mind a similar proposal concerning psychotherapy and Joseph Weizenbaum's (1976) ELIZA program. ELIZA was a simple program designed to demonstrate that a computer could be made to respond to natural language comments entered by a user. There was no pretense made that ELIZA actually *comprehended* what was entered by the user, or that its responses were anything but mindlessly rote in nature. About ELIZA, Weizenbaum wrote:

> ELIZA was a program consisting mainly of general methods for analyzing sentences and sentence fragments, locating so-called key words in texts, assembling sentences from fragments, and so on. It had, in other words, no built-in contextual framework or universe of discourse. This was supplied to it by a "script." In a sense ELIZA was an actress who commanded a set of techniques but who had nothing of her own to say. . . . The first extensive script I prepared for ELIZA was one that enabled it to parody the responses of a nondirective psychotherapist in an initial psychiatric interview. I chose this script because it enabled me to temporarily sidestep the problem of giving the program a data base of real-world knowledge. (pp. 188-189)

Weizenbaum was shocked and horrified to learn that a psychoanalyst who learned of his work actually made the suggestion that ELIZA might be profitably used to automate psychiatry, and that such programs would soon be able to handle several hundred patients per hour! Of this suggestion, he wrote:

> What must a psychiatrist who makes such a suggestion think he is doing while treating a patient, that he can view the simplest

mechanical parody of a single interviewing technique as having captured anything of the essence of a human encounter? (p. 6)

The same might be asked of Mr. Guilbeau, concerning his 5-minute IEP meetings.

The psychotherapy suggestion referred to above should not be viewed as an antiquated remnant of an unenlightened past. As recently as 1986, Eberly and Cech suggested that computerized counseling programs could be helpful, and that "Interpersonal interaction as such may not be necessary for positive personal changes" (p. 19). In light of such suggestions, the above question by Weizenbaum seems as relevant now as it did in 1976.

We find the use of most interpretation programs to be inappropriate at this time. They encourage the use of assessment instruments by personnel who are not fully competent in their use, and they apply a simplistic paradigm (IF-THEN) to the solution of complex human assessment problems. Weizenbaum came to a similar conclusion about the application of computers to any unstructured human problem:

What emerges as the most elementary insight is that, since we do not now have any ways of making computers wise, we ought not now to give computers tasks that demand wisdom. (p. 227)

We recommend caution in the use of interpretation programs. We believe their disadvantages generally outweigh their advantages, and we believe they have great potential for computer abuse. When computer interpretation programs such as those used with the Minnesota Multiphasic Personality Inventory (MMPI) are used, the resulting computer interpretation is probably no worse than other "cook book" approaches to interpreting such tests. The question is, Should any cook book approaches be used?

Production of Test or Assessment Reports

We see few problems with computer assistance in the production of reports, so long as such reports do not usurp professional judgment by involving computer *interpretation*. Word processors, for example, can be used as valuable and appropriate aids to the production of reports. Word-processing templates (blank forms stored on diskette) can be produced using school district or other human service agency forms. Users then fill in the blanks on their computers and print as many copies as needed.

Storage of Test Scores or Other Assessment Data

Our concern with computer storage of assessment information is related to problems of ensuring *privacy* and *confidentiality*. With respect to these issues, the principal rule should be that the assessment professional is responsible for ensuring that the individual has the right to approve or disapprove the gathering of information, and the right to control who is allowed access to that data (Meier & Geiger, 1986). Johnson (1979) provides us with a chilling, Orwellian suggestion that serves as an illustration of the potential for abuse in this regard by suggesting that physiological monitoring equipment be teamed with automated testing to check the truthfulness of a testee's responses!

Jacob and Brantley (1987) have also expressed concern about these issues. These researchers surveyed 268 school psychologists and found that 3% indicated they had experienced problems of unauthorized access to records, and 6% suggested that schools they were associated with had failed to notify parents of the existence of computerized pupil records. More telling, perhaps, 35% and 40% indicated they *expected future problems* in these two areas, respectively. Other, related problems were "Failure to maintain adequate back-up copies of computer records to assure that pupil information is not lost in the event of equipment problems" and "Use of computerized records for employee accountability studies without the knowledge and consent of personnel involved" (p. 73).

The above problems are indicative of unaddressed philosophical issues, especially those related to ethics. There are other, more practical concerns, however. We do not recommend that assessment data or other personal data be placed on hard disk drives or file servers. Hard disk drives are usually accessible to anyone who uses the computer, and file servers are often accessible to all members of the computer network. Although security systems are available for use with these devices, they are often cumbersome, and none is foolproof. Such data should be saved on floppy diskettes, the diskettes should be duplicated, and both copies kept under lock and key. Of course, a record should be kept of all those allowed access to this data. If data *are* kept on hard disk drives or file servers, code numbers should be substituted for names, the key to the code numbers should be kept secure in a separate location, and at least one floppy disk or hard copy should be made.

Another problem is created by public attitudes about data displayed on computer monitors. Many people seem to view such data as public information. Although such individuals would probably never pick up and read the contents of a file folder located on another professional's desk, they may have no qualms about reading data displayed on another's computer screen. It is hoped that this attitude will change as computers become more common and we begin to extend the courtesy of privacy to computer displays. Until then, computer users should develop the habit of switching off their computer monitors when colleagues or others approach, or when the computer will be left unattended. Turning off the monitor will have no effect on any programs that are running, and the monitor can be switched back on and work resumed at any time.

CONCLUSIONS

Although computers hold considerable promise for enhancing the assessment process, they also contain the potential for abuse. In this chapter, we have presented our position that computers are appropriately used to perform rote tasks and data storage, and that they are inappropriately used when they usurp expert judgment. We have attempted to make this point with reference to assessment. Dreyfus and Dreyfus (1988) do a good job of summing up this position with respect to the business world: "It turns out, then, that at every level of business from the factory floor to the board room, wherever skills are involved, formal models fail to capture human expertise" (p. 189).

What then, is the solution? Should we rebel mindlessly against computers in general? There are modern-day Luddites, both inside and outside the human services professions, who are engaging in such a rebellion. The *Whole Earth Review* recently published a "computer as poison" special issue (Dreyfus & Dreyfus, 1988). In the early 1980s, I thought I could detect the beginning of a backlash against educational computing, and I began a file for copies of anti–educational computing articles. I have three of these files now, each more than 1" thick, and it will soon be time to begin file number four.

Such reactionism will not succeed. The computer is here to stay. Indeed, it is destined to proliferate enormously. It is such a powerful tool that pressure for implementation has become an irresistible force. Those who wish to abolish the computer will fail. The question is not whether to involve computers in assessment, but how to do so intelligently. As we work toward that end, we would do well to heed these remarks by Dreyfus and Dreyfus (1988):

What we do now will determine what sort of society and what sort of human beings we are to become. We can make such a decision wisely only if we have some understanding of what sort of human beings we already are. If we think of ourselves only as repositories of factual knowledge and of information processing procedures, then we understand ourselves as someday to be surpassed by bigger and faster machines running bigger and more sophisticated programs. . . . But fortunately, there are other possibilities. We can use computers to track the vast array of facts and law-governed relationships of our modern technological world, yet continue to nurture the human expertise that inference engines cannot share by encouraging learners to pass from rule following to experience-based intuition. If we do so, our experts will be empowered by their computer aids to make better use of their wisdom in grappling with the still unresolved problems of technological society. The chips are down, the choice is being made right now. (pp. 205-206)

A FUTURISTIC EXAMPLE OF BEST PRACTICES IN COMPUTER-ASSISTED ASSESSMENT

George Smith, a computer-using school psychologist, has just received a referral on Sue Jones, a 4th-grade student. George has met with two of Sue's teachers, talked to Sue's parents, and observed Sue in the classroom. Sue was referred because both her parents and teachers are concerned that she is not keeping up in her school work. Sue seems bright enough, but is not completing assignments and is scoring poorly on tests. Because there is mixed opinion among parents and teachers as to the cause and remedy of Sue's problem, George has decided to conduct a thorough assessment, including a battery of tests that he believes will provide important information.

In cases like this, George usually administers three standardized tests: an extensive norm-referenced achievement test, a criterion-referenced achievement test, and a general intelligence test. The information he gathers from these three tests along with other information he has gleaned is then analyzed and condensed into a report that forms the basis for the Individual Education Plan.

The first test administered is a criterion-referenced achievement test. The administration of this test can be very cumbersome because it requires the test administrator to weave through a massive amount of test items and keep track of a large number of facts in order to focus in on those portions of the test that are best suited to the level of the subject. George uses his computer to make this a much smoother and more efficient experience. Although the actual test items are administered in the traditional manner, George uses his computer to keep track of Sue's performance and to help him focus on those sections of the test that will provide the most fruitful information. This allows George more freedom to observe and make notes about such things as Sue's problem-solving strategies.

The second test is a computer-administered intelligence test. This test has been normed for computer administration, and George is familiar enough with the test that he has confidence in the results it yields. He feels the reliability of the test is enhanced by the increased objectivity of the computer administration. While Sue is taking the test, George is able to observe carefully and take notes about how she interacts with the test items. The computer scores as well as administers this test.

The final test is a norm-referenced achievement test. This test is administered one-on-one with George again making careful notes while scoring the test. The computer only comes into play on this test after the testing session is completed. When all of the clerical work is done by hand, this test can take up to 2 hours to convert raw scores into various derived scores and to arrange all of the derived scores into a meaningful profile. Armed with a scoring program in which he has complete confidence, George is able to manipulate the scores quickly and accurately. The computer program will then print out various types of profiles and score comparisons depending on the options George chooses.

The most difficult part of George's job is to pull all the information he has collected together in an organized manner that will begin to form a picture of why Sue is falling behind in her school work. George uses the computer in two ways at this point in his work. First, he enters into a data base pertinent information that he has gathered through interviews, observations, and testing. The data base is designed to assist in organizing the information so it can be efficiently analyzed and woven into a final report. Next George uses a special expert system program that helps him consider a wide variety of options in making sense of the information he has gathered. George harbors no illusions that the computer can make decisions about Sue or arrive at useful conclusions about the cause and treatment of her problem. What his expert system program can do is expand the range of options to be considered beyond what he might consider on his own. The program does this by comparing a summary of the information gathered on Sue with similar cases and allows George to review what other school psychologists have concluded and recommended. George realizes that this information is only suggestive in nature and cannot supplant his own clinical expertise. He does find, however, that sometimes his attention is focused on aspects of the case that he would not have thought of and that need to be explored as options. This program allows George to do something that is akin to consulting with his colleagues and discussing Sue's case—a luxury that is not otherwise possible.

Once George has gathered information, organized it, and analyzed it, he is ready to put it all together in a well-organized, useful report that will form the basis for an IEP that will be prepared by an IEP committee. At this stage, the computer becomes an essential tool for George. Using a format template with his word processor, he can select items of information he has stored in the data base for inclusion in the report. He can add, delete, and modify the contents of the report until he is thoroughly satisfied that it is the best summarization he can provide. A final polish can be placed on the report by running it through a word processor and a grammar checker. George has learned to use his computer as a clerical aid and has found that the quality of his reports is superior to those he submitted before the computer was available.

Finally, George saves his report in a data base of cases. This data base serves as both a storage facility and a diagnostic aid for George. Besides being able to store many cases in a very small space, he can retrieve designated cases quickly and efficiently. Beyond these obvious advantages, however, George can use the data base in a more powerful way. Because the information is organized into records and categories, a wide variety of searches and sorts can be performed on the entire data base. George can, for example, call up all children he has tested who have an intelligence test pattern similar to Sue's or he can review all the cases where the child has been diagnosed as learning disabled.

In this futuristic example, we have spoken in generalities and have not used specific test or computer program names. This was done by design. Our intent in this example is to illustrate the ideal uses of a computer in assessment. As is clearly indicated in the chapter, we do not believe that tests, computer software, and assessment strategies are advanced to the point that the example we have provided is totally possible. Our example, however, is based on what we think constitutes the wise use of the computer in assessment that, if not possible now, will certainly be so in the near future.

REFERENCES

American Psychological Association Committee on Professional Standards and Committee on Psychological Tests and Assessment. (1986). *Guidelines for computer-based tests and interpretations.* Washington, DC: Author.

Becker, H., & Schur, S. (1986). Advantages of using microcomputer-based assessment with moderately and severely handicapped individuals. *Journal of Special Education Technology, 8*(2), 53-57.

Boocock, S. S. (1980). *Sociology of education: An introduction* (2nd ed.). Boston: Houghton Mifflin.

Burke, R. L. (1982). *CAI sourcebook.* Englewood Cliffs, NJ: Prentice-Hall.

Criswell, E. L. (1989). *The design of computer-based instruction.* New York: Macmillan.

Dreyfus, H. L., & Dreyfus, S. E. (1988). *Mind over machine: The power of human intuition and expertise in the era of the computer.* New York: The Free Press.

Eberly, C. G., & Cech, E. J. (1986, April). Integrating computer-assisted testing and assessment into the counseling process. *Measurement and Evaluation in Counseling and Development, 1*, 18-28.

Eller, B. F., Kaufman, A. S., & McLean, J. E. (1986). Computer-based assessment of cognitive abilities: Current status/future directions. *Journal of Educational Technology Systems, 15*(2), 137-147.

Gayeski, D. (1989). Why information technologies fail. *Educational Technology, 22*(9), 9-17.

Green, B. F. (1988). Critical problems in computer-based psychological measurement. *Applied Measurement in Education, 1*(3), 223-231.

Guilbeau, J. J. (1984). Micros for the special ed administrator: PROFILE: A Louisiana district's network of special educators. *Electronic Learning, 3*(5), 43.

Halpern, M. (1986, Winter). Evolving trends in testing. *Education Libraries, 11*, 12-15.

Jacob, S., & Brantley, J. C. (1987). Ethical-legal problems with computer use and suggestions for best practices: A national survey. *School Psychology Review, 16*(1), 69-77.

Johnson, J. (1979). Technology. In T. Williams & J. Johnson (Eds.), *Mental health in the 21st century* (pp. 7-9). Lexington, MA: D.C. Heath.

Kneller, G. F. (1965). *Educational anthropology: An introduction.* New York: John Wiley and Sons.

Kramer, J. J. (1988). Computer-based test interpretation in psychoeducational assessment: An initial appraisal. *Journal of School Psychology, 26*, 143-153.

Krug, S. E. (1984). *Psychware.* Kansas City, MO: Test Corporation of America.

Maddux, C. D. (1984). Breaking the Everest Syndrome in educational computing: An interview with Gregory Jackson and Judah L. Schwartz. *Computers in the Schools, 1*(2), 37-48.

Maddux, C. D., Johnson, L., & Willis, J. (1992). *Educational computing: Learning with tomorrow's technologies.* Boston: Allyn and Bacon.

Madsen, D. H. (1986, April). Computer-assisted testing and assessment in counseling: Computer applications for test administration and scoring. *Measurement and Evaluation in Counseling and Development, 1*, 6-14.

Meier, S. T., & Geiger, S. M. (1986, April). Implications of computer-assisted testing and assessment for professional practice and training. *Measurement and Evaluation in Counseling and Development, 2*, 29-37.

Moe, K. C., & Johnson, M. F. (1988). Participants' reactions to computerized testing. *Journal of Educational Computing Research, 4*(1), 79-86.

Olsen, J. B., Maynes, D. D., Slawson, D., & Ho, K. (1989). Comparisons of paper-administered, computer-administered and computerized adaptive achievement tests. *Journal of Educational Computing Research, 5*(3), 311-326.

Osguthorpe, R. T., & Zhou, L. (1989). Instructional science: What is it and where did it come from? *Educational Technology, 29*(6), 7-17.

Papert, S. (1980). *Mindstorms: Children, computers, and powerful ideas.* New York: Basic Books.

Pressey, S. L. (1926). A simple apparatus which gives tests and scores—and teaches. *School and Society, 23*, 373-376.

Pressey, S. L. (1927). A machine for automatic teaching of drill material. *School and Society, 25*, 549-552.

Ronau, R. N., & Battista, M. T. (1988, Spring). Microcomputer versus paper-and-pencil testing of student errors in ratio and proportion. *Journal of Computers in Mathematics and Science Testing, 7*, 33-38.

Sampson, J. P. (1986). Computer technology and counseling psychology: Regression toward the machine? *The Counseling Psychologist, 14*(4), 567-583.

Sarvela, P. D., & Noonan, J. V. (1988). Testing and computer-based instruction: Psychometric considerations. *Educational Technology, 28*(5), 17-20.

Schuerholz, L. J. (1984-1985). The use of technology and media in the assessment of exceptional children. *Diagnostique, 10*, 197-208.

Skinner, B. F. (1954). The science of learning and the art of teaching. *Harvard Educational Review, 24*, 86-97.

Skinner, B. F. (1958). Teaching machines. *Science, 128*, 969-977.

Skinner, B. F. (1986). Programmed instruction revisited. *Phi Delta Kappan, 68*(2), 103-110.

Sternberg, R. J. (1986, Fall). The future of intelligence testing. *Educational Measurement: Issues and Practice*, 19-22.

Travers, R. M. (1967). *Essentials of learning* (2nd ed.). New York: Macmillan.

Turner, G. A. (1987). Computers in testing and assessment: Contemporary issues. *International Journal of Instructional Media, 14*(3), 187-197.

Walker, N. W., & Myrick, C. C. (1985). Ethical considerations in the use of computers in psychological testing and assessment. *Journal of School Psychology, 23*, 51-57.

Watkins, M. W., & Kush, J. C. (1988). Assessment of academic skills of learning disabled students with classroom microcomputers. *School Psychology Review, 17*(1), 81-88.

Weizenbaum, J. (1976). *Computer power and human reason.* New York: W. H. Freeman.

Wise, S. L., & Plake, B. S. (1989, Fall). Research on the effects of administering tests via computers. *Educational Measurement: Issues and Practice, 8,* 5-10.

7 NEUROPSYCHOLOGICAL ASSESSMENT

Lawrence E. Melamed

INTRODUCTION

A Unique History

Neuropsychological assessment is perhaps unique as an assessment area in psychology. Its deepest roots are not in psychometric or psychological theory, but rather in 19th-century behavioral neurology. When Broca or Jackson or Lichtheim, to name a few of the "immortals," argued about the nature of the cognitive deficit experienced by a particular patient, their arguments were ordinarily buttressed by acute clinical observations denoting the circumstances under which the deficit occurred. Often these clinically derived observations of behavior led to models of cognitive processes that are remarkably similar to those found in current work in cognitive psychology or, more accurately, cognitive neuropsychology. It is certainly impressive that in the 19th century, Lichtheim (1885) was postulating a speech system that included a motor speech center, an auditory speech center, and a concept center. With lesions specific to centers or the connecting pathways, the common clinical syndromes of aphasia could be explained (e.g., disconnection of the auditory speech center and concept center would lead to transcortical sensory aphasia in which repetition is preserved but comprehension of such speech is poor).

It might be expected that in the century or so since the seminal work on aphasic syndromes appeared, psychometric roots might now be evident in neuropsychological assessment. Although a few very recent instruments (e.g., the Wechsler Memory Scale - Revised; Wechsler, 1987) demonstrate a major concern with psychometric properties, most instruments in use have been developed without an apparent primary interest in these matters. As Reynolds (1989) points out, "Problems of statistical methods and design in test development in clinical neuropsychology have been noted with increasing frequency. . . . It is a monument to the clinical acumen and tenacity of clinical neuropsychologists, and perhaps also the insensitivity of many medical practitioners to behavioral changes, that the field has survived and in fact prospered over the last 50 years" (p. 148).

Aside from tests appropriated from other domains (e.g., the WAIS-R), most neuropsychological assessment instruments still appear to have their source in clinical acumen (e.g., Benton Revised Visual Retention Test; Benton, 1974) or in conceptualizations of functional neuroanatomy that have evolved over the past several decades, such as from the contributions of Luria (1980), Goldstein (1944), and Halstead (1947). The value of these instruments was, until recently, considered to be in their success at denoting brain damage or in localizing sites of injury rather than in conceptualizing functional consequences as in the early work in behavioral neurology. There has been a resurgence of interest in the latter issue in the past decade or so in clinical neuropsychology, as remediation and rehabilitation planning have become core elements of the assessment task. Recently, there has been some movement in incorporating constructs from experimental psychology and cognitive science into neuropsychological test design in a more fundamental way than had been done previously. Important examples of such instruments are the California Verbal Learning Test (Delis, Kramer, Kaplan, & Ober, 1987) and the Recognition Memory Test (Warrington, 1984).

Distinguishing Characteristics

Probably the most distinguishing feature of neuropsychological testing compared to other psychological assessment is its breadth or thoroughness. Instruments are employed that examine highly integrative cognitive functions such as those found in intelligence tests as well as those that are focused on more limited cognitive operations such as visual, auditory, and tactual perception; linguistic functions; and memory. Additionally, most assessment batteries in neuropsychology have extensive components dealing with attentional processes and motor functions. Specific suggestions on instruments for evaluation in these various areas will be presented later. It is obvious from the breadth of this testing that strategies for integrating assessment data and making inferences about the nature of neuropsychological deficits are of primary concern.

A second distinguishing feature of neuropsychological assessment is its increasingly closer ties to fundamental research in experimental psychology and other life and behavioral sciences. The influence of basic science is extensive. As indicated earlier, models from cognitive science are being used in the design of neuropsychological instruments. There are continuing advances in the development of cognitive rehabilitation procedures that are based on models of normative functioning. These models, in turn, often have their origin in research in cognitive neuropsychology, which involves the study of cognitive functioning in individuals with brain lesions. As McCarthy and Warrington (1990) note, "The functional analysis of patients with selective deficits provides a very clear window through which one can observe the organization and procedures of normal cognition. No account of 'how the brain works' would even approach completeness without this level of analysis" (p. 1).

It can be argued that one of the most important components of one's work in clinical neuropsychology is staying abreast of work in cognitive psychology and cognitive neuropsychology. Not only does this help us understand what our, generally, clinically derived tests measure, but we are often provided with reasonable hypotheses for conceptualizing cognitive deficits and with possible remediation strategies. Notable in this regard would be the work of Posner (1989) on selective attention and Baddeley (1986) on working memory.

A final distinguishing feature of neuropsychological assessment is the "neuro" component. This aspect of the assessment requires that very direct ties to the medical community and its knowledge base exist. It is necessary to develop a working knowledge of a wide range of illnesses and their treatment. Certainly, one must be reasonably informed about current diagnostic procedures such as EEG, CT scan, and MRI. It is axiomatic that familiarity with neuroanatomy is required along with an understanding of the physical effects of various types of brain damage. Probably no neuropsychologist feels terribly secure in his or her medically related information but instead must continually upgrade this information. An additional influence of the "neuro" orientation is the help it provides in conceptualizing the nature of the deficits the individual is experiencing. At times it is much easier to conceptualize deficits (e.g., as left hemispheric or frontal) than it is to place them within a functional framework. Even when working with a nonacquired disorder such as a learning disability, an analysis that takes cognizance of functional neuroanatomy can be very helpful although its speculative nature precludes giving it any more status than that of a working hypothesis. It is the manner in which neuropsychological hypotheses integrate seemingly disparate data that gives them their force.

Applications of Neuropsychological Assessment

Neuropsychological assessment is being employed in an ever-increasing set of circumstances. Traditionally, it has been employed in two major areas, the first being the need to characterize the cognitive consequences of, for example, head injury, stroke, or diseases that affect neural tissue in order to facilitate rehabilitation planning and decisions on employment and living arrangements. This is probably still the fastest growing area of clinical neuropsychology given the growth of rehabilitation medicine and the aging of the population. The second traditional application has been in answering the question of "organicity" posed generally by psychiatrists. This question is presented in a wider variety of situations today. Examples would be (1) discriminating between dementia and pseudodementia or depression, (2) attempting to classify schizophrenia as Type I or Type II where the latter involves negative symptoms such as flattened affect and may be related to structural changes in the brain, or (3) in offering information about the neuropsychological profile of an individual who has known organic deficits coexisting with a major emotional disorder and therefore presents many complicated social service questions.

There are two newer areas of neuropsychological assessment today that show considerable growth. One is in the area of forensic application where neuropsychologists are called upon to offer assistance in myriad ways. Common questions have to do with evaluating the cognitive complaints that clients report after motor vehicle or industrial accidents or in medical malpractice suits. Very complicated issues in criminal cases can arise such as questions about the effect of a brain injury, after the commission of a crime, on the individual's behavior during a trial or probationary evaluation.

The other area in which application of neuropsychological assessment strategies has become more widespread is in the evaluation of learning disabilities. Child neuropsychology has been a particularly active area of research and it includes considerable work on learning disabilities. This research has been primarily focused on two issues. One has been the prediction of academic achievement using neuropsychological variables. Several longitudinal studies have demonstrated the efficacy of early assessment in predicting level of success several years hence (Fletcher & Satz, 1980; Melamed & Rugle, 1989; Rourke & Orr, 1977). This research argues for the application of neuropsychological assessment strategies in the kindergarten screening process. The other issue is that of subtype analysis. This has been an exceedingly active area in which several strategies have been employed to determine if reliable subtypes of children with learning disabilities can be discerned from the assessment data. These strategies have included clinical evaluations of profiles (e.g., Mattis, French, & Rapin, 1975) as well as a wide variety of statistical procedures such as cluster analysis (e.g., Watson, Goldgar, & Ryschon, 1983). Hynd, Connor, and Nieves (1988) present a very thorough review of this literature from 1963–1986. Although this literature does indicate that more than two subtypes of learning disabled children can be reliably discriminated, Hynd et al. point out that the tests used to create these subtypes are generally not useful in furthering an understanding of the nature of the deficits that define the subtypes. This understanding would be very important for remediation. For a highly critical analysis of the application of neuropsychological assessment to learning disabilities, the reader is referred to the at times cogent, at times very overdrawn, comments of Reschly and Gresham (1989).

As evaluating learning disabilities, both in adults and children, is increasingly common in neuropsychological assessment and will be a focus of the assessment examples presented later in this chapter, it seems useful to indicate the situations in which such an assessment would be advisable given the time commitment and expense of these procedures. First of all, a neuropsychological assessment would be warranted in almost all situations in which the child or adult has a history of head injury, even if relatively mild. This would also be true for a history of stroke, seizure disorder, and various systemic and genetic disorders. Additionally, even if the individual's history is negative for the above factors, the presence of an appreciable number of "soft" signs such as very delayed language development and severe motor immaturity would warrant the neuropsychological approach. An additional indication, not often considered, is the failure of academic intervention for reasons that are not evident. This circumstance can be masking an inadequate conceptualization of the disorder. Obvious examples are the continued application of language experience or phonics programs in reading after years of little or no progress by the student. Further, a neuropsychological approach can often alleviate the stress for the child or family that can build up from the reality or perception of being offered only incomplete or poorly focused information about the correlates of the learning disorder.

BRAIN–BEHAVIOR RELATIONSHIPS

Probably nothing is more self-evident in the practice of neuropsychological assessment than the need for familiarity with functional neuroanatomy (i.e., brain–behavior relationships). The starting point in developing this knowledge is getting acquainted with brain anatomy. At a beginning level this means becoming familiar with the major landmarks (i.e., gyri and fissures) of the cerebral cortex and the denoting of the lobes. Figure 7.1 is a simplified lateral view of the left cerebral cortex. Besides denoting the four lobes, the sulci used in defining their boundaries are given. Subsequent study would require becoming familiar with the wide range of landmarks that have become relevant to understanding various disorders (e.g., the angular gyrus in alexia). Of course, study would not be limited to structures evident on the lateral views of the cortex but would require familiarity with those observed from bottom (ventral) or central (medial) views. Additionally, knowing the location and expected size and shape of the fluid-filled cavities of the brain, the ventricles, is important for understanding the effects of many disease processes and injuries on the brain. Becoming familiar with all these elements of neuroanatomy is best met by an investment in a brain atlas such as the photographic one compiled by DeArmond, Fusco, and Dewey (1989). Further, it could even be argued today that becoming familiar with CT scans and MRI studies of the brain should be an aspect of one's preparation for neuropsychological practice. A helpful book for this purpose is that of Bigler, Yeo, and Turkheimer (1989). Once all this neuroanatomical material is familiar, the next step is to connect it to the existing lore on functional significance. Typically, this knowledge base relating function to cortical location uses partitions based on hemisphere and/or lobe. Compendia of this lore can be found in Lezak (1983) and in Kolb and Whishaw (1990).

FIGURE 7.1. *Lobes and Important Landmarks of the Cerebral Cortex*

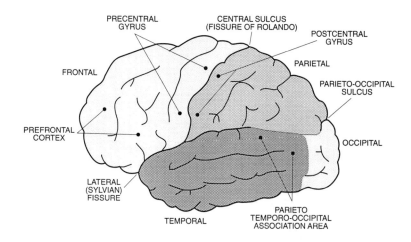

Note. Adapted from *Neuropsychological Assessment* (p. 63) by M. Lezak, 1983, New York: Oxford University Press. Copyright 1983 by Oxford University Press. Used by permission.

Another very important aspect of cortical anatomy is the distribution of the major arteries. Figure 7.2 is a medial view of this distribution. In understanding the cognitive consequences of an ischemic event such as a stroke, one has to consider the area irrigated by the blood vessel whose flow is decreased or interrupted. An excellent discussion of these cerebrovascular disorders can be found in Funkenstein (1988).

Although specifying cortical site by lobe and/or prominent landmark may appear to be rather exacting localization, it is in actuality not fine grained enough for many purposes. In neuroscience in general, and in many neuropsychological applications, anatomical localization within the neocortex is specified by Brodmann numbers, a system established over 80 years ago. In Figure 7.3, these numbers are presented for both a lateral and a medial view of the cortex. In this scheme, neighboring areas with discernibly different cell types are given different numbers. It can be seen that each lobe is divided into many different areas by this method. The frontal lobe is remarkable in its apparent diversity. It is interesting to note that there are sizable areas that overlap traditionally designated lobes, such as area 39 which appears to border on the parietal, occipital, and temporal lobes.

FIGURE 7.2. *A Medial View of the Cortical Arteries*

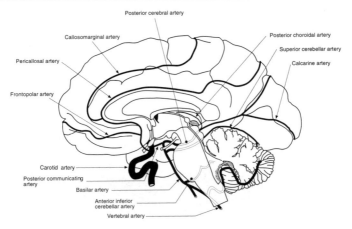

Note. Adapted from *Structure of the Human Brain: A Photographic Atlas* (p. 189) by S. J. DeArmond, M. M. Fusco, and M. M. Dewey, 1989, New York: Oxford University Press. Copyright 1988 by Oxford University Press. Used by permission.

FIGURE 7.3. *Brodmann Cortical Map*

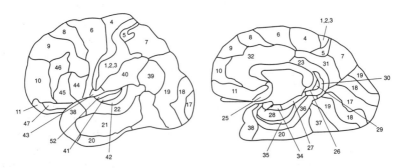

Note. Adapted from *Fundamental Neuroanatomy* (p. 310) by W. J. H. Nauta and M. Feirtag, 1986, New York: W. H. Freeman and Company. Copyright 1986 by W. H. Freeman and Company. Used by permission.

One very prominent approach to understanding the functional significance of this extraordinary diversity of cortical areas is the model proposed by the great Russian pioneer in neuropsychology, Luria (1980). Luria proposes three functional units underlying cortical activity. The first, the *unit for regulating tone and waking and mental states*, involves the arousal level and is dependent upon subcortical and brain stem mechanisms and is therefore not within the focus of our concern here. The second unit, that for *receiving, analyzing, and storing information*, involves the posterior neocortex, beyond the central sulcus. This can be thought of as the sensory cortex and is involved in processing visual, auditory, and somesthetic information. The third functional unit is that located anterior to the central sulcus and is described as the motor unit. More formally, it is the unit *for programming, regulation, and verification of activity*. For Luria, this final unit serves to organize conscious activity. It deals with the development of intentions and the planning and programming of activity and its verification.

In addition to the designation of these functional units, Luria proposed that there is a hierarchical structure that is characteristic of all regions of the cortex. For the posterior or sensory system, *primary* cortex contains cells that are for the most part modality specific and respond to the elementary features of stimulation. Examples, in terms of Brodmann numbers, would be area 17 for vision and area 41 for audition. *Secondary* "zones" receive projections from the primary ones. Luria sees these as less modality specific and more integrative, producing the organization evident in perceptual experiences. For vision, the secondary areas include 18 and 19, whereas areas 22 and 42 are examples for audition. At the pinnacle of the hierarchical structure for the sensory cortex, according to Luria, are the *tertiary* zones. These are areas in which the great majority of neurons are multimodal and process "general" features such as spatial arrangement. Most important, these tertiary regions serve to translate the visual experience into a symbolic one for higher order cognitive functioning. Large areas of the posterior cortex are tertiary in function. These include areas 7, portions of 22, 37, 39, and 40. Many of these areas are at the boundary of the parietal, temporal, and occipital lobes—the P-T-O junction. It should be apparent that Luria's system leads to an understanding of the qualitative differences in deficits that occur when, for example, area 17 is damaged compared to area 37—the difference between the occurrence of a blind spot in the visual field and an inability to recognize faces.

For the anterior or motor cortex, the primary area is Brodmann area 4, a motor command area for fine movements. The secondary is area 6, the premotor area in which motor programs are generated that are executed by the primary cortex. The anterior tertiary zone includes areas 9, 10, and 11 as well as others. This prefrontal cortex is decisive, according to Luria, in the formation of intentions and programs for behavior as well as in the regulation and verification of this behavior.

Luria's formulation of functional neuroanatomy is widely respected and employed but not, as might be expected, without critics. A particularly cogent analysis is presented by Kolb and Whishaw (1990).

ASSESSMENT FUNDAMENTALS

In this section, an introduction to the various strategies for creating a neuropsychological battery and for conducting the assessment will be presented. In particular, Kaplan's (1989) very stimulating suggestions on how an assessment might be conducted to facilitate an evaluation of a patient's compensatory strategies will be covered. Additionally, normative batteries for comprehensive adult and child evaluations will be described along with a discussion of the contents of specialized or briefer batteries that may be employed for assessment of, for example, dementia or learning disability.

Assessment Strategies

In general, there seem to be three denotable approaches to neuropsychological assessment. The first is that termed *fixed* by Kaplan (1989) or *actuarial* by Lezak (1984). In this approach, there is a relatively systematic use of the same set of tests from individual to individual. Interpretation of the test results depends upon there being a body of knowledge relating specific test profiles and "pathognomonic" signs to various organic or functional criteria. There are two widely employed examples of this approach to neuropsychological assessment, the Halstead-Reitan Battery (Reitan & Wolfson, 1985) and the Luria-Nebraska Neuropsychological Battery (Golden, 1981). These are very different instruments, with the former based on experimental investigations into frontal lobe function by Halstead (1947) and the latter on an attempt to make-over a masterfully conducted examination from behavioral neurology (cf. Christensen, 1975) into an instrument with scales denoted (e.g., "memory"), quantitative measurement, and, potentially, specifiable patterns and pathognomonic signs for various diagnostic purposes. Although space limitations do not allow an overview of the Halstead-Reitan instrument, some of the tests are often incorporated into the flexible batteries emphasized in this chapter and will be introduced later. The Luria-Nebraska instrument has been the source of much contention in the neuropsychological assessment literature and is generally given a negative evaluation by those not in the "camp." The problems enumerated concern methodological issues, validity concerns, as well as statistical and psychometric problems (Spiers, 1982; Stambrook, 1983).

Several criticisms of the fixed battery approach have been raised. Probably the major problem has been that the tests employed are often extremely difficult to interpret in terms of the cognitive skills being evaluated. Partly it is an issue of the measure tapping into many functions (i.e., of being overdetermined). Without additional measures exploring more fundamental skills, it is very difficult to understand the message in the test results. Further difficulty of interpretation comes about because of weak construct validity. When measures of language or memory or perception are present, they are often only tenuously related to the level of theoretical development in cognitive science or they only tap into a very limited portion of the component processes that need to be evaluated. Both the Halstead-Reitan and the Luria-Nebraska are very weak in their assessment of memory, perceptual functions, and language processes. The practical difficulty of using instruments with weak construct validity and hard-to-interpret procedures is that test results do not readily lead to the formulation of remediation or rehabilitation strategies. At this point, one might question the value of the fixed battery approach in general. It is necessary to point out that this approach retains considerable usefulness when questions of "organicity" are dominant. The overdetermination of test procedures, or, more positively, their dependence on integration of functions, makes them very sensitive to brain damage. With a broadening of appreciation of neuropsychological evaluation by allied medical professions, however, even this positive aspect may become less meaningful in the future.

Perhaps the polar opposite of the fixed battery approach is what Kaplan (1989) terms the *clinical investigative approach*. This is best exemplified by the work of Luria (1980) in its original form. Luria was very critical of psychometric tests because of the inability to evaluate performance on them clinically (i.e., qualitatively). His attack was to focus on how a problem was solved rather than on determining the number of correct answers. Although a wide range of tests would be employed, from those investigating sensory functions to those focusing on more complex integrative functions, the strategy of assessment was paramount. Luria was most concerned with the "structural dynamics" of a response. Tasks were continuously modified, made harder or different, so as to converge on the most adequate interpretation of the functional deficit and its physiological basis. The limitation of the strong clinical approach represented by Luria's work is in its aversion to quantification and the resulting difficulty in then elaborating procedures so that others can duplicate them. Christensen's (1975) attempt to do this with Luria's work is clearly commendable. A related approach that is becoming very influential is the process orientation of Edith Kaplan (1989). This approach also focuses on the strategies that the patient employs in solving tasks. In using this approach, some common instruments such as the WAIS-R (Kaplan, Fein, Morris, & Delis, 1991) are administered and scored in novel ways, at times with new or extended components. Unlike Luria's approach, qualitative aspects of performance are quantified and norms are produced. Procedures can be standardized so that others can reproduce them. It is likely that these innovations of Kaplan's will become a common aspect of neuropsychological assessment over the next decade. The power of this approach becomes apparent when evaluating patients with cerebral vascular accidents (CVAs), or other localized lesions, for cognitive rehabilitation.

The third strategy in neuropsychological assessment is the individualized approach, which has perhaps been best formulated by Lezak (1984), in which the assessment is ". . . tailored to the patient's problems, limitations, and situations" (pp. 29-30). This procedure uses standardized instruments but considers the individual's social and medical history, mental status, and the purpose of the assessment (e.g., rehabilitation planning, differential diagnosis). Although there may be considerable overlap in the testing battery established for assessing the results of, say, a closed head injury and that established for investigating, for example, an apparent learning disability in an adult, there will be differences in the range and depth of testing in the various areas and also a much greater interest in early medical history in the learning disability case. Lezak (1984) describes the conceptual structure of the individualized approach to be *deficit measurement*. Deficits are considered with reference to both normative information and the patient's history. Thus, an average WAIS-R Similarities score may appear to indicate a deficit for an individual who graduated from a prestigious university. When a pattern of impairment is established from the deficit analysis, the examiner, according to Lezak, uses his or her knowledge of brain function and disease, along with information about the patient's background and present situation, to produce an interpretation that allows for diagnostic inferences, predictions, management, and rehabilitation of the patient.

The strategy favored by the present author is the individualized approach of Lezak (1984). The application of this strategy will be demonstrated in a later section of this chapter. There is a modest difference in emphasis between the strategy presented in this chapter and the manner in which Lezak introduces this approach. The difference is found in the direct acknowledgment of the role of hypothesis testing in the current presentation. This multifaceted role includes "tailoring" and adjusting the final assessment battery as well as interpreting the pattern of deficits. As an example, when establishing a test battery for a person who has experienced a closed head injury as a result of a motor vehicle accident, there are certain expectations that guide the choice of evaluative instruments so that measures of executive functions and attentional processes usually dominate. On the other hand, it may appear likely to the investigator that problem-solving deficits are only modest in this individual; that, for example, compromised language skills or memory deficits are more primary in understanding this individual's functional deficits. These hypotheses would have to be followed up both by using appropriate language and memory test instruments and by adjusting the manner in which executive functions are examined to see if performance improves when memory or language skills are less essential to task performance.

The Problem of Norms

Psychologists are very familiar with tests that have an advanced level of norming, instruments such as the Wechsler tests or achievement batteries such as the Woodcock-Johnson or personality instruments such as the MMPI-2. When getting started in neuropsychological assessment, the generally poor quality of norms comes as a shock. Eventually, one is simply pleased to find norms on a sample of at least modest size that has some characteristics of the people one is assessing. Very few exceptions exist (e.g., the Wechsler Memory Scale – Revised comes to mind). Even there, the sample size at any age range is only 50. Newer instruments do often have norms (e.g., the California Verbal Learning Test or the Boston Naming Test), but samples are small and very little in the way of sophisticated examinations of reliability and measurement error have been conducted. The reasons for this situation are likely complex. One factor is the long history with clinical investigative methods in this field. It should be noted that psychometric procedures have made little inroad into behavioral neurology. Second, it is very expensive and time consuming to norm tests, and most investigators do not have the resources to conduct extensive norming research. Perhaps most important is the fact (or realization) that an investigator is primarily looking for obvious impairment. Lezak (1984) uses a 2 standard deviation from expectancy criterion in defining a significant deficit. In clinical practice, deficits are often so discrepant from expectancy that percentile ranks are far below the first percentile and standard scores are obviously distorted, being 4 or more SDs below the norming sample. Finely graded performance distinctions are less important under such circumstances.

Practitioners in neuropsychology find it necessary to develop files of norms from published articles and books. Two journals often publish norms that have been created in various clinical settings. These are *The Clinical Neuropsychologist* and *Developmental Neuropsychology*. Lezak's (1983) assessment text, an article by Bornstein (1985), and a recent book by Spreen and Strauss (1991) are other good sources.

A COMPREHENSIVE ADULT BATTERY

The purpose of this section is to present the contents of a comprehensive adult neuropsychological test battery assuming that an individualized or flexible battery approach is being employed. Useful instruments for the different assessment areas will also be introduced. The number of tests or procedures employed in any one area would depend upon the purpose of the assessment, the individual circumstances of the client, and the effort required to arrive at an acceptable characterization of the nature of the deficit that the client is experiencing. The purpose of the assessment can often include such items as rehabilitation planning or a vocational evaluation. *Circumstances* refers to the nature of the injury or illness as well as the person's premorbid medical and social history. An individual may have suffered a stroke but, in addition, has a history of long-term alcohol abuse. Diffuse brain damage such as in closed head injuries and certain dementias demand elaborate assessment.

The several areas of investigation in a comprehensive neuropsychological assessment are listed below. References are given for the less familiar instruments. The sequence in which they are presented here is not meaningful, although it is probably customary to begin with the intellectual (cognitive ability) measures because of their breadth and because certain subtests of the Wechsler instruments lend themselves to an elaboration by the process approach (Kaplan, 1989) or some related procedure.

Only a portion of the tests listed in each area here would be given in any assessment, no matter how comprehensive. In practice, most assessments are comprehensive with respect to breadth of areas explored. How elaborate testing will be in any one area, as indicated earlier, will depend upon the degree to which it is necessary to characterize an individual's cognitive profile finely in order to bring closure to the hypothesis testing in which the investigator has been engaged.

Cognitive Ability
>   WAIS-R
>   Raven Progressive Matrices
>   Shipley Institute of Living Scale

Attention/Concentration
>   Knox's Cube Test (Stone & Wright, 1980)
>   Trail Making A,B (Reitan & Wolfson, 1985)
>   Wechsler Memory Scale - Revised—Mental Control Subtest
>   Stroop Test (Trenerry, Crosson, DeBoe, & Leber, 1989)
>   Visual Search and Attention Test
>   (Trenerry, Crosson, DeBoe, & Leber, 1990)
>   Paced Auditory Serial Addition Test (Lezak, 1983)

Language Functions
>   Multilingual Aphasia Examination (Benton & Hamsher, 1983)
>   Boston Naming Test (Kaplan, Goodglass, & Weintraub, 1983)
>   Boston Diagnostic Aphasia Examination
>   Token Test
>   Peabody Picture Vocabulary Test

Visual Perceptual/Visual Motor
>   Rey-Osterreith Complex Figure Test (Lezak, 1983)
>   Hooper Visual Organization Test
>   Facial Recognition (Benton, Hamsher, Varney, & Spreen, 1983)
>   Judgment of Line Orientation (Benton et al., 1983)
>   Visual Form Discrimination (Benton et al., 1983)

Executive Functions
>   Wisconsin Card Sorting Test
>   Category Test (Reitan & Wolfson, 1985)

Porteus Maze Test
WISC-R Mazes

Memory: General Batteries
Wechsler Memory Scale - Revised
Memory Assessment Scales (Williams, 1991)

Memory: Restricted
California Verbal Learning Test (Delis et al., 1987)
Recognition Memory Test
Rey Auditory Verbal Learning Test (Lezak, 1983)
Benton Visual Retention Test
Learning Efficiency Test (LET; Webster, 1981)
Selective Reminding Test (Buschke & Fuld, 1974)

Motor
Grooved Pegboard Test
Finger Oscillation
Lateral Dominance Examination

Academic Skills
Wide Range Achievement Test
Gray Oral Reading Test - Revised

A COMPREHENSIVE CHILDREN'S BATTERY

In creating a neuropsychological battery for children, a number of issues are of relevance. It is very desirable that the instruments used be sensitive to developmental changes in cognitive function. The domain of functions assessed by a neuropsychological instrument should reflect the findings of more basic research on cognitive development. Very few instruments, whether developed originally in neuropsychology or for other purposes, such as in the fields of speech pathology or educational testing, meet this requirement today. Perhaps it is best to think of this requirement as a goal for future test development. A related and more manageable concern is that of the availability of norms. Norms are probably more important in child assessment than in adult work, particularly because the purpose for assessment can be the evaluation of learning disabilities or attentional difficulties, which can vary widely in degree and expression.

Additionally, these are problems for which there is no identified cortical lesion and, therefore, very little likelihood of predictable and extremely severe deficits occurring that have obvious clinical significance.

It is also necessary to consider that the purpose of a neuropsychological assessment with children almost always involves remediation which, in turn, means educational programming. Cognitive rehabilitation (e.g., for unilateral neglect) may also be required and employ procedures that differ little from those used with adults. Because of this need for remediation, coordinated planning with the schools is a must. School personnel such as the school psychologist are likely to be reading the assessment report and it must therefore be seen as relevant by them and as sensitive to their requirements for treating the child. Here, treatment means more than placement recommendations. It also includes suggestions for instruction and social guidance.

Two minor points should be noted. First, the assessment battery will have to have within it widely accepted, quality measures of academically pertinent skills. One cannot simply use the WRAT-R and expect to be able to come up with many educationally relevant recommendations for classroom instruction. Second, in conducting the neuropsychological assessment, a series of relatively brief sessions, especially for younger children, is most appropriate. It is not unusual to have the assessment take place all in one day with a few breaks interspersed, especially in hospital settings. It would seem that much more accurate data could be obtained by having several sessions scheduled during the time of day when the child is best able to perform intellectual tasks. This is especially important for observing executive functions and academic skills.

In presenting the elements of the comprehensive child's battery below, it is assumed that an individualized approach to assessment is being employed. It will be noted that the component areas of the child's battery are basically the same as in the adult battery. Wider choices exist in the child's battery in cognitive ability, language, and visual perceptual assessment. More restricted choices are evident for the attention/concentration and memory areas. Executive function and motor measures are very similar in the two batteries. In the latter areas, and selectively in others, the same test is used as with adults because of the existence of child norms. At times, the child's test is a simplified or reduced version of the adult test (e.g., the Category Test). It will be noted in the listings below that some common educational and psychological tests are suggested. The use of such tests is a common practice in child neuropsychological assessment. Telzrow (1989) argues that this approach allows the clinician to select tasks more appropriate to the functioning level and response limitations of the child. She further notes that the use of common instruments allows for a description of the neuropsychological assets of the child in a way that is understandable to school personnel. It also avoids an emphasis on descriptions of brain impairment, which is certainly appropriate in LD cases and even, perhaps, in those where the child has an acquired disorder but where referral issues primarily concern remediation. Of course, at least passable norms exist for such instruments. For many traditional instruments in child neuropsychology, such as for those derived from the Halstead-Reitan Battery, this is not the case. Two helpful sets of norms for such instruments are those of Knights and Norwood (1980) and of Spreen and Gaddes (1969).

Cognitive Ability
    WISC-R/WAIS-R
    Raven Colored Progressive Matrices
    Raven Standard Matrices

Attention/Concentration
    Knox's Cube Test
    Trails A,B
    Seashore Rhythm Test (Reitan & Wolfson, 1985)
    WISC-R Freedom from Distractibility Quotient
    Continuous Performance Test
    Token Test—response pattern

Language Functions
    TOLD-2P, TOLD-2I, TOAL-2
    TOWL-2
    Fullerton Language Test for Adolescents
    Token Test
    Expressive/Receptive One Word Picture Vocabulary Tests
    Wepman Auditory Series
    Multilingual Aphasia Examination
        (Schum, Sivan, & Benton, 1989)
    McCarthy Scales/Selected Verbal Subtests

Visual Perceptual/Visual Motor
   Bender Gestalt
   Developmental Test of Visual Motor Integration
   Motor-Free Visual Perception Test
   Jordan Left-Right Reversal Test
   Test of Visual-Perceptual Skills
   Bieger Test of Visual Discrimination (Bieger, 1982)
   McCarthy Scales/Selected Perceptual Subtests

Executive Functions
   Category Test
   Wisconsin Card Sorting Test
   Porteus Mazes
   WISC-R Mazes

Memory
   Wechsler Memory Scale - Revised
       (Older Adolescents)
   Wepman Visual Series
   McCarthy Scales/Selected Memory Subtests
   Learning Efficiency Test
   Children's Auditory Verbal Learning Test
   Selective Reminding Test
       (Clodfelter, Dickson, Wilkes, & Johnson, 1987)
   Wide Range Assessment of Memory and Learning

Motor
   Finger Oscillation
   Grooved Pegboard
   Lateral Dominance Examination

Tactual Perceptual
   Elements of Halstead-Reitan Sensory Perceptual Exam

Academic Achievement
   Various standardized instruments including
       diagnostic reading tests.

INTERPRETIVE STRATEGIES

Once the assessment is completed, the data must be evaluated for meaningfulness or interpretability, summarized, and integrated. The result of this process is the formation of a hypothesis or set of hypotheses that are consistent with the assessment findings and the current neuropsychological literature on brain–behavior relationships in general. The emphasis in one's conclusions today is more likely to be on functional interpretations of the assessment data and their significance in rehabilitation planning than on neurologically oriented specifications of the disorder. In this section, two separable tasks are denoted in the summarizing process. The first is the actual analysis of the test results. The second concerns the strategies for synthesizing these findings.

Analyzing Test Results

In analyzing test results, the most common procedure, which cuts across all assessment strategy approaches, is a level of performance or deficit analysis technique. Here, an individual's performance is compared to norms or cutoff scores. When norms are poorly constructed and/or when evaluating child data, this procedure can lead to the observation of more "pathology" than is justified given the variability and unreliability of the comparison data. Further, the discrepancies from expectation based solely on norms do not take into account an individual's unique background. For instance, deficits of less than a standard deviation from the mean on some measure (e..g., a problem-solving task) can be highly informative when it is likely that premorbid functioning was at a superior level (e.g., when the patient is a physicist). In general, the background factors to be considered would be the person's native language, handedness, occupation, and premorbid cognitive ability (Orsini, VanGorp, & Boone, 1988). Related to deficit analysis is the use of pathognomonic signs such as hemispatial neglect or moderate to severe anomia. These "markers" for brain damage are important to note even in the flexible battery approach to assessment where one's interest is less likely to be on confirming or identifying lesions and more on describing cognitive functions. Intervention planning, the primary goal of this approach, often makes such deficits the initial target of rehabilitation efforts.

Two other common procedures employed in summarizing test results are pattern analysis and the evaluation of lateralizing signs. In the latter case, such factors as asymmetrical deficits in motor speed or tactual perception are used to infer a generalized hemispheric "weakness" or locus of deficit. The variables employed are generally not at a pathognomonic level. Pattern analysis has been most widely developed in child neuropsychological assessment for learning disabilities. This "subtype" analysis has generated a very large literature with considerable consistency in findings (Hynd et al., 1988). Practical application with respect to remediation has been limited, but there are some promising starts (Lyon, Moats, & Flynn, 1988). It is not surprising that this type of analysis has evolved in the learning disability area. In this area, the diagnostic focus can only be a pattern of functional strengths and weaknesses. All brain–behavior interpretations are secondary and often problematic. The major handicap in employing subtype analysis is the variability of within-subtype profiles. Hynd et al. (1988) make the further point that the variables used in constructing the profiles frequently show weak correlations at best with academic skill deficits.

Synthesizing/Interpreting Test Information

As has already been noted, the flexible battery approach is recommended here for most assessment purposes. Most typically, one identifies a pattern of "intraindividual variability" in performance (Telzrow, 1989) and a list of pathognomonic signs from analyzing the test results. It is then necessary to attempt to characterize any evident neuropsychological impairment *and* develop recommendations for intervention. How does one integrate assessment data to produce this interpretation or characterization? The process involved requires the use of medical information and knowledge concerning premorbid functioning, education, work history, and cultural-linguistic background. Even information on test-taking behavior is essential to consider as fatigue, impulsive responding, and potential feigning of deficit all have to be considered. The actual synthesizing of the data follows one of two tracks—separately or simultaneously. The first is the investigation of hypotheses derived from knowledge of brain and behavior relationships from clinical research or from that conducted in cognitive neuropsychology. The cognitive deficits are seen as a pattern related to parameters of brain damage. In this way they are "explained." Their severity and mode of expression are still a unique element and require their own elaboration for purposes of remediation.

The second technique for synthesizing neuropsychological assessment data follows what has been termed the "strong inference methods" by Fennell and Bauer (1989) because of its association with the model of inductive inference created by Platt (1964). This approach is especially appropriate and efficient when attempting to characterize the functional deficits of the individual. Basically, one creates a series of related hypotheses to explain the result of an assessment task such as poor copying in a visual-constructional task. These hypotheses have to be such that data from another task will support some hypotheses and disconfirm others (e.g., in examining a child it may be noted that he or she does well on nonmotoric tests of visual perception, thus ruling out a visual-sensory or visual perceptual explanation for the constructional deficits on the drawing test). One continues the process of considering hypotheses until only one, or perhaps more realistically, only a small set remains viable (i.e., not disconfirmed). In the present example, one would need to consider test data on motor skills independent of visual guidance and on frontal lobe–type tasks that examine planning and organizing skills to track down the deficit appearing on the drawing task. A more formal presentation of this approach for perceptual testing is found in Melamed and Melamed (1985).

REMEDIATION AND REHABILITATION

The results of both procedures for integrating data and characterizing a person's neuropsychological profile, as outlined above, would be used in creating a program of cognitive rehabilitation or, in the case of an LD child, academic remediation. Recovery from brain damage is ordinarily described as involving two processes (Rothi & Horner, 1983). The first is a physiological event in which pathways regain function and active inhibition of cortical areas is lessened or terminated. The second process is termed substitution by Rothi and Horner and results from a *reorganization* of the functional system underlying the skill, in Luria's (1980) terms, by adding new subroutines and dropping impaired aspects. One can also include the use of assistive devices in this mode of recovery. Cognitive rehabilitation for acquired brain damage generally focuses on both the use of these assistive devices and the fostering of the development of new functional systems. At times, particularly in the early stages of recovery, an attempt to stimulate certain functions, such as sustained attention, may be attempted. On the other hand, for disorders such as learning disabilities or attentional deficits, which are not approached as "acquired" deficits in most circumstances, the use of assistive devices and compensatory strategies dominates in neuropsychologically based interventions. For instance, Hartlage and Telzrow (1983) suggest both matching treatment to learner aptitudes (following the lead of Cronbach and Snow, 1977) and employing assistive devices. Here, aptitudes are the neuropsychological strengths from the child's assessment profile. A very interesting approach to educational remediation is offered by Hynd (1986), who uses a compensatory strategy that combines the use of the child's strengths with an interpretation of the process of reading based on models developed from research in neurolinguistics and cognitive neuropsychology. Thus a visual-spatial whole word approach to vocabulary building such as the Edmark Reading Program would be recommended for a phonological dyslexic (i.e., a child who can read familiar words well, especially nouns, but has difficulty with phoneme-to-grapheme correspondence rules).

A CASE EXAMPLE: CHILD WITH CVA

This case has all the elements that make an assessment very difficult. The case concerns a 7-year-old boy (W.E.) who suffered a right-hemispheric infarct following cardiac surgery at age 4. A recent CT scan indicated that such structures as the middle frontal gyrus, right lentiform nucleus, and external capsule were involved. The child has left hemiplegia and recurring partial complex seizures, although their severity has decreased. He is considered very hyperactive by his family and physician. The remainder of W.E.'s medical history is unremarkable. As this child's lesion occurred early in life, there is no really useful premorbid school or testing history with which to compare current findings. W.E. was brought for assessment because he was making little progress in his 1st-grade work and the school was considering having him repeat 1st grade. His mother was concerned that W.E. required specialized educational intervention that was tailored to his unique cognitive and behavioral profile and that he would not benefit by simply repeating 1st grade.

The most prominent aspect of W.E.'s behavior during assessment was his constant motion. He demonstrated significant difficulty in both engaging and sustaining his attention. He could be echolalic, repeating words voiced by the examiner and then perseverating on them. It was possible to get valid data by using a reward system for time on task and by gaining W.E.'s attention through the examiner randomly modulating his voice and changing his seating pattern.

A Full Scale WISC-R IQ of 78 was obtained with Verbal and Performance IQs of 75 and 85, respectively. Scatter was from 3 (Information, Block Design) to 10 (Picture Arrangement, Object Assembly). Because this test was given by the school psychologist, no information was available about W.E.'s strategies on some of these tasks. His performance on the Raven's test was somewhat higher (IQ = 80) than might be expected by his score of 3 in Block Design, indicating that the motor requirements of the latter task likely interfered with his performance. W.E.'s academic achievement, using the WRAT-R, was very limited. He knew only his uppercase letters. He was unable to read any word and could not make reasonable guesses. He did not demonstrate any decoding strategies. With respect to arithmetic, he did not consistently respond correctly to the + and - symbols. He could do single-digit addition problems orally, that he could not do in written form, as long as the sum remained below 7.

With respect to visual perceptual skills, W.E. performed very poorly whether or not a motor response was required (comparing DTVMI and Bender drawings with performance on the Motor-Free Test of Visual Perception). He appeared to have great difficulty with visual analysis, finding it very difficult to discriminate individual form features. Using subtests from the McCarthy battery and spatial memory tests such as the one by Wepman demonstrated spatial confusion, poor immediate visual memory, and severe visual-motor deficits. His performance level was typically at about the 5-year level, except for more complex reasoning tasks where he was typically at about a 6-year level of performance. Several strategies for assessing unilateral spatial neglect were used and failed to demonstrate its occurrence.

A wide range of language tests were employed with W.E. given his poor performance on the WISC-R Verbal scale and the fact that there is a rather large research literature on the linguistic consequences of unilateral right-hemisphere lesions in childhood. Most of the instruments employed were standard ones such as the McCarthy Verbal subtests, the TOLD-2P, Token Test, and the EOWPVT and ROWPVT. Additionally, measures of fluency and phonemic discrimination were employed. W.E. showed a pattern of results that was consistent with the research literature: adequate grammatical skills and articulation, reduced confrontational naming, some dysfluency, and occasional stuttering. Overall, receptive language skills were superior to expressive ones. W.E. was marginally better dealing with semantic aspects compared to syntactic features.

The final area of testing concerned tactual perceptual skills and motor behavior. Instruments employed were primarily from the Reitan Battery for Young Children. W.E. could only employ his right hand and was able to demonstrate good fine motor skills on a pegboard task, adequate ballistic speed, good tactual form perception, and normative spatial localization.

In the case of W.E., the major source of hypotheses about his deficits came from knowledge of his illness and the research literature on the cognitive consequences of such lesions. Additionally, testing was very thorough in the perceptual and language areas in order to aid in the development of a strategy for educational intervention at his beginning reading level. Because of W.E.'s attentional deficits, the overall testing was limited in scope with memory evaluation being most affected. In the final report to the school, W.E.'s neuropsychological profile was presented in considerable detail with the deficits indicated above presented very clearly along with somewhat of an explanation of how they are related to his illness. It was argued in this report that W.E. would need an individualized educational plan that is tailored to his complex neuropsychological profile and a classroom environment that can minimize his attentional drift and allow for the involved and adaptable programming that will be required to help him. Instructional recommendations included suggestions for increasing his verbal fluency and clarifying his perception of other children's feelings. With respect to reading, the suggestion was made to use a multisensory approach given the limitations he shows in visual perception and phonemic discrimination. His adequate tactual perceptual skills should benefit him in this approach. Given his severe visual-constructional deficits, it was suggested that he begin on computer work very soon, particularly if writing instruction remains frustrating and offers little success. The strategy suggested for arithmetic was based on a substitution strategy in which he verbalizes arithmetic operations as he performs them.

CONCLUSIONS

Neuropsychological assessment is a field that has deep roots in both the clinical science of behavioral neurology and experimental cognitive science. It is a field that requires an interest in both neuroscience and behavior. In this chapter it has been demonstrated how a continuous process of development has been taking place in clinical neuropsychology in which constructs from these two fields have been combined to produce effective strategies for assessing and interpreting the effects of brain damage or anomalous development on behavior. What is most promising is the accelerated rate at which new assessment instruments have been created that reflect the constructs being developed in the cognitive science area. Perhaps equally important has been the progress in the development of assessment strategies, such as the process approach, and the clarification of the advantages of the use of a flexible assessment battery, as the focus of clinical neuropsychological practice has shifted to intervention. It is in this last area where progress has not been altogether satisfactory. Progress in the development of cognitive rehabilitation strategies and research on their effectiveness has not kept pace with advances in assessment. Given the close association between assessment and treatment that is desired today, this relative neglect of rehabilitation is likely to lessen in the near future.

REFERENCES

Baddeley, A. D. (1986). *Working memory*. Oxford: Clarendon Press.

Benton, A. L. (1974). *The Revised Visual Retention Test*. New York: The Psychological Corporation.

Benton, A. L. & Hamsher, K. deS. (1983). *Multilingual Aphasia Examination*. Iowa City: AJA Associates.

Benton, A. L., Hamsher, K. deS., Varney, N. R., & Spreen, O. (1983). *Contributions to neuropsychological assessment: A clinical manual*. New York: Oxford.

Bieger, E. (1982). *Bieger Test of Visual Discrimination*. Chicago: Stoelting.

Bigler, E. D. (1990). Neuropathology of traumatic brain injury. In E. D. Bigler (Ed.), *Traumatic brain injury* (pp. 13-49). Austin, TX: Pro-Ed.

Bigler, E. D., Yeo, R. A., & Turkheimer, E. (1989). *Neuropsychological function and brain imaging*. New York: Plenum Press.

Bornstein, R. A. (1985). Normative data on selected neuropsychological measures from a nonclinical sample. *Journal of Clinical Psychology, 41,* 651-659.

Buschke, H., & Fuld, P. A. (1974). Evaluating storage, retention, and retrieval in disordered memory and learning. *Neurology, 24,* 1019-1025.

Christensen, A. (1975). *Luria's neuropsychological investigation: Text*. New York: Spectrum.

Cronbach, L. J., & Snow, R. E. (1977). *Aptitudes and instructional methods*. New York: Irvington.

Clodfelter, C.J., Dickson, A. L., Wilkes, C. N., & Johnson, R. B. (1987). Alternate forms of selective reminding for children. *The Clinical Neuropsychologist, 1,* 243-249.

DeArmond, S. J., Fusco, M. M., & Dewey, M. M. (1989). *Structure of the human brain: A photographic atlas* (3rd. ed.). New York: Oxford University Press.

Delis, D. C., Kramer, J. H., Kaplan, E., & Ober, B. A. (1987). *California Verbal Learning Test.* New York: Harcourt Brace Jovanovich.

Fennell, E. B., & Bauer, R. M. (1989). Models of inference in evaluating brain-behavior relationships in children. In C. R. Reynolds & E. Fletcher-Janzen (Eds.), *Handbook of clinical child neuropsychology* (pp. 167-177). New York: Plenum Press.

Fletcher, J. M., & Satz, P. (1980). Developmental changes in the neuropsychological correlates of reading achievement: A six year longitudinal follow-up. *Journal of Clinical Neuropsychology, 2,* 23-37.

Funkenstein, H. H. (1988). Cerebrovascular disorders. In M. S. Albert, M. B. Albert, & M. B. Moss (Eds.), *Geriatric neuropsychology* (pp. 179-207). New York: The Guilford Press.

Golden, C. J. (1981). A standardized version of Luria's neuropsychological tests. In S. Filskow & T. J. Boll (Eds.), *Handbook of clinical neuropsychology* (pp. 608-642). New York: Wiley-Interscience.

Goldstein, K. (1944). The mental changes due to frontal lobe damage. *Journal of Psychology, 17,* 187-208.

Halstead, W. C. (1947). *Brain and intelligence: A quantitative study of the frontal lobe.* Chicago: University of Chicago Press.

Hartlage, L. C., & Telzrow, C. F. (1983). The neuropsychological bases of educational intervention. *Journal of Learning Disabilities, 16,* 521-528.

Hynd, C. R. (1986). Educational intervention in children with developmental learning disorders. In J. E. Obrzut & G. W. Hynd (Eds.), *Child neuropsychology: Clinical practice* (pp. 265-297). New York: Academic Press.

Hynd, G. W., Connor, R. T., & Nieves, N. (1988). Learning disability subtypes: Perspectives and methodological issues in clinical assessment. In M. G. Tramontana & S. R. Hooper (Eds.), *Assessment issues in child neuropsychology* (pp. 281-312). New York: Plenum Press.

Kaplan, E. (1989). A process approach to neuropsychological assessment. In T. Boll & B. K. Bryant (Eds.), *Clinical neuropsychology and brain function: Research, measurement, and practice* (pp. 129-167). Washington DC: American Psychological Association.

Kaplan, E., Fein, D., Morris, R., & Delis, D. C. (1991). *The Wechsler Adult Intelligence Scale - Revised as a neuropsychological instrument.* San Antonio: The Psychological Corporation.

Kaplan, E., Goodglass, H., & Weintraub, S. (1983). *Boston Naming Test.* Philadelphia: Lea & Febiger.

Knights, R. M., & Norwood, J. A. (1980). *Revised smooth normative data on the neuropsychological test battery for children.* Ottawa: Knights Psychological Consultants.

Kolb, B., & Whishaw, I. Q. (1990). *Fundamentals of human neuropsychology.* New York: W. H. Freeman.

Lezak, M. D. (1983). *Neuropsychological assessment* (2nd ed.) New York: Oxford University Press.

Lezak, M. D. (1984). An individualized approach to neuropsychological assessment. In P. E. Logue & J. M. Schear (Eds.), *Clinical neuropsy-*

chology: A multidisciplinary approach (pp. 29-49). Springfield: C. C. Thomas.

Lichtheim, L. (1885). On aphasia. *Brain, 7*, 433-484.

Luria, A. R. (1980). *Higher cortical function in man* (2nd ed.). New York: Basic Books.

Lyon, G. R., Moats, L., & Flynn, J. M. (1988). From assessment to treatment: Linkage to interventions with children. In M. G. Tramontana & S. R. Hooper (Eds.), *Assessment issues in child neuropsychology* (pp. 113-144). New York: Plenum Press.

Mattis, S., French, J. H., & Rapin, I. (1975). Dyslexia in children and young adults: Three independent neuropsychological syndromes. *Developmental Medicine and Child Neurology, 17*, 150-163.

McCarthy, R. A., & Warrington, E. K. (1990). *Cognitive neuropsychology: A clinical introduction.* New York: Academic Press.

Melamed, L. E., & Melamed, E. C. (1985). Neuropsychology of perception. In L. C. Hartlage & C. F. Telzrow (Eds.), *The neuropsychology of individual differences* (pp. 61-91). New York: Plenum Press.

Melamed, L. E., & Rugle, L. (1989). Neuropsychological correlates of school achievement in young children: Longitudinal findings with a construct valid perceptual processing instrument. *Journal of Clinical and Experimental Neuropsychology, 11*, 745-762.

Nauta, W. J. H., & Feirtag, M. (1986). *Fundamental neuroanatomy.* New York: W. H. Freeman.

Orsini, D. L., Van Gorp, W. G., & Boone, K. B. (1988). *The neuropsychology casebook.* New York: Springer-Verlag.

Platt, J. R. (1964). Strong inference. *Science, 146*, 347-353.

Posner, M. I. (1989). Structure and functions of selective attention. In T. Boll & B. K. Bryant (Eds.), *Clinical neuropsychology and brain function: Research, measurement, and practice* (pp. 173-202). Washington, DC: American Psychological Association.

Reitan, R. M., & Wolfson, D. (1985). *The Halstead-Reitan Neuropsychological Test Battery: Theory and clinical interpretation.* Tucson, AZ: Neuropsychology Press.

Reschly, D. J., & Graham, F. M. (1989). Current neuropsychological diagnosis of learning problems: A leap of faith. In C. R. Reynolds & E. Fletcher-Janzen (Eds.), *Handbook of clinical child neuropsychology* (pp. 503-519). New York: Plenum Press.

Reynolds, C. R. (1989). Measurement and statistical problems in neuropsychological assessment of children. In C. R. Reynolds & E. Fletcher-Janzen (Eds.), *Handbook of clinical child neuropsychology* (pp. 147-16). New York: Plenum Press.

Rothi, L. J., & Horner, J. (1983). Restitution and substitution: Two theories of recovery with application to neurobehavioral treatment. *Journal of Clinical Neuropsychology, 5*, 73-81.

Rourke, B. P., & Orr, R. L. (1977). Prediction of the reading and spelling performance of normal and retarded readers: Four-year follow-up. *Journal of Abnormal Child Psychology, 5*, 9-20.

Schum, R. L., Sivan, A. B., & Benton, A. R. (1989). Multilingual Aphasia Examination: Norms for children. *The Clinical Neuropsychologist, 3*, 375-383.

Spiers, P. A. (1982). The Luria-Nebraska Neuropsychology Battery revisited: A theory in practice or just practicing? *Journal of Consulting and Clinical Psychology, 50*, 301-306.

Spreen, O., & Gaddes, W. (1969). Developmental norms for fifteen neuropsychological tests for ages 6 to 15. *Cortex, 5*, 171-191.

Spreen, O., & Strauss, E. (1991). *A compendium of neuropsychological tests: Administration, norms, and commentary*. New York: Oxford University Press.

Stambrook, M. (1983). The Luria-Nebraska Neuropsychological Battery: A promise that *may* be partly fulfilled. *Journal of Clinical Neuropsychology, 5*, 247-269.

Stone, M. H., & Wright, B. D. (1980). *Knox's Cube Test*. Chicago: Stoelting.

Telzrow, C. F. (1989). Neuropsychological applications of common educational and psychological tests. In C. R. Reynolds & E. Fletcher-Janzen (Eds.), *Handbook of clinical child neuropsychology* (pp. 227-246). New York: Plenum Press.

Trenerry, M. R., Crosson, B., DeBoe, J., & Leber, W. R. (1989). *The Stroop Neuropsychological Screening Test*. Odessa, FL: Psychological Assessment Resources.

Trenerry, M. R., Crosson, B., DeBoe, J., & Leber, W. R. (1990). *Visual Search and Attention Test*. Odessa, FL: Psychological Assessment Resources.

Warrington, E. K. (1984). *Recognition Memory Test*. Windsor: Nelson.

Watson, B. U., Goldgar, D. E., & Ryschon, K. L.(1983). Subtypes of reading disability. *Journal of Clinical Neuropsychology, 5*, 377-399.

Webster, R. E. (1981). *Learning Efficiency Test*. Novato, CA: Academic Therapy.

Wechsler, D. A. (1987). *Wechsler Memory Scale - Revised*. New York: Harcourt Brace Jovanovich.

Williams, J. M. (1991). *Memory Assessment Scales*. Odessa, FL: Psychological Assessment Resources.

8 BEST USES OF THE WISC-III

Donald R. Jones and Susan James

WHY USE INTELLIGENCE TESTS?

The testing of intelligence has been the target of controversy since the time Binet first constructed his "mental" test in 1905. Criticisms have ranged from moral indictments against damaging individuals by giving them labels, to deliberate or accidental cultural bias, to accidental or intentional misuse of test results. These criticisms have both helped and hindered the process of measuring the intellectual functioning of children and adults. By this time, it is evident that although there are many valid criticisms of the current practices utilized in intelligence testing, there are also many valid reasons for continuing to measure intellect.

One of the principal reasons for the continued use of intelligence tests is their accuracy in predicting future behaviors (notably academic functioning). The IQ does not reflect a global summation of the brain's capabilities, nor yield an index of genetic potential, but it is the best predictor of school achievement (when used as described in this chapter). Typical correlations between scores and achievement range from the .70s in elementary years to the .50s in high school (Sattler, 1974). Furthermore, coefficients of a similar magnitude are generally reported for both White children and/or minority youngsters. Recent studies indicated that the WISC-R predicted an extremely wide number of variables accurately (Applebaum & Tuma, 1982; Matarazzo & Herman, 1984; Ryan & Rosenburg, 1983; Sutter & Bishop, 1986). Early research on the WISC-III suggests that it is similar to the WISC-R and is equally predictive of many significant behaviors (Wechsler, 1991).

IQs obtained from the WISC-III and similar standardized intelligence tests are extremely helpful in work with handicapped and nonhandicapped children. Intelligence tests provide a measure of the child's developmental strengths and limitations, thus enabling teachers and parents to plan and develop individualized programs that utilize the child's various levels of development. The results of tests such as the WISC-III are standardized procedures whereby a person's performance in various areas can be compared with that of his or her age-related peers. In addition, and most important, the child's own pattern of intellectual strengths and weaknesses can be ascertained. The WISC-III and other individually administered tests provide the administrator with a structured and relatively standardized situation within which a variety of behaviors can be observed. This enables a skilled diagnostician to form an impression of the cognitive style of the examinee as well as his or her behavioral idiosyncrasies, anxieties, social skills, attitudes, and motivation.

TEST ADMINISTRATION

The importance of proper test administration cannot be overstated, as the results of the most carefully constructed tests are only valid under proper testing conditions. To safeguard proper testing conditions and administration, an effective examiner should be especially concerned with the following: (1) establishing rapport, (2) physical and psychological considerations, (3) proper management of children, (4) observation of behavior, and (5) influence of the examiner. These are thoroughly discussed in Aiken (1987), Sattler (1988), and Wechsler (1974) and are summarized here.

Establishing Rapport

Through rapport, the examiner encourages the child to perform at his or her very best in order to yield an index of maximum performance and accurate measurement of capability. As an initial step in establishing rapport, it is a good idea to engage the child in informal conversation for up to 10 minutes. Though there are many ways to develop rapport with a child, smiles, nods, and a friendly demeanor help to convey the acceptance and warmth needed to place the child at ease. The successful examiner is courteous, understanding, and observant, attending to proper behavior and ignoring improper behavior when possible. Praising is desirable during testing but it is *effort*, not actual performance, that should be praised.

The test manual should always be consulted for permissible variations in the phrasing of test items. Some examiners, in their desire to maintain rapport, will unwittingly introduce extraneous material into the phrasing of the test items. This additional information may confound or aid a particular child; in either case, bias is thus introduced that may seriously influence test results, yielding an inaccurate measurement of the child's functioning.

Variation is permitted when dealing with children who have special needs. Hyperactive children may need to move about at points during the session and require less restriction from the examiner. Gifted children may require a quicker pace from the examiner where other children may require a slower pace. It is up to the examiner to adjust to the pace set by the child. These adjustments still generally aid in maintaining rapport and result in greater interest of the child in the task at hand.

Maintaining rapport is one way of creating a pleasant experience for all involved. Another way is to finish the test with some easy items that will leave the child and parent, if in attendance, with a good feeling. If proper rapport has not been developed to the point where the child is at ease and compliant with instruction, accurate measurement and valid test interpretation may be seriously affected. Testing may, therefore, need to be discontinued and/or rescheduled if it becomes an unpleasant experience for either the examiner or examinee.

Physical and Psychological Considerations

Some physical and psychological considerations apply to all test examinees, whereas others apply specifically to children. All examinees require a well-lit, properly ventilated room with minimal distraction. Children, additionally, require consideration based upon age, such as length and scheduling of sessions. In considering length of the session, it is suggested that preschoolers be tested for no longer than 30 minutes, elementary students for no more than 1½ hours. If longer tests such as the Wechsler Preschool and Primary Scale of Intelligence (WPPSI-R) are used, it may be necessary to administer them in two sessions.

Scheduling considerations include scheduling the test session during appropriate times when the child will most want to participate. Inappropriate scheduling for a young child would include scheduling a test session during lunch, naptime, or playtime or scheduling the test when peers are engaged in play activities nearby. The age of the child should be taken into consideration when scheduling tests before or after major holidays or after extended absences, as children may have difficulty concentrating during those times.

Research has shown that for both children and adults, performance is enhanced when testing takes place in familiar surroundings (Aiken, 1987). It has been hypothesized that strange, unfamiliar places may create tension and anxiety sufficient to reduce test scores. When children are being tested, familiarity with surroundings can make the difference between a child who is relaxed and ready to work, and one who is anxious and distracted by his or her new surroundings. Therefore, familiarity with surroundings becomes an additional factor to consider in scheduling test sessions for children.

It is the responsibility of the examiner to be alert for physical or psychological conditions that may adversely affect a child's performance. In such instances, it may be necessary to discontinue testing and reschedule it for another time when more suitable conditions may exist.

Management of Children

Development of rapport with the child is the first step in child management, which basically entails being friendly but firm. As mentioned previously, it is important to attend to the child and adjust to his or her pace. Younger children, especially, will need continuous guidance. Encouraging reassurance of effort along with supportive comments where needed are helpful in gaining the cooperation of the child.

Children respond well to first-name greetings; soft, simple sentences; and appropriate facial expressions. A statement such as, "We're going to do some things that are fun together" will generally elicit more cooperation than asking, "Do you want to do some things that are fun together?" With the latter, the choice for participation is left up to the child, whose choice must then be honored.

Additional factors to consider in the management of children include:

1. Keep gestures and use of materials clear and precise. Exaggerations of movement may be helpful in dealing with babies, such as firmly patting a dolly and motioning for the baby to do the

same. With children, the tone of voice and actions used can help the child in knowing when a response is expected.

2. Gross motor skill testing may be administered as a break from verbal item testing in lieu of a formal break.

3. Always strive to redirect work in a way that is most consistent with the child's motives and interests.

4. Accept each child as he or she is, realizing that there are reasons for the ways he or she feels and behaves. Attempt to find appropriate outlets for children's feelings and strive to meet their needs.

With good child management, an atmosphere may be provided in which the child can feel competent and will want to participate in the tasks you have planned. In the event that fatigue should occur or the child cannot be properly engaged, testing should be discontinued, at least temporarily.

Observation of Behavior

The child should be observed as unobtrusively as possible so as not to embarrass or intimidate him or her. The observations should be accurately recorded instead of trusted to memory. Throughout the observation period, particular attention should be paid to the nature of the rapport that has been established with the child and to reactions the examiner has toward the child. Inferences made during the observation period will be used in recording and interpreting responses that the child makes as well as in formulating a general impression of the youngster. Useful information from which inferences can be drawn may be obtained through observation of:

1. the physical condition of the child (clothing, neatness, hygiene);

2. the cooperativeness of the child (degree and nature of effort and attention the child expresses);

3. attitude toward the test (positivism/negativism, child's abilities, dependence and reaction to authority);

4. speech (articulation, irregularities, immaturity, and appropriateness or vocabulary level);

5. responses to test situation (adjustment, responses to both failure and success);

6. activity level (pace, regularity, and distractibility);

7. problem-solving approach (randomness or plan of action, perfectionism, impulsivity);

8. anxiety (tenseness or relaxation, mood change);

9. fine and gross motor control (indications of neuropsychological problems).

A detailed list of behavioral cues is contained in Table 8.1.

TABLE 8.1. *List of Behavior Cues*

Attitudinal Features

Attitude Toward You, the Examiner
1. How does the child relate to you (and how do you relate to the child)?
2. Is the child shy, frightened, aggressive, or friendly?
3. Is the child negativistic, normally compliant, or overeager to please?
4. Does the child's attitude toward you change over the course of the test?
5. Does the child try to induce you to give answers to questions?
6. Does the child watch you closely to discover whether his or her responses are correct?

Attitude Toward Test Situation
1. Is the child relaxed and at ease, tense and inhibited, or restless?
2. Is the child interested or uninvolved?
3. Does the child seem confident of his or her ability?
4. Is the child an eager or reluctant participant?
5. Are the tasks viewed by the child as games, as opportunities to excel, or as threatening sources of failure?
6. How well does the child attend to the test?

7. Is it necessary to repeat instructions or questions? If yes, does this need for repetition suggest a hearing problem, limited understanding of English, attention difficulties, poor comprehension, or an effort on the child's part to obtain more time to think about the question? Asking the child to repeat the question may provide clues about what factors account for the behavior.

8. Is it easy or difficult to regain the child's attention once you lose it?

9. Does the child appear to be making his or her best effort?

10. Does the child try only when urged by you?

11. Does the child give up easily, or does he or she insist on continuing to work on difficult items?

12. Does the child's interest vary during the examination?

13. How does the child react to probing questions (for example, does the child reconsider the answer, defend the first answer, quickly say "I don't know," or become silent)?

Attitude Toward Self

1. Does the child have poise and confidence?

2. Does the child make frequent self-derogatory or boastful remarks, or is he or she fairly objective about his or her achievement?

3. How aware is the child of the adequacy of his or her answers?

Work Habits

1. Is the child's work tempo fast or slow?

2. Does the child appear to think about and organize answers, or does he or she give them impulsively or carelessly?

3. Does the child revise any answers?

4. Does the child think aloud or only give final answers?

5. Does the child write out answers on the table with a finger, continually ask you for clarification, or use other means to solve the problems?

Reaction to Test Items

1. What type of test item produces reactions such as anxiety, stammering, or blushing?

2. Are there any areas of the test in which the child feels more or less comfortable?

continued

3. Is the child more interested in some types of items than in others?

4. Does the child block on some items ("I know, but I just can't think")? If blocking occurs, is it on easy items, difficult items, or all items?

5. Does the child need to be urged to respond? If yes, does the urging lead to a response? Does the response indicate that the child had the knowledge to respond correctly and merely wanted to be coaxed?

Reaction to Failure

1. How does the child react to difficult items? Does the child retreat, become aggressive, work harder, try to cheat, become evasive, or openly admit failure?

2. If the child becomes aggressive, toward whom or what does the child direct the aggression?

3. How does the child react to failure?

4. Does the child apologize, rationalize, brood, accept failure calmly, or become humiliated?

5. If humiliated, does the child express impotence or perplexity, suggesting loss of ability?

6. Can the child accept reassurance?

Reaction to Praise

1. How does the child react to praise?

2. Does the child accept praise gracefully or awkwardly?

3. Does praise motivate the child to work harder?

Language

1. How clearly does the child express himself or herself? Is the child's speech fluent, halting, articulate, inexact, or precise?

2. How accurately does the child express himself or herself? Are the child's responses direct and to the point, vague, evasive, free-associative, perseverative, or bizarre?

3. Do the responses reflect personal concerns or egocentrism?

4. Are the responses grossly immature?

5. If the child gives extraneous information, does this information suggest a compulsive need to cover all possibilities or is it completely irrelevant?

6. Does the child converse spontaneously or only in response to questions?

7. Does the child's conversation appear to derive from friendliness or from a desire to evade the test situation?

Visual-Motor

1. Are there any movements the child makes with his or her hands, feet, and face that are worth noting?

2. Is the child right or left handed?

3. Is the child's reaction time fast or slow?

4. Does the child proceed systematically or in a trial-and-error manner?

5. Is the child skillful or awkward?

6. Does the child execute bilateral movements skillfully or awkwardly?

7. Is the child aware of time limits on timed tasks? If yes, how does this awareness affect his or her behavior?

8. Does the child verbalize while performing tasks? If yes, are the verbalizations congruent with his or her actions?

Comparison of Verbal and Nonverbal Tasks

1. Are there differences in the child's reaction to verbal and nonverbal tasks (for example, is the child more anxious or more at ease with one type of task)?

2. Does the child understand the instructions for the verbal and nonverbal tasks equally well?

Note. From *Assessment of Children* (3rd ed.) (pp. 88-90) by J. M. Sattler, 1988, San Diego: Author. Copyright 1988 by Jerome K. Sattler. Reprinted by permission.

Along with observing the child, an effective examiner will also be sensitive to a child's individual needs, such as a drink of water or a trip to the bathroom, and will be alert to signs of discomfort, fatigue, motivation, anxiety, and distractibility, all of which should be taken into account during the interpretation of the results. In addition to observational skills acquired through training and practice, observational competence also depends on an understanding of the ways in which an examiner may affect an examinee.

Influence of the Examiner

The influence of the examiner upon a child's performance and test scores will in large part depend upon the personality of the examiner, his or her ability to develop rapport, and his or her management of the child. Although examiner personality will affect his or her ability to empathize, show genuine concern, and relate warmth and respect for the child, which helps in developing rapport, judgment and administrative skills are also important factors that affect test scores. Test scores may also be affected by the examiner's knowledge of a child prior to testing. For instance, if an examiner is informed that a particular child is bright, the examiner may be predisposed toward favorable recording, interpretation, and scoring. Studies by Hersh (1971), Larrabee and Kleinsasser (1967), and Schroeder and Kleinsasser (1972) found that positive expectance, called the "halo effect," led to higher scores being given. However, other researchers, such as Dangel (1972), Ekren (1962), Gillingham (1970), Saunders and Vitro (1971), and Sneed (1976), found that prior information did not affect the examiner's ability to remain unbiased. Sattler (1988) concludes that examiners can overcome the halo effect through awareness, vigilance, and attentiveness to actual test scores.

There are many studies indicating that examiners score identical responses in different ways (Sattler, 1988). These same reports also showed that an examiner's experience is minimal in contributing toward the variability. Other studies showed that examiners occasionally elicit different responses, and some studies found that better performance was obtained with use of a female examiner (Sattler, 1988).

The examiner's job is an extremely important one in order to enable the child to do his or her best and to ensure that unbiased administration occurs. Being properly trained, maintaining familiarity with specific test manuals, and adhering to standardized testing procedures will keep extraneous variables to a minimum. Following guidelines for proper administration and keeping abreast of ongoing research will aid in competency of administration and increase the probability of valid test results.

INTERPRETATION

Interpreting a child's performance on the WISC-III requires a synthesis of the following data: (1) test scores, (2) background information, and

(3) observation (interpretation) of the child's behavior during the administration of the test. Test scores, in and of themselves, have limited utility. For example, it is difficult to determine the significance of an IQ of 110 for a specific child. One can say that the score suggests that the child's performance places him or her in the high average range of functioning, in comparison with peers. But this information is extremely limited in predicting specific academic performances in various classes, determining intellectual strengths or weaknesses, or in deciding if the child has more potential than the scores indicate. A test score alone indicates performance but does not explain how or why the child obtained it. In order to explain results, one must utilize other information. A valid interpretation requires more than a listing of scores.

Interpretation of WISC-III results should be both from a normative and an idiographic framework. When working from this perspective, the examiner uses both normative scores (e.g., IQs and scaled scores) and idiographic personal information to generate hypotheses regarding the significance of the results for the child. Hypotheses derived from WISC-III results, behavioral observations, and background data, in combination, form the basis for making relevant recommendations. Individualizing WISC-III interpretation requires skill and experience. Cautious WISC-III interpretation by well-trained and insightful examiners enables true *individual* intelligence testing and reduces test abuse. The results of the WISC-III should be analyzed in a step-by-step procedure similar to the approach suggested by Sattler (1988). This approach enables the examiner to utilize both normative data and idiographic information and recommendations for each child. (See Table 8.2.)

Step One

Analysis begins by considering the Full Scale, Verbal, and Performance IQs. An examinee's Full Scale IQ provides a starting point for evaluating other scores. It is generally the most reliable score. The Full Scale IQ gives the child's relative standing in comparison with his or her age-related peers and provides a global estimate of his or her current intellectual functioning (a normative estimate). However, this score by itself masks variation in intellectual functioning that is always present. In order to begin analysis of variation in intellectual functioning, the examiner should consider the Verbal and Performance IQs, noting especially the difference between them. Early factor-analytic studies of the WISC-III

TABLE 8.2. *Wechsler Intelligence Scale for Children*

Classification of WISC-III Deviation IQ Categories and Percentage of Standardization Sample in Each Category

IQ	Classification	Percentage included in standardization sample
130 and above	Very superior	2.1
120-129	Superior	8.3
110-119	High average	16.1
90-109	Average	50.3
80-89	Low average	14.8
70-79	Borderline	6.5
69 and below		1.9

The percentages are for Full Scale IQ and are based on the total standardization sample ($N = 2,200$).

Note. From *Wechsler Intelligence Scale for Children - III: Manual* (p. 32), by D. Wechsler, 1991. New York: The Psychological Corporation. Copyright 1991 by The Psychological Corporation. Reprinted by permission.

suggest that the Verbal IQ (VIQ) measures verbal comprehension and freedom from distractibility whereas the Performance IQ (PIQ) measures perceptual organization and processing speed (Wechsler, 1991). If there is a significant difference between VIQ and PIQ, then the clinician should attempt an explanation for the reasons why the difference occurred.

There is some controversy about the magnitude of the VIQ–PIQ difference that should be considered "significant" and therefore interpretable. However, many clinicians regard a difference of 15 points or greater as safely significant (this difference is statistically significant at the .01 level). It should be noted, however, that 24% of the WISC-III standardization sample obtained a Verbal–Performance difference of 15 points or greater. This means that although a 15-point difference is statistically significant, it alone does not indicate pathology. It does, however, suggest the possibility of a problem.

Two children may have identical V–P discrepancies of 15 points in the same direction and yet each may have entirely different reasons for the discrepancy. Sattler (1988) has discussed possible interpretations of V–P discrepancies including: cognitive style, interests, education, emotional disturbances, brain damage, and sensory deficits. Interpretation of the discrepancy must consider personal background and the examinee's behavior in the testing situation. For example, a child in a family where reading and verbal skills are valued is likely to have a higher VIQ than PIQ. The information that the child comes from a verbally oriented family aids in interpreting the meaning of the VIQ–PIQ discrepancy.

Step Two

After consideration of the IQs and their differences, the clinician should examine the scaled score results to ascertain (1) if there are significant differences among the results of the tests; (2) if there is a significant difference in a specific test from the mean scaled score of all tests, the verbal tests, or the performance tests; or (3) if there are profile patterns that add meaning to the examinee's results. This step allows the examiner to analyze the child's cognitive strengths and weaknesses and is usually referred to as profile analysis or *intertest* analysis. The goal of the profile analysis is to describe the child's unique ability pattern. Ascertaining which tests the child handles best may help in planning educational programs that utilize strengths and compensate for weaknesses. Some profiles show extreme variability, some moderate variability, and others little variability. A flat and significantly above-average profile generally indicates that a child is gifted; conversely, a flat and significantly below-average profile generally indicates limited intellectual functioning. Profiles with considerable variation are generally indicative of strengths and weaknesses that may suggest clues about courses of action to help the child utilize his or her cognitive style more effectively.

The interpretation of intertest variability (profile analysis) is complex and controversial. Intertest variability may result from temporary problems, permanent incapacities, school experience, family background, or psychological disturbances. Which of these interpretations is (are) appropriate must be determined on an individual basis. This interpretation *must* take into account other data (especially life history information, observation of the child's behavior during testing, and interviews with his or her teacher).

Psychologists generally believe that the greater the variability of test scores, the greater the likelihood of pathology. It should be noted, however, that minimal variability does not eliminate pathology, nor does great variability necessitate pathology. These patterns do serve to alert the clinician about *possible* presence or absence of pathology. It should also be pointed out that subtests themselves have modest reliabilities. This implies that the clinician needs to consider seriously whether the variability between subtests is due to error variance or to variance in the cognitive abilities being measured.

This raises the issue of how much subtest scores should differ to be considered *significantly* different. Kaufman (1979) recommended the following procedure to deal with this concern.

1. Average all scaled scores for the Verbal subtests.

2. If a subtest is 3 or more scaled score points below the mean of Verbal subtests, it should be labeled a relative weakness.

3. If a subtest is 3 or more scaled score points above the mean of the Verbal subtests, it should be labeled as a relative strength.

4. Steps 1, 2, and 3 should be repeated for the Performance subtests. If no deviations occur, then no specific interpretation needs to be made.

5. Examine all strengths and weaknesses to determine whether or not there are patterns within the profile that may help in the explanation of the causes of the difference in the scores. This requires a thorough knowledge and study of the various abilities each subtest measures as well as other data such as personal background of the examinee.

Clinicians may also wish to examine intersubtest variability throughout all 12 subtests, rather than investigating differences of subtest scores only within the Verbal and Performance scales. A similar procedure to that described above can be used, except that each subtest score is compared with the mean scaled score obtained from the total of all subtests administered.

Step Three

Organizing the subtests into "factors" has frequently aided in generating useful hypotheses for interpreting the results. Research cited in the WISC-III manual (Wechsler, 1991) identified a four-factor organization as a profitable approach for analysis. These factors, previously alluded to, are (1) Verbal Comprehension (V–C), (2) Perceptual Organization (P–O), (3)

Freedom from Distractibility, and (4) Processing Speed. The subtest composition of each factor is given in Figure 8.1.

FIGURE 8.1. *Subtest Composition of WISC-III Factors*

Verbal Comprehension	Perceptual Organization	Freedom from Distractibility	Processing Speed
Information Similarities Vocabulary Comprehension	Picture Completion Picture Arrangement Block Design Object Assembly	Arithmetic Digit Span	Coding Symbol Search

Mean scores for the factors can be computed and examined for significant differences. Scaled score differences of 3 or greater are considered worthy of explanation. The V–C and P–O factors reflect cognitive functioning, whereas the Distractibility factor reflects behavioral or affective functioning. Explanations of significant differences among the mean scores of the factors must take into account what the factors measure.

Interpretation of the significance of high or low V–C or P–O factors is similar to interpretation of the Verbal and Performance scales, respectively. Interpretation of the Distractibility factor is based on several processes that seem to underlie this factor. A high Distractibility score suggests good attention, good short-term memory, numerical ability, and sequencing ability. A low Distractibility factor suggests difficulty in sustaining attention, distractibility, anxiety, short-term memory deficits, and poor rehearsal strategies.

The Distractibility factor should be investigated when one of the component subtests deviates from its respective mean Verbal or Performance score (Kaufman, 1979). For example, when either the Arithmetic or Digit Span scaled scores deviate significantly from the Verbal mean score or when the Coding scaled score deviates significantly from the mean Performance score, it indicates that this factor is operating differently from Verbal Comprehension and/or Perceptual Organization. This suggests that the clinician should attempt to find an explanation of the cause(s). Also, the Processing Speed factor needs to be interpreted when it deviates from other factors or when either the Coding or Symbol Search test deviates from the mean of the performance subtests.

Another possible factor organization was originally suggested by Bannatyne (1974). This organization may be applied to the WISC-III subtests as suggested in Figure 8.2.

FIGURE 8.2. *Alternative Factor Organization of WISC-III Subtests*

Verbal Conceptualization Ability	Spatial Ability	Sequencing Ability	Acquired Ability
Similarities Vocabulary Comprehension	Picture Completion Block Design Object Assembly Symbol Search* Mazes*	Arithmetic Digit Span Coding Picture Arrangement*	Information Arithmetic Vocabulary
*These subtests are added by the author			

Many researchers and clinicians have found this factoring organization especially beneficial in educational settings for planning individualized educational programs. There is evidence that reading disabled children (Rugel, 1974; Smith, Coleman, Dokecki, & Davis, 1977) score highest on the Verbal Conceptualization factor and third highest on the Sequencing factor. A similar pattern is frequently reported for learning disabled children. There is also evidence that learning disabled children perform poorly in the Acquired Knowledge factor.

Step Four

After examining the IQ results, the profile, and possible factors for patterns as well as for significant differences, the clinician may wish to derive more meaning from the child's performance on the WISC-III by performing a content or qualitative analysis of the child's responses to items contained in some of the subtests. An examination of the content of responses on Information, Vocabulary, Comprehension, and Similarities is often quite revealing. Responses to these subtests can be analyzed in a "projective sense." The clinician may logically assume that the child projects concerns, anxieties, and defenses with these responses, much as he or she would with a commonly used projective test. The presence of unique, highly personal, or unusual responses can often indicate significant clinical information regarding the child's intellectual or personality functioning. For instance, responses may suggest aggression, dependency, anxiety, or negativism as well as cognitive style.

Utilization of this step is an excellent technique for showing the relationship between cognitive functioning and affective functioning. One of the principal reasons for using an individual mental test, rather than a group test, is to examine this relationship, and use the results of the examination to aid in diagnosis and remediation for the child. This approach enables the development of a plan that includes information about the "whole child," not just the cognitive performance of the child.

This type of analysis of content is illustrated by a case where one of the authors was testing a 9-year-old girl who responded to an item on the Comprehension subtest which asks the examinee, "What is the thing to do when you cut your finger?" She responded by stating that she would tell her daddy. Background information had been obtained indicating a very close relationship between the girl and her father. Also, the girl's behavior during the administration of the test suggested an unusual degree of dependence. The response to the item along with other data confirmed a diagnosis of unusual dependency on the part of this child (especially with her father).

Step Five

Another step can involve examining for possible patterns of performance in answering items correctly or incorrectly for each subtest. This procedure (*intratest* analysis) makes for a more detailed and more individualized explanation of the results. The items on most subtests are arranged in an order of increasing difficulty. Thus the typical pattern would be for an examinee to pass the initial (easier) items and miss the later (more difficult) items. A more sporadic pattern should be investigated by the examiner with the objective of explaining the reasons for the unusual pattern. Unusual sporadic patterns may be the result of inattention, anxiety, poor educational background, memory deficits, or brain damage. An analysis of intratest scatter can provide information that is different from merely looking at the subtest scores.

An illustration of this type of analysis is to examine the child's scatter of correct/incorrect responses on the Information subtest. Sometimes a visual examination will reveal educationally significant information. For example, the analysis may indicate that the child has missed items that relate to a specific content area such as social studies or science. This could suggest that further testing may be indicated to determine academic proficiency in those areas and to aid in academic programming.

Step Six

Results of the WISC-III are frequently used as an aspect of neuropsychological evaluation of children. Obviously the WISC-III and other intelligence tests measure abilities that can be affected by brain damage. Some examples include memory, learning, perceptual organization, reasoning, and sensory-motor functioning.

Wechsler (1958) developed a scheme that he hoped would diagnose brain damage. His system involved a comparison of subtests he believed to be sensitive to dysfunction. He referred to the brain-sensitive tests as "no hold" tests. These included Digit Span, Digit Symbol, Similarities, and Block Design. The subtests he believed were resistant to neurological impairment were called "hold" tests. These included the Information, Object Assembly, Picture Completion, and Vocabulary subtests. This classification system has some truth, but when used by itself, without supporting data, can lead to misdiagnosis.

Recent research suggests there is no specific brain damage profile (Aram & Ekelman, 1986; Bornstein, 1983; Lezak, 1983). Brain damage may cause a general lowering on all or most subtests and may simply result in a lowering of specific subtests. Possibly the most general indicator of brain damage may be whether a person's scores are lower than would be expected for a person given previous indicators of cognitive and/or affective performance, and his or her current socioeconomic status, age, education, occupation, and other relevant personal information.

In spite of the above, an analysis of WISC-III results along the lines previously discussed can provide information that could be useful for neuropsychological purposes. For example, VIQ–PIQ differences of a magnitude greater than 15 are worthy of investigation for possible neurological dysfunction as well as for other pathologies (such as described previously). Attempts to use WISC-III Verbal–Performance Scale discrepancies have not been consistently successful. But this finding does not mean that VIQ–PIQ discrepancies are of no importance in neuropsychological assessment. The discrepancy still provides important information about the child's intellectual functioning that may be clinically significant if used in conjunction with other tests and background information. If the VIQ is 15 or more points lower than PIQ, you may consider the possibility of language impairment (Sattler, 1988). To develop this hypothesis, the examiner should analyze the child's verbal responses on the Comprehension, Similarities, and Vocabulary subtests. In addition, specialized tests of naming verbal fluency, and language comprehension may be needed to substantiate and diagnose the degree of and the specific areas of language impairment. A careful examination of the Arithmetic and Digit Span subtests can provide useful information about the ways in which the child's abilities to attend, concentrate, and deal effectively with numerical stimuli may be affecting his or her overall language functioning.

If the PIQ is 15 or more IQ points below the VIQ, the examiner should consider the possibility of impaired visual-spatial, constructional, or perceptual-organizational skills. An analysis of VIQ–PIQ differences is not sufficient to diagnose brain damage, but can alert the examiner to look for possible neurological dysfunctions. An examination of the performance on the Block Design, Object Assembly, and Picture Arrangement subtests may suggest a need for further assessment procedures to focus on this possibility.

It is generally accepted that brain damage in the left hemisphere is more likely to lower the Verbal scales, whereas right-hemisphere damage will result in lowered Performance scale scores. Reviews of this issue have shown that sometimes this laterality effect has occurred and at other times it has not (Aram & Ekelman, 1983); however, a VIQ–PIQ gap is consistent with this hypothesis.

It is also widely believed that brain damage is more likely to lower PIQ than VIQ. There is considerable theoretical support for this. The Performance subtests tend to be primarily a measure of fluid intelligence, which is physiologically based and therefore directly tied to intact brain tissue and is also more clearly related to problem-solving capabilities of the nature contained in Performance subtests. Thus, a destruction of brain tissue is more likely to affect fluid intelligence, which is likely to be reflected in lowered Performance subtest scores. There is evidence that the above assumptions are correct in many instances: however, there are many exceptions. For example, Russell (1979) reported that left-hemisphere damage resulted in a lowering of both Performance and Verbal subtests, whereas right-hemisphere and diffuse damage resulted in lowering of Performance subtest results.

One of the primary means of using WISC-III results for neuropsychological evaluation has been through profile analysis, much as discussed in Step Three. An analysis for possible brain damage is accomplished by examining for the presence of significant subtest deviations from other subtests. This analysis is an art and is dependent upon knowledge of brain function as it relates to performance on the subtests of the WISC-III. It also requires integration of information from (1) other psychometric data,

(2) knowledge of the child's development, and (3) observation of the child. Inferences about the meaning of intersubtest deviations are ultimately based on whether they make neuropsychological sense for the child being tested. Often, no clear scientifically based guidelines exist. However, one generally accepted principle is that intersubtest scatter is most likely to occur with focal lesions of recent origin (Groth-Marnat, 1990). In contrast, general lowering of all abilities (low subtest scatter) is more likely with either diffuse damage or chronic lesions. Clinicians may generate and test hypotheses about brain damage from profile analysis, if they keep in mind the limitations discussed above. It must be emphasized again that this sort of analysis is only one basis for neuropsychological assessment.

Research has generally supported the following conclusions about the relationship between subtests or patterns of subtests and possible neurological dysfunction:

1. Coding is the most sensitive subtest and can be lowered by lesions in any location. This subtest reveals information about sequencing, speed, associative learning, concentration, and visual-motor abilities. The child's performance is the end result of the integration of visual, perceptual, oculomotor, fine motor, and mental functions. Disturbance in any area of the brain regulating these functions may result in poor performance. (The author believes Symbol Search will also prove to be highly sensitive to neural dysfunction.)

2. Performance on Information, Vocabulary, Comprehension, and Picture Completion is generally least affected by brain damage. Picture Completion may be lowered by expressive language difficulties.

3. Similarities may reveal difficulties with verbal abstraction. In some cases children show extremely concrete reasoning. Lesions on the left temporal lobe are related to lowered performance on this subtest.

4. Digit Span may reveal attention and/or sequencing problems generally resulting from lesions in the left hemisphere. Also if large differences exist between Digits Forward and Digits Backward (3 or more), it may suggest a loss of flexibility.

5. Performance on Arithmetic reflects attention and concentration as well as cognitive reasoning. Lowered performance is related to lesions in the left parietal lobe and sometimes the right parietal lobe.

6. Picture Arrangement measures sequencing, step-by-step planning, and nonverbal social judgment and is very sensitive to damage in right frontal or right parietal lobes.

7. Block Design was very early recognized as a sensitive neuropsychological test that may reveal visual-spatial problems. Lesions in either the left or right parietal lobes generally lower scores on this subtest.

8. Object Assembly may also reveal visual-spatial organizational problems stemming frequently from lesions in the right parietal lobe.

In addition to a quantitative analysis of intersubtest differences, a clinician may also examine the child's responses to items on various subtests (especially Information, Vocabulary, Comprehension, and Similarities). A child's responses can provide useful information about the possibility of brain damage. Responses might suggest impairment leading to poor judgment or impulsivity. Frequently, damage in the left hemisphere causes or contributes to difficulty in abstracting; thus, the child's responses are very concrete. Note also if responses suggest the child once knew the answer. Diffuse brain damage may also cause a marked degree of intratest scatter (as discussed in Step Four). For example, the child may miss easy items and correctly answer difficult items. This pattern suggests the random loss of previously stored information, which sometimes accompanies diffuse brain damage.

DESCRIPTION OF THE SUBTESTS

To interpret the WISC-III, it is necessary to be aware of the major cognitive functions measured by each subtest. This section discusses the abilities measured, factors influencing performance, and possible meaning of high or low scores. The information given here is only to aid the clinician in establishing hypotheses about the child and should not be relied upon in the absence of other data (e.g., life history background).

Information

The Information subtest samples:

1. fund of knowledge;
2. intellectual curiosity;
3. long-term memory; and
4. acquired knowledge.

Performance is based on memory of information (facts) that the average person is exposed to and generally is able to acquire. Information and Vocabulary are two of the most stable subtests on the WISC-III. Information is a good measure of "g" (overall intellectual functioning) and correlates highly with educational attainment and with overall WISC-III results. Scores on Information and Vocabulary on the WAIS have also been found to predict college grade-point average as accurately as aptitude tests (Feingold, 1983). Anxiety seems to have little effect upon performance on the subtest. Results are influenced by quality of educational and cultural background.

High scores suggest good long-term memory, cultural and educational interests, and positive attitude toward school and intellectual endeavors. Low scores suggest lack of intellectual curiosity, poor educational background, and or cultural deprivation.

Similarities

This subtest measures:

1. verbal concept formation;
2. abstract reasoning;
3. verbal comprehension;
4. long-term verbal memory;
5. expressive vocabulary (verbal fluency); and
6. inductive reasoning.

Verbal concept formation and abstract reasoning are extremely influential in performance on the Similarities subtest. The more precise and abstract the responses, the higher the score. The examiner should note the level of abstraction or concreteness of the child's responses. As a rule, individuals with good insight and introspection tend to perform well on this subtest. Unusual (idiosyncratic) responses may suggest thought disorders.

Arithmetic

The Arithmetic subtest samples the following:

1. numerical reasoning;
2. numerical computation;
3. attention and concentration;
4. long-term verbal memory; and
5. educational background (especially arithmetic).

The Arithmetic subtest measures numerical reasoning (the ability to solve arithmetic problems). It also requires the ability to attend and to focus concentration. Arithmetic is stressful to many children because the tasks require focused attention and/or because the children may have experienced academic problems in the area of Arithmetic. However, examiners should establish whether the child's performance is lowered by lack of numerical skills or by anxiety. Data from life history and observation of the examinee's behavior should help in this respect. High scores suggest alertness, effective concentration, freedom from distractions, and a reasonably good education in arithmetic. Low scores are indicative of a poor educational background, lowered capacity for concentration, and/or possible anxiety (at least situational).

Vocabulary

The principal functions measured by this subtest are:

1. verbal comprehension;
2. verbal fluency;
3. verbal memory;

4. "g" factor; and

5. educational background.

Vocabulary is the best indicator of "g" (the individual's overall intellectual functioning). Vocabulary subtest scores correlate highly (.90) with Full Scale IQ. They are highly predictive of overall academic achievement. Vocabulary generally reflects the nature and effectiveness of the examinee's previous schooling. It is the most stable of all the subtests and, because of this stability, it is often used as an indicator of premorbid functioning in neuropsychological assessments. An examination of the content of Vocabulary responses is often beneficial and may reveal useful information about the child's thought processes, background, and significant emotional reactions.

High scores suggest high general intelligence, good long-term verbal memory, and verbal fluency. High scores also reflect positive attitudes toward intellectual endeavors, widespread reading, and good fund of information. Low scores suggest inept reading, poor or limited educational background, lack of familiarity with English, and/or possible negative attitudes toward education.

Comprehension

The Comprehension subtest samples:

1. social judgment;

2. knowledge of social expectancies;

3. ability to evaluate past experiences; and

4. conformity.

Comprehension has often been called a measure of social intelligence. It involves understanding situations and knowing what is the expected (proper) course of action. Responses indicate the extent to which an examinee either adheres to conventional standards or at least had knowledge of the standards and is willing to express them in a response. In evaluating an examinee's responses, it is important to distinguish between actually dealing with the situation to develop an original response and merely verbalizing overlearned socially acceptable responses. Content analysis of the responses again is frequently very informative. Many times children will reveal significant emotional problems by how and what they say. Emotions influence how individuals respond to environmental situations such as those that comprise many items on this subtest. More than any other subtest, Comprehension straddles intellectual and emotional functioning.

High scores suggest capacity for social compliance and good social judgment; low scores suggest poor social judgment, impulsiveness, and hostility (Weiner, 1966).

Digit Span

This subtest is a measure of:

1. short-term auditory memory;
2. attention and concentration;
3. sequencing; and
4. rote learning.

Although this is a supplementary test, it should be administered routinely because of the clinical information it can provide. Performance on this subtest requires the examinee to attend, encode information, decode (recall), sequence information, and vocalize information. A neurological dysfunction anywhere in this process can result in failure. In addition to neurological problems, emotional problems can affect responses. Performance can be greatly hampered by anxiety. The Digit Span subtest is considered to be one of the most susceptible to the effects of anxiety (along with Arithmetic and Digit Symbol).

High scores are indicative of good auditory short-term memory, good attention, and possibly relative freedom from situational anxiety. Low scores on Digit Span are suggestive of poor short-term auditory memory and/or poor concentration. Low scores may suggest anxiety and/or organic dysfunction. Also, a large discrepancy between Digits Forward and Digits Backward may suggest an organic deficit (Lezak, 1983).

Picture Completion

Picture Completion measures:

1. visual organization;

2. awareness of the whole in relation to its parts;

3. ability to ferret out essential from nonessential details; and

4. long-term visual memory.

Performance on Picture Completion involves recognition of the object depicted and detection of the portion missing. It is a test of visual analysis and requires concentration, visual alertness, visual organization, and long-term visual memory. The time limit places additional demands on the child, and performance also reflects previous cultural exposure. Responses are frequently indicative of emotional problems. For example, passive, dependent individuals may make mistakes because they need structure or support and they include this in their responses. Picture Completion is extremely resilient to brain damage and is, therefore, a good indicator of premorbid intelligence. High scores suggest good visual organization and alertness, whereas low scores may indicate poor visual organization, poor concentration, and/or impulsiveness.

Picture Arrangement

This subtest measures:

1. comprehension of a total situation;

2. sequencing;

3. planning (anticipating consequences of action); and

4. visual organization.

Picture Arrangement is viewed as a measure of planning ability and nonverbal visual organization. It requires the ability to anticipate events within a social context. Thus an individual's background can affect his or her performance on the test. Therefore, scores from persons of different cultural backgrounds should be interpreted with caution. This subtest measures social judgment, as each item requires the child to react to some interpersonal situation. Picture Arrangement requires the examinee to size up a situation before responding.

Persons who score high on Picture Arrangement are generally described as having high social intelligence and high ability to anticipate consequences of social actions. Low scorers are often described as having poor social judgment, unable to plan ahead, having a poor sense of humor, and ineffective interpersonal skills.

Block Design

This is a measure of:

1. nonverbal reasoning;

2. visual analysis and synthesis;

3. visual-motor coordination; and

4. perceptual speed.

Block Design is a measure of visual perception, including breaking down a design into component parts and then synthesizing (assembling) the parts to make a design. This subtest combines visual organization and visual-motor coordination. Performance involves application of nonverbal reasoning to spatial relationship problems.

The examiner should observe the examinee's method of responding. Some subjects are easily discouraged and give up, whereas others insist on completing the tasks, working even beyond the time limit. Also, some examinees approach the task randomly, whereas others are systematic. These approach styles are frequently revealing of personality traits.

Block Design is a relatively nonverbal, culture-free test with a low relationship to education. It can, therefore, be an important tool for assessing intellectual functioning of persons from divergent cultural backgrounds.

Research has also shown that performance on Block Design is very sensitive to brain damage. Lesions in the right hemisphere, particularly the right parietal lobe, affect performance on the test.

High scores are indicative of good visual-motor perception, good concentration, and good nonverbal reasoning. Low scores suggest poor perceptual functioning and problems in concentration.

Object Assembly

The Object Assembly subtest samples:

1. visual synthesis;
2. visual-motor coordination; and
3. visual organization.

This subtest involves skill at visual synthesis (putting parts together). Object Assembly also entails visual-motor coordination (activity-guided visual perception and sensory-motor feedback). Visual organization is also required to assemble an object out of parts that may not be recognized at first. The tasks require constructive ability as well as visual perceptual skill. Motivation is necessary when much trial and error is involved. Object Assembly is only moderately related to general intelligence. Its correlation with other subtests is generally low. It has also been noted that individuals with low IQs (60–75) frequently perform comparatively well on Object Assembly, whereas persons with high IQs can do quite poorly.

As on Block Design, clinicians should observe the examinee's problem-solving approach. Observations may reveal a wide variety of clinically significant behaviors: for example, reactions to frustration; indications of rigidity, perseveration, impulsiveness; and whether the approach is insightful or random. Also, it should be noted that performance on Object Assembly is sensitive to lesions, most notably right posterior, and occasionally in the frontal lobes.

Individuals who score high tend to show good perceptual-motor coordination, visual synthesis, and mental flexibility, whereas low scorers often show poor visual-motor coordination and concreteness.

Coding

This subtest taps:

1. short-term visual memory;
2. visual-motor coordination;
3. associative learning;
4. attention and concentration; and
5. perceptual speed.

The significant function measured by Coding is perhaps psychomotor speed. This test requires the child to learn an unfamiliar task that involves eye–hand coordination, attention, short-term visual memory, and the ability to work under pressure. Performance can obviously be affected by difficulties with any of these skills. Thus Coding is extremely sensitive to the effects of neurological dysfunction or emotional impairment. Psychologically disturbed and brain-damaged patients often have a difficult time with this subtest. Research has indicated that Coding is the most sensitive of any subtest to brain injury regardless of location of the damage (Lezak, 1983).

High scores suggest excellent visual-motor coordination, capacity for associative learning, and good perceptual speed. Low scores are suggestive of reduced short-term visual memory, lower associative learning, impaired motor functioning, and difficulty in attention or concentration.

Mazes

Mazes measures the following:

1. visual planning ability;
2. visual-motor coordination;
3. visual perceptual organization; and
4. short-term auditory memory.

Performance on this subtest requires a child to attend to directions and execute a task that involves remembering directions, displaying visual-motor coordination and resisting disruptive effects of performing under time constraints. Mazes is often useful with nonverbally oriented children or when a further assessment of sequencing and perceptual planning skills is needed.

Individuals who score high on Mazes usually possess good planning ability, mental flexibility, and ability to resist impulsive action. Low scores may reflect poor visual-motor coordination, poor visual planning, or neurological impairment, particularly to frontal lobes.

Symbol Search

Symbol Search measures:

1. visual organization;

2. short-term auditory memory;

3. attention and concentration; and

4. perceptual speed.

It is somewhat early to be precise regarding the significance of high and low scores on this subtest. It is believed that this test will prove to be extremely sensitive to neurological dysfunction and anxiety. This test should also be helpful with nonverbally oriented children and with examination of visual-perceptual organization.

DIAGNOSIS

The WISC-III can be used as one criterion for diagnosing learning disability (LD), educable mental retardation (EMR), giftedness, dyslexia and reading disorders, attention deficit hyperactivity disorders, conduct disorder, autism, and visual/hearing impairments, as well as nonspecific behavior disorders. In this section the focus of concern will be on discussing the use of the WISC-III in the diagnosis of the first three conditions: LD, EMR, and giftedness.

The diagnosis of learning disability is a complex task involving formal and informal assessment of a child's gross academic functioning as well as assessment of affective, perceptual-motor, and cognitive functioning. Thus it should be kept in mind that intelligence measurement of cognitive functioning is but one area that should be assessed for the diagnosis of LD.

In discussing LD, one should be cognizant of the controversies surrounding the definition of the term itself. Regardless of whether one adheres to the guidelines set forth in Public Law 94-142 as to the definition and diagnosis of LD, or to the National Joint Committee for Learning Disabilities (NJCLD) definition and emphasis (which are two of the more widely recognized sources of such information), the main consensus regarding definition is that LD results in major discrepancy between the expected and obtained academic levels of a child. Additionally, the learning problem should not be a primary or direct result of visual, hearing, or motor handicaps; mental retardation; emotional disturbance; or environmental, cultural, or economic disadvantage. For detailed information on the nature of the controversy surrounding the LD term, the reader is referred to Reynolds and Kamphaus (1900), Sabatino, Miller, and Schmidt (1981), and Sattler (1988).

Several uses can be made of the estimation of the child's general intelligence from test scores. One is to determine whether the child possesses the capability for high achievement despite present or past performance. Thus, if a child scores average or above on an intelligence measure while performing substandard work, this would be cause for investigation. Next, intelligence scores can be used as a criterion for excluding mental retardation as a primary cause of learning problems. Because the definition of mental retardation is an IQ score that is 2 or more standard deviations below the mean, an IQ score greater than 2 or more standard deviations below the mean would rule out mental retardation. Scores from distant subtests or areas of intelligence are helpful in identifying both strengths and weaknesses useful in remediation programs and identification of possible areas of LD.

The reader is cautioned that without a readily operationalized definition of LD, one is confronted with myriad opinions regarding what should be included in the diagnosis and evaluation of LD. Therefore, criticisms have been leveled at the manner in which IQ scores are used in the assessment of LD. In establishing a discrepancy between achievement (performance) and intelligence (ability), problems may emerge. One involves the case where a child exhibits a very superior IQ, for example 145, on the WISC-III, and standard scores of 125–130 on the WRAT-R spelling, reading, and arithmetic subtests. Although a discrepancy exists between IQ and academic achievement, this child is clearly superior in both areas of ability and performance. Should it be concluded that this child needs special help to remediate a disability? There are those who propose that LD should not include children with average or better scores in achievement and intelligence despite this discrepancy, and there are those who disagree. The measured factors on achievement and intelligence tests overlap; thus, the same processing difficulties that affect the child's achievement test scores may also affect intelligence test scores. Children who demonstrate no discrepancy in achievement and intelligence scores may not be diagnosed as learning disabled even though a processing difficulty may affect the child's functioning in both areas.

Although problems exist with classification, assessment of the level of intelligence as well as assessment for patterns of cognitive efficiency are utilized, and for these purposes, the WISC-III is the preferred measurement choice. This measure is intended for use with children ages 6 through 16 years 11 months, the ages during which most children are identified as learning disabled.

Despite numerous attempts to find profiles unique to the learning disabled child, none has proven entirely successful. For a discussion of patterns and profiles along with an analysis of Bannatyne (1974) recategorization of WISC-III subtests, the reader is referred to Berk (1983), Clampit and Silver (1990), Dean (1983), Reynolds and Kamphaus (1990), and Sattler (1988). Although there is no pattern that is consistently diagnostic of LD or reading disability, research has shown that the four most difficult subtests for reading disabled children are Arithmetic, Coding, Information, and Digit Span.

In conclusion, research suggests that although the WISC-III alone is not sufficient for the diagnosis of LD, it is a tool that when used in conjunction with other psychometric devices, can be useful in diagnosing various learning disabilities.

The WISC-III can also be used for the assessment of intellectual functioning in the assessment of mild mental retardation, although it cannot reliably distinguish between the brain-injured and non-brain-injured child by itself. IQ scores in the range of 50 to 69 are generally considered indicative of mild retardation. As with assessing learning disabled children, areas besides intelligence need to be taken into account. In diagnosing mental retardation, adaptive behavior and developmental processes need to be thoroughly assessed as well as general intellectual functioning. (See Table 8.3.)

Gifted children may have creative talents, exceptionally high IQs (over 130), or both. In identifying gifted children, intelligence, achievement, and behavior are areas that need to be assessed. The WISC-III can be used to assess the upper limits of a child's intellectual ability; however, for children under the age of 6, other instruments such as the Wechsler Preschool and Primary Scale of Intelligence (WPPSI-R) are recommended.

As the 21st century nears, increased legal responsibility placed on the school system to provide special education will result in increasing demands being placed on the diagnostician to choose appropriate assessment devices for the diagnosis of various members of our population. Meeting this demand will require not only that the diagnostician possess the knowledge and skill required to administer psychometric instruments properly, but that he or she be knowledgeable of the new assessment devices as they become available. For an idea of what form intelligence tests may take in the future, we will now turn to a discussion of some future trends in intelligence testing.

TABLE 8.3. *Levels of Adaptive Behavior for the Mentally Retarded*

Level	Preschool age: birth to 5 years	School age: 6 to 21 years	Adult: over 21 years
Mild Retardation	Can develop social and communication skills; minimal retardation in sensorimotor areas; rarely distinguished from normal until later age.	Can learn academic skills to approximately 6th-grade level by late teens. Cannot learn general high school subjects. Needs special education, particularly at secondary school age levels.	Capable of social and vocational adequacy with proper education and training. Frequently needs guidance when under serious social or economic stress.
Moderate Retardation	Can talk or learn to communicate; poor social awareness; fair motor development; may profit from self-help; can be managed with moderate supervision.	Can learn functional academic skills to approximately 4th-grade level by late teens if given special education.	Capable of self-maintenance in unskilled occupations; needs supervision and guidance when under mild social or economic stress.
Severe Retardation	Poor motor development; speech is minimal; generally unable to profit from training in self-help; little or no communication skills.	Can talk or learn to communicate; can be trained in elemental health habits; cannot learn functional academic skills; profits from systematic habit training.	Can contribute partially to self-support under complete supervision; can develop self-protection skills to a minimal useful level in controlled environment.
Profound Retardation	Gross retardation; minimal capacity for functioning in sensorimotor areas; needs nursing care.	Some motor development present; cannot profit from training in self-help; needs total care.	Some motor and speech development; totally incapable of self-maintenance; needs complete care and supervision.

Note. States may differ in their definition of these levels. From *Assessment of Children* (3rd ed.) (p. 426) by J. M. Sattler, 1988. San Diego: Author. Copyright 1988 by Jerome K. Sattler. Reprinted by permission.

FUTURE TRENDS IN INTELLIGENCE TESTING

In discussing future trends in intelligence testing one might first ask if the term *IQ* will continue to be used in the next century or be gradually replaced by terms some believe more suitably designate that which is being measured. Vernon (1979) has suggested that other terms, such as *vocabulary, general information,* and *syllogistic reasoning,* may more appropriately designate the tasks that comprise intelligence tests. Turnbull (1979) has proposed the use of tests that would provide separate scores on a variety of abilities. This call for measuring separate abilities is echoed by Horn (1979) who envisions measurement ranging from very elementary processes to that of broad but distinct dimensions of intelligence. Horn also proposes that tests in the future be used less often as measures of global intelligence to make invidious distinctions and more often to identify areas of intellectual strengths and weaknesses.

The identification of strengths and weaknesses becomes crucial when one is concerned, as Resnick (1979) is, with education and the application of intelligence and aptitude tests toward a systematic and refined matching of instructional treatments to aptitudes. Brown and French (1979), also concerned with education, have expressed the desire for an increased emphasis on the diagnosis and remediation of cognitive deficits, again requiring measurement of separate abilities, strengths, and weaknesses. They would like to see an extension of the predictive power of intelligence tests in order that school failure could be predicted prior to its occurrence. Along with Resnick, they see the possibility for school systems in the future to meet the needs of individuals more effectively with improved and more specific testing methods.

A related way in which researchers are attempting to meet the needs of individuals is through research on individual differences in information processing. The study of information processing involves focusing on ways in which individuals mentally represent and process information. Models formulated from such research categorize mental processes in terms of the different operations performed on the information. Thus, component analysis of tests involves isolating the information processing steps required to solve different types of problems. Such analysis has been conducted on tests of logical reasoning, inductive reasoning, and spatial visualization (Hunt, 1982). In the future, Hunt would like to see work done in this area applied to construct componential analysis of other types of tests, including paragraph comprehension tests in which individual items could be used to test different aspects of the comprehension process and arithmetic reasoning tests whereby the manner in which skills are used could be tested instead of merely testing the level of skill.

Hunt would also like to see future tests constructed to measure individual differences in three areas that he believes have been neglected in traditional testing. The first area involves testing for "time sharing" or "concentration." This tests the individual's ability to control attention during times of information overload. Hunt believes that the ability to control attention is an important component of intelligence and one that should be measured. (See Hunt, 1982, for a discussion of the concept and measurement of "time sharing.")

The second area that has not been adequately measured has been referred to as *motor control*. It involves the ability to think while making complex motor responses (one example of this would be driving a car). Hunt believes that tasks such as these requiring thought and motor response are components of intelligence and, as such, should be measured.

The third area that should be researched in the future involves tapping individual differences in the ability to organize a strategy to solve problems of long-term duration (lasting for hours, days, or months). These differences are important because, as Hunt notes, many individuals spend years contemplating solutions to problems. Hunt argues that traditionally, individual differences in long-term intellectual pursuits have been labeled "motivation." He believes these individual differences in long-term problem-solving strategies warrant future investigation as intellectual components themselves.

The future may also see the continued development of two methods of testing as possible alternatives to traditional intelligence tests—the learning potential testing method and the adaptive testing method. The learning potential testing method has been researched for over 20 years and is one method that many believe will be employed in the future. This concept is presented as offering a more positive assessment of the individual (potential for learning) than the traditional intelligence test offers (set developmental level or intelligence level).

This method involves (1) administering a pretest to determine the current level of cognitive functioning of the individual, (2) administering a training phase of "prompts," and (3) administering a posttest equal or similar (parallel form) to the pretest. Materials used in the pretest usually consist of standard tasks or problems administered in the usual way. The prompts consist of problem-solving strategies that may be taught in individual or group sessions. This training session can serve to explore the "zone of next development" as Vygotsky (1978) conceptualized it, or it may serve to reduce the influence of differences in prerequisite skills among students (e.g., understanding instructions; Wijnstra, 1984). From the posttest results, the learning potential may be assessed by comparing the difference between the initial developmental level of the child (pretest) with that of the potential development attained (posttest). Aiken (1987) notes that Vygotsky's concept of effective transfer from trial-to-trial, which would be indicated by a decreasing number of prompts, is indicative of a wide zone of potential development.

The adaptive testing method involves initially presenting the examinee with a screening or routing test to determine which item(s) should be administered thereafter. It differs from conventional testing in that the items administered to the examinee during the test are based or dependent on his or her responses to previous test items. This method assesses the examinee's maximum level of competence more quickly than can be achieved through conventional testing methods and, most important, allows for testing to be tailored to the capabilities of the examinee.

Hunt (1982) and Aiken (1987) anticipate that computer technology will greatly enhance the utility of the adaptive testing method, and Aiken foresees computer sites located throughout the United States equipped with such technology to test for college admissions, job qualifications, and military selection. Despite varying predictions for the future, there is general consensus that computer technology will become increasingly sophisticated and extensively utilized in the 21st century. This will present an ethical challenge to diagnosticians at all levels of competence. Although computers may be used to administer, score, and interpret tests, they cannot replace clinical judgment. It will be incumbent upon the diagnostician to recognize computer report limitations and to make decisions that are in the best interest(s) of the client. Therefore, the diagnostician will be called upon to take into account the examinee's unique clinical history in forming a complete assessment and to communicate results from computer reports to clients in a nontechnical manner. The new technology could be inappropriately used to lump people together or more appropriately used to research such areas as individual differences. It will be up to the individual diagnostician to adhere to ethical standards to ensure that computer technology is utilized to assure the best uses of intelligence tests in the future.

REFERENCES

Aiken, L. R. (1987). *Assessment of intellectual functioning*. Boston: Allyn and Bacon.

Appelbaum, A. S., & Tuma, J. M. (1982). The relationship of the WISC-R to academic achievement in a clinical population. *Journal of Clinical Psychology, 38*, 401-405.

Aram, D. M., & Ekelman, B. L. (1986). Cognitive profile of children with early onset unilateral lesions. *Developmental Neuropsychology, 2*, 155-172.

Bannatyne, A. (1974). A note on recategorization of the WISC scaled scores. *Journal of Learning Disabilities, 7*, 272-274.

Berk, R. A. (1983). The value of WISC-R profile analysis for the differential diagnosis of learning disabled children. *Journal of Clinical Psychology, 39*(1), 133-135.

Bornstein, R. A. (1983). Verbal I.Q.-Performance I.Q. discrepancies on the Wechsler Adult Intelligence Scale - Revised in patients with unilateral or bilateral cerebral dysfunction. *Journal of Consulting and Clinical Psychology, 51*, 779-789.

Brown, A. L., & French, L. A. (1979). The zone of potential development: Implications for intelligence testing in the year 2000. *Intelligence, 3*, 255-273.

Clampit, M. K., & Silver, S. J. (1990). Demographic characteristics and profiles of learning disability index subsets of the standardization sample of the Wechsler Intelligence Scale for Children - Revised. *Journal of Learning Disabilities, 23*(4), 263-264.

Dangel, H. L. (1972). Biasing effect of pretest referral information on WISC scores of mentally retarded children. *American Journal of Mental Deficiency, 77*, 354-359.

Dean, R. S. (1983). Intelligence as a predictor of nonverbal learning with learning-disabled children. *Journal of Clinical Psychology, 39*(3), 437-441.

Ekren, U. W. (1962). *The effect of experimenter knowledge of a subject's scholastic standing on the performance of a reasoning task*. Unpublished master's thesis, Marquette University, Milwaukee.

Feingold, A. (1983). The validity of the Information and Vocabulary Subtests of the WAIS for predicting college achievement. *Educational and Psychological Measurement, 43*, 1127-1131.

Gillingham, W. H. (1970). An investigation of examiner influence on Wechsler Intelligence Scale for Children scores. *Dissertation Abstracts International, 31*, 2178-A. (University Microfilms No. 70-20, 458).

Groth-Marnat, G. (1990). *Handbook of psychological assessment* (2nd ed.) New York: John Wiley & Sons.

Hersh, J. B. (1971). Effects of referral information on testers. *Journal of Consulting and Clinical Psychology, 37*, 116-122.

Horn, J. L. (1979). Trends in the measurement of intelligence. *Intelligence, 3*, 229-239.

Hunt, E. (1982). Towards new ways of assessing intelligence. *Intelligence, 6*(3), 232-240.

Kaufman, A. S. (1979). *Intelligence testing with the WISC-R.* New York: John Wiley & Sons.

Larrabee, L. L., & Kleinsasser, L. D. (1967). *The effect of experimenter bias on WISC performance.* Unpublished manuscript, Psychological Associates, St. Louis.

Lezak, M. (1983) *Neuropsychological assessment* (2nd ed.). New York: Oxford University Press.

Matarazzo, J. D., & Herman, D. O. (1984). Base rate data for the WAIS-R: Test-retest stability and VIQ-PIQ differences. *Journal of Clinical Neuropsychology, 6*, 351-366.

Resnick, L. B. (1979). The future of IQ testing in education. *Intelligence, 3*, 241-253.

Reynolds, C. R., & Kamphaus, R. W. (1990). *Handbook of psychological and educational assessment of children.* New York: Guilford Press.

Rugel, R. P. (1974). WISC subtest scores of disabled readers: A review with respect to Bannatyne's recategorization. *Journal of Learning Disabilities, 7*, 48-55.

Russell, E. W. (1979). Three patterns of brain damage on the WAIS. *Journal of Clinical Psychology, 35*, 611-620.

Ryan, J. J., & Rosenburg, S. J. (1983). Relationship between the WAIS-R and Wide Range Achievement Test in a sample of mixed patients. *Perceptual and Motor Skills, 56*, 623-626.

Sabatino, D. A., Miller, T. L., & Schmidt, C. (1981). *Learning disabilities.* Rockville, MD: Aspen.

Sattler, J. M. (1974). *Assessment of children's intelligence* (rev. ed.). Philadelphia: Saunders.

Sattler, J. M. (1988). *Assessment of children* (3rd ed.). San Diego: Author.

Saunders, B. T., & Vitro, F. T. (1971). Examiner expectance and bias as a function of the referral process in cognitive assessment. *Psychology in the Schools, 8*, 168-171.

Schroeder, H. E., & Kleinsasser, L. D. (1972). Examiner bias: A determinant of children's verbal behavior on the WISC. *Journal of Consulting and Clinical Psychology, 39*, 451-454.

Smith, M. D., Coleman, J. M., Dokecki, P. R., & Davis, E. E. (1977). Intellectual characteristics of school-labeled learning disabled children. *Exceptional Children, 43*, 352-357.

Sneed, G. A. (1976). An investigation of examiner bias, teacher referral reports, and socioeconomic status with the WISC-R. *Dissertation Abstracts International, 36*, 4367A. (University Microfilms No. 75-29, 943).

Sutter, E. G., & Bishop, P. C. (1986). Further investigation of the correlations among the WISC-R, PIAT, and DAM. *Psychology in the Schools, 23*, 365-367.

Turnbull, W. W. (1979). Intelligence testing in the year 2000. *Intelligence, 3*, 275-282.

Vernon, P. E. (1979). Intelligence testing and the nature/nuture debate, 1928-1978: What next? *British Journal of Educational Psychology, 49*, 1-14.

Vygotsky, L. S. (1978). *Mind in society: The development of higher psychological processes.* (M. Cole, V. John-Steiner, S. Scribner, & E. Souberman, Trans.). Cambridge: Harvard University Press.

Wechsler, D. (1958). *Measurement and appraisal of adult intelligence* (4th ed.). Baltimore: Williams & Wilkins.

Wechsler, D. (1974). *WISC-R manual.* New York: The Psychological Corporation.

Wechsler, D. (1991). *WISC-III manual.* New York: The Psychological Corporation.

Weiner, I. B. (1966). *Psychodiagnosis in schizophrenia.* New York: John Wiley & Sons.

Wijnstra, J. M. (1984, August). *Learning potential tests: An alternative to intelligence tests?* Paper prepared for the Inaugural European Conference on Developmental Psychology, Groningen, Netherlands.

9 ASSESSMENT FOR EFFECTIVE INSTRUCTION

Samuel A. DiGangi and
Suzanne P. Faykus

The title of this chapter, "Assessment for Effective Instruction," is likely to imply an assortment of purposes, intents, and content. *Assessment* refers to any number of issues related to testing, measuring, or evaluating student performance. *Effective instruction* refers to approaches such as informal assessment, teacher-made tests, curriculum-based measures, assisted assessment, or authentic assessment. In constructing this examination of best practices in assessment, we have attempted to address those areas of assessment that have a direct impact on decisions made about students. The assessment process is indeed a complex undertaking with regard to the tools or instruments used to conduct testing, as well as the diversity of beliefs held by those involved in making decisions that influence student performance. We have focused on the use of norm-referenced as well as criterion-referenced approaches, which are widely used in the schools to make decisions about students. This chapter explores the multifaceted nature of assessment of student performance: what we do, why we do it, and what, perhaps, we need to do.

WHY WE TEST

The need to measure student performance has been evident throughout the history of education. Assessment has served as the basis for teaching decisions (what to teach and how to teach), evaluation decisions (assignment of grades), and placement decisions (retention in grade, referral for special services, classification).

The use of testing to assist in making these decisions has evolved from early classroom-based procedures (Ayres, 1909) to intelligence testing (Binet & Simon, 1916), achievement measures (Linquist, 1951), process assessment, criterion-referenced assessment, and authentic assessment. Today, group-administered achievement tests are used throughout the country. Local newspapers publish the results of state and national testing. Student performance is compared to local and national norms as an indicator of the effectiveness of schools and teachers. Testing and evaluation remain controversial issues in the educational community. Individual views regarding "best practices" in testing and evaluation are as diverse as the methods and philosophies of instruction held by teachers and practitioners.

Although often used interchangeably, the terms *measurement, evaluation,* and *testing* refer to specific qualities in the investigation of student performance. Testing describes the *process* of collecting information about a student. This activity is conducted in the absence of judgments or comparisons regarding a student. Testing is merely the construction of a situation for gathering information. A *test* is a tool for collecting information about a student's performance. Measurement refers to the assignment of numbers to observations of student performance (Campbell, 1940). Scoring a test employs the process of measurement to the extent that an observation of the student's performance, collected through testing, is being quantified. Evaluation refers to a comparison of the observed behavior to a standard (Howell & Morehead, 1987). A sample of a student's behavior may be collected through testing, measured by examining and assigning a score to the student's performance on the test, and then evaluated by comparing the student's score on the test (behavior) to the score that was expected (standard). In noting the discrepancy between what the student did (the behavior) and what we wanted the student to do (the standard), we have conducted an evaluation. Purposes of testing, therefore, are best addressed by looking at what questions we hope to answer through *evaluation*. We will examine two primary purposes of testing: (1) placement of handicapped students and (2) instructional decision making.

Placement Decisions

Placement decisions refer to the assignment of students to groups based on measured ability and academic performance. This includes decisions regarding placement in special programs and special education services, assignment to a reading series, or assignment to a grade level within the school. Placement decisions are made with respect to norm-referenced performance. Norm-referenced tests yield information that compares an individual student to a group of other students called the normative sample. For example, if we were to administer a test to the class, rank order the students by score from highest to lowest, and then report the position of each student in the ranking, we would be making a norm-referenced comparison.

Although norm-referenced testing yields information with regard to ranking or class standing, a description of how the student performed on specific objectives in the curriculum is not addressed. For example, if Laura scored at the 75th percentile compared to her class, we know that Laura did the same as or better than 75% of the other students. We do not know how she performed on specific objectives. Placement decisions based on norm-referenced testing do not yield specific instructional information but are typically used to determine eligibility for special education services.

Eligibility

The enactment of Public Law 94-142, the Education for All Handicapped Children Act, mandated that all handicapped children are entitled to a free and appropriate public education regardless of their handicap. (See Table 9.1.) Although geared to handicapped students, PL 94-142 has affected the delivery of many educational services within the schools, including the ways in which student performance is assessed. The provision of least restrictive environment (LRE) states that to the maximum extent appropriate, handicapped children must be educated with nonhandicapped children in as normal an environment as possible. Eligibility for services, as well as type of service delivery, is determined through assessment. The appearance of categorical special education places emphasis on the ability of tests to "identify" students.

TABLE 9.1. *Major Provisions Under PL 94-142: The Education of All Handicapped Children Act (1975)*

Free and Appropriate Public Education

• All handicapped children are entitled to a free and appropriate public education regardless of their handicap.

Nondiscriminatory Assessment

• Procedures must be established to assure that testing and evaluation materials and procedures utilized for the purposes of evaluation and placement for children who are handicapped will be selected and administered so as not to be culturally or racially discriminatory.

Related Services

• Supportive services must be provided (speech pathology, psychological services, counseling, occupational therapy, etc.) when needed to assist a child who is handicapped to benefit from special education.

Individual Education Plan (IEP)

• A written IEP is required for all children who are handicapped that will include current level of achievement, annual goals and short-term objectives, specific educational services to be provided, dates of services, and criteria for evaluating the degree to which the objectives are being achieved.

Due Process

• Written notification to parents is required before an evaluation and before initial placement in a special education program.

• Written notification to parents is required when initiating or refusing to initiate a change in educational identification, evaluation, or placement.

• Parents have an opportunity to obtain an independent educational evaluation at public expense.

• Parents can request an impartial due process hearing.

Privacy and Records

- A child's educational and psychological records must remain confidential except to those individuals who are directly in- XX volved in a child's education and who have a specific reason for reviewing the records.
- Parents or guardians have the right to examine all relevant records with respect to identification, evaluation, and placement of their child.
- A child's educational records must be destroyed at the request of parents. (Exception: a permanent record of the child's name, address, grades, attendance records, and grade level completed may be maintained without time limitation.)

Least Restrictive Environment

- To the maximum extent that is appropriate, handicapped children must be educated with nonhandicapped children in as normal an environment as possible.

Swanson and Watson (1982) summarized requirements of PL 94-142 that pertain to evaluation of student performance:

1. Intellectual functioning, adaptive behavior, and school performance must be considered in assessing mental retardation.
2. Provision for the identification of all students with handicaps must be in place in each state.
3. Due process safeguards must be present. Parents are to be involved in all aspects of eligibility and placement.
4. The student must be evaluated prior to placement.
5. An individual educational plan must be developed prior to placement and, at minimum, revised annually.
6. The student must be placed in the Least Restrictive Environment.

The mandate set forth by PL 94-142, as well as related legislation (see Tables 9.2 and 9.3), has established parameters for the goals and objectives of student assessment. All states mandate specific rules and regulations XX regarding assessment procedures and eligibility criteria for special education services. There is significant variability among states with regard to these rules and regulations and numbers of students who receive special education services in various categories (Hallahan, Keller, & Ball, 1986; Ysseldyke & Algozzine, 1990).

Bias in Testing and Placement

Under PL 94-142, procedures must be established to assure that testing for purposes of evaluation and placement of children who are handicapped is conducted so as not to be culturally or racially discriminatory. In the identification of students for possible special education placements, several studies have demonstrated that sociocultural variables of students significantly influence teachers' referral decisions (Huebner, 1987; Ysseldyke & Algozzine, 1981; Zucker & Prieto, 1977). Student characteristics such as ethnic background, sex, and socioeconomic status (SES)

TABLE 9.2. *Features of PL 93-112 (1973), Section 504*

In 1977, Section 504 was implemented and was very similar to PL 94-142. It has been recognized as the civil rights law that ensured the implementation of PL 94-142 (Reynolds, Gutkin, Witt, & Elliot, 1984). Primary differences are:

- Section 504 includes several categories of persons who are handicapped that aren't included in PL 94-142 (e.g., individuals addicted to drugs and alcohol, conduct disorders, physical handicaps).

- In order to receive funds under PL 94-142, a child must be assigned a diagnostic label. Section 504 does not require a label; the child must be functionally handicapped.

- PL 94-142 requires an Individual Education Plan (IEP) of all children who are handicapped. Section 504 does not require an IEP, but it will satisfy the requirement of having an educational program that meets the individual needs of the child who is handicapped.

- Section 504 pertains to educational and employment opportunities, whereas PL 94-142 is restricted to educational opportunities.

- PL 94-142 includes services to non-public school children. Services are not provided under Section 504.

TABLE 9.3. *Major Provisions Under PL 101-476: The IDEA*

New Categories

- Autism has been included as a new eligibility category.

- Traumatic brain injury is a new eligibility category. Assessment of traumatic brain injury must provide appropriate neuropsychological, speech and language, and educational evaluations to provide accurate information for IEPs.

Transition Services

- Transition services (services that promote movement from school to postschool activities) must be included in a student's IEP by age 16.

- Related services (two new services have been added and Congress insists that schools do a better job implementing them)

    - *Rehabilitation counseling* is considered both a related and transition service. It is defined as "a counseling profession with a specific focus on disability, including career development and employment preparation of people with disabilities."

    - *Assistive technology service* is defined as "any item, piece of equipment or product system that is used to increase, maintain, or improve functional capabilities of individuals with disabilities." For many children the provision of assistive technology devices and services will redefine an appropriate placement in the least restrictive environment allowing children to participate in a normal educational setting and promote greater independence and productivity.

- Reemphasis on the need to provide recreation therapy as part of the IEP.

- *Social Work Services* has been in the regulations since 1977, but is now placed in statute itself. Many schools didn't consider social work services to be a related service. Congress now expects all schools to make these services available.

(continued)

Least Restrictive Environment

- Congress stresses the need for the least restrictive environment placement and has authorized a study to investigate how states are integrating the special education population and to gather information necessary for program improvements.

Residential Placements

- Congress has authorized grants to investigate the development of approaches to "reduce the use of out-of-community residential programs and increase school district-based programs."

---

influence teacher–student interactions, teacher decision making, and teacher formation of negative attitudes towards students (Algozzine, Mercer, & Countermine, 1977; Brophy & Good, 1970; Ysseldyke & Algozzine, 1982). A student's SES and ethnicity significantly affected a teacher's decision to refer for a psychoeducational evaluation (Argulewicz & Sanchez, 1983; Shinn, Tindal, & Spira, 1987; Ysseldyke & Algozzine, 1981), with higher referral rates among minority students and students from low socioeconomic backgrounds. Zucker and Prieto (1977) demonstrated that with all other information being equal, teachers were more likely to refer a Hispanic student than an Anglo student.

 Similarly, children from minority groups and low-SES environments were more likely to be recommended and placed into special education, once they performed poorly on an intelligence test (Mercer, 1971). Hall (1970) estimated that African-American children were placed into special education 15 times more often than Anglo children and were greatly overrepresented in the educable mentally retarded category (Dunn, 1973; Gelb & Mizokawa, 1986). Spanish-surnamed students were also reported to be overrepresented in educable mentally retarded classes (Dunn, 1973) and overrepresented by 300% in learning disabled classes (Ortiz & Yates, 1983). Gelb and Mizokawa (1986), in a national survey, demonstrated that low-SES status was positively related to an educable mentally retarded placement and negatively associated with a learning disability placement.

Intelligence Testing

Evaluation of students who are considered for special education services typically involves the administration of an intelligence test, coupled with other tests and information. Opponents of intelligence assessment argue that the tests are biased against certain groups of students and the information obtained is of little or no value in planning instructional interventions (Ysseldyke, Algozzine, & Thurlow, 1992). The use of intelligence tests in placement decisions has been legally challenged over the past 10 years (Reschly, Kicklighter, & McKee, 1988a,b), resulting in conflicting decisions with regard to test bias. For example, several court decisions (e.g., *PASE vs. Hannon*) ruled that traditional measures of intelligence were not biased if other safeguards were included in the placement process. Another court decision (*Larry P. vs. Riles*) has resulted in the ban on using intelligence tests in making eligibility decisions in some school districts and states. For example, in California, it is illegal to use intelligence tests to assess any student for the purpose of placement in special education.

Bias in intelligence testing is derived from several different sources and is most often expressed with regard to minority students. Considerable research was devoted to bias in the 1970s and 1980s which yielded complex results. First, there are multiple definitions of bias and results vary with definition used. Common definitions of types of bias include: mean differences, item bias, psychometric characteristics of tests, factor structure, atmosphere or examiner bias, and prediction. Second, as discussed in the previous section there has been disproportionate representation of minority groups in special education classes. Although this concern has been addressed in legislation, disporportionate numbers of minority students are *still* being placed into special education classes (Tucker, 1980; Ysseldyke et al.,1992).

Bias has been reported with regard to mean differences. It has been suggested that measured intelligence is a function of various sociocultural variables (Christianson & Livermore, 1970; Jensen & Reynolds, 1983; Mercer, 1977; Palmer, Olivarez, Willson, & Fordyce, 1989). Ethnicity has been found to affect differentially the results of measured intelligence and it has been reported that Anglo populations obtain significantly higher IQ scores than Blacks and Hispanics (Jensen, 1969, 1980; Nichols & Anderson, 1973; Shuey, 1966). In addition, a student's test performance varies as a function of geographic region and socioeconomic level. Tests of ability and achievement have demonstrated a positive relationship with regard to socioeconomic status (Ausubel, 1968; Barona, 1989; Deutsch, 1973; Haddad & Bardos, 1990; Marjoribanks, 1972; Zingale & Smith, 1978) in which children from more affluent backgrounds score significantly higher on intelligence and achievement measures than do children from impoverished backgrounds.

The Wechsler Intelligence Scale for Children - Revised (WISC-R; Wechsler, 1974) continues to be one of the most widely utilized intelligence measures in making decisions regarding special education placement. Research has suggested that sociocultural variables affect performance on the WISC-R. Several studies have confirmed that children of different minority groups perform differentially on the WISC-R (Mercer, 1970; Palmer et al., 1989; Taylor, Ziegler, & Partenio, 1984; Wechsler, 1974). For example, Palmer et al. (1989) reported WISC-R IQ measures evidenced bias across three ethnic groups (African American, Anglo, Hispanic) for both referred and nonreferred samples and concluded that this may lead to overidentification of pupils with a severe discrepancy. Cultural considerations may play a more profound mediating role than we have normally supposed in the determination of measured IQ scale differences in African-American adolescents (Asbury, Knuckle, & Adderly-Kelly, 1984). There is evidence, however, supporting the conclusion that there are no differences on the WISC-R when one studies psychometric properties of the test with different ethnic groups (Gutkin & Reynolds, 1980; Oakland & Feigenbaum, 1979; Reschly, 1978; Ross-Reynolds & Reschly, 1983; Taylor & Ziegler, 1987; Vance, Hankins, & Brown, 1988).

Research has indicated that most intelligence tests are not biased according to conventional definitions of item bias, psychometric characteristics, factor analysis, prediction, and atmosphere bias. For example, on the WISC-R, construct validity has been demonstrated not only for Anglo students but also for African-American students (Gutkin & Reynolds, 1981; Johnston & Bolen, 1984; Reschly, 1978; Sandoval, 1982; Vance & Wallbrown, 1978), and Hispanic students (Dean, 1979, 1980; Gutkin & Reynolds, 1980; Reschly, 1978; Sandoval, 1982). The WISC-R has also demonstrated little or no differences in Anglo versus minority students' prediction of achievement (Mishra, 1983; Naglieri & Hill, 1981; Reynolds & Gutkin, 1980; Oakland, 1983). Although research on construct validity suggests that the WISC-R measures the same basic abilities for minority students as for Anglos, and the predictive validity data indicate that the IQs are equally effective in predicting school success, there are no available data to support the use of the WISC-R for placement decisions. Intellectual assessment has little use in developing education programs or other interventions for students with learning and behavior problems.

Achievement Tests

In addition to intelligence instruments, achievement tests are norm-referenced measures used to make placement decisions. Achievement tests are administered by school psychologists, special education resource teachers, consultant teachers, psychometrists, or regular classroom teachers. Table 9.4 contains a review of the most commonly used achievement tests.

An evaluation of several studies examining the activities performed by school psychologists showed that approximately 55% of the psychologists' time was spent on activities related to assessment (Smith, 1984). The types of information generated by academic assessment are often viewed as being of little use in making instructional decisions about student progress (Smith, 1982). Fuchs and Fuchs (1986) presented the following recommendations for enhancing the assessment of student performance:

- School psychologists must expand their roles to include assessment-related activities that provide information directly relevant to instructional decision making.

- Direct assessment that is idiographic, repetitive, ecologically sensitive, and valid with respect to the curricula should be incorporated.

- Once an instructional plan is developed, school psychologists should help validate it empirically through frequent monitoring of student performance.

- The trial and error nature of this approach encourages school psychologists to assume an inductive, empirical approach to data collection—to adopt a researcher's perspective. (p.322)

Treatment Decisions

Treatment decisions answer questions regarding "what to teach" and "how to teach" (Howell & Morehead, 1987). What to teach involves determining where the student is performing with respect to the hierarchy of instructional objectives. How to teach decisions are based on an assessment of the effectiveness of instruction.

TABLE 9.4. *Commonly Used Measures of Academic Assessment*

Woodcock-Johnson Psycho-Educational Battery—Revised: Tests of Achievement

Authors:	R. W. Woodcock and N. Mather
Publisher:	DLM Teaching Resources (1989)
Purpose:	Individually administered comprehensive measure of academic achievement including reading, mathematics, written language, knowledge, and a quick screening of broad skills achievement.
Target Population:	Persons from 24 months to 90 years of age.
Test Construction:	Good
Reliability:	Good
Validity:	Moderate to good
Standardization:	The normative sample included 6,359 persons from 100 geographically diverse communities stratified across sex, race, Hispanic ethnicity, level of education, and SES according to the U.S. 1980 census.
Administration Time:	Approximately 1 hour
Interpretive Scores:	Standard scores, age and grade equivalents, percentile ranks, and Relative Mastery Index
Limitations:	1. A relatively new instrument; more validity data are needed. 2. Writing Samples subtest is difficult to score.

Wide Range Achievement Test—Revised (WRAT-R)

Authors:	S. Jastak & G. Wilkinson
Publisher:	Jastak Associates, Inc. (1984)
Purpose:	The Wide Range Achievement Test—Revised is an individually administered academic achievement test in reading, math, and spelling.
Target Population:	There are two levels of the test. Level 1 is appropriate for children ages 5 years to 11 years 11 months. Level 2 is given to persons 12 years old through late adulthood.
Test Construction:	Difficult to assess. Items sample a rather narrow portion of content.

Reliability:	The test manual reports high reliability, but these estimates are artificially inflated due to samples consisting of two diverse age groups. Due to the incomplete nature of the test manual, reliability estimates are uninterpretable.
Validity:	Poor
Standardization:	The WRAT-R was normed on 5,600 persons—200 at each age group who were stratified on basis of sex, race, geographical region, urban/nonurban. Socioeconomic status and level of education was not included. The sample of non-White subjects are not defined.
Administration Time:	Approximately 10–25 minutes
Interpretive Scores:	Grade equivalents, standard scores, percentile ranks, stanines, T scores, and normal curve equivalents.
Limitations:	1. This test should only be used as a quick screening device. 2. It samples limited domains of behavior in each area.

Peabody Individual Achievement Test—Revised (PIAT-R)

Author:	F. C. Markwardt, Jr.
Publisher:	American Guidance Service (1989)
Purpose:	The PIAT-R is an individually administered, wide-range screening test consisting of General Information, Reading, Mathematics, Spelling, and Written Expression.
Target Population:	Children ages 5–18 years and grades Kindergarten through 12th grade.
Test Construction:	Good
Reliability:	Good overall reliability for all subject areas and moderate interrater reliability for written expression.
Validity:	Good
Standardization:	The normative sample included 1,738 students who were stratified across geographic region, sex, SES, and ethnicity according to most recent census data.
Administration Time:	Approximately 1 hour

(continued)

Interpretive Scores:	Age and grade equivalents, age and grade-based standard scores, percentile ranks, normal curve equivalents, and stanines. The Written Expression subtest can be converted into grade-based stanines and a developmental scaled score.
Limitations:	1. Interpret written expression with caution due to moderate reliability. 2. When administering the test the examiner uses the score obtained on previous test to determine starting point on next subtest. This procedure is not always accurate.

Woodcock Reading Mastery Tests—Revised

Author:	R. W. Woodcock Contributing authors: N. Mather and E. K. Barnes
Publisher:	American Guidance Service (1987)
Purpose:	Individually administered battery which measures reading achievement (Word Comprehension, Word Identification, Word Attack, Passage Comprehension), readiness (Visual-Auditory Learning, Letter Identification), and a supplementary checklist.
Target Population:	Appropriate for persons from Kindergarten to seniors in college. Norms are available for adults up to age 75 and older.
Test Construction:	Good
Reliability:	Good
Validity:	Moderate to Good
Standardization:	Normative data were gathered from 6,089 subjects in 60 geographically diverse U.S. communities using a stratified sample which controlled for sex, census region, community size, race, SES, and ethnicity according to the 1980 U.S. census reports. Subsets of the norming sample representing populations with very low percentages of occurrence in the U.S. were oversampled to ensure accurate contributions to the total norms (e.g., Asian Pacifics).

Administration Time:	Approximately 1 hour
Interpretive Scores:	Grade and age equivalents, relative performance index, percentile ranks, standard scores, and instructional range.
Limitations:	1. Scoring is time consuming 2. Validity measures with instruments other than tests developed by Woodcock are not reported in the test manual.

KeyMath—Revised

Author:	A. J. Connolly
Publisher:	American Guidance Service (1988)
Purpose:	Individually administered diagnostic test that assesses three areas of mathematical knowledge: basic concepts, operations, applications. The KeyMath-R is a criterion-referenced test with norms provided for further interpretation.
Target Population:	Children in grades Kindergarten through 9th grade.
Test Construction:	Good
Reliability:	Good
Validity:	Adequate
Standardization:	Normative sample contained 200 children at each grade level for Kindergarten through 8th grade and 50 children in 9th grade. Distributed proportionately across geographic region, sex, SES, and race according to 1985 census data.
Administration Time:	Approximately 35–50 minutes
Interpretive Scores:	Standard and scaled scores, percentile ranks, age and grade equivalents, stanines, and normal curve equivalents.
Limitations:	1. Administration time may be lengthy in higher grades. 2. Small normative sample size for grade 9. 3. Some subtests contain primarily either high or low range of item difficulty thereby lacking a moderate range of difficulty.

(continued)

Peabody Picture Vocabulary Test—Revised (PPVT-R)

Authors:	L. Dunn & L. Dunn
Publisher:	American Guidance Service (1981)
Purpose:	PPVT-R is reported by authors to measure receptive vocabulary of standard American English.
Target Population:	The test is appropriate for ages 2 years 6 months into adulthood (norms through 40 years).
Test Construction:	Most technically adequate of picture vocabulary tests.
Reliability:	Moderate
Validity:	Poor to moderate, no validity data are reported in test manual.
Standardization:	This test was normed on 4,200 children and 828 adults who were stratified across geographic region, race, sex, community size, and parental occupation according to the 1970 census.
Administration Time:	Approximately 10–20 minutes
Interpretive Scores:	Standard score equivalents, percentile ranks, stanines, and age equivalents.
Limitation:	1. Some items are culturally biased. 2. Use this instrument only as a screening measure.

What to Teach?

This question has a straightforward answer—the curriculum. Determining what to teach requires a comparison of performance to the curriculum objectives. What to teach decisions should be based on measures of student *performance*. Performance measures sample a student's skills at a given point in time. Performance measures examine a student's relative standing with regard to the curriculum objectives. A student's position in the array of curriculum objectives must be assessed in order to determine exactly where instruction will begin. This evaluation is conducted in consideration of two factors: (1) the student's current level of performance and (2) the curriculum. Reschly et al. (1988 a, b) highlighted the need for assessment that is directly useful in designing instruction, evaluating the effectiveness of interventions, and monitoring student performance. Curriculum-based assessment and task analysis techniques meet these requirements (Shinn, Rosenfield, & Knutson, 1989).

Curriculum-Based Models

Curriculum-based assessment (CBA) is defined as any measurement procedure that employs "direct observation and recording of a student's performance in the local curriculum as a basis for gathering information to make instructional decisions" (Deno, 1987, p. 41). Curriculum-based monitoring is an approach to analyzing student performance over time. It employs a means for analyzing performance using systematic procedures with brief measures of academic performance. Direct and frequent assessment procedures appear to be effective, as well as meeting the calls for reform in educational evaluation.

Task-Analytic Model

Task analysis provides a structure for determining "what to teach." In the task-analytic model, skills are viewed as a combination of subskills and strategies (Howell, 1983). Task analysis is the process of breaking down a skill into its components (subskills and strategies). When a student does not demonstrate a necessary skill, that skill is task-analyzed and the student's performance on the necessary subskills and strategies is assessed. If a student has not mastered the requisite subskills and/or strategies, they become instructional objectives.

Sensitivity of Testing

Central to each of the issues raised above regarding instructional decision making is the idea that whatever tests and measures are being employed, they must be sensitive to instructional gain—the student's performance must be measurable with the test that is chosen. Measures employed to assess academic performance must be sensitive to changes in behavior and must be capable of frequent repetition (Shapiro & Lentz, 1985). Standardized achievement tests are not designed to be used in this manner. Shapiro and Lentz presented several assumptions that underlie the development of a methodology for the assessment of academic problems.

1. Assessment must reflect an evaluation of the behavior in the natural environment.
2. Assessment should be idiographic rather than nomothetic.
3. What is taught should be what is tested.

4. Strong links must be present between the results of assessment and behaviors targeted for intervention.

5. The assessment methods must be capable of providing ongoing evaluation.

6. Measures chosen for use in assessment must be empirically validated.

7. Examination of both performance and skill deficits must be included.

Assessment must involve direct observation of students' academic behavior, utilize work samples produced in the classroom setting, provide operational definitions of the goals of the intervention, be based on empirical research, and examine environmental variables, according to Shapiro and Lentz (p. 3).

IF THIS APPROACH WORKS

If traditional methods of assessment (i.e., norm-referenced tests) are fraught with the problems detailed above, why don't we stop using them? Overton (1992) proposed the following factors of ineffective assessment:

N B.
↓

1. Using instruments in the assessment process solely because those instruments are stipulated by school administrators.

2. Regularly using instruments for purposes other than those for which they have been validated.

3. Taking the recommended use at face value.

4. Using the quickest instruments available even though those instruments may not assess desired areas of concern.

5. Using currently "popular" instruments for assessment.

6. Failure of the examiner to document behaviors of the examinee during assessment that may be of diagnostic value.

7. Failure of the examiner to adhere to standardized administration rules including failure to follow starting rules, failure to follow basal and ceiling rules, and omission of actual incorrect responses on the protocol that could aid in error analysis and diagnosis.

8. Various scoring errors following test administration that may include simple counting and subtraction errors.

9. Ineffective interpretation of assessment results for educational program use. (pp. vii–viii)

Several researchers have examined reasons why more specific methods of assessment are not widely recognized in the classroom. Wesson, King, and Deno (1982) surveyed 136 teachers of students with learning disabilities and noted that 82% had received instruction on these approaches. Over 46%, however, reported that they do not use these procedures in the classroom. Time constraints are frequently cited as the reason that data-based techniques are not widely used, although Wesson and colleagues found teachers who use data-based decision-making procedures report that only 10% of their time is taken up by these procedures. DiGangi (1990) examined the data-based decision-making skills of teachers across level of expertise. He found that less than 12% reported actually employing procedures such as continuous monitoring of student performance in the classroom. Eighty-six percent of the teachers reported that they (1) did not have time given the constraints of the classroom and (2) this type of activity was not directly supported by the building-level administration.

Several studies have examined the relationships between content covered in published instructional programs and student performance on standardized tests. Jenkins and Pany (1978) investigated differences between objectives covered in published reading series and scores on standardized reading achievement tests and found significant differences in the match between published instructional programs and standardized tests. Jenkins, Deno, and Mirkin (1979) examined differential scores of reading measures on students when they were exposed to different tests. A student who mastered 1st-grade Reading 360 vocabulary would obtain a SORT grade equivalent of 1.4. If the same student had received instruction in Keys to Reading, he or she would receive a score of 2.2. A beginning 3rd-grade student who had been taught in the Keys to Reading series would score at 50% or more below grade level on the MAT subtests, but at or above grade level on the PIAT, SORT, and WRAT, respectively.

Shapiro and Derr (1987) examined five basal reading series and four achievement tests. They found significant differences between the curriculum objectives and the tests. Overlap between the curricula and the basal reading series decreased markedly with successive grade levels, with a dramatic drop after 3rd grade.

Nitko (1989) identified several undesirable consequences of using tests that are not clearly linked to instruction:

a. teachers and students might be inappropriately informed about students' learning progress and learning difficulties;

b. students' motivation for learning could be reduced;

c. critical decisions about students (awarding diplomas) might be made unfairly;

d. the effectiveness of instruction may be evaluated incorrectly. (p. 447)

Assessment in the Content Areas

Knowledge of the curriculum is an important factor in conducting assessment for effective instruction. An often overlooked aspect of curriculum-based evaluation is the curriculum. "Curriculum" refers to a prespecified set of learning outcomes resulting from instruction (Johnson, 1967). It is composed of those objectives that either lead to goals that have been determined to be important or are, in and of themselves, valued objectives.

Ysseldyke (1987) conducted an extensive review of the literature, concluding that the current classification systems do not work—and that there are reasonable alternatives. He contrasted the "state of the art" (what we know) with the state of practice (what we do). Reynolds (1984) urged a move from test-based classification and labeling toward classification that focuses on progress in the curriculum and is oriented to problems of instruction. Reynolds and Larkin (1987) identified several environmental characteristics predicting educational effects. Among those related directly to assessment considerations are:

- *Curricula linking instruction to current academic status*: A student performs at a higher level when instruction is based on objective assessment of his or her current academic status and when there is continuity in curriculum placement as the student moves through grade levels.

- *Curricula providing frequent checkpoints of progress*: Students exhibit higher achievement through curricula that provide frequent checks on learning for the purposes of feedback, providing additional instruction, and planning for next steps through a sequence of skills.

N . B

- *Curricula that focus on mastery of critical basic skills*: Effective curricula tend to focus on basic academic skills that assure the mastery of prerequisite skills before introducing new skills/concepts.

How to Teach

How to teach decisions are based on progress data. Instructional decisions must be linked to students' performance in the curriculum (placement) and progress through the curriculum (instruction). Several measures of student performance may be compared over time to indicate the extent of the student's progress in the curriculum. How to teach decisions are then based on assessment of the rate of student progress through the curriculum. The use of curriculum-based or criterion-referenced measures has clear implications for instructional delivery. Fuchs, Fuchs, and Hamlett (1989) investigated the use of curriculum-based measurement to enhance instructional reading programs. When teachers collected curriculum-based measurement (CBM) data and used that data to evaluate the effectiveness of their programs, and to make instructional decisions, student achievement was enhanced.

Daily measurement of student performance. Central to the assumptions of curriculum-based measures is the direct and daily measurement of student performance. *Direct* refers to the measurement of exactly what is being taught.

For example, if the student is being taught vowel teams, the assessment device would be composed of vowel teams. The methodology involved with curriculum-based approaches has been questioned. Several criticisms have centered on the lack of items represented in curriculum-based measures. As noted by Howell and DiGangi (1988), in a 1-minute sample at the 2nd-grade computation level, CBE provides the opportunity for a student to respond to 20 items that are directly relevant to instruction the student is receiving. On the WJ-R, the same student would be exposed to only 2 items that are instructionally relevant. This indicated that for any given 2nd-grade student 95% of the skills on the WJ-R are *not* instructionally relevant (the student has not been taught the objectives—and is not expected to know them yet). A typical psychoeducational evaluation report details information regarding placement and classification. The Case Example outlines an approach for making instructional decisions. In addition to requisite norm-referenced testing information, specific examples of curriculum-based assessment procedures for the areas of mathematics, reading, and written language are provided.

Psychoeducational Report

Andy
Birthdate: 5-11-79
Age: 11 years, 9 months

Reason for Referral

Andy was referred for a 3-year psychoeducational reevaluation in accordance with state and federal guidelines for continuing services in special education. A reevaluation is required to determine appropriateness and future educational needs of Andy's program.

Background Information

Additional information may be obtained from Andy's psychological file.

Health History: Information was supplied by Andy's mother by completing a Developmental Checklist. Andy's mother reported that she smoked cigarettes during pregnancy. Andy's reported birth and neonatal history were unremarkable, and developmental milestones were reached within normal limits. Andy's mother noted that Andy was a restless sleeper. Current school health records indicate that he is in good health.

Vision and Hearing: According to the school nurse, Andy passed a vision and hearing screening on 10-8-90.

Social History

According to Andy's classroom teacher, Mrs. Smith, Andy is well liked by other students and maintains good adult relationships. He exhibits excellent classroom behavior. Mrs Smith stated that lately he has not completed homework. Andy's playground behavior is reported to be appropriate when he is with a "good" peer group.

Educational History: Andy attended Kindergarten at Peaks School where he was evaluated (October, 1984) and placed in a Level 1 self-contained EMH classroom (January, 1985) with adaptive PE and speech services. During the 1987–1988 school year Andy was moved to a Level 2 self-contained EMH classroom. In February, 1988, Andy was reevaluated and qualified as a Learning Disabled student. He has received special education services in oral and written expression, reading comprehension, basic reading skills, and math calculation and reasoning with continued speech services under the classification of Learning Disabled since March, 1988.

Andy has consistently received superior and above average grades in his LD classes and average grades in Science, Social Studies, and Health.

Andy's school attendance has been excellent. This year he has been absent a total of 5 days. Causes other than educational, cultural, or environmental disadvantage are judged to be primary reasons for Andy's school difficulties.

Assessment Procedures

Records Review

Behavioral Observations

Woodcock-Johnson Psycho-Educational Battery, Tests of Achievement—Revised (WJ-R)

Beery Developmental Test of Visual-Motor Integration (VMI)

Wechsler Intelligence Scale for Children - Revised (WISC-R)

Assessment Results

Behavior During Testing: Andy was quiet, polite, and cooperative during all testing sessions. Rapport was easily established. Andy attempted all verbal and nonverbal tasks and did not display frustration when the task became more difficult. He appeared to be slow to respond on several subtest items. He responded appropriately to verbal praise for his efforts. The testing environment was well lighted and free from distraction. It is believed that these results are a valid estimate of Andy's current functioning.

Psychometric Results: Intellectual assessment indicates that Andy is functioning in the borderline range of intellectual ability. On the WISC-R, Andy achieved a Verbal Scale IQ of 75 (5th percentile), a Performance Scale IQ of 86 (18th percentile), and a Full Scale IQ of 79 (8th percentile). On the Verbal subtests, he demonstrated significant weaknesses on tasks that sampled his (a) knowledge of general information and (b) ability to define specific words, possibly due to his poor language ability. Andy's performance on the nonverbal subtests was more consistent. He displayed a significant strength on the Mazes subtest.

Visual-motor development was measured using the Developmental Test of Visual Motor Integration. Andy scored in the 29th percentile, with an age equivalent of 9 years 11 months.

Academically, on the WJ-R Tests of Achievement administered by his LD teacher, on 1-24-91, Andy scored at his anticipated level in reading (SS = 88; 21st percentile), mathematics (SS = 86; 18th percentile), and written language (SS = 80; 9th percentile). These results are higher than Andy's previous academic assessment (2-16-88) on the WJ-R Tests of Achievement (Reading: SS = 75; Math: SS = 74; Written Language: SS = 72). Andy's higher achievement scores are judged to be a result of special education services.

A speech and language progress report (January, 1991) by Andy's speech and language pathologist indicates that Andy has continued to work multiple meanings. She has introduced homophones which he can use in sentences with 85% accuracy. Andy is reported to be capable of identifying and using irregular plural nouns with 95% accuracy when shown a picture. She recommends continued speech services.

Summary

Andy is an 11-year-old 5th-grader who was reevaluated as part of his continuing services in special education. Intellectual assessment revealed that Andy is functioning within the borderline range of intelligence. Academically, Andy is achieving within his expected range in reading and math and below his anticipated level in written expression. It was agreed upon by the multidisciplinary evaluation team that Andy continues to qualify for special education as a learning disabled student.

Eligibility

Andy continues to qualify for special education and related services as a learning disabled student in the areas of: oral and written expression, basic reading skills, reading comprehension, and math calculation and reasoning. It was the opinion of the multidisciplinary evaluation team that continued resource assistance is necessary for Andy to maintain and make further gains academically. His educational difficulties cannot be remediated without special education services.

Recommendations

1. Current results of the evaluation should be presented to the multidisciplinary team to assist in designing an appropriate educational program for Andy.

2. It is recommended that Andy continue to receive special education services to improve oral and written expression, math, and reading skills.

3. It is recommended that Andy continue to receive speech and language therapy.

4. The following teaching strategies are recommended: (a) allow additional time for Andy to complete tasks, (b) encourage Andy to use newly learned words when speaking, (c) continue to work on multiple word meanings, (d) use visual cues, (e) present visual cues and in a simple format, and (f) encourage family activities to help expand Andy's repertoire of general information.

5. To determine "what to teach" and "how to teach," student performance should be assessed and monitored using the curriculum-based evaluation techniques detailed below.

Curriculum-Based Evaluation Techniques

Math

Assessment of math through 2-minute administrations

1. Establish a criterion for acceptable performance.

2. Select math problems that sample a broad range of computation and problem-solving objectives. Select items that are taught at the student's current grade level in which the student has received instruction. Place the sheets in front of the student.

3. Give the student the following instructions: "The sheets in front of you are math facts and problems. I want you to work as quickly and carefully as you can. If you cannot answer a problem, skip it and go on to the next problem. Keep working until I tell you to stop. Please begin."

4. Use a stopwatch to time the 2-minute interval. At the end of 2 minutes, tell the student to stop working.

5. *Scoring*: count the number of problems and digits correct.

6. Develop a list of assumed causes.

7. Verify assumed causes by using specific-level testing. For example, if you wanted to check accuracy and fluency on basic facts:

a. construct a test sampling basic facts

b. tell the student to answer each question carefully

c. score responses and summarize error patterns.

Reading

Assessment of reading through 1-minute passage reading.

1. Establish a criterion for acceptable performance.

2. Use passages of approximately 250 words from tests the student is currently using in the classroom. Choose a passage that is closest to the student's reading level. Place one copy of the passage in front of the student and use a separate copy to record student errors.

3. Give the student the following instructions: "I want you to read this out loud. Try to read each word. Read it as quickly and carefully as you can. If you come to a word that you do not know, I will tell it to you. Be sure to do your best reading. Please begin."

4. Use a stopwatch to record the 1-minute time interval.

5. Mark all errors on the examiner copy of the passage. Place a slash through words that are read incorrectly. If a student struggles with a word for 3 seconds, tell the student the word and mark it incorrect. Place a bracket after the last word read in the interval and allow the student to complete the passage.

6. *Scoring*: Count the total number of words read, number of words read correctly, and the number of errors during the 1-minute time interval.

7. Develop a list of assumed causes. For example, a content checklist can be constructed where the examiner would generate a list of errors and then mark the content category it falls under (e.g., consonant blends).

8. Verify assumed causes by using specific-level testing. For example, you might check for the purpose for reading.

   a. Tell student you want to find out how long it takes to read the passage correctly.

   b. Emphasize the importance of accuracy.

   c. Note if accuracy improves.

Written Language

Assessment of written expression through 3-minute administrations.

1. Establish a criterion for acceptable performance.

2. Select an appropriate story starter.

3. Give the student the following instructions: "You are going to write a story. I will read a sentence to you and I would like you to write a story about what happens next. You will have 1 minute to think about the story and 3 minutes to write the story. Do your best work. If you don't know how to spell a word you should guess how to spell it. For the next minute think about. . ." (story starter).

4. After 1 minute tell the student to begin writing. At the end of 3 minutes tell the student to stop working.

5. *Scoring*: Count the total number of words written, correct writing sequence, words spelled correctly, and total letters written.

6. Develop a list of assumed causes.

7. Verify assumed causes by using specific-level testing. For example, Videen, Dino, and Marston (1982) developed a procedure to measure writing fluency:

   a. Obtain samples of students' writing.

   b. Score the samples using the following criteria: (a) appropriate beginning word, (b) each subsequent word spelled and sequenced correctly, and (c) appropriate ending word.

   c. Summarize information.

   d. Compare information to established performance criteria by comparing scores with classmates who are judged to be fluent writers.

CONCLUSION

Identifying "best practices" in assessment involves consideration of many conflicting theoretical approaches. These differing views toward assessment reflect the precarious nature of our understanding of handicapping conditions.

Reschly (1987) presented several paradoxes apparent in the literature on education of students with learning problems:

- Mildly handicapped students, particularly LD, are actually any students that someone wishes to diagnose as such. Others claim that vast differences separate students classified as LD from classroom averages.

- Regular educators suggest less mainstreaming because of insufficient time to meet the needs of mildly handicapped learners. The Regular Education Initiate presents total mainstreaming for mildly handicapped students.

- Assessment for designing and monitoring instruction is universally endorsed, but commonly used assessment procedures with mildly handicapped students are sharply disputed. Some claim that traditional methods are irrelevant, unreliable, and invalid. Others claim that the newer direct measures are excessively narrow, limited, and superficial.

- Distinctions between categories (LD, mild or educable mental retardation, SED) are viewed as essential, and also irrelevant.   xx

- Matching instructional methods to a student's strengths is viewed as essential and worthless. (pp. 36-37)   xx

This chapter examined various factors in assessment for effective instruction. Regardless of theoretical perspective, research has demonstrated the merit of a direct approach to evaluation. "Best practices" in assessment will result from the elimination of testing procedures that:

- cover content that is not in the curriculum;

- omit content that is in the curriculum;

- require the student to respond under conditions that are not equivalent to the conditions of instruction;

- sample a segment of material that differs in size or complexity from the segment a teacher is attempting to teach;

- reference students' performance on a standardization group that receives different instruction under different circumstances.

Attempts to distinguish between classification and treatment decisions are relatively unproductive. Classification of students carries with it the implication that the assigned category has some utility (Robbins, 1966).   N.B. Effective assessment will carefully examine the type(s) of decisions required within the context of the intended intervention. As Heller, Holtzman, and Messick put it, "the purpose of the entire process—from referral for assessment to eventual placement in special education—is to improve instruction for children" (1982, pp. x-xi). From this perspective, all educational decision making should be based on *assessment for effective instruction.*

The authors recognize the contribution of Jane Lea Chipman, who assisted in the preparation of the manuscript and compilation of the case example.
Recommended evaluation techniques were adapted from Howell & Morehead (1987).

RECOMMENDED READING

Howell, K. W., & Morehead, M. K. (1987). *Curriculum-based evaluation for special and remedial education.* Columbus, OH: Charles E. Merrill.

Salvia, J., & Hughes, C. (1990). *Curriculum-based assessment: Testing what is taught.* New York: Macmillan.

Salvia, J., & Ysseldyke, J. E. (1991). *Assessment* (5th ed.). Boston, MA: Houghton Mifflin.

Shapiro, E. S. (1989). *Academic skills problems: Direct assessment and intervention.* New York: Guilford.

Shinn, M. R. (Ed.). (1989). *Curriculum-based measurement: Assessing special children.* New York: Guilford.

Tindall, G. A., & Marston, D. B. (1990). *Classroom-based assessment.* Columbus, OH: Charles E. Merrill.

REFERENCES

Algozzine, B., Mercer, C., & Countermine, T. (1977). Labeling exceptional children: An analysis of expectations. *Exceptional Children, 44,* 131-132.

Argulewicz, E. N., & Sanchez, D. (1983). The special education evaluation process as a moderator of false positives. *Exceptional Children, 49,* 452-454.

Asbury, C. A., Knuckle, E. P., & Adderly-Kelly, B. (1984). Effectiveness of selected neuropsychological and sociocultural measures for predicting WISC-R discrepancy group membership. *Educational and Psychological Research, 7,* 47-58.

Ausubel, D. P. (1968). *Educational psychology: A comparative view.* New York: Holt, Rinehart, & Winston.

Ayres, L. P. (1909). *Laggards in our schools.* New York: Russell Sage Foundation.

Barona, A. (1989). Differential effects of WISC-R factors on special education eligibility for three ethnic groups. *Journal of Psychoeducational Assessment, 7,* 31-38.

Binet, A., & Simon, T. (1916). *The development of intelligence in children* (E. S. Kit, Trans.). Baltimore: Williams & Wilkins.

Brophy, J. E., & Good, T. L. (1970). Teachers' communication of differential expectations for children's classroom performance. *Journal of Educational Psychology, 61,* 365-374.

Campbell, N. R. (1940). *Final report, Committee of the British Association of Advancement of Science on the problem of measurement.* London: British Association of Advancement of Science.

Christianson, T., & Livermore, G. (1970). A comparison of Anglo-American and Spanish-American children on the WISC-R. *Journal of Social Psychology, 81,* 9-14.

Deno, S. L. (1987). Curriculum-based measurement. *Teaching Exceptional Children, 20,* 41.

Deutsch, C. P. (1973). Social class and child development. In B. M. Caldwell & H. N. Ricciuti (Eds.), *Review of child development research* (Vol. 3, pp. 57-86). Chicago: University of Chicago.

Dean, R. S. (1979). Distinguished patterns of Mexican-American children on the WISC-R. *Journal of Clinical Psychology, 35,* 790-794.

Dean, R. S. (1980). Factor structure of the WISC-R with Anglos and Mexican-Americans. *Journal of School Psychology, 18,* 234-239.

DiGangi, S. A. (1990). *Visual analysis of data: The effect of applied behavior analysis training on teacher decision making.* Unpublished doctoral dissertation, Arizona State University, Tempe, AZ.

Dunn, L. M. (1973). Children with moderate and severe general learning disabilities. In L. M. Dunn (Ed.), *Exceptional children in the schools* (2nd ed.). New York: Holt, Rinehart, & Winston.

Federal Register. (1977). Regulations implementing Education for All Handicapped Children Act of 1975 (PL 94-142), *42,* 42474-42518.

Fuchs, L. S., & Fuchs, D. (1986). Linking assessment to instructional intervention: An overview. *School Psychology Review, 15,* 318-323.

Fuchs, L. S., Fuchs, D., & Hamlett, C. l. (1989). Effects of instrumental uses of curriculum-based measurement to enhance instructional programs. *Remedial and Special Education, 10,* 43-52.

Gelb, S. A., & Mizokawa, D. T. (1986). Special education and social structure: The commonality of "Exceptionality." *American Educational Research Journal, 23,* 543-557.

Gutkin, T. B., & Reynolds, C. R. (1980). Factorial similarity of the WISC-R for Anglos and Chicanos referred for psychological services. *Journal of School Psychology, 18,* 34-39.

Gutkin, T. B., & Reynolds, C. R. (1981). Factorial similarity of the WISC-R for white and black children from the standardization sample. *Journal of Educational Psychology, 73,* 227-231.

Haddad, F. A., & Bardos, A. N. (1990). Differential effects of socioeconomic status and gender on the Matrix Analogies Test-Expanded and the Wide Range Achievement Test-Revised with above-average elementary school students. *Journal of Psychoeducational Assessment, 8,* 133-138.

Hall, E. (1970). The politics of special education. In *Inequality in education* (pp. 17-22). Cambridge, MA: Harvard Center for Law and Education.

Hallahan, D. P., Keller, C. E., & Ball, D. W. (1986). A comparison of prevalence rate variability from state to state for each of the categories of special education. *Remedial and Special Education, 7(2),* 8-14.

Heller, K. A., Holtzman, W., & Messick, S. (1982). *Placing children in special education: A strategy for equity.* Washington, DC: National Academy Press.

Howell, K. W. (1983). Task analysis and the characteristics of tasks. *Journal of Special Education Technology, 6,* 5-14.

Howell, K. W., & DiGangi, S. A. (1988). Additional comments on Lombard. *NASP Communique, 16,* 4.

Howell, K. W., & Morehead, M. K. (1987). *Curriculum-based evaluation for special and remedial education.* Columbus, OH: Charles E. Merrill.

Huebner, E. S. (1987). Teachers' special education decisions: Does test information make a difference? *Journal of Educational Research, 80,* 202-205.

Jenkins, J. R., Deno, S. L., & Mirkin, P. K. (1979). Measuring pupil progress toward the least restrictive alternative. *Learning Disability Quarterly, 2,* 81-91.

Jenkins, J., & Pany, D. (1978). Standardized achievement tests: How useful for special education? *Exceptional Children, 44,* 448-453.

Jensen, A. R. (1969). How much can we boost IQ and scholastic achievement? *Harvard Educational Review, 39,* 1-123.

Jensen, A. R. (1980). *Bias in mental testing.* New York: Free Press.

Jensen, A. R., & Reynolds, C. R. (1983). Sex differences on the WISC-R. *Personality and Individual Differences, 4,* 223-226.

Johnson, M. (1967). Definitions and models in curriculum theory. *Educational Theory, 7,* 127-140.

Johnston, W. T., & Bolen, L. M. (1984). A comparison of the factor structure of the WISC-R for blacks and whites. *Psychology in the Schools, 21,* 42-44.

Larry P. vs. Wilson Riles et al. (1974). United States District Court, Northern District of California, Case No. C-71-22270 RFP.

Linquist, E. F. (Ed.). (1951). *Educational measurement.* Washington, DC: American Council on Education.

Marjoribanks, K. (1972). Environment, social class, and mental abilities. *Journal of Educational Psychology, 63,* 103-109.

Mercer, J. R. (1970). The ecology of mental retardation. *Proceedings of the first Annual Spring conference of the Institute for the Study of Mental Retardation* (pp. 55-74). Ann Arbor, MI: ISMR.

Mercer, J. R. (1971). Sociocultural factors in labeling mental retardates. *Peabody Journal of Education, 48,* 188-203.

Mercer, J. R. (1977). The struggle of children's rights: Critical juncture for school psychology. *School Psychology Digest, 6,* 4-19.

Mishra, S. P. (1983). Validity of WISC-R IQs and factor scores in predicting achievement for Mexican-American children. *Psychology in the Schools, 20,* 442-444.

Naglieri, J. A., & Hill, D. S. (1981). Comparison of WISC-R and K-ABC regression lines for academic prediction with black and white children. *Journal of Child Clinical Psychology, 15,* 352-355.

Nichols, P. L., & Anderson, V. E. (1973). Intellectual performance, race, and socioeconomic status. *Social Biology, 20,* 367-374.

Nitko, A. J. (1989). Designing tests that are integrated with instruction. In R. Linn (Ed.), *Educational measurement* (3rd ed., pp. 447-474). New York: Collier Macmillan.

Oakland, T. (1983). Concurrent and predictive validity estimates for the WISC-R IQs and ELPs by racial-ethnic and SES groups. *School Psychology Review, 12,* 57-61.

Oakland, T., & Feigenbaum, D. (1979). Multiple sources of test bias on the WISC-R and the Bender Gestalt Test. *Journal of Consulting and Clinical Psychology, 46,* 417-422

Ortiz, A. A., & Yates, J. R. (1983). Incidence of exceptionality among Hispanics: Implications for manpower planning. *NABE Journal, 7,* 41-54.

Overton, T. (1992) *Assessment in special education: An applied approach.* New York: Macmillan.

Palmer, D. J., Olivarez, A., Wilson, V. L., & Fordyce, T. (1989). Ethnicity and language dominance—Influence on the prediction of achievement based on intelligence test scores in nonreferred and referred samples. *Learning Disability Quarterly, 12,* 261-274.

Parents in Action on Special Education (PASE) vs. Hannon. 506 F. Suppl. 831 (N. D. Ill. 1980).

Reschly, D. (1978). WISC-R and factor structures among Anglos, Blacks, Chicanos, and Native American Papagos. *Journal of Consulting and Clinical Psychology, 46,* 417-422

Reschly, D. J. (1987). Learning characteristics of mildly handicapped students: Implications for classification, placement, and programming. In M. C. Wang, M. C. Reynolds, & H. J. Walberg (Eds.), *Handbook of special education research and practice* (pp. 35-58). New York: Pergamon.

Reschly, D. J., Kicklighter, R. H., & McKee, P. (1988a). Recent placement litigation Part II, minority EMR overrepresentation: Comparison of Larry P. (1979, 1984, 1986) with Marshall (1984, 1985), and S-1 and implications for future practices. *School Psychology Review, 17,* 37-48.

Reschly, D. J., Kicklighter, R. H., & McKee, P. (1988b). Recent placement litigation Part III: Analysis of differences in Larry P. Marshall, and S-1 and implications for future practices. *School Psychology Review, 17,* 37-48.

Reynolds, C. R., & Gutkin, T. B. (1980). Stability of the WISC-R factor structure across sex at two age levels. *Journal of Clinical Psychology, 36,* 775-777.

Reynolds, M. C. (1984). Classification of students with handicaps. *Review of Research in Education, 2,* 63-92.

Reynolds, M. C., & Larkin, K. C. (1987). Noncategorical special education: Models for research and practice. In M. C. Wang, M. C. Reynolds, & H. J. Walberg (Eds.), *Handbook of special education research and practice* (pp. 331-356). New York: Pergamon.

Robbins, L. L. (1966). An historical review of classification of behavior disorders and current perspective. In L. D. Eron (Ed.), *The classification of behavior disorders* (pp. 1-37). Chicago: Aldine.

Ross-Reynolds, J., & Reschly, D. J. (1983). An investigation of item bias on the WISC-R with four sociocultural groups. *Journal of Consulting and Clinical Psychology, 51,* 144-146.

Sandoval, J. (1982). The WISC-R factorial validity for minority groups and Spearman's hypothesis. *Journal of School Psychology, 20,* 198-204.

Shapiro, E. S., & Derr, T. F. (1987). An examination of the overlap between reading curricula and standardized achievement tests. *The Journal of Special Education, 21,* 59-67.

Shapiro, E. S., & Lentz, Jr., F. E. (1985). Assessing academic behavior: A behavioral approach. *School Psychology Review, 14,* 325-338.

Shinn, M. R., Rosenfield, S., & Knutson, N. (1989). Curriculum-based assessment: A comparison of models. *School Psychology Review, 18,* 299-315.

Shinn, M. R., Tindal, G. A., & Spira, D. A. (1987). Special education referrals as an index of teacher tolerance: Are teachers imperfect tests? *Exceptional Children, 54,* 32-40

Shuey, A. M. (1966). *The testing of Negro intelligence* (2nd ed.) New York: Social Science.

Smith, D. (1984). Actual and desired professional activities of school psychologists. *Professional Psychology: Research and Practice, 15,* 798-810

Smith, M. L. (1982). *How educators decide who is learning disabled: Challenge to psychology and public policy in the schools.* Springfield, IL: Charles C. Thomas.

Swanson, H. L., & Watson, B. I. (1982). *Educational and psychological assessment of exceptional children.* St. Louis, MO: C. V. Mosby.

Taylor, R. L., & Ziegler, E. W. (1987). Comparison of the first principal factor on the WISC-R across ethnic groups. *Educational and Psychological Measurement, 47,* 691-694.

Taylor, R. L., Ziegler, E. W., & Partenio, I. (1984). An investigation of WISC-R verbal-performance differences as a function of ethnic status. *Psychology in the Schools, 21,* 437-441.

Tucker, J. A. (1980). Ethnic proportions in classes for the learning disabled: Issues in nonbiased assessment. *Journal of Special Education, 14,* 93-105.

Vance, B., Hankins, N., & Brown, W. (1988). Ethnic and sex differences on the Test of Nonverbal Intelligence, Quick Test of Intelligence, and Wechsler Intelligence Scale for Children-Revised. *Journal of Clinical Psychology, 44,* 261-265.

Vance, H. B., & Wallbrown, F. H. (1978). The structure of intelligence for black children. *Psychological Record, 28,* 31-39.

Videen, J., Deno, S., & Marston, D. (1982). *Correct word sequences: A valid indicator of proficiency in written expression.* (Research Rep. No. 84). Minneapolis: University of Minnesota, Institute for Research on Learning Disabilities.

Wechsler, D. (1974). *Wechsler Intelligence Scale for Children - Revised.* New York: The Psychological Corporation.

Wesson, C. L., King, R. P., & Deno, S. L. (1982). Direct and frequent measurement of student performance: If it's good for us, why don't we do it? *Learning Disability Quarterly, 7,* 45-48.

Ysseldyke, J. E. (1987). Classification of handicapped students. In M. C. Wang, M. C. Reynolds, & H. J. Walberg (Eds.), *Handbook of special education research and practice: Vol. 1. Learner characteristics and adaptive education* (pp. 253-271). New York: Pergamon.

Ysseldyke, J. E., & Algozzine, B. (1981). Diagnostic classification decisions as a function of referral information. *Journal of Special Education, 15,* 429-435.

Ysseldyke, J. E., & Algozzine, B. (1982). Bias among professionals who erroneously declare students eligible for special services. *Journal of Experimental Education, 50,* 223-228.

Ysseldyke, J. E., & Algozzine, B. (1990). *Introduction to special education* (2nd ed.). Boston: Houghton Mifflin.
Ysseldyke, J. E., & Algozzine, B. (1992). *Critical issues in special education* (2nd ed.). Boston: Houghton Mifflin.
Zingale, S. A., & Smith, M. (1978). WISC-R patterns for learning disabled children at three SES levels. *Psychology in the Schools, 15,* 199-204.
Zucker, S. H., & Pietro, A. G. (1977). Ethnicity and teacher bias in educational decisions. *Instructional Psychology, 4* (3), 2-5.

10 ASSESSMENT OF SOCIAL SKILLS AND PEER RELATIONS

Kenneth W. Merrell

Social competence is a complex, multidimensional construct that consists of a variety of behavioral and cognitive variables, as well as different aspects of emotional adjustment, that are useful and necessary in developing adequate social relations and obtaining desirable social outcomes. Gresham (1986) conceptualized the domain of social competence as comprising the following three subdomains: (a) *adaptive behavior*, (b) *social skills*, and (c) *peer acceptance*.

A widely accepted definition of adaptive behavior is that it is "the effectiveness or degree with which the individual meets the standards of personal independence and social responsibility" (Grossman, 1983, p. 1). Adaptive behavior is assumed to be a developmental construct, in that expectations for independent and responsible behavior vary based upon age (Reschly, 1990). It is also important to consider that adaptive behaviors must be viewed within cultural and environmental contexts, in that expectations and demands for independence and responsibility also vary based upon the specific culture or subculture in which the individual resides (Reschly, 1990). The assessment of adaptive behavior is a critical aspect in the classification of developmental delays and mental retardation, and the current definition of mental retardation by the American Association on Mental Deficiency (AAMD) includes the construct of adaptive behavior (Grossman, 1983).

Social skills have been defined a number of ways, including cognitive, behavioral, and ecological definitions (Merrell, Merz, Johnson, & Ring, 1992). For purposes of this chapter, a good working definition of social skills is that they are specific behaviors that, when initiated, lead to desirable social outcomes for the person initiating them. From a behavioral standpoint, initiation of social skills increases the probability of reinforcement and decreases the probability of punishment or extinction based upon one's socially related behavior (Gresham & Reschly, 1987a). For children and youth, examples of classes of behavior representing social skills include academic and task-related competence, cooperation with peers, reinforcement of peers' behavior, and social initiation behaviors.

Although peer acceptance (which is referred to hereafter by a more generic label, *peer relations*) has been considered to be the third overall component or domain of social competence, it is often thought of as a *result or product* of one's social skills. This view of peer relations is reasonable, in that one's social reputation and quality of social relations are in great measure a result of how effectively one interacts socially with peers (Landau & Milich, 1990; Oden & Asher, 1977). Positive peer relations are associated with peer acceptance, whereas negative peer relations are linked with peer rejection.

Because the assessment of adaptive behavior is touched upon elsewhere in this book, and because such assessment is often for different purposes and may require different qualitative approaches than the assessment of social skills and peer relations, it will not be covered in this chapter. In addition to rating scale and sociometric assessment, children's social skills and peer relations can also be evaluated using methods such as direct behavioral observation interviews, and analogue/role-play situations. However, developing an adequate understanding of these other three techniques would require a substantial and separate treatment of each, which is beyond the scope of this chapter. Therefore, the treatment of the subject of assessing social skills and peer relations will be limited to behavior rating scale and sociometric methods.

SOCIAL SKILLS AND PEER RELATIONS IN CHILDHOOD

A growing body of literature in the fields of child development, education, and psychology collectively points to the conclusion that the development of adequate social skills and peer relationships during childhood has important and far-reaching ramifications. It has been established that development of appropriate social skills is an important foundation for adequate peer relationships (Asher & Taylor, 1981). There is also evidence that childhood social skills and consequent peer relationships have a significant impact on academic success (Walker & Hops, 1976) during the school years. In reviewing the literature on peer relations, Hartup (1983) demonstrated that it is well-established that the ability to relate effectively to others provides an essential contribution to the progress and development of the child.

Given that adequate social skills and peer relations are an important foundation for various types of success in life, it stands to reason that inadequate development in these areas is related to a variety of negative outcomes. A classic and frequently cited study by Cowen, Pederson, Babigian, Izzo, and Trost (1973) involving an 11- to 13-year follow-up study of 3rd-grade students provided convincing evidence that early peer relationship problems are strong predictors of mental health problems later in life. These researchers found that "peer judgment (using a negative peer nomination procedure) was, by far, the most sensitive predictor of later psychiatric difficulty" (p. 438). Other frequently cited studies have suggested that inadequate social skills and poor peer relations during childhood may lead to a variety of other problems later in life, such as later juvenile delinquency, school dropout, being fired from jobs, conduct-related discharge from military service, chronic unemployment and underemployment, and psychiatric hospitalizations (Loeber, 1985; Parker & Asher, 1987; Roff & Sells, 1968; Roff, Sells, & Golden, 1972).

As the literature on the social, emotional, and behavioral characteristics of children with disabilities continues to grow, it has become increasingly clear that these children are at significantly heightened risk for developing social skills deficits and experiencing peer rejection. Students identified as learning disabled have been found to experience high rates of social rejection by other children (Bryan, 1974; Cartledge, Frew, & Zacharias, 1985; Sater & French, 1989), to be rated by teachers as having poor interpersonal behavior (Gresham & Reschly, 1987b), and to exhibit maladaptive social behaviors in instructional settings (Epstein, Cullinan, & Lloyd, 1986; McKinney & Feagans, 1984; McKinney, Mc- Clure, & Feagans, 1982). Students identified as mentally retarded have been found to exhibit deficits in adaptive-social competencies (Gresham & Reschly, 1987b), experience high rates of peer rejection (Gresham, 1982), and receive inadequate amounts of social support (Park, Tappe, Cameto, & Gaylord-Ross, 1990). Likewise, students identified as having behavior disorders have been found to be readily discriminated from nonhandicapped students by their maladaptive social-emotional behav- iors (Merrell et al., 1992; Stumme, Gresham, & Scott, 1982; Vaughn, 1987) and to experience significant rates of social rejection by other children (Hollinger, 1987). Therefore, clinicians who work with dis- abled and other at-risk children should be especially aware of the social problems these children face and keep up to date on appropriate meth- ods of assessment.

ASSESSMENT WITH BEHAVIOR RATING SCALES

Rating Scale Technology: An Overview

Behavior rating scales utilize summative paper-and-pencil judgments about a child by an informant who knows the child well, most often a teacher or parent. These judgments are made using a standardized rating format, which yields scores that allow comparison between the subject and a normative group. Most rating scales now use an *algebraic* rating format, where the rater selects a number or other value that best represents the student's performance on the particular characteristic. For example, an algebraic response format for the item "Is physically aggressive" might have the rater select the value 0 if the statement is not true, 1 if the statement is sometimes true, and 2 if the statement is frequently true. Then, after completing the rating scale, the numerical value of the ratings would be added and compared in different configurations to those of a norm group. This type of format is more sophisticated and sensitive to behav- ioral change or intensity than a checklist format, which is *additive* in nature, in that the rater simply circles or checks items that seem to be true for the subject, and then adds the number of items checked. Rating scales have gained wide popularity in educational and clinical settings, particu- larly for behavioral assessment.

Rating scales have become widely used because they offer several advantages as an assessment method. Whereas direct behavioral observation is a potentially excellent method for assessing social competence, rating scales are less expensive in terms of professional time and training required and are capable of providing data on low-frequency but important behaviors that might not be seen in a limited number of direct observation sessions (Sattler, 1988). When compared to other assessment methods such as projective techniques and interviews, rating scales provide more objective and reliable data (Martin, Hooper, & Snow, 1986). Rating scales can be used to assess subjects who cannot readily provide information about themselves or be easily observed (e.g., very young children or adolescents in "lock-up" units in hospitals or juvenile detention centers). Rating scales also capitalize on observations from the student's normal environment (school and home) and the observations of expert informants (teachers and parents).

In spite of the popularity and advantages of rating scales, there are certain problems associated with their use that need to be considered in order to use them effectively. Two types of problems with rating scales have been discussed by Martin et al. (1986). The first type of problem is referred to as *bias of response*, meaning that the way that informants complete rating scales may create additional error in the resulting scores. Three types of response bias are particularly problematic, including: (a) *halo effects* (e.g., a teacher rating a student as having good behavioral characteristics because that student does well on academic work); (b) *leniency or severity* (the tendency of some raters to be overly generous or overly critical in their ratings of all subjects); and (c) *central tendency effects* (the tendency of raters to select midrange rating points and avoid extreme ratings such as "never" or "frequently"). The second type of problem is that rating scale scores are subject to four different kinds of *variance*, including: *source variance* (the way that ratings vary between different raters); *setting variance* (the way that ratings might differ across different classroom settings, or between school and home); *temporal variance* (the way that behavior ratings change over time based on changes in the rater or the subject); and *instrument variance* (different results obtained by using different rating scales). The recommended way of dealing with these two types of problems in rating scales is to use a multisource, multisetting, multi-instrument assessment design, which reduces the chance for bias and error by obtaining ratings of the subject from different informants, in different settings, and using different types of rating scales (Martin, 1988).

Behavior Rating Scales for Assessing Social Skills and Peer Relations

Until the mid-1980s, there was a dearth of nationally standardized rating scales for assessing social skills and peer relations. Most rating scales developed prior to this time were designed for the express purpose of assessing behavior problems, and there was a much smaller body of research on children's social competence (Achenbach & Edelbrock, 1983). However, during the past several years there has been a significant increase in interest and research in children's social competence, and one of the results of this increase has been the development of several psychometrically sound standardized assessment instruments. This section of the chapter will provide an overview of four behavior rating scales useful for assessing social competence and peer relations: (a) the Child Behavior Checklist, (b) the School Social Behavior Scales, (c) the Social Skills Rating System, and (d) the Walker-McConnell Scales of Social Competence and School Adjustment. These four instruments do not represent all that is currently available in this area, but they were selected for inclusion in this chapter because they all are: (a) norm-referenced using nationwide standardization groups, (b) psychometrically acceptable, (c) designed to be specifically useful for assessment of social skills and peer relations, and (d) commercially published and thus widely available. A brief overview of each of these instruments, in alphabetical order, follows.

The Child Behavior Checklist

The Child Behavior Checklist (CBCL) system, developed by Achenbach and his colleagues, is considered to be the most sophisticated problem behavior rating scale system currently available (Martin, 1988). The system includes a parent checklist, a self-report form for older children and adolescents, and a direct behavioral observation form. Although the rating scales in this system are best known and best used as instruments for the assessment of child psychopathology, the version for use by parents and parent surrogates, the Child Behavior Checklist (Achenbach & Edelbrock, 1983), also includes a social competence scale that is useful in social skills assessment in conjunction with problem behavior assessment. The rating scale version for teachers, the Teacher's Report Form (TRF) (Achenbach & Edelbrock, 1986), includes a series of non–behavior problem items conceptually similar to the Social Competence scale of the CBCL, which is referred to as the Adaptive Functioning scale. However, the items on this scale of the TRF are almost entirely related to academic achievement and adjustment and are thus not designed to be a complete measure of social skills or peer relations; therefore, only the Social Competence scale of the CBCL will be overviewed in this chapter. Because the Behavior Problem scales of the CBCL are reviewed elsewhere in this book, they will not be covered in this chapter.

The CBCL was designed as a rating scale for parents of 4- to 16-year-old children. The Social Competence scale of the CBCL is located on the first and second pages of the CBCL, just after the demographic information section and before the Behavior Problem scales. The Social Competence scales include 20 items in seven sections wherein the child is rated on participation in various activities such as sports, hobbies, organizations, jobs, and chores and is rated as to the quality and quantity of relationships with siblings and peers. For children age 6 and older, the parent also provides a rating of the child's performance on academic tasks and behavioral adjustment in school.

Unlike the Behavior Problem scales of the CBCL, the Social Competence items do not utilize a common standard rating format for each item; the rating format for each section differs somewhat depending on the nature of the rating task. For example, in sections I and II, the parent lists up to three sports in which the child most likes to participate (section I) and up to three hobbies, activities, or games other than sports in which the child most likes to participate (section II). The parent then provides an estimate of how much time the child spends at each activity compared to other children (ranging from "less than average" to "more the average") and an estimate of how well the child is able to perform each activity in comparison to same-age peers (ranging from "below average" to "above average"). In sections III and IV the parent lists up to three organizations or clubs to which the child belongs (section III) and up to three jobs or chores the child routinely does (section IV) and then compares the child's participation and effectiveness in these areas to that of same-age peers, ranging from "below average" to "above average." Section V asks the parent to list how many close friends their child has (with rating points ranging from none to four or more) and then to estimate how well the child gets along with peers and parents, as well as plays and works independently. The remaining sections of the Social Competence scale, VI and VII, ask the parent to rate the child's performance in different academic subjects (ranging from "failing" to "above average") and then to respond in a yes-no manner to questions related to specific academic issues and problems.

Items on the CBCL Social Competence scales are scored using the scoring system outlined in the CBCL manual. The directions must be followed carefully, as procedures for scoring items in each of the seven sections vary somewhat. Raw scores are then calculated for three designated areas (Activities, Social, and School) as well as a Social Competence Total. After these area and total raw scores have been calculated, they are converted to normalized T scores ($M=50$, $SD=10$), based on the CBCL normative samples of each sex at different age levels (4-5, 6-11, and 12-16). Higher scores reflect more positive social competence attributes, whereas lower scores reflect poorer social competence.

The CBCL was standardized using a sample of 1,442 "normal" children in the Washington, DC, metropolitan area and surrounding regions and a clinic-referred sample of 2,300 children from the eastern United States. At the time this chapter is being written, the CBCL is in the process of being revised to include a broader standardization sample. Extensive information on the technical aspects of the CBCL standardization is provided in the scale manual, and the psychometric properties of the Social Competence scales are adequate to excellent. Test-retest reliability coefficients by gender and age range at 1-week intervals range from .68 to .98 for the three area scores, and from .76 to .92 for the total score. Mean rs based on gender and age-level breakdowns for stability coefficients at 6- and 18-month intervals are .47 to .76. Interrater reliability coefficients for interparent agreement on the combined age and gender samples range from .44 to .81 on the area scores, and are reported at .59 for the total score.

The Social Competence scales of the CBCL differ from the other scales reviewed in this section of the chapter in that they consist of fewer rating items (20) and provide a different format for rating, but they should still be considered a useful screening tool for assessing social competence. The main limitation of using this part of the CBCL for assessing social skills and peer relations is that the number and scope of items is limited, and it thus does not represent the broader domain of social competence in as much detail as some other instruments. However, this instrument has the advantage of being linked to the Behavior Problem scales of the CBCL, which are highly regarded for their sophistication in assessing child psychopathology. Thus, the CBCL is useful as a screening device for social competence, particularly when the referral issues include the existence of severe behavior problems.

The School Social Behavior Scales

The School Social Behavior Scales (SSBS) (Merrell, in press) is a social behavior rating scale for use by teachers and other school personnel in assessing both social competence and antisocial problem behaviors of students in grades K–12. It includes two separate scales with a total of 65 items that describe both positive and negative social behaviors that commonly occur in educational settings. Items are rated using a 5-point scale ranging from 1 = "never" to 5 = "frequently." Each of the two scales of the SSBS yields a total score using a raw to standard score conversion with a mean of 100 and standard deviation of 15. The two scales each have three subscales, with scores reported as four different Social Functioning Levels, including "High Functioning," "Average," "Moderate Problem," and "Significant Problem."

Scale A, Social Competence, includes 32 items that describe adaptive, prosocial behavioral competencies as they commonly occur in educational settings. Subscale A1 (Interpersonal Skills) includes 14 items measuring social skills that are important in establishing positive relationships with and gaining social acceptance from peers (e.g., "Offers help to other students when needed" and "Interacts with a wide variety of peers"). Subscale A2 (Self-Management Skills) includes 10 items measuring social skills relating to self-restraint, cooperation, and compliance with the demands of school rules and expectations (e.g., "Responds appropriately when corrected by teacher" and "Shows self-restraint"). Subscale A3 (Academic Skills) consists of 8 items relating to competent performance and engagement on academic tasks (e.g., "Completes individual seatwork without being prompted" and "Completes assigned activities on time").

Scale B, Antisocial Behavior, includes 33 negatively worded items that describe problematic behaviors that are either other-directed in nature, or are likely to lead to negative social consequences such as peer rejection or strained relationships with the teacher. Subscale B1 (Hostile-Irritable) consists of 14 items that describe behaviors considered to be self-centered, annoying, and that will likely lead to peer rejection (e.g., "Will not share with other students" and "Argues and quarrels with other students"). Subscale B2 (Antisocial-Aggressive) consists of 10 behavioral descriptors relating to overt violation of school rules and intimidation or harm to others (e.g., "Gets into fights" and "Takes things that are not his/hers"). Subscale B3 (Disruptive-Demanding) includes 9 items that reflect behaviors likely to disrupt ongoing school activities and place excessive and inappropriate demands on others (e.g., "Is overly demanding of teacher's attention" and "Is difficult to control").

A number of studies and procedures are reported in the SSBS manual concerning the psychometric properties and validity of the instrument. The scales were standardized on a group of over 1,200 K–12 students from the United States, with each of the four U.S. geographical regions represented in the standardization process. The percentage of handicapped students in various classification categories in the standardization group very closely approximates the national percentages of these figures. Various reliability procedures reported in the SSBS manual indicate the scales have good to excellent stability and consistency. Internal consistency and split-half reliability coefficients range from .91 to .98. Test-retest reliability at 3-week intervals is reported at .76 to .83 for the Social Competence scores and .60 to .73 for the Antisocial Behavior scores. Interrater reliability between resource room teachers and paraprofessional aides ranges from .72 to .83 for the Social Competence scores and .53 to .71 for the Antisocial Behavior scores.

Validity of the scales has been demonstrated in several ways. Moderate to high correlations between the SSBS and three other behavior rating scales (including the 39-item version of the Conners Teacher Rating Scale, the Waksman Social Skills Rating Scale, and the adolescent version of the Walker-McConnell Scale of Social Competence and School Adjustment) suggest that the scale has good criterion-related validity. Other findings indicate the scales can adequately discriminate between gifted and average (Merrell & Gill, in press), handicapped and regular education (Merrell, in press), and behavior-disordered and other handicapped students (Merrell, 1991), suggesting that the SSBS has good construct validity. The factor structure of the two scales is very strong, with all items having a factor loading into their respective subscale of .50 or greater, and no items being duplicated across subscales.

The SSBS appears to be useful as a school-based rating scale that provides norm-referenced data on both positive social skills and antisocial problem behavior. It has satisfactory to good psychometric properties, is easy to use, and the items and structure are highly relevant to the types of behavioral issues encountered by school-based professionals. It should be noted that the Antisocial Behavior scale is designed specifically to measure behavior problems that are directly social in nature, or that would have an immediate impact on strained relations with peers and teachers. The scale was not designed to measure overcontrolled or internalizing behavior problems such as those associated with depression and anxiety, nor was it designed to measure behavior problems associated with Attention Deficit Hyperactivity Disorder. If these types of problem behaviors are a significant issue on an assessment case, the assessment should be bolstered by the addition of an appropriate measure designed specifically for these behaviors.

The Social Skills Rating System

The Social Skills Rating System (SSRS) (Gresham & Elliott, 1990) is a multicomponent social skills rating system that focuses on behaviors that affect parent–child relations, teacher–student relations, and peer acceptance. The system includes separate rating scales for teachers and parents, as well as a self-report form for students. Each component of the system can be used alone or in conjunction with the other forms. Separate instruments and norms are provided for each of three developmental groups, which include preschool level (ages 3–5), elementary level (grades (K–6), and secondary level (grades 7–12). Because a detailed description and review of each of the several SSRS forms is beyond the scope of this chapter, an overview of only the elementary-level teacher rating form will be provided herein. Because there are considerable conceptual similarities between the different forms and age level versions in the system, this description will provide the reader with an understanding that generalizes in many ways to the different forms within the system.

The elementary-level teacher rating form of the SSRS consists of 57 items divided over three scales, Social Skills, Problem Behaviors, and Academic Competence. For Social Skills and Problem Behaviors, teachers respond to items using a 3-point response format based on how often a given behavior occurs (0 = "never," 1 = "sometimes," and 2 = "very often"). On the Social Skills items, teachers are also asked to rate how important a skill is (on a 3-point scale) to success in the classroom. The importance rating is not used to calculate ratings for each scale but is used for planning interventions. On the Academic Competence scale, teachers rate students as compared to other students on a 5-point scale. Scale raw scores are converted to standard scores ($M=100$, $SD=15$) and percentile ranks. Subscale raw scores are converted to estimates of functional ability called Behavior Levels.

The Social Skills scale consists of 30 items that rate social skills in the area of teacher and peer relations. This scale contains three subscales, which include Cooperation, Assertion, and Self-Control. The Cooperation subscale identifies compliance behaviors that are important for success in classrooms (e.g., "Finishes class assignments on time" and "Uses time appropriately while waiting for help"). The Assertion subscale includes initiating behaviors that involve making and maintaining friendships and responding to actions of others (e.g., "Invites others to join in activities" and "Appropriately questions rules that may be unfair"). The Self-Control subscale includes responses that occur in conflict situations like turn taking and peer criticism (e.g., "Cooperates with peers without prompting" and "Responds appropriately to teasing by peers").

The Problem Behaviors scale consists of 18 items that reflect behaviors that might interfere with social skills performance. The items are divided into three subscales, including Externalizing Problems, Internalizing Problems, and Hyperactivity. The Externalizing Problems subscale items reflect inappropriate behaviors that indicate verbal and physical aggression toward others and a lack of temper control (e.g., "Threatens or bullies others" and "Has temper tantrums"). The subscale Internalizing Problems includes behaviors that indicate anxiety, sadness, and poor self-esteem (e.g., "Shows anxiety about being with a group of children" and "Likes to be alone"). The Hyperactivity subscale includes activities that involve excessive movement and impulsive actions (e.g., "Disturbs ongoing activities" and "Acts impulsively").

The third scale, Academic Competence, includes nine items that reflect academic functioning, such as performance in specific academic areas, student's motivation level, general cognitive functioning, and parental support (e.g., "In terms of grade-level expectations, this child's skills in reading are:_____" and "The child's overall motivation to succeed academically is:_____"). Behavior is rated on a 5-point scale that corresponds to percentages, ranging from 1 = lowest 10% to 5 = highest 10%.

The SSRS was standardized on a national sample of more than 4,000 children representing all four U.S. geographical regions. The demographic information is difficult to interpret because the manual does not provide an adequate normative breakdown based on the different test forms. However, given the overall large number of subjects who were rated in the SSRS national standardization, it should most likely be assumed that the norms for each rating form in the system were developed using a sufficient number of cases.

The scale manual states that overall psychometric properties obtained during scale development ranged from adequate to excellent. For the teacher scale, reliability was measured using internal consistency (i.e., alpha coefficients ranged from .74 to .95), interrater, and test-retest (i.e., .75 to .93 correlations across the three scales) procedures. Criterion-related and construct validity were established by finding significant correlations between the SSRS and other rating scales. Subscale dimensions were determined through factor analyses of each scale. Items that met a criterion of a .30 or greater factor loading were considered to load on a given factor.

The SSRS has the distinct strength of consisting of an integrated system of instruments for use by teachers, parents, and students. The manual is extremely well written, and the rating instruments have been designed to be easily usable and understandable. The sections of the instruments that measure social skills are very comprehensive and useful. The sections measuring problem behaviors and academic competence are quite brief, and should be considered as short screening sections to be used in conjunction with a social skills assessment.

The Scales of Social Competence and School Adjustment

The Walker-McConnell Scales of Social Competence and School Adjustment (SSCSA) (Walker & McConnell, 1988; Walker, Steiber, & Eisert, 1991) are social skills rating scales for teachers and other school-based professionals. Two versions of the scale are available—an elementary version for use with students in grades K–6 and an adolescent version for use with students in grades 7–12. The elementary version contains 43 positively worded items that reflect adaptive social-behavioral competencies within the school environment. The items are rated using a 5-point scale ranging from 1 "never occurs" to 5 "frequently occurs." The scale yields standard scores on three subscales ($M=10$, $SD=3$) as well as a total score ($M=100$, $SD=15$), which is a composite of the three subscales. Subscale 1 (Teacher-Preferred Social Behavior) includes 16 items that measure peer-related social behaviors that are highly valued by teachers and reflect their concerns for empathy, sensitivity, self-restraint, and co-operative, socially mature peer relationships (e.g., "Is considerate of the feelings of others" and "Is sensitive to the needs of others"). Subscale 2 (Peer-Preferred Social Behavior) includes 17 items that measure peer-related social behaviors highly valued by other children and reflect peer values that involve social relationships, dynamics, and skills in free-play settings (e.g., "Spends recess and free time interacting with peers" and

"Invites peers to play or share activities"). Subscale 3 (School Adjustment Behavior) includes 10 items reflecting social-behavior competencies that are especially important in academic instructional settings, such as having good work and study habits, following academic instructions, and behaving in ways conducive to classroom management (e.g., "Attends to assigned tasks" and "Displays independent study skills").

The adolescent version of the scale is very similar to the elementary version, in that it was designed as an upward extension of it. The adolescent version includes the 43 items from the elementary version (with 9 of the scale items having been revised to better reflect adolescent behavioral content) plus an additional 10 items designed to measure *self-related* social adjustment based on content from an adolescent social skills training curriculum (Walker, Todis, Holmes, & Horton, 1988). The factor structure of the adolescent version includes the same three factors found on the elementary version, plus a fourth subscale containing 6 items that is labeled as the Empathy subscale. This fourth factor includes items designed to measure sensitivity and awareness in peer relationships such a "Listens while others are speaking" and "Is considerate of the feelings of others." The adolescent version of the scale uses the same rating format and scoring system as the elementary version, and the four subscale scores are summed into a total score.

Extensive information on the standardization data and psychometric properties of the two versions of the SSCSA are reported in the scale manual. The scales were standardized on groups of approximately 2,000 students representing all four U.S. geographical regions. Studies undertaken during the development of the scales that are cited in the scale manual indicate adequate to excellent psychometric properties.

Reliability of the scales was established using test-retest (e.g., .88 to .92 correlations over a 3-week period with 323 subjects), internal consistency (e.g., alpha coefficients ranging from .95 to .97), and interrater (e.g., a .53 correlation between teachers' and aides' ratings on the total score in a day treatment facility) procedures. Validity of the scales was assessed using a variety of procedures. Discriminant validity was established in studies that found the SSCSA to differentiate among groups of students who would be expected to differ behaviorally (behavior-disordered and normal, antisocial and normal, behaviorally at risk and normal, and those with and without learning problems). Criterion-related validity was demonstrated by finding significant correlations between the SSCSA and a number of criterion variables, including other rating scales, sociometric ratings, academic achievement measures, and a systematic behavioral screening procedure. Construct validity of the scales was demonstrated by, among other procedures, finding strong correlations between evaluative comments of subjects by their peers and teacher ratings on the scales, and by finding low social skills ratings to be strongly associated with the emergence of antisocial behavior in a longitudinal study of elementary-age boys. A number of other psychometric validation studies are reported in the test manual that substantiate the reliability and validity of the scale. Subsequent investigations have found the SSCSA to correlate highly with other behavioral rating scales (Merrell, 1989) and to discriminate accurately groups of students referred for learning problems from average students (Merrell et al., 1992; Merrell & Shinn, 1990). The six-item Empathy subscale from the adolescent version of the SSCSA has been found to discriminate between a group of antisocial subjects with a record of arrests and an at-risk control group (Walker et al., 1991). The factor structure of the SSCSA scales has been shown to be very strong.

Both versions of the SSCSA are brief, easy to use, and contain items that are highly relevant for assessing social skills in educational settings. The research base behind the scales is truly exemplary, particularly when considering that the scales have only been recently published. Because neither version of the SSCSA was designed to measure problem behaviors, these instruments should be supplemented with an appropriate problem behavior assessment if the referral issues warrant it.

ASSESSMENT WITH SOCIOMETRIC PROCEDURES

The essence of sociometric assessment procedures is obtaining information from within a peer group (usually in a classroom setting) concerning the social dynamics in that group. The key feature in these procedures is that assessment data on various aspects of social status of persons within the peer group *is obtained directly from its members*, rather that through teacher ratings or observations by an impartial outside evaluator. These types of procedures allow the evaluator to tap directly into the ongoing social dynamics of a group, which is an obvious advantage, as there tend to be many things that go on within a classroom environment that students are more aware of than the teacher is (Worthen, Borg, & White, in press). Sociometric procedures have a long history of use in psychology and education and allow for assessment of such varied qualities as level of popularity, acceptance or rejection status, and attribution of specific positive and negative characteristics such as leadership ability, athletic or academic prowess, aggressiveness, and social awkwardness.

Early researchers in the use of sociometrics tended to view social status in a fairly unidimensional manner (Landau & Milich, 1990). However, more recent efforts in this area have led investigators to conclude that the construct of social status is both complex and multidimensional. For example, Coie, Dodge, and Cappotelli (1982) used peer preference questions in a sociometric technique with a large number ($n = 537$) of elementary and middle school–aged children and analyzed the obtained data to develop five different social status groups: popular, rejected, average, neglected, and controversial. An analysis of characteristics of the students indicated that although there was some overlap between categories, each had some distinct features. Popular children were those who were rated by peers as being cooperative, having leadership ability, and engaging in very little disruptive behavior. Rejected children were rated as frequently fighting and being disruptive and as not being cooperative or having leadership traits. Neglected children were those who were largely ignored by other children and were seen as being socially unresponsive. The fourth nonaverage group, controversial children, tended to exhibit features of both the popular and rejected group, being considered disruptive and starting fights, but also being perceived as being assertive leaders. This conceptualization of social status ratings into five groups, which has been backed up by subsequent research, shows how complex social dynamics within peer groups can be and suggests that sociometric procedures can indeed provide complex and useful social assessment data.

Unlike many other assessment methods, including rating scales, sociometric procedures are usually not norm referenced or commercially published. Instead, they tend to consist of different variations of a few relatively simple methods originally developed for use by researchers but fully capable of being translated into school or clinical practice. The technical and psychometric aspects of these procedures have been researched in several studies and have generally shown favorable evidence of technical soundness. Temporal stability of sociometric assessments has been shown to be relatively high, at both short- and long-term stability periods (Hartup, 1983; Roff et al., 1972). Landau and Milich (1990) reviewed several studies of interrater correspondence in sociometric procedures, and noted that moderate to high levels of correspondence between raters have generally been found. However, there is one interesting and peculiar finding in this regard—a gender difference on social convergence in ratings wherein both boys and girls tend to attribute more positive characteristics to members of their own sex, and more negative characteristics to members of the opposite sex. Validity of sociometric assessment procedures has been established in several studies (such as the previously reviewed studies by Cowen et al., 1973, and Ross et al., 1972) wherein social status ratings were predictive of various types of social adjustment and maladjustment later in life. In sum, although sociometric assessment procedures tend not to be standardized or commercially published like most other tests used by psychologists, they have nonetheless been demonstrated to have generally favorable technical properties and should be viewed as a potentially useful method of assessing peer relations and social status.

Four General Sociometric Procedures

It is difficult to divide sociometric procedures into distinct categories, because they tend to be nonstandardized and have considerable overlap. However, there are certain similarities and differences between different methods that make a general categorization possible. This section provides an overview of four general types of sociometric procedures: (a) peer nomination procedures, (b) picture sociometric techniques, (c) guess who measures, and (d) the class play. In some cases these categories involved general descriptions common to many methods within the category. In other cases, the categorical description is rather unique to a specific procedure that has been developed.

Peer Nomination Procedures

The oldest and most widely used sociometric approach, which is the basis for most other types of sociometric measures as well, is the nomination method, which was originally introduced by Moreno (1934). The basis of the peer nomination technique is that students are asked to nominate or name classmates that they prefer according to specific positive criteria. This approach typically involves the student naming three classmates he or she would most like to study with, play with during free time, work with on a class project, or participate with in some other positive way. For children with sufficient reading and writing ability, peer nomination procedures can be administered by either an item-by-peer matrix or a questionnaire wherein they fill in names of classmates on blank lines following questions.

The item-by-peer matrix consists of having the names of all children in the class across the top of the page, and the social interaction items listed vertically on the left side of the page. The students are instructed to put an "x" under the name(s) of the other students to whom they think the item applies (e.g., "Which three students would you most like to have as your best friends?"). Use of a questionnaire format accomplishes essentially the same thing (e.g., "Write the names of three students in your class that you would most like to have as your best friends" followed by three numbered blank lines).

Scoring of peer nominations is typically done by totaling the number of nominations that each child receives. Worthen et al. (in press) suggest that the results of positive peer nomination procedures can be classified and interpreted according to a frequently used set of criteria. *Stars* are individuals who are frequently chosen. *Isolates* are individuals who are never chosen in the process. *Neglectees* are those who receive only a few nominations. The results can also be plotted on a "sociogram," which shows the patterns of choice for each student, which helps in identifying not only frequently and never nominated students, but is useful in showing cliques or small groups. A *mutual choice* occurs when an individual is chosen by the same student that he or she selected. A *cross-sex choice* occurs when a boy chooses a girl or a girl chooses a boy. A *clique* is identified by finding a small group of students who choose each other and make few or no choices outside of that group. *Cleavage* is said to occur when two or more groups within the class or social unit are identified that never choose someone from the other group(s). Using these scoring and classification criteria, one can easily see how a procedure as deceptively simple as the peer nomination method can yield information that is both striking and complex.

Although the peer nomination technique has historically most often involved the use of positive items indicative of high social status, many practitioners and researchers have used variations of this method by employing negative nominations, using items that are created to identify students who are socially rejected by peers (e.g., "Who would you least like to play with?" or "Who would you never want to be friends with?"). The use of negative peer nomination procedures has proved to be controversial, with ethical questions being raised about the potential for negative effects. Although there is research indicating that sociometric assessment has no consequence on peer interactions (Hayvren & Hymel, 1984), many educators and parents are disapproving of the use of these procedures when negative nominations are involved.

Picture Sociometric Techniques

Picture sociometric techniques involve an individual presenting each child in a classroom with an arbitrary assortment of photographs of each child in the class, and then asking the child to answer a series of questions by pointing to or selecting a photograph of a peer. This method is an adaptation of other peer nomination methods that is useful for work with preliterate subjects. Landau and Milich (1990) state that it is the preferred method for preschool through 2nd-grade level subjects. Examples of questions that have been used with this technique include "Who do you like to play with the most?" "Who is your best friend?" and "Who is the best student in your class?" As with most other sociometric techniques, specific questions can be developed based on clinical or research questions, and these questions can be produced to indicate either social acceptance or social rejection.

The original picture sociometric technique and minor variations of it are scored based on totaling the number of times each child was nominated by classmates based on questions indicating positive social status. Using this scoring scheme, rejected or neglected children would have significantly lower scores than accepted children with higher social status. Of course, variations in scoring procedure would be needed if there were any significant deviations in administration methods from the original study by McCandless and Marshall (1957). For example, questions that reflect both positive (e.g., "Who do you most like to do schoolwork with?") and negative (e.g., "Who are you afraid to be around on the playground?") social status could be mixed, and the scoring system could be divided into positive and negative status categories.

The use of picture sociometrics was first reported by McCandless and Marshall (1957), and has subsequently been utilized in a number of other published studies. The psychometric properties of picture sociometric techniques have been shown to be quite good, with relatively high interrater reliability, very high short-term test-retest reliability, and adequate long-term test-retest reliability. (See Landau & Milich, 1990.) Validity of the picture sociometric method has been demonstrated by producing significant discriminations between groups of aggressive, aggressive-withdrawn, and normal boys (Milich & Landau, 1984). It is interesting to note that this technique has been shown to produce more effective discriminations of social status than information provided by teachers.

Guess Who Measures

The "guess who" technique is a sociometric approach wherein brief descriptions are provided to students, who are asked to write down names of a few other students (usually three or fewer) that they think best fit the descriptions. For example, the students might be asked to respond to descriptions such as "Guess who is often in trouble?" "Guess who does the best job on schoolwork?" "Guess who no one knows very well?" or "Guess who is often angry at other children?" The descriptions can be provided to the students either verbally or in written format. The content of the "guess who" items can be made up by the teacher, clinician, or researcher based on specific characteristics they are interested in identifying. Scoring of these types of measures is done by making simple frequency counts of each question/description. More elaborate scoring methods are also possible, such as grouping descriptions into categories of similar content (e.g., antisocial behaviors, helping characteristics, peer popularity) and obtaining frequency counts within each broader category.

An example of a "guess who" measure that has been used with a large number of students and has been carefully investigated is the Revised PRIME Guess Who Measure, which was developed for use in Project PRIME, a large-scale investigation of mildly handicapped students who had been integrated in regular education classrooms for part of their instructional day (Kauffman, Semmell, & Agard, 1974). The original instrument consisted of 29 questions/descriptions and was administered to over 13,000 students in grades 3–5. Factor analytic procedures conducted on the instrument divided the items into four major factors, which were labeled "disruptive," "bright," "dull," and "well behaved." A revised scale including 20 items (the 5 items contributing the most to each factor) was developed by Veldman and Sheffield (1979), who reported reliability coefficients ranging from .56 to .77 for each factor score and developed a satisfactory concurrent validity procedure for the instrument by correlating the instrument items with teacher ratings along similar dimensions.

In sum, the "guess who" technique is flexible, easy to administer and score, has been used in a large number of studies and projects, and has been found to have satisfactory technical properties. Clinicians and investigators desiring an adaptable, easy-to-administer sociometric measure may find "guess who" techniques a useful choice in assessment instrumentation.

The Class Play

The Class Play procedure was first utilized and described by Bower (1969) and has been further revised by Masten, Morrison, and Pelligrini (1985). It is a frequently used sociometric technique that has been employed in several large-scale investigations, including the classic 11- to 13-year follow-up study of elementary-age children by Cowen and his colleagues (Cowen et al., 1973). The basis of this procedure is that children are asked to assign their peers to various roles (usually both positive and negative roles) in an imaginary play. The original Class Play described by Bower (1969) included both positive (e.g., "someone who will wait their turn") and negative (e.g., "someone who is too bossy") roles, but consisted of a scoring procedure wherein only a single score (negative peer reputation) was derived, which was done by calculating the number of negative roles given to a child and dividing that by the total number of roles given to the child. Large percentages are supposed to indicate a high degree of peer rejection, whereas low percentages are meant to indicate that the child has higher social status. As is the case with most sociometric approaches, the specification of roles in the Class Play procedure (as well as the method of scoring) can be manipulated by the clinician or researcher to suit their goals. It should be noted that the scoring system advocated by Bower (1969) has been criticized as being on empirically shaky ground (Landau & Milich, 1990).

The use of Class Play procedures of sociometric assessment is attractive for two reasons other than the measurement capabilities it may have. One advantage is that children (particularly younger children) appear to enjoy participating in make-believe plays and casting their peers into the various roles. The second advantage is that teachers and administrators seem to view this type of procedure more positively than some other sociometric methods and, as such, it is more likely to be supported and approved than some other approaches. Masten et al. (1985) suggest that because of the diversity of roles needed in a play, this procedure will reduce any probability of disapproving labeling of children with high negative scores by other children in the rating/casting process.

Some Final Comments on Sociometric Procedures

The sociometric assessment approaches overviewed in this chapter, as well as other types of sociometric measures, have a great deal of appeal to clinicians and researchers and have a long history of use with psychology and education. However, these approaches are not without controversy. Many sociometric methods involve negative ranking or nomination procedures, or having children single out peers based on negative characteristics. Largely because of the use of these negative nomination procedures, parents (and some teachers and administrators) are often hesitant (or outright angry) at the possibility of their children participating in sociometric assessments, for fear of their child or other children being singled out by peers and further ostracized because of it. Although there is little empirical evidence to warrant this assertion completely, and some evidence to the contrary (Hayvren & Hymel, 1984), there seems to be a common concern that children will compare their responses after the assessment to find out which children were singled out for negative nominations, and this process will end up in increased isolation or social exile for the children who were commonly perceived in negative terms. The author is personally familiar with two separate research projects that had to undergo major methodological modifications because of threats by parents and some educators to "shut down the study" because of outrage over the use of negative peer-ranking or nomination procedures. Whether such concerns are founded or not, clinicians and researchers desiring to utilize sociometric approaches would do well to pick the most appropriate method for their purposes carefully, communicate closely and carefully with their constituent groups, and educate those involved on the purposes and procedures involved. In the meantime, additional research on any potential peer effects of sociometric measurement involving negative ranking or nomination should be conducted.

A CASE STUDY IN ASSESSING SOCIAL SKILLS AND PEER RELATIONS

In order to illustrate how the assessment procedures discussed in this chapter might be utilized in school or clinical practice, a case study report is presented. This case study is based on an actual client on whom the author conducted an assessment. In order to protect the confidentiality of the case, the client's name and some identifying details have been changed.

Only some of the actual assessment data that were obtained are reported in this case study. The actual assessment involved comprehensive intellectual, academic, and social-behavioral evaluation, much of which is tangential to an illustration of the assessment techniques discussed in this chapter.

Identifying Information

Name: Kayla S.
Age: 13 years, 2 months
Grade: 7

Reason for Referral

Kayla S., a 13-year-old female student, was referred for this assessment as part of her 3-year special education reevaluation. Kayla is currently placed in the 7th grade at a junior high school in an urban area in the state of Utah, where she receives special education services as behavior disordered under state and federal law. In making the request for this assessment, personnel from the school district specifically requested opinions on the follows questions: (a) Should Kayla continue to receive special education services under her current eligibility category? and (b) What types of intervention programming are most warranted at the present time?

Background Information

Information pertinent to Kayla's academic and behavioral background was obtained through a review of her special education file, and through interviews with her parents and her special education teacher. Kayla has a long history of special education placement for behavioral and learning problems. Reports from as early as her kindergarten year indicate the presence of significant social-behavioral problems, including consistent reports of noncompliance, outbursts and tantrums, refusal of requests from school personnel, and strained peer relations. Kayla's parents voluntarily had her placed in a psychiatric hospital for 2 weeks when she was 7 years old, after her noncompliant behavior and other social-behavioral problems had escalated to the point where they were extremely difficult to control. Previous assessment and programming data also indicate that Kayla's intellectual ability is in the borderline range (with her most recent WISC-R Full Scale IQ score being 76), and that she has academic learning problems in most areas, with mathematics being the most difficult academic task for her. She currently is placed in a self-contained special education classroom 4 hours per day and participates in a regular education classroom (reading and written language block) for 2 hours per day, where she is accompanied and assisted by a special education classroom aide.

Kayla's ethnic/cultural background is Caucasian, and English is the only language spoken in her home. She lives with both of her parents and her younger brother. Mr. and Mrs. S. have been closely involved in Kayla's education and are reported to be supportive of the school program as well as strong advocates for Kayla's educational needs. Her younger brother is currently 10 years old and is not reported to have any significant behavioral or academic problems at school. Kayla's parents report that she and her brother get along fairly well, though she frequently instigates fights with him.

Assessment Procedures

The following social-behavioral assessment procedures were conducted for this assessment:

Direct Behavioral Observation in the Special Education Classroom

Child Behavior Checklist (completed by parents and two teachers)

School Social Behavior Scales (completed by special education teacher)

Peer Nomination Sociometric Procedures in Both Classrooms

Diagnostic Interview with Kayla

Assessment Results and Interpretation

Kayla was observed in her special education classroom for a 30-minute period. The observation took place during the presentation of a unit on personal health. The observation consisted of a interval-recording procedure designed to identify significant social and academic interactions in 20-minute intervals and included social comparison information on the average behavior data of two other students who were alternately observed during the period. None of Kayla's social or emotional behaviors appeared especially problematic or differed from the comparison students during the observation period. However, Kayla's number of requests for help and clarification from the teacher and classroom assistant were twice as high as those of anyone else in the classroom, and she appeared to lack independent work skills and constantly required interaction from adults in the classroom.

The Child Behavior Checklist (CBCL) was completed jointly by Kayla's parents. On the Behavior Problems scales, significant elevations were present on the internalizing (T=79), externalizing (T=78), and Total (T=87) broad-band scores. Behavior problems were rated as significant across all narrow-band domains, with no isolated problem patterns. On the Social Competence scales of the CBCL, Kayla's scores were in the normal range on the Activities area (T=40), but in the problem range in the Social (T=25) and School (T=18) areas. An inspection of the items in these areas revealed that she was rated as having peer relationship problems, has no close friends, and is below average in all academic areas. Kayla's social competence total score (T=25) is also well below the normal score range.

The Teacher Report Form (TRF) of the CBCL was completed on Kayla by both her regular and special education teachers. The rating form completed by her regular education teacher did not indicate any narrow or broad-band behavioral problem scores in the "clinical" range (sum T=64), but several items were endorsed indicating peer relationship problems (e.g., "gets teased a lot" and "is not liked by other children"). It should be noted that Kayla is in this teacher's classroom only 2 hours per day and is accompanied by a special education aide, which likely helps reduce the occurrence of social-behavioral problems. The TRF completed on Kayla by her special education teacher indicated a more severe pattern of problems. Both of the broad-band T scores (Internalizing = 68, Externalizing =71) and the Sum T score (76) were at or close to the "clinical" range, and significant elevations were found on five of the nine narrow-band scores. An inspection of the pattern and endorsed items on the narrow-band scales was indicative of a pattern of problems involving oppositional-defiance, poor peer relationships, social immaturity, and inattentiveness during academic tasks.

Scores from the School Social Behavior Scales, which were completed on Kayla by her special education teacher, indicated an overall pattern of significant social skills deficits, accompanied by moderate elevations in antisocial behaviors. On the Social Competence scale, all three subscale scores (Interpersonal Skills, Self-Management Skills, and Academic Skills) were rated at the "significant problem" level, and the Social

Competence Total score of 66 (which is at the first percentile or lower) showed a significant pattern of generalized social skills deficits. All three of Kayla's Antisocial Behavior subscale scores (Hostile-Irritable, Antisocial-Aggressive, and Demanding-Disruptive) were rated at the "moderate problem" level, and her Antisocial Behavior Total score of 112 (78th percentile) indicated moderate levels of problem behavior excesses.

Sociometric assessment data were obtained earlier in the school year in both of Kayla's classrooms, through the use of a peer nomination technique that included items describing both positive and negative social status. Scoring of these procedures was done by obtaining separate sums of positive and negative status items for each student. In terms of positive nominations, Kayla was nominated by no students in the regular classroom, and by only one student in the special education classroom. On the negative items, Kayla received more nominations than any other student in her regular classroom (specifically on the items "Who would you not want to be best friends with?" and "Who has problems with their schoolwork?"). In the special education classroom, Kayla's scores on positive items were within the average range for that class, but her negative nomination scores were among the highest in the class, particularly on the item "Who is always in trouble with the teacher?" These patterns from the sociometric assessment are indicative of low social status and show a moderate to significant degree of social rejection by peers.

During the diagnostic interview with Kayla, several areas of questioning relevant to social skills and peer relations were pursued. Although she is rated by both teachers and students as having peer relationship problems, Kayla seems to have only a minor amount of insight about this. She stated that she gets along with most other students "just fine" and said that she has "lots of" friends, though she had difficulty naming them. She did admit that when other students tease her she sometimes calls them "dirty names," which usually results in an escalation of the situation. Kayla stated that she liked both of her teachers and her special education classroom aide, but acknowledged that when she gets tired or is in a bad mood, she likes to "tell them what I think about them" and becomes uncooperative. The general impression of the interviewer was that Kayla wants to have more friends and to be teased less by other students but does not seem to recognize either how to go about accomplishing this or the extent to which her negative behaviors affect her relationships with others.

Summary and Recommendations

Kayla S., who has a long history of receiving special education services as behavior disordered, was referred for a 3-year eligibility reevaluation. This case study involves only the social-behavioral aspects of the assessment. A moderate to significant pattern of behavior problems, social skills deficits, and social isolation and rejection was found through the results of the assessment process. It is the opinion of the examiner that Kayla should continue to qualify for special education services under her current classification, due to a longstanding pattern of inappropriate social-emotional behaviors, coupled with significant social skills deficits and peer relationship problems.

Although Kayla's current educational placements and IEP goals appear to be appropriate and their continuation is warranted, some additional intervention recommendations are offered, based on the social assessment data, in order to remediate some of these concerns:

1. Kayla's intervention goals could be modified to include a plan for increasing her ability to work independently on academic tasks, without constant interaction from teachers. To implement this plan successfully, Kayla will likely need specific training in monitoring her own behavior, developing independent cognitive thinking strategies, and learning a series of steps to follow when she is having difficulties.

2. Kayla could benefit from additional intervention training in the area of self-management skills, specifically aimed at helping her learn alternatives to tantruming and oppositional behavior. To implement a goal in this area successfully, Kayla would likely need to work on developing and practicing a list of appropriate alternatives to these negative behaviors, and her progress in these areas should be reinforced through an appropriate reward system.

3. Kayla is in need of some specially designed social skills training. The particular areas in which she appears to need the most training, modeling, and practice in are friendship-making skills, developing appropriate alternatives to antisocial statements to peers, and skills to increase her awareness of and sensitivity to other persons.

BEST PRACTICES IN ASSESSMENT

This chapter concludes with a discussion of best practices in the assessment of social skills and peer relations, and an outline of suggested steps to consider in improving the quality and utility of assessments. Two areas of discussion are included. First, best practical issues relating to improving the technical quality and integrity of the assessment process are examined. Then, best practice issues pertaining to the process of linking social-behavioral assessment with interventions are overviewed.

Assessment Procedures

The first set of issues and recommendations discussed for suggested best practices relates to the overall quality of the assessment process. Through the incorporation of careful planning and the implementation of certain procedures, the technical quality and overall utility and success of the assessment process can be greatly enhanced. Four specific suggestions in this area are offered as follows:

1. *Use rating scales and sociometrics routinely for early screening.* Effective screening practices involve being able to pick out systematically and with a high degree of accuracy students who are in the early stages of developing social-behavioral problems. The identified students are then evaluated more carefully to determine whether their social-behavioral problems warrant special program eligibility and intervention services. The purpose of screening for social-behavioral problems is usually for *secondary intervention*, which is the prevention of the existing problem from becoming worse (Kauffman, 1989). Screening for early intervention is one of the best uses of social skills rating scales and sociometric approaches, as they can potentially cover a wide variety of important behaviors or characteristics and usually take very little time to administer and score. For screening purposes, the general criterion is to include students whose rating scale scores are one or more standard deviations above instrument normative means in terms of social competence deficits or problem behavior excesses. Although sociometric techniques are generally not standardized to this extent, they can be used in screening by including students in the screening pool who show moderate or greater levels of social rejection or social neglect. This practice will narrow the screening pool down to a small to moderate percentage of the overall student population, and this selected group can then be evaluated more comprehensively.

2. *Use the "aggregation principle."* When using behavior rating scales for purposes other than routine screening, obtaining aggregated rating scale data is suggested in order to reduce bias of response and

variance problems in the assessment. In practice, using aggregated measures means obtaining rating evaluations from different raters in different
settings, and using more than one type of rating scale to accomplish this
(Martin et al. 1986).

3. *Use multimethod assessment procedures.* When rating scales or
sociometrics are utilized for purposes such as assessment for program
eligibility or intervention planning, they should be used in conjunction
with other assessment methods. In addition to behavior rating scales, direct
behavioral observation, objective self-report data, and problem-identifica-
tion interviews with teachers and parents are recommended for a comprehensive, multimethod assessment. A social skills or peer relations
assessment using this method is not only technically strengthened, but
may provide a better basis for forming intervention hypotheses, as some
methods of assessment may yield information on social-behavioral problems that other methods do not.

4. *Work closely with constituent groups when using sociometric assessment methods.* This chapter has already alluded to the controversy
surrounding the use of certain sociometric techniques (particularly those
using negative nomination procedures), and the hesitance or resistance
often encountered from parents or other professionals when attempting to
obtain these types of data. One way of avoiding misunderstandings and
heated discussions about the assessment process is to work very closely
with constituent groups every step of the way. These constituent groups
would typically include parents of the children to be assessed and the
teachers, specialists, and school administrators involved. Through the
process of education and open and frank communication, resistance may
be minimized, and the outlook for a successful assessment process may be
enhanced.

Linking Assessment to Intervention

Although the process of assessing social skills and peer relations has
many potential purposes, one of the most important of these purposes is
using the data to develop appropriate social-behavioral intervention plans.
Unfortunately, there is evidence that in many cases where assessment data
are obtained on students with special needs, the focus of the assessment
process is misdirected to the point where little intervention benefit to the
student is derived from it (Fuchs & Fuchs, 1986; Howell, 1986). With this
problem in mind, the following four suggestions are offered for using

assessment data from rating scales and sociometric approaches within an intervention framework:

1. *Recommended treatments should be matched to problems.* One of the problems often seen in social-behavioral assessment reports is the tendency for examiners to make generic recommendations such as "this student would benefit from social skills training." Such a broad and vague recommendation does very little to tie assessment data to an effective intervention. One of the major characteristics of effective practices for working with students who have emotional or behavioral problems is that treatments should be closely matched to problems (Peacock Hill Working Group, 1991). When social skills and peer relationship data suggest that a student has deficits in these areas, the suggested approach is identifying the specific problem areas (e.g., interacting appropriately with peers, accepting criticism, showing self-restraint) and then making recommendations for social skills training or other interventions that specifically address the key problems.

2. *Develop IEP goals by modifying rating scale items.* One of the advantages of using rating scale assessments is that they provide student performance data on a number of standardized items that reflect specific behaviors important to successful social adjustment. By carefully analyzing subtest score patterns and individual items where social-behavioral problems seem to be especially severe, individual items can be selected and reworded in developing IEPs or other intervention plan goal statements. For example, if a student had very low scores on the Interpersonal Skills subscale of the School Social Behavior Scales, and a careful content examination revealed that items 4 and 19 were rated as especially problematic, these items could be reworded into general goal statements such as "Steven will increase his level of providing help to other students when it is appropriately needed" and "Steven will increase his number of interactions with classmates in the classroom and on the playground."

3. *Continuously assess progress during intervention.* It has been demonstrated that continuous assessment and monitoring of student progress following the initial assessment and intervention is very important in successful implementation of behavioral and academic intervention (Howell & Morehead, 1987; Kerr & Nelson, 1989). Progress toward behavioral goals developed from social skills and peer relations assessment data could be easily assessed on a weekly or semiweekly schedule using appropriate rating scales or nonintrusive and simple sociometric

approaches. There are a number other simple ways of assessing daily progress, such as using student performance records.

4. *Follow-up intervention with further assessment.* Additional assessment following the intervention can also be a useful process. The main reason for follow-up assessment is to determine how well the intervention effects have been maintained over time (e.g., after 3 months) and how well the behavioral changes have generalized to other settings (e.g., the home setting and other classrooms). In actual practice, a follow-up assessment might involve having teacher(s) and parent(s) complete social competence rating scales on a student or conducting sociometric assessments after a specified time period has elapsed following the student's participation in a social skills training program. The data obtained from this follow-up assessment can be used to determine whether or not follow-up interventions seem appropriate and may be useful in developing future intervention programs if it is determined that social-behavioral gains are not being maintained over time or generalized across specific settings.

REFERENCES

Achenbach, T. M., & Edelbrock, C. (1983). *Manual for the Child Behavior Checklist and revised Child Behavior Profile.* Burlington, VT: University of Vermont, Department of Psychiatry.

Achenbach, T. M., & Edelbrock, C. (1986). *Manual for the teacher's report form and teacher version of the Child Behavior Profile.* Burlington, VT: University of Vermont, Department of Psychiatry.

Asher, S. R., & Taylor, A. R. (1981). The social outcomes of mainstreaming: assessment and beyond. *Exceptional Children Quarterly, 1,* 13-30.

Bower, E. (1969). *Early identification of emotionally handicapped children in school* (2nd ed.). Springfield, IL: Charles C. Thomas.

Bryan, T. (1974). Peer popularity of learning disabled children. *Journal of Learning Disabilities, 7,* 261-268.

Cartledge, G., Frew, T., & Zacharias, J. (1985). Social skills needs of mainstreamed students: Peer and teacher perceptions. *Learning Disability Quarterly, 8,* 132-140.

Coie, J. D., Dodge, K. A., & Cappotelli, H. (1982). Dimensions and types of social status: A cross-age perspective. *Developmental Psychology, 18,* 557-570.

Cowen, E. L., Pederson, A., Babigian, H., Izzo, L. D., & Trost, M. A. (1973). Long-term follow-up of early detected vulnerable children. *Journal of Consulting and Clinical Psychology, 41,* 438-446.

Epstein, M. H., Cullinan, D., & Lloyd, J. W. (1986). Behavior problem patterns among the learning disabled: III - Replication across age and sex. *Learning Disability Quarterly, 9,* 43-54.

Fuchs, L. S., & Fuchs, D. (1986). Linking assessment to instructional intervention: An overview. *School Psychology Review, 15*, 318-323.

Gresham, F. M. (1982). Misguided mainstreaming: The case for social skills training with handicapped students. *Exceptional Children, 48,* 422-433.

Gresham, F. M. (1986). Conceptual issues in the assessment of social competence in children. In P. Strain, M. Guralnick, & H. Walker (Eds.), *Children's social behavior: Development, assessment, and modification* (pp. 143-179). New York: Academic Press.

Gresham, F. M., & Elliott, S. N. (1990). *The Social Skills Rating System.* Circle Pines, MN: American Guidance Service.

Gresham, F. M., & Reschly, D. J. (1987a). Dimensions of social competence: Method factors in the assessment of adaptive behavior, social skills, and peer acceptance. *Journal of School Psychology, 25,* 367-381.

Gresham, F. M., & Reschly, D. J. (1987b). Issues in the conceptualization, classification and assessment of social skills in the mildly handicapped. In T. Kratochwill (Ed.), *Advances in school psychology* (pp. 203-264). Hillsdale, NJ: Lawrence Erlbaum.

Grossman, H. J. (Ed.). (1983). *Classification in mental retardation.* Washington DC: American Association on Mental Deficiency.

Hartup, W. W. (1983). Peer relations. In E. M. Hetherington (Ed.), *Handbook of child psychology (Vol. 4): Socialization, personality, and social development* (pp. 103-198). New York: Wiley.

Hayvren, M., & Hymel, S. (1984). Ethical issues in sociometric testing: Impact of sociometric measures on interaction behavior. *Developmental Psychology, 20,* 844-849.

Hollinger, J. D. (1987). Social skills for behaviorally disordered children as preparation for mainstreaming: Theory, practice, and new directions. *Remedial and Special Education, 11,* 139-149.

Howell, K. W. (1986). Direct assessment of academic performance. *School Psychology Review, 15,* 324-335.

Howell, K. W., & Morehead, M. K. (1987). *Curriculum-based evaluation for special and remediation education.* Columbus, OH: Merrill.

Kauffman, J. M. (1989). *Characteristics of behavior disorders of children and youth* (4th ed.). Columbus, OH: Merrill.

Kauffman, J. M., Semmell, M. I., & Agard, J. A. (1974). PEIMW: An overview. *Education and Training for the Mentally Retarded, 9,* 107-112.

Kerr, M. M., & Nelson, C. M. (1989). *Strategies for managing behavior problems in the classroom* (2nd ed.). Columbus, OH: Merrill.

Landau, S., & Milich, R. (1990). Assessment of children's social status and peer relations. In A.M. LaGreca (Ed.), *Through the eyes of the child* (pp. 259-291). Boston: Allyn & Bacon.

Loeber, R. (1985). Patterns of development of antisocial child behavior. *Annals of Child Development, 2,* 77-116.

Martin, R. P. (1988). *Assessment of personality and behavior problems.* New York: Guilford Press.

Martin, R. P., Hooper, S., & Snow, J. (1986). Behavior rating scale approaches to personality assessment in children and adolescents. In H. M. Knoff (Ed.), *The assessment of child and adolescent personality* (pp. 309-351). New York: Guilford Press.

Masten, A. S., Morrison, P., & Pelligrini, D. S. (1985). A revised class play method of peer assessment. *Developmental Psychology, 21,* 523-533.

McCandless, B., & Marshall, H. (1957). A picture sociometric technique for preschool children and its relation to teacher judgments of friendship. *Child Development, 28,* 139-148.

McKinney, J. D., & Feagan, L. (1984). Academic and behavioral characteristics of learning disabled children and average achievers: Longitudinal studies. *Learning Disability Quarterly, 7,* 251-264.

McKinney, J. D., McClure, S., & Feagans, L. (1982). Classroom behavior of learning disabled children. *Learning Disability Quarterly, 5,* 45-52.

Merrell, K. W. (1989). Concurrent relationships between two behavioral rating scales for teachers: An examination of self-control, social competence, and school behavioral adjustment. *Psychology in the Schools, 26,* 267-271.

Merrell, K. W. (1991, November). *The utility of the School Social Behavior Scales in differentiating behavior disordered students from other handicapped students.* Paper presented at the TECBD Conference on Severe Behavior Disorders of Children and Youth, Tempe, AZ.

Merrell, K. W. (in press a). Development and validation of the School Social Behavior Scales. *School Psychology Review.*

Merrell, K. W. (in press b). *The School Social Behavior Scales.* Brandon, VT: Clinical Psychology Publishing Company.

Merrell, K. W., & Gill, S. J. (in press). Social and behavioral characteristics of gifted students: A comparative study. *Gifted Child Quarterly.*

Merrell, K. W., Merz, J. N., Johnson, E. R., & Ring, E. N. (1992). Social competence of mildly handicapped and low-achieving students: A comparative study. *School Psychology Review, 21,* 91-109.

Merrell, K.W., & Shinn, M.R. (1990). Critical variables in the learning disabilities identification process. *School Psychology Review, 19,* 74-82,

Milich, R., & Landau, S. (1984). A comparison of the social status and social behavior of aggressive and aggressive/withdrawn boys. *Journal of Abnormal Child Psychology, 12,* 277-288.

Moreno, J. l. (1934). *Who shall survive?* Washington DC: Nervous and Mental Disease Publishing.

Oden, S. L., & Asher, S. R. (1977). Coaching children in social skills for friendship making. *Child Development, 48,* 496-506.

Park, H. S., Tappe, P., Carmeto, R., & Gaylord-Ross, R. (1990). Social support and quality of life for learning disabled and mildly retarded youth in transition. In R. Gaylord-Ross, S. Siegel, H. S. Park, S. Sacks, & L. Goetz (Eds.), *Readings in ecosocial development* (pp. 293-328). San Francisco: Department of Special Education, San Francisco State University.

Parker, J. G., & Asher, S. R. (1987). Peer relations and later personal development: Are low-accepted children "at-risk"? *Psychological Bulletin, 102,* 357-389.

Peacock Hill Working Group. (1991). Problems and promises in special education and related services for children and youth with emotional or behavioral disorders. *Behavioral Disorders, 16,* 299-313.

Reschly, D. J. (1990). Best practices in adaptive behavior. In A. Thomas & J. Grimes (Eds.), *Best practices in school psychology - II* (pp. 29-42). Washington DC: National Association of School Psychologists.

Roff, M. (1963). Childhood social interactions and young adult psychosis. *Journal of Clinical Psychology, 19,* 152-157.

Roff, M., & Sells, S. (1968). Juvenile delinquency in relation to peer acceptance-rejection and sociometric status. *Psychology in the Schools, 5,* 3-18.

Roff, M., Sells, B., & Golden, M. (1972). *Social adjustment and personality development in children.* Minneapolis: University of Minnesota Press.

Sater, G. M., & French, D. C. (1989). A comparison of the social competencies of learning disabled and low-achieving elementary age children. *The Journal of Special Education, 23,* 29-42.

Sattler, J. M. (1988). *Assessment of children* (3rd ed.). San Diego: Jerome M. Sattler.

Stumme, V. S., Gresham, F. M., & Scott, N. A. (1982). Validity of social behavior assessment in discriminating emotionally disabled and nonhandicapped students. *Journal of Behavioral Assessment, 4,* 327-341.

Vaughn, S. (1987). TLC—Teaching, learning, and caring: Teaching interpersonal problem-solving skills to behaviorally disordered adolescents. *The Pointer, 31,* 25-30.

Veldman, D. J., & Sheffield, J. R. (1979). The scaling of sociometric nominations. *Educational and Psychological Measurement, 39,* 99-106.

Walker, H. M., & Hops, H. (1976). Increasing academic achievement by reinforcing direct academic performance and/or facilitating nonacademic responses. *Journal of Educational Psychology, 68,* 218-225.

Walker, H. M., & McConnell, S. R. (1988). *The Walker-McConnell scale of social competence and school adjustment.* Austin, TX: Pro-Ed.

Walker, H. M., Steiber, S., & Eisert, D. (1991). Teacher ratings of adolescent social skills: Psychometric characteristics and factorial replicability. *School Psychology Review, 20,* 301-314.

Walker, H. M., Todis, B., Holmes, D., & Horton, G. (1988). *The Walker social skills curriculum: The ACCESS program (adolescent curriculum for communication and effective social skills).* Austin, TX: Pro-Ed.

Worthen, B. R., Borg, W. R., & White, K. R. (in press). *Measurement and evaluation in the schools: A practical guide.* White Plains, NY: Longman.

11 BEST PRACTICES IN ASSESSING ACADEMIC ACHIEVEMENT

Belinda Lazarus

Academic achievement is the most frequently evaluated aspect of learning in educational settings. Educators rely on group-oriented and individualized strategies to summarize students' present levels of performance, to guide instruction, and to evaluate program effectiveness. Various kinds of assessment data provide the foundation for making educational decisions. In this chapter, after a brief discussion of historical and theoretical aspects of academic assessment, the following areas will be covered: commonly used tests and strategies, emphasizing practical classroom and clinical applications; case studies demonstrating practical applications of various strategies with specific groups of special needs students; and issues associated with effective practices in assessing academic assessment.

HISTORICAL AND THEORETICAL PERSPECTIVES

Academic achievement is a widely recognized indicator of school success. For generations educators, parents, peers, and society in general have gauged an individual's personal progress and future potential to contribute to society with a variety of academic performance variables ranging from grades to levels of education. Students who earned above-average grades and graduated from high school, college, and/or postgraduate programs were expected to succeed in life and become contributing members of society. However, students who failed to gain basic reading, language, and math skills through traditional educational means were considered inherently slow and lacking in the ability to benefit from education. Cultural, economic, instructional, and health factors were seldom considered as possible causes for school failure.

Few educational alternatives existed for students who experienced problems with the general school curriculum. Students who experienced repeated failure were tolerated in the elementary grades and often advised to drop out of school and join the armed services, get married, or learn a trade as soon as they reached adolescence. Prior to PL 94-142, parents of handicapped students were even discouraged from sending their children to school and often resorted to private schools, comprehensive-care institutions, or home schooling, all at their own expense. In the rare instances when students were "tested" to ascertain the cause of their learning problems, one test was administered (usually an intelligence test) and the results were used to classify and isolate or exclude the student from the mainstream. In fact as late as 1919, The Wisconsin Supreme Court, in the case of *State ex. rel. Beattie v. Board of Education of City of Antigo* (Wis.), supported a school district's denial of educational services to a child with cerebral palsy because the condition produced "a depressing and nauseating effect on the teachers and children and that (the student) required an undue portion of the teacher's time" (p. 154).

In 1954, Judge Warren's ruling on the *Brown v. Board of Education* case, a class action suit petitioning for equal educational opportunities for Black school children, stated, "it is doubtful that any child may reasonably be expected to succeed in life if he is denied the opportunity of an education" (*Brown v. Board of Education*, 1954, p. 493.). Judge Warren's decision served as a catalyst for a series of events that would redefine the American educational system and generate controversies for decades to come. Subsequent litigation and legislation established educational opportunities for all school-aged American children at the public's expense and linked multidisciplinary assessment and achievement as an interrelated process needed to plan, monitor, and evaluate student gains.

Pubic Law 94-142, or the Education for All Handicapped Children Act of 1975, occasioned the strongest linkage between assessment and academic achievement. Several major provisions of PL 94-142 mandate mul-

tidisciplinary assessment to identify students needing special education N.B
services and require an individualized education program that is based on
and monitored by assessment. The mandate further specifies that in order
to qualify for special services, assessment data must show that the nature
and severity of the student's handicapping condition prevent adequate
academic achievement in the regular classroom.

ACHIEVEMENT TESTS AND STRATEGIES

Assessment of academic achievement falls into two categories: formal
tests and informal strategies. Formal tests are standardized assessments
with specific administration procedures. These norm-referenced tests
compare an individual student's or group's performance to a normative
sampling of individuals who share common characteristics such as gender,
age, grade level, geographic region, and socioeconomic status. Informal
strategies assess student and environmental factors that affect achievement
and compare the student to a predetermined standard (e.g., grade-level
expectancies, developmental milestones). A comprehensive evaluation of
academic achievement requires a combination of approaches. The following section describes formal, group-oriented, and individually administered tests and informal strategies in current use.

Group-Administered Tests

Group-administered, standardized tests are most often used by regular
classroom teachers. These tests provide normative data that allow teachers
to compare their class's achievement levels with a national normative
sample composed of same-age or grade peers. The tests also screen the
class for low-achieving students who may need a more comprehensive ←
evaluation. Two popular group-administered tests, the California Achievement Tests and the Metropolitan Achievement Tests, are described below.

California Achievement Tests

The California Achievement Tests (CAT; CTS/McGraw-Hill, 1985)
measure reading, spelling, mathematics, language, science, social studies,
and study skills of students in grades K through 12. The purposes of the
CAT include screening for grouping, further assessment needs, instruc- N.B

tional planning, and program evaluation. This timed test requires between 2½ hours and 6 hours 48 minutes to administer.

The CAT offers several scoring and interpretation options. The test yields percentile ranks, stanines, grade equivalents, normal curve equivalents, and scaled scores. Scores may be displayed in individual test records, graphic frequency distributions, summary reports, error analyses, and class test records. Interpretations of scores include group or individual mastery of criterion-referenced objectives, normative data comparing pupil performance to national norms, and demographic norm reports that compare class or school achievement levels to demographically similar school districts across the nation. The tests may be hand scored or submitted to the publisher for machine scoring.

Metropolitan Tests of Achievement

The Metropolitan Tests of Achievement, Sixth Edition (Mat6) contain two components, the Survey Battery (SB) and the Diagnostic Battery (DB), each designed for different, but related, purposes. The SB (Prescott, Balow, Hogan, & Farr, 1984) provides a global evaluation of skill acquisition for students in grades K through 12.9 in five academic areas: reading, mathematics, language, social studies, and science. The major purposes of the SB are general screening, monitoring group performance, and evaluating the general instruction program. Administration is timed and requires between 1 hour 35 minutes and 4 hours 14 minutes.

The DB includes the Reading Diagnostic Test (Farr, Prescott, Hogan, & Balow, 1986), the Mathematics Diagnostic Test (Hogan, Farr, Prescott, & Balow, 1986), the Language Diagnostic Test (Balow, Hogan, Farr, & Prescott, 1986), and an optional Writing Test. The subtests in each diagnostic battery represent an expansion of the SB subtests and provide teachers with a detailed analysis in specific skill areas to aid in instructional planning. Each diagnostic battery can be interpreted in a norm-referenced or a criterion-referenced manner and assesses students in grades K.5 to 12.9. Administration requires from 1 hour 19 minutes (one battery) to 3 hours 45 minutes (all batteries).

The conjunctive use of the SB and DBs provides a multidimensional view of group and individual achievement. Scoring options include norm-referenced data: scaled scores, percentile ranks, grade equivalents, normal curve equivalents, and performance indicators. Criterion-referenced data provided are independent, instructional, and frustration reading levels and instructional mathematic levels. The MAT6 may be hand scored or computer scored by the publisher. Summary reports and norm-referenced or criterion-referenced analyses of classes and individuals are also available from the publisher.

Formal Individually Administered Tests

Individually administered, multiple-skill tests are frequently used to determine a student's eligibility for special education services and to monitor program effectiveness. The tests usually include reading, language, mathematics, and knowledge subtests; occasionally science and social studies subtests are included. Multiple-skill achievement measures are frequently a part of the multidisciplinary assessment battery mandated in the identification and service of handicapped students. A description of three individually administered, norm-referenced tests in current use—the Peabody Individualized Achievement Test—Revised, the Kaufman Test of Educational Achievement, and the Woodcock-Johnson Tests of Achievement—Revised—follows.

Peabody Individual Achievement Test—Revised

The Peabody Individual Achievement Test—Revised (PIAT-R; Markwardt, 1989) represents a major revision of the original PIAT (Dunn & Markwardt, 1970). The PIAT-R is intended to screen, assist in determining eligibility for special education services, and facilitate the development of the individual education program. All of the subtests are untimed and require approximately 1 hour to 1½ hours to administer. The PIAT-R includes five required subtests (General Information, Reading Recognition, Reading Comprehension, Mathematics, and Spelling) and two optional Written Expression (WE) subtests, Level I for grades K through 2 and Level II for grades 3 through 12.

Scoring options for the required subtests include age and grade equivalents, standard scores, normal curve equivalents, percentile ranks, and stanines. For the WE subtests, raw scores may be converted to grade-based stanines or developmental scaled scores. Student responses to each subtest item and derived scores are recorded in an Individual Student Test Record. Derived scores are recorded in tabular and graphic formats that facilitate an examination of intraindividual differences. Composite scores are available for Reading (Reading Recognition + Reading Comprehension),

Total Test (add all required subtest raw scores), and Written Language (WE + Spelling). Hand scoring the PIAT-R is tedious; however, a "user-friendly" and efficient computer scoring disc is available from the publisher, according to Edwards (1989).

Kaufman Tests of Educational Achievement

The Kaufman Tests of Educational Achievement (K-TEA; Kaufman & Kaufman, 1985a,b,c) consist of two forms: the Comprehensive Form (CF) and the Brief Form (BF). Although both forms are recommended for program placement, planning, and evaluation, the KTEA-BF is recommended for screening purposes and the KTEA-CF is intended for determining intraindividual strengths and weaknesses. The forms may be used separately or conjunctively with students in grades 1 through 12.1. The KTEA-CF contains reading decoding, reading comprehension, mathematic applications, mathematic computation, and spelling subtests. The BF contains reading, mathematics, and spelling subtests.

The KTEA-CF and BF offer numerous scoring options. Age- and grade-based scores for either spring or fall include standard scores, age and grade equivalents, percentile ranks, stanines, and normal curve equivalents for each subtest and three composites: reading, mathematics, and total test. Further, the KTEA-CF offers teachers qualitative information through a detailed error analysis of each item in each subtest. All scores along with the error analyses are contained in individual student test protocols. Both forms may be hand or computer scored.

Woodcock-Johnson Psycho-Educational Battery—Revised

The Woodcock-Johnson Psycho-Educational Battery—Revised (WJ-R; Woodcock & Johnson, 1989) is a diagnostic series that includes measures of cognitive and academic functioning for children and adults from ages 5 to 78. The series includes the Tests of Achievement (TA-R) and the Tests of Cognitive Ability (TCA-R). This chapter addresses the TA-R, which include a standard battery of 9 required subtests and a supplemental battery consisting of 5 additional subtests designed to supply additional information. Numerous achievement and basic skill composites are available by combining subtest raw scores in a variety of ways. Table 11.1 lists the 14 achievement subtests and composite options.

TABLE 11.1. *The Relationship Between Woodcock-Johnson Tests of Achievement and Composite Score*

Tests of Achievement	Early Development	Reading — Broad Reading	Reading — Basic Skills	Reading — Comprehension	Mathematics — Broad Mathematics	Mathematics — Basic Skills	Mathematics — Reasoning	Written Language — Broad Written Language	Written Language — Basic Skills	Written Language — Expression	Written Language — P.S.U.	Handwriting	Broad Knowledge	Skills	Intra-Achievement Discrepancies
STANDARD BATTERY															
22. Letter-Word Identification	•	•	•										•		•
23. Passage Comprehension		•		•											•
24. Calculation					•	•									•
25. Applied Problems	•				•		•						•		•
26. Dictation	•							•	•		•		•		•
27. Writing Samples								•		•	•				•
28. Science	•												•		•
29. Social Studies	•												•		•
30. Humanities	•												•		•
SUPPLEMENTAL BATTERY															
31. Word Attack			•												
32. Reading Vocabulary				•											
33. Quantitative Concepts						•									
34. Proofing									•		•				
35. Writing Frequency										•					

Note. Reprinted from *Woodcock-Johnson Tests of Achievement Standard and Supplemental Batteries Examiner's Manual* (Woodcock & Mather, 1989, p.12). Used by permission of DLM.

The TA-R offer several scoring options familiar to teachers: age and grade equivalents, standard scores, and percentile ranks for content clusters. However, derived scores for individual subtests are unavailable. Age- and grade-level instructional ranges are constructed to encompass the student's instructional and frustration levels in content cluster areas. A comparison of the student's performance on each cluster and the average achievement of students with the same cognitive ability yields information about the student's actual and expected performance. This Relative Mastery Index is presented as a ratio and is the only score that may be unfamiliar to teachers. Hand scoring is time consuming, complicated by numerous tables, and may lead to error; however, a computer scoring program is available.

Case Study 1: Formal Tests

As the school district's special education consultant, Mr. Williams was asked to collect academic achievement data to assist the multidisciplinary assessment team in determining Kim's eligibility for special education services. Kim, a 12-year-old, 6th-grade girl, began exhibiting skill lags in language and reading in the 3rd grade. Even with extra assistance, she is currently failing all reading-related subjects and barely passing English. On the MAT6-SB that was recently administered to her 6th-grade class, Kim earned scores similar to a student aged 8-3 in reading and aged 9-7 in language areas. As a result, her 6th-grade teacher referred her for a comprehensive evaluation.

After consulting with the school psychologist, Mr. Williams discovered that Kim's level of cognitive functioning as measured by an individually administered intelligence test fell within the average range with a Full Scale score of 110. Former and current teachers reported that Kim's parents were cooperative, helped Kim at home, and even hired a tutor; however, Kim's progress remained minimal. Because the assessment team felt that both general and specific information about Kim's levels of academic functioning were needed, it was decided that the KTEA-CF, which provides normative data and criterion-referenced data through error analysis, would provide the best analysis of Kim's skills.

Kim cooperated throughout the administration of the KTEA-CF. Her attention span, oral language, and interaction skills impressed Mr. Williams. However, Kim's performance on the reading, language, and spelling subtests revealed severe discrepancies between her cognitive functioning and performance in these academic areas. In his report, Mr. Williams listed the following scores:

SUBTEST	AGE EQUIVALENTS	GRADE EQUIVALENTS	STANDARD SCORES	PERCENTILE RANKS
Reading Decoding	9-10	4.6	88	42
Reading Comprehension	8-1	3.1	70	32
Mathematic Applications	11-1	5.8	97	57

Mathematic Computation	10-8	5.6	93	53
Spelling	8-4	3.2	71	34

When the team convened and compared data, all of the team members agreed that learning disabilities in reading and language affected Kim's academic performance in the regular classroom. As a result, the team first recommended direct services for Kim for reading and language in the (special education resource room) Second, they suggested that Kim remain in the regular classroom for nonacademics, content subjects, and mathematics, with reading and writing support from the (resource teacher) in content areas. After considering the error analysis available on the KTEA-CF, the team recommended that resource room goals focus on building Kim's sight word and written vocabulary; improving her literal, interpretive, and evaluative comprehension skills; and teaching creative and critical writing skills.

Informal Assessment Strategies

Informal strategies are frequently used and offer teachers a flexible means of assessing academic achievement. In fact, many of the assessment areas mandated by PL 94-142 in the identification of handicapping conditions cannot be measured unless informal strategies are used. The qualitative information supplied by informal techniques lends a contextual perspective to the austere, numeric data produced by formal tests. Informal data transform the "statistical student" into a person with real-world relationships and experiences. Systematic observation, response and error analysis, interviews, checklists and rating scales, inventories, criterion-referenced tests, and curriculum-based assessment are among the frequently employed informal strategies.

Systematic Observation

Systematic observation requires planning but allows teachers to observe students in a variety of settings along with the environmental factors that occasion and reinforce the target behaviors. To develop a systematic observation plan, first define the target behavior in terms that limit the need for interpretation. Then, select convenient measurement, recording, and reporting systems that best describe the behavior. Observations may be conducted by the teacher, paraprofessional, psychologist, or any other trained individual.

Response and Error Analysis

Teachers frequently use response and error analysis to evaluate the permanent products (e.g., worksheets, tape-recorded responses) produced by students. Response analysis focuses on both the correct and incorrect responses produced by the student. Paper grading, in which incorrect responses are marked and correct responses are left unmarked, is a form of response analysis typically used by teachers. Error analysis considers only the incorrect responses for the purposes of establishing a consistent, meaningful pattern of errors (e.g., consistent mispronunciation of words containing a silent "e"). McLoughlin and Lewis (1990) advise that to establish a student's typical pattern of responding, a number of permanent products should be analyzed across time.

Interviews

Interviews can be as simple or complex as desired. The primary purpose of an interview is to obtain information that is often unavailable by other assessment means. Interviews are composed of questions designed to address a specific area such as educational history. Teachers may interview former teachers, supplemental service teachers, parents, and others regarding a student's academic achievement in other settings.

Checklists and Rating Scales

Checklists and rating scales are often used to guide interviews or may be completed independently by the student or an informant who is familiar with the student. Both are listings of behaviors (e.g., "knows addition facts") that require answers from informants. Checklists are less subjective, requiring a simple "yes" or "no" response, whereas rating scales require a subjective ranking of specific skills (e.g., "uses addition facts to solve everyday problems") usually ranging from "always" or "never" on a 5-point Likert-type scale.

Inventories

Inventories are the most popular informal strategy used by teachers. As the name implies, inventories "take stock" of what students know or do not know. Spelling tests, sight word lists, and math fact tests represent a few of the many academic areas assessed by inventories. Numerous commercial inventories are available or teachers can construct their own.

Criterion-Referenced Tests

Criterion-referenced tests contain numerous items addressing the same skill and provide an in-depth assessment of multiple academic domains. Basic reading, mathematic, and language areas are analyzed into all the subordinate skills composing the domain. The student's performance is compared to a prespecified criterion (usually grade level) based on a hypothesized or actual curriculum. Specifically, the criterion represents skill mastery at a particular grade level. Initially, criterion-referenced tests require a considerable amount of time to administer; however, subsequent administrations can be completed quickly.

Curriculum-Based Assessment

Curriculum-based assessment (CBA) contains items derived directly from the student's curriculum. As Salvia and Hughes (1990) succinctly define it, CBAs test what is taught. Although commercial CBAs exist, more relevant measures addressing a school's or student's curriculum are constructed by educators within the student's instructional environment. ✗✗ These CBAs are considered the fairest and most content relevant measures of students' levels of academic performance.

Case Study 2: Informal Assessment

Joseph, a 14-year-old freshman in Mrs. Gilmore's class for educable mentally retarded (EMR) students, has struggled with academics throughout school. Because Joseph is beginning his first year of high school, Mrs. Gilmore is unfamiliar with the specifics regarding Joseph's academic needs. The individualized educational program (IEP) accompanying him listed his Full Scale IQ on the Wechsler Intelligence Scale for Children (WISC-R; Wechsler, 1984) as 62. His performance on the PIAT-R earned age-equivalent scores ranging between 9-11 and 10-2 in reading skills, 8-3 and 9-7 in math calculations and applications, and 8-1 and 8-6 in spelling. However, goals and objectives listed on the IEP focused on 1st- and 2nd-grade skills such as recalling addition facts. Mrs. Gilmore felt that primary-level skills were too easy for Joseph. However, after evaluating work samples produced in her EMR class in math and reading, Mrs. Gilmore was startled to learn that Joseph missed most math problems and could not remember anything he read. She decided that she needed more specific information regarding the skills Joseph had mastered and those skills needing further instruction. Because the results of the PIAT-R provided only general information, Mrs. Gilmore decided to use several informal strategies to pinpoint the specific skills needed by Joseph.

To establish Joseph's sight word and comprehension skill levels, Mrs. Gilmore devoted 30 minutes to administering reading inventories that contained a list of sight words and three short stories that yielded independent, instructional, and frustration reading ranges. Joseph's recognition of sight words closely paralleled his performance on the PIAT-R; however, his instructional range in factual and interpretive kinds of comprehension fell at the primer level. Mrs. Gilmore also interviewed Joseph to ascertain his prior knowledge of the content addressed in the three comprehension stories. After discovering that Joseph's prior knowledge relating to the stories was limited, she asked Joseph to read a fourth story and supplied him with prior knowledge relating to the key concepts. His comprehension immediately improved. As a result of the informal assessment of Joseph's reading skills, Mrs. Gilmore established a list of specific sight words for Joseph to practice and learned that, when prior knowledge was supplied for him in prereading activities, his comprehension more closely paralleled his sight word vocabulary.

The following day, Mrs. Gilmore gave Joseph several math fact worksheets and a variety of addition and subtraction problems to complete while she taught a reading group. The results of the math facts inventories revealed that Joseph knew all of his addition, subtraction, and multiplication facts. Response and error analysis of his addition and subtraction worksheets showed that he did not consistently read operational signs appropriately, could not carry beyond the 100s place, and did not borrow correctly when a subtraction problem contained a 0. However, Mrs. Gilmore was pleased to note that Joseph knew when to carry and borrow. As a result of the mathematics assessment, Mrs. Gilmore planned long-term strategies and activities to remediate Joseph's deficits.

Although professionals often consider informal strategies to be time consuming, the preceding case study shows that with a little planning, a wealth of useful information can be obtained in an efficient manner. Many informal strategies do not need to be monitored by the teacher or can be conducted by a trained paraprofessional. Assessment results address specific information that is needed to remediate specific skill deficits exhibited by individual students.

PRACTICAL APPLICATIONS

Classroom Applications

By far, the major purpose of academic assessment is improving student performance in the classroom. However, the "Educational Reform" movement created a demand for accountability that also requires teachers to demonstrate effectiveness through assessment. Assessment practices in the classroom assume many forms. Formal tests that compare students with other students are administered to rank and quantify students' academic strengths and weaknesses. However, informal strategies are needed to gather specific information that translates into instructional strategies and activities for daily use. Frequently, the use of multiple strategies is needed to establish fully the range of students' instructional needs.

Current conceptualizations of assessment recognize the inextricable relationship between assessment and instruction. For planning, monitoring, and evaluating academic achievement, an assessment-instructional process is needed. Figure 11.1 depicts the cyclical nature of the relationship between assessment and instruction. The cycle is based on a derivative model in which each component of instruction evolves from the preceding component. The cycle begins with the selection and use of assessment strategies that produce the kind of data desired. Goals are based on assessment data; objectives are derived from the goals; and instructional strategies, activities, materials, and student response modes are selected in a sequential manner. Student responses are assessed and the cycle begins again. As a result, all components of instruction are linked in a never-ending cycle that is driven by assessment. The following example demonstrates the practical application of the model.

FIGURE 11.1. *Assessment-Instruction Cycle*

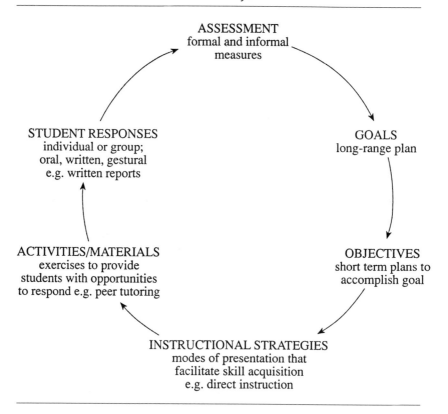

Case Study 3: Assessment-Instruction Cycle

Mrs. McKenna has become increasingly concerned about Ken, a 10-year-old boy in her 4th-grade class. Ken has always disliked reading and his performance on the California Achievement Tests indicated that he was functioning on a 2nd-grade level in all academic areas—even mathematics, his best subject. Mrs. McKenna considered Ken a bright, personable boy with many friends and wanted to develop strategies to improve his performance before referring him for special education assessment.

Ken's overall achievement on the CAT became Mrs. McKenna's immediate concern. On daily tasks, Ken excelled in mathematics and Mrs. McKenna felt certain that his CAT mathematic scores were inaccurate. She decided that more assessment information was needed to plan instruction and asked the special education teacher to administer the Woodcock-Johnson Tests of Achievement—Revised. Sure enough, Ken scored in the 96th percentile rank in mathematics. His language skills were a little below average at the 46th percentile, and his reading was his lowest score at the 33rd percentile with his performance equal to a child aged 8-3. After analyzing Ken's responses to each reading and language subtest item, Mrs. McKenna noted that word attack, sight vocabulary, and spelling skills were Ken's lowest scores. An interview with Ken's kindergarten and 1st-grade teachers confirmed that he had experienced problems with sight-sound correspondences from his earliest school experience. A hearing test revealed that Ken's acuity was normal. Finally, an inventory of alphabet letter sounds, assessment sound clusters, and syllables showed that Ken recalled all letter and consonant cluster sounds, but syllables containing variations of vowel sounds confused him.

Based on the assessment data, Mrs. McKenna established three goals for Ken: (1) to improve Ken's recognition of syllables containing vowels; (2) to improve Ken's sight word vocabulary; and (3) to increase spelling skills to practical writing. Because Mrs. McKenna wisely realized that students need to operationalize skills on a variety of levels of learning, she decided to establish several multidimensional objectives to accomplish each goal. To launch Ken's remediation program, Mrs. McKenna derived the following objectives from each goal:

GOAL: to improve Ken's recognition of syllables containing vowels.

1. When presented with written single syllables containing short or long vowel sounds, Ken will state the syllable with 90% accuracy on three consecutive trials.

2. When presented with written single syllables containing various vowel digraphs, Ken will state the syllable with 90% accuracy on three consecutive trials.

3. When presented with familiar words containing 2 and 3 syllables, Ken will first syllabicate and then pronounce the syllables and finally the word with 85% accuracy.

4. After studying unfamiliar words containing up to three syllables for a maximum of 10 seconds, Ken will state the word with 85% accuracy.

5. Upon encountering unfamiliar words in text appropriate for Ken's instructional reading skill level, he will use syllabication skills to help him pronounce the words with 85% accuracy.

GOAL: to improve sight word vocabulary

1. When presented with isolated sight words derived from Ken's reading and content area texts, Ken will state the word within 3 seconds with 95% accuracy.
2. When presented with sentences containing sight words addressed in Objective 1, Ken will orally read the sentence pronouncing each word correctly with 100% accuracy on 3 consecutive trials.
3. Upon encountering sight words in reading assignments, Ken will correctly identify the sight words with 100% accuracy each time he is called upon to read.

GOAL: to increase spelling skills in everyday writing

1. Upon request, Ken will write or say number words, months, days of the week, and weekly spelling words with 90% accuracy.
2. In free writing assignments Ken will spell familiar words with 90% accuracy.

After establishing the preceding objectives, Mrs. McKenna realized that direct instructional strategies were the most effective way to teach these skills. Although direct instruction requires a large amount of time with the student, Mrs. McKenna knew that Ken always finished his math assignments 15 to 20 minutes before most other students, so she decided to take advantage of that extra time. She enlisted the assistance of a paraprofessional and a classmate and developed flash cards to practice syllables, sight words, and sentences. She also developed spelling word lists based on the objectives. She then divided the responsibility for Ken's remediation among herself, the para, and the student. Each was assigned activities ranging from guided practice to peer review, informed of appropriate response modes, and provided with efficient ways to monitor Ken's progress. After 3 weeks of instruction, Mrs. McKenna administered a curriculum-based assessment device and discovered that Ken was steadily gaining skills toward each goal. Satisfied that the goals, objectives, strategies, and activities were appropriate, Mrs. McKenna decided to reassess Ken's progress every 6 weeks and adjust the goals and objectives according to the reassessment results. She also decided that the referral for special education assessment would be premature until Ken had a chance to benefit from extra assistance in her class.

Case Study 3 shows one of many possible applications of the Assessment-Instruction Cycle. Whether the cycle is applied to the regular or special education classroom, effective instruction requires teachers to address each component *starting* with assessment and working in a clockwise direction with each component evolving from the former. Unfortunately teachers often plan backwards, starting with the materials "on hand" and planning activities, teaching strategies, and tests based on materials instead of student needs. Ultimately, material-driven models of instruction limit both students' and teachers' opportunities to reach beyond the boundaries of convenience and attempt exciting, new strategies based on student needs. As Mrs. McKenna's case demonstrated, however, creative use of resources that are frequently available to teachers allows for departures from conventional methods to serve students who need extra help.

CLINICAL APPLICATIONS

Assessment of academic achievement facilitates treatment in several clinical settings. Psychologists, counselors, speech/language pathologists, and, increasingly, pediatric treatment teams routinely administer norm-referenced screening tests to establish a client's levels of academic functioning. Although classroom application of assessment strategies focuses primarily on data collection to guide instruction and facilitate skill acquisition, clinicians include measures of academic achievement in assessment batteries primarily designed to diagnose and treat antisocial behaviors, conduct disorders, psychological problems, or medical problems. From a clinical perspective, some professionals view academic achievement as a subordinate skill needed by clients to participate in their treatment programs. However, the majority of clinicians also regard academic achievement as an integral part of a student's growth and often provide parents and educators with corroborating evidence to support or dispute school-based decisions.

N.B.   A due process provision in PL 94-142, allowing for dispute resolution
through student evaluation that is independent of educational agencies, has
occasioned numerous referrals to private clinics. Parents who disagree
with the school-based team's decisions regarding placement and/or educational programming for their child often seek assistance from professionals outside the school district. Professionals in private practice are viewed
as unbiased sources of information and usually attempt to duplicate and
extend the school district's evaluation to provide a second opinion that
may or may not corroborate school-based findings. This important safeguard is a cost-free option for parents and frequently prevents inappropriate identification of handicapping conditions by encouraging school-based
professionals to plan and implement assessment strategies carefully and
thoughtfully.

The application of assessment strategies to measure academic achievement in clinical settings reflects the advantages and disadvantages inherent
in clinical settings. The most obvious advantage of clinical applications is
objectivity. Private practitioners seldom benefit or lose by gathering and
interpreting educational data to provide an independent second opinion.
Because many clinical practitioners rarely have prior experience with a
particular client, they may be unaware of the student's history, or reputation, and can approach the student with a minimum of preconceptions. As
a result, they have the luxury of maintaining a clinical neutrality that may
appeal to schools and parents alike. A second point is that clinicians are
frequently extremely well trained in the administration and, perhaps most
important, the interpretation of a variety of assessment instruments. Many
have formal training in psychometrics, descriptive and inferential statistics, and test construction and, consequently, interpret test results with a
clear conception of a particular test's strengths and limitations. Finally,
clinical practitioners often maintain more flexible schedules than teachers
and other school personnel. As a result, clinicians can devote as much time
as is needed by individual clients and can schedule testing at times that
may be more conducive to the optimal performance of clients.

Assessment of academics in clinical settings poses several disadvantages for clinical practitioners. First, clinicians may lack extensive experiential background with students in educational settings and must rely on
informants to supply information about the multitude of environmental
factors that either reinforce or punish behaviors. Even clinicians having a
longstanding therapeutic relationship with a client do not experience the
kinds of relationships commonly found in educational settings (e.g., peer

interactions, teacher–student interactions, class climate, teacher–student–administrator relationships and, certainly, the "culture" of the school ecosystem). Clinicians occasionally conduct classroom observations and/or analyze students' work samples; however, this limited exposure to the client's educational environment may provide superficial informa- XX tion that leads clinicians to inappropriate conclusions. Day-to-day inter-actions among students and teachers during structured academic instruction, unstructured independent study, nonacademic activities, and recess elude outside clinicians who can seldom afford the necessary time to observe for extended periods of time. However, clinicians can suggest assessment areas and strategies for educators to use. Second, clinical evaluations are expensive and may be beyond a school district's or parent's budget. As a result, schools may simply give in to parental demands to avoid the expense and, consequently, deny crucial services to needy students. Finally, private clinicians often do not have to "live with" their recommendations within the contingencies prevalent in contemporary N.B classrooms. Classroom teachers may view suggestions made by clinicians as unrealistic in terms of the resources available in school settings.

Case Study 4: Clinical Applications

Dr. Leonard, a counseling psychologist in private practice, worked with Rudy Perdue and his parents to solve several behavior problems that have plagued Rudy since he was a preschooler. Rudy, currently a 14-year-old 8th-grader, had several emotional problems and conduct disorders that caused discipline problems at home and school. At school, Rudy engaged in aggressive behavior with other children and at home he refused to comply with rules established by his parents. Once, during a temper tantrum, he even bit his father. The school coped with Rudy by diagnosing him as emotionally disturbed and placing him in a special education class for most of the day. However, the school refused to consider counseling as a part of Rudy's IEP, so his parents sought outside assistance from Dr. Leonard. After almost 2 years of weekly counseling sessions, Rudy had gained sufficient self-management skills to control his behaviors at home. His parents and siblings were relieved and now considered Rudy "cured." As a result, Mr. and Mrs. Perdue asked the school to put Rudy back into the regular classroom.

Unfortunately, although Rudy's behavior had also improved at school, he exhibited skill deficits in all academic areas. A re-evaluation precipitated by the parents' request to place Rudy back in the regular classroom revealed that he was functioning several grade levels below his 8th-grade status. Although the assessment team recognized Rudy's improved behavior, they refused to consider a full-day placement in the regular classroom and, instead, recommended a gradual transition starting with one class at a time. Mr. and Mrs. Perdue felt that they had gone to great expense and worked hard to improve Rudy's behaviors and were angry and disappointed at what seemed like a lack of cooperation and appreciation for their efforts from the school. They also felt that, because Rudy had established a reputation for poor behavior at school, the school personnel were prejudiced against Rudy. With high school in Rudy's immediate future, Mr. and Mrs. Perdue accused the school of failing to provide Rudy with the skills he will need to succeed. After consulting a community advocacy group for parents of handicapped children, Mr. and Mrs. Perdue decided to request a due process hearing that would most likely include an evaluation of Rudy's academic skills by an impartial third party.

During an introductory meeting with the hearing officer assigned to their case, Mr. and Mrs. Perdue described the counseling with Dr. Leonard that they had secured for Rudy and expressed their gratitude and respect for the doctor's skills. As a result, the hearing officer wisely selected Dr. Leonard to conduct an independent psychological and academic assessment of Rudy. The results of the doctor's assessment established Rudy's level of cognitive functioning at well above average and corroborated the school's findings. To Mr. and Mrs. Perdue's surprise, Dr. Leonard's assessment of Rudy's academic skills also agreed, at least in part, with the school's findings. Because the school had administered the KTEA-CP, Dr. Leonard selected the Woodcock-Johnson Tests of Achievement—Revised to establish skill ranges. The results showed that Rudy functioned between a 9-3 and 11-4 age level in mathematics, an 11-3 and 13-1 age level in reading, and a 10-8 and 12-4 age level in language. From his prior counseling experiences with Rudy, Dr. Leonard also knew that Rudy acquired and generalized skills easily. However, in his report, Dr. Leonard agreed with the school district's position that full-time mainstreaming would put too much pressure on Rudy. He recommended a compromise that involved integrating Rudy into regular classes in which Rudy might experience immediate success (e.g., reading and content courses). Dr. Leonard also recommended that school personnel and the parents develop an integration and evaluation plan aimed toward full-time placement in the regular classroom based on Rudy's progress. The district and Rudy's parents agreed to try Dr. Leonard's plan and, as a result, avoided further controversy.

Although Rudy's case study is admittedly idealized, it highlights a productive and frequent use of clinical professionals. When independent assessments are needed, the use of a similar, but different, test serves as a "check" and may provide additional kinds of data. The use of a professional who is familiar to parents and respected in the academic community increases the probability that all parties involved in a dispute will fairly consider the independent professional's results and recommendations. Finally, settling disputes efficiently may save resources and energy that can be focused on the student's needs.

ISSUES AFFECTING ASSESSMENT OF ACADEMICS

Longstanding and contemporary concerns relating to assessment of academic achievement necessitate a cautious approach in the use and interpretation of data produced by both formal and informal strategies. Several analyses of formal, norm-referenced tests challenge the adequacy of instruments commonly used to determine program eligibility and instructional planning for handicapped students (Johnson, 1984; Maddus, Kellaghan, Rawkow, & King, 1979; Ysseldyke & Shinn, 1981). The exclusion of or unaccounted for representation of handicapped, low socioeconomic, or minority populations in the norming procedures of many norm-referenced tests prevents informed selection of tests that produce unbiased comparisons of an individual's performance with peers sharing similar backgrounds (Fuchs & Fuchs, 1986; Fuchs, Fuchs, Benowitz, & Barringer, 1987). Further, examiner errors in selecting, administering, and scoring tests (Bennett, 1983) and misinterpretation and misuse of assessment data by examiners (Ross, 1990) produce inaccurate and misleading results.

Informal strategies frequently lack information about the technical adequacies of each strategy. These strategies are frequently developed by educators for use in a specific situation. As a result, rigorous analyses of the strategy's reliabilities, validities, and use of consistent administration procedures are seldom available. Some degree of error is always present in any measurement system. However, the amount and kinds of measurement error present in informal assessment strategies remain unknown. As a result, the examiner is left with the knowledge that the assessment data are inaccurate to an unknown degree. To minimize the effects of these technical inadequacies, McLoughlin and Lewis (1990) recommend employing multiple measures in a variety of settings, standardizing administration procedures of informal strategies, evaluating content validity in terms of the activities and curriculum used in the classroom, and describing strategies in objective language that enhances consistent application across various examiners.

Contemporary concerns about assessment of academics relates to reconceptualizations of each academic domain. Recent analyses of multiple-skill and specific-skill measures currently used to measure reading, mathematics, and language skills in regular and special settings show that most norm-referenced tests measure only superficial aspects of each academic domain. Even the most recently revised editions of various tests do not reflect established and emerging theories pertaining to the actual skills regarded as essential in reading, mathematics, and language skill acquisition. For example, reading comprehension is currently viewed as an integrative process that involves prior knowledge, intersentential integration, and prose organization (Johnson, 1984; Shanahan, Kamil, & Tobin, 1982; Wixson & Lipson, 1991). The one-sentence or short passages commonly found in reading comprehension subtests are insensitive to the integrative processes known to contribute to reading comprehension. Unfortunately, test developers have failed to address contemporary theories underlying academic achievement, and publication of instruments that are misaligned with present-day theory continues.

SUMMARY

Regardless of various concerns surrounding assessment of academic achievement, measures of academic performance remain the cornerstone of education. Various strategies are used to monitor student progress, evaluate instructional strategies, and describe the effectiveness of the American educational system. Formal and informal strategies are needed to provide a multidimensional view of students' strengths and weaknesses. Although numerous tests exist, a few tests usually emerge as "favorites" and are described in this chapter. However, consumers are advised to select instruments that best suit the purpose of the assessment and the needs of the student. Informal strategies that teachers use frequently are also described. The use of multiple measures across time and various settings represents the best safeguard available to increase the accuracy of results.

REFERENCES

Balow, I. H., Hogan, T. P., Farr, R. C., & Prescott, C. A.(1986). *Metropolitan Achievement Test 6: Language Diagnostic Tests.* San Antonio, TX: The Psychological Corporation.

Bennett, R. E. (1983). Research and evaluation priorities for special education assessment. *Exceptional Children, 50,* 110-117.

Brown v. *Board of Education of Topeka.* (1954). 547 U.S. 483.

CTS/McGraw-Hill. (1985). *California Achievement Test.* Monterey, CA: Author.

Dunn, L. M., & Markwardt, P. C. (1970). *Peabody Individual Achievement Test.* Circle Pines, MN: American Guidance Service.

Edwards, J. (1989). Test review: Peabody Individual Achievement Test—Revised. *Journal of Psychoeducational Assessment, 7,* 264-271.

Farr, R. C., Prescott, G. A., Hogan, T. P., & Balow, I. H. (1986). *Metropolitan Achievement Test 6: Reading Diagnostic Tests.* San Antonio, TX: The Psychological Corporation.

Fuchs, D., & Fuchs, L. S. (1986). Test procedure bias: A meta-analysis of examiner familiarity effects. *Review of Educational Research, 56,* 243-262.

Fuchs, D., Fuchs, L., Benowitz, S., & Barringer, K., (1987). Norm-referenced tests: Are they valid for use with handicapped students?. *Exceptional Children, 54,* 263-271.

Hogan, T. P., Farr, R. C., Prescott, C. A., & Balow, I. H. (1986). *Metropolitan Achievement Test 6: Mathematics Diagnostic Tests.* San Antonio TX: The Psychological Corporation.

Johnson, P. (1984). Prior knowledge and reading comprehension test bias. *Reading Research Quarterly, 14,* 219-239.

Kaufman, A., & Kaufman, N. (1985a). *Kaufman Test of Educational Achievement, Brief Form manual.* Circle Pines, MN: American Guidance Service.

Kaufman, A., & Kaufman, N. (1985b). *Kaufman Test of Educational Achievement, Brief Form manual.* Circle Pines, MN: American Guidance Service.

Kaufman, A., & Kaufman, N. (1985c). *Kaufman Test of Educational Achievement, Comprehensive Form manual.* Circle Pines, MN: American Guidance Service.

Maddus, G. F., Kellaghan, R., Rawkow, E. A., & King, D. J. (1970). The sensitivity of school measures. *Harvard Educational Review, 49,* 207-230.

Markwardt, F. D. (1989). *Peabody Individual Achievement Test—Revised.* Circle Pines, MN: American Guidance Service.

McLoughlin, J. A., & Lewis, R. B. (1990). *Assessing special students.* Columbus, OH: Charles E. Merrill.

Prescott, G. A., Balow, I. H., Hogan, T. R., & Farr, R. C. (1984). *Metropolitan Achievement Test 6: Survey Battery.* San Antonio, TX: The Psychological Corporation.

Ross, R. P. (1990). Consistency among school psychologists in evaluating discrepancy scores: A preliminary study. *Learning Disabilities Quarterly, 13,* 209-219.

Salvia, J., & Hughes, C. (1990). *Curriculum-based assessment: Testing what is taught.* New York: Macmillan.

Salvia, J., & Ysseldyke, J. E. (1988). *Assessment in special and remedial education.* Boston, MA: Houghton Mifflin.

Shanahan, T., Kamil, M. L., & Tobin, A. W. (1982). Cloze as a measure of intersentential comprehension. *Reading Research Quarterly, 17,* 229-255.

State ex. rel. Beattie v. Board of Education of City of Antigo (Wis.). (1919). 172 NW 153.

Wechsler, D. (1974). *Wechsler Intelligence Scale for Children - Revised.* New York: The Psychological Corporation.

Wixson, K. K., & Lipson, N. Y. (1991). *Assessment and instruction of reading disability: An interactive approach.* New York: Harper Collins.

Woodcock, R. W., & Johnson, M. B. (1989). *Woodcock-Johnson Psycho-Educational Battery—Revised.* Allen, TX: DLM.

Woodcock, R., & Mather, N. (1989). *Woodcock-Johnson Tests of Achievement Standard and Supplemental Batteries examiner's manual.* Allen, TX: DLM.

Ysseldyke, J. E., & Shinn, M. R. (1981). Psychoeducational evaluation. In J. M. Kauffman & D. P. Hallahan (Eds.). *Handbook of special education* (pp. 249-278). Englewood Cliffs, NJ: Prentice Hall.

12 BEST PRACTICES IN THE ASSESSMENT OF ADAPTIVE BEHAVIOR

MaryAnn Demchak and Sarah Drinkwater

Adaptive behavior refers to the ability of an individual to meet the demands of the everyday environment and encompasses self-sufficiency as well as social competence. In recent years, the importance of adaptive behavior in assessment and program planning has increased due to stringent assessment mandates of PL 94-142 and a stronger emphasis on the adaptive behavior component in the definition of mental retardation. Because adaptive behavior is distinct from intelligence and academic ability (Bruininks & McGrew, 1987), assessment of adaptive behavior provides unique information to the multidisciplinary assessment process (Keith, Fehrmann, Harrison, & Pottebaum, 1987). This unique information contributes to both classification of and instructional programming for individuals with disabilities.

HISTORICAL PERSPECTIVES

Adaptive behavior is grounded in the history of the treatment and identification of individuals with mental retardation. Horn and Fuchs (1987) discuss this history with an emphasis on the role of adaptive behavior. During the early years (i.e. prior to 1820), adaptive behavior was used primarily to identify those individuals unable to function in society. This assessment was informal and focused on those who were physically deformed or behaviorally deviant. The middle 19th century (i.e., 1820–1890) saw an emphasis on training programs that targeted skills needed for meeting the social demands of the larger community. Adaptive behavior took a minor role in identification of and intervention planning for individuals with mental retardation in the early 20th century (i.e., 1890–1940). During this time the primary emphasis was on intelligence scores. In recent years (i.e., 1940–present), a greater emphasis has been placed on adaptive behavior for the purposes of identification and program planning. It was during this last period that systematic assessment of adaptive behavior began to be stressed. Edgar Doll (1935), one of the primary advocates for emphasizing adaptive behavior, developed a measure of social maturity (i.e., adaptive behavior) to be used in conjunction with intelligence tests in identifying individuals as mentally retarded.

Contributions of Edgar Doll

Edgar Doll is the major pioneer in the assessment of adaptive behavior. His views that the primary criterion of "mental deficiency" must address social incompetence led to the development of the Vineland Social Maturity Scale (Doll, 1935). He stressed that it was important to look at the whole person and not simply at intelligence; it was insufficient to define mental retardation according to intelligence test scores alone (Doll, 1940). The scale was developed as a means of assessing social adequacy in terms of self-sufficiency, which becomes more complex with increasing age. Thus, the scale provided a means of investigating problems in the area of mental retardation that were previously not researched due to the lack of instrumentation. In addition to viewing adaptive behavior as developmental in nature, another of Doll's contributions is the recognition of the importance of environmental demands and opportunities. These expectations and opportunities influence the development of skills in adaptive behavior. For example, if an individual is never expected to perform a particular skill or provided with opportunities to perform the behavior, it is unlikely that the individual will develop that particular skill in that setting. Even though his specific categories are no longer used, Doll also established the perception of adaptive behavior as encompassing a variety of areas (e.g., self-help dressing, locomotion, occupation, self-direction)

(Doll, 1935, 1953, 1965). Another continuing contribution relates to methodology used to assess adaptive behavior, Doll's scale required the use of significant others as respondents in providing information regarding a person's performance in the area of social competence. Adaptive behavior instruments continue to use this format today.

The Increasing Emphasis of Adaptive Behavior in Mental Retardation Definitions

Although Doll advocated for a number of years that it was insufficient to assess only intelligence in the identification of individuals with mental retardation, it was not until 1959 that the American Association on Mental Deficiency (AAMD) included adaptive behavior in its definition of mental deficiency. Heber (1959, in Patton & Jones, 1990) defined mental retardation as "subaverage general intellectual functioning which originates during the developmental period and is associated with impairment in adaptive behavior" (p. 46). Thus, a person with a low IQ score who did not display significant limitations in the area of adaptive behavior could not be identified as mentally retarded. The 1973 AAMD definition of mental retardation included a stronger emphasis on adaptive behavior by stating that deficits in adaptive behavior must exist concurrently with significantly subaverage general intellectual functioning and must be evident during the developmental period (Grossman, 1973, in Patton & Jones, 1990). Grossman (1983) further expands the definition of mental retardation to recognize that significantly subaverage general intellectual functioning can result in or be associated with concurrent impairments in adaptive behavior. Once again, these impairments must be displayed during the developmental period.

In addition to defining mental retardation, the AAMD also clarified each of the key components of their mental retardation definition. Initially, definitions of adaptive behavior did not include a recognition that adaptive behavior is relative to one's age and culture. However, Grossman (1983) incorporated these important emphases in his definitions, stating that impairments in this area are reflected in marked limitations in meeting the requirements for personal independence and social responsibility expected for the age and cultural group of the individual.

Unfortunately, adaptive behavior assessment did not become a standard part of school assessment until the mid-1970s (Reschly, 1982). Even then, little guidance was offered to school psychologists regarding adaptive behavior definition, criteria, and assessment instruments (Patrick & Reschly, 1982). These authors also noted the absence of guidelines for combining the results of intelligence and adaptive behavior tests in classification decisions.

OVERVIEW OF ADAPTIVE BEHAVIOR

Although there are various definitions of adaptive behavior, the most commonly cited is that of the AAMD. "Adaptive behavior is defined as the effectiveness or degree with which individuals meet the standards of personal independence and social responsibility expected for age and cultural group" (Grossman, 1983, p. 1). Key components of adaptive behavior emphasize (a) typical performance and not ability, (b) increasing complexity as a function of age, (c) cultural expectations, (d) personal independence and social skills, and (e) environmental demands.

Typical Performance

Whereas assessment of intelligence focuses on a person's abilities, assessment of adaptive behavior stresses an individual's typical performance. What is important is actual behavior and not abilities or constructs that are believed to underlie behavior. The emphasis of adaptive behavior lies within meeting everyday demands of the individual's environment (Grossman, 1983). Thus, an individual would be scored deficient in a particular area if he or she possesses a skill, but does not routinely perform it. For example, a young man possesses the skills to complete purchases at a store independently but instead allows care providers to make his purchases for him. Although this man has the necessary skills, he would be identified as being deficient in this particular area because he does not typically perform this task. For the person to be considered competent, the skill must be completed *by* the individual not *for* the individual (Schmidt & Salvia, 1984).

Increasing Complexity with Age

What is viewed as appropriate adaptive behavior varies as a function of age. Expectations for a preschool child are much different from what is expected of a school-aged child, adolescent, or an adult. Grossman (1983) identifies changing areas of emphasis for various age groups:

During INFANCY AND EARLY CHILDHOOD in:

1. Sensorimotor Skills Development
2. Communication Skills (including speech and language)
3. Self-Help Skills
4. Socialization (development of ability to interact with others)

During CHILDHOOD AND EARLY ADOLESCENCE in AREAS 1 through 4 and/or

5. Application of Basic Academic Skills in Daily Life Activities
6. Application of Appropriate Reasoning and Judgement in Mastery of the Environment
7. Social Skills (participation in group activities and interpersonal relationships)

During LATE ADOLESCENCE AND ADULT LIFE in AREAS 1 through 7 and/or:

8. Vocational and Social Responsibilities and Performance (p. 25)

As can be seen, the criteria for judging adaptive behavior change with the age of the individual, becoming increasingly more complex. There is an increasing emphasis on meeting the demands of the environment. By the time an individual reaches adulthood, adaptive behavior examines the degree to which the individual is independent in the community and in a vocation. Increasing social participation and conforming to community standards is also examined.

Cultural Expectations

In addition to meeting age expectations, a person must also satisfy cultural expectations. Behaviors considered to be adaptive, or appropriate, will vary from culture to culture as well as within subcultures in the same country. For example, in many areas of the United States an important personal hygiene skill involves shaving. However, in some subcultures in the United States and Europe, shaving facial hair for men and body hair for women is not expected. It is particularly important to examine cultural expectations when evaluating social functioning (i.e., items focusing on interpersonal relationships) (Reschly, 1989). It should be noted that cultural demands are not static; social expectations change with time (Schmidt & Salvia, 1984).

Personal Independence and Social Skills

The AAMD definition stresses meeting the standards of personal independence and social responsibility that comprise the larger domain of social competence (Gresham & Elliott, 1987). Even though the AAMD definition is viewed as the authoritative source, it neglects to identify specific domains of adaptive behavior. Hence, a variety of adaptive behavior domains and subdomains have been used in adaptive behavior scales and research. Although a salient concept does not exist, adaptive behavior is a unique construct which does not overlap with intellectual and academic abilities (Bruininks & McGrew, 1987).

Holman and Bruininks (1985) analyzed existing adaptive behavior instruments and research, and identified 10 broad clusters and 45 more specific areas of adaptive behavior. These clusters and specific skills (summarized in Table 12.1) encompass personal independence and social skills. Although there are a large number of adaptive behavior domains and the names can vary, Reschly (1989) summarizes this information in four general domains: (a) independent functioning (e.g., toileting, self-feeding, self-dressing, use of leisure time, environmental mobility), (b) social functioning (e.g., avoiding inappropriate behaviors, appropriate sharing, appropriate communication), (c) functional academics (e.g., money handling, following a schedule), and (d) vocational responsibilities and performance (e.g., searching for a job, specific job skills). Although broad domains are sufficient for classification purposes, greater detail is necessary when assessing adaptive behavior for instructional planning. There does seem to be consistent agreement that adaptive behavior refers to meeting the demands of daily life to achieve personal and social self-sufficiency. This general agreement is reflected in the fact that adaptive behavior scales are fairly similar and typically include the same basic domains of behavior (Reschly & Gresham, 1988).

Environmental Demands

This last key component addresses situational specificity of adaptive behavior. The varying environmental demands are unique to the individual and incorporate interactions with others at school, at home, and in the

TABLE 12.1. *Holman and Bruininks' Domains and Subdomains of Adaptive Behavior*

Self-Help, Personal Appearance	Health Care, Personal Welfare
Feeding, eating, drinking	Treatment of injuries,
Dressing	health problems
Toileting	Prevention of health
Grooming, hygiene	problems
	Personal safety
Physical Development	Child-care practices
Gross motor skills	
Fine motor skills	Consumer Skills
	Money handling
Communication	Purchasing
Receptive language	Banking
Expressive language	Budgeting
Personal, Social Skills	Domestic Skills
Play skills	Household cleaning
Interaction skills	Property maintenance, repair
Group participation	Clothing care
Social amenities	Kitchen skills
Sexual behavior	Household safety
Self-direction,	
responsibility	Community Orientation
Leisure activities	Travel skills
Expression of emotions	Utilization of community
	resources
Cognitive Functioning	Telephone usage
Pre-academics	Community safety
(e.g., colors)	
Reading	Vocational Skills
Writing	Work habits and attitudes
Numeric functions	Job search skills
Time	Work performance
Money	Social vocational behavior
Measurement	Work safety

Note. From "Adaptive Behavior and Mental Retardation" by R. H. Bruininks, M. Thurlow, & C. J. Gilman, 1987, *The Journal of Special Education, 21*, p. 74. Copyright 1987 by PRO-ED, Inc. Reprinted by permission.

community. Any assessment of adaptive behavior must take into consideration performance in these various settings. It is inappropriate to assess behavior in one setting while excluding others; level of independence can vary markedly from one environment to another. This variability occurs as a result of unique expectations and demands of significant others in assorted settings. In addition, these variable expectations and demands can influence the overall development of adaptive behavior (Bruininks & McGrew, 1987). Finally, knowledge of environmental demands provides crucial information for programming purposes. What is adaptive, or appropriate, in one setting may not be so in another setting or at another time; that is, adaptive behavior is dynamic and dependent on time and place, rather than static (Horn & Fuchs, 1987).

RELATIONSHIP OF MALADAPTIVE BEHAVIOR TO ADAPTIVE BEHAVIOR

Maladaptive behavior (e.g., self-injurious behaviors, stereotypic behaviors, physical and verbal aggression, disruptive and destructive behaviors), a two-dimensional construct, is typically labeled as social (i.e., externally directed) or personal (i.e., internally directed) (Bruininks & McGrew, 1987). Although maladaptive and adaptive behavior are distinct constructs (Bruininks & McGrew, 1987), it is beneficial to assess the presence of maladaptive behaviors because they interfere with achieving adaptive behaviors (Sparrow & Cicchetti, 1987). In their review of research on adaptive behavior and mental retardation, Bruininks, Thurlow, and Gilman (1987) showed that not only does maladaptive behavior interfere with attaining adaptive behavior, it also limits integration into schools, interferes with family acceptance, limits employment, and interferes with integration into social settings. According to Bruininks et al. (1987), successful identification of and intervention with these behaviors is vital if the individual is to develop more adaptive behaviors and is to be integrated fully within society. In recent adaptive behavior scales (e.g., Vineland Adaptive Behavior Scales, Scales of Independent Behavior), the relationship between adaptive and maladaptive behaviors is addressed in ascertaining the individual's proficiency in meeting the demands of his or her environment (Bruininks et al., 1987).

Recent approaches to intervening with maladaptive behaviors place more of an emphasis on the relationship between adaptive and maladaptive behaviors than did past approaches. Currently, an emphasis is placed on conducting a functional assessment prior to designing intervention procedures (Lennox & Miltenberger, 1989). One aspect of functional assessment is identifying appropriate and functionally equivalent behaviors that can be targeted as alternatives to the maladaptive behavior(s). These alternative behaviors frequently fall in the adaptive behavior domains of communication, recreation, and social skills; the maladaptive behavior occurs because the individual does not have the appropriate adaptive behavior for the situation (Meyer & Evans, 1989). Discussing the methodology for completing functional assessments of maladaptive behaviors is beyond the scope of this chapter. (See Demchak, in press; Lennox & Miltenberger, 1989; O'Neill, Horner, Albin, Storey, & Sprague, 1990.)

OVERVIEW OF ADAPTIVE BEHAVIOR INSTRUMENTS

Vineland Adaptive Behavior Scales

One of the most well-known adaptive behavior instruments, the Vineland Adaptive Behavior Scales (Harrison, 1985; Sparrow, Balla, & Cicchetti, 1984a,b), a revision of the Vineland Social Maturity Scale (Doll, 1935, 1965), is composed of three versions: the Survey Form, the Expanded Form, and the Classroom Edition. Each of these versions contains items in the following domains: communication, daily living skills, socialization, and motor skills. Additionally, the Expanded and Survey Forms also assess maladaptive behavior. Scoring options include usually performed (scores 2 points), sometimes/partially performed (1 point), never exhibited (0 points), no opportunity for performance, and don't know. This scoring system allows credit for emerging skills and behaviors that are partially performed. According to the authors, the major purposes of the Vineland are diagnostic evaluation, program planning, and research. Each form of the Vineland may be more appropriate for one or more of these functions based on its organization, content, and comprehensiveness.

The Survey Form (Sparrow et al., 1984b), which utilizes a semistructured interview format, consists of 297 items and targets individuals from birth through 18 years or low-functioning adults. It is designed to be used for general assessment purposes highlighting strengths and areas of need. This form can be completed in 20 to 60 minutes.

The Expanded Form (Sparrow et al., 1984a), containing all items in the Survey Form plus additional items for a total of 577, is a more comprehensive assessment instrument designed ultimately to develop educational or habilitative plans. It also uses a semistructured interview format (requiring 60 to 90 minutes) with a caregiver or parent and is appropriate for use with the same individuals as the Survey Form. In addition, the Expanded Form includes a Program Planning Profile that provides an in-depth illustration of an individual's capabilities. This profile assists the practitioner in pinpointing particular skills for intervention. Those areas with the highest scores provide a base for expanding behaviors, whereas weaker domains identify potential behaviors for acquisition training.

The Classroom Edition (Harrison, 1985) is composed of 244 items assessing adaptive behavior in the classroom. This edition contains some items from the Survey and Expanded Forms plus additional items related to academic functioning. Unlike the other versions of the Vineland, this edition employs a questionnaire completed independently by the teacher in approximately 20 minutes. Even though the teacher completes the questionnaire, a trained examiner will likely need to score it and interpret the results. The Classroom Edition is appropriate for students 3 years through 12 years of age.

To the authors' credit, the Vineland is one of the most psychometrically sound adaptive behavior instruments available. Each of the three versions summarizes research on standardization, reliability, and validity in its own technical manual. The standardization sample involved over 3,000 participants representing a cross-section of the United States population and including individuals with disabilities. A review of the reliability and validity research illustrates technical adequacy. (See Salvia & Ysseldyke, 1988.)

Scales of Independent Behavior

Another well-known adaptive behavior instrument is the Scales of Independent Behavior (SIB) (Bruininks, Woodcock, Weatherman, & Hill, 1984). The SIB, a comprehensive measure (226 items) of adaptive behavior and functional independence, is composed of four broad domains: motor skills, social and communication skills, personal living skills, and community living skills. These four areas are further divided into 14 subscales which further delineate specific skills and behaviors (40–50 minutes administration time). Overall performance of an individual is summarized with a broad independence score, indicating a combined total score. Additional components of the SIB are a short-form version consisting of 32 items for screening (10–15 minutes administration time), an early development scale of 32 items for use with young children (10–15 minutes), and a scale of problem behaviors (8–10 minutes) which targets maladaptive behavior. The scoring options include a score of 0, which indicates the individual never performs the behavior; 1, which reflects the individual does the task but not well; 2, indicating the individual performs the task fairly well; and 3, illustrating the task is performed very well. The SIB is intended for a variety of assessment, program-planning, and evaluation purposes with individuals from infancy through adulthood.

Assessors can generate five profiles from the results of the SIB. Two percentile rank profiles, based on age, illustrate an individual's performance compared with that of others the same age. One of these percentile rank profiles also includes a comparison of level of intelligence. The subscale profile enables an interviewer to plot an individual's raw scores and to compare the individual's subscale scores. The fourth profile, the training implications profile, contains information on the individual's relative performance index based on age, level of functioning, and suggested training range. Last, the problem behaviors profile outlines the frequency and severity of the individual's problem behaviors.

Salvia and Ysseldyke (1988) provide a summary of the technical adequacy of the scale, detailing reliability and validity information, as well as norming information. The SIB appears to be quite valid, with variable reliability statistics.

Inventory for Client and Agency Planning (ICAP)

The ICAP (Bruininks, Hill, Weatherman, & Woodcock, 1986) is an adaptive behavior measure composed of 77 items and designed to assess comprehensively the status (e.g., diagnosis, marital status, medical characteristics), adaptive behavior, and needs of clients (20 minutes administration time). Its primary purpose is to aid interventionists in screening, monitoring, managing, and evaluating services provided to clients. The ICAP should be completed by a respondent who has known the client for a least 3 months and also sees the client on a daily basis. Domains included in the ICAP are: motor skills, social and communication skills, personal living skills, and community living skills.

Examiners score each item individually using a quality descriptor score. A score of 0 indicates that the client never performs the task, and a score of 1 reflects a poor performance of the task. If an individual performs a behavior fairly well, a score of 2 is recorded, and a score of 3 indicates that the individual does the task very well. Similar to the SIB, overall adaptive behavior performance is summarized within the broad independence score. The ICAP also includes a problem behavior scale (8–10 minutes) for assessing difficult behaviors that may affect personal and community adjustment.

Technical information on the psychometric adequacy of the ICAP is contained in the examiner's manual. Norming standards, as well as the sampling procedures used with the 1,764 subjects, are discussed. Several reliability and validity studies were conducted with the subjects and indicate adequate psychometric properties.

Comprehensive Test of Adaptive Behavior (CTAB)

The CTAB (Adams, 1986), another measure of adaptive behavior (kindergarten to adult), is designed primarily for use by special educators, psychologists, and teachers. It is a comprehensive instrument that provides both descriptive and prescriptive information in the areas of self-help skills, home-living skills, independent-living skills, social skills, sensory and motor skills, and language concepts and academic skills. The CTAB contains 497 male behaviors and 527 female behaviors that are sequenced from easiest to hardest based on the testing of 6,000 individuals with disabilities.

There are four components of the CTAB. The test manual describes the instrument and delineates each item, including criterion and testing procedures. Items are scored either "yes" or "no," based on what the individual does each day, not on what the individual can do. The parent/guardian survey is a questionnaire given to parents or significant others to verify the presence of behaviors not regularly observed by examiners. The parent/guardian survey uses a three-pronged scoring system: "yes," "no," or "don't know." Similar to the previously described instruments, the CTAB also provides a profile (called a record form) to summarize, in grid format, an individual's performance.

The CTAB technical manual contains information pertinent to the development and standardization, as well as the technical adequacy of the instrument. As mentioned above, the CTAB was standardized on 6,000 individuals with disabilities from a variety of programs and schools. Validity studies reflect the adequacy of the CTAB to measure adaptive behavior. In addition, reliability studies indicate high levels of interrater reliability, as well as test-retest consistency. Overall, the CTAB is a well-developed instrument for use in assessing adaptive behavior.

APPLICATION OF ADAPTIVE BEHAVIOR ASSESSMENT
TO IDENTIFICATION AND CLASSIFICATION

The major functions of adaptive behavior assessment encompass descriptive and prescriptive purposes (Adams, 1986). Descriptive assessment addresses identification and classification issues, whereas the prescriptive purpose focuses on programming issues. Regardless of the purpose of assessment, it is essential that the adaptive behavior instrument selected is psychometrically sound. Many adaptive behavior scales do not have adequate reliability and validity information (Kamphaus, 1987). Scales that are norm-referenced are more appropriate for use in supporting classification decisions, whereas criterion-referenced inventories are better suited to program planning (Browder, 1991; Reschly, 1989).

Assessment of adaptive behavior is an essential component when identifying individuals who are mentally retarded. If deficits in adaptive behavior do not exist concurrently with significantly subaverage general intellectual functioning, the person cannot be classified as mentally retarded (Grossman, 1983). Although adaptive behavior is viewed as an essential component in identifying individuals with mental retardation, no precise cut-off scores are provided by the AAMD for use in this identification (Reschly, 1989). Thus, clinical judgment plays an important role in applying the results of standardized adaptive behavior instruments to identification and classification.

Although assessment of adaptive behavior is not essential for identification of other disabilities, it has implications for other areas (e.g., emotional disorders, learning disabilities, physical handicaps). Reschly and Gresham (1988) recommend screening for deficits in adaptive behavior for all students with mild disabilities. The form of this assessment should include use of a standardized adaptive behavior scale and observations in different settings and with different respondents in order to develop a comprehensive picture of the individual. According to Reschly (1989), more appropriate classification decisions will be made and more appropriate program selection will result when adaptive behavior is assessed and considered in these decisions. In the following paragraphs we discuss the application of adaptive behavior assessment to identification and classification of individuals with behavior disorders, learning disabilities, physical disabilities, and sensory impairments.

Sparrow and Cicchetti (1987) found that impairments in adaptive behavior positively correlate with severity of psychological disturbance.

These authors also found that specific deficits occurred in interpersonal skills, coping strategies, and leisure skills. Major difficulties were found to exist in socialization and maladaptive behavior. Assessment of adaptive behavior will help to differentiate children with behavior problems from their nondisabled peers and, thus, should be an integral component of the whole assessment process (Sparrow & Cicchetti, 1987).

Adaptive behavior scales are not often used in classification decisions in the area of learning disabilities because the emphasis tends to be on academics. Additionally, students with learning disabilities tend to be treated as a homogeneous group. However, results from adaptive behavior instruments reveal that subgroups may exist and this information may influence classification decisions. Weller and Strawser (1987) reviewed the performance of students classified as learning disabled and found that they could be further divided into five subgroups that focused on specific adaptive behavior deficits (e.g., poor independent work habits, socialization). Knowing that these subgroups exist can impact how these students are identified and classified and can subsequently influence programming.

Assessment practices with those with physical handicaps, similar to assessment of students with learning disabilities, have also neglected adaptive behavior. With these students the emphasis tends to be on medical issues (e.g., occupational therapy, physical therapy), intelligence, and academic progress (Pollingue, 1987). Pollingue (1987) suggests that adaptive behavior scales can provide valuable knowledge that may influence classification and placement issues by contributing information on amount and type of assistance needed in meeting demands of daily living.

Last, the use of adaptive behavior measures with low-incidence populations (i.e., hearing and visual impairments) is in its infancy due to complex issues. These issues include impaired sensory input, appropriate assessment techniques, and adapted scoring procedures (Meacham, Kline, Stovall, & Sands, 1987). Even though these issues have not been resolved, adaptive behavior scales can provide useful information on the adaptive efforts of individuals with sensory impairments.

The above categorical descriptors are typically applied to school-age children and older individuals; however, it is not always appropriate to apply these labels to preschoolers. The label typically used with this population is "developmentally delayed." Developmental delays may be displayed in self-help, motor, cognition, social, and/or communication domains. Assessment of adaptive behavior has particular relevance with preschoolers because it may help practitioners to identify delays in these domains. Identification of these delays may help to qualify a child to receive special services; that is, adaptive behavior assessment may be one component of the multisource assessment.

There are several reasons for the increased emphasis on adaptive behavior in all disability areas and across all ages of individuals. First, the expansion of the AAMD definition of mental retardation to include adaptive behavior has had a major influence on the assessment of adaptive behavior. Second, litigative and legislative decisions have influenced the use of adaptive behavior scales. For example, various court cases (e.g., *Larry P. v. Riles, Diana v. the Board of Education*) contributed to the nondiscriminatory evaluation components of PL 94-142 and PL 99-457. As a result, there are more stringent assessment guidelines to be followed: (a) Tests cannot be racially or culturally discriminatory; (b) tests must be administered in native language or mode of communication; (c) no single evaluation can be used as a sole criterion; (d) trained personnel must administer tests; (e) tests must be validated for the purpose used; and (f) accommodations must be made for physical and sensory disabilities. Additionally, assessment must be conducted in all areas related to the suspected disability and must utilize multisource measures. This variety of sources can include teacher observations, parent report, and aptitude and achievement tests, as well as adaptive behavior scales. Not only is multifactored assessment required by current law, it also provides a more holistic approach to classification decisions (Reschly, 1981). Thus, more emphasis must be placed on adaptive behavior to describe typical patterns of behavior. Last, PL 94-142 and PL 99-457 recognize the importance of including parents in the educational decision-making process. A key way to involve parents in assessment is in the area of adaptive behavior. Parents and significant others are often the respondents on adaptive behavior measures and have vital information pertaining to their child's performance.

APPLICATION OF ADAPTIVE BEHAVIOR ASSESSMENT TO INSTRUCTIONAL PROGRAM PLANNING

Educational program planning involves delineating individual goals and objectives to address students' strengths and areas of need. Adaptive behavior measures can provide valuable information for programming for individuals who are physically handicapped (Pollingue, 1987), learning disabled (Weller & Strawser, 1987), sensory impaired (Meacham et al.,

1987), and mentally retarded (Langone & Burton, 1987). Additionally, there are programming implications for individuals with mild disabilities (Horn & Fuchs, 1987; Reschly, 1989) to severe disabilities (Horn & Fuchs, 1987; Langone & Burton, 1987) and for preschool children (Harrison, 1991), as well as school-aged children, adolescents, and adults.

General Program Planning

Program planning requires the use of instruments that thoroughly cover relevant areas. Unfortunately, most current adaptive behavior scales provide only an overview of the individual's adaptive perform-ance (Reschly & Gresham, 1988). The results are best used as a guide to identify general strengths, areas mastered, and needs for future independence. This global picture of an individual can be especially beneficial for the practitioner who is unfamiliar with the person who was assessed. Although more in-depth assessment will be needed when planning for an unfamiliar person, the adaptive behavior results can narrow the amount of additional assessment by helping the practitioner to identify priority areas. The results also provide a common basis for communication between professionals providing services to the indi-vidual (Snell & Griss, 1987).

To conduct a comprehensive evaluation, appropriate assessment prac-tices require the use of multiple sources (e.g., parents, teachers), multiple settings (e.g., home, school, community), and multiple methods (e.g., interview, observation). Especially important, for comparative purposes, is the use of at least one standardized adaptive behavior inventory for identifying deficits in this area (Reschly, 1989). When adaptive behavior deficits are used as part of the justification for special education classifi-cation, it is imperative that adaptive behavior goals are included in the individual education plan (Reschly, 1989).

Planning for Specific Instructional Programs

Although broad goals can be identified from the results of stand-ardized adaptive behavior inventories, specific instructional objectives require more in-depth assessment in the form of ecological, or environ-mental, inventories. These inventories are completed in the individual's current and future environments in order to identify specific skills needed in those settings. Conducting ecological inventories paired with providing

instruction in the natural settings enhances the probability of skill generalization and maintenance. Although the methodology for completing
ecological inventories has been emphasized in the area of severe disabilities (Brown et al., 1979), these procedures have been used infrequently in
the area of mild disabilities. However, this methodology has valuable
implications for individuals with either severe or mild disabilities.

Severe Disabilities

One of the best practices in severe disabilities is a functional curriculum that is developed using ecological inventories (Meyer, Eichinger, &
Park-Lee, 1987). The process for completing these inventories is delineated by Brown et al. (1979) as follows: (a) identify functional curricular
domains (i.e., domestic, community, leisure, vocational), (b) identify current and future environment, (c) identify subenvironments within each
environment, (d) specify activities that occur within each subenvironment,
and (e) delineate the skills required to complete each activity. Useful
strategies for obtaining this information include interviews, conducted by
the primary service provider, with significant others, future teachers, and
potential employers. (See Table 12.2 for examples of interview questions.)
Additionally, the practitioner may visit the home, future school placement,
and various community sites (e.g., restaurants, stores, parks, and possible
places of employment). Table 12.3 provides an example of a completed
ecological inventory for one environment within the community domain.
Ecological inventories provide numerous potential goals for instruction
that need to be prioritized. The questions in Table 12.4 can be used to assist
the practitioner in selecting goals as priorities for instruction. For each
potential goal the practitioner would ask each of the questions listed in the
table. Those goals receiving the largest number of "yes" answers would be
higher priorities than other potential goals. However, further assessment
is needed in the areas targeted as priorities to identify specific skills needed
as well as to identify potential adaptations.

Discrepancy analyses (i.e., student repertoire inventories), which
compare the performance of individuals with disabilities to those without,
are used to target specific behaviors needed for successful performance of
the activity. The steps for conducting discrepancy analyses are as follows:
(a) identify the skills performed by nondisabled peers to complete a
specific activity, (b) observe the individual with disabilities and record
whether or not the person is able to complete the steps, (c) complete a

TABLE 12.2. *Sample Interview Questions for Program Planning for Individuals with Severe Disabilities*

GENERAL QUESTIONS
1. Does your child take any medication? For what?
2. Is your child allergic to anything? if so, what?
3. How does your child learn to do new things?

COMMUNICATION/LANGUAGE
1. What languages are spoken in your home?
2. What language is spoken most often in your home?
3. How does your child communicate his/her needs to you?
4. How does your child communicate displeasure, pain, or dislike to you?
5. How does your child communicate with family members and friends?
6. Does your child follow simple instructions (e.g., "Come here," "Sit down")?
7. Do you think your child would learn skills more easily if taught in English or another language?

BEHAVIOR
1. Does your child exhibit any behaviors that you feel are inappropriate or that bother you or members of the family?
2. What do you or others do when this behavior occurs?
3. What do you do to comfort or calm your child?
4. What do you do to discipline your child or show disapproval?
5. Does your child adapt easily to changes in routine?

DOMESTIC/SELF-HELP SKILLS
1. Is your child able to feed her- or himself? If so, how did she learn to do this?
2. What are your child's favorite and least favorite foods?
3. Is your child able to dress her- or himself?
4. What personal hygiene skills would you like your child to learn?
5. Which self-help skill is most important to you for your child to learn?

COMMUNITY
1. What places in the community do you take your child to (e.g., shopping mall, restaurants, relatives' homes, others)?
2. How does your child behave when you take him/her to these places?

continued

RECREATION/LEISURE
1. What are your child's favorite activities and toys at home?
2. What does your child do after school?
3. Does your child play with siblings and neighborhood friends?
4. Does your child enjoy playing by him/herself?
5. In what way does your child move about the house?

VOCATIONAL
1. What jobs does your child help with at home (e.g., putting away toys, cleaning up spills and messes)?
2. Do you have any suggestions as to the type of work your child might be able to do when he or she is older?
3. Have you thought of any skills that your child might enjoy that would lead to work preparation (e.g., clerical work, gardening, janitorial)?

FUTURE
1. What places do you think your child might go to when he is older?
2. In the future, where do you see your child living (e.g., supervised apartment, group home, home)?

Note. From "Assessment Strategies" by M. A. Falvey in M. A. Falvey (Ed.), *Community-Based Curriculum: Instructional Strategies for Students with Severe Handicaps*, 1989, p. 42. Baltimore: Paul H. Brookes. Copyright 1989 by Paul H. Brookes Publishing Co. Reprinted by permission.

TABLE 12.3. *Sample Ecological Inventory for the Community Domain*

Domain: Community	**Environment:** Fast Food Restaurant
Subenvironment: Counter area	**Skills:** Go to eating area Scan for empty table Go to empty table and sit down Eat meal Collect trash on tray or in bag
Activity: Ordering	
Skills: Go to the counter Stand in line Move forward with line Place order when asked Pay for order when asked Pick up tray or bag and leave counter	**Subenvironment:** Trash area
	Activity: Throwing away trash
Subenvironment: Eating area	**Skills:** Go to trash area Throw trash in receptacle Place tray on top of receptacle
Activity: Eating meal	

TABLE 12.4. *Factors to Consider in Prioritizing Goals*

1. Is the targeted activity appropriate for the chronological age of the individual?

2. Can the targeted activity be taught using materials appropriate for the chronological age of the individual?

3. Is the targeted activity needed on a daily basis?

4. Can the targeted activity be taught regularly across settings and using different materials?

5. Will performance of the targeted activity increase interactions with nonhandicapped peers?

6. Is the targeted activity needed in current and future environments?

7. Is the targeted activity a critical activity (i.e., if the individual is not taught to perform the activity someone else will need to do it for him/her)?

8. Can the targeted activity be taught in the natural context in which it will be needed?

9. Is it a preference of the family or caregivers that the individual be taught the targeted activity?

10. Is it a preference of the individual to learn the targeted activity?

11. Can the individual partially (or independently) participate in the targeted activity?

discrepancy analysis of the person's behavior to identify why the person is unable to perform the step (e.g., unable to state what is desired because the person is nonverbal and lacks a communication system), and (d) specify what should be done (i.e., teach the skill directly, develop an adaptation, teach a related skill). For the person who is nonverbal, the targeted option may be to provide the person with communication cards and to then teach the person to use those cards to place his or her order. Table 12.5 provides an example of a completed discrepancy analysis. Completing discrepancy analyses addresses an area that Langone and Burton (1987) believe to be the cornerstone for assessing learner progress: comparison to persons without disabilities.

TABLE 12.5. *Sample Discrepancy Analysis for the Community Domain*

Student:	Domain:	Subenvironment:
Linda	Community	Counter Area
Date:	**Environment:**	**Teacher:**
May 15, 1991	Fast Food Restaurant	Thomas Smith

Nonhandicapped person inventory	Student inventory	Discrepancy analysis	What-to-do options
Activity: Ordering			
Skills:			
1. Go to the counter	+		
2. Stand in line	+		
3. Move forward with line	-	Stands in same place	Teach to take a step forward when person in front of her moves forward
4. Place order when asked	-	Is nonverbal and does not respond in any way	Teach to present a communication card that specifies her order
5. Pay for order when asked	-	Gives wrong amount of money	Teach to use next dollar strategy to pay for order
6. Pick up tray or bag and leave counter	+		

Code: + = correct response; - = incorrect response.

Mild Disabilities

With individuals with mild disabilities (e.g., mild mental retardation, learning disabilities, behavior problems), adaptive behavior, if assessed, is done so with an emphasis on identification as opposed to an emphasis on programming. However, adaptive behavior has valuable implications for planning for reintegration into regular education classrooms and for transition to postsecondary activities. Reintegration of students with mild disabilities may be more successful if practitioners employ environmental analyses to identify appropriate goals and objectives. By surveying the future environment (i.e., the regular education classroom) to delineate specific activities and skills, the teacher can target the behaviors relevant for success in that environment. If teachers neglect to conduct ecological inventories, it is likely that skills targeted in the special education environment will not be those that are most important for success in the mainstream setting (Horn & Fuchs, 1987). Targeting relevant goals and objectives may result in smoother transition to the mainstream setting and may also lead to more positive attitudes of regular educators (Horn & Fuchs, 1987).

Anderson-Inman, Walker, and Purcell (1984) suggest using methodology similar to ecological inventories for program planning with students with mild disabilities. Their process, referred to as transenvironmental programming, emphasizes preparing students placed in resource room programs for entry into mainstreamed classrooms. The first step focuses on assessing the target environment (i.e., the regular classroom) to identify critical behavioral expectations of the setting to ensure that students entering the class can meet these expectations. These authors provide examples of two instruments that can be used to identify behavioral and academic demands of the regular classroom. Step two stresses intervening in the special education environment to prepare the student for the regular class. Thus, it is necessary to teach, systematically, the social and academic skills as well as skills related to academic success (e.g., asking for help, following directions) necessary for success in the mainstream environment (i.e., those behaviors identified in step one). Generalization of skills across settings is the emphasis of step three. Specific strategies for enhancing generalization of behavior (e.g., using natural contingencies, programming common stimuli, self-management procedures, general case instruction) are discussed elsewhere (Albin & Horner, 1988; Stokes & Baer, 1977; Stokes & Osnes, 1988). The final step of the transenvironmental programming model emphasizes the importance of evaluating student performance in the target environment. This evaluation provides critical information as to the success of the intervention and also provides ongoing data for altering the intervention program if it has not been successful.

Environmental analyses are also beneficial in planning for community-based instruction and transition to postsecondary activities. Conducting ecological inventories can result in functional goals and objectives that may lead to greater skill generalization following completion of school. In the past the importance of transition was primarily emphasized for those individuals with more severe disabilities. However, with the recent reauthorization of PL 94-142 (PL 101-476, now referred to as the Individuals with Disabilities Education Act), transition services must be part of the IEP process for all students with disabilities by the age of 16 years and annually thereafter. For successful transition planning, practitioners cannot rely on what is thought to be needed but must address the interests and preferences of the student and move beyond traditional teaching approaches in the classroom. Langone (1990) outlines methodology that can be used to develop appropriate curricula for students with mild to moderate disabilities. He stresses that it is important to apply the principle of "community validity" in determining whether or not particular goals and objectives are meaningful for a specific student. To determine if curriculum content is community valid, Langone recommends completing a community needs assessment by (a) interviewing parents, guardians, students, and employers (Table 12.6 provides examples of interview questions pertaining to individuals with mild disabilities); (b) having these same individuals complete questionnaires; and (c) conducting direct observations. Observations, conducted in community environments, are organized in a format similar to the ecological inventories previously described. The environments are broken down into subenvironments; the observer indicates the specific activities that occur there and the skills needed to complete the activities. The practitioner can identify specific objectives for a particular student by subsequently completing discrepancy analyses. By employing this methodology with students with mild disabilities prior to developing the IEP, it is likely that teachers will develop more appropriate goals and objectives that emphasize teaching individuals meaningful skills needed for successful independent living upon completion of school. If skills are not community valid, they would not be given a high priority in the IEP (Langone, 1990). This approach to assessment and subsequent teaching also emphasizes moving beyond the instruction in the classroom and teaching in the community where the particular skills are, and will be, needed.

By following this approach, it is also likely that teachers will move beyond traditional approaches for teaching academics to students with mild disabilities. Instead, more of an emphasis will probably be placed upon "functional academics." Functional academics refers to those skills

TABLE 12.6. *Sample Interview Questions for Program Planning for Students with Mild Disabilities*

Student Questions

    1. What are your goals related to obtaining a job?

    2. How would you find a job in this area?

    3. What besides academics does school offer you? What are you interested in?

    4. Do you need a college degree or further education to attain your job goals?

    5. How do you spend your free time?

    6. With whom do you spend your free time?

Questions for Former Students

    1. Do you have problems in social situations?

    2. Do you have transportation difficulties in getting to your job (e.g., public transportation schedules, fares)?

    3. What do you think was the best/most important thing that you learned in school?

    4. What was the least helpful?

    5. What skills did you have to learn in order to live on your own?

    6. Are there any jobs you would rather do?

    7. Why have you not tried to get these jobs?

Questions for Employers

    1. What does an individual need to know for this job?

    2. What could stop you from hiring an individual with a disability?

    3. Is the site accessible?

    4. How do you feel about a job coach being on site?

    5. What are the specific job skills needed?

    6. Is there a dress code?

    7. Are there benefits with the job?

    8. Would you hire this individual for long-term or short-term employment?

Parent/Caregiver Questions

1. Does your son/daughter use time concepts for daily activities?
2. What do you anticipate for your son/daughter in the future after schooling is completed?
3. What basic or functional academic skills do you think your son/daughter needs for the future?
4. Are there any academic skills that, if your son/daughter could do them, would be directly usable at home or in the community?
5. Does your son/daughter interact with same-age peers in the neighborhood?
6. What kind of family recreational activities do you do?
7. What responsibilities does your son/daughter have at home?
8. What jobs or personal hygiene/grooming skills would you like your son/daughter to perform independently at home?
9. Can your son/daughter go to a store, buy something, and get change?
10. Can your son/daughter recognize signs within the community?

---

necessary for basic literacy and basic knowledge of concepts of time and number (Reschly, 1989). With this approach to teaching academics there is an emphasis on teaching reading, writing, and mathematics as they relate to everyday demands. Academic skills would be taught in the context of functional activities (e.g., managing own bank account, grocery shopping for self or family, planning menus, reading and following recipes/directions), using natural materials, and in the context of a variety of natural environments. The previously discussed strategies of ecological inventories (i.e., community or environmental inventories) and discrepancy analyses are once again the means for determining the specific academic content meaningful for a particular student. Table 12.7 provides an example of how to apply the ecological inventory approach to develop reading content. The questions in Table 12.8 provide guidelines for a practitioner to use when selecting reading vocabulary. The ecological inventory approach can also be used to identify functional mathematics content. Following implementation of the basic steps of the strategy (i.e., identifying the curriculum domains, environments, subenvironments, and activities), the practitioner reviews the activity to identify the (a) money concepts needed to perform the activity, (b) time concepts needed for independent performance, (c) essential measurement concepts, and (d) necessary problem-solving skills (Ford et al., in Grenot-Scheyer, Eshilian, & Falvey, 1989). Table 12.9 provides an example of an ecological inventory that incorporates functional academics (i.e., reading and mathematics) in ordering a meal in a restaurant. Once again, a discrepancy analysis would be completed to identify the specific skills needed by the student.

TABLE 12.7. *Ecological Inventory to Develop Reading Content*

Domain: Vocational

Environment: Junior High School

Subenvironment: Woodshop

Activity: Working on Wood Projects

ECOLOGICAL INVENTORY SEQUENCE/DEVELOPMENT OF KEY VOCABULARY:

1. List objects (nouns) used in activity.
   a. Equipment names: jigsaw, vise, workbench
   b. Tool names: Sandpaper, ruler, file
   c. Safety signs: "Flammable," "Do not touch," "Exit"
2. List actions (verbs) performed in activity.
   a. Working: sand, cut, file, rasp
   b. Cleaning: sweep, dust, put away, wash
3. List modifiers and descriptors (adjectives and adverbs) used in activity.
   a. Adjectives: hard, rough, smooth
   b. Adverbs: smoothly, quickly
4. List prepositions used in activity
   a. Working: rasp around, gauge in
   b. Cleaning: sweep behind, clean under
5. List titles used in activity
   a. Names of woodshop teacher, aides, peers

Note. From "Functional Academics" by M. Grenot-Scheyer, L. Eshilian, and M. A. Falvey in M. A. Falvey (Ed.), *Community-Based Curriculum: Instructional Strategies for Students with Severe Handicaps*, 1989, p. 297. Baltimore: Paul H. Brookes. Copyright 1989 by Paul H. Brookes Publishing Co. Reprinted by permission.

TABLE 12.8. *Questions to Ask to Determine Reading Vocabulary*

1. What reading vocabulary will be taught?
   a. Is the vocabulary functional?
   b. Is the vocabulary chronological-age appropriate?
   c. Will the vocabulary meet the current and subsequent needs of the student?
   d. Can the vocabulary cross environments?
   e. Is the vocabulary similar to vocabulary that nonhandicapped peers use?
   f. Does the vocabulary promote independence?
   g. Will the vocabulary meet the largest variety of student needs?
   h. Does the vocabulary consider the cultural/familial needs and characteristics?
   i. Can the vocabulary be used frequently?
2. How will the vocabulary be taught?
   a. Can the vocabulary be used with a variety of reading strategies?
   b. Is the vocabulary motivating to the student?
   c. Can the vocabulary be taught in accordance with the student's preferred learning modality?
   d. Can the vocabulary be taught with, by, or in the presence of nonhandicapped peers?
3. Where will the vocabulary be taught?
   a. Will the vocabulary be taught in the natural context in which it occurs?
   b. Can the vocabulary be taught/used by a variety of people in the student's environment?
   c. Can the student use the vocabulary to communicate across a wide variety of environments?

Note. From "Functional Academics" by M. Grenot-Scheyer, L. Eshilian, and M. A. Falvey in M. A. Falvey (Ed.), *Community-Based Curriculum: Instructional Strategies for Students with Severe Handicaps,* 1989, p. 301. Baltimore: Paul H. Brookes. Copyright 1989 by Paul H. Brookes Publishing Co. Reprinted by permission.

Preschoolers with Disabilities

The use of adaptive behavior scales with preschoolers with disabilities is not a widespread practice. However, appropriate and functional programming for preschoolers with severe disabilities is an issue for many

TABLE 12.9. *Sample Ecological Inventory Incorporating Functional Academics*

Domain: Community	**Environment:** Fast Food
Subenvironment: Counter Area	Restaurant
	Activity: Ordering
Skills: Go to counter	Place order when asked
Stand in line	Pay for order when asked
Check time to determine	Determine appropriate
appropriate menu board	amount of money to give
(e.g., breakfast or lunch)	counterperson
Read menu board to select	Wait for change
desired item(s)	Count change
Determine if have enough	Pick up tray or bag and leave
money for desired item(s)	counter
Move forward with line	

early interventionists. Ecological inventories and discrepancy analyses, previously discussed, provide a framework for identifying appropriate goals and objectives, including participation in ongoing activities in the integrated preschool setting. Similar to Anderson-Inman et al.'s (1984) transenvironmental programming approach, Vincent et al. (1980) and Salisbury and Vincent (1990) have contributed the criterion of the next environment model for planning for preschoolers with disabilities. This model enables practitioners to evaluate early childhood programs to determine relevant skills for programming to enhance success in current and future environments. To ascertain relevant survival skills for smoother transitions, four strategies are recommended: (a) kindergarten tryouts, (b) follow-up of children who have already transitioned, (c) kindergarten teachers generate skills, and (d) direct observation of potential classrooms for integration. Assessing adaptive behavior is an ongoing process that only begins in the preschool years.

Summary of Best Practices

It is most important that assessment of adaptive behavior be relevant for all individuals with disabilities, regardless of type or severity, and for individuals preschool-age through adulthood. Successful use of adaptive behavior assessment in general and specific program planning for students with mild to severe disabilities requires implementation of a variety of best practices. Third-party respondents must be people who know the individual well in a variety of settings so that they do not resort to guessing about an individual's typical performance. It is insufficient to base assessment of adaptive behavior on only performance in classroom or program situations. Rather, performance in home and community environments must also be considered for a comprehensive profile of the individual. Also necessary for this complete profile is consideration of information from various sources: standardized adaptive behavior instruments, interviews with significant others, and direct observation of the individual in the natural environment. Results from this multisource assessment have implications both for classification and instructional programming. If assessment of adaptive behavior is used as part of the multisource assessment process for identification and classification, it is imperative that psychometrically sound instruments are used. Although the global score obtained from adaptive behavior scales may contribute to classification decisions and general goals, more information is needed for developing specific objectives for instructional programming. If results from an adaptive behavior scale contribute to classification and placement decisions, adaptive behavior, generally or in specific domain(s), should be addressed within the individualized program plans for the individual. Using standardized instruments that are comprehensive in addressing various domains and that include items ranging from low to high in complexity and skill development (Cone, 1987) can narrow the amount of subsequent detailed assessment needed. However, designing instructional objectives and programs requires more specific assessment (e.g., ecological inventories, transenvironmental programming) in the natural environment.

Placing an emphasis on adaptive behavior in specific program planning for students with mild to severe disabilities leads to a variety of best educational practices. Subsequent instruction pertaining to the goals and objectives developed through assessment emphasizing adaptive behavior requires use of natural environments and materials to be most successful. Additionally, the targeted skills should be taught in the context of meaningful activities, and not in isolation, to ensure maximum success. As is evident from the above discussion, it becomes necessary to target different goals and objectives for students with mild disabilities than have been typically targeted in the past (Reschly, 1989). By following these guidelines, the probability is enhanced that individuals with mild to severe disabilities will be more likely to generalize and maintain skills; that is, they will be more successful in meeting the demands of their everyday environment(s).

ISSUES AND FUTURE DIRECTIONS

Although the above strategies and procedures are documented as best practices, there continues to be a need to encourage practitioners to implement them in many situations. For example, assessment of adaptive behavior, relevant for individuals with all types of disabilities, tends to be emphasized only for those who are mentally retarded. It is recommended that practitioners utilize assessment of adaptive behavior for classification and programming decisions for other types of disabilities (e.g., learning disabilities, behavior disorders, sensory impairments, physical disabilities). In addition, adaptive behavior assessment is appropriate for individuals of all ages, including preschoolers.

One important role of adaptive behavior measurement is use in planning for future educational placements, employment, and living arrangements. More emphasis needs to be placed on strategies such as (a) Anderson-Inman et al.'s (1984) approach to planning for reintegration of students with mild disabilities, (b) use of the criterion of the next environment model with preschoolers with disabilities (Salisbury & Vincent, (1990), (c) planning for transition from school to postschool activities, and (d) targeting functional academics with students with mild disabilities. Finally, more work needs to be done to bring the methodology of ecological inventories and discrepancy analyses to all practitioners who work with individuals with severe disabilities in order to help these individuals participate more fully in their communities.

In addition to the above issues that involve practitioner implications, there are standardization and adaptive behavior construct concerns that continue to need attention. Although many of the recent, well-known adaptive behavior instruments include preschool children in their norming sample, the numbers may not be adequate. For example, the CTAB includes only 77 preschoolers (5 years of age) in its norming sample. Also, as early childhood special education is a relatively new field, the content of adaptive behavior items should be reviewed to be sure they are ecologically valid and appropriate for young children.

Another major area of concern relates to the issue that there is no clear concept of adaptive behavior (Bruininks & McGrew, 1987; Kamphaus, 1987; Schmidt & Salvia, 1984). Numerous definitions of adaptive behavior contribute to wide variability in the number of domains and subdomains on individual adaptive behavior instruments affecting validity. If domains are inadequately covered on a particular instrument, this inadequacy could unfairly influence classification or programming decisions.

CONCLUSION

Adaptive behavior is a dynamic construct influenced by the individual's age, environment, and culture. Assessing adaptive behavior provides a useful, overall profile of the individual with implications for classification and instructional programming. Including adaptive behavior as part of the multisource assessment process will contribute to sounder classification and placement decisions. According to Reschly (1981), assessment of adaptive behavior is essential in order to guarantee that educational programs for students with disabilities are functional and effective rather than "dead-end and inferior." Because we can effectively modify and teach adaptive behavior, it is imperative that we do so to enhance the likelihood that individuals with disabilities will be successful in present and future environments.

REFERENCES

Adams, G. L. (1986). *CTAB/NABC technical manual*. San Antonio: The Psychological Corporation.

Albin, R. W., & Horner, R. H. (1988). Generalization with precision. In R. H. Horner, G. Dunlap, , & R. L. Koegel (Eds.), *Generalization and maintenance: Life-style changes in applied settings* (pp. 99-120). Baltimore: Paul H. Brookes.

Anderson-Inman, L., Walker, H., & Purcell, J. (1984). Promoting the transfer of skills across settings: Transenvironmental programming for handicapped students in the mainstream. In W. L. Heward, T. E. Heron, D. S. Hill, & J. Trap-Porter (Eds.), *Focus on behavior analysis in education* (pp. 17-37). Columbus, OH: Merrill.

Browder, D. M. (1991). *Assessment of individuals with severe disabilities: An applied behavior approach to life skills assessment* (2nd ed.). Baltimore: Paul H. Brookes.

Brown, L., Branston-McClean, M. B., Baumgart, D., Vincent, L., Falvey, M., & Schroeder, J. (1979). Using the characteristics of current and subsequent least restrictive environments in the development of curricular content for severely handicapped students. *AAESPH Review, 4,* 407-424.

Bruininks, R. H., Hill, B. K., Weatherman, R. F., & Woodcock, R. W. (1986). *Examiner's manual, Inventory for Client and Agency Planning.* Allen, TX: DLM Teaching Resources.

Bruininks, R. H., & McGrew, K. (1987). *Exploring the structure of adaptive behavior* (Report Number 87-1). Minneapolis: University of Minnesota, Department of Educational Psychology.

Bruininks, R. H., Thurlow, M., & Gilman, C. J. (1987). Adaptive behavior and mental retardation. *The Journal of Special Education, 21,* 69-88.

Bruininks, R. H., Woodcock, R. W. , Weatherman, R. F., & Hill, B. K. (1984). *Interviewer's manual, Scales of Independent Behavior.* Allen, TX: DLM Teaching Resources.

Cone, J. D. (1987). Intervention planning using adaptive behavior instruments. *Journal of Special Education, 21,* 127-148.

Demchak, M. A. (in press). The functional assessment of problem behaviors in applied settings. *Intervention in School and Clinic.*

Doll, E. A. (1935). A genetic scale of social maturity. *The American Journal of Orthopsychiatry, 5,* 180-188.

Doll, E. A. (1940). The social basis of mental diagnosis. *Journal of Applied Psychology, 24,* 160-169.

Doll, E. A. (1953). *The measurement of social competence: A manual for the Vineland Social Maturity Scale.* Circle Pines, MN: American Guidance Service.

Doll, E. A. (1965). *Vineland Social Maturity Scale: Condensed manual of directions.* Circle Pines, MN: American Guidance Service.

Falvey, M. A. (1989). Assessment strategies. In M. A. Falvey (Ed.), *Community-based curriculum: Instructional strategies for students with severe handicaps* (pp. 35-61). Baltimore: Paul H. Brookes.

Grenot-Scheyer, M., Eshilian, L., & Falvey, M. A. (1980). Functional academics. In M. A. Falvey (Ed.), *Community-based curriculum: Instructional strategies for students with severe handicaps* (pp. 285-320). Baltimore: Paul H. Brookes.

Gresham, F. M., & Elliott, S. N. (1987). The relationship between adaptive behavior and social skills: Issues in definition and assessment. *The Journal of Special Education, 21,* 167-181.

Grossman, H. J. (1983). *Classification in mental retardation.* Washington, DC: American Association on Mental Deficiency.

Harrison, P. L. (1985). *Vineland Adaptive Behavior Scales: Classroom education manual.* Circle Pines, MN: American Guidance Service.

Harrison, P. L. (1991). Assessment of adaptive behavior. In B. Bracken (Ed.), *The psychoeducational assessment of preschool children* (pp. 168-186). Boston: Allyn & Bacon.

Holman, J. G., & Bruininks, R. H. (1985). Assessing and training adaptive behaviors. In K. D. Lakin & R. H. Bruininks (Eds.), *Strategies for achieving community integration of developmentally disabled citizens* (pp. 73-104). Baltimore: Paul H. Brookes.

Horn, E., & Fuchs, D. (1987). Using adaptive behavior in assessment and intervention: An overview. *The Journal of Special Education, 21,* 11-26.

Kamphaus, R. W. (1987). Conceptual and psychometric issues in the assessment of adaptive behavior. *The Journal of Special Education, 21,* 27-35.

Keith, T. Z., Fehrmann, P. G., Harrison, P. L., & Pottebaum, S. M. (1987). The relation between adaptive behavior and intelligence: Testing alternative explanations. *Journal of School Psychology, 26,* 31-43.

Langone, J. (1990). *Teaching students with mild and moderate learning problems.* Boston: Allyn & Bacon.

Langone, J., & Burton, T. A. (1987). Teaching adaptive behavior skills to moderately and severely handicapped individuals: Best practices for facilitating independent living. *The Journal of Special Education, 21,* 149-165.

Lennox, D. B., & Miltenberger, R. G. (1989). Conducting a functional assessment of problem behavior in applied settings. *The Journal of the Association for Persons with Severe Handicaps, 14,* 304-311.

Meacham, F., Kline, M. M., Stovall, J. A., & Sands, D. I. (1987). Adaptive behavior and low incidence handicaps: Hearing and visual impairments. *The Journal of Special Education, 21,* 183-196.

Meyer, L. H., Eichinger, J., & Park-Lee, S. (1987). A validation of program quality indicators in educational services for students with severe disabilities. *The Journal of the Association for Persons with Severe Handicaps, 12,* 251-263.

Meyer, L. H., & Evans, I. M. (1989). *Nonaversive intervention for behavior problems: A manual for home and community.* Baltimore: Paul H. Brookes.

O'Neill, R. E., Horner, R. H., Albin, R. W., Storey, K., & Sprague, J. R. (1990). *Functional analysis of problem behavior: A practical assessment guide.* Sycamore, IL: Sycamore.

Patrick, J. L., & Reschly, D. J. (1982). Relationship of state educational criteria and demographic variables to school-system prevalence of mental retardation. *American Journal of Mental Deficiency, 86,* 351-360.

Patton, J. R., & Jones, E. D. (1990). Definition, classification, and prevalence. In J. R. Patton, J. S. Payne, & M. Beirne-Smith (Eds.), *Mental retardation* (3rd ed., pp. 33-75). Columbus, OH: Merrill.

Pollingue, A. (1987). Adaptive behavior and low incidence handicaps: Use of adaptive behavior instruments for persons with physical handicaps. *The Journal of Special Education, 21,* 117-125.

Reschly, D. J. (1981). Psychological testing in educational classification and placement. *American Psychologist, 36,* 1094-1102.

Reschly, D. J. (1982). Assessing mild mental retardation: The influence of adaptive behavior, sociocultural status, and prospects for nonbiased assessment. In C. R. Reynolds & T. B. Gutkin (Eds.), *The handbook of school psychology* (pp. 209-242). New York: John Wiley & Sons.

Reschly, D. J. (1989). Incorporating adaptive behavior deficits into instructional programs. In G. A. Robinson, J. R. Patton, E. A. Polloway, & L. R. Sargent

(Eds.), *Best practices in mild mental disabilities* (pp. 39-63). Reston, VA: Council for Exceptional Children.

Reschly, D. J., & Gresham, F. M. (1988). Adaptive behavior and the mildly handicapped. In T. R. Kratochwill (Ed.), *Advances in school psychology* (Vol. 6, pp. 249-282). Hillsdale, NJ: Lawrence Erlbaum.

Salisbury, C. L., & Vincent, L. J. (1990). Criterion of the next environment and best practices: Mainstreaming and integration 10 years later. *Topics in Early Childhood Special Education, 10*(2), 78-89.

Salvia, J., & Ysseldyke, J. E. (1988). *Assessment in special and remedial education* (4th ed.). Boston: Houghton Mifflin.

Schmidt, M. W., & Salvia, J. (1984). Adaptive behavior: A conceptual analysis. *Diagnostique, 9*, 117-125.

Snell, M. E., & Grigg, N. C. (1987). Instructional assessment and curriculum development. In M. E. Snell (Ed.), *Systematic instruction of persons with severe handicaps* (3rd ed., pp. 64-109). Columbus, OH: Merrill.

Sparrow, S. S., Balla, D. A., & Cicchetti, D. (1984a). *Vineland Adaptive Behavior Scales: Interview Edition Expanded Form manual.* Circle Pines, MN: American Guidance Service.

Sparrow, S. S., Balla, D. A., & Cicchetti, D. (1984b). *Vineland Adaptive Behavior Scales: Interview Edition Survey Form manual.* Circle Pines, MN: American Guidance Service.

Sparrow, S. S., & Cicchetti, D. V. (1987). Adaptive behavior and the psychologically disturbed child. *The Journal of Special Education, 21*, 89-100.

Stokes, T. F., & Baer, D. M. (1978). An implicit technology of generalization. *Journal of Applied Behavior Analysis, 10*, 349-367.

Stokes, T. F., & Osnes, P. G. (1988). The developing applied technology of generalization and maintenance. In R. H. Horner, G. Dunlap, & R. L. Koegel (Eds.), *Generalization and maintenance: Life-style changes in applied settings* (pp. 5-19). Baltimore: Paul H. Brookes.

Vincent, L. J., Salisbury, C., Walter, G., Brown, P., Gruenewald, L. J., & Powers, M. (1980). Program evaluation and curriculum development in early childhood/special education: Criteria of the next environment. In W. Sailor, B. Wilcox, & L. Brown (Eds.), *Methods of instruction for severely handicapped students* (pp. 303-328). Baltimore: Paul H. Brookes.

Weller, C., & Strawser, S. (1987). Adaptive behavior of subtypes of learning disabled individuals. *The Journal of Special Education, 21*, 101-115.

13 PSYCHOEDUCATIONAL ASSESSMENT OF RACIAL/ETHNIC MINORITY CHILDREN AND YOUTH

Margaret R. Rogers

This chapter is designed to provide an overview of best practices in assessing racial/ethnic minority children and youth. The main focus is to assist psychologists and educational diagnosticians in considering the legal, ethical, psychometric, and ecological/cultural influences that contribute to effective practices in evaluating minority children and to describe the strengths and limitations of current assessment technology in applications with these populations. The chapter is written as a professional resource and guide for practicing school psychologists, regular and special educators, and graduate students who are training to become psychologists or educational diagnosticians.

It should be noted that the assessment of minority children, and particularly linguistic minority children, presents a special challenge to evaluators because the technology as a whole has not kept pace with the needs for ecologically valid and methodologically sound procedures in this area. Although significant advancements have been made in the last decade in the technical adequacy of some of the most popular and widely used assessment measures, overall there is a paucity of appropriate instrumentation. In addition, empirical evidence supporting the use of specific assessment practices is underdeveloped. As the knowledge base in this area expands and changes, so will ideas about what constitutes best practices in providing assessment services to minority children.

DEFINITIONS

The focus of this chapter is on working with racially, ethnically, culturally, and linguistically diverse youngsters. The term *racial/ethnic minority* children and youth will refer to individuals belonging to African-American, Hispanic (e.g., Mexican-American, Latino, Puerto Rican), Pacific Islander (Samoan, Hawaiian), native American (e.g., Sioux, Cherokee), Asian-American (Chinese, Japanese, Vietnamese, Cambodian, Korean), or biracial groups. The children and adolescents who represent these groups have been born and raised in the United States, have immigrated to this county, or may be refugees. It is clear that whereas minority group members may share a number of similarities, considerable heterogeneity and diversity exists among these groups as well. The characteristics that distinguish members of one group from those of another can range from physical attributes (e.g., skin pigmentation, facial features) to cultural experiences (e.g., similar family origins, social and political histories and activities, religious beliefs). Members of these groups are considered to be culturally different to the extent that they share cultural backgrounds and experiences different from those of the dominant culture.

Culturally different children may also be linguistically different in that their native language may not be English. Limited-English-proficient (LEP) children are those who speak a language other than English in addition to demonstrating some English language skills. LEP children's proficiency and competency in speaking their native language and English ranges from mastery over both languages, to mastery over one and limited fluency in the other, to mastery over neither language. LEP children frequently come from home environments in which a primary language other than English is spoken and use of English within the home varies considerably.

The focus here will be on the psychoeducational assessment of racially/ethnically, culturally, and linguistically diverse children. First, the demographic changes that are taking place in the United States and in our public schools will be addressed. Second, the legal, ethical, and psychometric factors that shape assessment practices will be discussed. The assessment process will extend from prereferral activities to follow-up. The process will emphasize a systematic approach to data gathering using the most psychometrically sound and ecologically valid procedures available. Special attention will be given to promoting an ecological approach to assessment that considers the cultural and linguistic context of each child. Because all human experiences occur within a context, it is crucial that we consider how children's behavior, attitudes, and values are defined and shaped by the cultural context in which they occur.

CHANGING U.S. DEMOGRAPHICS

Over the last two decades, the United States has witnessed steady changes in its demographic makeup. Recent estimates from the U.S. Bureau of the Census (1989b) suggest that from 1980 to 1990, the number of Whites grew by only 7.7%, whereas the proportion of African Americans rose by 15.8%, and Hispanics by 34.5%. These statistics suggest that proportionately, minority groups are growing at a substantially faster pace than is the White "majority" group. It has been estimated that these differential growth rates will continue to the year 2000, with the number of Whites increasing by 5.2%, African Americans by 12.8%, and Hispanics by 26.8% (U.S. Bureau of the Census, 1989b).

A number of reasons have been offered to help explain this shift in the country's demographic composition. Ponterotto and Casas (1991) point to rising immigration and fertility rates among the nation's minorities as two of the more important factors influencing current and future demographic trends. In comparing the 1980 birthrates against the projected birthrates for the year 2000 across White, African-American, and the combined native American, Asian, and Pacific Islander populations, it is evident that there have been and are expected to be significant differences between these groups in the number of births over the 20-year period (U.S. Bureau of the Census, 1989a). The overall number of White births is clearly decreasing while the combined number of African-American, native American, Asian, and Pacific Islander births is steadily rising.

For the schools, these changing demographics mean that minority children are present and will continue to appear in growing numbers among public school enrollments. In 1985, Hodgkinson reported that the

25 largest city school systems in the United States already contained majorities of minority students. Ponterotto and Cases (1991) estimate that by the year 2000, one third of all school-age children will belong to a racial-ethnic minority group. Similar proportions of minorities are expected among preschool enrollments, as well. Children who speak a language other than English are also represented in significant numbers in the public schools, and estimates suggest that one out of every eight school children is linguistically different (Plisko, 1984).

Overall, these data clearly suggest that evaluators are providing and will continue to provide assessment services to a racially/ethnically, culturally, and linguistically diverse clientele. The challenges the public schools face in meeting the educational and psychological needs of these children are complicated by the fact that many minority youngsters live in poverty. In 1988, the poverty rate for White children under the age of 18 was 14.6%, for African Americans 44.2%, and Hispanics 37.9% (U.S. Bureau of the Census, 1988). Living in poverty exerts a pervasive influence on children's development. Children raised in lower income settings are at heightened risk for exposure to environmental toxins, inadequate pediatric care, high parental illiteracy rates, and limited intellectual stimulation within the home environment (Zill & Schoenborn, 1990). These children may not have their needs for food, shelter, medical care, and clothing routinely met. Ultimately, all of these factors have the potential to influence children's performance in the classroom and during the assessment process and need to be considered when interpreting their achievements, behaviors, and skills.

LEGAL CONSIDERATIONS

To a large extent, considerations regarding best practices in assessing and educating minority children are guided by federal, state, and local legislation and litigation outcomes. Over the last few decades, the courts and Congress have become increasingly more active in influencing the direction of educational and psychological services within the schools. The impact of these legal proceedings on the education of children in general, and minority children in particular, is tremendous. Because of the profound influence these cases and legislative acts have had in shaping current educational policies and assessment practices that pertain to culturally and linguistically diverse children, it is important that those who work with minority children understand the legal precedents that are involved. By becoming aware of these legal influences and changes, professionals will be better equipped to provide assessment services within the prescribed legal parameters. For the present purposes, only a handful of the most important court cases and legislative acts have been selected to be highlighted.

Perhaps the most important case in its time to argue for the educational rights of minority children was *Brown v. Board of Education* (1954). In that case, the Supreme Court ruled that segregated schools were not providing equal educational opportunities for minority children and ordered schools to desegregate. This landmark ruling was felt across the nation as public schools were forced for the first time to provide an education to all children, regardless of color.

A decade later, the Civil Rights Act of 1964 represented another major achievement in the advancement of human rights. During the early 1960s, the social and political climate was changing as minority groups organized themselves politically on a national level. What became known as the civil rights movement represented a time of heightened social and political activism for both minorities and civil rights activists. One of the most important outcomes of this movement was the Civil Rights Act, which prohibited federally funded institutions from engaging in discriminatory practices on the basis of a person's color, race, or national origin. One intention of this legislation was to ensure educational equity for all children attending federally funded schools. As such, the Civil Rights Act represented a major milestone in the legal history of the nation. It was the first time the federal government struck down discriminatory practices on a broad and sweeping scale. This legislation was closely followed by a handful of significant court cases.

Once racial/ethnic minority children were allowed access to the schools, the courts began to evaluate educational assessment and placement practices in *Hobson v. Hansen* (1967). This case involved a Washington, DC, school system in which large numbers of African-American children were represented in the lower educational track. The court ruled that the schools' overreliance on information about students' performance on standardized ability tests when making educational tracking decisions needed to stop because such practices resulted in a disproportionate number of minority students being placed in lower tracks. The court reasoned that the standardized tests were invalid and culturally inappropriate when used with African Americans and lower-socioeconomic class students because the tests had been normed on a predominately middle-class and White sample.

Therefore, the practice of placing minority and lower-SES students in the lower tracks on the basis of test performance constituted adverse impact on those students. This case was particularly noteworthy because it was the first time the courts called into question the use of conventional assessment practices with minority youngsters.

Diana v. Board of Education (1970) also proved to be a key decision in shaping assessment practices employed with minority children. This case involved representatives of nine Spanish-speaking Mexican-American children from California who claimed that the children were being inappropriately placed in special education classes for the mentally retarded on the basis of evaluations conducted in English. In this case, the plaintiffs argued that the placements were discriminatory and inappropriate because the children were evaluated in their nonnative language, then deemed eligible for special education services. The plaintiffs also claimed that the testing materials used in the assessments were culturally biased.

In the end, the schools agreed to: (1) conduct evaluations in children's native language as well as in English; (2) stop using unfair verbal items on tests; (3) develop intelligence tests based on Mexican-American cultural experiences and standardization samples; and (4) conduct reevaluations of all the misidentified children. The practical outcomes of this case included the requirement that children who speak a language other than English be evaluated both in English and in their native language, the sanctioning of the use of nonverbal assessment devices, and the growing awareness of the need for tests based on locally derived norms.

In another case involving the rights of linguistic minority youngsters, the Supreme Court ruled in *Lau v. Nichols* (1974) that by requiring Chinese-speaking students to learn English in order to participate fully in their education, the San Francisco schools were discriminating against the students. The Lau decision called for schools to redesign the educational services provided to LEP children. Specifically, it required schools to establish procedures for identifying, assessing, and instructing linguistically different children and suggested that LEP children receive instruction in their native language to benefit from the educational experience.

Around the same time the courts were struggling with assessment and placement cases and having a significant impact on evaluation protocol, the federal government enacted the Rehabilitation Act of 1973 and the Education of All Handicapped Children Act (PL 94-142) of 1975, both designed to provide protection from discriminatory practices. PL 94-142 legislated that all handicapped students had the right to a free and appropriate education and included several provisions calling for nondiscriminatory assessment and placement practices. These provisions include three elements of primary importance to minority youngsters: All children have the right to an assessment conducted in their native language; multiple rather than single evaluation procedures need to be employed when assessing a child's skills and abilities; and children need to be protected from racially and culturally discriminatory practices in the selection and administration of assessment devices.

In 1990, Congress amended PL 94-142 and renamed it the Individuals with Disabilities Education Act (PL 101-476), which, among other things, places a priority on meeting the educational needs of disabled minority children. With this new emphasis on minorities, PL 101-476 replaces PL 94-142 in helping to guide best practices in assessing minority children today.

The final two court cases are highlighted because they underscore the courts' increasing involvement in decisions regarding the use of standardized intellectual assessment instruments with minority children. In *Larry P. v. Riles* (1979), African-American children from California who had been evaluated with intelligence tests and placed in classes for the mentally retarded claimed the tests were culturally biased. They also claimed the tests led to a disproportionate number of African-American children being placed in special education. After lengthy expert testimony, the courts ruled that the schools had engaged in discriminatory evaluation practices because the intelligence tests used during the evaluation contained culturally inappropriate items and materials, were not validated on the minority group being assessed, and were the primary determinant for placement. This judgment captured the attention of evaluators across the nation and led to dramatic changes in the delivery of assessment services in California.

In contrast to the outcome of Larry P., the ruling in a similar case, *PASE v. Hannon* (1980), was very different. Even though PASE and Larry P. both involved the issue of whether intelligence tests were appropriate to use in assessing African-American children's eligibility for special education classes, the judgments rendered by the courts in these two cases were markedly different. Unlike the Larry P. ruling, the PASE court decided that although the intelligence tests contained some items that may be construed as biased, their overall effect on the outcome of African-American children's evaluations would be minimal and, therefore, they were not discriminating against the children. Practically, this meant that the courts condoned the use of intelligence tests with minority children in the Chicago schools when they were part of a psychoeducational assessment battery.

Taken together, these court decisions and legislative acts have had enormous consequences for the way racial/ethnic/linguistic minority children are evaluated and educated in the schools. Many of the rulings serve as safeguards for effective assessment practices. Specifically, the evaluation of minority children now must be based on (1) multidisciplinary assessments involving information gathered from a variety of sources and methods, (2) assessments conducted in the child's native language as well as English, (3) assessments that protect children from selection and administration practices that are racially and culturally discriminatory, (4) clearly specified procedures for assessing linguistically different children, and (5) informed parental consent and informing parents of their rights to due process.

ETHICAL CONSIDERATIONS

Psychologists performing psychoeducational evaluations are guided not only by legal mandate, but also by the ethical standards and principles developed by the National Association of School Psychologists (NASP) and the American Psychological Association (APA), and by the testing standards outlined in the Standards for Educational and Psychological Testing (American Educational Research Association, American Psychological Association, & National Council on Measurement in Education, 1985). The Standards serve as the authoritative document on the development, use, interpretation, and evaluation of tests and are a useful resource for professionals who assess minority children because they clearly specify characteristics of tests that evaluators should consider when selecting and using assessment instruments. The Standards contain one entire chapter (Chapter 13) exclusively devoted to testing linguistically different youngsters that is crucial reading for those who work with these populations.

Both APA's and NASP's ethical guidelines provide psychologists with general standards that help to define and regulate various aspects of professional practice and conduct. In addition, APA recently developed and published more specific principles to help guide service delivery with minorities in the Guidelines for Psychological Practice with Ethnic and Culturally Diverse Populations (Myers, Wohlford, Guzman, & Echemendia, in press). These guidelines are summarized in the following nine principles:

1. Psychologists educate their clients to the processes of psychological intervention, such as goals and expectations; the scope and, where appropriate, legal limits of confidentiality; and the psychologists' orientations.

2. Psychologists are cognizant of relevant research and practice issues as related to the population being served.

3. Psychologists recognize ethnicity and culture as significant parameters in understanding psychological processes.

4. Psychologists respect the roles of family members and community structures, hierarchies, values, and beliefs within the client's culture.

5. Psychologists respect clients' religious and/or spiritual beliefs and values, including attributions and taboos, since they affect world view, psychosocial functioning, and expressions of distress.

6. Psychologists interact in the language requested by the client and, if this is not feasible, make an appropriate referral.

7. Psychologists consider the impact of adverse social, environmental, and political factors in assessing problems and designing interventions.

8. Psychologists attend to as well as work to eliminate biases, prejudices, and discriminatory practices.

9. Psychologists working with culturally diverse populations should document culturally and sociopolitically relevant factors in the records. These may include, but are not limited to:

a. number of generations in the country

b. number of years in the country

c. fluency in English

d. extent of family support (or disintegration of the family)

e. community resources

f. level of education

g. change in social status as a result of coming to this country (for immigrant or refugee)

h. intimate relationship with people of different backgrounds

i. level of stress related to acculturation.

For the complete version of these principles, readers are referred to the Guidelines for Psychological Practice with Ethnic and Culturally Diverse Populations (Myers et al., in press). It should be noted that although these principles help to guide the services of doctoral-level psychologists, in terms of best practices it makes sense for nondoctoral psychologists and educational diagnosticians to adhere to them as well.

PROFESSIONAL PREPARATION AND QUALIFICATIONS

Given the specialized nature of assessment practices with minority children, it is suggested that those learning how to perform and those already conducting psychoeducational evaluations receive extensive instruction in areas that relate to quality service delivery with culturally and linguistically diverse clients. Evaluators need to be well informed about a range of topics including language development, second-language acquisition, nonbiased assessment techniques, and culturally sensitive evaluation procedures in order to provide optimal services. Each of these topics is considered to be vitally important in preparation for work with minority children and their families. In addition to content knowledge, prepared evaluators need competencies in three important areas.

First, evaluators should have extensive coursework and training in the construction, selection, use, and interpretation of tests. Any good psychological tests and measurement text (e.g., Anastasi's *Psychological Testing*, 1988) along with the Standards for Educational and Psychological Testing (American Educational Research Association, American Psychological Association, & National Council on Measurement in Education, 1985) should be required reading. It is strongly believed that better training in testing and measurement will prevent the inappropriate use of tests with all children.

In addition to specialized training in tests and measurement, evaluators need to develop a knowledge base in cross-cultural psychology to be able to provide culturally sensitive assessment services. Research has indicated that individuals from diverse cultures may show differences in terms of their values, communication styles, beliefs about causality, and deference to authority (Sundberg & Gonzales, 1981). According to Nuttall,

De Leon, and Valle (1990), one way that psychologists can become more sensitive to cultural issues is by evaluating their own value systems and cultural backgrounds to understand better how these processes influence their practices. Learning more about the environmental characteristics and the psychosocial climate of the child's home and community can provide the evaluator with a broader and more complete understanding of the child's experiential base and how those experiences affect academic achievement and interpersonal adjustment. Evaluators interested in learning more about the unique social, political, and familial characteristics of different cultural and ethnic groups are encouraged to consult one of a number of excellent resources (e.g., Nuttall et al., 1990; Taylor Gibbs & Nahme Huang, 1989).

Third, as part of the training process it is vitally important that students have first-hand exposure and supervised casework experience with racial/ethnic and linguistic minority children during practice and internship. Through structured practical experiences students will be able to synthesize information drawn from coursework with hands-on experiences to develop their multicultural competencies. Special attention during the applied component of training should be paid to learning how to locate, secure, and tap into community, home, and/or school-based resources. Information from these sources will help to place each child's evaluation within its appropriate cultural context.

PSYCHOMETRIC CONSIDERATIONS

A critical skill in assessing minority children is being sensitive to and knowledgeable about the psychometric characteristics of assessment procedures. Best practices dictate that evaluators use the most well-developed, objective, reliable, valid, and systematic data-gathering methods available. Special attention must be focused on carefully selecting appropriate instrumentation given the nature of the presenting problem along with considerations regarding the child's racial/ethnic, cultural, linguistic, and socioeconomic background.

Part of the reason the evaluators need to be particularly careful in the selection and administration of assessment procedures with minority children is because of the long and controversial history psychological tests have had in applications with these populations. Few subjects in the testing movement have captured the heightened emotional debate as has the use of traditional testing devices with culturally and linguistically diverse youngsters (Reynolds & Brown, 1984). At the heart of much of the debate has been the issue of whether or not standardized tests are discriminatory and biased when used with racial/ethnic minority children. In part, these arguments have been propelled by the fact that children from different racial/ethnic groups have historically been overrepresented, or in some cases underrepresented, among special education populations, allegedly as the result of bias inherent in tests.

As a consequence, the technical adequacy of tests has come under intense scrutiny. Experts in testing (e.g., Anastasi, 1988; Salvia & Ysseldyke, 1991) have pointed out a number of problems in measuring the abilities and skills of minority children. Problems with inadequate representation among standardization groups, inappropriate test content, and questionable item relevancy have all been cited as significant difficulties with traditional standardized tests (Fradd, Barona, & Santos de Barona, 1989). The technical characteristics that have proved to be most problematic will be highlighted so that evaluators will be cognizant of features of assessment devices that need to be evaluated when selecting an instrument for use with a culturally diverse youngster.

Adequate Representation Within the Standardization Sample

One concern arises when tests and test data are used as if the test norms adequately reflect the individual or group being assessed. Some instruments have excluded African Americans, Hispanics, and other minority groups in the norming process and sampled only Whites when standardizing the instrument. This practice limits the applicability of the test norms to the White group only. Other tests have included minorities during the norming process, but underrepresented their overall numbers.

Further, some test developers have included minority groups in adequate numbers, but have not evenly sampled these groups in terms of other major population characteristics such as socioeconomic status (SES). Over- or underrepresenting lower-, middle-, or upper-SES minorities in the standardization group sacrifices the accuracy of the test norms. A norm-referenced test designed to represent the current demographics of children in the United States needs to include samples of minority and majority group members in proportion to the latest data from the U.S. Bureau of the Census in terms of age, sex, race, SES, size of community, and geographic location. A good rule of thumb is that tests selected for use should have norms that were developed within the last 15 years. Salvia and

Ysseldyke (1991) recommend that test publishers develop new norms for tests every 15 years. Given the rapidly changing demographics in the United States, this suggestion seems warranted.

Test Content

The content of a test can be problematic when different groups perform differently on test items. When groups can be distinguished on the basis of their performance on test items such that some items are more difficult for members of different groups, those items are considered to be biased (Reynolds & Kaiser, 1990). Two methods have been employed to eliminate item bias. First, test developers and publishers have appointed expert review teams to scrutinize test content for objectionable and potentially biased items. Then, identified items have been removed from the item pool. This approach has received more support from a public relations perspective than it has from an empirical point of view (Reynolds & Kaiser, 1990).

The second, more methodologically sound approach, has been to subject test items to statistical analysis during test development and modify or discard items from the final item pool that evidence race or gender bias. Careful evaluators will need to review test manuals to ensure that item bias procedures have been undertaken and that selected instruments have empirically demonstrated a lack of bias across minority groups. Choosing tests that have eliminated biased items will effectively minimize this source of error from the evaluation process.

A second way that test content can be problematic concerns the testing materials. Anastasi (1988) points out that a test may contain pictures, words, or illustrations that exert an undesirable influence on the testing situation for the minority child. For example, a test may contain stereotypical pictures, offensive words, or pictures that depict only one racial group. Exposure to these stimuli during a standardized test administration could affect a minority child's motivation to perform at optimal levels.

A third, though indirect, way that test content can be problematic is when the test results are misused to predict a child's future potential but the child has not been exposed to and has not had an opportunity to learn the material that is the subject of the test. This is particularly problematic with achievement testing. Generally speaking, it is not appropriate to use test results gathered under these conditions for predictive purposes. By thoroughly reviewing test materials and stimuli for potentially objectionable characterizations and questionable or irrelevant content before conducting an assessment, an evaluator can more carefully screen and select instruments accordingly.

Construct Validity

The construct validity of a test may also be a concern when the test evidences factorial invariance across racial/ethnic minority groups. Test developers and publishers need to report empirical evidence in the test manual that attests to the stability of the factor structure of a test for various majority and minority groups.

Other Test-Related Concerns

In addition to the technical qualities of tests, Anastasi (1988) recommends that evaluators consider other test-related factors that influence the validity of an assessment and have an impact on the meaningfulness of test results of minority children. Such factors as previous exposure to standardized testing situations, motivation to perform well, and the rapport established between test taker and evaluator are all variables that may have an impact on test validity. To deal with these effects, she proposes several suggestions. First, evaluators should retest children with alternate versions of the test in cases where the validity of the test administration is questioned. Second, evaluators should provide test takers with an adequate period of time to become oriented to the test procedures and environment before beginning formal testing. Third, evaluators should provide children with opportunities to practice test-taking skills. It should be noted that some of the more recently developed individually administered intelligence tests and academic achievement measures have responded to these suggestions by including sample "practice" items and by developing and publishing alternate test forms. Many of these instruments will be highlighted in the section of this chapter dealing with critical components of the assessment process.

To summarize, it is important for practitioners to evaluate carefully the technical merits and qualities of an instrument before selecting it for use with a particular minority child. Tests must have representative and appropriate norms, must contain test materials that sensitively reflect multicultural experiences, and should not exhibit item bias or factorial invariance. Also, evaluators should consider the recommendation of

Anastasi (1988) when planning assessments with culturally and/or linguistically different children.

CRITICAL COMPONENTS OF THE ASSESSMENT PROCESS

This section serves as a practical guide for evaluators to follow in performing culturally sensitive, appropriate, and accurate assessments with racially, ethnically, culturally, and linguistically diverse clients. Special attention is devoted to minimizing and/or eliminating possible sources of bias at each step in the assessment process. Alternatives to the more traditional assessment devices are described. The most important components of the assessment process are prereferral activities; pre-assessment multidisciplinary team meetings; record review; environmental, language proficiency, cognitive, adaptive behavior, fine motor, academic achievement, and social/emotional assessments; postevaluation team meetings; report writing; and follow-up activities. Each of these steps, with the exception of fine motor, adaptive behavior, and social/emotional assessments, is discussed.

Prereferral Activities

Evaluators can assist their school systems in preparing to meet the educational and psychological needs of minority children in two important ways: by educating and upgrading the skills of those who provide services to minority youngsters and by participating in school-based prereferral teams.

Educational Efforts

A primary objective of practitioners working in multicultural and multilingual settings is to engage in ongoing educational efforts (e.g., inservices and workshops) with the school faculty and staff about the cultural and social characteristics of the diverse groups of minority children in their schools. It is also helpful to identify individuals in the community who because of their experiences and/or training are familiar with the cultural characteristics of various minority groups and can serve as cultural consultants to the schools. One purpose of the inservices should be to increase awareness about cultural and psychosocial factors operating within children's home environments that promote or hinder academic and social development. Another purpose should be to explore how a minority child's home environment and culture differ in relation to the school culture. Finally, the information disseminated at the inservices needs to inform educators and administrators of the legal, ethical, and psychometric considerations associated with assessing minority children.

Prereferral Teams

Another objective of the evaluator is to participate in and contribute to the school-based prereferral team. The prereferral team is usually the first group to speak with the referring teacher or parent. If teacher referred, it is a good idea to contact the child's parent(s) during the prereferral phase to gather supplementary information and enlist support in helping to solve the problem. Through contacts with the family, the evaluator has an opportunity to become better acquainted with the sociocultural context of the home and the factors that influence the child's social and academic development.

When a minority child is initially referred to the team, close attention needs to be paid to the reasons for the referral. In a meta-analysis of the teacher expectation research, Dusek and Joseph (1983) report that teacher expectations about students' academic and social skills are frequently based on initial impressions about the student's race, social class, and physical attractiveness. Reasons for referral based on these variables alone in the absence of objective data are never sufficiently justified. When these types of referrals arise, consultation with the referral source is recommended to help clear up misperceptions and revise stereotypical or biased thinking.

Presenting problems that survive this process will proceed through the problem-solving activities employed by the prereferral team. The goals of the team are to define clearly and prioritize presenting problems, gather and review baseline data, identify solutions that have been tried but have failed, pinpoint alternative solutions, monitor the implementation of interventions, and help the teacher to evaluate intervention effectiveness. When dealing with culturally and linguistically different children, the problem-solving process is crucial in supplying valuable information about instructional strategies that have and have not worked. Test-teach-test techniques are strongly recommended as part of the data collection process. If the interventions attempted at this level are not successful and the team has eliminated teacher bias as the basis for the referral, the child will be referred to the multidisciplinary team for a more in-depth evaluation.

Pre-Assessment Multidisciplinary Team Meeting

Once a minority child has been referred to the multidisciplinary team, team members need to review the referral information and supplementary data collected by the prereferral team objectively and decide if a more thorough and comprehensive assessment appears warranted. If the team decides to proceed with further assessments, the child's parent(s) need to be notified formally. Keep in mind that these early meetings with the parents will set the tone for future interactions, and every effort should be made to treat them in a culturally sensitive manner. Poorer families may not have a telephone, and some parents may be illiterate or may not speak English. In these cases, a home visit with the evaluator, parents, and cultural consultant and/or interpreter is recommended. Prior to the meeting, the evaluator will need to make sure that the cultural consultant and interpreter understand that all interactions with the family are confidential.

The early meetings with the parents are an excellent opportunity to obtain information about the family's customs and language preferences. For culturally different children, Miller (1984) recommends that evaluators use this opportunity to find out the name the child prefers to be called during the evaluation. He notes that cross-cultural differences exist in terms of how a person prefers to be addressed and points out the importance of ascertaining the family's customs about names to prevent misunderstandings. For linguistically different children, Sattler (1988) advises evaluators to use a home language survey with the parents to gather information about the languages used between the child and his/her siblings and parents at home. He suggests that evaluators inquire about the languages depicted in the television programs the child watches and the language the parents use when reading to the child. Gathering this type of information at this stage will help guide interactions with the child and his/her family during the remaining portions of the assessment.

Parents who have recently arrived in the United States, or are new to the school district or to special education procedures, will have a high need for information regarding the evaluation process and the implications of the process. Therefore, during the meeting the evaluator will need to ensure that the parents are completely informed of their legal rights and options as well as what an assessment entails. The notification of plans to evaluate should be written in language the parents understand and should specify (a) the type of evaluation(s) that will be carried out, (b) the parents' legal options and rights to due process, and (c) a request for their written consent to the evaluations.

Once parental consent has been secured, the multidisciplinary team needs to decide how the assessments will be organized. Experienced evaluators have pointed out the advantages of extending the different assessments over a multiday period. For example, Chamberlain and Medinos-Landurand (1991) suggest that when linguistically different children require multiple evaluations, the assessments should be carried out in a sequential, rather than simultaneous, manner. This allows children time to become accustomed to the demands of one-to-one assessments and reduces the likelihood that they will feel overwhelmed. Employing a less intensive assessment schedule also affords the various specialists time to analyze the child's performance after each assessment and to make decisions about the need for continued data collection (Chamberlain & Medinos-Landurand, 1991).

Review of Records

If the records have not already been examined during prereferral, the next step in the assessment process is to review the child's cumulative folder. Children who immigrate to the United States may have school records from their native country and these should be requested. In reviewing the file, pay close attention to the child's school history. For example, note interruptions in schooling, location and number of schools attended, grades enrolled in and completed, language(s) used in former classrooms, report card grades and achievement test scores, history of retentions, and special services previously received. Any information about the educational system and curricula the child has been exposed to along with specific academic skills the child has mastered are helpful to ascertain. Additional information regarding the child's developmental and medical history as well as current health status should be noted, and appropriate referrals for vision and hearing screening should be made.

Environmental Assessment

When performing psychoeducational assessments of culturally and linguistically different children, an environmental assessment is a critical component of the process and includes a systematic analysis of the characteristics of the home, school, and community environments in which the child functions. Behavior that may be considered to be appropriate within the context of the home or community may not be construed similarly within the classroom and it is important to identify and document the cultural similarities and differences within the settings so that the child's performance can be interpreted within an appropriate cultural framework.

Minority children may be exposed to cultural practices at school that are embedded in the majority culture orientation of the school they attend and curriculum they are exposed to but that are not consistent with their home and community experiences (Garber & Slater, 1983). These cultural mismatches in norms and expectations between the home and school create confusion for the children and can affect their assessment performance as well as their day-to-day functioning in the classroom.

For example, research has suggested that cultural mismatches between the participation structures of children's home and school environments can affect academic success. Participation structures refer to rules that define acceptable behavior in different situations. Au and Mason (1981) studied the reading achievement of Hawaiian children and found that the children experienced significant gains in reading skills after the participation structures of the classroom were changed to be more compatible with those operating at home. They found that the children's home environments were characterized by overlapping interactions where family members freely interrupted each other when conversing. When reading instruction at school was modified to accommodate this overlapping conversational style, reading achievement improved. This research underscores the value and importance of collecting information from the home and school environments of culturally different children.

Many of the techniques employed in environmental assessments are similar to the methods used by ethnographers in the study of diverse cultures. The techniques include but are not limited to interviews, observations, checklists, and peer nomination techniques. Interviews and observations will each be examined more closely in turn.

Interviews

Pre-observation interviews with the child's teacher provide an opportunity to gather further information about the reasons for the referral and help to operationalize the presenting problems. In clarifying the nature of the concerns, the evaluator will want to determine problem frequency, severity, and duration and gather antecedent and consequent information. These interviews can also be used to ascertain the extent of the teacher's previous experiences with culturally or linguistically different children.

Interviews with the child and parent(s), and sometimes extended family members, are also important in contributing to an understanding of the child's cultural and linguistic background. Catarino (1991) recommends conducting part of the parent interview with the child present so the evaluator will be able to observe parent–child conversations and make note of any differences that exist in the child's linguistic skills or communicative style within the home and school environments.

In speaking with the parent(s), the evaluator will want to gather information regarding the family's origins as well as cultural background. For example, if a family has recently immigrated to the United States the evaluator will want to determine the length of time the family has lived at their present residence, the locations of previous residences, and the extent of their involvement with their new community. This will give an indication of the degree of their acculturation to the new area and prevailing culture. Has the family left their native country because of war? Are there any social or political forces that are having an impact on their child's situation? Has the child lost relatives or witnessed acts of war? Did the parents experience a change in job status when they moved? What do the parents do for a living? Have there been family separations? Do extended family members live with them? All of these considerations will have an impact on the child's psychological functioning and will need to be considered as factors that may be influencing school behavior and academic performance.

The evaluator will also want to assess the parents' attitude towards education. Do they value an education? What are their own educational backgrounds and experiences? What are their expectations for their child's education? Do the parents help the children with homework assignments? What are the child's study habits? Is there evidence that the family spends time together? Do the parents read to themselves or to their children? What are the consequences for school success or failure? Answers to these questions give an indication of the child's psychosocial environment and the parents' attitudes towards achievement.

Information about the family's social functioning and the child's medical and developmental history also needs to be gathered. Were developmental milestones met? Has the child had any significant medical problems? Questions concerning previous diagnosis will be important when dealing with children from some racial/ethnic groups because of their high-risk status (e.g., native Americans and fetal alcohol syndrome). How does the family treat medical problems? What are the parents' attitudes towards children with handicaps or illnesses? What is the child's place in the birth order? How many siblings does the child have? Are there opportunities to play with same-age and same-language peers? What is the child's age? Miller (1984) advises that there are variations among cultures regarding how a child's age is calculated and suggests that reports about a child's age may need to be verified through appropriate channels.

Does the child have any chores or household responsibilities? What is the division of labor in the home? Does the family value cooperation or competition more? Is the child encouraged to become independent? Are there noticeable differences in the way sons and daughters are treated? What are the roles of the mother and father in the family? How is the child disciplined? Finally, the evaluator will want to assess informally the communication mode and style between the parents and their children. Is it mostly nonverbal or verbal? Is eye contact important? What language is used? Accurate documentation of this information will help the evaluator to a better understanding of the sociocultural and linguistic context of the child's home environment.

Observations

Careful collection of observational data throughout the assessment will provide information about how the child functions across settings. Some combination of one-to-one assessment and classroom, school, home, and community observations will typically be desired. The evaluator will want to pay special attention to any indications of cultural mismatches between home/community and school environments and the ways the child copes with the inconsistencies. Evidence of the child's motivational and cognitive styles should also be noted.

To increase the precision and accuracy of the collected data, structured observations of operationalized target behaviors are recommended. The evaluator should make sure that data are collected within a variety of instructional contexts. Does the child work well independently and in small and large groups? Also, how does he or she relate to peers and teachers? It is advisable that these observations include comparisons with same-age culturally/linguistically similar and cultur-ally/linguistically different peers. The observations will provide a wealth of information about the match between the child's behaviors and the behaviors of others within his or her environment. To gather information about how the child fits in with his or her community, Correa (1989) recommends that the evaluator attend social events and community-based meetings in the child's home environment.

ONE-TO-ONE ASSESSMENTS

There is considerable variation in the reasons for carrying out psy-choeducational evaluations. There are, however, features of psychometri-cally sound and valid assessments that should be remembered regardless of the purpose of the evaluation. First, the most reliable, valid, and appropriate instruments should be selected for use during the evaluation. Depending on the purpose of the assessment, appropriate instruments may be screening or diagnostic tools and may be based on locally or nationally derived norms. Second, bilingual children will need to have each assess-ment performed separately in both languages with instruments that are technically appropriate in each language. When technically adequate pro-cedures are not available, the evaluator will need to use single-subject design methodology to collect baseline, intervention, and postintervention data to help determine the child's strengths and weaknesses.

Third, to ensure that assessments are an accurate reflection of the child's competencies and skills, it is desirable to have the parents observe the evaluations through a one-way mirror, if the setting permits. The parents should be asked to render their judgment about the validity of the child's performance. Did the child demonstrate what he or she is capable of doing? Is this the way the child usually behaves? These questions are important in establishing the validity of the assessment and must be asked. A fourth practice that will enhance the validity of the minority assessment is the use of testing of limits (TOL) procedures (Sattler, 1988). Once the standardized test administration is completed, the evaluator can employ TOL to determine the strategies the child used to solve incorrectly an-swered questions. TOL procedures are especially useful with children who have little experience with the demands of one-to-one assessments and with those who have not been taught a specific skill being assessed.

Language Proficiency Assessment

The assessment of language proficiency needs to be the very first one-to-one evaluation conducted with linguistically different youngsters because the language(s) used for all subsequent assessments and the interpretations made of the test results are based on the competencies shown during this initial evaluation. Generally speaking, children who are clearly monolingual should be evaluated in their dominant language, whereas bilingual children need to be evaluated in both languages. Current legal and ethical guidelines dictate that bilingual children should have all assessments performed in their native language and in English by a specialist fluent in both languages.

Whoever (usually the speech and language specialist) conducts the language proficiency evaluation needs to be aware of current research and theory regarding the acquisition of first and second languages. She or he should perform a thorough assessment of the child's speaking, writing, and reading skills and receptive and expressive abilities using both informal and formal data collection techniques. Fradd et al. (1989) suggest collecting three 15-minute oral language samples as part of the informal assessment and point out that the child's teacher may be in the best position to obtain these samples because he or she has the most sustained contact with the child. Both the teacher and the specialist who performs the assessment will want to pay close attention to and document any idiosyncrasies in the child's speech that reflect differences in dialect or regional variations in speech patterns. Close collaboration between the specialist, parents, teacher, and psychoeducational evaluator will help to define the child's linguistic abilities.

The purpose of the language proficiency evaluation is to determine the extent of the child's fluency in English and in the home language. The evaluation will distinguish children whose native language skills are intact and well developed, but whose English skills are just emerging, from children who show delays in native language skills and in learning skills. Children who are bilingual will show a range of linguistic competencies and their expertise in either language will be dependent on their age, ability level, language(s) of instruction, and amount of exposure to their native language and English. Clinical observations suggest that younger children generally take less time than older children to acquire a second language (Cummins, 1984). Also, because of differences in ability level and rate of learning, mentally retarded children usually take longer than normal children to learn a second language and gifted children may learn to speak a second language at an accelerated pace.

Cummins (1984) has noted that most bilingual children acquire the ability to converse in a second language before they can use the second language on more academic or cognitively demanding tasks. He has suggested that children's ability to converse in a second language appears within the first 2 years of exposure to the language, whereas the ability to use a second language to function effectively in an academic setting takes from 5 to 7 years. Cummins' studies suggest that speech and language specialists will need to assess both conversational and more academically focused language skills during the language proficiency evaluation in order to gather information that will be most predictive of the child's language abilities in academic settings. The specialist will need to be thoroughly familiar with the specific skills various instruments are designed to assess in order to accomplish this objective.

Other researchers have suggested that as children acquire a second language, they experience a period of regression in their first language skills (Fradd et al., 1989). These findings suggest that as bilingual children grow and change, frequent assessments of their language skills are warranted. In fact, Ortiz et al. (1985) recommend against using the results from language proficiency assessments that are more than 6 months old because of the variability seen in the children's language skills when they are acquiring a second language.

Use of Interpreters

Evaluators who are monolingual will need to refer bilingual children to a well-trained and qualified bilingual specialist for this phase and, if needed, for the remaining portions of the evaluation. Ethically and legally, this is the most prudent action to take. In the past, monolingual evaluators who have been confronted with referrals of bilingual children have questioned the feasibility of using test interpreters rather than bilingual specialists. In these cases, Figueroa (1990) recommends against the use of poorly trained interpreters and views the use of well-trained interpreters as problematic.

Interpreters may not be trained in test administration procedures, may substitute words, may speak a different dialect, or may engage in subtle prompting behaviors that exert an influence on the child's responses (Nuttall, Medinos-Landurand, & Goldman, 1984). In addition, translating a test that has been developed and normed in English may not yield a technically equivalent form of the test. Translators may substitute words that are more difficult than the original words and this will influence the psychometric properties of the test. Overall, Figueroa (1990) calls into question the validity of evaluations conducted by interpreters because of the lack of empirical evidence supporting the use of interpreters. Therefore, it is advisable that monolingual evaluators locate bilingual specialists in their area and employ their services when a bilingual child has been referred for an evaluation.

Cognitive Assessments

The information provided by the environmental and language-proficiency assessments will help to tailor the cognitive and educational evaluations to fit the unique characteristics of the referred minority child. An evaluation for special education eligibility will need to be based on a carefully selected combination of cognitive, academic achievement, and behavioral measures because no one instrument will provide an adequate sample of the child's skills and competencies. The next two portions of the chapter draw attention to the advantages and disadvantages of some of the most widely used assessment devices in applications with culturally and linguistically different children and youth. First, a sample of the major intellectual assessment devices (e.g., Kaufman Assessment Battery for Children, Stanford-Binet Intelligence Scale—IV, Wechsler Intelligence Scale for Children - Third Edition, Wechsler Preschool and Primary Scale of Intelligence - Revised) used with preschool and school-age youngsters will be reviewed and will be followed by a discussion of alternatives to these more conventional measures. Then, some of the more popular academic achievement instruments will be reviewed. All reviews emphasize the technical dimensions of the instruments that are relevant to assessing minority children and that have the potential to affect the validity of the evaluation.

Specifically, each test was analyzed with respect to the following characteristics:

1. Does the test contain an adequate and representative standardization sample?

2. Have the test authors employed a minority panel and/or statistical item analysis procedures to detect biased items?

3. Is the reliability and validity of the scale established and documented?

4. Are diverse racial/ethnic groups represented in the test materials through pictures and other illustrations?

5. Does the test contain sample or practice items?

6. Is a parallel or alternate form available?

7. Is there empirical evidence supporting the use of the instrument with English-as-a-Second-Language (ESL) students?

8. Has a Spanish version of the test been developed and properly normed?

Kaufman Assessment Battery for Children

The Kaufman Assessment Battery for Children (K-ABC) (Kaufman & Kaufman, 1983) is a test of intelligence and achievement appropriate for use with children between the ages of 2-5 and 12-5. The scale contains 10 mental processing subtests and 6 supplementary achievement subtests. It yields a total Mental Processing Composite (MPC) score that has a mean of 100 and a standard deviation of 15. It has been lauded for including normal, exceptional, and gifted children in the standardization sample and is considered to be one of the most user friendly of the major intelligence scales. The K-ABC was also the first in the most recent generation of intelligence tests that attempted to respond to many of the criticisms of traditional intellectual measures vis-à-vis uses of the scales with minority children. In applications with minority populations, the K-ABC has many attractive and distinctive features.

First, in comparison to other major intelligence tests, the K-ABC contains many tasks that do not require expressive language skills. This is a positive feature for evaluators concerned with the impact of regional or dialectical speech differences on test performance. A second important feature is that a Spanish version of the scale is available for use with Spanish-speaking Mexican children that was normed on a Mexican sample. A third desirable feature is that test items were analyzed during test development by both a panel of minority experts and by statistical procedures to identify biased items. As a result, objectionable items were revised or eliminated from the final version of the scale, and test stimuli reflect pictures of diverse multicultural groups.

Fourth, each of the mental processing subtests is preceded by an unscored sample item, and the first two scored items are designated as teaching items to help familiarize children with task demands and provide experience in test taking. Fifth, the mean MPC yielded by the scale for minority groups comes closer to the mean MPC for Whites than do the full scale quotients of other similarly developed intelligence instruments. The 15-point discrepancy between minority groups and Whites on the Wechsler Intelligence Scale for Children - Revised is narrowed to 0 to 7 points on the K-ABC. The largest discrepancy on the K-ABC occurs between African-American school-aged children and Whites (African-American mean MPC = 93.7, White mean MPC = 100), followed by Navajo Indians (mean MPC = 94.2), and Hispanics (MPC = 97.5). A mean MPC reported for a small sample of Sioux Indians (100.6) most closely approximates the White sample MPC. A sixth attractive feature of the K-ABC is that the manual provides sociocultural norms by SES and race (African American and White) for those interested in comparing the test taker's performance with other children from similar racial and SES groups.

The K-ABC also has a number of shortcomings in its applications with minorities. Although the norm group approximated the 1980 U.S. Census data in terms of Whites, African Americans, Hispanics, and other (native Americans, Pacific Islanders, Asians) groups, the sample underrepresented Hispanics and African Americans at the lower-SES level and overrepresented both groups at the upper-SES level. This upward bias may contribute to the closer approximations seen between Whites' and minority groups' MPCs. The SES imbalance also suggests that the scale is most representative of African Americans and Hispanics at the middle-SES levels.

Two other limitations of the K-ABC are concerned with the test authors' recommendations for adapting the scale for use with non-English-speaking children. First, the authors suggest that the English version of the scale can be used with non-English-speaking children with the aid of an interpreter. Towards that end, the manual provides Spanish directions as well as English directions. However, there is no evidence that the Spanish instructions or interpreters were part of the test development or standardization process, and LEP and/or bilingual children were not included in the norm groups. Therefore, this recommendation is not based on sound assessment principles. In addition, the authors promote the Nonverbal scale (composed of a selection of mental processing subtests) as an alternative for use with non-English-speaking children aged 4-0 to 12-5; but, again, since the norms did not include LEP children, the comparisons with this population would be of limited usefulness. Therefore, caution should be used in employing the English version of the K-ABC with non-English-speaking children.

Stanford-Binet Intelligence Scale: Fourth Edition

The Stanford-Binet Intelligence Scale: Fourth Edition (SB-IV) (Thorndike, Hagen, & Sattler, 1986) represents the latest revision in the long and distinguished history of Binet intelligence scales. It is used with children, adolescents, and young adults between the ages of 2 and 23. This revision contains 15 subtests, 6 new and 9 retained from the previous version. Several steps were taken during the development and standardization of the scale to respond to the special characteristics of racial/ethnic minority children.

For instance, items from the Stanford Binet Intelligence Scale L-M criticized for ethnic bias were removed from the latest version and the test now contains a sampling of pictures that represent ethnically diverse people. In addition, two independent panels of minority experts analyzed test items for possible bias while the scale was being revised. Moreover, statistical procedures identified biased items and the items that evidenced bias were eliminated from the final version of the scale. Many of the subtests begin with sample items. Finally, concurrent validation studies reported in the manual that support this type of validity were based on samples that adequately represented minority group members.

Despite these efforts, three major concerns have been expressed about the psychometric qualities of the scale. First, the accuracy of the norms has been questioned (Cronbach, 1989). Although the standardization sample approximated the 1980 U.S. Census data on the basis of ethnicity, and the norm group includes Whites, African Americans, Hispanics, Asians, Pacific Islanders, and native Americans, the upper-SES level was oversampled for these groups and weighting procedures were needed to adjust for the effects. Thus, the norms are not considered to be an accurate reflection of the populations they are supposed to mirror.

Second, the reliability of the scale has yet to be determined using large and representative samples of minority youngsters. The test-retest reliability studies reported in the manual did not include adequate numbers of

minority children. Third, the construct validity of the scale and, specifically, the stability of the factor structure across minority groups, has not
yet been demonstrated. In order to conclude that the scale is measuring the
same constructs for different groups of people, empirical evidence in this
area is needed.

There are a number of other, less technical, concerns about the SB-IV
that may limit its usefulness with minority individuals. Like the Wechsler
scales, the SB-IV requires verbal skills on at least half of its subtests.
Evaluators concerned about testing children who speak a different dialect
will need to pay close attention to the children's verbal responses to reduce
the likelihood of scoring errors. Also, to date, a Spanish version of the
scale has not been developed and marketed.

Wechsler Intelligence Scale for Children - Third Edition

The Wechsler Intelligence Scale for Children - Third Edition (WISC-
III) (Wechsler, 1991) is the latest version of the WISC scale to be revised
and renormed and is appropriate for use with youngsters ages 6-0 to 16-11.
It contains a total of 13 subtests; 12 of the subtests were retained from the
WISC-R and include modifications, and the 13th subtest is the new
Symbol Search scale. The WISC-III has a number of laudable features.
First, the test developers not only employed a panel of minority experts to
review the items for bias but also used item analysis procedures on the test
results of an oversample of more than 400 ethnic minority children to
identify biased items. Items that showed bias were either eliminated or
reworded. Second, the manual specifically states that evaluators who use
the test with culturally or linguistically diverse youngsters should receive
formal training with similar populations. Third, to reduce the verbal
demands placed on the test taker at the beginning of testing, the subtests
have been resequenced so that the introductory subtest is now a Performance one rather than a Verbal subtest. In addition, three subtests (Similarities, Picture Arrangement, and Object Assembly) begin with sample items.

The standardization sample approximates the 1988 U.S. Census data
in terms of proportional representation of Whites, African Americans,
native Americans, Aluets, Asian Americans, Pacific Islanders, Hispanics,
and other minority groups. Seven percent of the sample was classified as
handicapped, 5% gifted, and only English-speaking children were represented in the standardization group. The test does not contain a parallel

form or alternate Spanish version nor does it provide administration instructions and normative data for use with ESL students.

Wechsler Preschool and Primary Scale of Intelligence - Revised

The Wechsler Preschool and Primary Scale of Intelligence - Revised (WPPSI-R) (Wechsler, 1989) is a completely renormed, downward and upward extension of the original WPPSI scale and is appropriate for use with children between the ages of 3-0 and 7-3. The WPPSI-R contains 12 subtests; 6 representing the Verbal subtests and the remaining 6 making up the Performance subtests. The scale contains several noteworthy advancements over its predecessor. For example, a panel of minority experts reviewed each item for bias and made recommendations for item revision or exclusion. Also, items were statistically analyzed for bias using data compiled from 400 minority children and biased items were eliminated. Two of the subtests contain pictures of racial/ethnic children, and all but one of the subtests include a sample item.

The standardization sample is excellent and approximates 1986 U.S. Bureau of the Census data regarding sex, age, geographic region, ethnicity, and parental occupation and education characteristics. Altogether, the sample is composed of Whites (70.1%), African Americans (15.3%), Hispanics (11.2%), and other (3.4%) minority groups. However, there is no evidence that LEP children were included in the sample, and a Spanish version of the scale is not available. Evidence for internal, interrater, and test-retest reliability of the scale suggests that the highest reliabilities are for the full scale. Construct, concurrent, and predictive validity studies area also reported in the manual.

Alternative Cognitive Measures

Alternative cognitive instruments have been employed to supplement, and in some cases replace, conventional assessment techniques. Depending on the instrument, these alternative tools can be useful in providing further information about the child's present functioning and potential for future learning. A handful of intelligence instruments have been translated into Spanish (e.g., the K-ABC and the WISC-R) and are available for use with Spanish-speaking children. Other scales that have been used with minority children to supplement more conventional techniques include a group of nonverbal scales that primarily measure reasoning skills. They are the Test of Nonverbal Intelligence (Brown, Sherbenou, & Johnson, 1982), the Columbia Mental Maturity Scale (Burgemeister, Blum, & Lorge, 1972), the Raven's Progressive Matrices (Court & Raven, 1986), and the Leiter International Performance Scale (Leiter, 1948).

These nonverbal scales have been targeted for use with culturally and linguistically different children for a number of reasons. One reason is that evaluators have assumed that nonverbal scales are more culture fair than conventional intelligence scales because they eliminate the culture "loading" dimension of tests that rely on verbal abilities. The culture loading of more traditional tests has often been cited as the reason minorities perform less well than majority children on the scales. However, Anastasi (1988) cites a number of studies showing that minority children achieve higher overall scores on the more traditional scales than on the nonverbal devices. Another reason that nonverbal scales have been used with linguistically different children is because they do not require verbal responses and have been considered to be appropriate for assessments with LEP children. However, none of the nonverbal scales has been normed on LEP youngsters which makes using the scales for normative comparisons inappropriate.

Two major disadvantages of nonverbal scales limit their usefulness with minority children. First, the scales exhibit a number of psychometric weaknesses. For example, the norms for the Leiter are not only quite dated, but are based on a very small and homogeneous sample of 289 children. Second, little evidence exists that suggests a relationship between performance on nonverbal tests of intelligence and academic success in the classroom. Therefore, evaluators are urged to exercise caution in the use of nonverbal devices with minority children; and, when these devices are employed, they should not be used in isolation.

Two other alternative intelligence measures that have been discussed in the literature as supplementary devices are the Cartoon Conservation Scales (De Avila & Havassy, 1975) and the Learning Potential Assessment Device (LPAD) (Feuerstein, 1979). The Cartoon Conservation Scales are based on Piaget's theory of cognitive development and require the child to demonstrate an understanding of conservation concepts on a series of paper-and-pencil tasks. The LPAD is based on a test-teach-test assessment paradigm in which the evaluator engages in a teach-assess-teach-assess loop. Unfortunately, although both approaches appear promising, neither has been systematically employed or researched. They thus cannot be recommended for use until more empirical evidence is presented.

Academic Achievement Assessment

Depending on its purposes, the educational achievement evaluation is best accomplished through a combination of norm-referenced, criterion-referenced, and curriculum-based procedures. In this section, some of the major individually administered academic achievement norm-referenced tests will be discussed. Special attention will be devoted to the qualities of the tests that are relevant when assessing minority children.

Kaufman Test of Educational Achievement

The Kaufman Test of Educational Achievement (K-TEA) (Kaufman & Kaufman, 1985) is a test of academic achievement composed of five subtests: Mathematics Applications, Mathematics Computation, Reading Decoding, Reading Comprehension, and Spelling. The K-TEA is used with children and adolescents aged 6-0 to 18-11. The standardization group approximated the 1983-1984 U.S. Bureau of the Census data in terms of proportionately representing Whites, African Americans, Hispanics, native Americans, Alaskans, Asians, and Pacific Islanders. During test development, test items were statistically analyzed for bias and many that showed bias were eliminated. However, 12 items that showed race or gender bias were incorporated into the final version of the scale in a counterbalanced manner. Internal and test-retest reliability estimates of the scale are satisfactory. The content and construct validity also appear to be adequately established.

Drawbacks of this scale in its use with minority groups include the lack of a parallel form, the lack of a Spanish version of the test, and the lack of sample items. In addition, unlike the colorful and attractive stimuli comprising the K-ABC, all of the K-TEA pictures are achromatic and do not seem inviting. A handful of the pictures depict the physical characteristics of multicultural children.

Woodcock-Johnson Psycho-Educational Battery – Revised

The Woodcock-Johnson Psycho-Educational Battery – Revised (WJ-R) (Woodcock & Johnson, 1989) is an updated, expanded, and renormed version of the original 1977 scale. It consists of nine standard subtests and five supplementary subtests that assess reading, mathematics, written language, and knowledge skills of people aged 2–90. The WJ-R has a number of advantages over the K-TEA in applications with minority youngsters. First of all, it contains parallel forms A and B, and both forms have pictures of minority children, use multicultural names in the test stimuli, and contain colorful and appealing illustrations. Second, item bias procedures were employed to detect items that proved to be more difficult for members of minority groups. Six of the subtests begin with sample or practice items. The standardization sample did not include anyone with less than 1 year of experience with English and the test authors caution against using the scale with ESL children. They also clearly state that the scale should not be used with an interpreter and recommend using the Bateria Woodcock Psycho-Educativa en Español (Woodcock, 1982) for Spanish-speaking youngsters.

The methods employed to standardize the scale were impressive. Although the standardization sample approximated 1980 U.S. Census data, minority groups were slightly overrepresented among the 6,359 subjects. The norm group was composed of White (78.6%), African-American (16.9%), Hispanic (9.3%), Asian/Pacific Islander (3.2%), and native American (1.3%) individuals. Stringent SES selection procedures were also employed to ensure adequate representation in terms of parental and community characteristics.

KeyMath – Revised

The KeyMath – Revised (Connolly, 1988) is an expanded version of the original KeyMath test and assesses mathematics skills within the three broad areas of Basic Concepts, Operations, and Applications. Alternate forms A and B are designed to be used with youngsters in grades K–9. Test pictures and wordings reflect a multicultural influence, and the manual reports that test items were reviewed for possible bias during a national calibration study. Those items identified as biased were then revised or excluded from the final scale. However, the manual is unclear whether this review process was based on subjective or statistical procedures. The scale contains no sample items. Stratified sampling procedures were employed to match 1985 Census data and although Whites, African Americans, Hispanics, native Americans, Pacific Islanders, and Asians were represented in appropriate numbers, there was a slight underrepresentation of individuals from the Southwestern and Northeastern portions of the United States. The content validity and construct validity of the scale have been demonstrated, as have internal and alternate form reliability.

Test of Written Language – 2

The Test of Written Language – 2 (Hamill & Larsen, 1988) is designed to assess mechanical and more substantive aspects of written language skill in youngsters ages 7 to 17. The scale contains parallel forms A and B, each of which are composed of 10 subtests. Sample items begin a handful of these subtests. The manual does not report the use of any item analysis procedures to reduce or eliminate racial or gender bias. The norm sample approximates the Statistical Abstract of the U.S. in terms of ethnicity (e.g., White, 84%; African American, 12%; Hispanic, 9%; American Indian, 3%; Asian, 1%; and other groups, 4%). The test authors recommend against the use of the scale with non-English-speaking youngsters and instead suggest the Pruebo de Lectura y Lenguaje Escrito (Hamill, Larsen, Weiderholt, & Fountain-Chambers, 1982), which assesses written Spanish skills and was normed on 2,300 children ages 8–16 residing in Mexico and Puerto Rico.

Woodcock Reading Mastery Test – Revised

The Woodcock Reading Mastery Test – Revised (WRMT-R) (Woodcock, 1987) contains the Word Identification, Word Attack, Word Comprehension, Passage Comprehension, Visual Auditory Learning, and Letter Identification subtests designed to assess the reading skills of kindergartners to individuals aged 75 and older. The WRMT-R is a revision and renorming of the 1973 Woodcock Reading Mastery Test. Several subtests begin with sample items and alternate forms G and H are available for retesting purposes. During test development, statistical procedures were used to detect biased items. The norm group for youngsters in grades K–12 matches the 1980 Census data and Whites, African Americans, native Americans, Asians/Pacific Islanders, and Hispanics are adequately represented. A minor disadvantage of the WRMT-R is that all of the illustrations are achromatic and do not seem to depict minorities. In fact, the physical characteristics of those shown in the pictures are quite dated and remind the reviewer of hairstyles from the 1950s–1960s.

Postevaluation Multidisciplinary Team Meeting

After the various assessments have been conducted, the multidiscipli-nary team will reconvene with the school administrator, regular and special education teachers, bilingual teacher, speech and language specialist, psychoeducational evaluators, parents, cultural consultant, and any other personnel involved with the case in attendance. If the child's parents speak a language other than English and the team members do not all speak the other language, a well-trained interpreter who is sensitive to the dynamics and requirements of multidisciplinary team meetings should attend.

The purposes of the postevaluation meeting are to discuss the results of the evaluations, provide feedback to the parents about their child's performance, and determine the child's educational and psychological needs. Care will need to be taken to interpret the assessment results within an appropriate linguistic and cultural context. If the child received lower scores on the assessments than were expected, Anastasi (1988) and Cham-berlain and Medinos-Landurand (1991) advise evaluators to consider carefully reasons why the low scores occurred. For example, was the child tested on material that was unfamiliar or that had not been taught? Was the content of the test inconsistent with the child's cultural experiences? Were techniques used to familiarize the child with the testing environment? Were technically adequate tests chosen and used? Did the child seem motivated during the assessments? If the parents had an opportunity to observe the assessments, did they feel that the child's performance accu-rately reflected the child's true abilities?

The results of all evaluations and the implications of them should be simply and clearly communicated to the parents in language they under-stand. During the meeting, the parents will need to be given enough time to formulate and ask questions and process the feedback they receive. If the child is eligible for special education services, the parents' input should be sought and incorporated into the team decision-making process. The practical and legal ramifications of any decisions made during the meeting should be clearly delineated.

Report Writing and Follow-up Activities

After the child's strengths and weaknesses have been identified, rec-ommendations for intervention will need to be developed and imple-mented. The evaluator should periodically monitor the child's progress and consult with teachers and family members on an ongoing basis. Both successful and unsuccessful interventions should be documented in the child's records. Careful documentation will assist the multidisciplinary team in building a data base on each child so that intra- and interindividual comparisons of academic progress can be made.

A written report should be generated for each evaluation. The psychoeducational assessment report should indicate the race/ethnicity of the child and his or her parents, the languages spoken at home and during the assessments, and any deviations in standardization that occurred during the administration of norm-referenced instruments. The specific instruments and techniques that were used should be clearly indicated, and the dates of administration along with the time each test required should be documented. In addition, any steps that were taken by the evaluator to improve the validity of the assessments should be noted. In general, the report should contain sufficient detail so that readers will understand the exact protocol that was followed during the assessment.

SUMMARY AND CONCLUDING REMARKS

The major aim of this chapter has been to assist psychologists and educational diagnosticians in performing technically sound and culturally sensitive assessments with diverse children and youth. Based on legal, ethical, and psychometric considerations, several recommendations for conducting assessments with culturally and linguistically different children appear warranted. First, evaluators working in multicultural and multilingual schools need to make sure that each psychoeducational assessment they perform is tailored to meet the unique cultural and linguistic features of the diverse children they work with. Evaluation results should be interpreted within their appropriate cultural context. Decisions regarding a child's educational and psychological needs must be based on data derived from multiple sources, methods, and settings. Second, when choosing norm-referenced measures, test manuals need to be reviewed carefully to ensure that psychometric indicators are suitable for the individual test taker. The norms must contain a representative sample that matches the characteristics of the referred child and the reliability and validity of the scale should be documented. In select cases, locally normed instruments may be the measures of choice.

Third, assessment procedures used with minority children need to reflect current research. Ethically, it is the evaluator's responsibility to be aware of available research in the field and translate the empirical evidence into professional practice. Finally, the evaluator needs to develop a network of professional and community contacts and resources that will assist in providing culturally relevant assessments to minority children. The chapter closes with a case study in which the guidelines for best practices in assessing minority children are illustrated.

CASE STUDY

Reason for Referral and Review of Records

Carlos is a 6-year, 8-month-old Mexican-American male, referred for an evaluation by his 1st-grade teacher because of concerns over his limited motivation and poor progress in the reading curriculum. As a 1st-grader, he can identify the letters of the alphabet but has difficulty with some sound–symbol associations, and reading and understanding words in text. His teacher primarily relies on large group and self-instructional techniques to teach reading and places a priority on independent seatwork. She graphs each child's weekly progress in reading on the bulletin board. Before she referred him for an evaluation, she worked with the prereferral team to operationalize the problems and identify possible interventions. She tried individualizing his instruction over a month-long period but did not notice an appreciable difference in his reading acquisition. She did, however, find that his attention to task improved dramatically.

Environmental Assessment

An interview with his parents was conducted with the help of an interpreter. The interpreter was present because even though both parents speak English and Spanish with each other and with their children at home, Carlos' mother prefers to speak Spanish and is more proficient in it. Carlos speaks fluent English at school and converses at home in Spanish and English. Carlos' parents are originally from Mexico and moved to the United States along with his maternal grandparents and three older brothers and sisters when Carlos was 1 month old. He currently resides along with his parents and siblings in an apartment downstairs from his grandparents. Although neither of his parents graduated from high school, they value their children's education and schooling. Carlos' father works in a nearby plant and holds a second job in the evenings. His mother is not employed outside the home and has very little contact with people outside of her extended family.

Carlos' parents are a traditional couple and believe in a division of labor within the family along gender lines. The family is also very cooperative and frequently pool their energies along with extended family members to accomplish something for the good of the group. The family clearly values group achievements over individual accomplishments.

Carlos' developmental and medical histories were normal. His records suggest that vision and hearing abilities were intact when he was screened 4 months ago. He is in good physical health.

Classroom observations indicate that he is on task about 60%–80% of the time during reading instruction in comparison to a same-age Mexican-American classmate. His attention seems to vary depending on the structure of the task. He attends most during large and small group activities but is frequently off task when working independently. Socially, no problems are noted in his relationships with peers or adults.

Pre-Assessment Multidisciplinary Team Meeting

The team met to decide whether Carlos' referral warranted a complete evaluation. Once the decision was made to proceed with an assessment, a home visit with Carlos' parents was arranged to discuss the purpose of the assessments, possible implications of the evaluations, and to secure parental consent. Consent forms were presented in Spanish and English.

One-to-One Assessments

Because he has received instruction for the last 2 years in English and is fluent in it, his psychoeducational evaluation was conducted in English. Carlos' cognitive functioning was assessed using the WPPSI-R. Academic abilities were assessed using curriculum-based strategies and the WJ-R. Given his ethnic, linguistic, and socioeconomic background, these norm-referenced instruments were selected as most appropriate for his evaluation. TOL procedures were used to assess his ability to respond to alternative instructions and to gather information about his approach to problem solving.

Summary and Recommendations

The results suggest that he is functioning within the low average range of intellectual abilities in comparison to same-age peers in the areas assessed by the measure. His skill development in reading was in the low average to borderline range of abilities. He could identify printed and cursive letters in isolation, read and define about 60% of the words from his 1st-grade reader, but showed poor comprehension of context-reduced material. A significant discrepancy between intellectual functioning and reading skills was not noted. His attention to tasks improved during group and individualized instructional activities and suffered during independent seatwork. Based on these findings along with information received from his parents and teacher, the following recommendations are made:

1. Given his positive response to group instructional strategies, coupled with his skill development needs in reading, a trial period of small group reading instruction using direct instruction techniques is recommended. Carlos seems to benefit from the added structure and feedback that group instruction affords him and concentrates best under these conditions. His teacher will want to collect baseline, intervention, and postintervention data on his progress during the trial period. The evaluator will consult with his teacher, monitor his progress on a periodic basis, and maintain contact with his parents so that they are kept abreast of any successes or developments.

2. In comparison to his classmates, Carlos is experiencing difficulty acquiring vocabulary words. To improve his vocabulary, it is suggested that his teacher present vocabulary words in word families. For example, *ray, lay, say,* and *way* all belong to the same word family. This will help him to see the relationships between the words while he is learning them.

3. Carlos enjoys working along with other people in a cooperative atmosphere. Any instructional techniques that his teacher can employ that are structured in a cooperative rather than competitive manner would be beneficial.

REFERENCES

American Educational Research Association, American Psychological Association, & National Council on Measurement in Education. (1985). *The standards for educational and psychological testing.* Washington, DC: American Psychological Association.

Anastasi, A. (1988). *Psychological testing.* New York: Macmillan.

Au, K. H., & Mason, J. M. (1981). Social organization factors in learning to read: The balance of rights hypothesis. *Reading Research Quarterly, 17,* 115-152.

Brown v. Board of Education, 347 U.S. 483 (1954).

Brown, L., Sherbenou, R. J., & Johnson, S. K. (1982). *Test of Nonverbal Intelligence.* Austin, TX: Pro-Ed.

Burgemeister, B., Blum, L. H., & Lorge, I. (1972). *Columbia Mental Maturity Scale.* New York: The Psychological Corporation.

Catarino, L. C. (1991). Step-by-step procedures for the assessment of language minority children. In A. Barona & E. E. Garcia (Eds.), *Children at risk: Poverty, minority status, and other issues in educational equity* (pp. 269-282). Washington, DC: National Association of School Psychologists.

Chamberlain, P., & Medinos-Landurand, P. (1991). Practical considerations for the assessment of LEP students with special needs. In E. V. Hamayan & J. S. Damico (Eds.), *Limiting bias in the assessment of bilingual students* (pp. 111-156). Austin, TX: Pro-Ed.

Connolly, A. J. (1988). *KeyMath—Revised.* Circle Pines, MN: American Guidance Service.

Correa, V. I. (1989). Involving culturally diverse families in the educational process. In S. H. Fradd & M. J. Weismantel (Eds.), *Meeting the needs of culturally and linguistically different students: A handbook for educators* (pp. 130-144). Boston: College-Hill.

Court, J. H., & Raven, J. (1986). *Manual for Raven's Progressive Matrices and Vocabulary Scales: Coloured Progressive Matrices.* London: Lewis.

Cronbach, L. J. (1989). Review of the Stanford-Binet Intelligence Scale: Fourth Edition. In J. V. Mitchelle, Jr. (Ed.), *Tenth mental measurements yearbook* (pp. 773-775). Lincoln, NB: Buros Institute of Mental Measurement.

Cummins, J. (1984). *Bilingualism and special education: Issues in assessment and pedagogy.* San Diego, CA: College-Hill.

DeAvila, E. A. & Havassy, B. (1975). *Cartoon Conservation Scales.* Corte Madera, CA: Linguametrics Group.

Diana v. Board of Education, Civil Action No. C-70 37 RFP (N.D.Cal. January 7, 1970).

Dusek, J. B., & Joseph, G. (1983). The bases of teacher expectancies: A meta-analysis. *Journal of Educational Psychology, 75,* 327-346.

Feuerstein, R. (1979). *The dynamic assessment of retarded performers: The learning potential assessment device, theory, instruments, and techniques.* Baltimore, MD: University Park Press.

Figueroa, R. A. (1990). Best practices in the assessment of bilingual children. In A. Thomas & J. Grimes (Eds.), *Best practices in school psychology II* (pp. 93-106). Washington, DC: National Association of School Psychologists.

Fradd, S. H., Barona, A. & Santos de Barona, M. (1989). Implementing change and monitoring progress. In S. H. Fradd & M. J. Weismantel (Eds.), *Meeting the needs of culturally and linguistically different students: A handbook for educators* (pp. 63-105). Boston: College-Hill.

Garber, H. L., & Slater, M. (1983). Assessment of the culturally different preschooler. In K. D. Paget & B. A. Bracken (Eds.), *Psychoeducational assessment of preschool children* (pp. 443-472). New York: Grune & Stratton.

Hamill, D. D., & Larsen, S. C. (1988). *Test of Written Language—2 manual.* Austin, TX: Pro-Ed.

Hamill, D. D., Larsen, S. C., Wiederholt, J. L., & Fountain-Chambers, J. (1982). *The Pruebo de Lectura y Lenguaje Escrito.* Austin, TX: Pro-Ed.

Hobson v. Hansen, 269 F. Supp. 401 (D. D.C. 1967).

Hodgkinson, H. L. (1985). *All one system: Demographics of education, kindergarten through graduate school.* Washington, DC: Institute for Educational Leadership.

Kaufman, A. S., & Kaufman, N. L. (1983). *Kaufman Assessment Battery for Children manual.* Circle Pines, MN: American Guidance Service.

Kaufman, A. S., & Kaufman, N. L. (1985). *Kaufman Test of Educational Achievement comprehensive form manual.* Circle Pines, MN: American Guidance Service.

Larry P. v. Riles, 495 F. Supp. 926 (N.D. Cal. 1979).

Lau v. Nichols, 414 U.S. 563 (1974).

Leiter, R. G. (1948). *Leiter International Performance Scale.* Chicago: Stoelting.

Miller, N. (1984). The case history in a cross-cultural milieu. In N. Miller (Ed.) *Bilingualism and language disability: Assessment and remediation* (pp. 169-176). San Diego: College-Hill.

Myers, H. F., Wohlford, P., Guzman, L. P., & Echemendia, R. (Eds.). (in press). *Ethnic minority perspectives on clinical training and services in psychology.* Washington, DC: American Psychological Association.

Nuttall, E. V., De Leon, B., & Valle, M. (1990). Best practices in considering cultural factors. In A. Thomas & J. Grimes (Eds.), *Best practices in school psychology II* (pp. 219-233). Washington, DC: National Association of School Psychologists.

Nuttall, E. V., Medinos-Landurand, P., & Goldman, P. (1984). A critical look at testing and evaluation from a cross-cultural perspective. In P. C. Chinn (Ed.), *Education of culturally and linguistically different exceptional children* (pp. 42-62). Reston, VA: The Council for Exceptional Children.

Ortiz, A. A., Garcia, S. B., Holtzman, W. H., Jr., Polyzoi, E., Snell, W. E., Jr., Wilkinson, C. Y., & Willig, A. C. (1985). *Characteristics of limited English proficient Hispanic students in programs for the learning disabled: Implications for policy, practice and research.* Austin, TX: The University of Texas, Handicapped Minority Research Institute on Language Proficiency.

PASE v. Hannon, 506 F.2d. 831 (N.D. IL 1980).

Plisko, V. W. (Ed.). (1984). *The condition of education.* Washington, DC: U.S. Department of Education, National Center of Education Statistics.

Ponterotto, J. G., & Casas, J. M. (1991). *Handbook of racial/ethnic minority counseling research.* Springfield, IL: Charles C. Thomas.

Reynolds, C. R., & Brown, R. T. (1984). Bias in mental testing: An introduction to the issues. In C. R. Reynolds & R. T. Brown (Eds.), *Perspectives on bias in mental testing* (pp. 1-39). New York: Plenum Press.

Reynolds, C. R., & Kaiser, S. M. (1990). Test bias in psychological assessment. In T. B. Gutkin & C. R. Reynolds (Eds.), *The handbook of school psychology* (pp. 487-525). New York: John Wiley & Sons.

Salvia, J., & Ysseldyke, J. E. (1991). *Assessment* (5th ed.). Boston: Houghton Mifflin.

Sattler, J. M. (1988). *Assessment of children: Third edition.* San Diego: Author.

Sundberg, N. D., & Gonzales, L. R. (1981). Cross-cultural and cross-ethnic assessment. In P. McReynolds (Ed.), *Advancement in psychological assessment* (pp. 460-541). San Francisco: Jossey-Bass.

Taylor Gibbs, J., & Nahme Huang, L. (1989). *Children of color: Psychological interventions with minority youth.* San Francisco: Jossey-Bass.

Thorndike, R. L., Hagen, E. P., & Sattler, J. M. (1986). *The Stanford-Binet Intelligence Scale: Fourth Edition.* Chicago, IL: Riverside.

U.S. Bureau of the Census. (1988). *Money, income and poverty status in the United States: 1988.* Current Population Reports, Series P-60, No. 166. Washington, DC: Government Printing Office.

U.S. Bureau of the Census. (1989a). *Projections of the population of the United States by age, sex, and race: 1988-2080.* Current Population Reports, Series P-25. No. 1018. Washington, DC: Government Printing Office.

U.S. Bureau of the Census. (1989b). *Statistical abstract of the United States: 1988* (109th ed.). Washington, DC: Government Printing Office.

Wechsler, D. (1989). *Wechsler Preschool and Primary Scale of Intelligence - Revised manual.* San Antonio: The Psychological Corporation.

Wechsler, D. (1991). *Wechsler Intelligence Scale for Children - Third Edition manual.* San Antonio: The Psychological Corporation.

Woodcock, R. W. (1982). *Bateria Woodcock Psycho-Educative en Español.* Allen TX: DLM Teaching Resources.

Woodcock, R. W. (1987). *Woodcock Reading Mastery Test—Revised manual.* Allen, TX: DLM Teaching Resources.

Woodcock, R. W., & Johnson, M. D. (1989). *Woodcock Johnson Psycho-Educational Battery—Revised manual.* Allen, TX: DLM Teaching Resources.

Zill, N., & Schoenborn, C. A. (1990). Developmental, learning, and emotional problems: Health of our nation's children, United States, 1988. *Advance Data from Vital and Health Statistics of the National Center for Health Statistics,* 1-11.

14 ASSESSMENT OF CONDUCT PROBLEMS, ATTENTION-DEFICIT HYPERACTIVITY DISORDER, AND ANXIETY DISORDERS IN CHILDREN AND ADOLESCENTS

Steven K. Shapiro

There is general agreement among diagnosticians of childhood psychological dysfunction that assessment practices have suffered from many conceptual and methodological shortcomings. Historically, for example, many epidemiological studies have used nonstandardized criteria and nebulous terms such as "severe disorders," "emotional disturbance," and "need for services" in describing various aspects of problems in children that were considered to impair daily functioning (Kazdin, 1989). Furthermore, the rates and characteristics of childhood dysfunction frequently vary on parameters of age, gender, type of disorder, ethnicity, family history and demographics, and geographical region (Gould, Wunsch-Hitzig, & Dohrenwend, 1980; Graham, 1977; Langner, Gersten, & Eisenberg, 1974; Rutter, Cox, Tuping, Berger, & Yule, 1975). Conceptualizations of the dysfunction based solely on consensual validation, ill-defined sample characteristics, and psychometrically inadequate measures adversely affect diagnostic integrity.

Besides general conceptual and procedural problems that have hampered the development of diagnostic practices, the impact of many special characteristics of children and adolescents on assessment practices also must be considered. Although the intended focus of this chapter precludes a comprehensive coverage of these factors (Kazdin, 1989; Sattler, 1988; Tuma & Elbert, 1990), a few points are worth mentioning.

Developmental considerations impact greatly on the manifestation and perceived clinical significance of childhood behavior disorders. For example, empirical findings seem to suggest that not all problematic behaviors in childhood result in serious psychological dysfunction in adulthood. Many behaviors deemed "problematic" are somewhat common in childhood (Lapouse & Monk, 1958) and may wax and wane with the developmental process. Also, Levitt (1971) coined the term "developmental symptom substitution" to describe the observation of changing manifestations of the same underlying clinical problem with development (e.g., aggressive behavior manifesting itself through teasing and shoving in childhood versus fighting and weapon use in adolescence). Therefore, as articulated by Kazdin (1989), one task is to decide which behavior problems will remit over the course of "normal development" and which ones require evaluation and formal intervention. Another obstacle confronting childhood psychopathology research and diagnostic techniques has been assumptions about the limits of children's psychological development and what children can and cannot experience. The impediment created by these assumptions is particularly evident in the investigation of childhood depression (Cantwell & Carlson, 1983; Kazdin, 1989; Quay, Routh, & Shapiro, 1987; Ryan et al., 1987), where agreement regarding its diagnostic validity is far from unanimous.

The manner in which children are referred also brings special challenges to the assessment process. Unlike adults, children usually do not refer themselves for evaluation or therapy. Instead, parents (independently or upon the recommendation of medical or school personnel) typically initiate the referral process. In general, children typically attribute their problems to factors over which they believe they have little responsibility. Adolescents are more likely to consider "internal" factors (e.g., thoughts, feelings, and the role *they* play) when they are developing attributions about their emotional or behavioral problems.

Even when parents initiate the evaluation process, several investigators have shown that parental personality, expectations regarding child behavior, the degree of marital discord, reported stress in the home, and the degree of parental social contacts impact on a parent's perception of deviance and reported information about their child's presumed behavior problem (Forehand, Lautenschlager, Faust, & Graziano, 1986; Mash & Johnston, 1983; Rohrbeck & Twentyman, 1986). Occurrences of abuse and neglect frequently reduce the probability that a child will be referred by his or her parent, unless there is physical or behavioral evidence that comes to the attention of other support systems to which the child has access.

Clearly, therefore, the assessment of psychological dysfunctions in children and adolescents presents many challenges that are created due to developmental, familial, and social factors that make this population unique. Despite these formidable obstacles, there have been major advances in the assessment of childhood dysfunctions. The purpose of this chapter is to provide a review of empirically based techniques for evaluating behavioral problems. Although there is no consensus on what constitute the "best" assessment procedures, this chapter will focus on a "multiaxial" assessment model and a "normative-developmental" approach represented in the developmental psychopathology literature. In this context, assessment of childhood dysfunctions typically involving disruptive, undercontrolled behaviors and more "internalized," overcontrolled behaviors will be outlined.

ASSESSMENT PARADIGMS

In discussing the history and "structural revolution" of science, Kuhn (1970, 1977) defined a paradigm as a conceptual model for organizing ideas and information. These paradigms provided both a focal point and a foundation to help scientists choose a problem to study, the methods to use, and guidelines for interpretation of their findings. Although the development of these paradigms may have precluded attention to certain conceptual approaches, they also provided a crucial role in defining objectives, and accumulating and organizing scientific knowledge. Achenbach (1985) illustrated the impact that various paradigms have had on our conceptualization and assessment of childhood psychopathology. These assessment paradigms, each representing different objectives and methods, include: (1) medical, (2) psychodynamic, (3) psychometric, and (4) behavioral paradigms.

The "medical assessment" paradigm, also referred to as the "neurobiological model" (Knoff, 1986), represented the view that mental disorders were disease entities and were thus explainable in terms of an organic etiology. The goal of assessment, therefore, was to provide "laboratory" test findings that were presumed to represent the biological variables that define the disorder. As Achenbach (1985) noted, this medical paradigm was vital in "rescuing the study of disordered behavior from demonology and superstition" (p. 30). Focusing on systematic documentation of symptom patterns, physical correlates, course, and outcome has aided in the identification of organic correlates of certain disorders (e.g., mental retardation caused by thyroid deficiencies, chromosomal abnormalities, or inborn metabolic dysfunctions). However, the etiology of many disorders remains unknown, even though some seem to represent organic etiology more than others. Even if a specific organic etiology was found, this would not preclude the need for other nonmedical approaches to address the multifaceted nature of some disorders (e.g., autistic disorder).

The origin of the "psychodynamic assessment" paradigm can be traced back to organic medicine's failure to explain hysterical symptoms, which defied basic anatomical principles (Achenbach, 1985). This assessment paradigm contributed to the development of projective techniques which, due to the presentation of ambiguous stimuli, were presumed to reflect underlying needs, desires, motivation, affects, and conflicts (Reynolds & Kamphaus, 1990). These inferential constructs are then used in developing "idiographic" (i.e., detailed portrayal of the individual as a unique entity) formulations. Although psychodynamic assessment approaches are still strongly represented among diagnosticians, numerous criticisms of this technique have been raised. For example, Chapman and Chapman (1967) noted the clinicians' tendencies to perpetuate erroneous principles of interpretation advanced by those who popularized the test, despite strong evidence to the contrary. In addition, due to the inferential nature of psychodynamic assessment techniques, external validation is difficult at best. How can information on complex psychodynamic inferences be reliably obtained? Even if reliable data could be obtained, how can we determine unconscious versus conscious factors, or differentiate between motives, structures, and defenses (Achenbach, 1985)? Presumably in response to some of the many criticisms about the idiographic assessment approaches, there has been a recent effort to develop more nomothetic systems (i.e., the formulation of general or universal laws and principles) for scoring projective techniques, applied to both adults and children.

The psychometric assessment paradigm originates from efforts to *measure* psychological traits. This approach is best represented by the long history of intelligence testing. (See Sattler, 1988.) Emphasizing a more pragmatic approach to the assessment of intelligence, Binet and Simon (1903/1916) sought reliable and valid measures of cognitive processes — items that would reflect the kinds of judgment and reasoning used in school. This approach emphasized the "normative-developmental" approach, which evaluated performance and children's abilities relative to their age-matched peers. This early approach is well-represented in "objective" measures where there are standardized administration and scoring rules, where a quantitative score is derived from each trait which is described by multiple items, and where the meaning of the score depends on and is compared to a particular normative or reference group (Achenbach, 1985). Overall, therefore, the psychometric assessment paradigm emphasizes the identification of individual differences in functioning, rather than emphasizing particular causes of these differences, which characterizes the medical and psychodynamic approaches.

The "behavioral assessment" paradigm originates largely from Watson's (1913) supposition that human behavior is explainable entirely in terms of observable stimuli and responses. This approach avoids hypothetical constructs that are utilized by the aforementioned paradigms and makes no inferences about underlying organic or mental variables. Instead, behavioral assessment focuses on the individual child and the environmental contingencies that serve to maintain the behavior. Viewing behavior as situationally determined and due to environmental consistencies, observations of these behaviors occur in the natural environment. A clear benefit of this approach is that the assessment techniques have a direct link to intervention strategies. The assessment is viewed as an intrinsic component of treatment, rather than as preceding and separate from treatment (Achenbach, 1985; Mash & Terdal, 1988). However, problems arise when behaviors are refractory to direct assessment (e.g., due to reactivity to observation, infrequency of the behavior, or situational diversity of the behavior). Other concerns have to do with the difficulty in detecting *patterns* of behavior that may be more appropriate targets for change rather than emphasis on the molecular response level, and the relating of knowledge accumulated from one child to similar children in other times and places.

A MULTIAXIAL MODEL OF ASSESSMENT

Stemming largely from the influential work of Achenbach and his colleagues (Achenbach, 1982, 1985, 1990a,b; Achenbach & Edelbrock, 1983; Achenbach & McConaughy, 1987; Achenbach, McConaughy, & Howell, 1987), "developmental psychopathology" has been widely accepted as an approach which views psychopathology in relation to developmental transitions and maturation throughout the life cycle. The focus on maladaptive deviations in the context of milestones and sequences in physical, cognitive, social-emotional, and educational development (Achenbach, 1990a,b) encourages the adoption of a perspective which goes beyond any one particular theoretical orientation. That is, Achenbach (1990a,b) suggests that developmental psychopathology can be viewed as a "macroparadigm"—a way of integrating various theoretical approaches so as to facilitate the convergence of several variables, methodologies, and explanations. In this context, the assessment paradigms described earlier, as well as sociological, family systems, and cognitive approaches (Achenbach, 1990a,b), represent "microparadigms" because they deal with a *portion* of information relevant to developmental psychopathology. Achenbach (1990a,b) points out that although researchers focus on a particular microparadigm, our understanding of psychopathology can be enhanced by integrating these specific paradigms with the hopes of stimulating approaches which converge on salient topics. Therefore, as stated by Achenbach (1900a), "the concept of developmental psychopathology is broader than can be exemplified by any single study, theory, or explanation" (p. 3).

Children's behavior varies from one situation to another. Therefore, in order to obtain information that will have the most practical utility, multiple assessment procedures and informants should be utilized. The need for this strategy is best exemplified by Achenbach et al. (1987) who found only modest agreement between reports by different informants. Specifically, average correlations of .60 were found between ratings by informants seeing children under similar conditions (e.g., pairs of teachers or parents); considerably lower average correlations were found between ratings by different types of informants seeing children under different conditions (e.g., parents vs. teachers; teachers vs. mental health workers), as well as between children's self-reports and reports by others. Instead of discounting certain sources as more or less valid, based on one's own theoretical or methodological bias, the assessment process is facilitated by an intrinsically multiaxial approach. The purpose of this approach then becomes the delineation of strengths and weaknesses of children's functioning in multiple areas, and to reveal information specific to issues of different interaction patterns that may have intervention implications. Thus, as stated by Achenbach (1990a):

> Because the child's functioning may really differ from one area to another, the goal is not to determine which assessment procedure yields a singular truth about the child but to use what each one reveals about needs for help in particular areas. In some cases, multiaxial assessment may reveal that certain interaction partners, such as parent or teacher, need changing more than the child does. In other cases, multiaxial assessment may show that one type of intervention is needed for one context but a different type is needed for another context. (p. 11)

Achenbach (1985; see also Achenbach & McConaughy, 1987; McConaughy & Achenbach, 1988) outlined five axes that are relevant to the assessment of a child in the context of developmental psychopathology. The selection of procedures included in each of the axes is based primarily on the availability of adequate psychometric properties or the potential of obtaining such information. The various axes include: (1) parent report of developmental history and behavioral characteristics; (2) teacher report of academic and behavioral characteristics; (3) cognitive (e.g., intellectual, academic) assessment; (4) physical (medical) assessment; and (5) direct assessment of the child through behavioral observation techniques, clinical interviews, and/or self-report. A focus on techniques that are based on standardized, empirical, normative-developmental procedures appears crucial in order to provide a valid and reliable system of information. Validity will determine the degree to which the system can serve the function of (1) providing nomenclature necessary for communication; (2) furnishing a basis for description and information retrieval; (3) providing a basis for making predictions; and (4) providing the basic concepts for theory formation about etiology, pathology, prognosis, and response to treatment (Blashfield, 1984; Quay, 1986a). Implicit in the above discussion is the attempt to merge two models of behavioral classification: (a) the empirical/dimensional approach, which utilizes statistical techniques to isolate interrelated patterns of behavior, and (b) the categorical approach, in which diagnostic entities are derived by clinical consensual validation through clinicians noting which characteristics occur together. The remainder of the chapter will focus on reviewing the "best" (i.e., valid, reliable, clinically useful) instruments available to evaluate the diagnostic categories that have been associated with the dimensions of overcontrolled or internalizing behavior problems (Anxiety Disorder) and undercontrolled or externalizing behavior problems (Conduct Disorder and Attention-Deficit Hyperactivity Disorder). These diagnostic categories represent those which are found in the revised third edition of the *Diagnostic and Statistical Manual of Mental Disorders* (DSM-III-R; American Psychiatric Association [APA], 1987). Readers interested in a more thorough discussion of issues in the classification of child and adolescent psychopathology are directed toward Achenbach, Conners, Quay, Verhulst, and Howell (1989), Cantwell and Baker (1988), and Quay (1986a).

ATTENTION-DEFICIT HYPERACTIVITY DISORDER (ADHD)

Representing the most prevalent disruptive behavior disorder, ADHD comprises a heterogeneous group of children who manifest developmentally inappropriate levels of inattention, impulsivity, and/or overactivity for a period of at least 6 months, with an age of onset prior to age 7 (for specific ADHD criteria, see DSM-III-R, APA, 1987). Consistent with a polythetic approach (i.e., no single specific symptom or set of symptoms is necessary or sufficient criteria for diagnosis), DSM-III-R no longer delineates subtypes that were outlined in DSM-III (APA, 1980; ADD with hyperactivity, ADD without hyperactivity, and ADD residual type). The decision to drop the provisions for identifying diagnostic subtypes of attention-deficit has met with much criticism. For example, Werry (1988) has stated that the new ADHD criteria "jettison the data of 17 years for thousands of cases . . . in favor of a hastily-derived largely untested Johnny-come-lately set of criteria" (p. 139). Barkley (1991) provides a more favorable critique of current diagnostic criteria and outlines suggestions for future revisions.

Research has continued to identify meaningful subgroups within this heterogeneous category, in light of the presence of a diversity of related or comorbid psychiatric symptoms (learning disability, conduct disorder), family backgrounds, developmental characteristics, and treatment responses. (See Barkley, DuPaul, & McMurray, 1990; Cantwell & Baker, 1988; Hinshaw, 1987.) Aside from issues related to subtypes, Barkley (1990) has recently provided a definition of ADHD to include "developmental deficiencies in the regulation and maintenance of behaviors by rules and consequences. These deficiencies give rise to problems with inhibiting, initiating, or sustaining responses to tasks or stimuli, and adherence to rules or instructions, particularly in situations where consequences for such behavior are delayed, weak, or nonexistent" (p. 71). Providing a rich and useful description of ADHD from a transactional perspective, Henker and Whalen (1989) describe the social dysharmony that characterizes ADHD children:

> Hyperactive children tend to be perceived as annoying and aversive or, by more benign judges, as immature and maladroit. Either by design or by default, these children scamper through their days in what appears to be a free-wheeling fashion, relatively uncurbed by the social codes and situational cues that guide actions of others. . . . Hyperactive children are socially busy, continually seeking and prolonging interpersonal contacts . . . these high-impact youngsters serve as social catalysts, accelerating inappropriate interactions in siblings, peers, parents, and teachers. . . . ADHD children are soundly and roundly rejected by peers. . . . Although unanswered questions abound, it is clear that hyperactivity is a transactional disorder, located in the interface between the child and his social world. Part and parcel of the social problems encountered by hyperactive children are the responses they elicit from others. Peers resent the intrusion and lament the unpleasantness, often worrying that an ADHD child will get them into trouble as well. (p. 217)

There has been an increased recognition that problems associated with ADHD do not disappear following puberty. Follow-up studies have documented interpersonal difficulties, impulsive restless behavior, relatively high rates of job changes, legal problems, antisocial activity, conduct disorder, and substance abuse (Henker & Whalen, 1989; Lambert, 1988). Treatment strategies have included pharmacologic and nonpharmacologic methods, although not surprisingly, drawbacks and discouraging outcome data exist for most approaches (Henker & Whalen, 1989).

With regard to assessment of ADHD, Barkley (1990) has identified the clinical interview, the medical examination, and the use of behavior rating scales to be the most important components in a comprehensive evaluation. Supplemental techniques including objective tests of attention and direct behavioral observation techniques are also highly recommended.

Clinical Interview

As an assessment method, interviewing represents a shared practice among clinicians of various orientations, although the exact procedures will differ depending on theoretical orientation (LaGreca, 1983). In no other form of assessment does the clinician have the degree of flexibility to structure questions, response options, and the content areas covered than is possible through the clinical interview (Morris & Collier, 1987). As described earlier, the child brings special circumstances and issues to the assessment process, which necessitates gathering information from multiple sources. This information gathering focuses on the *content* of the interview, whereas others may focus on the *process* of the interview in order to enhance the relational aspects of the face-to-face interview. Although the different foci may yield somewhat different information, it is the combination of these two approaches which seems most beneficial. Because the focus of this chapter precludes a detailed coverage of the interview process, those interested in more specific discussion are directed to Barkley (1990), Bierman (1990), Greenspan (1981), Kanfer, Eyberg, and Krahn (1983), LaGreca (1983), Morris and Kratochwill, 1983a, and Sattler (1988). Nonetheless, therapist warmth and acceptance are seen as crucial to establishing a therapeutic rapport during the interview. In the context of this relationship, information regarding the child's thoughts, perceptions, and feelings as well as those of his or her parents will assist in the process of problem identification and treatment planning. It is this delicate balance which makes the process of interviewing both an art and a science (Barkley, 1990).

Parent Interview

In the context of a procedural outline for evaluating a child for ADHD, Barkley (1990) provides a highly useful and applied discussion of interviewing the parent. Barkley outlines several purposes of including this source of information. First, interviewing the parents establishes the necessary working relationship between the clinician and members of the family for subsequent assessment and intervention. Second, due to the parents' vast knowledge regarding the child and the family, valuable descriptive information that may represent different parental viewpoints can be obtained. Third, the parental interview can provide information regarding their own psychological functioning (e.g., degree of family stress associated with the child's problem; personality or psychiatric problems) which will be crucial to consider when formulating a treatment plan. Fourth, hypotheses can be formed regarding parent–child interaction styles by observing the child's behavior and the parental response (if the child is present during the parental interview). Fifth, the interview can serve as a preparatory phase to parent training issues, changing the focus from presumed historical or developmental causes of the child's behavior to an emphasis on identifying immediate antecedents and consequences of the behavior. Sixth, the interview can assist in formulating a diagnosis and treatment recommendations. Regarding the former, clinicians may choose to describe the child in terms of developmental or behavioral deficits, avoiding a diagnostic label. However, Barkley (1990) points out that the diagnosis of ADHD, if accurate, carries with it useful information regarding developmental course, prognosis, special education placement eligibility, and selection of potential response to treatment options. Finally, the seventh purpose of the parent interview is to provide the parents with an opportunity to be "understood" and to share their feelings of frustration and distress.

Although the utility of meeting with the parent is obvious on many levels, the major purpose of the parental interview is to obtain detailed information about the child. It is recommended that this be done in a semistructured manner, following a format that guarantees the coverage of pertinent domains in a relatively standard manner but that also allows for procedural deviations to consider unique child/family characteristics and to maintain rapport. In the context of outlining the procedures followed in the ADHD clinic at University of Massachusetts Medical Center, Barkley (1990) provides recommendations for conducting a structured psychological parent interview. Such an outline can be applied to most referral questions and is not specific to the evaluation of ADHD. This interview covers information regarding prenatal (e.g., health, maternal age, substance or medication use during pregnancy), perinatal (e.g., labor and delivery information), and postnatal (e.g., temperamental characteristics and health of the infant) history, and developmental milestones (e.g., age at which child sat, crawled, walked, spoke single words or word combinations, was toilet trained). Current medical information should also be obtained (e.g., hearing; eyesight; fine and gross motor coordination; speech; chronic health problems; history of childhood diseases, accidents, and hospitalization; suspicions of substance use and physical/sexual abuse; sleeping patterns; nocturnal bladder and bowel control; appetite), as well as psychological and pharmacological treatment history. School history should also be discussed in terms of academic and social progress; special education program placement; occurrences of suspensions, expulsions, or grade retentions; and instructional modifications. Questions related to social history will provide information regarding the child's relationship with siblings and the ability to establish and maintain friendships. Following the opportunity for the parent(s) to express primary and related concerns about their child's behavior, information regarding behavior management strategies, compliance with parental commands, and the occurrence of stressful events can be obtained. For purposes of obtaining specific diagnostic information, questions related to psychiatric conditions for which the child may meet criteria should be presented. Finally, family history should be obtained as it relates to marital chronology and stability, and basic psychological information on paternal and maternal relatives as well as the child's siblings. Throughout this structured interview, follow-up questions can be posed as they relate specifically to the precipitating or concurrent issues that appear relevant to the cognitive, social, and emotional manifestation or sequelae of ADHD symptoms.

Child Interview

Assuming that the child was present during the parent interview, the clinician likely had an opportunity to observe the child's behavior and the characteristics of the parent–child interaction. One must be cautious in using such information as exclusionary criteria of ADHD, because research has indicated that children rarely misbehave during office evaluations and office-based behaviors are unrepresentative of behavior that occurs in naturalistic settings (Costello, Edelbrock, Costello, et al., 1988; Sleator & Ullman, 1981). Such is also the case regarding office-based observations of the child's developmental characteristics. Compounding the problem is the finding that correlations between information provided by the child and other informants are modest at best (Achenbach et al., 1987) but improve with age (Bierman, 1983; Edelbrock & Costello, 1984). Barkley (1990) points out that "The more specific and publicly observable the event is that a child is being asked to report on, the greater the likelihood that the report may prove reliable and hence valid" (p. 249). However, Barkley (1990) also notes that ADHD children typically under-report their difficulties, which is reflected by the minimal degree of validity in ADHD adolescents' self-reports.

Following an initial phase of determining the child's perceptions of the purpose of the evaluation and a period of interaction designed to put the child at ease (e.g., topics including pasttimes and favorite activities), a diplomatic approach to questioning the child about behavior problems and interpersonal conflicts can begin. Elaborations on this discussion can follow a format similar to the parent interview, making note of the child's perceptions of his or her problems and the impact of these on his or her daily functioning. An important part of the child interview is to determine what the child would like to have "different" in his or her environment or for him- or herself. Children of various ages readily respond to the interviewer's request to state three wishes that can be used to improve himself/herself or any other individual(s) (Barkley, 1990). Other techniques to maximize the child's comfort with the interviewing situation and to provide an optimal environment for expression of feelings should also be utilized. Closing the interview with neutral topics in order to minimize the discomfort that may have resulted from discussing affect-laden topics is recommended.

Structured psychiatric interviews have also been employed in the assessment of ADHD and other psychiatric diagnostic categories. Although these interviews have been designed to provide more precise and quantifiable information, and can be used with parents and their children, many limitations have been expressed (Edelbrock & Costello, 1984). Barkley (1990) states that these interviews are likely more useful in the research context than in clinical practice, due to the lack of normative, actuarially based data and the dependence on the current DSM-III-R diagnostic system (which is in the process of being modified for DSM-IV). Nevertheless, familiarity with some of these measures would be useful.

The reader is directed toward literature pertaining to the Child Assessment Schedule (CAS; Hodges, Cools, & McKnew, 1989; Hodges, Gordon, & Lennon, 1990; Hodges, Kline, Stern, Cytryn, & McKnew, 1982; Hodges, McKnew, Burbach, & Roebuck 1987; Hodges & Saunders, 1989), the Diagnostic Interview Schedule for Children (DISC; Costello, Edelbrock, Dulcan, Kalas, & Klaric, 1987; Edelbrock & Costello, 1988; Williams, McGee, Anderson, & Silva, 1989), and the Semistructured Clinical Interview for Children (SCIC; Achenbach & McConaughy, 1989). The SCIC, unlike the former two schedules, is based on empirically established scales rather than "keyed" to consensually derived psychiatric taxonomies, and can be compared to information obtained from parent and teacher report forms (see below).

Teacher Interview

The observations and opinions of the child's teacher(s) should be considered a critical component of the ADHD evaluation. Personal interviews or contact by phone can provide first-hand information regarding school achievement and behavior towards nonparental authority figures and peers in structured and unstructured school situations. Teachers can also provide useful information regarding parental motivation to pursue treatment, parental misperception about the child's school problems, as well as information regarding the degree of "uncooperativeness, insensitivity, or naivete of the school personnel" in managing the child's behavior (Barkley, 1990, p. 254).

Behavior Rating Scales

The use of a well-standardized behavior rating scale has become an integral part of evaluating psychopathology in children, particularly in those with conduct problems and globally defined hyperactivity. This method allows for a quantification of responses to a set of questions regarding behavior problems, based on norm-referenced criteria. The ease with which rating scales can be implemented creates both advantages and disadvantages. The advantages rest on the amount of information that can be gathered across many situations; the potential for collecting information on "rare" behaviors that may not occur during in vivo evaluation procedures; cost/time considerations; the multidimensional coverage of psychopathology; and the "filtering out" of situational variations, among others (Barkley, 1990). A disadvantage in using rating scales is the potential overreliance of such procedures at the exclusion of adjunct evaluation techniques and considering the psychometric adequacy of the rating scales. Barkley (1900) outlines several factors pertaining to issues of reliability and validity upon which he has based his selection of appropriate instruments:

1. The items should be clearly worded and, whenever possible, be specific and operational;

2. The items within each scale should adequately sample the domain of the construct of interest, with the least number of items required (i.e., parsimony);

3. Response choices should allow discrimination of frequency or severity of the behavior being rated, so as to sample the range of the symptom adequately within the targeted population;

4. The item should reflect the construct of interest by correlating significantly with measures of the same construct taken by other means, sources, and in the natural setting (i.e., "face validity," "concurrent validity");

5. The scale should discriminate between samples of subjects that are known to have different behaviors or symptoms (i.e., "discriminant validity");

6. Predictive validity is demonstrated (and clinically useful) when the scale correlates significantly with the same scale or similar measures taken at a later time in development;

7. Scales should also have adequate test-retest (the readministration of the scale within weeks or months) and interrater (ratings completed by two individuals) reliability;

8. Prescriptive utility is beneficial to clinical practice, since the scale would predict a person's differential response to different treatment modalities. (pp. 279–280)

Several rating scales have been used with ADHD, some for assessing treatment response and some for diagnostic purposes (although these are not mutually exclusive). The focus of the present review will be on psychometrically adequate measures used for the latter purpose. The reader is directed to more comprehensive reviews of behavior rating scales offered by Barkley (1990), Beck (1987), Morris and Collier (1987), and Witt, Heffer, and Pfeiffer (1990).

The Child Behavior Checklist (CBCL; Achenbach & Edelbrock, 1983) is considered by many to be the "Cadillac" of behavior rating scales, due to the quality of its empirical foundation, the content areas covered, and the amount of available information documenting its reliability and validity. The CBCL follows a normative-developmental approach by comparing the adaptive competencies and behavioral problems of the child to separate norms for boys and girls grouped into three ages (4-5; 6-11; 12-16). The informant is asked to rate a child on 118 behaviors using a 3-point scale for each item. Factor analytic studies have yielded two "broad-band" behavioral dimensions—externalizing and internalizing. Such analyses have also produced several "narrow-band" statistically derived syndromes that vary somewhat by age and gender. Social or adaptive competence is evaluated through a series of 20 items that assess the extent of the child's involvement in activities (e.g., sports, hobbies, jobs, chores), social interactions (e.g., through organizations and peers), and his or her school history. The extensive information regarding the reliability and validity of the CBCL has been reviewed elsewhere (Achenbach & Edelbrock, 1983; Barkley, 1990; Beck, 1987).

Serving as a potentially useful counterpart of the parent report form of the CBCL, Edelbrock and Achenbach (1984) have developed a teacher report form (CBCL-TRF). The CBCL-TRF is very similar in format to, and possesses the same positive features of, the parent version. The availability of reliability and validity information is not as extensive as for the CBCL, but there is little reason to believe that the CBCL-TRF will not attract the same positive regard as the parent version. The availability of a self-report form for adolescents (CBC-YSR; Achenbach & Edelbrock, 1987) and a direct observation form (CBCL-DOF; Achenbach, 1986) is also very attractive for clinical and research purposes.

Other well-developed behavior rating scales (although somewhat less well-established due to ongoing validation work or utility in assessing treatment response more so than for general diagnostic purposes) include the Revised Behavior Problem Checklist (RBPC; Quay & Peterson, 1987) and the Conners Rating Scales (Conners, 1990).

Barkley (1990) reports on two recently revised behavior rating scales designed to assess situational factors associated with a child's attention and concentration problems. The Home Situations Questionnaire—Revised (HSQ-R; DuPaul, 1990b) has satisfactory test-retest reliability and concurrent validity with parent ratings of hyperactivity and has also been shown to be sensitive to treatment effects (Barkley, 1990). Ongoing studies will clarify the incremental utility of this scale as a measure of situational-specific (i.e., home, public places) problems suggestive of ADHD. Similar comments apply to the School Situation Questionnaire—Revised (SSQ-R; DuPaul, 1990b).

Barkley (1990) also recommends the use of other rating scales to obtain more specific information about the referred child's academic performance (Academic Performance Rating Scale: APRS; DuPaul, Rapport, & Perriello, 1990), symptoms of ADHD included in DSM-III-R (ADHD Rating Scale; DuPaul, 1990a), the degree of parent–adolescent conflict (Conflict Behavior Questionnaire: CBQ; Robin & Foster, 1989), and common issues that lead to conflict between parents and their teenagers (Issues Checklist: IC; Robin & Foster, 1989). Again, a more detailed discussion of rating scales that have been used in the evaluation of ADHD is offered by Barkley (1990).

Laboratory Measures

There has been considerable growth in the development of objective measures to assess ADHD symptoms, although few, if any, have been recommended for widespread clinical use (Barkley, 1990). More promising laboratory tests (in terms of the adequacy of their psychometric properties) are reviewed below.

Vigilance and Sustained Attention Tests

The Continuous Performance Test (CPT) has received widespread attention for almost 40 years (Rosvold, Mirsky, Sarason, Bransome, & Beck, 1956), particularly with the availability of microprocessors and personal computers. Although many "home grown" versions of the basic CPT paradigm exist, most suffer from a lack of standardization and normative information. However, their strength lies in their ability to provide an objective and convenient measure of sustained attention with good discriminant validity. Clearly, exclusive use of these measures is unwise, and instead they should be used as part of a battery of procedures to obtain information from multiple sources using multiple methods.

The Gordon Diagnostic System (GDS; Gordon, 1983) is a commercially available battery of clinical assessment tools. The attractiveness of the GDS is based on its portable, childproofed, microprocessor-driven design and acceptable psychometric properties (e.g., standardized administration procedures; normative data; validity and reliability). The CPT of the GDS requires the child to press a button each time a specified number or numerical sequence occurs in a stream of randomly presented numbers. Measures of hit rate (targets correctly identified), commissions (responses to nontargets), and performance across time are generated. Support for the utility of the GDS version of the CPT includes findings of test-retest reliability, concurrent and discriminant validity, and sensitivity to drug effects. Somewhat detracting from its diagnostic power are findings of a 15%–35% false-negative rate (i.e., "normal" performance by ADHD children); however, the false-positive rate of 2% (non-ADHD children performing poorly) is encouragingly low (for details, see Barkley, 1990). Other CPT methods have also been shown to be helpful in identifying subtypes of ADHD (August & Garfinkel, 1989, 1990; Halperin et al., 1990) although replication is still required.

Impulse Control

Three measures have been used to measure the degree of impulsivity of behavioral disinhibition in children and adolescents. The Matching Familiar Figures Test (MFFT; Kagan, 1966) has an extensive history of being used as a match-to-sample test, although findings regarding its reliability, discriminant validity, and sensitivity to drug effects (as well as incomplete normative information) detract from its clinical utility.

Researchers have begun to document the utility in distinguishing between different types of commission errors made on the CPT. For example, Halperin et al. (1988) have found significant correlations between behavior ratings of impulsivity and an "A-Not X" commission error rate; ratings of inattention were correlated with an "X-only" commission error rate.

The Delay Task, which is part of the GDS, is based on the paradigm of differential reinforcement of low rates (DRL). This task requires the child to inhibit responding in order to gain a point. If a child waits at least 6 seconds before responding, feedback will be provided through a counter and a light-flash. If the child responds before the 6-second interval has elapsed, the timer resets and no points are recorded. Normative and discriminant validity information is available (McClure & Gordon, 1984) as well as adequate test-retest reliability (Gordon & Mettelman, 1988).

Barkley (1990) suggests that additional research is required on its clinical utility, due to the task's insensitivity to drug effects and modest correlations with ratings of hyperactivity (Barkley, Fisher, Newby, & Breen, 1988).

Reflecting a recent focus on the neuropsychological functioning of ADHD children, the Stroop Word-Color Association Test (Stroop, 1935) has been shown to discriminate between ADHD and normal children (Grodzinsky, 1990) and ADD children with and without hyperactivity (Barkley, Grodzinsky, & DuPaul, 1990). This task also possesses test-retest reliability and sensitivity to frontal lobe dysfunctions in adults (Lezak, 1983). Barkley (1990) states that this task's discriminating ability is likely due to its ability to measure impulsivity (as a result of it being a measure of the ability to suppress or inhibit automatic responses). Evaluation procedures based on a neuropsychological foundation will likely be an area of continued interest, due to current views that ADHD involved an orbital-frontal-limbic origin (R. A. Barkley, personal communication, March, 1991).

Direct Observation Techniques

Unlike the more indirect assessment techniques that include rating scales or interviews using the identified child or an informant, direct behavioral assessment techniques provide an opportunity to conduct formal observations of diagnostically relevant behaviors in natural (e.g., home or school) or analogue (e.g., clinic playroom) settings. Again, the reader is directed to Barkley (1990) for a detailed discussion of techniques, procedures to maximize the "ecological validity" of the behavioral observations, and precautions to keep in mind when evaluating an ADHD child. Other extensive reviews of general issues pertaining to behavioral assessment are offered by Morris and Collier (1987), Gettinger and Kratochwill (1987), and Shapiro and Skinner (1990).

Observations Conducted in Natural Settings

Designed specifically for determining the frequency and severity of ADHD symptoms, the Hyperactive Behavior Code (Jacob, O'Leary, & Rosenblad, 1978) and the Classroom Observation Code (Abikoff, Gittelman-Klein, & Klein, 1977) are among the more commonly used. Although these procedures have demonstrated discriminant validity and high correlations with teacher ratings on the Conners Teacher Rating Scale, they have been criticized for not systematically determining the antecedents and consequences of behavior and neglecting to observe teacher and peer interactions (Barkley, 1981).

As mentioned earlier, Achenbach (1986) has developed a direct observation form that includes items comparable to those contained in the CBCL parent and teacher version. The CBCL-DOF contains six scales that were factor-analytically derived from 96 items (Withdrawn-Inattentive, Nervous-Overactive, Depressed, Hyperactive, Attention-Demanding, and Aggressive) using classroom observations of 287 children. Interobserver reliability and concurrent and discriminant validity have been demonstrated (McConaughy & Achenbach, 1988; McConaughy, Achenbach, & Gent, 1988). Clearly, this version of the CBCL offers many advantages over other currently available classroom observation procedures, including the wide array of behaviors assessed, the availability of normative data, the use of an empirical approach to determine how in vivo behaviors statistically relate, and its discriminant validity. Barkley (1990) states that "school personnel should be encouraged to adopt such a system as part of their standard evaluation of children for consideration for special education, *rather than relying so heavily on traditional projective methods of assessing behavior and personality* [emphasis added]" (p. 341).

Observations Conducted in Analogue Settings

Behavior coding systems developed for use in clinic playroom settings have been described extensively in the literature (Barkley, 1981). Observations are usually conducted through a one-way mirror while the child is attempting to complete a task (usually academic in nature) with various environmental distractors available. Standardized procedures can be used to structure the environment, implement different coding periods (e.g., habituation and actual coding), and operationalize target behaviors. Barkley (1990) describes the ADHD Behavior Coding System, which can be utilized in the clinic or in school (with certain procedural changes). Operationalized definitions are offered for behaviors such as "off task," "fidgeting," "vocalizing," "plays with objects," and "out of seat." Although Barkley holds little hope for the development of normative information, if the assessment is being used within the classroom, other children could be used as a normative reference point. Regardless, Barkley (1990) reports high intercoder agreement, and high correlations with teacher ratings of ADHD symptoms and measures of academic accuracy and productivity (DuPaul et al., 1990).

In closing, it should be apparent that the evaluation of suspected ADHD is a task requiring a considerable time commitment on the part of the diagnostician, the child, and significant others in the child's environment. All too frequently, children do not receive the proper treatment because of an inadequate diagnostic process. An example of this is an inappropriately strong reliance on the WISC-R Freedom from Distractibility factor isolated by Kaufman (1975) as a diagnostic procedure in evaluating inattention and distractibility, coupled with a hastily administered checklist completed by one informant. Unfortunately, there are many more unvalidated and unreliable measures purporting to be useful in the evaluation of ADHD than there are psychometrically and clinically sound instruments. Clearly, the diagnostician must be an educated consumer and frequently resist the lure of marketing claims or regionally or institutionally popular instruments.

CONDUCT DISORDER (CD)

DSM-III-R (APA, 1987, p. 53; see pp. 55-56 for specific diagnostic criteria) characterizes Conduct Disorder (CD) as a "persistent pattern of conduct in which the basic rights of others and major age-appropriate societal norms and rules are violated." Two primary subtypes of CD are specified: Solitary Aggressive Type and Group Type. These subtypes represent a change from DSM-III (APA, 1980), which specified subtypes of conduct problems presumably differing on the extent of manifested aggression and socialization. Although at the present time, the reliability and validity of the new DC criteria have not been established (except for results from a field trial of disruptive disorder presented by Spitzer, Davies, & Barkley, 1990), the DSM-III-R subtypes would appear to be quite consistent with findings from several multivariate studies. (For a review, see Quay, 1986b.) An additional DSM-III-R diagnosis of Oppositional Defiant Disorder appears to be a less severe variant of CD, has received little empirical validation as a separate diagnostic entity, and thus is seen by many to simply introduce "diagnostic noise." (See Reeves, Werry, Elkind, & Zametkin, 1987.)

Overall, several studies have provided consistent evidence that "aggression is indeed a valid and in fact the cardinal symptom of CD which affects or coexists with impaired interpersonal relationships and low popularity" (Quay et al., 1987, p. 499). It is for this reason, as well as others, that many favor a continuous dimensional approach to the definition of CD. In fact, much attention has been given to identifying the prevalence, associated and discriminating characteristics, prognosis/stability, antecedents, and response to treatment of aggression itself. (For a review of these components, see Martin & Hoffman, 1990; Quay, 1986b; Quay et al., 1987; Routh & Daugherty, in press.) Such an approach has provided the impetus for developing assessment measures for aggressive conduct problems ("antisocial" behavior) that have had a direct impact on treatment programs. It should be pointed out that the failure to distinguish between CD and ADHD has been a chronic methodological problem. However, Hinshaw (1987) has provided a comprehensive review of multivariate studies which, taken together, emphasizes that these disorders represent distinct entities that frequently occur together (i.e., they are comorbid). In fact, Barkley (1990) states that over 60% of clinic-referred ADHD children also display oppositional and defiant behavior. The simultaneous presence of CD and ADHD appears to forbode a worse outcome, and is associated with an earlier onset and severity of behavior problems, and the presence of parental psychopathology. (For details as well as other comorbid psychopathology, see Routh & Daugherty, in press.)

There are many similarities between ADHD and CD with regard to the assessment procedures used. First, subscribing to the multimethod, multiinformant approach, no one single source of information should be relied upon. Second, due to their wide coverage of child and adolescent psychopathology, many of the same assessment instruments adequately evaluate aggressive and "delinquent" behavior.

Parent and Child Interviews

Most of the issues related to the clinical interview and content areas outlined earlier in this chapter have similar importance to the assessment of CD. With regard to the structured parent interviews, several include questions concerning symptoms of CD—Child Assessment Schedule (CAS; Hodges et al., 1982), Diagnostic Interview Schedule for Children (DISC; Costello et al., 1987), Diagnostic Interview for Children and Adolescents (DICA; Herjanic & Campbell, 1977), and the Schedule for Affective Disorders and Schizophrenia for School Age Children (K-SADS; Puig-Antich & Chambers, 1978). The ultimate utility of these interviews will be the degree to which they are revised to keep up with the current psychiatric taxonomic system. Routh and Daugherty (in press) indicate that the DISC seems to be the most popular for use with children above age 10. For younger children, the semistructured CAS may be more appropriate due to factors of task demand and pacing. (See Hodges & Cools, 1990.) With regard to child interviews, the K-SADS, DICA, and CAS have shown good concordance (agreement) with child-reported CD (Carlson, Kashani, Thomas, Vaida, & Daniel, 1987; Hodges et al., 1987). Kazdin and Esveldt-Dawson (1986) have reported on the development and psychometric properties of the Interview for Antisocial Behavior (IAB), although the utility of this measure as a standardized parent interview has not yet been fully explored.

Behavior Rating Scales

The three most widely used behavior rating scales for parents and teachers are the Child Behavior Checklist (CBCL; Achenbach & Edel-brock, 1983; Edelbrock & Achenbach, 1984), the Conners Rating Scales (Conners, 1990), and the Revised Behavior Problem Checklist (RBPC; Quay & Peterson, 1987). The CBCL questionnaire is probably the most commonly used, and the Conners Scale was originally developed to document medication effects for hyperactivity. However, inherent to labeling practices of factor-analytic subscales, each rating scale includes a scale that quantifies conduct disorder–related symptoms. In an attempt to develop a "second generation" instrument, Achenbach, Conners, and Quay (1983) have designed a rating scale that includes items that tap into 12 syndrome constructs that have been hypothesized through previous multivariate efforts. Field testing is ongoing. (See also Achenbach et al., 1989.)

Peer Nominations and Ratings

Among the valid and reliable techniques used to elicit behavioral and social competence information from peers are those techniques referred to as sociometric measures. As pointed out by Routh and Daugherty (in press), these techniques are frequently not approved by human subjects committees (and schools) due to their elicitation of negative comments about children's peers. However, findings by Bell-Dolan, Foster, and Sikora (1989) do not provide support for the negative effect byproduct hypothesis. Nonetheless, as with any measure, reactivity effects should be recognized, safe guarded, and/or evaluated based on whether such measures have any incremental utility in the assessment of a child's social competence (Hughes, 1990).

Peer nomination techniques are essentially those in which each child is asked to identify a restricted number of children in their class/grade whom they "like the most," "are best friends with," or "most like to play with" (positive nominations), and "like the least" (negative nominations). Although many systems of derived scores have been used to characterize children, among the more well-researched systems is one proposed by Coie, Dodge, and Cappotelli (1982). Combining standardized scores of positive and negative nominations (i.e., the number received by each child) to produce a "social preference" and "social impact" has been used to form "social status" groups—popular, average, controversial, neglected, and rejected.

Peer rating techniques involve having children in a group (e.g., class, grade, camp, or psychiatric inpatients) rate each other on a Likert-type scale on the basis of the degree of liking. Procedural modifications can be made depending on the developmental level of the group (e.g., the use of a "happy-neutral-sad" continuum rather than presenting numbers; presenting pictures of each child to be rated). Although ratings and nominations scores have been found to be significantly correlated (e.g., Asher, Singleton, Tinsley, & Hymel, 1979), Schofield and Whitley (1983) suggest that ratings provide information on a child's peer acceptance or likability, whereas nominations reflect friendship patterns. Researchers have frequently combined the two procedures. (See Asher & Dodge, 1986.)

Information on the extent to which peer nomination is valid and reliable reinforces its usefulness as a research instrument and clinical tool. For example, the behavioral interaction style of children has been deemed to be the "cause of [social] status and not just a result" (Hughes, 1990, p. 428). As it relates to conduct problems, "rejected" children tend to engage in aggressive and inappropriate behavior (Dodge, 1983) and were described as such by peers (Asher & Coie, 1990; Coie & Dodge, 1983; Coie & Kupersmidt, 1983; Dodge, Coie, & Brakke, 1982). However, recent studies (Bierman, 1986, 1987; Hodgens & McCoy, 1989) have questioned the homogeneity of this rejected group. For example, Hodgens and McCoy (1989) isolated a rejected-aggressive and rejected-nonaggressive group of junior high school students who differed in the degree of social initiations made and received, and the duration of sustained interactions. Rabiner, Lenhart, and Lochman (1990) found that both aggressive and nonaggressive rejected boys generated fewer verbal assertion and conflict-escalating responses as solutions to hypothetical social problems than did nonrejected boys, but only under conditions designed to evoke automatic response tendencies. Under conditions designed to elicit reflective reasoning tendencies, aggressive rejected boys continued to provide fewer verbal assertion responses and more adult help-seeking responses, whereas the nonaggressive rejected boys responded in a manner similar to that of nonrejected boys. These findings suggested that nonaggressive rejected boys have an adequate repertoire of appropriate problem-solving strategies but fail to access these strategies when quick responding is required (Rabiner et al., 1990). Such group characteristics were thought to indicate different intervention approach requirements—impulse-control training for nonaggressive rejected boys (e.g., Kendall, 1986) and repertoire-building *plus* impulse control training for aggressive rejected boys.

A testimonial to the clinical meaningfulness of social status information is found in previous findings related to the degree of stability associated with the rejected group and later personal adjustment. Researchers have consistently documented the stability of the rejected group membership (Coie & Dodge, 1983) and the increased risk these children have in experiencing serious adjustment problems in later life (Cowen, Pederson, Babigian, Izzo, & Trost, 1973; Parker & Asher, 1986; Roff, Sells, & Golden, 1972). These findings have contributed to a continuing focus on descriptive and intervention research. (See Asher & Coie, 1990.)

Cognitive-Behavioral Assessment of Aggression

Over the past several years, there has been increased attention given to social-cognitive aspects of aggressive behavior. Under this framework, cognitive behavior therapy is directed toward children's deficiencies and distortion in their cognitive processing of events. The former is characterized by an insufficient amount of cognitive activity, whereas the latter involves misperceptions. Driven by the work of Novaco (1978) and Dodge (1986), Lochman, White, and Wayland (1990) present a social-cognitive model of anger and aggression:

> The child encounters a potentially anger-arousing stimulus event, but the emotional and physiological reaction is due to the child's perception and appraisal of the event rather than due to the event itself. These perceptions and appraisals can be accurate or inaccurate, and are derived from prior expectations which filter the

event, and from the child's selective attention to specific aspects, or cues, in the stimulus event. If the child has interpreted the event to be threatening, provocative or frustrating, the child can then experience physiological arousal, and also will become engaged in another set of cognitive activities directed at deciding upon an appropriate behavioral response to the event. The internal arousal has a reciprocal interaction with the individual's appraisal processes, since the child has to interpret and label the emotional connotations of the arousal. . . . Reactions from others can then become stimulus events which back into the model, becoming recurrent, connected behavioral units. (pp. 29-30)

Through a series of questions regarding vignettes describing or displaying children involved in hostile, benevolent, or neutral situations, certain social cognitive characteristics of aggressive children have been delineated. These questions and vignettes are designed to operationalize the five stages of Dodge's (1986) social information processing model—cue utilization, attributions about others' intention, generation of alternative solutions, consideration of consequences of solutions, and behavioral implementation of solutions. Lochman et al. (1990) provide a useful review of findings pertaining to measures of cognitive appraisals and deficiencies of aggressive children. (See also Lochman, Meyer, Rabiner, & White, in press.) For a direct application to the diagnostic category of Conduct Disorder, see Dodge, Price, Bachorowski, and Newman (1990).

Behavior Observations

Despite the many limitations of direct behavioral observation techniques (e.g., time-consuming, cumbersome, expensive; issues of reactivity to observation and low base rates of behavior), information obtained from these procedures can provide a measure of validation (e.g., for bias-prone rating scales) and data that are useful for the implementation of intervention programs. Patterson's program of research (1977, 1982, 1986; Patterson, Dishion, & Bank, 1984) exemplifies the use of behavioral coding procedures in the analysis of "coercive" exchanges between children exhibiting antisocial behavior and members of their family. Patterson (1982) described this process of coercion in the context of avoidance conditioning—the child reacts in a manner aversive to the parent in response to an aversive behavior by the parent; the child's behavior results in the termination of the aversive stimuli, which reinforces and amplifies noncompliance.

Other behavioral coding systems and procedures pertinent to the quantification of aggressive, defiant, and noncompliant behavior are discussed above and detailed in Barkley (1990).

Although there is a high degree of concurrence between CD and ADHD, several assessment techniques enable the diagnostician to measure the contribution of both groups of symptoms to the manifestation of disruptive behavior. Unfortunately, the inadequacy with which many test developers have defined their groups has resulted in a plethora of studies that make erroneous conclusions about supposedly distinct characteristics of CD and ADHD (such is also the case for ADHD and LD). However, with an increasing understanding of the correlates (e.g., cognitive, social, biological, familial), etiology, outcome/prognosis, and response to treatment of these frequently coexisting disorders, the evaluation process will likely become more specific. Indeed, the development of measures based on social-information processing models has been instrumental in the assessment of aggressive conduct problems and the development of intervention approaches.

ANXIETY DISORDER

Multivariate statistical approaches to classification have consistently yielded two broad-band dimensions of deviant behavior in children—externalizing (undercontrolled) and internalizing (overcontrolled). Although not without their criticism, the empirical basis of the externalizing behaviors (e.g., conduct problems, attentional problems) has been supported, which is at least partly reflected in DSM-III-R. Multivariate studies have supported the existence of an internalizing dimension termed "anxiety-withdrawal" (AW) which is characterized by indicators of anxiety, depression, and social withdrawal. However, as Quay and LaGreca (1986) note, the diagnostic reliability of subcategories of this dimension found in DSM-III-R has been less than favorable.

Perhaps in response to this lack of reliability, increased attention has been given to the development of more specific and potentially more valid and reliable assessment procedures that go beyond parent and teacher behavior rating scales. It is beyond the scope of this chapter to review adequately the advances in the understanding of symptoms represented in the anxiety-withdrawal (and depression) dimension. Literature pertaining to the diagnostic and assessment issues in childhood depression will not be reviewed here. Readers interested in childhood depression are referred to reviews by Kazdin (1990) and Kendall, Cantwell, and Kazdin (1989). The focus on anxiety disorders in the present chapter is based on the perception that characteristics of anxiety (e.g., behavioral avoidance, social withdrawal) have particular relevance to educational settings. In addition, the consensus of the DSM-III-R nosologists is that there are few characteristics of depression that are unique to children (although more recent empirical studies provide contrary evidence), whereas some DSM-III-R anxiety disorders are described as specific to childhood or adolescence.

Perhaps the best way to gain an appreciation for the difficulties involved in assessing anxiety is to discuss basic definitional issues. Terms that have typically been used to describe anxiety in children are *fear, anxiety,* and *phobia.* Although the clinical utility and heuristic value of these terms have been questioned (Morris & Kratochwill, 1983b), definitions of and distinctions between them have been offered by many. Kendall and Ronan (1990) describe *fear* as a "discriminative response to a perceived environmental threat involving behavioral avoidance, cognitive distress, and physiological arousal" (p. 224). Francis and Ollendick (1987) consider *anxiety* as a "set of physiological reasons, subjective feelings of distress, and avoidance behaviors that occur without obvious precipitating external threats or clear antecedent stimulus events" (p. 374). Childhood *phobias* are viewed as specific fears that are "disproportional to the degree of threat posed by the feared stimulus" (Francis & Ollendick, 1987, p. 374). More specifically, Kendall and Ronan (1990) describe *phobias* as "behavioral reactions to specific environmental stimuli that have attained a level of clinical significance in terms not only of motoric reactivity, but also of various concomitant cognitive and physiological changes" (p. 224). Despite these seemingly useful definitions, agreement about conceptual and clinical distinctions is lacking. Kendall and Ronan (1990) suggest, for example, that the functional analysis of avoidant behavior could be improved "by extending the pristine behaviorist interpretation of stimulus conditions" by examining the "cognitive conditions (factors in information processing) leading to, maintaining, and/or remediating children's fearful or anxious behavior" (p. 224). For example, fear and anxiety would be distinguished on the basis of the cognitive representation of concrete external and abstract internal threat, respectively. Therefore, in addition to the consensual agreement on the importance of placing fears or anxieties in the context of developmental appropriateness (Graziano, DeGiovanni, & Garcia, 1979; Morris & Kratochwill, 1983b), behavioral avoidance could be better understood if cognitive information-processing factors are examined (Kendall & Ronan, 1990).

Like its predecessor, DSM-III-R offers three presumably distinct types of anxiety disorders of childhood or adolescence: separation anxiety disorder, avoidant disorder, and overanxious disorder. Whereas the first two are characterized by situation-specific anxiety, anxiety with the latter is generalized to various situations. The age of onset of the first two is typically, but not exclusively, during or before the early school years. The essential feature of separation anxiety disorder is an excessive anxiety regarding separation from those to whom the child is attached. Miller, Boyer, and Rodoletz (1990) suggest that "adverse separation experiences will be evident when the child is younger, is insecurely attached to the caregiver, and is exposed to unpredictable and uncontrollable separation conditions" (p. 192). Specifically relevant to school settings, there has been renewed interest in school phobia as a potentially meaningful separate diagnostic category. Researchers have suggested that anxiety about attending school can stem from separation problems or from excessive fear specific to school attendance. (See Last & Francis, 1988.)

Avoidant disorder is characterized by an excessive shrinking from contact with unfamiliar people to the extent that it interferes with peer relationships. This occurs despite the desire for and satisfying relations with family members or familiar figures. Miller et al. (1990) point to the need for considerably more research regarding the diagnostic validity, treatment responsiveness, course, and outcome of this disorder.

Overanxious disorder is characterized by excessive worrying that is generalized to a variety of situations and is not linked to an identifiable stressor. Specific symptoms may include excessive or unrealistic worry about future events, past behaviors, or competence; somatic complaints; marked self-consciousness; excessive need for reassurance; marked feelings of tension or inability to relax. Mattison and Bagnato (1987) have provided evidence for this disorder's convergent and discriminant (Dysthymia and ADHD) diagnostic validity.

Readers interested in recent reviews of issues related to the nature, development, treatment, and outcome of the above anxiety disorders are directed to Crowell and Waters (1990), Miller et al. (1990), Quay and LaGreca (1986), and Wenar (1990).

Interview Methods

Similar to most other behavior problems in children, the clinical interview is the most commonly used technique for evaluating primary and associated characteristics of anxiety. The potential benefits and drawbacks of using various versions representing different degrees of structured formats apply to the assessment of anxiety. As already indicated, examples of structured interviews include the K-SADS, DICA, DISC, and CAS. Specific to the evaluation of anxiety, the Interview Schedule for Children (ISC; Kovacs, 1983) is a semistructured interview which has been shown to produce reliable anxiety disorder diagnoses (Last, Hersen, Kazdin, Finkelstein, & Strauss, 1987).

As indicated by Francis and Ollendick (1987), questions phrased in specific and simple ways may facilitate responses from the timid, shy, unresponsive, and anxious child. Anchoring questions in behavioral terms for the parents (e.g., examples of behaviors that suggest the child is anxious) can also be helpful. In the context of a cognitive-behavioral assessment, Kendall and Ronan (1990) encourage the use of structured interview formats. These authors suggest that such an approach can (1) elicit information on the child's social-cognitive reasoning abilities; (2) identify specific fears/anxieties which can form the basis of an assessment of situations in which the child can/cannot cope; and (3) examine anxiety and fear across three "response channels"—behavioral, physiological, and cognitive.

Rating Scales and Checklists

Among the more frequently used rating scales completed by parents or teachers that include subscales associated with children's fears and anxieties is the CBCL (Achenbach & Edlebrock, 1983) and the RBPC (Quay & Peterson, 1987). The manuals which accompany these well-constructed instruments discuss research findings relevant to anxiety and social withdrawal.

Self-report measures are also frequently used in the assessment of child and adolescent anxiety. The revised Children's Manifest Anxiety Scale (RCMAS; Reynolds & Richmond, 1978) is one of the more widely used self-report measures specific to anxiety. Factor analysis has yielded three subscales: physiological anxiety, worry and sensitivity, and concentration anxiety (e.g., inattentiveness and preoccupation); the RCMAS also includes a Lie Scale. Reynolds and his colleagues (Reynolds, 1982; Reynolds & Paget, 1983; Reynolds & Richmond, 1979) have provided information on the psychometric adequacy of the RCMAS on the basis of its internal consistency, test-retest reliability, convergent and discriminant validity, and normative data on children ages 6 to 19.

The State-Trait Anxiety Inventory for Children (STAIC; Speilberger, 1973) and the Fear Survey Schedule for Children—Revised (FSSC-R; Ollendick, 1983) are two other commonly used self-report measures of anxiety. Findings on the psychometric adequacy of the STAIC have been inconsistent, particularly with regard to the state-trait distinction in children (Kendall & Ronan, 1990). The FSSC-R assesses specific fears in categories of school, home, social, physical, animal, travel, classical phobia, and miscellaneous. Ollendick (1983) noted the utility of the FSSC-R in selecting children for treatment, assessing pre-post treatment effects, and in investigating children's fear sensitivities. Kendall and Ronan (1990) recommend additional research to establish the empirically supported utility of the FSSC-R. Several other situation-specific scales are available to the clinician/researcher. (See Kendall & Ronan, 1990; Miller et al., 1990.)

Social anxiety in children has received increased attention, primarily due to its moderating role in children's social skills and their peer acceptance (Quay & LaGreca, 1986). Responding to the need for a valid assessment of children's social anxiety, LaGreca and her colleagues have developed the Social Anxiety Scale for Children (SASC; LaGreca, Dandes, Wick, Shaw, & Stone, 1988) and its revision (SASC-R; LaGreca, 1989; LaGreca & Stone, in press). Factor analysis has yielded three factors related to a child's fear of being negatively evaluated and generalized or situation/peer-specific social avoidance and distress. Concurrent measures have included peer ratings; other self-report measures regarding anxiety; perceived competence/self-worth, and depression; and teacher ratings of behavior.

A related but sufficiently distinct approach to the self-report of anxiety includes techniques that attempt to measure associated cognitive characteristics. This cognitive-behavioral approach focuses on assessing self-statements, irrational beliefs, current concerns, images, problem-solving capacities, expectancies, and attributions that may relate to the etiology, maintenance, or remediation of anxiety and fears (Kendall & Ronan, 1990). Specific assessment techniques, which have been reviewed by others (Kendall & Braswell, 1982a,b), include self-monitoring techniques, unobtrusive recordings of spontaneous speech and verbalizations following "think aloud" instructions, role playing, imagery assessment, thought-sampling and thought-listing methods, interviews, and endorsement measures (Kendall & Ronan, 1990). Research conducted within the last 10 years has documented anxious children's tendencies to exhibit more negative self-talk (i.e., cognitive distortions), negative expectancies, and affective arousal compared to their nonanxious peers. Kendall and Ronan (1990) also report on initial psychometric characteristics of the Children's Anxious Self-Statement Questionnaire (CASSQ), which has been shown to have utility as a treatment outcome measure due to its high test-retest reliability and discriminant validity.

The popularity of self-report measures of anxiety should be viewed in the context of cautions and issues frequently raised. Kendall and Ronan (1990, p. 234) outline four major issues: (1) self-report measures do not adequately measure the situation-specific aspects of anxiety and fear in children; (2) specific fear schedules may not always reflect specific and individualized fears; (3) many measures lack adequate psychometric data for certain ages and genders; (4) self-reports may not always accurately reflect internal states. The authors call for further investigations regarding the convergence of agreement across alternate sources of information and response channels, and the predictive validity of the measures.

Behavioral Observation Techniques

In addition to the above commonly cited drawbacks of symptom checklists, another potential limitation is that most ratings are based on retrospective information (Miller et al., 1990). Behavioral methods of observation provide a direct and relatively noninferential way to assess anxiety as it actually occurs. The Behavioral Avoidance Tests (BAT; Lang & Lazovik, 1963) measure the motoric aspects of an anxiety response, and involve presenting or imagining the presence of the feared object. Objective measures of fear include proximity to the feared object, and the number and latency of approach responses. The BAT has been criticized due to the lack of standardized procedures and psychometric information (Barrios, Hartmann, & Shigetomi, 1981). However, the advantages of the BAT are that the assessment takes place in a more structured environment and can be conducted by nonprofessionals. Idiosyncratic and/or motoric, nonavoidant responses (e.g., trembling, facial expressions) may provide treatment-relevant information (Barrios et al., 1981). Kendall and Ronan (1990) indicate that the potential utility of the BAT is in examining the relationship between behavioral approach-avoidance and cognitive-behavioral measures (e.g., self-statements, think-aloud procedures).

Other techniques of behavioral observation would involve direct observation of a child in a naturalistic setting (e.g., school, medical/dental situations). One of the few standardized and valid procedures for use in the school is the Preschool Observation Scale of Anxiety (POSA; Glennon & Weisz, 1978). The POSA assesses 30 specifically operationalized, time-sampled behaviors associated with separation anxiety. Glennon and Weisz (1978) have reported on studies documenting favorable interrater agreement and validity.

Ratings of direct observation are not without their drawbacks, of which few are specific to the assessment of anxiety. For example, expectational biases, reactivity, lack of standardized formats and manuals, observer drift, cost of training and equipment, and lack of reliability and validity have been cited as factors by which direct observation rating scales are deemed potentially problematic (Miller et al., 1990).

Peer Nominations and Ratings

A common approach used to evaluate social deficiencies in children is to measure the sociometric status using peer nomination and peer ratings. Described earlier in this chapter, peer nomination and ratings have been found to be moderately reliable and consistently valid. Strauss and colleagues have conducted several studies based on methodologically rigorous procedures. For example, Strauss, Lahey, Frick, Frame, and Hynd (1988) used DSM-III criteria to identify clinic-referred anxious children who were compared with a nonreferred control group and a clinic-referred comparison group with conduct problems. Evaluation procedures included well-validated independent measures of anxiety and peer adjustment. Findings indicated that anxiety-disordered children were liked significantly less than normal children, but anxious and conduct-disordered children did not differ from each other. The anxious group received lower social impact scores (total like-most and like-least nominations) of any group and were likely to fall in the socially neglected category of peer status. Additional analyses suggested that the lack of popularity of children with anxiety disorder may be limited to those with concurrent depression. For a comprehensive review of literature pertaining to social deficits of children with internalizing disorders, the reader is referred to Strauss (1988).

Physiological Measures

Physiological assessment of anxiety requires a level of equipment and skill sophistication that precludes its use as a standard technique employed by diagnosticians. However, measures of cardiovascular responsivity (e.g., heart rate) and electrodermal indices (e.g., skin conductance and skin resistance) could represent the physiological response channel in a multimethod assessment battery, the other two response channels being observable motor responses (e.g., direct behavioral observation) and cognitive responses (e.g., self-statements, etc.). Although the potential utility of physiological assessment is encouraging (Himadi, Boice, & Barlow), 1985; Kendall & Ronan, 1990), the lack of systematic normative data with children as well as the expense involved precludes its regular use in clinical practice and suggests the need for more basic research (Francis & Ollendick, 1987).

Not unlike other behavior problems in children, many researchers advocate a multimethod measurement approach to assessing anxiety in children and adolescents. Interviews, symptom checklists, and rating scales completed by the child and his or her caregiver can provide useful retrospective information. Procedures designed to shed light on the cognitive processes associated with the development, maintenance, and treatment responsivity of anxiety can also be useful for those espousing a cognitive-behavioral orientation. Behavioral measures can be useful, primarily as a treatment outcome measure (Miller et al., 1990). Basic research involving physiological measures may provide a better understanding into how best to incorporate these techniques into clinical practice. With an increased recognition for the potential debilitating effects of anxiety and social withdrawal, more specific assessment measures have been developed. Continued efforts are likely to result in a better understanding of anxiety in children, its relationship with other child behavior problems, and what type of intervention techniques may facilitate better adjustment.

CONCLUSIONS

This chapter has presented an introduction to salient issues in the assessment of behavior problems in children, and measures designed to evaluate these problems in valid and reliable ways. Consistent with the initial discussion of various assessment models and a multimethod, multiinformant strategy espoused by many diagnosticians, the review of assessment practices has focused on the use of interviews, symptom checklists and rating scales, sociometric measures, behavioral observation techniques, and laboratory-based measures. In the same way that heterogeneity exists between groups of children exhibiting developmentally inappropriate behavior, important differences exist within the categories of assessment techniques. Assessment techniques differ in the degree to which they represent clinically or statistically derived taxonomy; whether they are specific to a disorder or multidimensional in nature; whether it is a self-, parent-, teacher-, or peer-report measure; and the response "channel" they are evaluating (i.e., behavioral, physiological, cognitive). Although such a diversity of assessment tools might suggest a highly refined system of describing the behavior problem in terms of antecedent and etiology, primary and associated characteristics, response to treatment, and prognosis and outcome, this is not the case. Findings that may seem contradictory, when evaluated at face value, pose a particular challenge to child clinical and educational diagnosticians. Instead, the orientation of developmental psychologists and diagnosticians pursuing a multiaxial view of assessment facilitates the incorporation of various theoretical orientations and the recognition that method or rater variance should not always be assumed to reflect a lack of reliability or validity. Instead, particularly for children, situation-specificity, interpersonal factors, and differences in interpretation should be taken into account when formulating an interpretation of the assessment findings and developing an intervention plan.

The purpose of this chapter was to provide a foundation for understanding and structuring the assessment process with children who are exhibiting behavior problems. Special attention was given to the evaluation of attention-deficit hyperactivity disorder, due to its high prevalence and relevance to school situations. Interviews and rating scales reviewed as tools for an ADHD evaluation are also used for the evaluation of other behavior problems, due to the multidimensional nature of these procedures. At the same time, much of the gain in our understanding of child psychopathology has been the result of more specific measures of the behavior in question (e.g., cognitive assessment of anxiety). Although the present view has focused on valid and reliable measures of certain categories or dimensions of psychopathology, several other techniques and measures have been maintained as "standard" devices, despite questionable validity or limited incremental utility of the information obtained. Several of these measures fall under the heading of projective techniques, which have been popular historically, but have either not received the attention of empirically oriented diagnosticians or have not been found to be empirically valid by researchers. Examples of projective techniques frequently used with children include creative drawings, thematic apperception techniques, sentence completion techniques, and the Rorschach technique. Reviews by Allen and Hollifield (1990), Chandler (1990), Haak (1990), Knoff (1990), and Worchell and Dupree (1990) offer useful discussions of the major projective techniques. Not without their merit, these procedures *may* provide information regarding self-image (for a more objective measure of perceived competence and self-worth, see Harter, 1985, and Marsh, 1990); interpersonal relations; current concerns, motivations, needs, threats, and a perception of significant others; perceptual-cognitive aspects; cognitive style; behavioral tendencies; and psychodynamic information (Chandler, 1990). Although empirical support for such a list is not well established, these clinical methods are frequently used to generate working hypotheses that may be validated by other means. Furthermore, as any individual working with children will attest, these indirect measures may provide a "window" into the anxious, angry, noncommunicative, and/or defensive child. One might argue that the degree of efficiency and productivity possessed by an instrument is as important as sound empirical evidence based on behavioral principles. On the other hand, if there is any area of diagnostic practice with children that need not be maintained, it is the illusory interpretations generated from the blind use of projective techniques. Thus, as with any measure of human behavior, a healthy balance of curiosity and skepticism appears warranted with these indirect, subjective techniques.

Obviously, certain assessment practices are more well developed than others. Although various instruments have been found to be valid and reliable, the result of this psychometric refinement is frequently a higher degree of instrument complexity, expensive equipment and/or impractical settings, the need for more comprehensive evaluations, and loss of ecological validity. Instead of viewing this as a detraction and reason to digress to the persistent use of unvalidated assessment procedures or methods of interpretation, it should encourage an interdisciplinary approach as well as the necessity for diagnosticians, regardless of their orientation and level of training, to continually *update and expand* their knowledge base, even if it means going beyond the "boundaries" of their traditional training. Such is the challenge for students of clinical and educational diagnostic practices.

REFERENCES

Abikoff, H., Gittelman-Klein, R., & Klein, D. (1977). Validation of a classroom observation code for hyperactive children. *Journal of Consulting and Clinical Psychology, 45*, 772-783.

Achenbach, T. M. (1982). *Developmental psychopathology* (2nd ed.). New York: Wiley.

Achenbach, T. M. (1985). *Assessment and taxonomy of child and adolescent psychopathology*. Beverly Hills, CA: Sage.

Achenbach, T. M. (1986). *Manual for the Child Behavior Checklist - Direct Observation Form*. Burlington, VT: University of Vermont, Department of Psychiatry.

Achenbach, T. M. (1990). Conceptualizations of developmental psychopathology. In M. Lewis & S. Miller (Eds.), *Handbook of developmental psychopathology* (pp. 3-14). New York: Plenum.

Achenbach, T. M., Conners, C. K., & Quay, H. C. (1983). *The ACQ Behavior Checklist*. Burlington, VT: University of Vermont, Department of Psychiatry.

Achenbach, T. M., Conners, C. K., Quay, H. C., Verhulst, F. C., & Howell, C. T. (1989). Replication of empirically derived syndromes as a basis for taxonomy of child/adolescent psychopathology. *Journal of Abnormal Child Psychology, 17*, 299-323.

Achenbach, T. M., & Edelbrock, C. (1983). *Manual for the Child Behavior Checklist and Revised Child Behavior Profile*. Burlington, VT: University of Vermont, Department of Psychiatry.

Achenbach, T. M., & Edelbrock, C. (1987). *Manual for the Child Behavior Checklist - Youth Self-Report*. Burlington, VT: University of Vermont, Department of Psychiatry.

Achenbach, T. M., & McConaughy, S. H. (1987). *Empirically based assessment of child and adolescent psychopathology: Practical applications*. Newbury Park, CA: Sage.

Achenbach, T. M., & McConaughy, S. H. (1989). *Semistructured clinical interview for children aged 6-11*. Burlington, VT: University of Vermont, Department of Psychiatry.

Achenbach, T. M., McConaughy, S. H., & Howell, C. T. (1987). Child/Adolescent behavioral and emotional problems: Implications of cross-informant correlations for situational specificity. *Psychological Bulletin, 101*, 213-232.

Allen, J. C., & Hollifield, J. (1990). Using the Rorschach with children and adolescents: The Exner Comprehensive System. In C. R. Reynolds & R. W. Kamphaus (Eds.), *Handbook of psychological and educational assessment of children: Personality, behavior, and context* (pp. 168-186). New York: Guilford.

American Psychiatric Association. (1980). *DSM-III: Diagnostic and statistical manual of mental disorders* (3rd ed.). Washington, DC: Author.

American Psychiatric Association. (1987). *DSM-III-R: Diagnostic and statistical manual of mental disorders* (3rd ed., rev.). Washington, DC: Author.

Asher, S. R., & Coie, J. D. (1900). *Peer rejection in childhood.* New York: Cambridge University Press.

Asher, S. R., & Dodge, K. A. (1986). Identifying children who are rejected by their peers. *Developmental Psychology, 22*, 444-449.

Asher, S. R., Singleton, L. C., Tinsley, B. R., & Hymel, S. (1979). A reliable sociometric measure for preschool children. *Developmental Psychology, 15*, 443-444.

August, G. J., & Garfinkel, B. D. (1989). Behavioral and cognitive subtypes of ADHD. *Journal of the American Academy of Child and Adolescent Psychiatry, 28*, 739-748.

August, G. J., & Garfinkel, B. D. (1990). Comorbidity of ADHD and reading disability among clinic-referred children. *Journal of Abnormal Child Psychology, 18*, 29-45.

Barkley, R. A. (1981). *Hyperactivity: A handbook for diagnosis and treatment.* New York: Guilford.

Barkley, R. A. (1990). *Attention-Deficit Hyperactivity Disorder: A handbook for diagnosis and treatment.* New York: Guilford.

Barkley, R. A. (1991). A critique of current diagnostic criteria for Attention Deficit Hyperactivity Disorder: Clinical and research implications. *Journal of Developmental and Behavioral Pediatrics, 11*, 343-352.

Barkley, R. A., DuPaul, G. J., & McMurray, M. B. (1990). Comprehensive evaluation of Attention Deficit Disorder with and without Hyperactivity as defined by research criteria. *Journal of Consulting and Clinical Psychology, 58*, 775-789.

Barkley, R. A., Fischer, M., Newby, R., & Breen, M. (1988). Development of a multimethod clinical protocol for assessing stimulant drug responses in ADHD children. *Journal of Clinical Child Psychology, 17*, 14-24.

Barkley, R. A., Grodzinsky, G., & DuPaul, G. J. (1990). *A comprehensive evaluation of Attention Deficit Disorder with and without Hyperactivity. III. Neuropsychological measures.* Manuscript submitted for publication, University of Massachusetts Medical Center, Worcester.

Barrios, B., A., Hartmann, D. P., & Shigetomi, C. (1981). Fears and anxieties in children. In E. J. Mass & L. G. Terdal (Eds.), *Behavioral assessment of childhood disorders* (pp. 259-304). New York: Guilford.

Beck, S. (1987). Questionnaires and checklists. In C. L. Frame & J. L. Matson (Eds.), *Handbook of assessment in childhood psychopathology: Applied issues in differential diagnosis and treatment evaluation* (pp. 79-106). New York: Plenum.

Bell-Dolan, D. J., Foster, S. L., & Sikora, D. M. (1989). Effects of sociometric testing on children's behavior and loneliness in school. *Developmental Psychology, 25*, 306-311.

Bierman, K. L. (1986). The relationship between social aggression and peer rejection in middle childhood. In R. Prinz (Ed.), *Advances in behavioral assessment of children and families* (Vol. 2, pp. 151-178). Greenwich, CT: JAI.

Bierman, K. L. (1987). The clinical significance and assessment of poor peer relations: Peer neglect versus peer rejection. *Journal of Developmental and Behavioral Pediatrics, 8*, 233-240.

Bierman, K. L. (1990). Using the clinical interview to assess children's interpersonal reasoning and emotional understanding. In C. R. Reynolds & R. W. Kamphaus (Eds.), *Handbook of psychological and educational assessment of children: Personality, behavior, and context* (pp. 204-219). New York: Guilford.

Binet, A., & Simon, T. (1916). *The development of intelligence in children.* Baltimore: Williams & Wilkins. (Original work published 1905)

Blashfield, R. K. (1984). *The classification of psychopathology. Neo-Kraepelinian and quantitative approaches.* New York: Plenum.

Cantwell, D. P., & Baker, L. (1988). Issues in the classification of child and adolescent psychopathology. *Journal of the American Academy of Child and Adolescent Psychiatry, 27*, 521-533.

Cantwell, D. P., & Carlson, G. A. (Eds.). (1983). *Affective disorders in childhood and adolescence: An update.* New York: Spectrum.

Carlson, G., Kashani, J., Thomas, M., Vaida, A., & Daniel, A. (1987). Comparison of two structured interviews on a psychiatrically hospitalized population of children. *Journal of the American Academy of Child and Adolescent Psychiatry, 26*, 645-648.

Chandler, L. A. (1990). The projective hypothesis and the development of projective techniques for children. In C. R. Reynolds & R. W. Kamphaus (Eds.), *Handbook of psychological and educational assessment of children: Personality, behavior, and context* (pp. 55-69). New York: Guilford.

Chapman, L. J., & Chapman, J. P. (1967). Genesis of popular but erroneous psychodiagnostic observations. *Journal of Abnormal Psychology, 74*, 271-280.

Coie, J. D., & Dodge, K. A. (1983). Continuities and changes in children's social status: A five-year longitudinal study. *Merrill-Palmer Quarterly, 29*, 261-282.

Coie, J. D., Dodge, K. A., & Cappotelli, H. (1982). Dimensions and types of status: A cross-age perspective. *Developmental Psychology, 18*, 557-570.

Coie, J. D., & Kupersmidt, J. B. (1983). A behavioral analysis of emerging social status in boys' groups. *Child Development, 54*, 1400-1416.

Conners, C. K. (1990). *Manual for Conners' Rating Scales.* North Tonawanda, NY: Multi-Health Systems.

480   BEST PRACTICES IN ASSESSMENT

Costello, E. J., Edelbrock, C. S., Costello, A. J., Dulcan, M. K., Burns, B. J., & Brent, D. (1988). Psychopathology in pediatric primary care: The new hidden morbidity. *Pediatrics, 82*, 415-424.

Costello, E. J., Edelbrock, C. S., Dulcan, M. K., Kalas, R., & Klaric, S. (1987). *Diagnostic Interview Schedule for Children (DISC)*. Pittsburgh: Western Psychiatric Institute and Clinic, School of Medicine, University of Pittsburgh.

Cowen, E. L., Pederson, A., Babigian, H., Izzo, L. D., & Trost, M. A. (1973). Long-term follow-up of early detected vulnerable children. *Journal of Consulting and Clinical Psychology, 41*, 438-446.

Crowell, J. A., & Waters, E. (1990). Separation anxiety. In M. Lewis & S. Miller (Eds.), *Handbook of developmental psychopathology* (pp. 209-218). New York: Plenum.

Dodge, K. A. (1983). Behavioral antecedents of peer social status. *Child Development, 54*, 1386-1399.

Dodge, K. A. (1986). A social information processing model of social competence in children. In M. Perlmutter (Ed.), *The Minnesota Symposium on Child Psychology: Vol. 18. Cognitive perspectives on children's social and behavioral development* (pp. 77-125). Hillsdale, NJ: Lawrence Erlbaum Associates.

Dodge, K. A., Coie, J. D., & Brakke, N. P. (1982). Behavior patterns of socially rejected and neglected preadolescents: The roles of social approach and aggression. *Journal of Abnormal Child Psychology, 10*, 389-410.

Dodge, K. A., Price, J. M., Bachorowski, J., & Newman, J. P. (1990). Hostile attributional biases in severely aggressive adolescents. *Journal of Abnormal Psychology, 99*, 385-392.

DuPaul, G. J. (1900a). *The ADHD Rating Scale: Normative data, reliability, and validity*. Unpublished manuscript, University of Massachusetts Medical Center, Worcester.

DuPaul, G. J. (1990b). *The Home and School Situation Questionnaire - Revised: Normative data, reliability, and validity*. Unpublished manuscript, University of Massachusetts Medical Center, Worcester.

DuPaul, G. J., Rapport, M., & Perriello, L. M. (1990). *Teacher ratings of academic performance: The development of the Academic Performance Rating Scale*. Unpublished manuscript, University of Massachusetts Medical Center, Worcester.

Edelbrock, C. S., & Achenbach, T. M. (1984). A teacher version of the Child Behavior Profile: I. Boys aged 6-11. *Journal of Consulting and Clinical Psychology, 52*, 207-217.

Edelbrock, C. S., & Costello, A. (1984). Structured psychiatric interviews for children and adolescents. In G. Goldstein & M. Hersen (Eds.), *Handbook of psychological assessment* (pp. 276-290). New York: Pergamon.

Edelbrock C. S., & Costello, A. J. (1988). Convergence between statistically derived behavior problem syndromes and child psychiatric diagnoses. *Journal of Abnormal Child Psychology, 16*, 219-231.

Forehand, R., Lautenschlager, G. J., Faust, J., & Graziano, W. G. (1986). Parent perceptions and parent-child interactions in clinic-referred children: A preliminary investigation of the effects of maternal depressive moods. *Behavior Research and Therapy, 24*, 73-75.

Francis, G., & Ollendick, T. H. (1987). Anxiety disorders. In C. L. Frame & J. L. Matson (Eds.), *Handbook of assessment in childhood psychopathology: Applied issues in differential diagnosis and treatment evaluation* (pp. 373-400). New York: Plenum.

Glennon, B., & Weisz, J. R. (1978). An observational approach to the assessment of anxiety in young children. *Journal of Consulting and Clinical Psychology, 46*, 1246-1257.

Gettinger, M., & Kratochwill, T. R. (1987). Behavioral assessment. In C. L. Frame & J. L. Matson (Eds.), *Handbook of assessment in childhood psychopathology: Applied issues in differential diagnosis and treatment evaluation* (pp. 131-161). New York: Plenum.

Gordon, M. (1983). *The Gordon Diagnostic System.* DeWitt, NY: Gordon Systems.

Gordon, M., & Mettelman, B. B. (1988). The assessment of attention: I. Standardization and reliability of a behavior based measure. *Journal of Clinical Psychology, 44*, 682-690.

Gould, M. S., Wunsch-Hitzig, R., & Dohrenwend, B. P. (1980). Formulation of hypotheses about the prevalence, treatment, and prognostic significance of psychiatric disorders in children in the United States. In B. P. Dohrenwend, B. S. Dohrenwend, M. S. Gould, B. Link, R. Neugebauer, & R. Wunsch-Hitzig (Eds.), *Mental illness in the United States: Epidemiological estimates* (pp. 9-44). New York: Praeger.

Graham, P. J. (Ed.). (1977). *Epidemiological approaches in child psychiatry.* New York: Academic Press.

Graziano, A. M., DeGiovanni, I. S., & Garcia, K. A. (1979). Behavioral treatment of children's fears: A review. *Psychological Bulletin, 86*, 804-830.

Greenspan, S. I. (1981). *The clinical interview of the child.* New York: McGraw-Hill.

Grodzinsky, G. (1990). *Assessing frontal lobe functioning in 6 to 11 year old boys with Attention Deficit Hyperactivity Disorder.* Unpublished doctoral dissertation, Boston College.

Haak, R. A. (1990). Using the Sentence Completion to assess emotional disturbance. In C. R. Reynolds & R. W. Kamphaus (Eds.), *Handbook of psychological and educational assessment of children: Personality, behavior, and context* (pp. 147-167). New York: Guilford.

Halperin, J. M., Newcorn, J. H., Sharma, V., Healey, J. M., Wolf, L. E., Pascualvaca, D. M., & Schwartz, S. (1990). Inattentive and noninattentive ADHD children: Do they constitute a unitary group? *Journal of Abnormal Child Psychology, 18*, 437-449.

Halperin, J. M., Wolf, L. E., Pascualvaca, D. M., Newcorn, J. H., Healey, J. M., O'Brien, J. D., Morganstein, A., & Young, J. G. (1988). Differential assessment of attention and impulsivity in children. *Journal of the American Academy of Child and Adolescent Psychiatry, 27*, 326-329.

Harter, S. (1985). *Manual for the Self-Perception Profile for Children.* Denver: University of Denver.

Henker, B., & Whalen, C. K. (1989). Hyperactivity and attention deficits. *American Psychologist, 44,* 216-223.

Herjanic, B., & Campbell, W. (1977). Differentiating psychiatrically disturbed children on the basis of a structured interview. *Journal of Abnormal Child Psychology, 5,* 127-134.

Himadi, W. G., Boice, R., & Barlow, D. H. (1985). Assessment of agoraphobia: Triple response measurement. *Behavior Research and Therapy, 23,* 311-323.

Hinshaw, S. P. (1987). On the distinction between attentional deficits/hyperactivity and conduct problems/aggression in child psychopathology. *Psychological Bulletin, 101,* 443-463.

Hodgens, J. B., & McCoy, J. R. (1989). Distinctions among rejected children on the basis of peer-nominated aggression. *Journal of Clinical Child Psychology, 18,* 121-128.

Hodges, K., & Cools, J. N. (1990). Structured diagnostic interviews. In A. M. LaGreca (Ed.), *Through the eyes of the child* (pp. 109-149). Boston: Allyn and Bacon.

Hodges, K., Cools, J., & McKnew, D. (1989). Test-retest reliability of a clinical research interview for children: The Child Assessment Schedule. *Psychological Assessment, 1,* 317-322.

Hodges, K., Gordon, Y., & Lennon, M. P. (1990). Parent-child agreement on symptoms assessed via a clinical research interview for children: The Child Assessment Schedule (CAS). *Journal of Child Psychology and Psychiatry and Applied Disciplines, 31,* 427-436.

Hodges, K., Kline, J., Stern, L., Cytryn, L., & McKnew, D. (1982). The development of a child assessment interview for research and clinical use. *Journal of Abnormal Child Psychology, 10,* 173-189.

Hodges, K., McKnew, D., Burbach, D. J., & Roebuck, L. (1987). Diagnostic concordance between the Child Assessment Schedule (CAS) and the Schedule for Affective Disorders and Schizophrenia for School-Age Children (K-SADS) in an outpatient sample using lay interviewers. *Journal of the American Academy of Child and Adolescent Psychiatry, 26,* 654-661.

Hodges, K., & Saunders, W. (1989). Internal consistency of a diagnostic interview for children: The Child Assessment Schedule. *Journal of Abnormal Child Psychology, 17,* 691-701.

Hughes, J. (1990). Assessment of social skills: Sociometric and behavioral approaches. In C. R. Reynolds & R. W. Kamphaus (Eds.), *Handbook of psychological and educational assessment of children: Personality, behavior, and context* (pp. 423-444). New York: Guilford.

Jacob, R. G., O'Leary, K. D., & Rosenblad, C. (1978). Formal and informal classroom settings: Effects on hyperactivity. *Journal of Abnormal Child Psychology, 6,* 47-59.

Kagan, J. (1966). Reflection-impulsivity: The generality and dynamics of conceptual tempo. *Journal of Abnormal Psychology, 71,* 17-24.

Kanfer, R., Eyberg, S. M., & Krahn, G. L. (1983). Interviewing strategies in child assessment. In C. E. Walker & M. C. Roberts (Eds.), *Handbook of clinical child psychology* (pp. 95-108). New York: Wiley.

Kaufman, A. S. (1975). Factor analysis of the WISC-R at eleven age levels between 6.5 and 16.5. *Journal of Consulting and Clinical Psychology, 43*, 135-147.

Kazdin, A. E. (1989). Developmental psychopathology. *American Psychologist, 44*, 180-187.

Kazdin, A. E. (1990). Childhood depression. *Journal of Child Psychology and Psychiatry, 31*, 121-160.

Kazdin, A. E., & Esveldt-Dawson, K. (198). The Interview for Antisocial Behavior: Psychometric characteristics and concurrent validity with child psychiatric inpatients. *Journal of Psychopathology and Behavioral Assessment, 8*, 289-303.

Kendall, P. C. (1986). Comments on Rubin and Krasnor: Solutions and problems in research on problem solving. In M. Perlmutter (Ed.), *Cognitive perspectives on children's social and behavioral development: The Minnesota Symposia on Child Psychology* (Vol. 18, pp. 69-76). Hillsdale, NJ: Erlbaum.

Kendall, P. C., & Braswell, L. (1982a). Assessment for cognitive-behavioral interventions in schools. *School Psychology Review, 11*, 21-31.

Kendall, P. C., & Braswell, L. (1982b). Cognitive-behavioral assessment: Model, measures, and madness. In J. N. Butcher & C. D. Speilberger (Eds.), *Advances in personality assessment* (Vol. 1, pp. 35-82). Hillsdale, NJ: Erlbaum.

Kendall, P. C., Cantwell, D. P., & Kazdin, A. E. (1989). Depression in children and adolescents: Assessment issues and recommendations. *Cognitive Therapy and Research, 13*, 109-146.

Kendall, P. C., & Ronan, K. R. (1990). Assessment of children's anxieties, fears, and phobias: Cognitive-behavioral models and methods. In C. R. Reynolds & R. W. Kamphaus (Eds.), *Handbook of psychological and educational assessment of children: Personality, behavior, and context* (pp. 223-244). New York: Guilford.

Knoff, H. M. (1986). The personality assessment report and the feedback and planning conference. In H. M. Knoff (Ed.), *The assessment of child and adolescent personality* (pp. 546-582). New York: Guilford.

Knoff, H. M. (1990). Evaluation of projective drawings. In C. R. Reynolds & R. W. Kamphaus (Eds.), *Handbook of psychological and educational assessment of children: Personality, behavior, and context* (pp. 89-146). New York: Guilford.

Kovacs, M. (1983). *The Interview Schedule for Children (ISC): Form C and the follow-up form.* Unpublished manuscript, University of Pittsburgh, Pittsburgh, PA.

Kuhn, T. S. (1970). *The structure of scientific revolutions* (2nd ed.). Chicago: University of Chicago Press.

Kuhn, T. S. (1977). *The essential tension.* Chicago: University of Chicago Press.

LaGreca, A. M. (1983). Interviewing and behavioral observations. In C. E. Walker & M. C. Roberts (Eds.), *Handbook of clinical child psychology* (pp. 109-131). New York: Wiley.

LaGreca, A. M. (1989, February). *Social anxiety in children: Scale development and validation.* Presented at the First Annual Meeting of the Society for Research in Child and Adolescent Psychopathology, Miami, FL.

LaGreca, A. M., Dandes, S. K., Wick, P., Shaw, K., & Stone, W. L. (1988). Development of the Social Anxiety Scale for Children: Reliability and concurrent validity. *Journal of Clinical Child Psychology, 17*, 84-91.

LaGreca, A. M., & Stone, W. L. (in press). Social anxiety in children: Relationship to peer, teacher, and self-ratings. *Journal of Clinical Child Psychology.*

Lambert, N. M. (1988). Adolescent outcomes for hyperactive children. *American Psychologist, 43*, 786-799.

Lang, P. J., & Lazovik, A. D. (1963). Experimental desensitization of a phobia. *Journal of Abnormal and Social Psychology, 66*, 519-525.

Langner, T. S., Gersten, J. C., & Eisenberg, J. G. (1974). Approaches to measurement and definition in the epidemiology of behavior disorders: Ethnic background and child behavior. *International Journal of Health Services, 4*, 483-501.

Lapouse, R., & Monk, M. A. (1958). An epidemiological study of behavior characteristics in children. *American Journal of Public Health, 48*, 1134-1144.

Last, C. G., & Francis, G. (1988). School phobia. In B. Lahey & A. Kazdin (Eds.), *Advances in clinical child psychology* (Vol. 11, pp. 193-222). New York: Plenum.

Last, C. G., Hersen, M., Kazdin, A. E., Finkelstein, R., & Strauss, C. C. (1987). Comparison of DSM-III Separation Anxiety and Overanxious Disorders: Demographic characteristics and patterns of comorbidity. *Journal of the American Academy of Child and Adolescent Psychiatry, 26*, 527-531.

Levitt, E. E. (1971). Research on psychotherapy with children. In S. L. Garfield & A. E. Bergin (Eds.), *Handbook of psychotherapy and behavior change: An empirical analysis* (pp. 474-494). New York: Wiley.

Lezak, M. (1983). *Neuropsychological assessment.* New York: Oxford University Press.

Lochman, J. E., Meyer, B. L., Rabiner, D. L., & White, K. J. (in press). Parameters influencing social-problem-solving of aggressive children. In R. J. Prinz (Ed.), *Advances in behavioral assessment of children and families* (Vol. 5). London: Kingsley.

Lochman, J. E., White, K. J., & Wayland, K. K. (1990). Cognitive-behavioral assessment and treatment with aggressive children. In P. C. Kendall (Ed.), *Child and adolescent therapy: Cognitive-behavioral procedures* (pp. 25-65). New York: Guilford.

Martin, B., & Hoffman, J. A. (1990). Conduct disorders. In M. Lewis & S. Miller (Eds.), *Handbook of developmental psychopathology* (pp. 109-118). New York: Plenum.

Marsh, H. W. (1990). *Self-Description Questionnaire.* San Antonio, TX: The Psychological Corporation.

Mash, E. J., & Johnston, C. (1983). Parental perceptions of child behavior problems, parenting self-esteem, and mothers' reported stress in younger and older hyperactive and normal children. *Journal of Consulting and Clinical Psychology, 51*, 86-99.

Mash, E. J., & Terdal, L. (Eds.). (1988). *Behavioral assessment of childhood disorders* (2nd ed.). New York: Guilford.

Mattison, R. E., & Bagnato, S. J. (1987). Empirical measurement of overanxious disorders in boys 8 to 12 years old. *Journal of the American Academy of Child and Adolescent Psychiatry, 26*, 536-540.

McClure, F. D., & Gordon, M. (1984). Performance of disturbed hyperactive and nonhyperactive children on an objective measure of hyperactivity. *Journal of Abnormal Child Psychology, 12*, 561-572.

McConaughy, S. H., & Achenbach, T. M. (1988). *Practical guide to the Child Behavior Checklist and related materials.* Burlington, VT: University of Vermont, Department of Psychiatry.

McConaughy, S. H., Achenbach, T. M., & Gent, C. L. (1988). Multiaxial empirically based assessment: Parent, teacher, observational, cognitive, and personality correlates of Child Behavior Profile types for 6- to 11-year-old boys. *Journal of Abnormal Child Psychology, 16*, 485-509.

Miller, S. M., Boyer, B. A., & Rodoletz, M. (1990). Anxiety in children: Nature and development. In M. Lewis & S. Miller (Eds.), *Handbook of developmental psychopathology* (pp. 191-207). New York: Plenum.

Morris, R. J., & Collier, S. J. (1987). Attention Deficit Disorder and Hyperactivity. In C. L. Frame & J. L. Matson (Eds.), *Handbook of assessment in childhood psychopathology: Applied issues in differential diagnosis and treatment evaluation* (pp. 271-321). New York: Plenum.

Morris, R. J., & Kratochwill, T. R. (1983a). *The practice of child therapy.* New York: Pergamon.

Morris, R. J., & Kratochwill, T. R. (1983b). *Treating children's fears and phobias: A behavioral approach.* New York: Pergamon.

Novaco, R. W. (1978). Anger and coping with stress: Cognitive-behavioral intervention. In J. P. Foreyet & D. P. Rathjen (Eds.), *Cognitive behavioral therapy: Research and application* (pp. 135-173). New York: Plenum.

Ollendick, T. H. (1983). Reliability and validity of the revised Fear Survey Schedule for Children (FSSC-R). *Behavior Therapy and Research, 21*, 685-692.

Parker, J. G., & Asher, S. R. (1987). Peer relations and later personal adjustment: Are low-accepted children at risk? *Psychological Bulletin, 102*, 357-389.

Patterson, G. R. (1977). Naturalistic observation in clinical assessment. *Journal of Abnormal Child Psychology, 5*, 309-322.

Patterson, G. R. (1982). *Coercive family process.* Eugene, OR: Castalia.

Patterson, G. R. (1986). Performance models for antisocial boys. *American Psychologist, 41*, 432-444.

Patterson, G. R., Dishion, T. J., & Bank, L. (1984). Family interaction: A process model of deviancy training [Special Issue]. *Aggressive Behavior, 10*, 253-267.

Puig-Antich, J., & Chambers, W. (1978). *The Schedule for Affective Disorders and Schizophrenia for School-Age Children (Kiddie-SADS).* New York: New York State Psychiatric Institute.

Quay, H. C. (1986a). Classification. In H. C. Quay & J. S. Werry (Eds.), *Psychopathological disorders in childhood* (3rd ed., pp. 1-34). New York: Wiley.

Quay, H. C. (1986b). Conduct disorder. In H. C. Quay & J. S. Werry (Eds.), *Psychopathological disorders in childhood* (3rd ed., pp. 35-72). New York: Wiley.

Quay, H. C., & LaGreca, A. M. (1986). Disorders of anxiety, withdrawal, and dysphoria. In H. C. Quay & J. S. Werry (Eds.), *Psychopathological disorders in childhood* (3rd ed., pp. 73-110). New York: Wiley.

Quay, H. C., & Peterson, D. R. (1987). *Manual for the Revised Behavior Problem Checklist.* Coral Gables, FL: University of Miami.

Quay, H. C., Routh, D. K., & Shapiro, S. K. (1987). Psychopathology of childhood: From description to validation. In M. R. Rosenzweig & L. W. Porter (Eds.), *Annual review of psychology* (Vol. 38, pp. 491-532). Palo Alto, CA: Annual Reviews.

Rabiner, D. L., Lenhart, L., & Lochman, J. E. (1990). Automatic versus reflective social problem solving in relation to children's sociometric status. *Developmental Psychology, 26,* 1010-1016.

Reeves, J. C., Werry, J. S., Elkind, G. S., & Zametkin, A. (1987). Attention deficit, conduct, oppositional, and anxiety disorders in children: II. Clinical characteristics. *Journal of the American Academy of Child and Adolescent Psychiatry, 26,* 144-155.

Reynolds, C. R. (1982). Convergent and divergent validity of the revised Children's Manifest Anxiety Scale. *Educational and Psychological Measurement, 42,* 1205-1212.

Reynolds, C. R., & Kamphaus, R. W. (1990). *Handbook of psychological and educational assessment of children: Personality, behavior, and context.* New York: Guilford.

Reynolds, C. R., & Paget, K. D. (1983). National normative and reliability data for the revised Children's Manifest Anxiety Scale. *School Psychology Review, 12,* 324-336.

Reynolds, C. R., & Richmond, B. O. (1978). What I think and feel: A revised measure of children's manifest anxiety. *Anxiety of Abnormal Child Psychology, 6,* 271-280.

Reynolds, C. R., & Richmond, B. O. (1979). Factor structure and construct validity of "What I Think and Feel:" the Revised Children's Manifest Anxiety Scale. *Journal of Personality Assessment, 43,* 281-283.

Robin, A. L., & Foster, S. L. (1989). *Negotiating parent-adolescent conflict: A behavioral family systems approach.* New York: Guilford.

Roff, M., Sell, S. B., & Golden, M. M. (1972). *Social adjustment and personality development in children.* Minneapolis: University of Minnesota Press.

Rohrbeck, C. A., & Twentyman, C. T. (1986). Multimodal assessment of impulsiveness in abusing, neglecting, and nonmaltreating mothers and their preschool children. *Journal of Consulting and Clinical Psychology, 54,* 231-236.

Rosvold, H. E., Mirsky, A. F., Sarason, I., Bransome, E. D., & Beck, L. H. (1956). A continuous performance test of brain damage. *Journal of Consulting and Clinical Psychology, 20,* 343-350.

Routh, D. K., & Daugherty, T. K. (in press). Conduct disorder. In S. R. Hooper, G. W. Hynd, & R. E. Mattison (Eds.), *Assessment and diagnosis of child and adolescent psychiatric disorders: Current issues and procedures.* Hillsdale, NJ: Lawrence Erlbaum Associates.

Rutter, M., Cox, A., Tupling, C., Berger, M., & Yule, W. (1975). Attainment and adjustment in two geographical areas: I. The prevalence of psychiatric disorder. *British Journal of Psychiatry, 126*, 493-509.

Ryan, N. D., Puig-Antich, J., Ambrosini, P., Rabinovich, H., Robinson, D., Nelson, B., Iyengar, S., & Twomey, J. (1987). Clinical picture of major depression in children and adolescents. *Archives of General Psychiatry, 44*, 854-861.

Sattler, J. M. (1988). *Assessment of children.* San Diego, CA: Author.

Schofield, J. W., & Whitley, B. E., (1983). Peer nomination vs. rating measurement of children's peer preference. *School Psychology Quarterly, 46*, 242-251.

Shapiro, E. S., & Skinner, C. H. (1990). Principles of behavioral assessment. In C. R. Reynolds & R. W. Kamphaus (Eds.), *Handbook of psychological and educational assessment of children: Personality, behavior, and context* (pp. 343-363). New York: Guilford.

Sleator, E. K., & Ullman, R. L. (9181). Can the physician diagnose hyperactivity in the office? *Pediatrics, 67*, 13-17.

Speilberger, C. (1973). *Manual for the State-Trait Inventory for Children.* Palo Alto: Consulting Psychologists Press.

Spitzer, R. L., Davies, M., & Barkley, R. A. (1990). The DSM-III-R field trials of disruptive behavior disorders. *Journal of the American Academy of Child and Adolescent Psychiatry, 29,* 690-697.

Strauss, C. C. (1988). Social deficits of children with internalizing disorders. In B. Lahey & A. Kazdin (Eds.), *Advances in clinical child psychology* (Vol. 11, 159-161). New York: Plenum.

Strauss, C. C., Lahey, B. B., Frick, P., Frame, C. L., & Hynd, G. W. (1988). Peer social status of children with anxiety disorders. *Journal of Consulting and Clinical Psychology, 56*, 137-141.

Stroop, J. R. (1935). Studies of interference in serial verbal reactions. *Journal of Experimental Psychology, 18*, 643-662.

Tuma, J. M., & Elbert, J. C. (1990). Critical issues and current practice in personality assessment. In C. R. Reynolds & R. W. Kamphaus (Eds.), *Handbook of psychological and educational assessment of children: Personality, behavior, and context* (pp. 3-29). New York: Guilford.

Watson, J. B. (1913). Psychology as the behaviorist views it. *Psychological Review, 20*, 158-177.

Wenar, C. (1990). Childhood fears and phobias. In M. Lewis & S. Miller (Eds.) *Handbook of developmental psychopathology* (pp. 281-290). New York: Plenum.

Werry, J. S. (1988). In memorium - DSM-III. Letter to the Editor. *Journal of the American Academy of Child and Adolescent Psychiatry, 27*, 138-139.

Williams, S., McGee, R., Anderson, J., & Silva, P. A. (1989). The structure and correlates of self-reported symptoms in 11-year-old children. *Journal of Abnormal Child Psychology, 17*, 55-71.

Witt, J. C., Heffer, R. W., & Pfeiffer, J. (1990). Structured rating scales: A review of self-report and informant rating processes, procedures, and issues. In C. R.

Reynolds & R. W. Kamphaus (Eds.), *Handbook of psychological and educational assessment of children: Personality, behavior, and context* (pp. 364-394). New York: Guilford.

Worchel, F. F., & Dupree, J. L. (1990). Projective storytelling techniques. In C. R. Reynolds & R. W. Kamphaus (Eds.), *Handbook of psychological and educational assessment of children: Personality, behavior, and context* (pp. 70-88). New York: Guilford.

15 BEST PRACTICES IN PRESCHOOL/ DEVELOPMENTAL ASSESSMENT

Steven W. Lee and Annette M. Iverson

The practice of psychoeducational assessment at the early childhood level continues to undergo significant changes. These changes include improvements in the quality and number of instruments available, new models of assessment (i.e., curriculum-based assessment), and legislative mandates (i.e., PL 99-457). It is hoped that this metamorphosis in the assessment of young children will lead to eclectic approaches in assessment that may capitalize on the most recent research, but will not neglect what we have learned in assessment over the past 90 years. The eclectic or ecological-interactive view endorsed here charges the clinician to be knowledgeable of the various models and techniques of assessment of young children and to use them to increase the probability of drawing accurate conclusions about the child in answer to the referral questions.

The chapter leads the reader through an overview of the trends in preschool/developmental assessment that have led us to this point in time. This is followed by a discussion of the salient assessment models that can be employed with young children, along with a brief discussion of some of the most popular tests/techniques in this arena. Of special emphasis is the ecological-interactive model, which can be used as an overarching framework that allows the inclusion of diverse procedures and techniques in the assessment process. The chapter concludes with a discussion of several key issues in the assessment of young children.

HISTORICAL/LEGISLATIVE OVERVIEW OF PRESCHOOL/DEVELOPMENTAL ASSESSMENT

Not unlike other disciplines, numerous events have shaped the movement toward increased and more accurate identification of educational/developmental handicaps in infants and preschool children. Historically, these events may be identified as having three sources: (1) the testing movement, (2) early intervention studies, and (3) federal programs/legislation.

The Testing Movement

The testing movement began in the early to mid-1800s in an attempt "to make a clear distinction between mental incapacity and mental illness" (Sattler, 1988, p. 38). The ball began rolling for the psychological (cognitive) testing movement with the publication of the 1905 Binet intelligence scale. As Brooks-Gunn and Weinraub (1983) state, "the 1905 scale revolutionized the testing movement" (p. 31). After several revisions, the Stanford-Binet test appeared in America in 1916. Although the first test for infants (birth to 3) was cited in 1887, there was a general "lack of interest in infant testing" (Brooks-Gunn & Weinraub, 1983, p. 33).

It wasn't until the mid-1920s that the first published tests for infants and preschool children appeared. Perhaps the most well known were Kuhlmann's downward extension of the Binet-Simon scale and the Linfert and Hierholzer standardized intelligence test for infants (Brooks-Gunn & Weinraub, 1983). At about the same time as these instruments were produced, Arnold Gesell at Yale was interested in normal growth and development in babies, toddlers, and preschool children. Gesell's investigations yielded the Gesell Developmental Schedules, which provided fundamental information on the behavioral development of infants and young children. The "Schedules" supplied the developmental norms upon which developmental scales could be constructed and based.

Early instruments developed in the 1920s and 1930s lacked good psychometric properties, but instruments like Cattell's Infant Intelligence Scale and Griffith's Mental Development scale improved on reliability indices, although they still lacked solid evidence of predictive validity (Brooks-Gunn & Weinraub, 1983). Within the past 20 years, the development of instruments like the Bayley Scales of Infant Development (Bayley, 1969) and the Battelle Developmental Inventory (Newborg, Stock, Wnek, Guidubaldi, & Svinicki, 1984) has provided greater promise for improved psychometric properties.

The impetus for social-emotional assessment of young children came from the realization that cognitive/developmental assessment yielded little information about children's social and emotional functioning. Although interviewing and direct observation had been used for some time, instruments designed to evaluate social-emotional abilities in young children have developed within the past 25 years. These tests, like the early Preschool Attainment Record (Doll, 1966), function as rating scales using a parent or teacher to estimate the young child's skills. Advances in these types of rating scales have led to instruments with better psychometric properties and more specific uses (Martin, 1986).

Although infant and preschool testing has lagged behind assessment of adults and school-aged children, this is not necessarily seen as a disadvantage. The focus on the disadvantages of normative testing in the late 1960s and early 1970s, which led to the public backlash against the testing movement, caused the pendulum to swing toward a more ecological perspective on psychoeducational testing. This perspective of the 1990s includes the use of informal and criterion-referenced tools, direct observation, interviewing, naturalistic inquiry, curriculum-based assessment, as well as the use of normative instruments to evaluate not only the child, but also his or her environment. Because few normative developmental instruments were available during the late 1960s and early 1970s, the area of preschool and developmental assessment has benefited from our increased awareness of the need for multisourced psychoeducational evaluations.

Early Intervention Studies

As Fallen and Umansky (1985) point out, the rationale for early education of young children came from many sources, including animal studies and work in the fields of medicine and child development. Similar findings from these heterogeneous studies seemed to lead to the conclusion that if poor and/or handicapped children could receive early educational intervention, they might be more proficient socially and educationally when they eventually enter school.

The initial results for early intervention programs suggested significant benefits to the participants (Ferry, 1981; Gottfried, 1973). More recent investigations and meta-analytic studies, however, have concluded that the results are mixed (Casto & Mastropieri, 1986; Haskins, 1989). Early intervention programs seem to result in immediate short-term benefit in intellectual performance and academic achievement, and reduced grade retention or placement in special education when the child enters school (Casto & Mastropieri, 1986; Haskins, 1989). Similar intellectual and academic gains are noted for children in Head Start programs; however, stable, long-term, positive effects of Head Start have yet to be realized (Haskins, 1989).

The emphasis on early intervention programs has naturally led to a perceived need to use psychoeducational instruments to do everything from determining which children qualify for which programs to evaluating the efficacy of the programs themselves (Spodek, 1982). Therefore, the need to provide information on the effects of early intervention programs spurred the growth of tests designed to evaluate the skills, abilities, and behaviors of young children.

Federal Programs/Legislation

The federal government's recognition of the need to provide medical, social, and educational services to handicapped citizens in the United States led to the development of many special programs for young children. Although the involvement of the federal government in special education was restricted prior to the 1960s (Fallen & Umansky, 1985), the passage of an important series of laws in the mid-1960s heightened awareness and provided funding for various types of programs that would aid medically, socially, and economically deprived children. These laws included the 1964 Maternal, Child Health and Mental Retardation Act, the 1965 Elementary and Secondary Education Act, and the 1964 Educational Opportunity Act which established Project Head Start (Lichtenstein & Ireton, 1984).

The passage of the Handicapped Children's Early Education Assistance Act of 1968 was the first legislation designed to provide educational programs for young handicapped children. In 1974, the passage of the Economic Opportunity and Community Partnership Act required Head Start programs to have at least 10% handicapped young children on their rolls (Fallen & Umansky, 1985). "By 1975, 61 federal laws related to the handicapped had been passed with Public Law (PL) 94-142 serving as the cornerstone" (Paget & Bracken, 1983, p. 12).

PL 94-142 required free, public education for *all handicapped* children within the least restrictive environment. This law defines eligible children as ranging from ages 3 to 21. The implementation of PL 94-142 for young children was frequently delayed as "priorities for serving children were established such that states must first serve school aged children who are in an inappropriate placement, and, finally, preschool children" (Fallen & Umansky, 1985, p. 4). The lag in the development of preschool programs for handicapped preschoolers, perceived problems with PL 94-142, and the lack of programs for handicapped infants and toddlers (birth to 2) led to the passage of PL 99-457, the Education for the Handicapped Act Amendments of 1986 (Part H).

The reforms specified in PL 99-457 focused on implementing a new eligibility system for services that provides for infants and toddlers who are experiencing developmental delays, or for those who are at risk for developmental delay due to medical conditions or environmental circumstances. In addition, PL 99-457 recognized the importance of family involvement and empowerment. By creating the Individualized Family Service Plan (IFSP), the involvement of the family is required in all educational programming. From another perspective, this legislation recognized the difficulties that families face while trying to cope with and manage a handicapped infant or toddler. PL 99-457 attempts to provide families with needed professional support through a defined link with the educational system (Gallagher, 1989).

It can be seen that the testing movement, early intervention studies, and federal legislation all played a significant and interactive role in the preschool/developmental testing movement. As a reaction to these trends, scholars in this area have responded by positing various models for psychoeducational assessment for young children that represent the most current trends in child assessment. These models and trends will be the focus of the next section.

OVERVIEW OF MODELS AND THEORIES OF PRE-SCHOOL/DEVELOPMENTAL ASSESSMENT

The newest models used for the assessment of young children, coupled with our older and more venerable methods, provide the knowledgeable clinician with an impressive array of techniques and procedures to assess cognitive functioning, evaluate social-emotional concerns, or identify interventions. This section will analyze various approaches/models of assessment for young children and attempt to detail the salient characteristics of each. In addition, attention will be given to the advantages of each approach with a bent toward what each approach may offer the clinician. Although each of these models is presented separately, many actually overlap with each other and share some common tenets and techniques. For example, when home or classroom observations are discussed within the behavioral model, it is recognized that these observations could also be called informal techniques. It is hoped that the reader will come away with an eclectic view of how best to evaluate psychological, educational, and developmental problems in infants, toddlers, and preschool children.

The Traditional Model

The traditional model of assessment is quite well known in psychology. It has medical model roots and posits that psychosocial problems of the individual are due to some intrapsychic disturbance or defective trait. The traditional approach makes the assumption of cross-situational constancy. For example, behaviors exhibited in one setting would also be shown in other settings. From an assessment perspective, observed behaviors are viewed as signs or indicators of the underlying psychological disturbance (Shapiro, 1987).

Because the nature of the problem is viewed as residing within the child, the focus of the evaluation would naturally include the child and would largely ignore surrounding environmental influences. The traditional model psychologist may use psychometric tests, but would also include interviews and projective techniques to identify signs denoting the nature of the underlying disorder. Diagnosis of the disorder follows a medical model orientation (Lee, 1991), and prescriptive treatment would focus on resolution of the underlying conflict. A traditional treatment of choice for young children might be play therapy.

Although few psychologists hold to a strict traditional view of assessment, there are elements of this position that warrant consideration. The traditional model has taught us the importance of the child's viewpoint on the problem. Discussion or interviews with the child (regardless of age) about the child's concerns are techniques that are sometimes lost with other models of assessment. The notion of "child study" comes from the traditional model of assessment. It connotes an *in-depth* examination of the child, including thoughts, behaviors, motivations, and emotions, which is most certainly of merit.

The Developmental Model

The developmental model as described here is defined narrowly and posits that children progress through stages or milestones of development. Stage theorists like Piaget and Erickson maintain that each child passes through these stages in a specific order (Brainerd, 1978). From a functional standpoint, infants and children show certain behaviors that are indicative of attainment of a milestone or certain stage-linked abilities. Most developmentalists believe that maturation occurs as a result of the interaction of the physically maturing child with his or her environment (i.e., parents, school).

Developmental assessment techniques have frequently used observation methods and parental interviews to document the degree to which a child has passed through a developmental stage. Instruments (Uzgiris & Hunt, 1975) have also been developed to assist the evaluator in determining the degree of stage or milestone attainment. The developmental model has been criticized as an inappropriate way to assess development for handicapped infants and preschoolers, as they do not routinely follow the normal developmental progression (Berkeley & Ludlow, 1989). Strict developmental assessment may also be criticized on the grounds that assessment results are not easily translated outside the bounds of the particular theory of development used for the evaluation. This is likely one of the reasons for the limited popularity of strict developmental (stage) assessment.

Developmental assessment teaches us that both informal and formal techniques may be used fruitfully to evaluate developmental progress in young children. In addition, the contribution of stages (theories) of development provides additional dimensions for clinicians to form and validate their hypotheses about the children they are evaluating. Finally, developmental theories provide a scaffold for abilities or behaviors that can be expected as the child grows and matures. Therefore, information about behaviors to be expected allows teachers and/or parents to assist more fully in the child's learning through planned environmental manipulations.

The Normative/Standardized Test Model

This familiar model of assessment assumes that the ability or behaviors of a child may best be evaluated by comparing each child's responses to standard stimuli (test questions or problems) with the responses of other children of the same age, sex, race, or handicap. These comparisons with the target child's norm group provide an indicator of the child's ability or behavior as compared to his or her peers. Comparisons with the normative group are frequently used to characterize the child's ability as below or above average, or mentally retarded or gifted. Within this model, high-quality tests are viewed as having good psychometric properties (i.e., reliability and validity). If a test reliably and accurately measures a construct (i.e., motor skills), proponents of this model believe that reliable conclusions may be drawn about the ability of the child in the measured domain.

Although this model is quite popular, it is not without criticisms. McLoughlin and Lewis (1981) point out that standardized tests collect only a small sample of behavior that cannot be expected to be representative. The use of standardized tests that lack reliability and validity leads to inaccurate conclusions and magnifies the problem of collecting such small samples of behavior. The lack of predictive accuracy of these tests for young children is well known; therefore, the prognostic value of these tests is limited.

Proponents of this model point out that because these tests are administered in a standardized format, they are more objective representations of the child's ability than makeshift testing that uses different materials and verbal prompts and may allow the child varying amounts of time to respond (Maloney & Ward, 1976). Standardized/normative tests summarize the child's skills and abilities in quantifiable terms, thus allowing for discrimination among children on the basis of ability or behavior.

This model strives toward the objective measurement of important skills and abilities in young children. The notion of comparing children's behavior or abilities with normative groups provides the basis for standardized/normative testing. If these tests are psychometrically viable, this model has much to offer in efficiency, economy, and predictive power (Maloney & Ward, 1976). Regardless of the psychometric properties of these tests, these tests are frequently administered outside the child's normal environment (i.e., classroom, home); therefore, generalizations to these environments should be made with great care.

The Behavioral Model

In the behavioral model, behaviors occur as a function of the antecedents and consequences surrounding the behavior. An analysis of these events in the natural environment, including the fluctuations in the frequency of the target behavior(s), is the form of behavioral assessment. Situational specificity is a hallmark of the behavioral model. The child's minute-to-minute behavior can be traced to the situational demands of the setting. Therefore, a thorough analysis of the environment should yield the key influences on the target behavior(s). It is not surprising that behavioral observations are the key tool of the behavioral model.

The popularity of behavioral assessment has not only led to its frequent use in psychoeducational testing, but also to criticisms of the behavioral model and its methods. Behavioral approaches to assessment have been viewed as too molecular, focusing on small behavior changes while ignoring the individual as a whole. In addition, parents and teachers have spurned behavioral change techniques because they are viewed as too manipulative.

The value of the behavioral model for assessment has been well outlined by Shapiro (1987). Behavior observations made in home, preschool, or day care settings are more ecologically valid, and inferences for the home or school setting are more easily made because the assessment took place in the target setting. The collection of behavioral data in a psychoeducational assessment provides baseline measurements (i.e., number frequencies) against which intervention programs may be compared. Finally, behavioral technology is relatively easy to use. With proper (and frequently minimal) training, persons may be trained to record behavior frequencies or duration accurately and implement behavior change programs.

The Judgment-Based Model

Judgment-based assessment (JBA) assumes that the members of the environments of a specific child each have their own perceptions and beliefs about the child. One may attain useful and valid information about a child by tapping these perceptions and beliefs.

Proponents of JBA believe that psychology's quantitative study of group behavior does not yield information about individual differences that is necessary for producing successful interventions for individual children (Hayes, 1990). JBA is consistent with the multisourced assessments that are required by PL 94-142 and 99-457, as they use rating scales, checklists, and observations gathered from many professionals, parents, and the child during the assessment. As suggested by Fleischer, Belgredan, Bagnato, and Ogonosky (1990), "the format characteristics of judgment-based measures provide the capability to focus also on wider ranging, often ambiguous variables such as reactivity, motivation, endurance, and temperament [response classes]. . . . [S]uch measures of response classes, when placed on a continuum, produce more accurate parental assessments" (Wolfensberger & Kurtz, 1981, p. 17).

The controversy surrounding clinical judgment versus statistical (actuarial) prediction has raged for many years (Holt, 1970; Sawyer, 1966). Meehl's (1954) book *Clinical Versus Statistical Prediction* ignited the controversy, as Meehl concluded in his review that actuarial predictions were superior to clinical judgments. Criticism of the judgment-based model stems from the assertion that clinical judgments are subject to constantly fluctuating beliefs, attributions, and physical variables of the judge that make objective judgments (ratings) inherently inaccurate. However, Hayes (1990), reports that ratings are frequently used in *all* psychoeducational assessment instruments, so assuming that judgments are not made on "objective" tests is inaccurate. There are beliefs that people hold that may only be evaluated using a judgment-based approach to assessment (Hayes, 1990).

JBA may be more important for evaluating young children than any other age students. Because young children lack language facility, their parents and teachers become extremely valuable sources of information on the day-to-day behavior of the infant or preschooler. In some cases, these ratings are the only feasible way to collect the needed information about the child. The clinician can gain valuable insight into the child's world when that world is viewed within the context of the familiar rater.

The Ethnographic/Naturalistic Inquiry Model

Naturalistic inquiry is an inductive approach to assessment for young children that features data collection by the evaluator as a "participant observer" into the environment of the youngster. Standardized and normative techniques are eschewed in favor of interviews and observations to view the child in the natural environment. Proponents argue that the open-ended nature of the assessment allows for rapport to be built easily, resulting in more natural responses from parents, teachers, and children (Odom & Shuster, 1986). The data and information obtained from naturalistic inquiry are viewed as rich, complete, and insightful.

Odom and Shuster (1986) report that dangers of this approach include becoming too involved with child or family and actually influencing events as they occur. In addition, the approach may be not be amenable to traditional time frames for psychoeducational assessment, as much time is needed with the family and child in order to develop rapport for gathering data on "naturally" occurring responses. Last, the amount of data collected may be too unwieldy and difficult to summarize or draw meaning from the information (Odom & Shuster, 1986).

Although there seem to be certain limitations associated with the use of data from naturalistic inquiry, there are elements of the approach that may add significantly to the collected assessment information. First, open-ended interviews provide the opportunity for the clinician to tailor the questions to the specific questions to be answered, or to the information the interviewee is able to provide. Second, the information collected when the clinician takes the time to develop adequate rapport is likely to be rich and more in depth and a more accurate representation of the child's abilities than quickly administered test batteries. Furthermore, clinicians who work with young children on a routine basis know the value of rapport building before *any* meaningful response may be elicited.

The Salient Responses Model

This model was developed as a result of dissatisfaction with the use of the developmental model with handicapped children. Numerous authors (Berkeley & Ludlow, 1989; Garwood, 1982; Switzky, Rotatori, Miller, & Freagon, 1979) have been critical of the developmental model on the grounds that handicapped children do not necessarily follow normal developmental progressions. Similarly, curricula based on the developmental model are inappropriate for handicapped infants and preschoolers. As a result of these (and other) concerns, Lewis and Starr (1979) advanced a model based on traits that may be observed across all domains of development. These attributes are dimensions of any response, including characteristics such as speed of response, quantity of responses, or quality of response. As pointed out by Berkeley and Ludlow (1989), "as the child develops, play changes with respect to salient response attributes: the amount of time the child spends engaged in play (quantity); the differentiation of the actions the child employs to play with different objects (quality); the length of time it takes the child to learn new play skills (speed of acquisition)" (p. 61). Proponents of this model believe that these general variables may provide a more accurate representation of ability and progress than developmental assessment and curricula (Berkeley & Ludlow, 1989).

The model has had limited use since it was proposed 12 years ago. Some reasons for this include some potential drawbacks of the model that have been suggested by Berkeley and Ludlow (1989). These limitations include the time necessary to implement the model, which may involve retraining of staff and the development of nonstandardized instruments for assessment. Communication with other professionals trained in the developmental model may be inhibited due to their inexperience with assessment of this sort.

Elements of the model offer valuable insight to professionals who have assumed that all children (including handicapped children) follow the same developmental path as they grow and mature. The salient responses model does not assume this to be true, resulting in an alternative assessment methodology based on key dimensions that span ages and developmental milestones. The use of Lewis and Starr's (1979) suggestions for assessing behavior variables that are "salient" may cast a new light on skills and abilities of young children that are not apparent through traditional psychoeducational assessment results. In addition, these behavioral dimensions may be a more sensitive measure of the unique educational growth and maturational characteristics of young handicapped children.

The Curriculum-Based Assessment (CBA) Model

Curriculum-based assessment fundamentally means that evaluation takes place on what the student has learned within the curriculum. Thus, assessment should include an analysis of the curriculum and the student's progress within it. Frequently CBA is ongoing, providing a moving picture of the student's progress rather than a snapshot of abilities at one point in time. This monitoring allows for more incisive and cogent interventions. Using the curriculum as its base, interventions based on CBA seem to have greater ecological and content validity resulting in better recommendations that match the child and the teaching environment.

In evaluating infants and preschool children, CBAs may focus on "curriculum-embedded" or "curriculum-referenced" assessment (Salvia &

Hughes, 1990). Curriculum-embedded assessment used an actual published curriculum as the vehicle for assessment. There are several published curricula for infants and preschool children that provide ongoing assessment tools in the package that relate very specifically to what is taught. Curriculum-referenced assessment denotes evaluation of developmental skills that underlie most of the developmental curricula commercially available. In this way, ongoing developmental assessment using developmental batteries provides results that can be translated into the child's skills on most developmental curricula.

Curriculum-based assessment has been widely embraced as an alternative to testing practices of the 1960s, 70s, and 80s that had little relevance to the consumers of psychological test results. However, CBAs have been criticized on their technical adequacy and lack of standardization (Shinn, Rosenfield, & Knutson, 1989). This does not seem to be a major concern, however, as CBAs are designed more as criterion-referenced measures than norm-referenced instruments. The degree to which CBAs relate to the curriculum seems to be more important than their traditional psychometric properties.

In the evaluation of infants and preschool children, CBA has much to offer the clinician and his or her clients. Ongoing monitoring of teaching and learning at the preschool level may be more important than any other age given the rapidity of change and growth at these formative ages. The CBA model provides a system for ongoing monitoring, especially when curriculum-embedded material is used. In addition, CBA offers the closest link between the assessment and the curriculum, allowing for relevant interventions with a greater probability of a close child–curriculum match.

The Informal Assessment Model

Informal assessment, as proposed by Abbott and Crane (1977), may not in fact be a model per se, but rather a set of heterogeneous techniques that warrant mention here because of their potential value in evaluating young children. Informal measures are non–norm-referenced, unstandardized instruments or techniques. Informal measures have value in their flexibility of use and content validity for the assessment at hand. Informal tools "used in early childhood education settings include anecdotal records, time samples, skills checklists, rating scales, product evaluation and coded observations" (Abbott & Crane, p. 122). Another less frequently used but valuable informal technique has been referred to as "informal process testing" (Lee & Elliott, 1988).

All of these tools have value in that they can be altered to help answer the referral questions and they yield information not usually attainable through other methods. Informal process testing (Lee & Elliott, 1988) is the evaluation of developmental skills through tasks that can be altered and are not standardized. Elements of informal process testing include techniques like *trial lessons*, in which the systematic manipulation of key learning factors (i.e., presentation of stimuli, physical materials, reinforcers) may be done to assess the way in which learning may best be stimulated. Fundamentally, approaches like these are flexibly administered and provide information on potentially fruitful, child-specific teaching methods.

Criticism of informal tools remains similar to that of other nonstandardized instruments (i.e., poor psychometric properties, no norms); however, it is the lack of these elements that makes informal testing an especially valuable adjunct to traditional or normative assessment (Lee & Elliot, 1988). The results obtained from informal testing can be closely related to the curriculum and specific teaching methods for a specific child. For young children, the variability of their responses to standardized/normative testing provides a niche for flexible assessment that allows for their individual competencies to come to the forefront.

The Ecological-Interactive Model

Perhaps the broadest model for viewing the assessment of young children may be the ecological-interactive model (EIM). The EIM, as proposed by Paget and Nagle (1986), posits that many interacting elements have played (and will continue to play) a role in the behavior and development of the young child. To understand the skills and abilities of any child, these elements and their interaction are the focus of the assessment. More specifically, the ecological-interactive model proposes that the child should be evaluated within the context of systems such as school, family, peers, and community that constantly interact with the child and with each other resulting in the behavior (competencies) shown by the young child. Although the clinician may begin by assessing the child, these other key elements of the child's life are also evaluated and considered.

The ecological-interactive model utilizes multidimensional assessment methods (Paget & Nagel, 1986). These methods would not rule out any or all of the techniques or instruments of the previously mentioned models. Indeed, the clinician who holds to this view might use some approaches to assessment of young children not previously mentioned. For example, family interviews (Wilson, 1986), evaluation of the day care or preschool environment, peer nominations or ratings, and a demographic evaluation of the community would undoubtedly provide helpful information about the context of the young child's behavior and abilities. From Paget and Nagle's (1986) viewpoint, instruments and methods of this sort "will contribute substantially to the creation of an ecologically-valid assessment methodology for use by school psychologists" (p. 159).

Summary of Models

The summary of models presented above sought to outline briefly the tenets, and highlight the techniques and approaches, of each model. Although each model has value in the assessment of young children, the ecological-interactive approach is an overarching model, under which an eclectic view of assessment may be formed. An eclectic view of assessment places an increased number of techniques at our disposal, thus providing added opportunities for making informed decisions for the infants, young children, and their parents whom we serve.

OVERVIEW OF TESTS

Based on a model of ecological-interactive assessment of young children and their families, brief reviews of tests are presented by category: screening, diagnostic assessment of developmental disabilities, family assessment, classroom environment assessment, developmental assessment, curriculum-based assessment/special populations, and social/emotional assessment. Reviews may include the following: name of instrument, author and date of publication, what the test measures, age range, mode of administration, scoring criteria, standardization population, appropriate populations to whom the test may be administered, and application/intervention links to the classroom and/or clinic.

Assessment of competence in young children necessarily involves a multimeasure/multisource approach (Bagnato, Neisworth, & Munson, 1989). Meaningful information about a child cannot be derived from the use of one measure in isolation from others. A thorough evaluation includes a careful selection from the full array of instruments to assess the child's developmental skill level, his or her functioning in the home and/or school environments, and the family's needs and leads to functional, developmentally appropriate goals for the home, school, or clinic.

Screening/Assessment

The primary purpose of screening is to identify children who appear to need special services to achieve their maximum potential (Lichtenstein & Ireton, 1984). Screening instruments are often used by professionals conducting Child Finds in which large numbers of children are evaluated. These instruments should not be used for diagnosis of developmental disabilities, development of interventions, or program evaluation. They also should not be used alone but should include careful observation of the child's behavior in home and school settings. Selected screening instruments that can be used in the school or clinic are summarized below.

1. Battelle Developmental Inventory Screening Test (Newborg, Stock, Wnek, Guidubaldi, & Svinicki, 1984). The Battelle consists of 96 items across five domains: personal-social, adaptive, motor, communication, and cognitive (birth through 8 years). It is individually administered via direct or naturalistic observation or parent interview. It was standardized on 800 children representative of the general population.

2. Denver Developmental Screening Test (Frankenburg, Dodds, Fandal, Kazuk, & Cohrs, 1975). The Denver consists of 105 items across four domains: gross motor, fine motor, adaptive language, and personal-social (2 weeks to 6.4 years). It is individually administered via direct testing and some parent interview. It was standardized on 1,036 children from the Denver area.

3. Developmental Profile II (Alpern, Boll, & Shearer, 1980). This test consists of 186 items across five scales: physical, self-help, social, academic, and communication (birth to 9 years). It is individually administered via interview and some direct testing. It was standardized on 3,008 children and underrepresents Oriental, Spanish-American, and mixed and rural backgrounds.

4. Developmental Indicators for the Assessment of Learning—Revised (Mardell-Czudnowski & Goldenberg, 1983). The DIAL-R consists of 24 items in three domains: gross and fine motor, concepts, and language (2 to 6 years). It also has 8 additional behavioral items. It can be individually administered by one assessor but is typically administered by a team

of assessors to large numbers of children, e.g. kindergarten screening. It was standardized on 2,477 children.

5. Minnesota Child Development Inventory (Ireton & Thwing, 1972). The MCDI consists of 320 items across eight scales: general development, gross motor, fine motor, expressive language, comprehension, conceptual situation comprehension, self-help, and personal-social (1 to 6 years). It is individually administered via a maternal report inventory. It was standardized on 796 children from a Minneapolis suburb.

Diagnostic Assessment

Norm-referenced assessment instruments provide for comparisons of a child's performance with that of other children the same age. Thus, these instruments are typically used for diagnostic and classification purposes. It is recommended that the assessor look beyond norm-referenced test scores to observations of behavior to understand processes children use to arrive at responses. Furthermore, it is often useful to administer tests under nonstandardized conditions, to modify test materials, and to accept nonstandard responses to truly understand children's strengths and weaknesses. Caution is suggested when interpreting differences in performance under standardized and nonstandardized conditions to parents and teachers. These instruments are typically criticized for their poor linkage to interventions that lead to improved outcomes for children. When an instrument is helpful in developing intervention plans and in evaluating progress of preschoolers, it is noted in the review. All of the instruments listed below are individually administered and are appropriate for diagnosis and classification in the school or clinic.

1. Battelle Developmental Inventory (Newborg et al., 1984). The Battelle yields scores across five domains: personal/social, adaptive, communication, motor, and cognitive (birth through 8 years). Separate portions or domain-specific subareas can be administered by professionals, including special educators and preschool and day care staff. Items may be scored through structured test format, naturalistic observation, and parent or teacher interview. The manual describes procedural adaptations for handicapped children (e.g., motor, visual, hearing, speech, emotionally impaired, and multiply handicapped), but separate norms are not available. Authors suggest using this measure to make placement decisions, monitor a child's progress, and develop intervention plans. However, caution is

recommended in using this norm-referenced test as a criterion-referenced assessment device (Boyd, 1989).

2. The Bayley Scales of Infant Development (Bayley, 1969). The Bayley consists of a mental and a motor index plus an interpretive social behavior record (1 to 36 months). It is individually administered via direct testing and some direct and naturalistic observation. It is widely used with low-functioning preschool-aged children and infants and toddlers and is recommended for diagnosis, prescriptive teaching, and repeated testing in evaluation of intervention/program outcomes (Haskins, Ramey, Stedman, Blacher-Dixon, & Pierce, 1978). In particular, it is a good instrument to use with the mentally retarded and visually impaired.

3. Hiskey-Nebraska Test of Learning Aptitude (Hiskey, 1966). The Hiskey-Nebraska consists of 12 subscales requiring motor responses (for children ages 3 through 17 years). It is a performance test that can be administered verbally or through pantomimed gestures. No verbal responses are required and, thus, it is useful with deaf children and many young mentally retarded children. It has been normed on deaf and normal children but normative data are relatively weak under age 5; also, a basal may not be attained for delayed 3-year-olds.

4. Kaufman Assessment Battery for Children (Kaufman & Kaufman, 1983). The K-ABC consists of four subscales: Sequential Processing, Simultaneous Processing, a Mental Processing Composite, and Achievement (2½ through 12½ years). The K-ABC was developed from a theoretical foundation that focuses on the individual's information-processing and problem-solving style. Recent research suggests that sequential-simultaneous interpretations may not apply to preschoolers (Keith, 1985). Keith's (1985) factor analysis suggests that a one-factor solution (a simultaneous factor) or a two-factor solution (a reasoning factor and a verbal memory factor) may best explain the data for the 5-year-old age group. Professionals are urged to study the extensive research conducted with the K-ABC and educate themselves in the most effective uses (Paget & Barnett, 1990).

5. McCarthy Scales of Children's Abilities (McCarthy, 1972). The McCarthy consists of a global measure of cognitive ability and measures of specific abilities: Verbal, Perceptual-Performance, Quantitative, Memory, and Motor (2½ to 8½ years). It lacks provision for children's refusals and has a limited floor, requiring extrapolated scores with the moderately and severely developmentally disabled. In addition, factor-analytic studies show that a quantitative factor does not appear for 3- and 4-year-olds

(Kaufman, 1975). Wide scatter is common and does not necessarily imply deficiencies. The manual asserts that it is useful for assessing children with mental retardation, sensory deficits, speech deficits, giftedness, and learning disabilities; however, none of these groups were in the normative sample. The McCarthy scales contain colorful and interesting materials useful for children with a short attention span and low frustration tolerance. The scales provide information regarding an individual's strengths and weaknesses and, thus, can be useful in long-range planning and in establishing short-term goals (Kahn, 1988).

6. The Stanford-Binet Intelligence Scale, Fourth Edition (Thorndike, Hagen, & Sattler, 1986). The Stanford-Binet consists of eight preschool subtests: Vocabulary, Comprehension, Absurdities, Quantitative, Pattern Analysis, Copying, Bead Memory, and Memory for Sentences (2 through 5 years). It was devised using a theoretical model of intelligence. Although it is possible to obtain a single score reflecting "general" ability, it also yields subscales termed Verbal Reasoning, Abstract/Visual Reasoning, Quantitative Reasoning, and Short-Term Memory. Thus, it separates abilities influenced by school-like experiences from those thought to depend less on such experiences. From an ecological perspective, this represents an improved method for assessing preschoolers with no preschool experience (Paget & Barnett, 1990).

7. Wechsler Preschool and Primary Scale of Intelligence - Revised (Wechsler, 1989). The recently revised WPPSI-R yields a global score of intellectual ability and Verbal and Performance subscales (3 years to 7 years 3 months). Originally, the WPPSI (Wechsler, 1967) was developed from a downward extension of items from the Wechsler Intelligence Scale for Children. However, the new revised edition uses colorful test materials, with a number of new test items. The WPPSI-R is used as a diagnostic tool, to identify and classify children with cognitive deficits, to make placement decisions, and to develop long-range educational goals.

Family Assessment

The expansion in family roles in early intervention programs shifts more emphasis onto the assessment of family needs and strengths. From assessment results the clinic or school professional can develop interventions to address family needs that have negatively impacted the family system and the preschool child. Specific descriptions of measures that assess varied aspects of family needs and resources follow.

1. The Survey of Family Needs (Bailey, 1988). This measure assesses six major categories: needs for information, support, explanation of child's handicapping condition to others, community services, financial help, and family functioning.

2. The Family Support Scale (Dunst, Jenkins, & Trivette, 1984). This measure assesses the availability of 18 possible sources of social support and the family's judgment of the helpfulness of each available support.

3. The Family Adaptability and Cohesion Evaluation Scale (Olson, Portner, & Lavee, 1985). The FACES III is a 20-item self-report scale that measures: family adaptability (flexibility) and cohesion (emotional closeness) as currently perceived and as ideal. The difference between the perceived and the ideal yields a measure of family satisfaction.

Assessment of Preschool Classrooms

In addition to family ecology, preschool classroom ecology has profound effects on children's behavior (Carta, Sainato, & Greenwood, 1988; Moore, 1987, 1988; Rogers-Warren, 1982; Rogers-Warren & Wedel, 1980; Twardosz, 1984). Knowledge of salient classroom features and resultant effects on children is important to access. From the results, a classroom manager can make adjustments in the classroom setting that encourage engagement in activities (i.e., learning, social). Listed below are assessment instruments developed to quantify the various components of preschool environments. These are appropriate for school use and for clinical use when children's referral problems may be related to school environments.

1. Planned Activity Check (Risley & Cataldo, 1973). The PLA-Check yields the percentage of children who are engaged and which materials, activities, people, or schedules generate the greatest amount of interest and participation. It yields a group level of engagement from which the professional may generate appropriate classroom interventions.

2. Caregiver Assessment of Child Engagement (McWilliam & Galant, 1984). The CACE yields engagement levels for individual children. Two types (attentional and active) and three categories (adults, peers, and materials) of engagement are measured on a rating scale of specific classroom activities such as snack time. Based on results, the classroom structure can be modified to increase appropriate engagement levels for a particular child.

3. Daily Engagement Rating Scale (McWilliam, Galant, & Dunst, 1984). The DERS is similar to the CACE except that it provides a daily measure of engagement for all activities taken together.

4. Early Childhood Environment Rating Scale (Harms & Clifford, 1980). The ECERS includes 37 items across seven subareas: personal-care routines, furnishings and display, language-reasoning experiences, fine and gross motor activities, creative activities, social development, and adult needs (3 to 6 years). Items are scored on a 7-point scale for provision of support. The ECERS yields an overall picture of preschool settings including how materials, space, child-level activities, classroom scheduling, and adult supervision are organized and used. This setting evaluation gives direction to professionals who wish to maximize the use of environmental resources.

5. Infant/Toddler Environment Rating Scale (Harms, Cryer, & Clifford, 1989). The ITERS is similar to the ECERS in its framework for environmental assessment. It assesses the quality of care provided for children under age 30 months.

6. Family Day Care Rating Scale (Harms & Clifford, 1989). The FDCRS includes 32 items across six categories: space and furnishings for care and learning, basic care, language and reasoning, learning activities, social development, and adult needs (infancy through kindergarten). Each item is described in four levels of quality: inadequate (does not even meet custodial care needs), minimal (meets custodial needs and, to some degree, basic developmental needs), good (meets developmental needs), excellent (high-quality personalized care). The FDCRS items assess each of the six CDA competency goals established by the Child Development Associate Family Day Care credential. It is a parallel of the ITERS and ECERS. It assesses the quality of care provided in family/home day care and is useful in self-evaluation by care providers, for supervision and monitoring, and for program evaluation.

7. Infant/Toddler Learning Project Observation System (Rogers-Warren, Santos-Colond, Warren, & Hasselbring, 1984, cited in Dunst, McWilliam, & Holbert, 1986). The ITLP includes 34 items across seven categories: physical environment, classroom scheduling, material availability, appropriateness of learning activities, behavior management, child-caregiver interactions, and classroom safety (birth to 2 years). Items are rated on a 5-point scale for attention to the classroom environment.

8. Preschool Assessment of the Classroom Environment Scale (Dunst et al., 1986). The PACE includes 70 items across four categories: program

organization, environmental organization, methods of instruction, and program outcomes (birth to 6 years). Items are scored on a 5-point rating scale. Lengthy administration includes observation of the environment, an interview of managers of classrooms, and a review of written materials. A five-step process results in developing and implementing changes in the classroom ecology.

Developmental Assessment

Ordinal scales have been developed from Piaget's theory to assess children's developmental stages. Piagetian-based tools are not norm-referenced and not frequently used for placement and classification decisions. They are useful in instruction and programming although recent evidence indicates that preschool-aged children can function better on certain cognitive tasks than Piaget's theory proposes. These scales may be more useful to the school clinician than to the professional in a clinical setting.

1. Albert Einstein Scales of Sensorimotor Development (Escalona & Corman, 1969). These scales have 54 items across three areas of sensorimotor functioning: prehension, object permanence, and space. They are recommended for assessment of the cognitive development of low-functioning preschoolers, leading to program initiatives.

2. Assessment in Infancy: Ordinal Scales of Psychological Development (Uzgiris & Hunt, 1975). This instrument consists of seven scales: visual pursuit and permanence of objects, means of obtaining desired environmental events, vocal imitation, gestural imitation, operational causality, construction of object relations in space, and schemes for relating to objects. The scales are useful in ascertaining appropriate types of materials and level of programming for mentally retarded individuals.

3. Concept Assessment Kit (Goldschmidt & Bentley 1968). This scale assesses development in Piaget's preoperational stage of cognitive development (4 to 7 years).

Curriculum-Based Assessment

Curriculum-based instruments yield results that transfer into curriculum and intervention recommendations (Fewell, 1984; Neisworth & Bagnato, 1986). Because curriculum-based scales vary in theoretical basis of items, inclusion of instructional strategies, modifications for handicap, and comprehensiveness, Bagnato, Neisworth, and Capone (1986) developed a five-category typology of CBA measures. There are a number of instruments across all five categories available on the market; only those developed to assess handicap-specific populations of preschoolers are listed in the following descriptions.

Autistic/Severely Handicapped

1. Autism Screening Instrument for Educational Planning (Krug, Arick, & Almond, 1979). The ASIEP consists of the following domains: vocal behavior, interaction assessment, educational assessment of functional skills, and prognosis of learning rate (preschool and school-aged). It is specifically developed to assess ability differences of the severely handicapped and autistic. It is more likely to be used in an educational setting than a clinic setting but is appropriate for either.

2. Individualized Assessment Treatment for Autistic and Developmentally Delayed Children (Schopler, Lansing, Reichler, & Waters, 1979). This instrument yields integrated assessment and curricular components (0 through 8 years). It is specifically developed to assess autistic and developmentally delayed children. The theoretical base of the instrument is behavioral and, thus, features instructional and behavioral strategy linkages for intervention. Thus, the instrument has applications for school settings.

Visually Impaired

3. Oregon Project for Visually Impaired and Blind Preschool Children (Brown, Simmons, & Methvin, 1979). This instrument includes domains of fine and gross motor, communication, social-emotional, self-help, and cognition (0 through 6 years). Guidelines for use with blind, low-vision, and multihandicapped children are provided. The Oregon assessment functions as a curriculum guide; specific goals and suggested activities are provided for teachers and parents. The instrument aids acquisition of first-grade skills, mobility, and Braille.

Hearing Impaired

4. Sequenced Inventory of Communication Development (Hedrick, Prather, & Tobin, 1984). The SICD includes the following subdomains of expressive and receptive language: discrimination, awareness understanding, oral-motor-vocal imitation, and vocal responsiveness in initiating conversations with others. It is administered in an informal play

atmosphere to children with hearing and communication disorders. It is appropriately used in the school or clinic setting.

5. The Callier-Azusa Scale: Assessment of Deaf/Blind Children (Stillman, 1974). This instrument includes domains of motor development, perceptual development, daily living skills, cognition, and communication (0 through 9 years). The test is appropriate for deaf/blind and severely and profoundly handicapped. It is particularly comprehensive at lower developmental levels and provides target treatment and goals.

Social/Emotional Assessment

Techniques in interviewing, direct observation, rating scales, and sociometry are currently available to assess the social and emotional functioning of preschool children. Only rating scales are reviewed below.

1. Achenbach Child Behavior Checklist (Achenbach & Edelbrock, 1983). The CBCL yields subscale scores for: social withdrawal, depressed, immature, somatic complaints, sex problems, schizoid, aggressive, and delinquent (4 through 16 years). Developed primarily for school-age children, the scale was extended downward for the preschool population resulting in difficulty or irrelevance of some test items. Caregivers rate the child on a 3-point scale. This scale is a helpful diagnostic tool in the school and the clinic. Examination of individual items yields direction for interventions.

2. Personality Inventory for Children (Wirt, Lachar, Klinedinst, & Seat, 1977). The PIC yields the following subscales: undisciplined/poor self-control, social incompetence, internalization/somatic symptoms, cognitive development, general adjustment, achievement screening, intellectual screening, developmental rate, somatic concern, depression, family relations, delinquency, withdrawal, anxiety, psychosis, hyperactivity, and social skills (3 through 16 years). It is helpful in diagnosis in the school and clinic. The preschool portion of this test is also the result of a downward extension, as was the CBCL (see above).

CASE STUDY

Aubrey, 2½ years of age, was brought to the local county Child Find by her mother. A team of nurses, optometrists, audiologists, preschool teachers, and school psychologists administered multidisciplinary screenings of Aubrey to identify possible needs for special services.

Presenting problems included inability to move into a sitting position or sit unsupported, no walking, very few self-help skills, and so forth. Aubrey's medical history revealed an Apgar score of 4 at the time of birth. However, she received no special interventions from the neonatal period to the time of the Child Find. The Child Find vision screening indicated a need for further assessment. Hearing screening results were within normal limits. The Denver Developmental Screening Test indicated that Aubrey was delayed in gross and fine motor and personal-social domains. Adaptive language was borderline. Results indicated possible cerebral palsy and comprehensive, diagnostic assessment was recommended to the mother. Appropriate medical referrals were made to a neurologist and ophthalmologist. Also, Aubrey's mother signed a consent form giving permission for the in-depth physical therapy, speech and language pathology, and school psychology diagnostic assessments to be conducted.

The physical therapist assessed gross and fine motor skills and the speech/language pathologist evaluated speech and language functioning. The school psychologist administered the Stanford-Binet to aid in differential diagnosis and classification. Results of the individually administered intelligence scale placed Aubrey in the Average range across verbal subtests. Those subtests requiring motor skills were delayed. The Survey of Family Needs yielded weaknesses in all six areas: needs for information, support, explanation of child's handicapping condition to others, community services, financial help, and family functioning.

Multidisciplinary team members diagnosed Aubrey as physically impaired (cerebral palsy). Recommendations included (1) physical therapy interventions; (2) home-based, itinerant preschool services focused on giving information about the handicapping condition, financial help, and community services; (3) training parents as teachers, especially in the motor development domain; and (4) improving family functioning.

EFFICACY OF AND ISSUES IN PRESCHOOL/ DEVELOPMENTAL ASSESSMENT

The issues in preschool/developmental assessment are many, but it is through consideration of these issues that clinicians can improve their assessment background and skills, leading, it is hoped, to better psychoeducational assessments for young children. Although there is not enough space here to cover the key issues in the area exhaustively, a broad sampling of the issues will be attempted by grouping them into three areas: (1) approaches to assessment, (2) the testing-placement sequence, and (3) PL 99-457 and family involvement.

Approaches to Assessment

As can be seen from the above discussion on models of assessment, an array of different models underlie the assessment approaches that we use. Each has its own value and a potentially important part to play in a complete ecological evaluation of the young child. In practical application, however, a variety of factors play a role in the number and type of psychoeducational instruments/techniques that a clinician might employ. These factors include elements such as time available for the assessment, tests on hand, behavior of the child/parents, and training background of the clinician.

The impetus of this chapter toward identifying improved practices in preschool/developmental assessment centers around expanding the clinician's view of assessment. This view should include a holistic (ecological) perspective on assessment that charges the clinician with *collecting various (diverse) bits of information* using a *multimodal* approach, resulting in more confidence in conclusions and recommendations about each child. Given the variability of behavior of young children, care must be taken to maximize the surety of every decision or conclusion made for children at this level. This is no easy task. Figure 15.1 shows an *example* of information collected for a parent referral question about their son's developmental skills. It shows that information has been collected using a variety of different models to maximize accuracy in answering the referral question. As is frequently the case, the data are not clear-cut. Even information from the same source (test, observation, etc.) may not be consistent. The clinician therefore draws conclusions on the strength of his or her conviction or confidence in the information collected.

So what is new about this you may ask? Fundamentally there are two new elements to conceptualizing testing of young children in this way. First is the emphasis that multiple bits of information are needed (rather than data from one or two standardized tests) to increase confidence in conclusions and recommendations. Second is the idea that approaches and techniques from various models may contribute to a

FIGURE 15.1. *Information Collection and Decision Making in Psycho-educational Assessment*

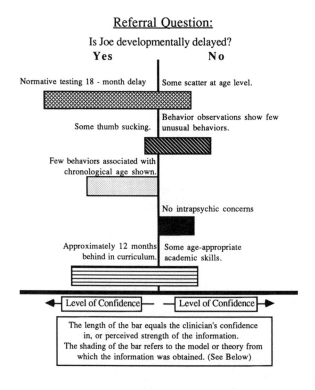

Referral Question:

Is Joe developmentally delayed?

Yes	No

Normative testing 18 - month delay | Some scatter at age level.

Some thumb sucking. | Behavior observations show few unusual behaviors.

Few behaviors associated with chronological age shown.

No intrapsychic concerns

Approximately 12 months behind in curriculum. | Some age-appropriate academic skills.

◄— Level of Confidence — — Level of Confidence —►

The length of the bar equals the clinician's confidence in, or perceived strength of the information.
The shading of the bar refers to the model or theory from which the information was obtained. (See Below)

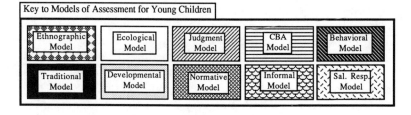

Key to Models of Assessment for Young Children

Ethnographic Model	Ecological Model	Judgment Model	CBA Model	Behavioral Model
Traditional Model	Developmental Model	Normative Model	Informal Model	Sal. Resp. Model

unique and richer perspective on the young child, the family, and the environment. Many clinicians may believe they do these things; however, the all too frequent use of the "standard battery" mediates against this approach.

The Testing-Placement Sequence

The issues in testing and placement are many, but there are several that are particularly important to consider for psychoeducational assessment of young children. There has been controversy over the predictability of assessment tools for preschool children and infants. Fundamentally, the older the child, the more accurate our predictions are considered to be (Paget & Bracken, 1983). The converse, of course, is that the younger the child, the more inaccurate are our predictions. To help counter this problem, utilize only those tests (when using standardized/normative tests) that have adequate reliability and validity for the child in question. In addition, the instrument should have good predictive validity for future academic or social performance. Multiple measures should be used to verify hypotheses about the child and to gain more specific information about what the child can and cannot do under certain circumstances. Routine follow-along evaluation of infants is an excellent practice, given the rapid changes in development, the variability of behavior during testing, and the lack of predictive ability of psychometric instruments for these children.

Considerations for educational placement of young children frequently begin with the educational diagnosis. Mallory and Kerns (1988) report that many states use the traditional categorical labels (i.e., MR, LD), whereas others have opted to use more generic terms such as "developmentally delayed." Concerns about categorical labeling center around the appropriateness of the label (i.e., specific learning disability) for young children who have little educational experience, the expectation of teachers and parents after categorical labeling (Mallory & Kerns, 1988), and the assumption of categorical labeling that children have only one area of need. Mallory and Kerns (1988) conclude that "consideration of categorical labeling of young children raises more questions than it answers. . . . [F]uture research should consider the practices that early intervention and preschool programs use to assess young children, to provide services based on individual needs rather than diagnostic categories" (p. 49).

PL 99-457 and Family Involvement

Consonant with the ecological-interactive theme of this chapter is PL 99-457. This law not only extends PL 94-142 to infants and preschool children, but specifies family involvement in the assessment and education of the young child. This recognition of the importance of the family to young children underscores the need to go beyond the testing room for relevant and crucial data. It appears that the Individualized Family Service Plan (IFSP) was developed with the intent of increasing parental involvement in the educational process, and developing intervention within the family context (Swanson & Watson, 1989). However, the best way to implement the IFSP has been the focus of much speculation (Harbin, 1988).

It is clear that increased involvement with the family will magnify the need for family assessment instruments. Interviewing skills along with instruments like the Survey of Family Needs (Bailey, 1988) and the Family Adaptability and Cohesion Evaluation Scale (Olson, Portner, & Lavee, 1985) may be used to attain a multifaceted look at the young child within the family context. However, key issues of intrusion into the family, and methods of involving less interested parents/families, are yet to be fully faced.

CONCLUSIONS

With the rapid change that is taking place in preschool/developmental assessment, there are various challenges facing both practicing clinicians and those in training. These challenges include learning new approaches for family assessment; staying current with new instruments on the market; understanding the requirements of PL 99-457 and how it may be implemented locally; and, perhaps most important, adopting an ecological model that allows the eclectic use of various approaches to assessment. The value of the ecological-interactive model lies in improved assessment conclusions through multimethod and multisourced assessment techniques.

The confidence that the clinician can place in his or her conclusions drawn from the data collected is paramount in the assessment endeavor. The focus of this chapter has been to acquaint or re-acquaint the reader with the numerous ways in which young children may be evaluated and with the value of using multiple approaches in the assessment process.

SUGGESTED READINGS

Abbot, M. S., & Crane, J. S. (1977). Assessment of young children. *Journal of School Psychology, 15,* 118-128.

Bagnato, S. J., Niesworth, J. T., & Capone, A. (1986). Curriculum-based assessment for the young exceptional child: Rationale and review. *Topics in Early Childhood Special Education, 6,* 97-110.

Bagnato, S. J., Neisworth, J. T., & Munson, S. (1989). *Linking developmental assessment and early intervention: Curriculum-based prescriptions* (rev. ed.). Rockville, MD: Aspen.

Brooks-Gunn, J., & Weinraub, M. (1983). Origins of infant intelligence testing. In M. Lewis (Ed.), *Origins of intelligence: Infancy and early childhood* (3rd ed., pp. 25-66). New York: Plenum.

Casto, G., & Mastropieri, M. A. (1986). The efficacy of early intervention programs: A meta-analysis. *Exceptional Children, 52,* 417-424.

Fewell, R. R. (1984). Assessment of preschool handicapped children. *Educational Psychologist, 19,* 172-179.

Haskins, R. (1989). Beyond metaphor: The efficacy of early childhood education. *American Psychologist, 44,* 274-282.

Lewis, M., & Starr, M. (1979). Developmental continuity. In J. D. Osofsky (Ed.), *Handbook of infant development* (pp. 653-670). New York: Wiley.

Lichtenstein, R., & Ireton, H. (1984). *Preschool screening: Identifying young children with developmental and educational problems.* Orlando, FL: Grune & Stratton.

Mallory, B. L., & Kerns, G. M. (1988). Consequences of categorical labeling of preschool children. *Topics in Early Childhood Special Education, 8,* 39-50.

Martin, R. P. (1986). Assessment of the social and emotional functioning of preschool children. *School Psychology Review, 15,* 216-232.

Odom, S. L., & Shuster, S. K. (1986). Naturalistic inquiry and the assessment of young handicapped children and their families. *Topics in Early Childhood Special Education, 6,* 68-82.

Paget, K. D., & Bracken, B. A. (Eds.). (1983). *The psychoeducational assessment of preschool children.* New York: Grune & Stratton.

Spodek, B. (Ed.). (1982). *Handbook of research in early childhood education.* New York: The Free Press-Macmillan.

Wilson, C. C. (1986). Family assessment in preschool evaluation. *School Psychology Review, 15,* 166-179.

REFERENCES

Abbott, M. S., & Crane, J. S. (1977). Assessment of young children. *Journal of School Psychology, 15,* 118-128.

Achenbach, T. M., & Edelbrock, L. S. (1983). *Manual for the Child Behavior Checklist and Revised Child Behavior Profiles.* Burlington, VT: Department of Psychiatry, University of Vermont.

Alpern, G., Boll, T., & Shearer, M. (1980). *Developmental Profile II manual.* Aspen, CO: Psychological Development.

Bagnato, S. J., Neisworth, J. T., & Capone, A. (1986). Curriculum-based assessment for the young exceptional child: Rationale and review. *Topics in Early Childhood Special Education, 6,* 97-110.

Bagnato, S. J., Neisworth, J.T., & Munson, S. (1989). *Linking developmental assessment and early intervention: Curriculum based prescriptions* (rev. ed.). Rockville, MD: Aspen.

Bailey, D. B. (1988). Assessing family stress and needs. In D. B. Bailey & R. J. Simeonsson (Eds.), *Family assessment in early intervention* (pp. 95-118). Columbus, OH: Merrill.

Bayley, N. (1969). *Bayley scales of infant development.* New York: The Psychological Corporation.

Berkeley, T. R., & Ludlow, B. L. (1989). Toward a reconceptualization of the developmental model. *Topics in Early Childhood Special Education, 9,* 51-66.

Boyd, R. D. (1989). What a difference a day makes: Age-related discontinuities and the Battelle Developmental Inventory. *Journal of Early Intervention, 13,* 114-119.

Brainerd, C. J. (1978). *Piaget's theory of intelligence.* Englewood Cliffs: Prentice-Hall.

Brooks-Gunn, J., & Weinraub, M. (1983). Origins of infant intelligence testing. In M. Lewis (Ed.), *Origins of intelligence: Infancy and early childhood* (3rd ed., pp. 25-66). New York: Plenum.

Brown, D., Simmons, V., & Methvin, J. (1979). *The Oregon project for visually impaired and blind preschool children.* Medford, OR: Jackson County Educational Service District.

Carta, J. T., Sainato, D. M., & Greenwood, C. R. (1988). Advances in the ecological assessment of classroom instruction for young children with handicaps. In S. L. Odom & M. B. Karnes (Eds.), *Early intervention for infants and children with handicaps* (pp. 217-240). Baltimore: Paul H. Brookes.

Casto, G., & Mastropieri, M. A. (1986). The efficacy of early intervention programs: A meta-analysis. *Exceptional Children, 51,* 417-424.

Doll, E. A. (1966). *Preschool attainment record.* Circle Pines, MN: American Guidance Service.

Dunst, C. J., Jenkins, V., & Trivette, C. M. (1984). The Family Support Scale: Reliability and validity. *Journal of Individual, Family, and Community Wellness, 1*(4), 45-52.

Dunst, C. J., McWilliam, R. A., & Holbert, K. (1986). Assessment of preschool classroom environments. *Diagnostique, 11,* 212-232.

Escalona, S. K., & Corman, H. H. (1969). *Albert Einstein Scales of Sensorimotor Development.* New York: Albert Einstein College of Medicine of Yeshiva University.

Fallen, N. H., & Umansky, W. (1985). *Young children with special needs.* (2nd ed.). Columbus, OH: Merrill.

Ferry, P. C. (1981). On growing neurons: Are early intervention programs effective? *Pediatrics, 67,* 38-41.

Fewell, R. R. (1984). Assessment of preschool handicapped children. *Educational Psychologist, 19,* 172-179.

Fleischer, K. H., Belgredan, J. H., Bagnato, S. J., & Ogonosky, A. B. (1990). An overview of judgment-based assessment. *Topics in Early Childhood Special Education, 10,* 13-23.

Frankenburg, W., Dodds, J., Fandal, A., Kazuk, E., & Cohrs, M. (1975). *Denver Development Screening Test reference manual.* Denver, CO: Ladoca Project and Publishing Foundation.

Gallagher, J. J. (1989). A new policy initiative: Infants and toddlers with handicapping conditions. *American Psychologist, 44,* 387-391.

Garwood, S. G. (1982). Misuse of developmental scales in program evaluation. *Topics in Early Childhood Special Education, 1,* 61-69.

Goldschmidt, M. J., & Bentley, P. M. (1968). *Manual: Concept Assessment Kit: Conservation.* San Diego: Educational & Industrial Testing Service.

Gottfried, N. W. (1973). Effects of early intervention programs. In K. S. Miller & R. M. Oregor (Eds.), *Comparative studies of blacks and whites in the U.S.* (pp. 102-131). New York: Seminar Press.

Harbin, G. (1988). Implementation of P. L. 99-457: State technical assistance needs. *Topics in Early Childhood Special Education, 8,* 24-36.

Harms, T., & Clifford, R. M. (1980). *Early Childhood Environment Rating Scale.* New York: Teachers College Press.

Harms, T., & Clifford, R. M. (1989). *The Family Day Care Rating Scale.* New York: Teachers College Press.

Harms, T., Cryer, D., & Clifford, R. M. (1989). *Infant/toddler Environment Rating Scale.* New York: Teachers College Press.

Haskins, R. (1989). Beyond metaphor: The efficacy of early childhood education. *American Psychologist, 44,* 274-282.

Haskins, R., Ramey, C. T., Stedman, D. J., Blacher-Dixon, J., & Pierce, J. E. (1978). Effects of repeated assessment on standardized test performance by infants. *American Journal of Mental Deficiency, 83,* 233-239.

Hayes, A. (1990). The context and future of judgment-based assessment. *Topics in Early Childhood Special Education, 10,* 1-12.

Hedrick, D. A., Prather, E. M., & Tobin, A. R. (1984). *Sequenced Inventory of Communication Development.* Los Angeles: Western Psychological Services.

Hiskey, M. (1966). *Hiskey-Nebraska Test of Learning Aptitude.* Lincoln, NE: Author.

Holt, R. R. (1970). Yet another look at clinical and statistical prediction: Or, is clinical psychology worthwhile? *American Psychologist, 25,* 337-349.

Ireton, H., & Thwing, E. (1972). *The Minnesota Child Development Inventory,* Minneapolis, MN: Behavior Science Systems.

Kahn, J. V. (1988). Cognitive assessment of mentally retarded infants and pre-schoolers. In T. D. Wachs & R. Sheehan (Eds.), *Assessment of young developmentally disabled children* (pp. 163-182). New York: Plenum.

Kaufman, A. S. (1975). Factor structure of the McCarthy Scales at five age levels between 2½ and 8½. *Educational and Psychological Measurement, 35,* 641-656.

Kaufman, A. S., & Kaufman, N. L. (1983). *Kaufman Assessment Battery for Children: Interpretive manual.* Circle Pines, MN: American Guidance Service.

Keith, T. Z. (1985). Questioning the K-ABC: What does it measure? *School Psychology Review, 14,* 9-12.

Krug, D. A., Arick, J., & Almond, P. J. (1979). Autism screening instrument for educational planning. In J. Gilliam (Ed.), *Autism: Diagnosis, instruction, management, and research* (pp. 67-82). Austin: University of Texas Press.

Lee, S. W. (1991). The family with a chronically ill child. In M. Fine (Ed.), *Collaboration with parents of exceptional children* (pp. 201-217). Brandon, VT: Clinical Psychology Publishing Company.

Lee, S. W., & Elliott, J. (1988, October). *Informal testing with preschool children.* Paper presented at the annual meeting of the Kansas Association of School Psychologists, Manhattan, Kansas.

Lewis, M., & Starr, M. (1979). Developmental continuity. In J. D. Osofsky (Ed.), *Handbook of infant development* (pp. 653-670). New York: Wiley.

Lichtenstein, R., & Ireton, H. (1984). *Preschool screening: Identifying young children with developmental and educational problems.* Orlando, FL: Grune & Stratton.

Mallory, B. L., & Kerns, G. M. (1988). Consequences of categorical labeling of preschool children. *Topics in Early Childhood Special Education, 8,* 39-50.

Maloney, M. P., & Ward, M. P. (1976). *Psychological assessment: A conceptual approach.* New York: Oxford.

Mardell-Czudnowski, C., & Goldenberg, D. (1983). Revision and restandardization of a preschool screening test: DIAL becomes DIAL-R. *Journal of the Division of Early Childhood, 8,* 149-156.

Martin, R. P. (1986). Assessment of the social and emotional functioning of preschool children. *School Psychology Review, 15,* 216-232.

McCarthy, D. (1972). *Manual for the McCarthy Scales of Children's Abilities.* New York: The Psychological Corporation.

McLoughlin, J. A., & Lewis, R. B. (1981). *Assessing special students* (2nd ed.). Columbus, OH: Merrill.

McWilliam, R. A., & Galant, K. (1984). *Caregiver Assessment of Child Engagement.* Unpublished rating scale, Family, Infant and Preschool Program, Western Carolina Center, Morganton, NC.

McWilliam, R. A., Galant, K., & Dunst, C. J. (1984). *Daily Engagement Rating Scale.* Unpublished rating scale, Family, Infant and Preschool Program, Western Carolina Center, Morganton, NC.

Meehl, P. E, (1954). *Clinical versus statistical prediction: A theoretical analysis and review of the evidence.* Minneapolis: University of Minnesota Press.

Moore, G. T. (1987). The physical environment and cognitive development in child-care centers. In C. S. Weinstein & T. G. David (Eds.), *Spaces for children: The built environment and child development* (pp. 41-72). New York: Plenum Press.

Moore, G. T. (1988). Theoretical perspectives on development and the environment: A paper in memory of Joachim Wohlwill. *Children's Environment Quarterly, 5,* 5-12.

Neisworth, J. T., & Bagnato, S. J. (1986). Curriculum-based developmental assessment: Congruence of testing and teaching. *School Psychology Review, 15,* 180-199.

Newborg, J., Stock, J. R., Wnek, L., Guidubaldi, J., & Svinicki, J. (1984). *The Battelle Developmental Inventory.* Allen, TX: DLM Teaching Resources.

Odom, S. L., & Shuster, S. K. (1986). Naturalistic inquiry and the assessment of young handicapped children and their families. *Topics in Early Childhood Special Education, 6,* 68-82.

Olson, D. H., Portner, J., & Lavee, Y. (1985). *FACES III.* St. Paul: University of Minnesota.

Paget, K. D., & Barnett, D. W. (1990). Assessment of infants, toddlers, preschool children, and their families: Emergent trends. In T. B. Gutkin & C. R. Reynolds (Eds.), *The handbook of school psychology: Second edition* (pp. 458-486). New York: John Wiley & Sons.

Paget, K. D., & Bracken, B. A. (Eds.). (1983). *The psychoeducational assessment of preschool children.* New York: Grune & Stratton.

Paget, K. D., & Nagle, R. J. (1986). A conceptual model of preschool assessment. *School Psychology Review, 15,* 154-165.

Risley, T. R., & Cataldo, M. F. (1973). *Planned activity check: Materials for training observers.* Unpublished manual, Center for Applied Behavior Analysis, Lawrence, KS.

Rogers-Warren, A. K. (1982). Behavior ecology in classrooms for young, handicapped children. *Topics in Early Childhood Special Education, 2(1),* 21-32.

Rogers-Warren, A. K., Santos-Colond, J., Warren, S. F., & Hasselbring, T. S. (1984, December). *Strategies and issues in quantifying early intervention.* Paper presented at National Center for Clinical Infant Programs Conference, Washington, DC.

Rogers-Warren, A. K., & Wedel, J. W. (1980). The ecology of preschool classroom for the handicapped. *New Directions for Exceptional Children, 1,* 1-24.

Salvia, J., & Hughes, C. (1990). *Curriculum-based assessment: Testing what is taught.* New York: Macmillan.

Sattler, J. M. (1988). *Assessment of children* (3rd ed.) San Diego: Sattler.

Sawyer, J. (1966). Measurement and prediction, clinical and statistical. *Psychological Bulletin, 66,* 178-200.

Schopler, E., Lansing, M., Reichler, R. J., & Waters, L. (1979). *Individualized assessment and treatment for autistic and developmentally disabled children.* Austin, TX: Pro-Ed.

Shapiro, E. S. (1987). *Behavioral assessment in school psychology.* Hillsdale, NJ: Lawrence Erlbaum.

Shinn, M. R., Rosenfield, S., & Knutson, N. (1989). Curriculum-based assessment: A comparison of models. *School Psychology Review, 18,* 299-316.

Spodek, B. (Ed.). (1982). *Handbook of research in early childhood education.* New York: The Free Press-Macmillan.

Stillman, R. D. (1974). *The Callier Azusa Scale: Assessment of deaf/blind children.* Reston, VA: Council for Exceptional Children.

Swanson, H. L., & Watson, B. L. (1989). *Educational and psychological assessment of exceptional children.* Columbus, OH: Merrill.

Switzky, H., Rotatori, A., Miller, T., & Freagon, S. (1979). The developmental model and its implications for assessment and instruction for the severely/profoundly handicapped. *Mental Retardation, 17,* 167-170.

Thorndike, R. L., Hagen, E. P., & Sattler, J. M. (1986). *Stanford-Binet Intelligence Scale: Fourth Edition.* Chicago: Riverside.

Twardosz, S. (1984). Environmental organization: The physical, social, and programmatic context of behavior. In M. Hersen, R. M. Eisler, & P. M. Miller (Eds.), *Progress in behavior modification* (Vol. 18, pp. 123-161). New York: Academic Press.

Uzgiris, I. C., & Hunt, J. (1975). *Assessment in infancy: Ordinal scales of psychological development.* Urbana: University of Illinois Press.

Wechsler, D. (1967). *Manual for the Wechsler Preschool & Primary Scale of Intelligence.* New York: The Psychological Corporation.

Wechsler, D. (1989). *Manual for the Wechsler Preschool and Primary Scale of Intelligence - Revised.* San Antonio: The Psychological Corporation.

Wilson, C. C. (1986). Family assessment in preschool evaluation. *School Psychology Review, 15,* 166-179.

Wirt, R. D., Lachar, D., Klinedinst, J. K., & Seat, P. D. (1977). *Multidimensional descriptions of child personality: A manual for the Personality Inventory for Children.* Los Angeles: Western Psychological Services.

Wolfensberger, W., & Kurtz, R. A. (1971). Use of retardation-related diagnostic and descriptive labels by parents of retarded children. *Journal of Special Education, 8,* 131-142.

16 FUTURE TRENDS IN ASSESSMENT

H. Booney Vance

If history is a predictor of future trends in assessment, testing is likely to see a combination of the old with the new. Many professionals such as psychologists, lawyers, politicians, and educators appear to be somewhat disillusioned by the area of assessment. This disillusionment or dissatisfaction often leads to concerns about how things might be in the future, what's new on the horizon, and other "what if" questions. It has been indicated that the researcher seems committed to advancing theory whereas the clinician accepts change with great reluctance (Perlman & Kaufman, 1990). It can be said, however, that social influence and legal decisions will continue to play a major role in test refinement and development, as well as in defining the purpose of assessment.

Many writers, including Resnick (1979), Sternberg (1979), Glasner (1981), and Snow (1980), have projected what they think intelligence testing and other assessment areas might be like in the 21st century. With the ever-changing political and social climate of our times, it becomes very difficult to predict what lies 20 years from now. As we know, it is far easier to predict short-term changes than long-term ones, and the short-term predictions are usually more valid. I would like to gaze into the "crystal ball" and suggest what the future might hold for the professional who works primarily in the assessment area.

In 1990 Merenda suggested that there will be a number of major issues facing psychological testing in the United States. These issues include computer-adaptive testing, matching of tests and curriculum, testing of the handicapped, and honesty in testing. In a 1990 article on judgment-based assessment (JBA), which appeared in the *Journal of Early Childhood Special Education*, Hayes (1990) suggested that three directions should be explored. Hayes emphasized the need to widen JBA to include judgments of abilities and emotional characteristics as well as developmental processes. In addition, Hayes suggested that assessment include judgment by others such as persons with disabilities, and he predicted that new methods for eliciting judgments such as response to videotaped segments of a child's behavior and content analyses of spontaneous vocalizations collected longitudinally will be major sources of assessment data in the future.

Adaptive testing will become more applicable to a wide range of tests. Adaptive testing enables a clinician to employ a statistical model that allows for the development of a pool of items scaled in terms of difficulty levels, discrimination indexes, and percentages of guessing indexes for administration by computer. According to Aiken (1987), "adaptive testing makes possible the presentation of only a fraction of the number of items required by the traditional testing practice in which an examinee answers all items" (p. 396). Adaptive testing procedures will increase the flexibility and facility with which tests can be given by computer–examiner interaction. A major advantage of interactive-adaptive testing is the use of a decision model that takes into account not only items and tasks of a test but also the levels of errors or accuracy in the examinee's responses (ceiling levels) and where to begin testing (basal levels). In addition, clearer and more accurate test scores can be determined by taking into account the statistical properties of the test items as well as the number of correct responses.

HOLISTIC ASSESSMENT

Since the conception of measuring intellectual abilities, clinicians have been aware that IQ tests measure more than just achievement and cognitive abilities. Little attention is often given by test developers to items that measure social competence, adaptation to one's world, socialization, or whatever you choose to call social competence (except for scales of adaptive behavior). Cattell and Schuerger's Objective-Analytic Test Battery (OATB) (1982) was designed to measure the interaction of cognition and affect by ten traits derived from Cattell's research (Institute of Personality and Ability Testing). Some of the tasks included in OATB are musical preference, criticalness of judgment, humor appreciation, and picture perception along with rigidity. Other authors, such as Scarr (1981) and Hayes (1962), strongly suggest that assessment of cognitive abilities should have an inseparable socialization/competence component. In fact, Scarr (1981) indicated that assessment should focus on competence/socialization rather than on intelligence. Such traits as emotional variability, self-image, creativity, adjustment, and perceptual skills will become more common in the development of assessment instruments that purport to measure intelligence. Emphasis will be placed on discovering solutions to complex problems or on problem-solving skills rather than just on achievement and learned activities. There will be a move from the narrow measurements of an intelligence quotient toward the holistic assessment of effectiveness of a person's adjustment to his or her society, according to Aiken (1987).

ASSESSMENT OF PERSON–ENVIRONMENT INTERACTION

The assessment of personal-environmental factors (attitudes) that influence and shape an individual's behavior is a recurrent one in psychology. Early theorists distinguished between two types of environment—the physical and psychological (Walsh & Betz, 1990). Such investigators as Kantor (1924), Luvin (1989), as well as Magnusson (1981b) have contributed to and influenced the notion of a personal-environmental interactive assessment model. This model assumes that human behavior tends to be influenced by many factors that reflect a combination of the person and the situation. Endler and Magnusson (1976b) suggested that there are four basic elements of the person-situational interactional model. According to Endler and Magnusson (1976b), these four basic elements are as follows:

1. Behavior is a function of a continuous process of multidirectional interaction between the individual and the setting he or she encounters.
2. The individual is an intentional, active agent in this interactional process.
3. Cognitive and motivational factors are essential determinants of behavior.

4. The psychological meaning of situations for the individual is the important determining factor. (p. 362)

Two perspectives that reflect Endler and Magnusson's theory are Holland's (1985) Personality Types and Model Environment and Pervin's Personal Environmental Theory (Pervin, 1977). Assessment policies in the future will probably utilize these models more frequently to assess, organize, and understand information about individuals and their environments.

FAMILY ASSESSMENT/EARLY INTERVENTION

Federal legislation in 1968 established the Handicapped Children's Early Education Program and provided recognition of intervention services and parent involvement. The necessary prerequisite for services is the comprehensive assessment of family strengths. Public Law 99-457 mandated that all states by school year 1990–1991 provide free and appropriate services to handicapped children ages 3 to 5 and requires that an individual education plan for preschoolers be included when appropriate and desired by parents. These plans would focus on how family strengths could enhance a child's development. Many families of young children have unique needs (strengths and weaknesses) and this is especially true for many families of young handicapped children. Bailey and Simeonsson (1988) indicate that family assessment is critical "because the approach taken and the measures used in assessing family needs and strengths will significantly shape the professional's view of the family, communicate messages to family members about the value and priorities of the professionals and ultimately influence family goals and services" (p. 9). Dunst (1985) suggested that the domains that are potentially important areas of family assessment include: critical events, sibling relationships, family strengths, and parent–child interactions. Each of these domains constitutes an important component of family-focused assessment and intervention.

This relatively new area of assessment will become even more important and crucial in light of federal laws and preschool intervention programs. Family assessment practices will rekindle many issues relating to professional and ethical standards and social issues in assessment. One of the first and more important considerations in family assessment is whether the technical quality of the instrument to be used is of sufficient merit that the test user can effectively evaluate, administer, utilize, and interpret the test (test standards, primary as well as secondary standards). Not only must a test be of high technical quality, but also the clinician must be qualified to administer it. It is not only the responsibility of the test user to be competent in administration and interpretation of family assessment instruments, but the organization or agency also has responsibilities. The issue of privacy and confidentiality regarding any means of gathering information becomes even more important because the data obtained during the family assessment become more accessible due to the number of individuals and agencies involved with the process.

BAYES' THEOREM

In the years ahead the inclusion of prior data with assigned importance or value will gain popularity and will be used in almost all assessment procedures, especially in the cognitive-achievement domain. This procedure will probably follow Thomas Bayes' Theorem about probability, which provides a basis for arriving at a final estimate of a person's status (posterior estimate) based on an initial estimate (prior estimate) and additional information, according to Thorndike, Cunningham, Thorndike, and Hagen (1991). Thorndike et al. (1991) suggested that an important application of this theory is to adaptive testing. Basically Bayes' theory is simple and, according to Thorndike et al. (1991), "what it says is that we should frequently—possibly always—take account of what we already know when interpreting new information about an individual or about a group" (p. 470). A major problem arising out of operationalizing this theory is deciding how much weight should be given to prior data. For the interested reader Thorndike (1982) provides a good introduction to Bayes' Theorem and Bayesian thinking.

FULL-SERVICE TESTING

Full-service testing by computer has been discussed in detail in Chapter 6 of this book. Ultimately many different assessment tools may be adaptively administered, scored, and interpreted by using diskettes containing a variety of programs. There is little doubt that computers will become more prominent in educational as well as psychological assessment in the future. This will add to many concerns raised previously in Chapter 6, such as ethics in testing, invasion of privacy, self-incrimination, and the right to rebuttal, as well as the issue of physical or psychological risk.

Within the arena of computer-assisted assessment advances in technology (machine), artificial intelligence will probably be able to develop a very sophisticated model of human intelligence. Research in biochemical as well as neurophysiological bases of intelligence will dramatically increase, with probable advances in psychopharmacology that could produce improvement in various domains of intellectual functioning.

LITIGATION AND ASSESSMENT OF SPECIAL POPULATIONS

Perhaps one of the most critical as well as unclear trends that may affect the future and practice of psychoeducational assessment is multicultural assessment. The Education of the Handicapped Act (PL 94-142) mandated racially and culturally nondiscriminatory assessment procedures be used in the identification of "handicapped" children to be served by federally funded programs. In addition, the Senate Report (No. 94-168, pp. 26-29) specifically stated that the law is concerned with the erroneous classification of children variously described as "non-English speaking, poor, minority and bilingual."

Cummings (1989) suggested that the underlying structure of the assessment process has remained essentially intact in that psychologists continue to test children until they find the disability that explains the student's apparent academic problems. Cumming goes on to suggest that the function of an assessment specialist working with multicultural children should be one of an advocacy orientation. In other words, according to many experts this proposed new role would require the psychologist to rely less on the traditional methods of psychological assessment and to broaden the conceptual basis for assessment beyond just the psychoeducational to include the entire learning environment (children's language and culture, school environment) and parent collaboration with school personnel.

Figueroa (1989) contends that "school psychology, conceivably the most test dependent and test defined profession, is the recipient of an inadequate technology and knowledge base, which exposes its growing bilingual clientele to needless levels of error and misdiagnoses" (p. 145). He suggests that school psychologists consider a paradigm shift in self-definition instead of continuing to conduct what some consider to be malpractice.

The assessment of bilingual/multicultural children continues to be a major problem for many psychologists and special educators. Cummings'

(1989) cognitive academic linguistic proficiency model fails to provide much of a guideline for clinicians. Mental processing on bilingual students has yet to receive much attention from researchers. Research regarding the use of interpreters in assessing bilingual children is negligible and inadequate. Many psychological as well as educational instruments that are translated from English to another language such as Spanish are usually for students with little or no sustained exposure to English. What is the validity for these tests when used with non-English-speaking children immersed in an English-speaking educational system? Questionable, at best! Even straight translation is problematic. According to Figueroa (1990), publishers fail to realize that the language systems of many bilingual/minority children are overlapping and distinct. For instance, The Psychological Corporation in 1982 published a Spanish version of the WISC-R without supportive normative data. This Spanish version of the WISC-R was based on one person's dissertation. I believe this area will become very important in the future given the population shift and growth of minorities in the United States. Issues such as how to redefine learning disabilities for multicultural children, how the translations of a test affect its psychometric properties with multicultural children, and how bilingual/minority children process information must be addressed if we are going to answer the question posed by Figueroa (1989): Are the technology and regulations governing the practice of psychology inadequate to meet the needs of linguistic minority children?

IMPROVEMENT IN TEST CONSTRUCTION

At some future time, will test instruments carry a hazard warning, as currently seen on cigarette packages, reading "this product could be hazardous to your future health and education"? Linn (1989) made a very interesting observation:

> . . . on inspection of three versions of a well-established standardized achievement battery, one published around the time of each of the three editions of Educational Measurement, 1951, 1971, 1981, one might easily wonder if there had been any progress in the field of educational measurement since the early 1950's. (p. 1)

If we were to look at the current revision of some of the more popular psychological (IQ) instruments, perhaps the same could be said about them except for the impact of computers on all aspects of assessment, new models of test development (item selection/analysis) based on item response theory, and the use of meta-analysis in test validation results.

In the near future there will likely be multiple changes in test construction. Classical test theory is being increasingly challenged by new statistical models and new psychometric theories. For instance, the use of meta-analysis will become more widespread as more researchers become familiar with the methodology. Item-test response theory (IRT) will likely increase, especially in the area of evaluating items used in test construction. In addition, the legal system is likely to mandate changes in test construction, especially in the critical areas of evaluation of current and potential test bias. The use of local norms will become more widespread and this factor will also influence test construction and assessment.

Many of the future trends projections are predicated on the fact that there will be professionals who will be looking for methods to improve tests and testing. As Golden, Sawicki, and Franzen (1990) aptly suggested, as public and political interest in tests and assessment continues to increase, that interest may be related to a desire to survive as well as a desire to improve.

As this chapter suggests, there are many new, exciting activities in assessment. Although it is impossible to predict every new trend that will take place in testing, these trends seem positive and we may look forward to more progress in the coming decade.

REFERENCES

Aiken, L. R. (1987). *Assessment of intellectual functioning.* Newton, MA: Allyn and Bacon.

Bailey, D. B., & Simeonsson, R. J. (1988). *Family assessment in early intervention.* Columbus, OH: Merrill.

Cattell, R. B., & Schuerger, J. M. (1982). *Objective-Analytic Test Battery.* Champaign, IL: Institute of Personality and Ability Testing.

Cummings, S. J. (1989). A theoretical framework for bilingual special education. *Exceptional Children, 2,* 111-119.

Dunst, C. J. (1985). Rethinking early intervention. *Analysis and Intervention in Developmental Disabilities, 5,* 165-201.

Endler, N. S., & Magnusson, D. (1976b). Personality and person by situation interactions. In N. S. Endler & D. Magnusson (Eds.), *Interactional personality and psychology* (pp. 1-27). New York: Wiley.

Figueroa, R. A. (1989). Psychological testing of linguistic minority students: Knowledge gaps and regulations. *Exceptional Children, 2,* 145-152.

Figueroa, R. A. (1990). Assessment of linguistic minority group children. In C. R. Reynolds & R. W. Kamphaus (Eds.), *Handbook of psychological and educational assessment of children: Volume 1. Intelligence and achievement* (pp. 148-191). New York: Guilford.

Glasner, R. (1981). The future of testing—a research agenda for cognitive psychology and psychometrics. *American Psychologist, 36*(9), 515-521.

Golden C. J., Sawicki, R. F., & Franzen, M D. (1990). Test construction. In G. Goldstein & H. Hersen (Eds.), *Handbook of psychological assessment* (pp. 21-40). New York: Pergamon Press.

Hayes, A. (1990). The context and future of judgment-based assessment. *Topics in Early Childhood-Special Education, 10,* 1-12.

Holland, J. L. (1985). *Professional manual for the Self-Directed Search.* Odessa, FL: Psychological Assessment Resources.

Kantor, J. R. (1924). *Principles of psychology* (Vol. 1). Bloomington, IN: Principia Press.

Lewin, K. (1935). *A dynamic theory of personality: Selected papers.* New York: McGraw-Hill.

Linn, R. L. (1989). Current perspectives and future directions In R. L. Linn (Ed.), *Educational measurement* (3rd ed., pp. 1-10). New York: Macmillan.

Magnusson, D. (1981b). *Toward a psychology of situation: An interactional perspective.* Hillsdale, NJ: Lawrence Erlbaum Associates.

Merenda, P. F. (1990). Present and future issues in psychological testing in the United States. *Evaluation-Psicological, 6,* 3-31.

Perlman, M. D., & Kaufman, A. S. (1990). Assessment of child intelligence. In G. Goldstein & M. Hersen (Eds.), *Handbook of psychological assessment* (pp. 59-78). New York: Pergamon Press.

Pervin, L. A. (1977). The representational design in person-situation research. In D. Magnusson & N. S. Endler (Eds.), *Personality at the crossroads: Current issues in interactional psychology* (pp. 371-384). Hillsdale, NJ: Lawrence Erlbaum.

Sternberg, R. J. (1979). The nature of mental abilities. *American Psychologist, 34,* 214-230.

Thorndike, R. L. (1982). *Applied psychometrics.* Boston: Houghton Mifflin.

Thorndike, R. M., Cunningham, G. K., Thorndike, R. L., & Hagen, E. P. (1991). *Measurement and evaluation in psychology and education.* New York: Macmillan.

Walsh, W. B., & Betz, N. E. (1990). *Test and measurement.* Englewood Cliffs, NJ: Prentice Hall.

AUTHOR INDEX

Bagnato, S. J., 469, 485, 498, 503, 510, 518, 519, 520, 522
Bailey, D. B., 508, 517, 519, 528, 532
Bailey, N., 519
Baker, L., 448, 449, 479
Ball, D. W., 277, 301
Balla, D. A., 373, 398
Balow, I. W., 344, 363
Bank, L., 466, 485
Bannatyne, A., 245, 262, 267
Bardos, A. N., 279, 301
Barker, R., 41, 63
Barkley, R. A., 448, 449, 450, 451, 453, 454, 455, 456, 457, 459, 460, 461, 462, 478, 487
Barlow, D. H., 474, 482
Barnett, D. W., 506, 507, 522
Barona, A., 279, 300, 410, 438
Barringer, K., 361, 363
Barrios, B. A., 472, 478
Bartel, N. B., 64
Battista, M. T., 184, 185, 199
Bauer, R. M., 222, 227
Baumgart, D., 395
Bayes, T., 529
Bayley, N., 115, 116, 144, 491, 506
Bayne, C. K., 73, 109
Becher, H., 185, 198
Beck, L. H., 486
Beck, S., 456, 457, 479
Becker, R. L., 87, 107
Behar, L. B., 132, 144
Belgredan, J. H., 498, 520
Bell, J., 117, 144
Bell, M. C., 155, 174
Bell-Dolan, D. J., 463, 479
Bellack, A. S., 64
Bender, L., 6, 26, 46
Benner, S. M., 41, 64
Bennett, R. E., 361, 363
Benowitz, S., 361, 363
Bentley, P. M., 510, 520
Benton, A. L., 202, 226
Berger, M., 442, 487

Berk, R. A., 116, 144, 262, 267
Berkeley, T. R., 495, 499, 500, 519
Bersoff, D., 2, 26
Betz, N. E., 527, 533
Bierman, K. L., 450, 453, 464, 479
Bigler, E. D., 206, 226
Bijou, S. W., 64
Binet, A., 153, 173, 272, 300, 445, 479
Bisconer, S. W., 110
Bishop, P. C., 231, 268
Blacher-Dixon, J., 506, 520
Blashfield, R. K., 448, 474
Bloom, B., 30, 64
Blum, I. L., 158, 171, 173, 424, 438
Boehm, A. E., 129, 144
Boice, R., 474, 482
Bolen, L. B., 280, 302
Boll, T., 504, 519
Bond, E. A., 154, 173
Boocock, S. S., 181, 198
Boone, K. B., 220, 228
Borg, T., 321, 337, 340
Bormuth, J. R., 47, 64
Bornstein, M. T., 42, 64
Bornstein, P. H., 42, 64
Bornstein, R. A., 214, 226, 248, 267
Bott, D. A., 64
Botterbusch, K., 80, 107
Bower, E., 327, 337
Bowman, M. L., 4, 26
Boyd, R. D., 519
Boyer, B. A., 469, 485
Boyer, E. G., 37, 67
Bradley-Johnson, S., 126, 144
Brady, J. E., 14, 26
Brainerd, C. J., 495, 519
Brakke, N. P., 464, 480
Brandon, T. L., 107
Bransome, E. D., 457, 486
Branston-McClean, M. B., 395
Brantley, J. C., 187, 190, 193, 198
Braziel, P. M., 85, 108
Breen, M., 459, 478
Brent, D., 480

SUBJECT INDEX